Global Politics

Ben Fugill
Jane Hirons
Brian Hull

To order, please visit www.hoddereducation.com or contact Customer Service at education@hachette.co.uk / +44 (0)1235 827827.

ISBN: 978 1 0360 0350 0

© Ben Fugill, Jane Hirons and Brian Hull 2024

First published in 2024 by
Hodder Education,
An Hachette UK Company
Carmelite House
50 Victoria Embankment
London EC4Y 0DZ

www.hoddereducation.com

Impression number   10 9 8 7 6 5 4 3 2 1

Year   2028 2027 2026 2025 2024

Cover photo © pathdoc - stock.adobe.com

Illustrations by Integra Software Services Ltd

Typeset in India by Integra Software Services Ltd

Produced by DZS Grafik, Printed in Slovenia

A catalogue record for this title is available from the British Library.

MIX
Paper | Supporting
responsible forestry
FSC™ C104740
FSC
www.fsc.org

Contents

ASSESSMENT

Introduction

Welcome to *Global Politics for the IB Diploma*. This textbook provides complete coverage of the new IB Global Politics Diploma syllabus, with first teaching from 2024 and first assessment in 2026.

The Diploma Programme Global Politics course aims to give students the opportunity to explore the world around them and engage with contemporary political issues that impact our global community. Students on this course have the unique opportunity to study the political issues and challenges that are of particular interest to them within the wider framework of the course concepts, content and context. *Global Politics for the IB Diploma* provides extensive support to both teachers and students of this course.

This textbook effectively explores the concepts, content and context of the IB Global Politics syllabus:

1 **Concepts:** power, sovereignty, legitimacy and interdependence are political concepts that are critically evaluated throughout the course and defined and used extensively within this book. 2 **Content:** the prescribed topics and content are clearly organized and the book provides in-depth examinations of power and global politics, as well as thematic studies on rights and justice, development and sustainability, and peace and conflict.	**Context:** Both concepts and content must be grounded in real-world examples and case studies, which can be found at the global, international, regional, national, sub-national, local and community levels; often more than one level may be involved. This textbook provides a good foundation by exploring several diverse cultural, geographic, economic and institutional case studies that effectively embed the concepts and content of the course.

Global Politics for the IB Diploma is designed to support the International Baccalaureate Diploma Programme Global Politics course at both the Standard level and the Higher level. The content of the textbook closely aligns to the prescribed content and concepts of the curriculum, while also providing contextualized real world examples and assessment support. It is a book that has been developed with great care and attention to meet the needs of a diverse community of educators and students.

The textbook is laid out sequentially:

Section 1: Core – Understanding power and global politics
Section 2: Thematic studies – Rights and justice
Section 3: Thematic studies – Development and sustainability
Section 4: Thematic studies – Peace and conflict
Section 5: Assessment – Guidance on the IA engagement project
Section 6: Assessment – Guidance for both SL and HL students on Papers 1, 2 and 3

◼ Digital materials

The textbook is also available as an e-Book, which contains interactive case studies as an additional feature.

How can students use this book?

Students can use *Global Politics for the IB Diploma* to supplement and expand on what they learn in the classroom. The textbook is clearly structured and provides an excellent overview of the essential elements of the course, including internal and external assessments. This book was primarily written to support the learning needs of students.

How can educators use this book?

1 Educators can follow the textbook sequentially, starting with Chapter 1, and be assured that the concepts and content will be thoroughly covered.

2 They may prefer to start the course with the thematic studies chapters (Chapters 2, 3 or 4) and integrate the core topics within the thematic studies as they arise.

3 They may choose to start with targeted global issues or specific case studies that are of particular interest to their students. They can then integrate the prescribed concepts and content from the core and thematic studies.

4 Also, if purchasing the eBook, they may use the online interactive case studies as an additional tool to help students development inquiry skills further.

No matter which approach is used, the many examples and case studies in this book will provide a good foundation from which more learner-centered inquiries can evolve. Additionally, the guidance on how to approach the Engagement Project and external assessment for both SL and HL students can be examined as needed.

Finally, both educators and students will appreciate the many features that support teaching and learning throughout the book, such as:

- activities
- key words and their definitions
- case studies
- discussion points
- profiles of key political theorists
- explanations and contextualized examples of political theories
- global politics extended essay tips
- common mistakes
- TOK links
- review questions.

 The 'In cooperation with IB' logo signifies the content in this coursebook has been reviewed by the IB to ensure it fully aligns with the current IB curriculum and offers high quality guidance and support for IB teaching and learning.

How to use this book

The following features will help you to consolidate and develop your understanding of global politics through concept-based learning.

Key terms

◆ Definitions appear throughout the margins to provide context and help you understand the language of global politics. There is also a glossary of all key terms at the end of the book.

SYLLABUS CONTENT

▶ This coursebook follows the exact order of the contents of the IB Global Politics Diploma syllabus.
▶ Syllabus understandings are introduced naturally throughout each topic.

Exploring solutions

This feature includes key inquiry statements to explore, presented with either context or more questions to consider.

Key theorist

Introduces key theorists as well as competing perspectives.

ACTIVITY

A range of activities to help you understand some of the most difficult global politics concepts.

Perspectives

In this feature you will explore different political issues and perspectives.

CASE STUDY

Real-world international examples and case studies are used to bring the subject to life.

Case studies form the basis of this course. The course encourages the use of inquiries, contemporary examples and case studies at a variety of levels, from the local to the global, as well as from smaller scale businesses to multinational ones. Throughout the coursebook, we have chosen case studies that reflect the context in which you are learning, as well as case studies that allow for comparisons across contexts.

Questions are often included to allow you to analyse and synthesize your understanding.

Discussion point

Questions to either discuss as part of a group in class or to think about individually. These will challenge you to apply some of the global politics concepts locally.

Common mistakes

These detail some common misunderstandings and typical errors made by students, so that you can avoid making the same mistakes yourself.

Extended essay

Investigate a topic of special interest, either through one of your six DP subjects or through an interdisciplinary approach. The EE helps you to develop the self-regulated research and writing skills that you need to fulfill your aspirations at university.

TOK

Links to Theory of Knowledge (TOK) allow you to develop critical thinking skills and deepen understanding by bringing discussions about the subject beyond the scope of the content of the curriculum.

Concepts

Independence, power, theoretical perspectives, legitimacy, sovereignty and international law underpin the IB Global Politics Diploma course and are integrated into the conceptual understanding of all units, to ensure that a conceptual thread is woven throughout the course. Conceptual understanding enhances your overall understanding of the course, making the subject more meaningful. This helps you develop clear evidence of synthesis and evaluation in your responses to assessment questions. Concepts are explored in context and can be found interspersed in the chapter.

HL extension

The HL extension boxes suggest possible areas for extended inquiries on the eight global political challenges: Borders, Environment, Equality, Health, Identity, Poverty, Security and Technology.

Chapter summary

At the end of each chapter, there is a summary of the key points addressed to help you to develop and understand the depth of knowledge you need to acquire for the course.

REVIEW QUESTIONS

Review questions are also included at the end of each chapter to allow you to consolidate your learning.

A bibliography listing all of the works referred to in this book is available at
www.hoddereducation.com/ib-extras

1 Understanding power and global politics

SYLLABUS CONTENT

By the end of this chapter, you should understand:
▶ how to distinguish between stakeholders and actors
▶ systems: structures and dynamics
▶ legal frameworks, norms and institutions.

1.1.1 Framing global politics

■ What is a political issue?

Political issues are at the heart of Diploma Programme (DP) Global Politics. But what is a 'political issue'? It is any situation or matter that deals with how power is distributed and how it operates in the real world. We can see this by looking at how people engage with issues that impact their lives, their community and the wider world. In fact, political issues are all around us, and it is a mistake to think they simply involve governments and politicians. We encounter political issues on a daily basis, whether that be in news sources or on social media, through to education and health care, taxes and following the law, or even when chatting with friends. All political issues involve *people*: actors and stakeholders.

The interaction of actors and stakeholders is at the centre of all global political issues. Questions to bear in mind when examining case studies and examples of these groups include:

● Who has power?

● Who are the powerless?

● Who is trying to bring about change?

● Who is resisting change?

● Who is impacted by these interactions?

All of these questions help us to better understand the world around us.

 TOK

The question 'what is a political issue' is, from a theory of knowledge perspective, related to the 'scope' of this particular form of knowledge. Different types of knowledge can be distinguished by their primary concern, or focus. The primary concern of global politics is knowledge about the distribution and application of power in the world. As this is a form of human behaviour, the study of global politics is considered to be part of the human sciences.

Other human science subjects include:
● economics, the study of the distribution of money and other resources
● psychology, the study of the relationship between human behaviour and human cognition
● sociology, the study of the development and interaction of social dynamics
● anthropology, the study of human cultures.

There is, of course, a lot of overlap between these subjects and other areas of knowledge (global politics has to consider, for example, the economic practices of states), but the primary concern of each subject is always unique.

How do we distinguish 'actors' from 'stakeholders'?

Actors	Stakeholders
When talking about political issues, we refer to those who have the power to bring about change as actors. Actors can be seen at all levels of our global society, from international to local. A worker holding up a sign demanding better wages is just as much an actor as the factory owner who has the power to give those higher wages. Both are exercising power in their own ways.	Sometimes political issues impact people who are not directly involved in the issue. These people may not be aware that they could exercise power, or they have no interest in doing so. Additionally, many people live in societies where it is unsafe to openly seek change. Often these people have little to no power to take action, but they are nonetheless impacted by those who do. In politics, we call these individuals 'stakeholders'. For example, the child of a striking factory worker who is able to attend university because their parent took action and received higher wages would be considered a stakeholder. They didn't actively participate in the political issue, but their life was impacted by it.

1.1.2 The state

There are many types of actors and stakeholders on the global political stage, but as a starting point it can be helpful to first consider what is arguably the most powerful actor in global politics: the state. In this section, you will be introduced to the state, the internal governance of a state and the global organizations that have states as their members.

What is a 'state'?

Our modern understanding of the state comes from the Treaty of Westphalia (1648) and the Montevideo Convention (1933) (see Table 1.1).

■ **Table 1.1** The Treaty of Westphalia and the Montevideo Convention

Treaty of Westphalia (1648)	Montevideo Convention (1933)
• Ended one of the most destructive conflicts in Europe's history, the Thirty Years War. • Named after Westphalia, an area of north-west Germany. • Set out to prevent future conflict by recognizing that states have certain rights and responsibilities.	• Agreement signed in Montevideo, Uruguay. • Established the standard modern definition of a state as a means to preserving peace. • The agreement requires that no state shall intervene in the domestic or foreign affairs of another state.

Based on both the Treaty of Westphalia and the Montevideo Convention, we can say that the characteristics of a state include:

- an independent government that has control over a clearly defined area – this area must have internationally recognized borders
- generally being seen as having absolute control over its own territory and people
- having the right to defend its territory within its borders and being recognized as a state by other states and actors
- systems of government, which can be national, regional and/or local, and some kind of legal system being in place

- having a permanent population
- having exclusive rights within its own territory including:
  - the use of force
  - control of the money and currency
  - laws and other requirements, such as taxes and rules surrounding citizenship.

What is a 'nation state'?

◆ **Diaspora** refers to a large group of people living somewhere that is not their original homeland. Sometimes these people have moved by choice, but other times they may have been forced to relocate.

There are important differences between a 'state' and a 'nation state'. A 'nation' is an ethnic or cultural group with a common, defined culture. Nation states may have a sovereign territory, or they may not.

Nation states with clearly defined borders are somewhat rare in our increasingly interconnected and globalized world, but examples include Japan, Albania and Iceland. Nations can, however, exist without a physical homeland and also include members of the nation who are in **diaspora**, which means they do not live in their original homeland. Some examples of stateless nations include the Kurdish people, Rohingya people and Roma people.

How do we determine what is a state and what is not?

States have traditionally been seen as the most important and powerful actors in global politics. They have control over national interests and also contribute to a kind of international community that exercises power in many contemporary global political issues.

States, therefore, continue to be seen as the primary actors in global politics, although in recent decades challenges to the supremacy of the state have emerged as more actors engage with political issues. Today, it can no longer be said that the international community is composed exclusively of states, but they may still be its strongest component.

Discussion point

Sealand is a Second World War offshore platform located in the North Sea off the coast of England. In 1967, a former British army major purchased Sealand and named himself Prince Roy of Sealand.

Sealand issues its own passports (which are not recognized outside of Sealand) and has its own stamps, flag, currency and government. Its website lists the population at 27, but this fluctuates. In recent years, many have accused Sealand of being a place where hackers, pirates and criminals operate freely.

Sealand has declared itself to be an independent sovereign state, but no other state recognizes it and most people don't take it seriously. Based on your understanding of the characteristics of a state, do you think Sealand qualifies?

■ **Figure 1.1** Sealand: an independent sovereign state?

Different systems of government found in different states

Although the Treaty of Westphalia and the Montevideo Convention provide us with a definition of the rights and responsibilities of a state, a quick look at the world we live in tells us that not all states function in the same way.

TOK Exhibition Question: 35. In what ways do values affect the production of knowledge?

Many of the differences between these different political systems can be discussed in terms of what each one values or regards as important. These values then lead people to take different views (or, in other words, construct different knowledge claims) on particular issues. Towards the left, you might find beliefs that economic equality is most important with an expectation that it's the government's role to ensure this occurs. Towards the right, you might expect to see less value given to governmental intervention in social and economic issues. For the TOK exhibition, you might find an object that appears to be non-political, but that different people at different points on this spectrum view in quite different ways.

There are many political systems and many different ways of representing them. You may come across different political systems presented as a linear diagram, as shown in Figure 1.2. Figure 1.3 is also linear.

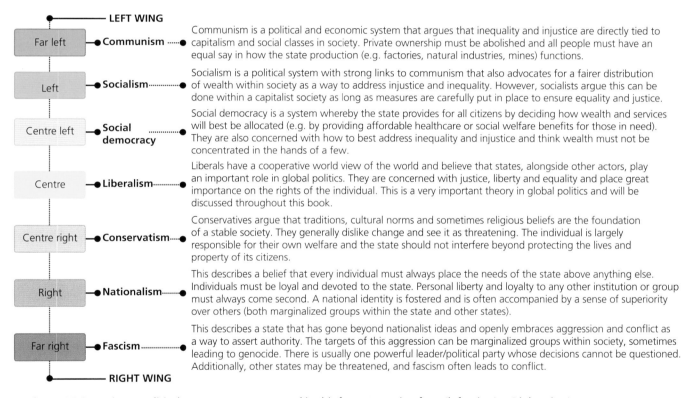

LEFT WING

Far left — **Communism** — Communism is a political and economic system that argues that inequality and injustice are directly tied to capitalism and social classes in society. Private ownership must be abolished and all people must have an equal say in how the state production (e.g. factories, natural industries, mines) functions.

Left — **Socialism** — Socialism is a political system with strong links to communism that also advocates for a fairer distribution of wealth within society as a way to address injustice and inequality. However, socialists argue this can be done within a capitalist society as long as measures are carefully put in place to ensure equality and justice.

Centre left — **Social democracy** — Social democracy is a system whereby the state provides for all citizens by deciding how wealth and services will best be allocated (e.g. by providing affordable healthcare or social welfare benefits for those in need). They are also concerned with how to best address inequality and injustice and think wealth must not be concentrated in the hands of a few.

Centre — **Liberalism** — Liberals have a cooperative world view of the world and believe that states, alongside other actors, play an important role in global politics. They are concerned with justice, liberty and equality and place great importance on the rights of the individual. This is a very important theory in global politics and will be discussed throughout this book.

Centre right — **Conservatism** — Conservatives argue that traditions, cultural norms and sometimes religious beliefs are the foundation of a stable society. They generally dislike change and see it as threatening. The individual is largely responsible for their own welfare and the state should not interfere beyond protecting the lives and property of its citizens.

Right — **Nationalism** — This describes a belief that every individual must always place the needs of the state above anything else. Individuals must be loyal and devoted to the state. Personal liberty and loyalty to any other institution or group must always come second. A national identity is fostered and is often accompanied by a sense of superiority over others (both marginalized groups within the state and other states).

Far right — **Fascism** — This describes a state that has gone beyond nationalist ideas and openly embraces aggression and conflict as a way to assert authority. The targets of this aggression can be marginalized groups within society, sometimes leading to genocide. There is usually one powerful leader/political party whose decisions cannot be questioned. Additionally, other states may be threatened, and fascism often leads to conflict.

RIGHT WING

■ **Figure 1.2** Sometimes, political systems are represented in this format, moving from 'left wing' to 'right wing'

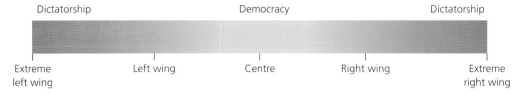

Dictatorship | Democracy | Dictatorship

Extreme left wing | Left wing | Centre | Right wing | Extreme right wing

■ **Figure 1.3** Another linear representation of political systems

These are, of course, very simplified versions of political systems and they have many limitations because real-world political systems are not necessarily on a 'neat spectrum'. However, the spectrums, and the terms within them, can help us to understand the complexities of real-world global political issues.

■ Political parties

Political parties are groups of people who have common views about how the government of a state should function. They are focused on political power; they either want it or want to hold on to it.

Additionally, in a well-functioning democracy, political parties who do not hold government power can challenge the decisions and policies of the political party that does have government power.

Political parties are often associated with democracies and elections, but they can be found in other systems of government too (see Table 1.2). Although the states in Table 1.2 represent a wide range of political systems, all have political parties. Some of these states, such as China, are one-party states, meaning there is only one legal political party allowed. Other states, such as the United States, have multiple political parties.

■ **Table 1.2** Examples of influential political parties within states

State	Party	Notes
China	Chinese Communist Party	The only political party in China.
India	Bharatiya Janata Party	One of two major political parties in India. The other major party is the Indian National Congress.
Russia	United Russia	This is by far the largest political party in Russia and has maintained power there since 2007.
North Korea	Workers' Party of Korea	The only political party in North Korea.
Singapore	People's Action Party	The major political party in Singapore, which has maintained power since 1965.
United States	Democratic Party	One of two major political parties in the United States, the other being the Republican Party.
Argentina	Justicialist Party	Has held power in Argentina off and on since 1946.
South Africa	African National Congress	Has held power in South Africa since 1994.

1.1.3 Political leaders

Leaders are individuals who are in charge of a group of people. A political leader is in charge of some form of government, whether that be state, sub-national or local governments. Some are elected by the people of the state and some are appointed by a political party or a more powerful political leader. Sometimes, leaders first elected by the people manage to increase their power and remain in control indefinitely. Some leaders inherit power by birth and some seize power by force.

Ultimately, political leaders come in many forms and make for interesting subjects of study in global politics.

Discussion point

Can you think of a real-world political leader who has seized power by force?

● Common mistake

Students often use historical examples in their answers. But remember, IBDP Global Politics is focused on the world as it is today, so make sure your example isn't 'historical'. The course is an examination of real-world global political events that are happening now and/or directly impacting our world today. As a general rule, use examples from your own lifetime.

1.1.4 Sub-national and local governments

Sometimes when we think of leadership and power within a state we concentrate only on those political leaders who we see as the public face of the state. However, presidents, prime ministers, monarchs and heads of state cannot effectively govern a state without the support of sub-national and local governments.

In most states, much of the authority for planning, managing and allocating resources is transferred from the central government to regional or local government departments. Sub-national and local officials in government are closest to the people, and are in a better position to understand how local communities function and how best to meet their needs. Local political leaders, for example, usually deal with issues that impact the daily life of citizens and stakeholders, such as access to childcare, sanitation concerns or traffic congestion. However, decisions or policies created by the state's central government can certainly impact the lives of these stakeholders.

In a stable and well-functioning country, sub-national and local governments ordinarily interact quite regularly with the more powerful central government of the state. The power of the central government may be controlled by one political party or, in the case of a democracy, there may be several parties. All of these actors also interact closely with many other stakeholders and actors from within the state and beyond the state borders.

In democratic states, national, sub-national and local leaders are chosen in elections. National, sub-national and local governments should work in partnership and not as adversaries, although in many real-world situations this is not always the case.

> **Discussion point**
>
> Choose a country you are familiar with and investigate how its sub-national and local governments are structured.

◼ Summary of actors closely connected to the internal operations of a state

Interactions between the following actors contribute to the governance of a state:

- the state
- political parties
- political leaders
- sub-national government(s)
- local government(s).

In a stable and well-functioning country, sub-national and local governments ordinarily interact quite regularly with the more powerful central government of the state. The power of the central government may be controlled by one political party, or several, in the case of a democracy. All of these actors also interact closely with many other stakeholders and actors, both from within the state and beyond the state borders.

From within, it is often sub-national and local governments who deal directly with the residents of the state. Local political leaders usually deal with issues that impact the daily life of citizens and stakeholders, such as access to childcare, sanitation and traffic congestion. However, decisions or policies created by the state's central government can certainly impact the lives of these stakeholders.

Concepts

Liberalism and realism

In our increasingly globalized world, it appears that states cannot function effectively in isolation. Some argue that this interdependence is evidence of a global community working towards improving the lives of all, and that the state's power and influence are on the decline. This viewpoint is fundamentally liberal.

Others argue that ultimately the state remains the key player in global politics; any apparent 'cooperation' only takes place if the state sees its own interests improve. This viewpoint is realist.

Table 1.3 summarizes the main characteristic of liberalism and realism. (Note: liberalism and realism are viewpoints or interpretations of real-world global political issues, and we will explore both in more depth in the thematic studies sections of this book.)

■ **Table 1.3** The main theories of liberalism and realism

Key theory	Key arguments
Liberalism	• It is the duty and obligation of all states to ensure the rights of citizens. States who ignore the rights and well-being of their citizens are unstable and unjust. • The fairest and most just government system is democracy. Other systems, such as monarchies or dictatorships, do not put the needs of the people first and are therefore problematic. • It is important to ensure that governments do not become too powerful through continual monitoring and, if necessary, challenging the power of the state if it is seen to violate the freedoms of the people. • Liberalism implies openness and open-mindedness and is concerned most with the rights of the individual.
Realism	• We live in a world of states working in their own best interests, much like the opponents in a game of chess. • States are the primary actors on the world stage; other actors are not really of much importance. • The world is in a state of anarchy and there is no 'global governance', so states must take care of themselves. • The world is a ruthless place where states must aggressively compete against each other to survive and maintain power.

Discussion point

In Global Politics, theories such as liberalism and realism are very complex and so it helps to examine them in relation to real-world examples. These theories, and many others, attempt to explain the reality of global politics. Why do you think real-world examples are so important in a course like IBDP Global Politics?

1.1.5 Intergovernmental organizations

Intergovernmental organizations (IGOs) consist of two or more states who promise that they will work together on political issues that are of common interest to all. They usually operate under a signed treaty, so that all states within the IGO are subject to international law and can be held accountable.

CORE: Understanding power and global politics

IGOs exist to create a place for states to successfully work together towards the common good of all. They focus on maintaining peace, economic development and global social issues. IGOs play a very important role in global politics as the world becomes more interdependent and globalized.

It is important to remember that states make up IGOs and therefore the decisions and actions taken by IGOs should reflect the decisions of the states involved.

As essentially a collection of states, IGOs obviously interact on an international level of global politics. However, they also interact with a wide range of other actors and stakeholders depending on the shared aims of the group. IGOs focused on development, for example, need to interact with other actors and stakeholders who have expertise in this area.

Many argue that world stability relies on states working together, and the most efficient way to facilitate cooperation is through IGOs. IGOs enable states to communicate openly and regularly and are therefore able to effectively address shared concerns. Additionally, issues that are not contained within the borders of states, such as climate change and pandemics, can be addressed collaboratively.

Although, as we have said, there is a general acceptance that no state shall intervene in the domestic or foreign affairs of another state, membership in an IGO can influence and change how a state operates.

Discussion point

Although IGOs are a collection of states and all states should be seen as equal within the organization, we know that in the real world some states are more powerful than others. In what ways could this impact the unity of IGOs?

■ Examples of intergovernmental organizations in global politics

The most well-known and powerful IGO is the United Nations (UN). The UN operates at the international level of global politics, and we will be exploring this IGO in greater detail later in this chapter.

Other well-known regional IGOs include the European Union (EU), the African Union (AU) and the Association of Southeast Asian Nations (ASEAN). These IGOs often cooperate with the UN, but they also provide an opportunity for representatives of the same region to address concerns that are of specific importance to them.

Finally, you will find smaller but powerful IGOs working towards specific goals, including:

- trade
- the environment
- infectious disease
- economic interests
- security.

Discussion point

Can you think of any IGOs that deal with issues related to infectious diseases and pandemics? How about economic interests?

For example, the World Trade Organization (WTO) deals with issues around trade, and the North Atlantic Treaty Organization (NATO) is an IGO concerned with international security.

Regardless of their size or purpose, IGOs are an example of collectivism, as the will of the group as a whole should take priority over the claims of any individual state. It is hoped that a collective of states is more powerful and more effective than states working in their own self-interest.

1.1.6 Organized civil society and non-governmental organizations

◼ What is organized civil society?

Civil society is a term we use to describe organizations or groups of people that are not linked to the government. These organized groups usually have some kind of common purpose and goal. Sometimes they want to make changes in society and can challenge existing problems, attitudes or beliefs. There are so many organized civil society groups it would be difficult to list them all, but they include churches, charitable groups, cultural institutions, professional associations and sometimes private businesses.

An active and engaged civil society is desirable in a democratic state, as it offers varying perspectives on how to improve society and provokes discussion and debate.

Civil society groups may be critical of government policies and hold governments to account over their actions. They may also:

- work towards ending poverty, corruption and economic inequality
- respond to crises (such as floods, earthquakes or fires) and help those in need
- promote law and order and prevent crime
- promote public freedoms
- advocate for transparency of government budgets
- protect the environment
- empower persons belonging to marginalized or disadvantaged groups
- deliver services to help disadvantaged groups in society
- fight against discrimination
- demand corporate social responsibility and accountability
- combat human trafficking
- empower women
- combat hate speech
- advocate for rights for the LGBTQ+ people
- empower youth
- advance social justice and consumer protection
- provide social services such as food kitchens and shelters.

As with most actors in global politics, civil society does not operate in isolation and interaction is frequent.

● HL extension: Environment

Examining how civil society impacts climate policies is one way to begin an investigation into environmental global political challenges at the local and national level. Investigating how different sectors of civil society provoke debate and discussion regarding the best approaches to dealing with our global climate crisis could lead to the development of an excellent HL case study.

◼ What are non-governmental organizations?

Non-governmental organizations (NGOs) may seem somewhat similar to organized civil society groups, and that's because they are! NGOs refers to a huge variety of organizations that also aim to help people. NGOs, however, always try to remain independent from any kind of government influence and are usually non-profit.

The goals and methods of different NGOs can vary, but generally speaking they work towards:

- improving human rights
- helping those in need
- social and economic development.

Some NGOs are smaller and work locally, while others operate regionally and yet others are international (see Figure 1.4). This is different from organized civil society, which may be influenced by regional and global trends but is generally focused on local society.

1	Community NGOs
2	City-level NGOs
3	National-level NGOs
4	International NGOs

■ **Figure 1.4** Types of NGOs based on the level of involvement

Figure 1.5 illustrates the different categories of NGOs. These involvement:

- **Charitable NGOs:** directed at meeting the needs of the vulnerable and disadvantaged. They may provide food and shelter, and help people in times of natural and human-made disasters. Generally, the 'receivers' of help do not have a role other than to accept what is offered.
- **Service NGOs:** provide people with some kind of service, for example family planning or education. Those receiving help are expected to actively participate in the process to help themselves.
- **Participatory NGOs:** provide people with tools, land or materials necessary for them to then go on to help themselves and the community.
- **Empowering NGOs:** aim to empower people by helping them to understand their social, political and economic rights as individuals and as communities.

Discussion point

What NGOs have you heard about? Are there any NGOs in your community that you could engage with or have already engaged with?

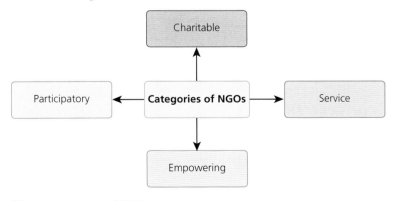

■ **Figure 1.5** Different categories of NGOs

1.1.7 Private actors and private companies

■ Private actors

Private actors in society are those who are not directly involved with the government but who have the ability to make change and influence people. A private actor could be a philanthropist, business leader or even a well-known athlete or celebrity. Or, a private actor may be any member of society who has somehow managed to influence the actions of others.

Table 1.4 examines two globally influential and well-known private actors: Jeff Bezos and Mark Zuckerberg.

■ **Table 1.4** Two influential private actors

Private actor	Background
Jeff Bezos, Amazon	Jeff Bezos founded Amazon in 1994. He donated more than $400 million worth of Amazon stock to multiple civil society organizations in 2022, though it's unclear which organizations received those shares. He owns the influential US newspaper the *Washington Post*. He also owns Blue Origin, an aerospace company that develops rockets, and he briefly flew to space in 2021.
Mark Zuckerberg, Facebook/Meta	Zuckerberg started Facebook at Harvard in 2004 at the age of 19. Facebook changed its name to Meta in November 2021 to enable a shift of the company's focus to the metaverse. In June 2021, anti-trust cases were filed against Zuckerberg by national and sub-national governments within the United States. Zuckerberg won.

Discussion point

Both Jeff Bezos and Mark Zuckerberg are enormously wealthy private actors who have been, or currently are, heads of powerful private companies. Why might some states see these wealthy private actors as threatening? Does the fact that Americans Zuckerberg and Bezos are famous globally reinforce the perception that Americans dominate the world economy? To what extent is this perception a reality? Why might other states welcome collaboration with such actors?

"WE WERE PRIVATIZED."

■ **Figure 1.6** This cartoon portrays ordinary people paying more for services that have been privatized

■ Private companies

Private companies are not directly involved with the government and are usually motivated by profit. However, in many countries, private companies are influencing public policy and traditionally state-run institutions like never before. Some people have expressed concern over the increasingly influential role of certain private actors and companies in recent decades. In particular, commercial technology firms, such as Facebook/Meta, have unprecedented access to citizens' private data.

Globally, we see the increasing involvement of private companies in services traditionally governed by the state, such as education, prisons, transportation systems and hospitals. This process, known as 'privatization', may mean governments are selling state-owned business to private companies.

We have previously mentioned that states like to have control over what happens within their borders and to their people, so why would they allow private companies to take over these services?

Many economists argue that state governments are inefficient when managing state-run companies. They argue that private companies increase efficiency and deliver a better 'product'. Often states are hopeful that privatization will benefit economic development. However, a growing number of real-world examples contradict this claim.

Discussion point

The cartoon in Figure 1.6 is critical of the privatization of essential services. It makes the claims that ordinary people will have to pay more for these services to ensure profits are made. What are the arguments against this claim?

1.1.8 Social movements

Social movements are groups of people who share a common concern about how society is functioning. These movements attempt to change attitudes and behaviour among the social community. In countries where expressing yourself is legal, you may see social groups organizing themselves to come together as a group and publicly discuss how society can improve. In countries where it's dangerous or illegal to publicly identify yourself as someone who wants change, these groups may communicate online or arrange private meetings to discuss common goals.

These groups can begin spontaneously without a formal structure, but they share a common outlook and a desire for change. Social movements cover a wide variety of societal problems, including dangerous and reckless driving, discrimination against women and attitudes towards LGBTQ+ people.

◼ Stages of social movements

Figure 1.7 examines the lifespan, or the stages, of typical social movements.

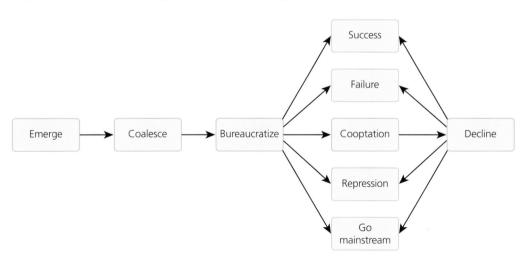

◼ **Figure 1.7** The stages of social movements (Wykis)

Discussion point

Why might a state 'repress' a social movement? Can you think of any real-world examples of this happening?

School Strike for Climate

In August 2018, Swedish school student Greta Thunberg began a school strike to bring attention to climate change. At first she was alone, but soon many other young people joined her.

In the weeks leading up to the Swedish elections the students sat outside the Swedish Parliament demanding that political leaders take action on the climate crisis. Her activism inspired a social movement and #FridaysForFuture started trending on social media.

Although the original point was to apply pressure on Swedish politicians, this social movement soon transformed into informing and motivating young people to become involved in the climate crisis. School Strike for Climate and Fridays for Future spread globally and saw students walking out of the classroom in many countries.

■ **Figure 1.8** Greta Thunberg, founder of Schools Strike for Climate

Discussion point

Have you heard of School Strike for Climate/Fridays for Future? If yes, would you say it is an example of a successful social movement? If no, do you think this is evidence that it failed? Can you justify your evaluation?

1.1.9 Resistance movements

Similar to social movements, resistance movements are groups of people who want change but whose complaints are more directed towards particular government policies, laws and leadership. Therefore, resistance movements provide more of a challenge to those in power than do social movements. However, in real-world situations, protest and social movements are often interconnected, as true change in society often involves changing both community attitudes and structural power.

In states where the freedoms of citizens are limited, it can be very dangerous to be part of a resistance movement because by doing so you are challenging the authority of the state. The US Department of Defense describes a resistance movement as 'an organized effort by some portion of the civil population of a country to resist the legally established government or an occupying power and to disrupt civil order and stability'. Clearly, this definition sees resistance movements as illegal and something to be feared. Others believe that, if laws or governments are oppressive or corrupt, resistance movements can bring positive change.

There are two types of resistance movements: those that use violence and those that don't.

Erica Chenoweth (1980–)

Erica Chenoweth is a professor at Harvard University and has authored several books and articles on mass movements, non-violent resistance, terrorism, political violence, revolutions and state repression.

Chenoweth has concluded that, if resistance movements are to succeed, they must be non-violent in nature. This is because the use of violence stops a lot of people from joining. The more people joining the resistance, the more severe the disruption to daily life and the greater impact. Also, if changes are achieved through violence, Chenoweth argues, the power structure that follows is often as oppressive as the one it replaced.

● Extended essay

In early 2020, a spate of non-violent demonstrations against the government of Prime Minister Prayut Chan-o-cha in Thailand erupted. The protesters' demands included the reform of the Thai monarchy, something previously unheard of.

Many young activists were arrested as the government attempted to shut down the movement. However, several of the activists, including Chonthicha 'Lookkate' Jangrew, have since decided to enter politics to attempt to make changes from within the system. She and other activists continue to attempt to reform the government and monarchy, despite multiple charges against them. They argue that the people of Thailand demand change.

Jangrew is just one of many young activists globally who are resisting government policies and laws peacefully. If you're thinking of writing an extended essay on social or resistance movements, examining the methods used by activists such as Greta Thunberg or Chonthicha 'Lookkate' Jangrew would be a good place to start. However, remember that a good extended essay must consider multiple perspectives, and always discuss your ideas and potential research questions with your extended essay supervisor.

■ Is a violent resistance movement the same as a terrorist group?

Regardless of whether they are successful or not in achieving change, violent resistance movements can cause destruction in and destabilize a society. The term 'non-violent resistance movement' is not particularly controversial, but resistance movements that use violence can be divisive.

There are dozens of definitions of the term 'terrorism'. Terrorism is subject to a lot of debate and study, not only concerning its definition but also regarding its causes and ways of combating it. Some argue that the way to distinguish a terrorist organization from a violent resistance movement is to examine the motives and goals of the group. Does it merely want to seize power? Is it carelessly hurting and killing innocent people in the process? Does it appear to want to create a society that would be even more corrupt, unfair or violent than the one it's fighting against?

TOK

You may hear the phrase 'one person's terrorist is another person's freedom fighter'. To what extent does the definition of terrorism depend on different perspectives?

● HL extension: Security

Violent resistance movements are a serious concern for both the government and the citizens of any state and are a global political challenge. An investigation of how a specific violent resistance movement threatens the security of a state, and the response of different actors as a result of this threat, could lead to the development of an excellent HL case study.

1.1.10 Interest and pressure groups

■ Interest groups

An interest group is a formally organized group of people that aims to influence public policy. Interest groups exist in all states, regardless of the system of government. There are thousands of types of interest groups, ranging from those representing the interests of certain industries, such as the pharmaceutical industry or dairy farming, to religious groups or those that focus on a particular issue, such as gun control.

■ Pressure groups

Pressure groups are very similar to social movements, and often the two terms are used interchangeably. They are usually found within interest groups, and they directly and openly work towards influencing those with power. Two prominent pressure groups active in global politics today are Black Lives Matter and People for the Ethical Treatment of Animals (PETA).

Both types of groups use a variety of tactics to draw attention, including:

- marches
- sit-ins
- petitions
- social media campaigns
- advertising through posters or billboards
- holding public meetings
- contacting local government
- staging some kind of stunt to attract attention.

■ **Figure 1.9** A Black Lives Matter march in Berlin, 2017

■ **Figure 1.10** Activists march for animal rights in Manhattan, 2017

1.1.11 Formal and informal political forums

In global politics, 'forums' refer to meetings of actors to discuss and debate different perspectives on a political issue. There are two main types of forum: formal and informal.

■ Formal forums

As the name suggests, formal forums are regulated and have a definitive structure, rules and regulations in place. For example, the UN frequently hosts different formal forums on a wide variety of political issues.

Within democratic states, formal forums are sometimes established to provide an opportunity for a range of actors and stakeholders to express their opinions about issues impacting their community or state.

Formal forums regulate the interactions between actors and tend to produce definitive approaches to political issues, but some people question whether the structure and formality of such forums limits their creativity.

■ Informal forums

Informal forums are gatherings of actors who meet to discuss and debate different perspectives on a political issue. An informal forum ranges from a group of residents of a city street meeting to discuss common concerns about crime, to regional or global meetings involving states and non-state actors.

Informal forums are not restricted by a complex structure and rules, which some people think leads to more creative solutions.

The World Economic Forum

The World Economic Forum is an informal forum based in Geneva, Switzerland. It hosts an annual meeting in the Swiss town of Davos, giving it its informal name.

A wide variety of actors from the fields of business, media, civil society, government and academia come together at Davos to discuss solutions to some of the world's most pressing problems in an informal setting, enabling different people representing different perspectives and skills to debate and propose innovative and creative solutions to global problems.

One criticism of Davos is that it is a meeting of the world's 'elite', as most of its participants are very wealthy and powerful men. Some question how a group that controls most of the world's wealth can find solutions to benefit all.

> ### Discussion point
>
> Formal and informal forums can be found at all levels of global politics, local to international. Why is it beneficial to bring together people with diverse opinions and perspectives?

1.1.12 The media

The media, including print, television and online, have long had an impact on political issues. Different news agencies may claim to be impartial, but achieving such a goal, even if the agency is sincere, is not always possible.

Social media has emerged as a powerful tool in global politics. Social media platforms can be relatively safe places for people to express opinions and be exposed to the opinions of others.

As we mentioned earlier, states like to have control over what happens within their borders and, to varying degrees, the actions of their own people. As a result, some states feel their power is threatened by social media and they attempt to restrict citizens' access to it. Additionally, in recent years the online world has become a place where states and other non-state actors spread disinformation in order to shape and manipulate public attitudes, opinions and issues of concern.

TOK

The impact of social media is huge and often we are not even aware of the ways in which we are influenced. Research the ways in which social media 'algorithms' curate consumers' experiences when viewing social media. Do you think that these algorithms provide a limited view of the world? How might our understanding of political issues be impacted by these algorithms?

The power of social media is demonstrated by the concern many states have expressed over its use. Table 1.5 is a partial list of states that have placed restrictions on or banned social media.

■ **Table 1.5** States that have banned or restricted access to social media

State	Reasons for ban/restrictions
Nigeria	For several months ending in 2022, Nigeria's government ordered telecommunications companies to block Twitter (now known as X) after a series of tweets started trending, criticizing President Muhammadu Buhari. The government claimed the tweets were a threat to national and economic security.
China	China began to block Facebook and other platforms in 2009, arguing that they threatened Chinese interests. We-chat, a multi-purpose messaging service, is allowed, as all data collected by We-chat are shared with Chinese authorities.
India	In 2020, India banned TikTok along with many other mobile apps, claiming that they were threatening state security and social stability.

Discussion point

To what extent do you agree that social media can threaten state security?

1.1.13 Systems and interactions in global politics

'Systems' in global politics refers to the structures in place that limit the actions of all the actors previously mentioned in this chapter. You have already seen that government systems and structures can influence whether or not certain actors are allowed to openly operate. We can clearly see that all states have sub-national and local governments and the vast majority of states belong to some kind of IGO. Rules, societal norms and institutions further regulate many of the other actors we have examined.

When you explore global political issues, always be on the lookout for these actors and stakeholders and consider what role they play in the issue. Be aware that not every political issue involves all of these actors and stakeholders.

By examining a real-world political issue, we can better understand the role actors and stakeholders play in global politics today. This is something you will undertake both with the support of your teacher and independently.

A deconstruction of a political issue: the Ebola virus breakout in West Africa, 2014

In 2014, the viral disease Ebola surfaced in Liberia, Guinea and Sierra Leone. At the time this region of West Africa was already facing political instability, unstable borders, a weak health care system and poverty.

> **Actors involved from the start:** the states of Liberia, Guinea, Sierra Leone, Nigeria, Mali and Senegal.
>
> **Stakeholders involved from the start:** the people living in those states and the wider regional and global community.

At first, local government health authorities in all three of the originally infected countries struggled to understand the disease, which was not unknown but incredibly rare.

States with Ebola infections authorized various methods to halt the spread of the disease. Sierra Leone made residents stay home for three days, while Liberia closed most of its borders. All of these actions further crippled the states' economies and did little to stop the spread of the disease, which quickly reached Nigeria, Mali and Senegal.

Despite these and other efforts, states quickly realized they needed the support of regional IGOs, the African Union (AU) and the Economic Community of West African States (ECOWAS) to deal with the crisis. Additionally, states and regional IGOs sought out the support of global IGO the World Health Organization (WHO). However, these organizations were later criticized for acting too slowly.

> **Regional and international actors:** the AU, ECOWAS and the UN became involved at the request of the states originally impacted.

Ebola was quickly recognized as a threat globally, and soon dominated news and social media posts around the world. Global and regional NGOs, particularly those associated with medical expertise, offered assistance, as did state actors, private actors and companies. The political issue of how to control and manage the Ebola crisis soon involved a huge range of actors too numerous to list.

The WHO and multiple NGOs initially determined that Ebola was being spread through local customs and burial traditions in West Africa. In West Africa,

it is customary for individuals to touch or hold their deceased loved ones before burial. However, this is when Ebola is most contagious. According to Guinea's Ministry of Health, 60 per cent of Ebola's cases were linked to traditional burial practices and the WHO estimated that 80 per cent of cases in Sierra Leone were tied to burial practices. As a result, these types of burial practices were banned, causing huge upset and mistrust within local communities.

Then, in 2014, the NGO Médecins Sans Frontières (or Doctors Without Borders) had to stop working in a treatment centre in Guinea after its members were attacked by those who believed that the organization had brought the virus with them. Health care workers from within West Africa also took great risks in helping those infected with Ebola and suffered violent attacks by community members who viewed them with suspicion. Additionally, many community stakeholders began to question whether the virus was real, and misinformation quickly spread.

As a result of these experiences, some experts have concluded that respecting community stakeholders should be the key to controlling any kind of disease outbreak. As the crisis evolved, a priority was placed on making burials safe and dignified, but was it too little too late?

> **Health care actors:** alongside local health care workers in West Africa, the WHO and state health agencies including the US Center for Disease Control and NGOs such as Médecins Sans Frontières (also called Doctors Without Borders) became involved in the crisis. Additionally, volunteer health care workers from many other countries offered assistance to Ebola clinics in West Africa.
>
> **The media:** the global media began reporting on the crisis as it evolved.

Eventually Ebola was brought under control and West Africa was declared Ebola-free in May 2015, after over 11,000 people lost their lives.

While we have covered some of the actors and stakeholders involved in addressing this political issue, It is important to remember that other individuals and collective actors played a role in these events – far too many to list in full. Many of these groups do not fall into the categories mentioned in this chapter. This is, however, yet more evidence that we live in an interconnected and globalized world.

Discussion point

Local governments and government officials are often the first actors to become aware of and respond to health emergencies. The local government health authorities in West Africa were quickly overwhelmed with concerns regarding the containment and treatment of this virus. Why would they turn to the central governments of their countries before seeking help from IGOs or other actors outside of the state?

Chapter summary

In this chapter we have covered:
- what is meant by the term 'global political issue'
- who actors and stakeholders are, and how they interact with each other and global political issues
- what is meant by 'the state'
- what types of systems make up a state
- the ways in which actors and stakeholders within systems interact and are involved in real-world political issues.

REVIEW QUESTIONS

Now that you have read this chapter, reflect on these questions:

- What is the difference between an actor and a stakeholder?
- What is generally accepted to be the definition of a state?
- Would a state be potentially more threatened by a resistance movement or a social movement? Why?
- What are some of the functions of intergovernmental organizations (IGOs)?
- Draw a diagram or mind map that shows the interactions between multiple actors and stakeholders involved in the 2014 Ebola crisis in West Africa.

CORE: Understanding power and global politics

By the end of this chapter, you should understand:
▶ the types and ways of understanding power
▶ classifications of power.

> *What is needed is the realization that power without love is reckless and*
> *abusive, and that love without power is sentimental and anaemic.*
>
> *Martin Luther King, Jr, Where Do We Go from Here?*

■ **Figure 1.11** Martin Luther King, Jr

While power can sometimes be perceived negatively, it is, in fact, a neutral notion that can, as explored by Martin Luther King, Jr, be utilized in various ways. Power encompasses many meanings depending on the context. For example, power is required to propel a vehicle forward, to coach a sports team effectively or to coerce an authoritarian leader so they stop persecuting a group within their borders. While there is value in considering the various types of power within the context of global politics, it is the third example that best describes the work those working in international relations theory are trying to do.

Whether power is defined as the ability to make or resist change or the ability to get what we want, power is at the very root of many structures in our society. However, in the context of global politics, it was perhaps best defined by key theorist Joseph Nye in 2021 as:

> *the capacity to do things, but more specifically in social situations, the ability to affect*
> *others to get the outcomes one wants. Many factors affect our ability to get what we*
> *want, and they vary with the context of the relationship.*

Key theorist

Joseph Nye (1937–)

Joseph S. Nye Jr is an American political scientist and diplomat who has made significant contributions in the field of international relations. He is professor emeritus at Harvard University's Kennedy School of Government.

Nye is best known for his work on the concepts of 'soft power' and 'smart power'. He defined soft power as the ability of a country to attract other countries through cultural, institutional and political values, rather than using military or economic means. He later expanded on this idea with the concept of smart power, which refers to the ability of a country to combine the use of both hard and soft power to achieve its foreign policy objectives.

■ **Figure 1.12** Joseph Nye

Nye has also served in various US government positions throughout his career, including being the assistant Secretary of Defense for International Security Affairs during the Bill Clinton administration.

1.2.1 Types and definitions of power

There are many types of power and, depending on how we explore the issue, we can take many different angles, even in global politics. However, drawing on the work of political scientist Joseph Nye, there seem to be at least three types of power – hard power, soft power and smart power.

Arguably, Nye's most significant contribution to international relations theory is the concept of soft power, which he introduced in the late 1980s. In contrast to hard power – elements like military and economic might – soft power emphasizes the influence a state can exert through attraction, culture, values and diplomacy. Nye revolutionized how scholars and policy makers perceive international influence by articulating the importance of these types of 'non-coercive' power resources.

Nye then expanded on these ideas through his notion of smart power – a strategic mix of hard and soft power.

Hard, soft and smart power are now central to discussions about effective foreign policy. Joseph Nye's innovative perspectives on power dynamics in international relations have contributed greatly to the field, making him one of the most influential global political scholars.

■ Hard power

Hard power, often called command power, includes using force and money to push a political actor into doing something they may not have otherwise done. For example, in 2021, the World Bank suspended funds being sent to Sudan to support their transition to a civilian government because of a military coup in October of that year. In this example, money was used in order to try to get the military to step back and allow the movement pushing for democracy and civilian rule to continue.

Hard power is often understood through the lens of so-called 'sticks', 'carrots' and 'sermons':

- A stick is something used to threaten an actor into doing something they would not otherwise do.
- A carrot is a desirable reward for acting in a way that one would have otherwise not acted.
- Sermons may include verbal warnings, directives or position statements sent directly to governments or as a speech condemning the actions of a state or non-state actor.

Either way, they can all be coercive, hard power tools.

Military power as hard power

While military force is often regarded as the ultimate stick in the realm of hard power in global politics, we must consider other components of power when discussing whether military power should be used. We can easily measure a country's military power by taking inventories of its weapons and the size of its armies, navies and air forces. However, this perceived strength can be misleading. An actor's military strength is not solely a function of the size of its military weapons or number of troops.

As Lawrence Freedman explains in *Foreign Affairs Magazine*, the enemy's resources are an important factor when weighing up the military strength of a state. No military operates in isolation, and the capabilities of its adversaries can drastically shape the outcome of conflicts. Also, contributions from allies or trusted partners can sway the balance of power and expand a state's military capabilities, whether this be through logistics, weapons or direct interventions.

Quantity is not the only factor in military power; the quality of equipment and its maintenance are also important. An extensive arsenal loses its advantage if the weaponry is old or poorly maintained. Furthermore, the effectiveness of any military tool, no matter how advanced, relies on the forces using it. A high degree of training and motivation can make a difference in critical combat scenarios.

There are times when military power is not really helpful at all. For example, when faced with global political issues such as climate change, a pandemic or an economic crisis, military power can do little to alleviate these challenges.

Other factors influencing military power

Beyond the battlefield, other factors influence how well a military can respond. These include:

- the ability of a state's logistical and economic frameworks to support the military
- the ability of an economy to sustain prolonged warfare
- the capacity of an actor to ensure that essential supplies consistently reach the front lines, a challenge that can grow as the conflict changes and morphs over time.

Also, we cannot overlook the significance of public and international support. The drive to continue a war effort is underpinned by both domestic and international backing. Establishing and preserving this support requires a government and other actors to craft compelling narratives explaining setbacks and celebrating victories. For example, during the Syrian civil war (2011), the dynamics of power extended beyond the battlefield. While military force was a significant aspect of the conflict, the ability to sustain the war effort and influence outcomes also depended on broader factors.

Economic power played a crucial role as various external actors, such as Iran, Russia and many Western countries, provided financial support, weapons and resources to different factions within the conflict. The economic capacity of these external actors to sustain their support had a direct impact on the duration and intensity of the war.

Public and international support were also instrumental. Different sides in the conflict sought to garner support both domestically and internationally through propaganda, media campaigns and diplomatic efforts. Public opinion and international alliances played a role in shaping the direction of the conflict and influencing negotiations.

The success, or failure, of hard power – including military power – is often determined by the context of the event itself.

As we saw earlier in the case of Sudan, money can be used as a stick and as a carrot. For example, in the case of foreign assistance, carrots can be used by wealthy states in order to reward less wealthy states for doing something they may not have otherwise done – highlighting that it is still coercive power. The wealthy state may provide technical assistance or a loan to a country (the 'carrot') in exchange for opening access to a raw materials market or providing free trade where the lower-income states do not apply taxes (tariffs) to imports or provide subsidies for the goods they export. In either case, the poorer country is doing something they wouldn't have done without the financial carrot.

Alternatively, wealthy nations may provide assistance during a humanitarian crisis or natural disaster. This may enhance the prestige of the donor state and provide a market that helps the farmers in the donor state. As Joseph Nye explains, 'A carrot is more effective than a stick if you wish to lead a mule to water, but a gun may be more useful if you aim to deprive an opponent of his mule'.

Economic power as hard power

In today's interconnected global economy, no one state is truly dominant, and countries can turn to suppliers around the world for essential goods and services, meaning economic power must be used alongside other states and non-state actors. Countries can also use these diverse sources to evade the use of economic power by one state, which is, in its own way, a form of economic power.

A defining characteristic of modern economic power is its precision. Economic measures, like sanctions, can be surgically designed to de-escalate a conflict. By targeting specific banks, businesses or politicians, states can place pressure on key decision makers and their political allies while potentially preserving the well-being of most citizens. This targeted approach to economic power differs from military power, where even the most advanced armies often struggle to avoid the unintended consequence of civilian casualties.

However, the success of economic power often relies on how the target state is governed. Authoritarian leaders often have a firm grip on the state's military, security and media. As a result, they can avoid pushback from citizens who are affected by other states' economic power.

Authoritarian leaders can also often ignore the pressures of public opinion. For instance, while the United States has frequently imposed economic sanctions against autocratic states like China, Cuba, Iran, Iraq and Russia, these sanctions have often struggled to achieve their objectives. Alternatively, economic measures are more effective when the targeted head of state is held accountable by other branches of government and functioning democratic institutions, where discontent can be clearly expressed.

Other factors influencing economic success

While using economic power as a tool of hard, coercive power significantly decreases the number of civilian casualties, there can be unintended consequences:

● The rich and powerful can evade forms of economic power, like sanctions.

● When economic measures are used against a major, interconnected economy, it can inadvertently cause disruptions that go well beyond the targeted state. For example, Russia's blockade of the Black Sea in response to sanctions has increased the cost of Ukrainian wheat in many African countries.

While economic power offers states a precise and strategic tool in global politics, its effectiveness and consequences are therefore shaped by the complexities of global interconnectedness and domestic structures.

■ Power conversion: resource power versus behavioural power

As Joseph Nye states, power is about the outcome, the 'end product'. Nye explains that this is down to an actor's ability to influence an outcome or another actor's behaviour. However, understanding power requires us to be precise about who is involved and what the issues at play are exactly.

Resource power

Resource power comes out of the assets an actor possesses. Traditional examples include a country's large population, its sizeable economy and a strong military. Resource power is valued because it is noticeable and often quantifiable (can be counted). However, possessing these resources does not ensure an actor can achieve the desired outcomes. For instance, a state might have a large economy but fail to use it strategically to achieve a desired outcome. Also, just because a state has a large population does not mean it contributes to its power. In fact, large populations may have the opposite effect. For example, trying to ensure all members of the population are fed and housed can create economic challenges that negatively impact a state's economic power.

Relational power

On the other hand, behaviour or relational power focuses on the actual outcome or influence that comes out of the resources. Nye calls this 'power conversion'. The emphasis is on the relational aspect of power, which sees resources as only the vehicles or raw materials used to change an actor's behaviour or relationship with another actor. This conversion of power considers how resources, when used in specific circumstances, produce (or fail to produce) the desired outcomes. Whether it is an actor's strategies or the context of the environment, it is not the resources that achieve the desired outcome, but how they are used or the circumstance within which they are used that is most important. Resources don't always equal having influence. The true measure of power lies in outcomes helped by paying attention to the circumstances and the strategies used for power conversion.

CASE STUDY

The Iran nuclear deal

We saw relational power in action as part of the diplomatic efforts of the United States and its allies to negotiate the Iran nuclear deal, formally known as the Joint Comprehensive Plan of Action (JCPOA). In this context, the US and its partners used their economic resources as a means to influence Iran's behaviour regarding its nuclear program. The resources, such as sanctions relief and access to the global economy, were viewed as vehicles or a means for changing Iran's behaviour and relationship with the international community. Through extensive negotiations and diplomacy, the participating nations aimed to shape Iran's actions by providing incentives for complying with the JCPOA's restrictions on its nuclear activities. In this case, the power of the negotiating states was evident not just in the resources they possessed but in the strategic use of the resources to achieve a desired outcome – to prevent Iran from developing nuclear weapons.

Reflect on the different aspects of hard power as discussed in the chapter and explain how the effectiveness of these forms of hard power can vary depending on the political, economic and cultural context of both the exerting and receiving countries. For example, can the success of one form of hard power be dependent on the presence or absence of another?

ACTIVITY

Choose a recent international incident where hard power was primarily used and analyse the incident, focusing on the specific forms of hard power employed. Evaluate the effectiveness of the hard power strategies by considering their purpose.

Relational power

In his book *The Future of Power*, Joseph Nye explains that relational power has three elements related to the behaviour of actors:

1 **Commanding change:** 'The ability to command others to change their behaviour against their initial preferences.'

2 **Establishing preferences:** 'If I can get you to want what I want, I will not have to force you to do what you do not want to do.'

3 **Controlling agendas:** 'If ideas and institutions can be used to frame the agenda for action in a way that makes others' preferences seem irrelevant or out of bounds, then it may never be necessary to push or shove them. In other words, it may be possible to shape others' preferences by affecting their expectations of what is legitimate or feasible. Agenda-framing focuses on the ability to keep issues off the table.'

■ Soft power

If power is the ability to affect others to get desired outcomes, we could ask a related question: how quickly do you want to affect others? In the short term, hard power is more effective than soft power. I can threaten you and force you to give me your new mobile phone. It doesn't matter that you don't want to, I get your phone immediately.

To convince you to give me your phone using soft power, I would need to persuade you that the best thing for you is to have you give me your phone. This will take time and may very well be ineffective.

According to Nye, soft power is the ability to affect change in others by 'framing the agenda' or establishing the norms or expectations. Once the norms and expectations are set, then having the ability to persuade others, or create attraction, so that actors behave along the lines of the established norms and expectations is soft power in action.

Soft power is when actors are neither pushed nor coerced into behaving a certain way but are instead drawn or pulled towards doing something because they are attracted or convinced of the outcomes or benefits of falling in line with the established norms.

In global politics, the effectiveness of hard power tends to be fast and visible. We can see how tanks and drones immediately impact wars. Similarly, we can see how hard power clearly influences the financial status of a country impacted by sanctions.

Alternatively, the effectiveness of soft power tends to be slow. The attraction of values and culture may be visible only in the long term, or not clearly visible. Sometimes, it is difficult to determine the extent to which soft power has impacted decision-making by an actor.

In the previous section, we saw how economic resources can produce hard power, but they can also lead to soft power. States with economic power may attract others to follow their example because the outcomes are beneficial. For example, the European Union (EU) has soft economic power in the form of its high gross domestic product as well as high levels of education and social services, which has led a number of European states to pursue membership. While there is undoubtedly hard, carrot-type power involved in gaining

■ **Figure 1.13** Movies made in Hollywood may help to promote American values and culture around the world

access to the EU – stop corruption in your country, or you won't be part of the club – there is also soft, attractive power at work. States are drawn to the collective economic and relational power of EU membership, and so they aim to create policies that align with the EU because they are attracted to the EU's successful example.

Soft power as cultural and social power

Soft power is closely related to both cultural and social power.

Cultural power

Cultural power can come from parts of a culture that gain international prominence and acceptance, such as language, fashion, cuisine, art, education or entertainment. For instance, Hollywood and Harvard are examples of cultural institutions that contribute to the soft power of the United States.

Hollywood, a centre for film production that creates movies widely watched and appreciated around the world, helps promote American values and culture. The result is that citizens and leaders of other countries are drawn towards American norms. But Hollywood's global influence is not just about film commerce: it is also about sharing certain values, lifestyles and perceptions.

Harvard is a prestigious university that attracts students from around the world and produces influential scholars, enhancing the United States' reputation as a centre for learning and intellectual excellence. In addition, international students who attend Harvard (or other equally prestigious universities) can take their experiences and ideas back to their home countries. They may go on to hold influential positions in government and business, potentially affecting the behaviour of states through their decision-making and leadership.

> ### Discussion point
>
> Research an example of how media, education or art from one country has influenced another country's culture or policy. How might the long-term effectiveness of soft power compared to the immediate effects of hard power be both beneficial and a challenge?

ACTIVITY

Choose a cultural product (film, music, art, sport, etc.) from any country. Analyse how it might contribute to that country's soft power. Consider aspects like global appeal, cultural messages and the ways in which it might encourage other countries to engage in similar practices.

■ **Figure 1.14** Harvard University attracts international students, who may then take their experiences and ideas back to their home countries

Social power

Social power in global politics can be closely connected to cultural power. Again, it extends its influence by establishing social norms and practices. For example, the idea of democracy and human rights, largely rooted in Western political thought, has significantly influenced global politics, affecting diplomacy, international treaties and even military or economic intervention.

Cultural and social values can influence other cultures and societies. Over time, this can change attitudes and behaviours in societies that adopt or adapt to these values, or norms. For example, the spread of certain educational models or the global popularity of English as an additional language reflects this social and cultural power.

Soft power is subtle and not always easy to pinpoint. However, these examples show soft power in action.

TOK

When exerting soft power, political leaders or parties might make use of the media – whether it be social media or traditional media. Can you find examples of politicians making use of social or traditional media to influence how their followers think about certain issues? This could be considered an example of how soft power is being used to shape the values and culture in such a way that in the longer term certain political aims are achieved.

■ Smart power

To counter the misperception that soft power could be used to the exclusion of hard power and still be an effective approach to foreign policy, in 2004, Nye developed the term 'smart power', which he defined as the 'ability to combine hard and soft power into successful strategies where they reinforce rather than undercut each other'.

Nye also felt that relying solely on military power is insufficient to achieve long-term security and prosperity in today's complex and interconnected world. He felt a more nuanced combination of hard military and economic power (hard power) alongside diplomacy and cultural influence (often soft power) was more likely to achieve foreign policy objectives.

Each state has a unique mix of hard and soft power. They use smart power in a manner that works best for them. For example, Norway likely relies more heavily on its soft power (it has been at or near the top of the Human Development Index for decades – see pages 226–227, where the Human Development Index is explained in detail). In contrast, while the United States has plenty of soft power, it can also lean heavily on its hard power (the United States has had by far the largest military budget of any country in the world for many decades). As Nye explained, the trick is effectively combining hard and soft power to achieve successful strategies.

Figure 1.15 illustrates how states combine hard and soft power to form smart power.

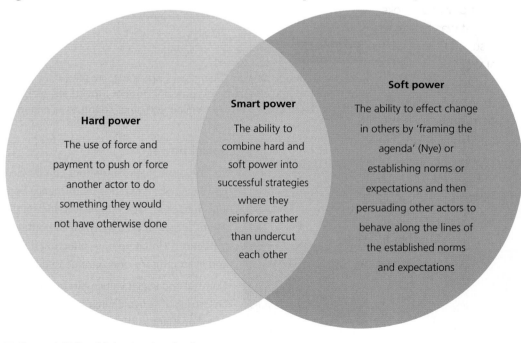

■ **Figure 1.15** Combining hard and soft power to create smart power

CORE: Understanding power and global politics

Ukraine

■ **Figure 1.16** President Zelensky speaking at the UN, December 2022

The war in Ukraine has proven to be a good example of the various aspects of power that we have explored so far in this chapter. First, there has been hard military power. Russia has attempted to coerce Ukraine, by military force, into, at the very least, regime change that would ensure Ukraine was within Russia's sphere of influence.

Russian government officials have also attempted to use soft power to evoke sympathy for the invasion by arguing it was to ensure Ukraine's neutral status. They have suggested the invasion was because:

- NATO has encircled Russia, directly threatening Russian security
- the West orchestrated the removal of a democratically elected Ukrainian president in 2014
- Russian-speaking residents of the Donbas region of Ukraine needed saving from a 'genocide'
- in President Putin's own words, 'drug addicts and neo-Nazis' run Ukraine, and it needs 'denazification'.

These arguments have been largely debunked. As a result, Putin's attempt to use soft power has been mostly unsuccessful.

Ukraine, too, has used hard military power to achieve its desire to defend itself and push the invading Russian troops out of the country. In addition to supplying Ukraine with various weapons systems, the international community has also used hard power to assist Ukraine through sanctions. Prominent Russians, including Vladimir Putin, have had assets outside Russia frozen so they could not be accessed. The country's banking, energy and manufacturing sectors, and access to global trade have also been targeted. Putin has also attempted to use hard power to force the EU and Germany, in particular, to walk back their support of Ukraine through sanctions of his own that have included cutting off most of the natural gas flows to Europe. In fact, due to Putin's hard power capabilities, the EU was initially reluctant to sanction Russian banks for fear of harming its own banks.

In the short term, the war is likely to be determined by military and/or economic hard power. However, soft power has also been at play. Ukrainian president Volodymyr Zelensky has been especially effective in this regard. Whether it has been his use of social media – his response on social media, when the United States offered to assist him in fleeing Ukraine was that he needed ammunition, not a ride – or his virtual visits to parliaments and universities around the world, his experience as a television actor has served him well in drawing support globally to the Ukrainian cause. In addition, reporting Russian atrocities against civilians in Bucha, a suburb of Kyiv, has increased Ukraine's soft power and reduced Russia's soft power. Not only has this resulted in sympathy towards Ukraine and its people, but it has also resulted in substantial contributions to the military effort. By using both soft and hard power – or smart power – Ukraine has given itself a chance to repel the Russian invasion.

Discussion points

When might it be necessary to combine hard and soft power? Provide an example from a current global politics issue.

What are the challenges or limitations in implementing smart power strategies?

TOK

Find media articles from different sources and showing different viewpoints about the war in Ukraine. Compare and contrast the articles in terms of how they seek to shape the narrative about the war, thereby exerting soft power in trying to shift the values and cultures of the views/readers/consumers of that media.

1.2.2 Further types of power

◼ Structural power

Structural power reflects the influence wielded by actors, often states or groups of states, but at times also includes influential corporations or international institutions. This power is exercised not necessarily by direct coercion or rewards but through the ability to shape and determine the structures of the global political system in a way that advances state interests. These could be strategic, economic or political. While it is a more subtle form of power when compared to military or economic power, it is deeply embedded within the frameworks that guide the interactions between state and non-state actors.

One central aspect of structural power is its ability to establish norms. For example, norms like sovereignty are key to the UN's structure. Principles like this profoundly influence the behaviour of member states. The same goes for the economic norms the World Trade Organization (WTO) or the International Monetary Fund (IMF) set out. By determining what is viewed as 'normal' or 'acceptable' in international relations – what Nye calls 'agenda-setting' – actors can guide the actions of other actors by referring to the structural norms. In summary, structural power sets the rules of the global politics game.

◼ Cyberpower

Cyberpower refers to using cyberspace to create advantages and influence events. Cyberspace includes the internet, computer networks, information technology and all our interconnected digital devices. Cyberpower can be seen in various forms, from cyber warfare to digital diplomacy and cyber espionage.

Many states now view cyberspace as a domain of warfare similar to traditional forms of warfare. Countries have developed cyber units to defend national infrastructures, gather intelligence and potentially disable the cyber infrastructures of those they are in conflict with. Cyberpower can also extend to non-state actors like terrorist groups, hacktivists and criminal gangs, who use it to disrupt services and steal information to further their goals.

Cyberpower is not limited to warfare, however. Cyber espionage has become a popular tool for states to gather intelligence on other state and non-state actors. It is cheaper and faster than traditional military and economic forms of warfare, and very difficult to catch those engaging in cyber espionage. For example, in 2023 China's Ministry of State Security said in a report that the US National Security Agency (NSA) carried out attacks on the servers of China's technology company Huawei in an effort to steal data.

The uneven distribution of cyber capabilities and access to digital resources can influence global political power dynamics. State and non-state actors with strong cyber capabilities can influence less digitally developed countries. As technology evolves and the world becomes more interconnected, the significance of cyberpower in international relations will only grow. Understanding this power dynamic is an increasingly important element of power in global politics.

Consider the effectiveness of hard, soft and smart power in the context of a current global political issue. Can you identify where one type of power might be more effective than the others?

ACTIVITY

Think of a situation in your own life or a recent event in the news where different types of power (hard, soft or smart) were evident. Write a brief analysis of the situation, identifying the types of power used and their effectiveness.

CASE STUDY

Use of cyberpower to create conflict

States use their cyberpower to manipulate opinions and create conflict in other states. This has implications for democratic processes and in recent years we have seen several alleged election interference campaigns.

Perhaps the most well-known instance was the 2016 US presidential election, which was characterized by a particularly polarized political divide. In January 2017, the US Intelligence Community released a report that concluded that Russian president Vladimir Putin had ordered a cyber-influencing campaign during the 2016 US presidential election. The report stated that the goals of the influencing campaign were to undermine the US election process, denigrate the Democratic presidential nominee, Hillary Clinton, and support the opposing Republican presidential candidate, Donald Trump.

To do this, Russian hackers were accused of infiltrating the Democratic Party's election committee's servers and leaking sensitive emails. The report also alleged social media manipulation. According to the report, the Internet Research Agency, a Russian company based in St Petersburg, shared politically divisive content on major social media platforms. It aimed to inflame already tense political conflict through ad campaigns and by creating fake accounts and pages that would be used to spread disinformation.

HL extension: Technology

Notions of cyberpower, cyberwarfare and cyber espionage could be excellent starting points for HL students to explore the global political challenge of Technology. Consider inquiring into its use by both state and nonstate actors. Choose a specific example and consider how they use it and why. The global political challenges of Borders and Security could also be linked to this inquiry.

Power-over, power-to, power-with

While Nye's notion of power is very popular within global politics, experts are starting to pay attention to the concepts of 'power-over', 'power-to' and 'power-with'. Power-over reflects an actor's relationship where one actor has power over another. Power-to involves the ability of an actor to carry out an act. In contrast, power-with is the ability of members of a group to work together to achieve a goal.

Mary Parker Follett was the first person to establish the notions of power-over and power-with. She described power-over and power-with as two opposite understandings of power, writing, 'So far as my observation has gone, it seems to me that whereas power usually means power-over, the power of some person or group over some other person or group, it is possible to develop the conception of power-with.' According to Follett, power-over should be understood as coercive while power-with is viewed as a cooperative, active form of power.

Interestingly, when Hannah Arendt considered power-over in her book *On Violence*, she suggested that every exercise of power of one person over another consists in a form of violence and should not be labelled as power. Instead, she argued that power deserves its name only when enacted as power-with.

The distinction between power-over and power-to was developed by Hanna Pitkin, who challenged the understanding of power as reflecting a social relationship and instead saw power as an ability. Pitkin saw the need to distinguish between situations where an actor has power over another actor, which occurs only when that actor gets the other to do something. Instead, she argued, there are situations in which an actor has the 'power to' accomplish something alone. She labelled this as power-to, the widely understood notion of power as 'being able to'.

These are not the only perspectives on power in the study of Global Politics. What is important is that you understand that power is the central component of this course. Whenever you are considering a political issue or global political challenge, you should return to the notion of power and consider how it is being used and manifesting itself in the context of your topic.

Chapter summary

In this chapter we have covered:
- power in global politics
- definitions and ways of understanding power
- classifications and types of power, including hard power, soft power, relational power, smart power, structural power, cyberpower, and power-over, power-to and power-with.

REVIEW QUESTIONS

Now that you have read this chapter, reflect on these questions:
- Define and differentiate between hard power, soft power and smart power. Provide real-world examples of how each type of power has been employed in global politics.
- Explain the distinction between resource power and relational power. How can a state possess many resources yet fail to exert significant influence in international affairs? Provide examples to support your explanation.
- Provide examples of how cultural and social power, such as language, education and shared values, can influence the behaviour of states and non-state actors in global politics.
- Explain how the concepts of structural power and cyberpower influence global politics. What do you think might be the long-term impact of cyberpower on global politics?
- How do the concepts of power-over, power-to and power-with challenge traditional understandings of power? Provide an example of each of the three forms of power.

■ **Figure 1.17** A painting of the peace treaties being signed between May and October 1648 in Osnabrück and Münster, Germany, ending the Thirty Years War

SYLLABUS CONTENT

By the end of this chapter, you should understand:
▶ traditional and modern notions of state sovereignty
▶ sources of sovereignty
▶ internal and external dimensions of sovereignty
▶ challenges to state sovereignty.

1.3.1 Traditional and modern notions of state sovereignty

Sovereignty is a key concept of the Global Politics course. It is essential that you understand this concept, as it relates to the global political issues of rights and justice, development, and peace and conflict. You should go beyond a 'dictionary understanding' of this concept and instead always be actively examining its significance in real-world examples as you make your way through this course. To begin, however, we should consider a basic definition of what we think of as 'sovereignty'.

Sovereignty is linked to the independence of a state. In our world today, states are supposed to have control over their territory and be able to provide an effective government for their residents.

● HL extension: Borders

Controlling the movement of people and goods across borders remains a top priority for most states. An interesting starting point for a case study about borders could be an examination of a particular state with challenging events taking place in relation to its borders. This closely links to the sovereignty of a state and border violations are a global political challenge with potentially wide-reaching implications both regionally and globally.

Some experts argue that the importance of sovereignty is declining as there are so many actors involved in modern global political issues. IGOs, civil society, private companies, social movements, resistance movements, formal and informal forums and the media all actively challenge the supremacy of the state in one way or another, some more forcefully than others.

Others argue that, although it may appear that the state's power and authority has weakened, this is just an illusion, as the state continues to have the final word on what happens within its own borders. States may join IGOs and seemingly cooperate with the demands of other actors, but, ultimately, the state is always working in its own best interest.

Concepts

Liberal and realist views on sovereignty

Liberals see that the world is becoming more interdependent and globalized. They therefore argue that sovereignty of the state has weakened.

Realists argue that the state remains the most important actor in global politics. They argue that sovereignty remains intact and states continue to exercise a great deal of control.

■ Peace of Westphalia

Where do our ideas about sovereignty and the role of the state come from? This question is complex, and students studying contemporary global politics should have some understanding of its origins. The Peace of Westphalia of 1648 is a good starting point to begin an examination of traditional and modern notions of state sovereignty.

The Peace of Westphalia was a collection of peace treaties that brought an end to a very violent and unsettling period in European history. The Thirty Years War was, in fact, a series of many wars throughout central Europe, during which different actors attempted to settle old disputes and gain territory. Like most peace treaties, Westphalia aimed to put measures in place to ensure that peace could be maintained.

After the Peace of Westphalia, old systems collapsed, and some argue a more modern concept of a nation state emerged. Whether that was a result of the treaties of Westphalia is debated, but when we read of 'Westphalian sovereignty' this is what is being referred to.

Two main principles were established by Westphalia. They provide a foundation to any definition of 'sovereignty':

1 States should have unchallenged control over what happens within their territory. Within the state, any other claims made by actors, such as cultural or religious groups, local governments or civil society, will always be secondary.

2 Globally, it is expected that all states respect the independence of each other and not, in any way, interfere with the internal workings of each other.

Historians will tell you that both of these principles have been frequently breached and that the ideals of the Treaty of Westphalia do not always match reality. Certainly the era of colonialism demonstrates that European states did not respect the principles of Westphalia in many places beyond the continent of Europe. However, despite this reality, the principles did take root and even today many see them as essential components of global politics.

Discussion point

Some experts claim that states are using the internet and social media to interfere with the internal affairs of other states. Can you think of any recent real-world examples that illustrate these concerns?

■ The colonial era

Although, as we have seen, the Treaty of Westphalia implies an acceptance of state sovereignty, in the centuries that followed many European countries did not define established societies located outside of the continent of Europe as 'states'. Therefore, they saw no reason to respect the independence of these places, resulting in the era of colonialism.

Colonialism can be defined as the domination and control of people or areas by an outside state or nation. This domination took two main forms:

● It sometimes involved the resettlement of people to the 'new' land, referred to as a 'colony' or a 'settlement' (as occurred in, for example, Canada, the United States, Australia and New Zealand). This is called a colony of settlement.

● It could also involve control over the economic and political systems of a society (as occurred in, for example, India, Democratic Republic of the Congo, Indonesia and Brazil). This is called a colony of rule.

We often see the word 'imperialism' mentioned alongside colonialism. Imperialism ordinarily refers to the European empires as a whole – both colonies of settlement and colonies of rule. Colonialism and imperialism are by nature exploitative and damaging, and the consequences of this period can be felt even today.

Concepts

Postcolonialism

Postcolonialism is a political viewpoint. It makes the claim that, just because the era of colonialism and European imperialism appears to be over, we are still experiencing its negative consequences, which continue to impact almost all aspects of daily life. Ideas of race, gender, class, education and politics continue to be shaped by a 'European' perspective, and non-Western perspectives are often seen as outside the global 'norm' and not treated with the same respect.

◉ TOK

Consider various political viewpoints as you study the historical events described in this chapter. Does it matter to your understanding of 'sovereignty' if you've applied a postcolonial viewpoint (prioritizing the negative effects of colonization on the indigenous or local populations)? Is there a 'neutral' way of exploring these important historical facts about the rise of the modern understanding of 'state'?

Self-determination and sovereignty re-examined

In the early twentieth century, particularly after the First World War, many people saw 'self-determination' as a pathway towards future peace.

Self-determination is closely related to sovereignty because it assumes that empires and colonies should be a thing of the past. No state should have the authority to take control of another. People should decide who they want to be their rulers.

By 1933, the only way to achieve self-determination was to be recognized as an independent state. The International Conference of American States took place in Montevideo, Uruguay in 1933. It represented states who had gained independence from colonizers. However, some felt uneasy and fearful that they could lose their independence unless they established clear criteria, and so they set about doing just that. The conference also hoped to inspire and support those who had not yet broken free from colonial rule.

As a result, they drew up a clear definition of the state. This convention has had a significant impact on our modern understanding of sovereignty.

■ **Figure 1.18** The countries that attended the Montevideo Convention

CORE: Understanding power and global politics

◆ **Genocide** refers to the deliberate killing of one ethnic, racial or religious group, with the aim of destroying that group.

◆ A **failed state** is a state that has lost the ability to govern but still has some sort of external sovereignty. There may be uncontrolled violence, government collapse and/or a general breakdown of systems within the state.

◆ A **rogue state** is a state threatening world peace and not cooperating with the international community.

Westphalia and Montevideo provide us with a fairly comprehensive explanation of traditional state sovereignty. As we have seen, a sovereign state has both rights and responsibilities. However, global politics is about contemporary global political issues, so how do these 'historical' documents impact our world today? For the most part, these traditional definitions of state sovereignty remain relevant today, despite facing increasing challenges in more recent years.

Modern notions of state sovereignty

While in the past it may have been widely accepted that states have a monopoly of power within their borders, this notion has been challenged as our world has become more globalized and interconnected (see Figure 1.19). It has been argued that a global era requires global engagement.

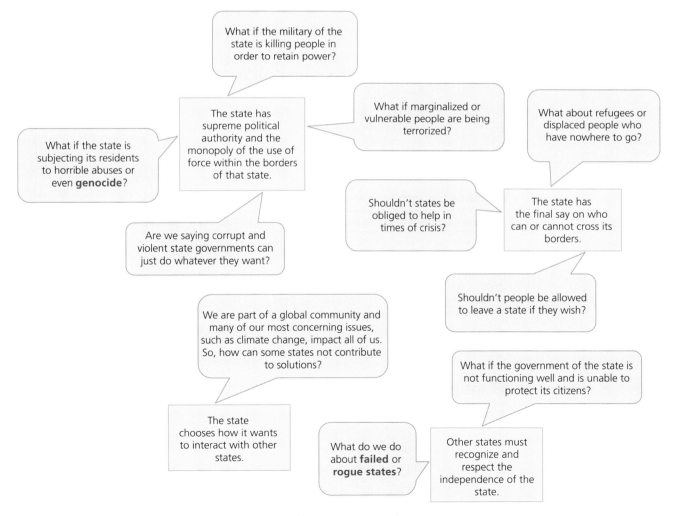

■ **Figure 1.19** Traditional notions of sovereignty and challenges to these notions

All of these challenges have led many to argue that traditional notions of sovereignty simply do not work in our modern political landscape.

Concepts

Social constructivism

Social constructivists would argue that the word 'sovereignty' itself depends very much upon the customs and practices of states and international systems. These can change over time and are flexible depending upon the unique circumstances of global political issues. They would argue that in the real world there is no set definition or meaning of sovereignty and there are many exceptions to this supposed global norm.

Discussion point

In what circumstances should international institutions such as the United Nations or more powerful states intervene with the internal affairs of another state?

This is not a question anyone can easily answer, and as you make your way through the IBDP Global Politics course you will see that this question arises frequently when looking at political issues involving rights and justice, development and sustainability, and peace and conflict. There are multiple actors, stakeholders and theories all offering varying perspectives you should consider.

1.3.2 Sources of sovereignty

Power is at the root of any discussion about sovereignty. How a state exercises its power and how all states interact with each other has much to do with this key concept.

■ The possession and use of force

Table 1.6 outlines the ways in which states use force to exert sovereignty.

■ **Table 1.6** The use of force within and against other states

The use of force within the state	The use of force against other states
The use of force is seen as a necessary component of state governance.	Most states maintain an armed force of some kind, but the use of force against other states is to be avoided.
Without the ability of the state to have the sole monopoly on the use of force, many argue that the state could not function and society would fall into chaos.	It is, however, generally agreed by the international community that, if a state suffers an armed attack by a foreign power, its sovereignty is breached, and in response the use of force could be justified.
States ordinarily have some sort of judicial system as well as one or several overarching national police forces. Depending on the size of the state there may be additional levels of police at the regional and local levels.	The idea of an armed attack is based on traditional ideas of warfare, which may or may not be present in modern conflicts.

■ International laws and norms

International laws are a set of agreements and treaties between different countries. States come together, often within the framework of an IGO such as the UN, and make rules they believe will be of benefit to all and preserve peace and security. These laws may evolve based on shifting global norms: what was once seen as a sovereign right of a state may now be seen differently, for example.

Because of sovereignty, no state can be forced to sign a treaty. They are free to accept or decline any international treaty or agreement. As you will see, international laws can be found in all of the thematic studies of the course, as they cover a wide variety of global political challenges.

International laws are meant to be **binding** so if a state has agreed to a law and then goes on to violate it, there will be consequences.

What do international laws normally cover?

International laws:

- attempt to maintain friendly and cooperative relations between states
- provide basic rights for all people
- attempt to solve international disputes and problems to prevent conflict
- limit the internal and external use of force
- attempt to regulate rules of trade and international shipping
- limit the development of weapons.

Discussion point

From the list above, can you see how international laws impact a wide range of political issues, including those associated with rights and justice, development and sustainability, and peace and conflict?

Is international law really law?

Some experts consider international law to be more of a moral code of conduct, but others strongly disagree and argue that states can and should face severe consequences for abuses. These consequences can include economic restrictions such as sanctions being placed on the state, and condemnation from other states. An example of economic sanctions and condemnation being imposed can be seen in the case of the EU openly condemning and imposing multiple economic sanctions against Russia, beginning in 2014.

The obstacle to the international community imposing more severe consequences for breaching international law is, of course, state sovereignty.

What is a global 'norm'?

A global norm is simply the shared expectations and understandings of states and other actors and stakeholders as to what is acceptable behaviour.

As we will see, global norms surrounding state sovereignty have been shifting and changing in recent decades. Many question the absolute authority of the state, particularly as the power and influence of other actors and stakeholders, such as IGOs, organized civil society, NGOs, private actors and companies, social movements, resistance movements, formal and informal forums and the media, continue to expand.

 TOK

How might the changing social and cultural beliefs of a population influence the changing political norms?

Global norms and understandings of 'sovereignty' change over time and have huge consequences. In what way do you think these changes have been influenced by 'non-political' (or at least not state-controlled) social and cultural values and beliefs?

You might consider how society is more aware of power-minorities or disadvantaged people or the institutionally disadvantaged, or the growing influence of social media or the internet to raise awareness of various injustices that might not have been widely known about in the past.

1.3.3 Internal and external dimensions of sovereignty

◼ Internal sovereignty

Internal sovereignty refers to the absolute authority of the state within its own borders. States that have strong internal sovereignty should have secure structures and systems of rule, which enable:

- the government of the state to have control over the people living within its borders
- the government to have the power to make decisions and enforce laws
- the peoples' acceptance of the authority of the state and its government.

Internal sovereignty is often seen as essential to having a well-functioning society, but in reality it might be difficult to find any state that has absolute internal sovereignty, since this implies absolute acceptance of the authority of the government.

Some may see democratic states as having more internal sovereignty than dictatorial ones because the people actively participate in the political process and elect their governments. And, although government decisions are frequently criticized and questioned in democracies, the mechanisms of the state and state authority would not be widely challenged if internal sovereignty is intact.

Concepts

Liberalism and internal sovereignty

Liberals believe that the people of a state must be in agreement with the will of the government in order to achieve internal sovereignty. The best way to achieve this is through the political system of democracy, in which people can actively participate in choosing the political leadership of their country.

In addition, liberals believe that any examination of internal sovereignty must consider the complex interactions of multiple actors and stakeholders, not simply the authority of the state government.

◼ External sovereignty

As the name suggests, this kind of sovereignty looks at the wider picture. External sovereignty refers to the ability of the state to act independently when dealing with actors and states from outside of its borders. It is the power a state has when interacting with other states and actors.

How do economics and the balance of power impact external sovereignty?

A quick glance at real-world global interactions clearly shows that some countries are perceived as being more powerful than others, and it could be said that they have great external sovereignty. Power is often measured in terms of a state's wealth and military strength. It is argued that these attributes allow powerful states to prioritize their own interests over that of others even within the context of our more globalized world.

A state-centric model of global politics (realist) sees states as independent and autonomous much like a series of balls, some more powerful than others. They may or may not collide with each other as they maintain a precarious but essential balance of power (see Figure 1.20). This theory is sometimes referred to as the Billiard Ball model.

Discussion point

To what extent do you agree that the wealthiest states have the strongest external sovereignty? What other factors strengthen external sovereignty?

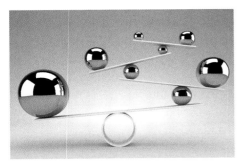

■ **Figure 1.20** Realists claim a delicate balance of power must be maintained between powerful and less powerful states to prevent conflict and crisis, much like the balance demonstrated here

1.3.4 Challenges to state sovereignty

■ Challenges to the monopoly of the use of force

When there is widespread and unrestricted violence within a state, sometimes caused by resistance groups, criminal gangs or terrorism, the state has clearly lost its monopoly on the use of violence. This kind of unchecked violence is without doubt at odds with the most fundamental responsibility and duty of the state to control violence and protect its people. In cases in which states have lost the capacity to control violence, it is not unusual that the government is unable to provide essential services to its people, such as policing, health care, education and sanitation. This often forces people to seek alternate forms of authority who they feel can at least help them with day-to-day necessities and governance. These alternate forms of authority may operate locally, regionally or even nationally, and they further erode the internal sovereignty of the state.

CASE STUDY

Somalia

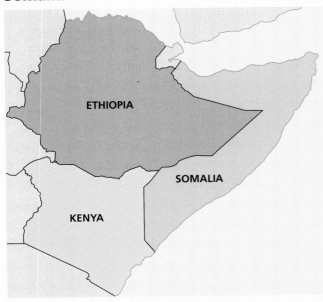

■ **Figure 1.21** Somalia, Ethiopia and Kenya

From the 1980s onward Somalia has been considered by many to be a failed state. Civil war, violent resistance movements and uncontrolled inflation all undermined the legitimacy of the central government. The United States and Ethiopia were two foreign states actively supporting the existing government during this period and this continues to the present day.

In 2006, al-Shabaab, a violent resistance movement, seized control over large areas of Somalia after the central government was unable to govern these areas effectively. The United States, long a supporter of the government of Somalia, began air strikes against al-Shabaab in 2007. By 2011 the group controlled parts of the capital city Mogadishu and, as a result, the African Union sent armed troops to Somalia under the African Union Mission in Somalia (ANISOM) to help restore the internal sovereignty of the Somali government. Neighbouring state Kenya, concerned about the threat al-Shabaab posed to its own interests, also sent troops. In response, al-Shabaab lost some of its controlled territory but also launched attacks against military and civilian targets in Kenya, killing hundreds.

As of 2023 al-Shabaab continues to conduct attacks both within Somalia and neighbouring countries.

ANISOM, the UN, Kenya, Ethiopia, the United States and other actors continue to work against them. The people of Somalia have suffered enormously for several decades of Somali turmoil. In addition, from 2022 to 2023 the worst drought in 40 years resulted in widespread famine, causing a crisis of severe malnutrition and death.

Discussion points

Review all you have learned about traditional notions of state sovereignty. In what ways does Somalia not meet the criteria of a sovereign state?

Increased global interdependence has meant there are many actors involved in this crisis. Who are the other actors either attempting to challenge or attempting to restore Somalia's internal sovereignty?

Extended essay

If you are interested in examining modern-day challenges to traditional notions of state sovereignty, a good place to start would be to investigate specific example(s) of how increased global interdependence has meant a wide variety of state and non-state actors frequently challenge the internal sovereignty of states in crisis. A good extended essay must consider multiple perspectives, and always discuss your ideas and potential research questions with your extended essay supervisor.

◼ Supranationality

Today, we can find many states working together as part of larger groups or collectives. Earlier in this chapter you were introduced to IGOs, which play a significant role at both the regional and international level of global politics. When states agree to join an IGO they are agreeing to work together with other states and come to collective decisions. The term 'supranationality' means that IGO institutions make decisions as a group. Individual state members may disagree with the majority in such circumstances, but the will of the institution will prevail. Therefore, an IGO by its nature is 'supranational', meaning 'over or above' individual states and, to a certain extent, joining one challenges the sovereignty of the state.

Why would states agree to give up some degree of sovereignty in order to join a supranational institution? Clearly they believe that the benefits outweigh the disadvantages (see Table 1.7).

Table 1.7 Commonly perceived benefits for states joining an IGO

Economic	Political	Security
A group of states that work together as a single market can be more efficient economically. The easy movement of goods, services and workers can benefit all.	Countries banding together can be perceived as more powerful and have a greater say in global political issues compared with single states acting independently.	States in an IGO are perceived as a united group and less vulnerable than isolated states.

Discussion point

In our globalized and interconnected world, a state operating in isolation is an anomaly and ordinarily signals something is wrong. Almost all states belong to one or more IGOs. Other than economic, political and security advantages, what are some other possible reasons a state might join an IGO despite the risk of losing some sovereignty? Do some online research to make sure your flag knowledge is up to date.

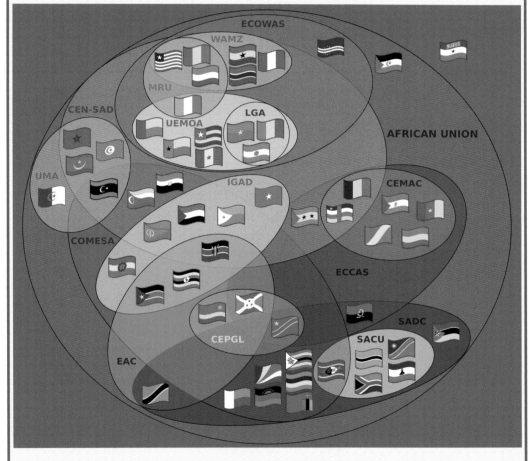

Figure 1.22 Some of the regional supranational organizations active in Africa

Supranational groups

Supranational groups are extensive and cover a wide variety of organizations. Many states belong to multiple supranational groups, as each may be perceived as offering unique advantages.

As you can see in Figure 1.22, most African states see that the advantages to joining regional IGOs outweigh any kind of reduction of sovereignty. These states are also members of many international IGOs not shown in the figure.

However, it is worth noting that states do sometimes distance themselves or remove themselves completely from IGOs due to perceptions that their sovereignty has been unacceptably diminished. One such case was when the UK voted to leave the EU in 2016, often referred to as 'Brexit'.

Perspectives

Rishi Sunak on Brexit

In 2016, the UK prime minister Rishi Sunak was quoted as saying that the UK would be better off if they left the European Union because they would be able to control their own immigration policies and justice systems as well as prosper economically.

Discussion point

According to Prime Minister Sunak, in what ways did belonging to the EU directly impact the UK's sovereignty?

◼ Indigenous land claims

◆ **Indigenous** refers to a person or people living in an area or a land from the earliest times, before the arrival of colonists.

Indigenous people are people who have lived in an area of land for a very long period of time. Over the course of centuries the land they lived on may have been taken over by other groups, who then created states and borders, usually without the informed consent of the earlier inhabitants.

● HL extension: Identity

There are many groups of people who are marginalized and treated unfairly because of their identity and in recent decades more and more people are standing up for equal rights. A good starting point for a global political challenge case study would be to examine how a specific group has challenged norms and brought about positive changes for its community.

There is growing recognition that advancing indigenous peoples' collective rights to lands, territories and resources not only contributes to their well-being but also to the greater good of the wider society by tackling problems such as climate change and the loss of biodiversity.

However, this is an obvious challenge to state sovereignty. Traditional definitions of state sovereignty assume that, within the state, any other claims made by actors, such as cultural or religious groups, local governments or civil society, will always be secondary to that of the state. As evidence that traditional notions of state sovereignty are evolving, it can be seen that many states have acknowledged that indigenous people have special claims to land ownership and use.

Indigenous people were directly impacted by colonialism as their lands and autonomy were taken from them. The group in Figure 1.23 are demanding we 'End Co$_2$lonialism'. Why do you think they have included a subscript '2' in the word 'Colonialism'?

■ **Figure 1.23** Indigenous people gather to protest at a climate march in New York City, 2014

Key theorist

Frantz Fanon (1925–61)

Frantz Fanon was a political philosopher and Marxist from Martinique, then under French colonial rule, whose works significantly influenced later Marxist and postcolonialist theories. In his book *The Wretched of the Earth* (1961) he details the suffering of the people who were colonized:

> *For a colonized people the most essential value, because the most concrete, is first and foremost the land: the land which will bring them bread and, above all, dignity.*

According to the UN Permanent Forum on Indigenous Issues, a global recognition of the land rights of indigenous people is improving:

- Although 20 per cent of land in Australia is owned by indigenous people, it tends to be in remote areas and is not particularly desirable.
- In Indonesia, indigenous communities who had been prevented from living in traditional forest lands were given greater access to these lands in 2013.

■ **Figure 1.24** Frantz Fanon

- In New Zealand, Maori people retained collective and individual rights over their traditional lands, forests and fishing rights.
- In Panama, five regions were recognized as being the lands of indigenous people.

We will explore indigenous rights in more detail in Section 2.

Extended essay

If you are interested in examining how indigenous land claims challenge traditional notions of state sovereignty it might be a good idea to begin by investigating claims made by specific indigenous groups in your own country or region. Remember, though, a good extended essay must consider multiple perspectives, and always discuss your ideas and potential research questions with your extended essay supervisor.

■ **Figure 1.25** Poster advertising the theatre production *The Melting Pot*, United States, 1916

■ Transnational cultural groups

Nationalism refers to a state where people have a strong belief and support for their nation. Residents of this kind of state often share a common language, history and a unified cultural identity. Nationalism is not necessarily negative, but it is often associated with a sense of arrogance and superiority, as states with a strong sense of nationalism usually put their own interests first, and this can lead to conflict. Historically, migrants moving into a state with a strong sense of nationalism were expected to 'fit in' and adopt the characteristics of that nation as quickly as possible in order to be accepted.

The 'melting pot'

The idea that new migrants joined a 'melting pot' in the United States was used as a metaphor for many years to explain American identity. In this scenario, migrants prioritize becoming American and their own languages, beliefs and culture become secondary characteristics. The children of these migrants normally abandoned the 'old ways' and therefore, theoretically, the unified 'national identity' remained intact.

The same situation can be seen in states where the unique cultural identities of migrants are de-emphasized and even actively discouraged.

◆ **Knowledge communities** are a group of people who share similar knowledge, beliefs, assumptions or opinions.

 TOK

The 'melting pot' is a powerful metaphor that gives people a way to think about how people, with their different identities and **knowledge communities** (including languages and practices), can share a vision of who they are at the national level. However, the metaphor de-emphasizes people's 'local' identities, and this is by design. But are all identities or cultures or cultural practices equally de-prioritized?

The question of what the 'national culture' looks like after this metaphorical process of 'melting together' has occurred is a challenging one, but one that sits at the heart of many of the social struggles within nations. How might educational institutions, 'official languages', forms of government and political ideologies actually prioritize a particular population within the 'melting pot', rather than equally de-emphasize particular cultures or knowledge communities in favour of a clear 'national identity'?

Transnationalism today

We live in a very different world in the twenty-first century, and ideas about the importance of nationalism are changing. Globalization and interdependence have made travel and migration much more commonplace. Additionally, access to the internet has made staying in contact with family, friends and associates from around the world easier. Transnationalism, as opposed to nationalism, can refer to migrants who maintain strong ties with their heritage and culture, while transnational cultural groups are groups of people who share a common sense of identity, values or culture but live in more than one state.

Are transnational groups a threat to state sovereignty?

Some experts argue that transnational groups are a threat to state sovereignty because residents of a country who have strong ties with religious groups, political events and cultural traditions of another place may not prioritize the interests of the state they currently live in. Traditional definitions of state sovereignty assume that within the state any other claims made by actors such as cultural or religious groups will always be secondary to that of the state. Therefore, the supremacy of the state could be potentially challenged by transnational cultural groups.

> **Discussion point**
>
> Based on what you have learned about realism so far, do you think realists see transnational cultural groups as threatening to state sovereignty? Why or why not?

As evidence to support this claim, some experts refer to violent transnational groups, such as Islamic State, which directly challenged the sovereignty of multiple states including Iraq, Syria, Yemen, Somalia and Libya. Additionally, by using propaganda and social media, Islamic State was able to recruit people from all over the world, many of whom belonged to transnational cultural groups.

The alternative perspective is that it's useless to try to hold on to rigid and old-fashioned principles of state sovereignty, which simply don't work in our interdependent globalized world. Liberalism emphasizes that transnationalism is almost always beneficial to all states as it leads to more diverse and vibrant societies and a stronger sense of living in a global community, thereby decreasing the likelihood of conflict. Liberals would argue that violent transnational groups such as Islamic State are extremely rare and not in any way typical. Therefore, the benefits far outweigh any risk.

■ Transnational companies

Transnational companies (TNCs), often referred to as multinational companies (MNCs), are companies that originated in one country but grew to have business operations in two or more additional countries. Some people argue that in our globalized world certain large TNCs are more powerful than state actors and are a direct threat to traditional notions of state sovereignty.

Transnational technology and media companies

Transnational companies with a focus on technology, such as Facebook/Meta, YouTube and Google, have immense authority and power. Sometimes the information found on social media platforms directly challenges government decisions and undermines the control the government has over the people living within a state's borders. This arguably diminishes the internal sovereignty of the state. Depending on the situation, though, some might argue that these challenges to the internal sovereignty of the state are beneficial, particularly if they connect and motivate people to make positive changes in their society.

> **Discussion point**
>
> How does the reliance of states on technology companies to monitor information challenge traditional notions of state sovereignty?

However, in recent years misinformation has been deliberately spread on multiple social media platforms with the goal of influencing elections at the national, sub-national and local government levels, and causing division and unrest in society. In response, states have had to rely on these same transnational technology companies to monitor and screen deliberately misleading and untruthful content. States are therefore shown to be reliant on the transnational technology companies to control the spread of misinformation, as they are unable to stop this themselves.

The immense wealth and power of TNCs

In 2019, transnational technology company Microsoft pledged $500 million to provide affordable housing to the people of Seattle, Washington. This is an example of a company taking on the responsibility of what, ordinarily, would be considered the sovereign responsibility of the state, and some would see this as a direct challenge to traditional notions of state sovereignty.

Some TNCs have a great deal of financial resources. One way to measure this is to look at the **gross domestic product (GDP)** of states and compare them with the **market cap** of TNCs. For example, Amazon's market cap is higher than the GDP of most countries in the world (Wallach).

◆ **Gross domestic product (GDP)** is the value of goods and services produced in a country in one year.

◆ The **market cap** refers to the total value of a company's shares of stock.

■ **Table 1.8** Countries with GDPs closest to Amazon's market cap

Amazon	$1.7 trillion
South Korea	$1.6 trillion
Australia	$1.4 trillion
Spain	$1.4 trillion
Mexico	$1.3 trillion
Indonesia	$1.1 trillion
Netherlands	$907 billion
Saudi Arabia	$793 billion
Turkey	$761 billion
Switzerland	$703 billion

With immense wealth comes power, and many TNCs are directly involved in the economies of less economically developed countries. Some of the positive outcomes of the involvement may include:

- providing employment
- contributing to community development projects
- providing industrial training to youth
- strengthening the local economy
- providing emergency assistance to disaster survivors
- environmental protection
- staff development
- providing the state with valuable tax revenue.

As a result, many states are willing to allow these kinds of TNCs to operate within their borders. For many there are clear benefits to this, as long as the state does not interfere with the process.

Are transnational corporations a threat to state sovereignty?

The extent to which TNCs challenge state sovereignty is debatable. If states willingly allow TNCs to operate freely within their borders some would say this does not challenge the sovereignty of the state.

However, others argue that the immense wealth of some TNCs enables them to get state governments to make changes to national laws and policies that favour the operations of the TNC. In particular, there are concerns that some TNCs exploit the human rights of workers and, as it is the responsibility of the state to protect its citizens, this could be seen as a challenge to sovereignty.

Ultimately, all TNCs are motivated by profit. Therefore, many experts question the true motivation of these companies when they invest in less economically developed states. Regardless of whether TNCs do more good than harm, we can agree that they challenge a 'state-centric' world view of global politics and traditional notions of state sovereignty.

We will look at different approaches and models of development more fully in Section 3 on development and sustainability.

ACTIVITY

Go to the UN Sustainable Development website and read 'What difference can a multinational make?' by Marcos Neto, October 2019: **www.undp.org/blog/what-difference-can-multinational-make**

Neto is claiming that 'internal barriers' are preventing MNCs from doing a lot of amazing things that will help low-income communities. To what extent do you think these 'internal barriers' are linked to internal sovereignty?

■ **Figure 1.26** Marcos Neto, director of the Sustainable Development Hub, UN Development Programme

Chapter summary

In this chapter we have covered:
- the nature of state sovereignty, which is rooted in historical treaties that outline both the characteristics and duties of a state
- how The Treaty of Westphalia and the Montevideo Convention helped to establish several characteristics of a state that are still considered relevant today
- the multiple challenges to state sovereignty in our increasingly interdependent world, including internal (for example, nationalist movements, indigenous land claims) and external (for example, TNCs, media or interference from other states)
- the extent to which norms of sovereignty are evolving and changing.

REVIEW QUESTIONS

Now that you have read this chapter, reflect on these questions:
- Write your own definition of state sovereignty using both the Treaty of Westphalia and the Montevideo Convention.
- What is the difference between an international law and an international norm?
- What are the main challenges to state sovereignty?
- What is an example of a violent non-state actor actively threatening state sovereignty?

Legitimacy in global politics

1.4

By the end of this chapter, you should understand:
▶ sources of state legitimacy
▶ challenges to state and government legitimacy
▶ sources of legitimacy of non-state actors
▶ legitimation processes and the loss of legitimacy of political actors.

1.4.1 What is state legitimacy?

◆ **Legitimacy** refers to conformity to the law or to rules.

In its simplest form, state **legitimacy** means people accept the state's right to rule over them. However, legitimacy involves more than complying or simply deferring to those in power.

Concepts

Legitimacy

Legitimacy refers to an actor or an action that is commonly considered acceptable to a population. It provides the fundamental rationale for all forms of governance and other ways of exercising power.

The most accepted contemporary form of state legitimacy is some form of democracy or constitutionalism, whereby the governed have a defined and periodic opportunity to choose who governs and exercises power. In states where this is not the norm, other sources of legitimacy might be expressed, such as hereditary or traditional leadership.

Within any proposed framework of legitimacy, individual actions by a state can be considered legitimate to a greater or lesser extent. Other actors in global politics, and their behaviour, can also be evaluated from the perspective of legitimacy. Evaluation can be based on the acceptance or recognition these actors are given by others in exercising certain roles or taking specific decisions.

When governments have legitimacy, they can usually overcome periods of dissatisfaction because there is a belief by members of the population that those in power are competent and will fix the problems or that they came to power through a legitimate process and have the right to rule. There is an underlying belief that those in power will seek to do better or, if it is a democracy, citizens will change those in power. In this case, legitimacy lies with the system and a belief that, if those in power underperform, the legitimate system will allow them to make changes. Even though there is frustration with the performance of a group or individual, citizens continue to comply with societal norms because they see the system as legitimate.

Legitimacy matters because there is likely to be conflict and disorder without it. States aim to create structure and orderliness for society (to varying degrees of success). Conflict and chaos will likely result if we do not agree to grant the state legitimacy. There will be times when citizens withdraw their consent to the legitimacy of a state, but that will vary depending on economic and political stability and cultural and social norms. If there is a constant withdrawal of the granting of legitimacy, the development of a state is likely to suffer.

■ Core elements of legitimacy

Citizens believe the state has the right to rule

Citizens are central to legitimacy because they have the numbers. There is always more of them than those in power. Throughout history, states have successfully suppressed citizens when they are unhappy. However, there have also been many instances of citizens who, despite facing violent risks, reject the legitimacy of both rules and systems and demand something better. In short, legitimacy does not operate independently of citizens' beliefs. While not all citizens have equal capacity to confer legitimacy, they must be satisfied that the government is capable and justified in charge of the state.

Legitimacy beliefs have their origins in social values

■ **Figure 1.27** A mother brings her baby to a routine vaccination at a health centre in Uttar Pradesh, India. States gain legitimacy through having functioning institutions, such as good health care

Any power arrangement must appeal to an underlying norm. Those in power must govern according to society's values. For example, some members of states tend to value freedoms, while others value collective social security, while still others value a religious ethic. States lose legitimacy when they fail to rule in a way that aligns with the social norms (generally speaking) of the state they govern.

While some experts agree with the idea that legitimacy stems from a state that reflects society's ideas and values of its citizens, others argue that legitimacy comes from functioning institutions. This could be a free and fair electoral system or providing good education and health care. Sometimes, the provision of quality institutions is not valued because people may not expect quality institutions from the state – the state has never provided quality institutions, so they simply do not expect that from the state.

Legitimacy determines how people behave towards the state

Suppose the government oversees unfairness or a deterioration in the standard of living. In that case, they are likely to be seen as illegitimate and should be replaced democratically or via rebellion and protest. In contrast, when citizens cooperate and do not resist the government's actions, this is a sign of legitimacy. Legitimacy makes citizens more likely to defer to the decisions and rules of those in power because they are considered fair. It also means that the capacity of states to preside over economic and social development increases. Legitimacy brings stability within society and in how people behave. When it breaks down, so do the stability and order of society.

Legitimation is a continuous process

No matter the governing system that is in place, leaders use the resources they have available to them to create and maintain the perception of legitimacy. This could be done through a variety of tools, such as the media, infrastructure projects, decreases in taxation and social services.

Sources of state legitimacy

There are no standard ways states gain legitimacy, and so there are several ways to look at sources of legitimacy. In this section, we will examine several of these ways for you to consider as you explore the notion of legitimacy.

The descriptions in this first section are largely framed in the positive: if these things are demonstrated, they will achieve legitimacy. However, the opposite is also true: if they fail to demonstrate or are not in line with the descriptions below, leaders or governments will fail to achieve legitimacy.

History and tradition

History in the form of tradition is a source of legitimacy as it sets norms and expectations for what is deemed acceptable. For example, monarchies often derive their authority from tradition and lineage. The role of history is continuity: if a monarchical dynasty has been in power for generations, their reign is seen as the natural order and provides a strong foundation for continued acceptance of the traditional or even natural order of things.

Ideology

Ideology is another source of legitimacy. Governments that have legitimacy through shared beliefs and values of the electorate draw their legitimacy from their ideological underpinnings. Citizens will rally behind leaders who share, uphold and advocate shared ideologies.

Growth and development

When governments can demonstrate economic growth, creation of jobs and a rise in the standard of living, they reinforce their legitimate status. People often equate economic success with competent leadership.

Similarly, and somewhat linked to ideology, governments that consider economic growth and social and environmental development can bolster legitimacy through long-term planning and concern for comprehensive societal well-being. Really, any effective leadership in areas such as these, as well as law enforcement, judicial proceedings, infrastructure, education and health care, will grow legitimacy

Leadership, international recognition and identity

Leaders who demonstrate effective and competent decision-making are respected, appreciated, supported and admired.

In addition, competent leadership in the international arena can also foster legitimacy when that leader is recognized and respected by other states. This might be done by cooperating with other states as part of international institutions.

Alternatively, leaders taking a stand or refusing to cooperate can add to their legitimacy at home: 'They won't be pushed around' or 'They stand up for our country' can help build legitimacy capital. This helps foster a strong sense of national identity and pride. Similarly, promoting culture, language or shared values within a country can also lead to greater legitimacy.

Freedom and fairness

Citizens expect accountability and transparency. When both exist, they bring legitimacy, and when citizens see or perceive that the government is corrupt and the cause of unfairness, that legitimacy quickly disappears.

Related to this is the principle of free and fair elections, which is fundamental in democratic societies. When citizens feel this is occurring, it can be a source of legitimacy. It assures citizens that their voice matters and they have a genuine role in the political process. However, on the other hand, a free and fair electoral system may add no extra legitimacy if this is the expectation.

Order and stability

Order and stability are essential, especially, but not only, in volatile regions. Even if some of the sources of legitimacy we listed above are lacking within a state, a government that can maintain peace, order and societal stability often earns a type of legitimacy from its citizens

---

Discussion point

Considering the various sources of state legitimacy, which source do you believe is the most important for maintaining state legitimacy?

Perspectives

Max Weber's conception of legitimacy

The basis of every system of authority, and correspondingly of every kind of willingness to obey, is a belief, a belief by virtue of which persons exercising authority are lent prestige.

Max Weber, The Theory of Social and Economic Organization

Max Weber (1864–1920) was a German sociologist, historian, lawyer and political economist. His statement regarding legitimacy highlights two critical elements: those who have the power of authority are granted this power by those they have power over. This may be given or accepted but, either way, unless those under the authority of those in power wish to challenge that power, they concede power to those in authority.

ACTIVITY

Choose a country and identify the primary source(s) of its legitimacy. Explain how this source has contributed to the stability and effectiveness of its government or, in contrast, its instability and ineffectiveness.

Legitimacy, then, refers to people's beliefs about political authority and, sometimes, political obligations.

Weber further explained that there are three main sources of legitimacy:

1 **Tradition:** there can be legitimacy because of tradition. The political or social order has existed for a long time, and members of society either grant it legitimacy simply because 'it has always been there' or because they have faith that the system ought to be the way it is.

2 **Charisma:** legitimacy can be a result of charismatic rulers. Members of society have faith in their capacity to rule because they are drawn to the leader and the leader's ability to rule effectively.

3 **Rational:** legitimacy may be granted to a political system because there is trust in its legality. Power has been legitimately acquired through a system that reflects the rule of law. A rational system further achieves legitimacy through three factors:

   i   an effective legal system where the rule of law is the norm

   ii an efficient and effective government system that meets the population's needs

   iii those in power are competent, capable and, as a result, can administer the political systems effectively.

■ **Figure 1.28** The rule of law is intertwined with the concept of legitimacy

The rule of law

The rule of law means that everyone is under or subject to the law. No member of society is above the law; no one can ignore the law without consequences. Everyone, from a common citizen to the highest government official, is subject to the same legal standards, fostering a sense of fairness and consistency. The rule of law is a safeguard against tyranny. Setting legal limits on what the government or any individual can and cannot do protects individuals from potential oppression.

The rule of law is intertwined with the concept of legitimacy. A system that does not maintain the rule of law will likely be unpredictable and unjust. This often erodes legitimacy and may ultimately result in a challenge to those in power who are aiming to ignore the law.

Discussion point

Discuss Weber's three main sources of legitimacy and provide a current example of each.

■ Input and output legitimacy

It has been suggested that input and output legitimacy are strong indicators of how states might gain legitimacy (Mcloughlin).

● Input or process legitimacy reflects how the state acquires power. The perceived fairness of the electoral system is a key indicator of when people will grant legitimacy.

● Output or performance legitimacy reflects how well the state exercises its power. The fulfilment of everyday well-being, including providing security and justice, is widely considered a key way the state can earn the right to rule.

Alternatively, output legitimacy could reflect the state effectively protecting the perceived identity or the standards of the majority religion.

Either way, the more effectively the state delivers on expectations – and performs well – the more legitimacy it will have.

ACTIVITY

Investigate a recent political event (for example, an election or a policy implementation) in a country of your choosing. Assess whether it demonstrates any issue of input or output legitimacy. Explain why.

▪ Top-down and bottom-up legitimacy

Top-down legitimacy is rooted in the idea that authority and legitimacy originate from a central authority or institution and flow towards the population, rather than emerging from the majority population. Typically, it is associated with hierarchical or centralized systems of governance. This might be a monarch, a religious figure, or a single leader or party. Decisions and policies originate from the central authority with little to no input from citizens.

Top-down legitimacy

For top-down legitimacy to remain unchallenged, the authorities achieve control through:

- the flow of information
- the suppression of dissent
- the creation of legal structures that concentrate power in the hands of the few.

This approach may ensure quick decision-making and fewer bureaucratic barriers to taking action on almost all issues. Of course, it also means limiting individual freedoms and rights. Also, decisions may end up being out of touch with the population's needs.

Sometimes, a top-down approach achieves legitimacy because citizens are simply resigned to there being no better alternative. Furthermore, they might believe that they would be worse off under a different system. This may mean they prefer a strong state capable of stamping out opposition because otherwise society would be chaotic.

A prime example of top-down legitimacy is Saudi Arabia. The Saudi government is a monarchy, where power is centralized in the hands of the royal family. Decisions and policies are predominantly made by the ruling monarch and his appointed officials, with limited input or participation from the general public. The legitimacy of the government is largely derived from traditional and religious authority, with the monarch seen as a guardian of Islamic traditions. This top-down approach allows for swift decision making and maintains social order, but it also limits public participation in governance.

Bottom-up legitimacy

On the other hand, bottom-up legitimacy originates through participation from the broader population and provides political power agency to a broad spectrum of society. This type of legitimacy is found in democratic systems where governance and power are born out of representation and participation. Participation can come from referendums, open forums and elections.

Bottom-up legitimacy tends to be more responsive to societal needs, as legitimacy is based on meeting the needs of the public. It demands transparency and accountability from elected officials and institutions.

However, one criticism of bottom-up legitimacy is that there is a risk of a so-called 'tyranny of the majority', through which dominant groups might overshadow minority interests. For example, if the majority of the population feels as though same-sex couples should not be permitted marriage rights, the majority impact negatively the legal rights of a minority group.

New Zealand is a good example of bottom-up legitimacy. It operates as a parliamentary democracy where the government is elected by the people. The legitimacy of the New Zealand government is rooted in its democratic process, where citizens have a significant say in governance through regular, free and fair elections. The government's policies are often responsive to the needs and opinions of the country's residents, and there is a strong emphasis on transparency and accountability with the government. This approach ensures that the legitimacy of the government is continually renewed and maintained through public participation and representation.

So, while there are a number of ways in which we can consider how legitimacy is established, it can be generally suggested that states are legitimate when citizens accept the right of the state to make decisions. Part of this agreement includes obeying these decisions, or they will face consequences. Many of these consequences would also be established by the state.

As we have seen, the reasons why citizens may accept a state's legitimacy to coerce them can vary significantly. It does seem, however, that legitimacy comes from bringing order to social relations and possibly the political process.

> ### Discussion point
>
> Analyse the strengths and weaknesses of both bottom-up and top-down approaches to legitimacy. Which approach do you think is more effective and why?

▪ Justification of coercive power as legitimacy

Another perspective on sources of legitimacy is that an actor is only legitimate if it can reasonably justify its coercive power. This could be thought of in two ways:

- First, the system that is in place is seen as legitimate. Those in power can then justify their legitimacy by pointing to the legitimacy of the system. By doing this, they can argue that they can now create laws that coerce the population.
- This leads to the second justification for coercion. The authorities, those creating the laws or demanding the population do as instructed, must convince the population that the laws and requirements created are reasonable.

An alternative view is that those in power do not need to justify the legitimacy of the system that granted them power or justify the laws they create. Instead, as long as members of society obey the laws created, they are legitimate.

Other experts, like Phillip Pettit, suggest that neither a legitimate system nor obedience is enough for state legitimacy. Instead, a state is legitimate only if it imposes a social order that promotes freedom and 'non-domination' for all its citizens. It is legitimate if it appropriately imposes a social order.

▪ Legitimation processes

As we have noted, the source of legitimacy can be related to the legitimation process itself. We have already seen some of the ways in which authoritarian states can gain legitimacy. Now we will look at some of the processes of the democratic methods of legitimacy.

Representative democracy

Representative democracy is a system where citizens elect representatives to make decisions on their behalf rather than being part of all the many decisions enacted in a state. Legitimacy in representative democracies comes from the mandate given by the electorate through regular, free and fair elections. By choosing their representatives, citizens trust them to act in their best interest. The periodic elections ensure accountability, as representatives who fail to deliver can be voted out. This process ensures that those in power remain accountable to the people, so upholding the democratic system's legitimacy.

The main types of representative democracies are presidential and parliamentary systems:

Presidential system

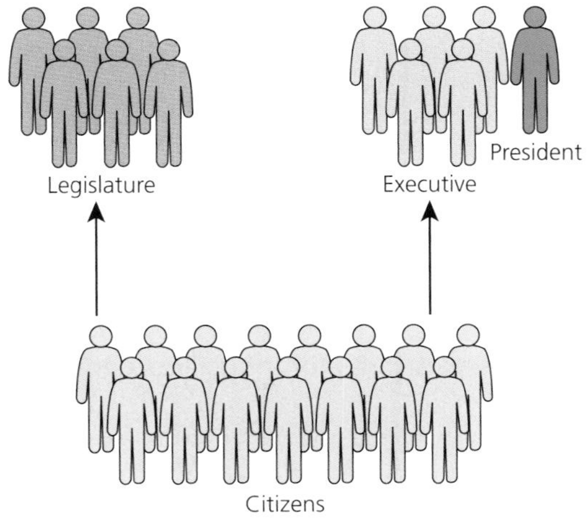

Legislature

Executive

President

Citizens

In a presidential or republic system, the executive exists separately from the legislature and the majority of representatives create and vote on laws. The president, who heads the executive, is elected independently of the legislature and is the head of state and the government, for example the United States and Brazil.

Parliamentary system

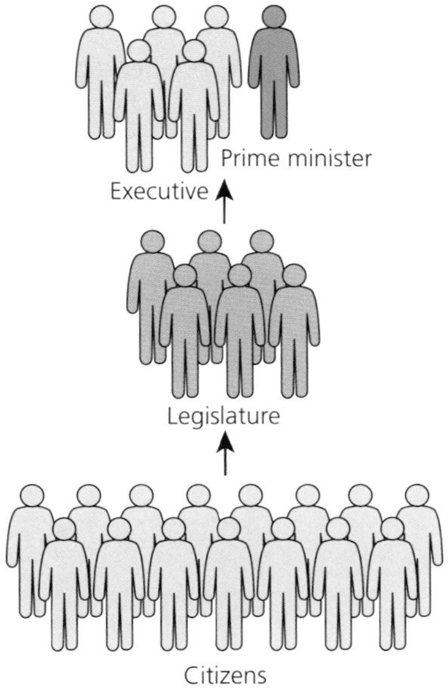

Prime minister

Executive

Legislature

Citizens

In a parliamentary system, the executive is accountable to the legislature. The head of government (often referred to as the prime minister) is typically a member of the political party with a majority in the legislature, while the head of state might be a monarch (in constitutional monarchies), for example the UK and Canada, or a president (in parliamentary republics), for example India.

■ **Figure 1.29** The presidential and parliamentary systems

There is also a hybrid of the two systems explained above. This system combines elements of both presidential and parliamentary systems. It has a president elected by the public and a prime minister who is responsible to the legislature. The president is the head of state, while the prime minister, often from the legislative majority, is the head of government, for example France or Finland.

Citizens' assemblies

While not a system unto itself, some systems employ citizens' assemblies. They are a deliberative democracy where citizens are brought together to discuss and recommend specific political or social issues. These assemblies are typically designed to reflect a representative population sample through random selection or stratified sampling, where subgroups are created based on their shared characteristics (race, gender, educational attainment, etc.). The assembly members meet to learn about the experts, discuss the issues and then develop recommendations. Facilitators are in place to guide the discussions to ensure they remain productive and inclusive.

Several countries have used citizen assemblies including:

- **Spain:** the assembly met in Madrid to discuss city planning and urban issues to help redesign areas of the city
- **Belgium:** the region of Ostbelgien established a permanent citizens' assembly in 2019 to make recommendations to its parliament.

CASE STUDY

Legitimacy indices

Several indices evaluate the levels of democracy in states across the world. These indices use various indicators, such as political participation, civil liberties and the functioning of government, to arrive at their rankings. Below are several examples that you may want to research further.

Democracy Index

Produced by the Economist Intelligence Unit, the Democracy Index ranks countries based on five categories:

1 electoral process and pluralism
2 civil liberties
3 the functioning of government
4 political participation
5 political culture.

Countries are then classified into one of four types: full democracies, flawed democracies, hybrid regimes, and authoritarian regimes.

Freedom in the World Report

Published by Freedom House, this report assesses political rights and civil liberties around the world. Countries are evaluated and rated on a scale from 'Free' to 'Partly Free' to 'Not Free'. Like the Democracy Index, this assessment is based on several indicators of political rights and civil liberties.

Varieties of Democracy or V-Dem

V-Dem is an initiative from the University of Gothenburg in Sweden that provides a multidimensional approach to assessing democracy. It aims to reflect the complexity of democracy beyond simply the presence of elections. It collects data to measure five principles of democracy:

1 electoral
2 liberal
3 participatory
4 deliberative
5 egalitarian measures.

1.4.2 External challenges to state legitimacy

Up to this point, we have explored various sources of state legitimacy and, while doing so, have addressed ways in which that legitimacy can be challenged or lost. However, there may also be challenges to legitimacy that occur outside of the state.

Below is a summary of several ways there can be external challenges to state legitimacy.

International recognition

The lack of recognition by significant international actors or bodies can delegitimize a state. Recently, coups in Myanmar, Afghanistan, Mali and Niger have resulted in regional organizations like the AU and ASEAN refusing to acknowledge the new leadership as the legitimate leaders of those countries. This has an impact on trade and participation in many international governmental organizations. Both the lack of recognition and economic challenges impact the legitimacy of those in power.

Economic or diplomatic sanctions

Economic or diplomatic sanctions imposed by the international community can erode the legitimacy of a state's leadership by highlighting human rights violations, military action and so on. Sanctions can cause economic hardships and result in a country's leader(s) losing legitimacy.

Transnational crime

Activities like drug trafficking, human trafficking and arms smuggling can challenge state legitimacy, especially when state actors are implicated or when the state appears powerless to prevent such activities.

Global media and information

Increasing interconnectedness means that human rights abuses or corruption can be quickly highlighted throughout the world. International non-governmental organizations (NGOs) and activists can challenge state legitimacy by highlighting and campaigning against abuses or corruption within a state, so impacting the legitimacy of the state.

Comparative governance and legal rulings

The success or effectiveness of governance in neighbouring or similar countries can pose a challenge to the legitimacy of the state. If citizens compare their state unfavourably to others, it may erode the perceived legitimacy of their government.

In addition, rulings against a state by international judicial bodies like the International Court of Justice or the International Criminal Court can affect state legitimacy.

> **Discussion point**
>
> Explain how international recognition, economic sanctions, transnational crime, global media and comparative governance each pose external challenges to state legitimacy.

ACTIVITY

Select two different types of countries and examine their rankings according to two of the legitimacy indices we have discussed. Explain what you think are the reasons behind the rankings and how each state's ranking reflects its legitimacy.

1.4.3 Legitimacy of non-state actors

States are not the only global political actors that can achieve legitimacy. Non-state actors also need and crave legitimacy. This can come from many sources and will depend on the type of non-state actor.

Below, we highlight some of the causes of legitimacy for non-state actors.

■ Movements or insurgencies

Local support is crucial for insurgent groups or movements. This support may come from shared ideologies, grievances against a common enemy, or providing goods and services.

■ Effective governance

In areas where the state has a limited presence, non-state actors that establish some form of governance, even if basic, can gain legitimacy. Their ability to maintain order and administer territories can be a significant source of legitimacy. This may manifest through offering services such as health care, education or welfare that the state failed to provide.

■ Non-governmental organizations

Initially, NGOs may derive legitimacy from a perceived moral high ground or ethical stance. However, if those NGOs are transparent and accountable about their operations, funding sources and decision-making processes, they can gain legitimacy, especially among international partners and governments.

NGOs can also achieve legitimacy simply by collaborating with other non-state actors.
For example, NGOs that partner with the UN or receive funding from major international donors gain legitimacy by working with or being supported by these well-recognized actors.

Finally, NGOs that can effectively achieve their stated objectives, whether humanitarian relief or advocacy goals, can gain credibility and legitimacy.

■ Multinational corporations

For non-state actors like multinational corporations (MNCs), economic strength can be a significant source of legitimacy, especially in regions that rely heavily on foreign investment and the jobs these corporations can provide.

It is important to highlight that legitimacy is often in the eye of the beholder. What might seem like a legitimate non-state actor to one group or individual might be viewed skeptically by another. Non-state actors operate in complex environments, so their legitimacy can often change based on various factors.

Chapter summary

In this chapter we have covered:
- what is meant by state legitimacy
- sources of state legitimacy
- challenges to state and government legitimacy
- sources of legitimacy of non-state actors
- legitimation processes and the loss of legitimacy of political actors.

REVIEW QUESTIONS

Now that you have read this chapter, reflect on these questions:
- ■ What is state legitimacy, and why is it important for the stability and functioning of a state?
- ■ Summarize Max Weber's three main sources of legitimacy. How do these sources contribute to a state's perceived right to govern?
- ■ What are some external factors that can challenge or erode the legitimacy of a state?
- ■ How do non-state actors, such as insurgencies, NGOs and multinational corporations, establish and maintain their legitimacy?

1.5 Interdependence in global politics

SYLLABUS CONTENT

By the end of this chapter, you should understand:
▶ global governance and international law
▶ achievements and limitations of the United Nations
▶ participation of intergovernmental organizations and non-state actors in global governance
▶ global interactions and networks.

1.5.1 Interdependence

◆ **Interdependence** can be defined as the mutual reliance between and among groups, organizations, geographic areas and/or states on access to resources that sustain living arrangements.

◆ **Global governance** refers to the systems and institutions of decision-making and cooperation among state and non-state actors that facilitate collective action on global political issues.

◆ **Globalization** describes how the growth and development of trade and technology, and the spread of social and cultural influences, have made the world (states, governments, economies and people) a more connected, interdependent place.

Interdependence is one of the four key concepts that underpin the IBDP Global Politics course. In this chapter, we will examine its role in **global governance** and interactions in global politics, but do remember that the impact of interdependence stretches beyond this chapter and into the three thematic studies that make up the course.

We can define interdependence as the mutual reliance between and among groups, organizations, geographic areas and/or states on access to resources that sustain living arrangements. We see this play out in a number of ways in global politics:

● Economic interdependence is expressed in trade agreements between states.

● Security interdependence is the reason why states sign defence treaties and form collective security alliances. The increase of transnational issues such as terrorism and climate change have forced states and non-state actors to acknowledge the growing need for interdependence, as clearly not all political issues can be solved by individual nation states alone.

● **Globalization** – promoted by rapid changes in technologies – and the development of a digital world have only served to accelerate the growing interdependence that characterizes contemporary global politics.

Liberal theorists, such as Joseph Nye (see Key theorist box, page 21), characterize these new forms of interdependence as complex interdependence, and argue that the impact on global politics and the way in which political actors, particularly states, conduct themselves has been significant.

1.5.2 Global governance and international law

▮ Governance versus government

In any discussion of global governance and international law, it is necessary to distinguish between government and governance. The easiest way to do this is to consider the scope of the two.

We can understand government as something that takes place primarily at a state level and involves defined actors – civil servants and elected politicians, for example – engaged in a relatively rigid set of activities to ensure the smooth running of a particular state or political entity that are bound by clearly defined rules or laws. Governance, on the other hand, is a much more wide-ranging process that involves a much broader range of institutions, rules and participants and occurs both within and beyond the level of the nation state. Governance is generally more focused around political issues while government is much more concerned with processes at a national level. For example, it makes sense for us to think of the UK government or the Indian government, but we are much more likely to talk of global governance rather than government when considering issues such as climate change and global trade.

This distinction will be referred to and developed throughout this chapter. Governance is an important idea in global politics because it is so closely related to the key concept of interdependence, which plays such a key role in the story told by liberal theorists (see Chapter 1.1).

Concept

Liberalism and interdependence

Interdependence refers to the way in which political actors relate to each other in a complex international system. Liberal theory suggests that the world is characterized by what they term 'complex interdependence'. We can understand complex interdependence to mean that there are multiple channels between multiple actors that impact on multiple issues.

Given the fact that we live in a world that is characterized by interdependence, it is reasonable to assume that the role played by the state is not perhaps as central to global politics as was once the case (although this is not to say that the state is now irrelevant). Global political issues require actors to work together to tackle them in a way that goes beyond states acting on their own. One of the ways in which actors, including states, do this is through the application and development of international law.

We can understand international law by distinguishing it from national law:

- National laws are created by states and generally only apply within the jurisdiction of those states. Laws are created by institutions including legislatures, such as national parliaments and national courts. Of course, much depends on the exact political system in a given country.

- International laws are laws created by states – usually through intergovernmental organizations such as the UN – that states agree to be bound by. International law is relevant to the discussion of global governance as it provides a framework that constrains states and other actors, within which they must act.

◼ Global governance

There are several examples of global governance in practice and you will see that these differ both in the political issues they attempt to address and in the political actors involved:

UN Security Council resolutions

UN Security Council (UNSC) resolutions are one way in which the international community can be seen to exercise global governance. They are distinct from other resolutions passed by UN organs, such as the General Assembly, as they are the only resolutions with the potential to be binding on UN member states.

◆ The **P5** is the five permanent members of the UN Security Council – China, France, Russia, the UK and the United States.

In order for a UNSC resolution to be passed, it must be agreed upon by a minimum of nine of the 15 members of the council and must not be vetoed by any of the five permanent members, commonly referred to as the **P5**. These member states are China, France, Russia, the UK and the United States.

Examples of resolutions passed by the UNSC include those relating to North Korea, in which the council imposed sanctions such as severe restrictions on imports and exports of non-essential goods in order to encourage Pyongyang to abandon its development of nuclear missile technology.

World Trade Organization

The World Trade Organization (WTO) and the trade agreements it makes are another example of global governance being led by intergovernmental organizations (IGOs).

In its own words, the WTO:

- 'provides a forum for negotiating agreements aimed at reducing obstacles to international trade and ensuring a level playing field for all, thus contributing to economic growth and development' – this shows us the importance of the role these types of IGOs play in a world characterized by interdependence

- 'provides a legal and institutional framework for the implementation and monitoring of these agreements, as well as for settling disputes arising from their interpretation and application' – this shows its important contribution to global governance.

The WTO was not the first organization to attempt to codify and establish an agreed structure for international trade, as it was preceded by the General Agreement on Tariffs and Trade (GATT) in 1947.

The WTO grew out of what has become known as the Uruguay Round. This was a seven-and-a-half-year negotiation that was launched in 1986 and, by the end, involved 123 countries and covered almost all trade, 'from toothbrushes to pleasure boats, from banking to telecommunications, from the genes of wild rice to AIDS treatments' (WTO).

However, as the world has continued to develop and is, in many respects, a very different place to the world of 1986, a second round, known as the Doha Round, was launched in Qatar in 2001. While this resulted in an agreement in 2013 regarding trade facilitation, many other issues are still currently being discussed and negotiated. This is significant, as it demonstrates both the importance of global governance in our interdependent world and the complexity of the issues that have resulted in such a long time frame for each round of WTO negotiations. Indeed, it raises questions about whether the WTO really is the best means by which we, as an international community, deal with issues of trade.

Global governance and climate change

The UNSC and the WTO are single actors working in a specific area of global governance. However, when we consider the political issue of climate change, we see the involvement of a much broader range and number of political actors.

Since its launch in Rio de Janeiro in 1992, the United Nations Framework Convention on Climate Change (UNFCCC) has been the major framework by which state and non-state actors and civil society participants have attempted to tackle climate change. The Conference of the Parties (COP) is the annual meeting of all parties to the convention, and meetings have taken place in a number of places, including Kyoto in 1997 (COP 3) and Paris in 2015 (COP 21).

Since the first summit in 1992, the number of non-state participants has steadily grown. COP 21 in Paris, for example, took place with more than 28,000 accredited participants, of whom 8,000 were registered as non-state observers (Bäckstrand et al.). Some experts suggest that this can be seen as a new form of multilateralism that goes beyond simply seeing multilateralism as cooperation between state actors. Bäckstrand terms this new form of multilateralism in global governance '**hybrid multilateralism**'.

Hybrid multilateralism is significant in any discussion of global governance for two reasons:

● First, it shows the role that non-state actors can play in holding states to account for pledges made in tackling global political issues such as climate change.

● Second, it acknowledges that effective global governance relies on non-state actors not simply as observers of the governance process but also as meaningful actors able to effect change in their own right.

■ International law

When we discuss issues of global governance – particularly given the realist view that states operate in an anarchic system – it is necessary to consider the role played by international law.

Discussion point

What do you think of when you think of international law? What exactly is it and how does it differ from national law? Where does it come from? Who is bound by it and what are the consequences for breaking it?

The English philosopher Jeremy Bentham (1748–1832) defined international law as a collection of rules governing relations between states and, while this is an important element of contemporary international law, it does not encompass the full reality of the concept in the interconnected global system of the twenty-first century. For example, Bentham's definition fails to mention either individuals or international organizations, both of whom are key actors impacted by contemporary international law.

When we discuss international law, it is important not to simply try and apply the principles of national law to an international context. As Christopher Greenwood, Professor of International Law and former judge at the ICJ, points out, there is no 'code of international law', nor does international law have any parliament or anything that can be considered as legislation in the same way as it is understood in the sense of domestic politics. Crucially, while there may be an International Court of Justice (ICJ) and other specialized courts and tribunals such as the International Criminal Court (ICC), their jurisdiction is dependent on the consent of states and therefore differs hugely from the jurisdiction possessed by national courts. You, for example, do not need to consent to be bound by the laws of your country in order to fall under the jurisdiction of your legal system.

There are several sources of international law and Greenwood proposes four major sources as a starting point:

1 treaties between states

2 customary international law derived from the practice of states

3 general principles of law recognized by civilized nations

4 judicial decisions and the writings of 'the most highly qualified publicists'.

1 Treaties between states

Treaties are, perhaps, one of the first things you thought of when taking part in the discussion activity above. A treaty is a formal agreement reached between two or more states. Treaties, by their very nature, are binding on states and as such they can be viewed as a source of international law, as they place conditions on states that they willingly agree to be bound by.

For instance, when seeking to settle disputes between states, the ICJ often makes reference to treaties signed by both states. For example, in its 2009 decision regarding the border dispute between Costa Rica and Nicaragua about navigational rights on the Colorado river bordering the two countries, the court reached its judgment with reference to the bilateral treaty of 1858 signed by both countries.

Treaties, therefore, are considered international law because they are essentially a written agreement between two or more countries as to what constitutes legal obligations in a particular case.

2 Customary international law derived from the practice of states

◆ **Customary international law** is formed not by written or codified laws, but by existing practices or customs accepted by international states.

Customary international law is not written or codified. Instead, it exists because it is based on existing practices of states. For example, traditionally, visiting heads of state have been granted legal immunity when visiting another state. Because this has been established practice among the vast majority of states for a significant length of time, it has become established as customary international law. To put it simply, the source of customary international law is the established custom of states.

3 General principles of law recognized by civilized nations

General principles, while not perhaps as common a source of international law as treaties or customary laws, are when an international body such as the ICJ wishes to adopt a legal principle that is widely recognized and accepted within national legal systems.

For example, the principle that corporations can have a legal personality, and are therefore entitled to diplomatic protection in the same way as individuals, was incorporated into international law following a ruling of the ICJ in 1970, when the court considered what was widely accepted in national legal systems.

4 Judicial decisions and the writings of 'the most highly qualified publicists'

◆ **Judicial precedent** refers to the lower courts having to follow the decisions of the higher courts. It is common in many national legal systems.

Finally, while there is no concept of **judicial precedent** in international law, in many cases the international courts, such as the ICJ and ICC, make reference to previous decisions by the court. Therefore, judicial precedent has a significant impact on the development and creation of law and can thus be considered a source of international law.

As we have seen, international law is not the only component of global governance, but it remains a significant framework in which both states and non-state actors must operate in the contemporary global system.

1.5.3 The United Nations

◼ UN Charter

The UN Charter marked the founding of the United Nations (UN) when, on 24 October 1945, it was ratified by the required number of signatory states. To this day, the UN Charter remains the document upon which the UN is based and is binding on all member states.

The UN Charter:

- sets out the rights and obligations of member states and, as such, is considered an instrument of international law
- sets out the aims of the organization as stated in the preamble, as well as the structure of the UN.

The UN is perhaps the major non-state actor in global politics and, as such, it plays an important role in the global governance regime. While the role played by the UN has developed since its founding, as UN Secretary-General Antonio Guterres points out:

> in the end, it comes down to values … We want the world our children inherit to be defined by the values enshrined in the UN Charter: peace, justice, respect, human rights, tolerance and solidarity.
>
> UN Secretary-General Antonio Guterres, 'United Nations: About us'

This is not to say that the UN has been consistently regarded as successful in its aims, and we will consider some of its achievements and limitations later on in this chapter.

Discussion point

Read the preamble to the UN Charter, which you can find on the UN website (**www.un.org**). To what extent do you believe the UN has achieved the aims set out in the charter?

■ Structure of the UN

The UN is made up of six major bodies – known as UN organs – all of which are set out in the UN Charter. They are the:

- UN General Assembly
- UN Security Council
- Economic and Social Council
- International Court of Justice
- Trusteeship Council
- UN Secretariat.

UN General Assembly

The UN General Assembly (UNGA) is the main forum of the UN. Every member state is represented and it operates on a one-state, one-vote basis.

The main functions of the UNGA are to:

- discuss any question relating to international peace and security (except when a dispute or situation is being discussed by the UN Security Council)
- make recommendations for the peaceful settlement of any situation that might harm the friendly relations among nations
- discuss and make recommendations on the powers and functions of any organ of the UN
- request studies and make recommendations to promote international cooperation, the development of international law, the protection of human rights and international collaboration on economic, social, cultural, educational and health issues
- receive and discuss reports from the Security Council and other UN organs

■ **Figure 1.30** The UN General Assembly Hall at the UN headquarters in New York City

- discuss and approve the UN budget
- elect non-permanent members of the Security Council, the members of the Economic and Social Council; to elect the judges of the International Court of Justice (jointly with the Security Council); and on the recommendation of the Security Council, to appoint the Secretary-General.

It is important, however, to note that the UNGA can only pass recommendations rather than binding resolutions. This means that a member state cannot be forced to abide by an UNGA recommendation. It could be argued that this makes the General Assembly an ineffective forum, particularly as a component of global governance. Nonetheless, its recommendations are a significant expression of global opinion and therefore carry a certain degree of moral weight, despite not being legally binding on states.

UN Security Council

The UN Security Council (UNSC) is a significant player in global politics and the global governance regime, primarily because the resolutions it passes are legally binding on UN member states, as stated in Article 25 of the UN Charter:

> *The Members of the United Nations agree to accept and carry out the decisions of the Security Council in accordance with the present Charter.*

The UNSC is made up of 15 states, five of which are permanent members with a veto power over any proposed resolutions. This means no resolution may be passed if one of the P5 (see page 62) either vetoes a resolution or does not vote. The other ten members are elected by the General Assembly to serve two-year terms.

The primary responsibility of the UNSC, as set out in the UN Charter, is the maintenance of international peace and security. The UNSC has significant powers compared to other UN organs, including the ability to authorize the use of peacekeepers or, as a last resort, to authorize the use of military force by a coalition of member states or a regional organization. Clearly, the ability to exercise hard power such as this has significant implications for global governance and has led to much debate about the make-up of the council. In particular, as we saw at the start of this chapter, the veto power of P5 members is a source of considerable controversy in some quarters and, it might be argued, gives these states excessive influence in the contemporary global governance regime.

ACTIVITY

As a class, role play the UN Security Council Reform from the Council on Foreign Relations at **https://modeldiplomacy.cfr.org/pop-up-cases/un-security-council-reform**. When you have done this, use the following prompts as a basis for either a group or individual reflection:
- To what extent is the UNSC out of date as a twentieth-century organization in a twenty-first century world?
- What are the alternatives? Who would the winners and losers be in any changes to the UNSC?

International Court of Justice

The International Court of Justice (ICJ) – the only one of the six UN organs to be based in The Hague rather than in New York City – is the UN organ responsible for settling legal disputes submitted to it by member states in accordance with international law.

The ICJ decides disputes between countries based on the voluntary participation of the states concerned, and states that agree to participate in proceedings are required to comply with the decision of the court. The ICJ also gives advisory opinions on legal questions referred to it by other UN organs and specialized agencies. The role of the ICJ in global governance, then, is obvious. It is not only a source of international law but also makes significant contributions to interpreting existing international law.

Given the importance of the ICJ to global governance, it is unsurprising that such care is taken over the selection of the 15 judges who make up the court. Each judge is elected for a nine-year term and must be elected by both the UNGA and the UNSC. There may be no more than one judge of the same nationality on the court.

You must be careful, however, not to confuse the International Court of Justice (ICJ) with the International Criminal Court (ICC), which is also based in The Hague but is a criminal court that prosecutes individuals, while the ICJ deals with disputes between states.

Economic and Social Council

The Economic and Social Council (ECOSOC) is the UN organ concerned with economic and social affairs. Its primary responsibility is to coordinate the economic and social work of the UN family of organizations. This means it has responsibility for a number of other UN bodies and institutions such as the various Food and Agriculture Organizations (FAOs) and International Labour Organizations (ILOs).

ECOSOC is made up of 54 members who are elected by the UNGA for three-year terms. As stated in the ECOSOC Handbook:

> ECOSOC is unique amongst the major UN organs in that it is not a universal body, like the General Assembly; it has no binding powers like the Security Council; and has no authoritative legal voice like the International Court of Justice.

Despite this, it has responsibility for a huge range of issues, including coordinating and guiding the UN development system, which covers a wide array of UN activities in the economic, social and environmental fields.

ECOSOC also follows up on major decisions on sustainable development and the Sustainable Development Goals (SDGs), and makes recommendations to the UNGA, UN member states and other UN agencies.

Trusteeship Council

The Trusteeship Council, for our purposes, is largely irrelevant as it suspended work in 1994. The role of the council was to provide supervision for 11 Trust Territories that had been placed under the administration of seven member states, in order to prepare them for self-government and independence.

Now that all of these territories have achieved independence or self-government, the Trusteeship Council has a limited role in global governance.

UN Secretariat

In simple terms, the UN Secretariat can be likened to the UN's civil service. Its role is to:

- gather and prepare background information on various issues so that government delegates can study the facts and make recommendations
- help carry out the decisions made by the different organs of the UN

- organize international conferences
- translate speeches into the UN's official languages and distribute documents
- keep the public informed about the UN's work.

The UN Secretariat is headed by the Secretary-General, who is elected by the UNGA, on the recommendation of the UNSC, for a five-year term.

■ Achievements and limitations of the UN

Since its inception in the immediate aftermath of the Second World War, the UN has undoubtedly had a significant impact on global politics. However, the extent to which the organization has managed to achieve its goals and objectives is debatable. It is certainly true that, to a significant degree, the UN has been successful in meeting one of its key aims. The phrase in the UN Charter, 'we the peoples of the united nations determined to save succeeding generations from the scourge of war which twice in our lifetime has brought untold sorrow to mankind' clearly refers to the two world wars of the twentieth century. There has not been a third world war and, to this extent, the UN has been successful. However, there has been no shortage of regional conflicts, both inter- and intrastate in nature, since the adoption of the UN Charter, and a cynic might argue that this means the UN has been unsuccessful in achieving its aims.

The same can be said of almost all of the UN's goals. Progress has been made, but this progress has been insufficient both to meet the aims of the organization as laid out in its founding charter and to meet the challenges of an increasingly interconnected twenty-first century world. It could be argued that many of the limitations of the UN arise from the unwieldy structure that is an inevitable result of an organization that seeks to be truly global and encompass all states, regardless of political and cultural tradition. This means that compromise is often difficult to achieve and can result in recommendations being made that fail to achieve much other than a generalized expression of good intent.

The UN can also be criticized for replicating the dominant position of certain states in the international system at the expense of less powerful states. Nowhere is this more obvious than in the fact that five countries hold a permanent position and veto power on the UNSC, arguably the most powerful UN organ.

It is important that, while you are familiar with the structure of the UN, you are able to consider and make links to the three thematic studies. Given that any detailed discussion of the strengths and weaknesses of the UN would take up a book on its own and is therefore beyond the scope of this textbook, we will briefly consider the achievements of the organization in the light of the three thematic studies of rights and justice, development and sustainability, and peace and conflict, and consider the role of different UN agencies and institutions.

Rights and justice

The UN Human Rights Council (UNHRC) is made up of 47 member states who are elected by the UNGA with seats distributed on a regional basis. One of the great strengths of the UNHRC is that its very existence is a statement by the UN that human rights matter to the extent that it is necessary to have a body whose mission is to protect and promote human rights around the world.

Additionally, special rapporteurs appointed by the council have been instrumental in bringing human rights abuses around the world to wider attention, for example in Belarus and Eritrea. The council has also been commended for its use of the universal periodic review (UPR) procedure, through which the human rights record of each UN member state is reviewed every four years.

As Zeid Ra'ad Al Hussein, UN High Commissioner for Human Rights, points out:

> *The UPR is one of the Human Rights Council's most innovative and striking achievements, with real potential for transformative action. It has set an important precedent by maintaining complete universality over its first two cycles.*
>
> *Quoted in UNHCR, 'What is the Human Rights Council?'*

However, this raises an obvious question. If the UPR is so successful, then why do so many of the UN's member states continue to carry out human rights violations with relative impunity?

The UNHRC has also been heavily criticized by Human Rights Watch and other civil society actors for allowing states with highly questionable human rights records to be elected to the council. Indeed, the US under the Bush administration refused to support the creation of the council in 2006 for this very reason, although this decision was subsequently reversed by President Obama. States with questionable human rights records elected to the council have included Saudi Arabia, China, Russia and the Philippines. As Louis Charbonneau of Human Rights Watch has pointed out, 'electing serious rights abusers like Cameroon, Eritrea, and the UAE sends a terrible signal that UN member states aren't serious about the council's fundamental mission to protect human rights'. The Human Rights Council, in the view of its critics, simply provides international cover and legitimacy to those states it should be calling out and challenging for abuses of human rights.

Discussion point

The Human Rights Council, in the view of its critics, simply provides international cover and legitimacy to those states it should be calling out and challenging for abuses of human rights. To what extent do you agree with this claim? What evidence might you use to support your view?

Development and sustainability

The UN Development Programme (UNDP) is the UN's global development network which, in its own words, 'advocates for change and connects countries to knowledge, experience and resources to help people build a better life'. In order to do this, the UNDP focuses its work on three main areas:

- sustainable development
- democratic governance and peacebuilding
- climate and disaster resilience.

It is clear that there has been some success in many of these areas, and especially in terms of sustainable development. While we will discuss progress towards the Sustainable Development Goals (SDGs) in more detail in Section 3 on development and sustainability, the fact remains that governments worldwide are working together and setting targets in order to achieve them. The fact that this may not be completely successful or that progress may not be as much as hoped for is, to an extent, irrelevant to the fact that the UNDP, along with other actors, has succeeded in changing the agenda and is bringing sustainability to the forefront of global governance.

The UNDP has also enjoyed successes that have not necessarily been widely publicized. For example, after many NGOs and other agencies withdrew from Afghanistan after the return to power of the Taliban in 2021, the UNDP took on responsibility for funding essential health services in the country, including paying the salaries of health workers (DeYoung).

ACTIVITY

Choose one UN committee, agency or programme to investigate in further detail, in order to create a shared class resource that addresses the question: 'To what extent is the UN an agent of positive change in the contemporary global governance regime?'

Peace and conflict

With regard to peace and conflict, the UN International Residual Mechanism for Criminal Tribunals exists to perform a number of essential functions that were previously carried out by the International Criminal Tribunal for Rwanda (ICTR) and the International Criminal Tribunal for the former Yugoslavia (ICTY). While both of these conflicts fall outside of the scope of global politics due to the contemporary nature of the subject, the international residual mechanism is significant because it is responsible for continuing the work of both of those tribunals. It is responsible for:

● ensuring those convicted serve their sentences

● apprehending and prosecuting remaining fugitives

● providing assistance to national jurisdictions where requested

● the continued protection of witnesses.

While tribunals following crimes such as those committed in Rwanda and the former Yugoslavia are discussed in more detail in the peace and conflict thematic study in Section 4, this is nonetheless indicative of the key role played by UN bodies in global governance.

1.5.4 Further interaction in global governance

■ Participation of IGOs and non-state actors in global governance

While it is sometimes easy to think of global governance in terms of interactions between state actors and the UN, it is important to acknowledge that IGOs other than the UN also play a significant role.

European Union

The European Union (EU), an IGO made up of 27 member states and with a population of over 400 million people, is a key player in this respect. The EU:

● creates laws that are binding on all member states

● has introduced regulations to standardize and promote trade within the bloc

● has made significant moves towards developing a common foreign policy in certain areas, known as the Common Foreign and Security Policy

● sets standards related to human rights: for example, states wishing to join the bloc must have abolished the death penalty and the union has its own court – the European Court of Human Rights – to which citizens of member states can bring cases, often against their own governments.

The impact of the EU on global governance can be seen in the aftermath of the UK's decision to leave the union. The complex negotiations that followed the referendum in 2016 before the actual withdrawal in 2020 ('Brexit') clearly showed the relative power of the EU as an IGO compared to the UK acting unilaterally. The UK needed to renegotiate at least 759 treaties with a diverse range of countries as a result of no longer being part of the EU (McLean). Additionally, British businesses wishing to continue to trade with the EU are now in the position of being bound by its rules without having any input into the creation of those rules. In an interdependent and interconnected world, IGOs have a significant impact on the framework within which we all live our lives.

While the EU is perhaps the most integrated of the intergovernmental political unions globally, the impact of others on global governance can also be seen. The example of the African Union (AU) and its unwillingness to cooperate with the International Criminal Court (ICC), despite 33

ACTIVITY

Investigate the challenges the UK faced in withdrawing from EU agreements and in renegotiating agreements with other states following Brexit. Remember, Brexit is a contentious issue and you should reflect carefully on the trustworthiness of the sources you choose to use.

of its member states also being parties to the Rome Statute of 1998, shows that IGOs are also able to hinder global governance when they feel it is not working in their best interests. In the case of the ICC, the AU claimed that the ICC is demonstrating racism against African leaders and thus, by extension, all Africans (Olufemi and Bello). This highlights one of the key issues surrounding any discussion of global governance, namely governance of whom, by whom and for whose benefit?

Multinational corporations

It is also worth touching, briefly, on the involvement of multinational corporations (MNCs) in global governance. This can be seen in both a positive and negative light.

From a positive point of view, it can be argued that MNCs are responsible for the vast majority of foreign direct investment, which supporters would argue promotes both economic and human development, so supporting the work of UN agencies such as the UNDP.

However, on the other hand, we might point to the way in which MNCs may seek to avoid areas where the reach of global governance is not as strong. For example, many Western companies have been criticized for locating production in countries where regulation of workers' rights is either lax or completely ignored. This has led to notable incidents such as the 2013 collapse of Rana Plaza in Bangladesh, in which over 1,000 garment workers making clothes for Western markets were killed. Additionally, the US subprime mortgage crisis that led to the global financial crisis of 2007–08 is a further example of the way in which reckless conduct by major companies can have global consequences that, in many ways, the global governance regime is not prepared to deal with.

Discussion point

To what extent is it in the interests of states to act against their own self-interest on occasion? What examples can you think of where this might be the case?

▪ Cooperation and competition between political actors

As you know, political actors both compete and cooperate in global politics. For example, the 27 member states of the EU cooperate on trade and various political issues to an unprecedented degree. Equally, states work together in tackling global political challenges such as conflict and climate change, as can be seen in the work of the UN. However, as realist theorists such as John Mearsheimer point out, the international system is, to a large degree, anarchic, and states must compete to ensure their own survival. They do this through both economic and military means, among others. This highlights one of the key challenges of global governance, which is the question of how to persuade states to act against their own short-term self-interest.

It is not just states who cooperate in the international system, however. Communities of cooperation exist in numerous spheres and include scientists working together across national boundaries to tackle shared challenges such as the development of COVID-19 vaccines, as well as civil society actors who cooperate on issues such as human rights around the world.

If we accept that we live in an increasingly interconnected and interdependent world – and it would be foolish to accept that this is not the case – then the question becomes whether this world is characterized primarily by cooperation or by competition. Undoubtedly, the answer is a combination of the two, but it will be up to you to make sense of your study of the IBDP Global Politics course to decide what the balance is between the two.

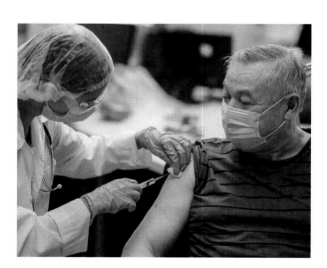

▪ **Figure 1.31** A patient receives a COVID-19 vaccine, the result of scientists working together across national boundaries to tackle the shared challenge of the COVID-19 pandemic

■ Treaties, collective security alliances and economic cooperation

Treaties, as discussed earlier in this chapter, are one of the more formal ways in which states agree to interact within a particular framework. Two examples of areas in which states may make treaties are when forming security alliances and fostering economic cooperation.

Collective security alliances

The North Atlantic Treaty Organization (NATO) is an obvious example of a collective security alliance. The organization was founded in 1949 with the signing of the North Atlantic Treaty by European and North American states in response to the perceived threat posed by the Soviet Union.

Essentially, at the heart of NATO is the principle, enshrined in Article 5, that an attack on one member of the alliance is, in effect, an attack on all members of the alliance. Since its founding, Article 5 has been invoked only once, by the United States following the September 11 terrorist attacks.

It is difficult to measure how successful NATO has been, but the accession of Finland in 2023, with Sweden likely to follow shortly after, in response to Russia's 2022 invasion of Ukraine, suggests that states still see much value in the principle of collective defence. Nonetheless, for those outside of the alliance, the view may be somewhat different. Russia, for example, lists planned NATO expansion as a threat to its sovereignty and interests as part of its justification for the invasion of Ukraine. It is a reasonable conclusion that military alliances benefit those within them and not so much those left on the outside.

Military cooperation also takes place in other contexts.

The Five-Eyes alliance of the UK, United States, Canada, Australia and New Zealand is intended to be an intelligence-sharing alliance between the five states that works in all of their interests.

The AUKUS alliance between the UK, US and Australia is an interesting example of the way in which states compete as well as cooperate. Initially Australia, as part of a move to update its submarine fleet, had agreed a deal with France to provide them. However, they reneged on this contract and went with an offer from the British and Americans to provide them with nuclear-powered submarines. From Australia's point of view, this made sense as it gave them a more significant military capacity. From the UK and US point of view it made sense too, as it formed part of a balancing act against the growing power of China in south-east Asia. However, the anger on the part of the French – who lost out on a contract worth $60 billion plus numerous jobs and associated economic benefits – was understandably great. As Charles Kupchan, writing for the Council on Foreign Relations, s, such a lack of transparency is inappropriate among close allies and represents a breach of trust. This serves to illustrate the difficult balancing act that states walk when cooperating with others, particularly in the area of defence and security.

Economic cooperation

States also cooperate on an economic level in a number of different ways, and there are numerous treaties that illustrate the importance of these trade relationships. Trade treaties may be bilateral or multilateral. The EU is an example of a multilateral or regional trade agreement, as is the

United States–Mexico–Canada Agreement (USMCA), which replaced the North American Free Trade Agreement. There are significant advantages to states cooperating in this way, not least of all the fact that countries can take advantage of specialization, as well as making it easier for cross-border trade to take place, as is the case with the lack of internal borders within the EU.

States also use economic cooperation as a means of competing with each other for power and influence. In recent years, China has surpassed the United States as Africa's largest trading partner and this growing investment and involvement in Africa has contributed to Chinese soft power on the continent. Research by Afrobarometer, a pan-African research network, shows that, since the creation of the Forum on China–Africa Cooperation – a Chinese-led vehicle for engagement in Africa – in 2000, 'the public holds generally favourable views of economic and assistance activities by China. Africans rank the United States and China No. 1 and 2, respectively, as development models for their own countries. Remarkably, in three of five African regions, China either matches or surpasses the United States in popularity as a development model. In terms of their current influence, the two countries are outpaced only by Africa's former colonial powers' (Lekorwe et al.).

■ Global interactions and networks

Global interactions and networks at a variety of levels also provide evidence of interaction in contemporary global politics, and much of this can be seen through the lens of globalization.

Globalization

Globalization is a highly contested concept both within and beyond global politics, but Brown et al. suggest that the most important single idea 'concerns the growing disjuncture between the notion of a sovereign state directing its own future, the dynamics of the contemporary global economy, and the increasing complexity of world society'. Globalization, therefore, is highly dependent on networks and interactions between actors in the international system at all levels.

While the Commonwealth – an organization of states, most of which used to be part of the British Empire – is often seen by some to be irrelevant, there are elements that support the view that our world is now characterized by networks and interactions that do not depend on physical space and that transcend national borders. For example, the Commonwealth of Learning is an intergovernmental organization (IGO) of the Commonwealth with the mandate to promote the use of open learning and distance education, knowledge, resources and technologies.

◆ **Digital government**, also known as e-government, is the use of technological communications, such as smartphones and the internet, to provide public services to citizens and other persons in a country or region.

Similarly, Digital Nations – an IGO made up of leading **digital governments** – is a collaborative network that seeks to share expertise in harnessing digital technology in order to improve the lives of citizens. Currently made up of Canada, Denmark, Estonia, Israel, Mexico, New Zealand, Portugal, South Korea, the United Kingdom and Uruguay, this is not only an example of states cooperating but also an acknowledgement of the role played by digital technologies in aiding the process of globalization.

Cultural exchanges

Cultural exchanges also play an important – if perhaps overlooked – role in global interactions and the development of networks. These may include education opportunities, such as the EU Erasmus scheme which, since its inception in 1987, has helped 3.3 million students to study abroad within the bloc.

Elsewhere, towns and cities around the world participate in city twinning arrangements and schools organize cultural and language exchanges.

While the benefits of such exchanges may be difficult to quantify, they undoubtedly contribute to the rich and complex web of interconnection that characterizes global interactions in the twenty-first century.

Chapter summary

In this chapter we have covered:

- what is meant by global governance and the distinction between governance and government
- the way in which global governance involves a number of different actors
- the role played by international law
- the structure of the United Nations and some of its achievements in relation to the three thematic studies.

REVIEW QUESTIONS

Now that you have read this chapter, reflect on these questions:

- To what extent is the international system characterized more by cooperation than by competition?
- Which actors have benefited from globalization and which have lost out?
- How does interdependence in global politics affect our understanding of the role of power and the way in which it is exercised?

By the end of this chapter, you should understand:
▶ theories, models and analytical frameworks in global politics
▶ the use and applicability of theories and models to political issues
▶ the bias and limitations of theories and models.

1.6.1 Theory in global politics
■ Defining theory

Before you explore some of the different theories of global politics in more depth, it is worth taking a moment or two to consider exactly what we mean by theory. What is a theory? What is it supposed to do? And why might we choose to use theories to make sense of the world around us?

We can start with a simple definition and say that we understand a theory to be a set of connected ideas and assumptions that attempts to explain why something happens the way it does and often to predict what may happen in a given situation or set of circumstances. This is, perhaps, not a very satisfactory definition of what a theory is and this is partly because theories in the social sciences – not just Global Politics – come in such diverse forms.

It is perhaps helpful to distinguish between different types of theories based on what they seek to do. Heywood and Whitham suggest that there are three types of theory according to this system of classification:

● Explanatory theories are those that attempt to explain why certain events happen and under what circumstances.

● Interpretive theories focus on the meanings that shape actions and institutions in global politics and the ways in which they do so. Interpretive theories, therefore, will often treat the world as a set of competing truths.

● Normative theory, rather than explaining how the world is, focuses on how it ought to be.

● TOK

One important feature of theories is that they provide their own set of concepts and language. You might think of a theory as a toolbox for building an understanding. Each theory, or toolbox, will provide certain concepts or tools with which to build knowledge and the instructions on how to do this. Concepts and arguments that are appropriate in one theory might not be relevant to another. The question then is which theory to use? How can we decide which theory provides the best explanation, interpretation or guidance?

We can also distinguish between what might be considered the foundational or traditional theories of global politics and critical responses to them. Given that theories in global politics largely reflect the concerns of policy makers and political scientists, it is unsurprising that the two major traditional theories of liberalism and realism focused on power and competition between states in the context of a twentieth century characterized by two world wars, and the Cold War between two major powers. These traditional theories have been refined and developed over time by different writers, in response partly to criticisms of them made by proponents of what are generally termed critical theories, such as postcolonialism and Marxism. Theories, therefore, should be understood in relation to other theories rather than in isolation.

It is important, before considering different theories of global politics in more depth, to bear in mind a couple of key points:

- No theory can possibly hope to offer an overarching answer to – or explanation of – all considerations in global politics. Theories differ in what is seen as important. As leading realist theorist John Mearsheimer points out, 'the world is enormously complicated and we need simple tools to make sense of that enormously complicated world. Those simple tools are theories and any time you come up with a theory it is a simplification of reality'.

- The majority of theories do not make moral judgements. Rather, theories such as realism attempt to explain why the world is the way it is. They do not comment on whether or not this is, in some sense, morally right.

TOK

The TOK framework might be a helpful tool to understand the similarities and differences between these different theories.

Divide a large sheet of paper into four equal sections, each with one of the following headings: Scope, Perspectives, Methods, and Tools and Ethics. Now divide each of the elements into sections for each of the theories. Take notes on the theories, adding your notes into the relevant section of the knowledge framework. Finally, review the notes for each of the elements and identify where the theories overlap, differ or actually conflict.

▇ Realism

One of the most significant theories of global politics is realism. It gets it name because its supporters claim it is realist in nature: it seeks to explain the world as it really is rather than as it should be. In that sense, realism is an explanatory theory. As Mearsheimer states, 'The sad fact is that international politics has always been a ruthless and dangerous business, and it is likely to remain that way.' This, in Mearsheimer's view, describes the world as it is rather than how we might want it to be.

Realism has often been referred to as a theory of power politics because its key focus and concern is on power in global politics. We can distinguish between two broad traditions of realist thought, classical realism and structural realism. Both seek to explain the role power plays in the way in which states act in the international system, and both are based on two assumptions:

- Humans are, by their nature, selfish and competitive.
- There is no higher authority than the state. We can describe this by saying states operate in an anarchic system. In this sense, anarchy refers to an ordering principle and can be considered as the opposite of hierarchy.

The major distinction between the two is that the classical realists are predominantly focused on human nature, seeing this as the major driver of state behaviour, while structural realists, as the name suggests, see the structure of the international system as the main factor determining why states behave in the way they do.

Classical realism

The key idea of classical realism – that the behaviour of states is largely determined by human nature – is not a new idea. Niccolò Machiavelli, writing about politics in the sixteenth-century republic of Florence, claimed that life was characterized by strife, which forced political leaders to rule through cruelty, cunning and manipulation. Thomas Hobbes, writing in the seventeenth century, supported these ideas, arguing that the strongest of all human desires is the desire for power. The problem, however, is that no single group is in a strong enough position to dominate society and establish a system of orderly rule, leading to what Thomas Hobbes referred to as a state of nature. Life in this state of nature, in Hobbes' own words, would be 'solitary, poor, nasty, brutish and short', and he suggests that the only solution to this would be the creation of a sovereign power.

This relates specifically to global politics if we consider the state of nature put forward by Hobbes as made up of states rather than individuals. If we accept, as classical realists do, that because we are human we are ego-driven and self-seeking, then conflict and competition are a natural feature of the international system. Essentially, our natural egoism as humans creates what can be termed state egoism, leading each state to pursue its own interests above all other things. Additionally, the fact that all states are led by people who are subject to an inherent desire to seek power for its own ends, leads states to pursue power. Classical realism, then, claims that it is human nature and the natural desire for power, that means states seek to pursue power at the expense of other states.

Structural realism

Structural realists, such as John Mearsheimer and Stephen Walt, accept the classical realist argument that the pursuit of power is the determining factor of state behaviour. However, they claim it is the structure of the international system that forces states to operate in this way rather than anything to do with human nature.

Structural realism as a theory is based on five key assumptions:

1 States operate in an anarchic global system.
2 All states possess at least some offensive military capability.
3 States can never know the intentions of other states.
4 The primary goal of all states is survival.
5 States are rational actors.

1 States operate in an anarchic global system

The international system, according to structural realists, is anarchic. This means that there is no higher authority than the state. For Mearsheimer, anarchy simply means 'that there is no centralized authority, no night watchman or ultimate arbiter, that stands above states and protects them' (quoted in Kaplan). This is important because it means that states must depend primarily upon themselves for survival, rather than being able to call on a higher authority to help them.

2 All states possess at least some offensive military capability

All states possess at least some offensive military capacity, which means that all states have the ability to inflict some degree of harm on other states. Obviously, different states have hugely different military capacities, but it is important to distinguish between military capacity and military organizations. So, while states such as Costa Rica do not have a military they do have the – albeit limited – capacity to inflict harm on other states through branches of the state such as police organizations.

HL extension: Security

The theory of structural realism places the security and survival of the state at the centre of the decision-making process of states. It may be interesting to explore this idea through real world case studies that allow you to consider how states balance against and ally with each other in order to maintain a balance of power that benefits both a stable world order and the goals of individual states. The invasion of Ukraine by Russia is one such example that could be explored in more depth.

3 States can never know the intentions of other states

This is fundamental to structural realism as a theory. While it is possible to know the capacity of other states through the size of their military or the number and types of weapons they possess, it can never be possible to truly know their intentions, as these are in the heads of policy makers and national leaders. It is, of course, possible to make educated and well-evidenced guesses as to their intentions but, as realist theorists would point out, this is not the same as knowing.

4 The primary goal of all states is survival

This is a logical assumption and does not overlook the fact that states have a number of different goals, such as, for example, economic growth or promoting a particular political or religious ideology. However, the assumption is based on the idea that, unless the state survives in the international system, then all other goals are irrelevant as it will not be around to achieve them.

5 States are rational actors

The final assumption made by structural realists is that states are rational actors, and this is important to remember in a world where political leaders may often be mocked for being backward or stupid. Rational, then, in this sense, means that states are capable of developing strategies that maximize their chances of survival. This does not mean that states – and political leaders – do not make miscalculations. Mistakes are inevitable in a structure where states operate with less than perfect information. However, the essential point remains: that states will generally make what they believe is the smartest decision because it will benefit them and their own self-interest.

◆ **Hegemony** occurs when one state is politically, economically and militarily dominant over other states.

So how do these five assumptions relate to power? The result of accepting the five assumptions upon which structural realism is based is that, in an anarchic international system, power is equal to safety. It makes sense, in order to ensure your own safety, that you are more powerful than other states in the system. States, therefore, should pursue **hegemony** through amassing power.

In theory, this means global hegemony but, as realists such as Mearsheimer have pointed out, this is not a realist aim and therefore the aim for states in an anarchic system should be twofold:

1 States should aim to be a regional hegemon in their own sphere of influence.

2 States should prevent any other state from becoming a regional hegemon in their region of the world.

The question then becomes, how much power should states attempt to gain in the international system? Is there a point where enough power becomes too much power? This is where the structural realists divide into two camps. On the one hand, we have the offensive structural realists, who argue that states should seek to maximize their power wherever possible. On the other hand, we have defensive structural realists, such as Kenneth Waltz, who argue that once states amass power beyond a certain point it can have negative consequences that will actually result in making a state less safe in the international system rather than more safe.

There are three reasons, in particular, why defensive realists argue that pursuing hegemony is a foolish strategy and that states should confine themselves to seeking what Waltz refers to as an appropriate amount of power:

● First, defensive realists argue that states will seek to balance against any state that attempts to achieve hegemony in the international system. This may take the form of strategic or military alliances that would result in the original state experiencing a decline in relative power compared to previously.

● Second, defensive realist theorists argue that the offence/defence balance will almost always favour a defending state. The balance refers to how easy it is to defend a state from attack compared to conquering a defending state. As defending states usually have the advantage, it is therefore probable that a state that wishes to significantly increase its power is likely to become engaged in wars that it will go on to lose. For defensive realists, this is an unappealing option for any state who would be better advised to focus on consolidating their position within existing power structures.

● Third, even if it is possible to conquer another country, the costs of doing so will very likely outweigh any benefits. Partly, this is due to nationalism, which often makes it impossible to fully subdue the conquered population, among other factors, and this can be seen in recent conflicts in Iraq and Afghanistan.

There is, however, agreement between defensive and offensive structural realists in some areas. For example, both agree that there is no advantage to using nuclear weapons in a conflict unless they are possessed by only one conflict actor. The reason for this is simple. If both sides have nuclear weapons (and therefore what is known as a survivable **retaliatory capacity**), then neither will benefit from striking first. This is the principle that underpins the nuclear theory of **mutually assured destruction**.

Key theorist

John Mearsheimer (1947–)

John Mearsheimer is an American political scientist and scholar of international relations who is widely regarded as one of the leading contemporary proponents of structural realism. In his book *The Tragedy of Great Power Politics*, Mearsheimer set out his theory of offensive realism. Subsequent books have explored what Mearsheimer has called the Great Delusion, by which he means the idea of liberal hegemony characterized by the desire to create democratic governments and promote liberally minded global institutions. Mearsheimer has attracted controversy in recent years with his analysis of the Russian invasion of Ukraine in which he argues the EU and NATO are largely to blame.

■ **Figure 1.32** John Mearsheimer

ACTIVITY

John Mearsheimer delivered a lecture at the University of Chicago titled 'Why is Ukraine the West's fault?' This lecture attracted a great deal of controversy, especially after the Russian invasion of Ukraine in 2022. Watch the lecture on YouTube and consider the extent to which Mearsheimer is able to use his theory of structural realism to predict and explain state behaviour.

■ Liberalism

Liberalism is another one of the major theories of international relations from the latter part of the twentieth century. It is perhaps best understood as a response to the ideas put forward by realist thinkers.

Liberals take issue with realist theory on a number of grounds, but there are three that are particularly important:

- Liberal theorists disagree that the international system is based around conflict. Rather, liberalism stresses the importance of cooperation in global politics.
- Where realism has relatively little to say of global politics below the state level, liberals argue that non-state actors, such as non-governmental organizations (NGOs), multinational corporations (MNCs) and intergovernmental organizations (IGOs) play an important role in the international system that is disregarded by realist theories.
- While the story told by realists is characterized by continuity, in the liberalist story global politics is characterized by rapidly occurring great change.

Like realism, liberalism is also underpinned by several key assumptions:

1 States are interdependent to such an extent that the way in which they relate to each other had changed by the latter half of the twentieth century.

2 What happens in one state can affect what happens in another state.

3 Relations between two states can have a significant impact on relations between other states.

We might consider, looking at these assumptions, that states have always been interdependent to some extent. However, liberal theorists such as Joseph Nye have argued that the form of interdependence that developed in post-Second World War global politics – known as complex interdependence – became the overriding characteristic by which the international system was defined.

This complex interdependence was made up of three main elements:

1 Multiple channels

2 Multiple issues

3 Decline in the effectiveness of military force as a tool of foreign policy

1 Multiple channels

Realists would argue that states are by far the most important actors in global politics and they pay relatively little attention to non-state actors or to domestic politics. Liberals do not dispute the importance of states, but they suggest that realists fail to take into account the important role played by non-state actors, such as MNCs and NGOs.

Interactions between these non-state, as well as state, actors form many of the multiple channels that exist in an international system characterized by complex interdependence. For example, MNCs operate in more than one state, as do international NGOs. IGOs, while made up of states, arguably operate on a level that is distinct from the state level, which is the focus of realists.

Additionally, liberals highlight the important role played by sub-state actors in global politics. For example, non-multinational businesses often do not operate in isolation from the international system as they import and export goods to other countries. Cities and provinces set up trade missions abroad. For example, the Canadian provinces of British Columbia sent 71 trade missions to Asia in the period 2010–2020 followed by Alberta and Saskatchewan with 54 and 27 missions respectively (Harrison et al.).

At a more individual level, students in international schools are likely to have friendships with those from other countries and cultures as well as travelling abroad themselves. In the story told by liberalism, these are all important multiple channels in our increasingly interconnected global system.

2 Multiple issues

Liberals also take issue with what they see as the realist claim that power is the currency of global politics. Instead, they argue that economic, ideological, religious and cultural issues all form part of the contemporary global agenda – what they call 'multiple issues'.

The result is that many of the issues that realists see as purely domestic in nature do, in fact, have a much more international dimension than we might at first suppose. For example, if a state chooses to adopt new environmental standards and introduces regulations or laws to support this, then this has an international dimension as it will almost certainly have an impact on trading partners if imports have to meet the new standards. This is one example of domestic policy having a foreign policy impact as a direct result of connections – or multiple channels between multiple actors – in the international system.

Liberals would also argue that the nature of many of the multiple issues facing the international community has changed. Climate change, for example, is arguably one of, if not the, biggest challenges facing the world today and it is simply not possible for states to tackle the issue individually.

ACTIVITY

In groups or individually, create a mind map that identifies and elaborates on multiple channels between multiple actors affected by and tackling multiple issues. Be sure to include specific real-world examples. You can use this mind map as a 'jumping off' point for exploring some of your chosen examples in more depth.

3 Decline in the effectiveness of military force as a tool of foreign policy

The issue of climate change also illustrates why a decline in the effectiveness of military power is an important component of liberal theory. Essentially, military power is not an effective response to many of the issues we face today. It is obviously not possible, for example, to attack a rise in ocean water temperature with bombs and guns. Even violent threats like terrorism are much harder to deal with through conventional military means when terror attacks are often carried out by those who live among us. In addition, liberals make the point that in a world characterized by complex interdependence, even in those circumstances where military action is possible or feasible, it will often harm the multiple interests of both state and non-state actors.

The question for liberals, then, is why do state and non-state actors cooperate, particularly if the international system is as anarchic and dangerous as realists claim it to be? In answering this, they come to the same explanation for state behaviour as realists: they do so because it is in their own self-interest to do so.

Liberals offer several reasons as to why this is the case:

1 States realize that any hostile actions – such as attempting to conquer a neighbouring state – are likely to harm their interests as much as the interests of a rival state.

2 States are constrained by the multiple channels characteristic of complex interdependence. Even if leaders want to use conflict to deal with perceived security threats, they often face resistance from public or powerful interest groups.

3 In democracies, in particular, citizens are more able to hold leaders to account, which may prevent them from engaging in conflict. This is not always the case, of course, as illustrated by the decision of the UK government to go to war in Iraq despite a million people marching in London as part of the Stop the War coalition.

4 The existence of nuclear weapons arguably provides a significant disincentive to the use of war as a foreign policy tool. One of the reasons for the United States' initial reluctance to meet all of Ukraine's demands for military materials and equipment in response to the 2022 invasion by Russia has been the desire to avoid escalating the conflict to one between nuclear powers. Ultimately, a nuclear power actually using the major tool in its arsenal risks huge damage to all of humanity.

5 The technological developments that have come about as a result of globalization, such as the falling cost of air travel and the digital information revolution and access to the internet, have resulted in a more connected world in which all actors feel there is more at stake as a result of conflict.

While it is sometimes tempting to see liberalism and realism as the opposites of each other – and each theory does certainly make criticism of the other – they are not in opposition. Most liberals, for example, accept the realist idea that the international system is essentially anarchic, while most realists are willing to accept that realism does not address important issues below state level.

Nevertheless, they both provide a good starting point to theory in global politics and many of the theories that have followed – often known as critical theories – have developed in response to the points put forward by these two traditional theories of global politics and international relations.

▩ Neo-Marxism

Marxist theory in global politics is based, as the name suggests, on the work of the German philosopher and economist Karl Marx (1818–83). Marx wrote extensively on his claim that production, distribution and consumption of goods in society – what he called the modes of production – were the major factor impacting social life.

The key issue for Marx was the relationship of individuals to the means of production. The bourgeoisie (owners of the means of production) benefit from the capitalist system and therefore go to great lengths to persuade the proletariat (those who do not own the means of production and are therefore required to sell their labour to the bourgeoisie) that capitalism works in their interest. The proletariat, on the other hand, are 'subjugated as wage labourers, living unhappy lives and carrying out what Marx called alienated labour in which they have little or no personal investment' (Whitham and Heywood). The conflict between the two classes is what lies at the heart of Marxist theory. However, where traditional Marxism is concerned with class conflict within countries, neo-Marxists focus on class conflict on a global scale. As stated by Kaarbo and Ray, 'the neo-Marxist perspective focuses on the international system of capitalism, the competition among economic classes, and the relationship of politics and society to capitalist production'.

Economic core and economic periphery

In order to fully understand neo-Marxist theory, it is necessary to consider the way in which the world came to be divided into what some writers claim are an economic core and an economic periphery. The imperialism of the great European powers led to the creation of a system in which the economic structures of the world benefit the wealthy states and populations (those in the economic core) at the expense of others (those in the economic periphery). For example, in countries such as Uganda and Kenya, agricultural economies focused around feeding the population were uprooted in favour of crops desired by the colonial powers, such as tea and coffee.

Dependency theory, which we will discuss in more detail in the thematic study on development – is an example of a neo-Marxist theory that suggests that powerful countries manipulate the economic periphery through their control of international organizations, development aid and unfair trading practices. They do this in order to maintain their control of the international system.

The elites

Neo-Marxists also focus on the role played by elites in the global system. They argue that elites in poorer countries have more in common with elites in the global core than they do with their own populations. The incentive for corruption and economic mismanagement, then, is high, provided the global elites feel that their own interests are being provided for.

The role of MNCs and TNCs

Neo-Marxists are also interested in the role MNCs and TNCs play in global politics. They do not see them as another – essentially benign (not harmful) – multiple channel between global political actors, as liberal theory might suggest. Rather, neo-Marxism focuses on the way in which many MNCs are able to influence state economic policy in order to create conditions in which they are then able to exploit local populations in order to maximize profits. Neo-Marxism, then, can be seen as not just an explanatory theory – although it certainly attempts to explain why the world functions in a particular way – but it also has a significant normative component. This means that, rather than explaining how the world is, it focuses on how the world should be.

In conclusion, neo-Marxism is critical of both realism and liberalism. It takes issue with realism's focus on military power, arguing instead that economic power is the main driver in global politics. On the other hand, neo-Marxists criticize liberalism as, while accepting there is a high degree of interdependence in contemporary global politics, they argue that this takes a particular form of exploitative interdependence based on inequality.

■ Postcolonialism

Postcolonialism has several similarities with neo-Marxist theory in that it sees the historical impact and legacy of colonialism as a significant – and in the case of postcolonialism, the decisive factor – impacting on global politics. As Sheila Nair points out, 'The use of "post" by postcolonial scholars by no means suggests that the effects or impacts of colonial rule are now long gone. Rather, it highlights the impact that colonial and imperial histories still have in shaping a colonial way of thinking about the world and how Western forms of knowledge and power marginalize the non-Western world' (McGlinchey et al.).

Discourse

One of the key terms used in postcolonialism, as well as other theories, is discourse. We can understand this to mean the ways in which we write and speak of things in global politics. Put simply, discourse is a way of thinking. Postcolonial theorists are concerned with discourse because they argue that much of how we understand the world is through Western discourses – particularly discourses of power – and these are a legacy of imperialism and colonization.

For example, traditional theories of global politics, such as realism and liberalism, focus on the concept of sovereignty and understand it in terms of a Westphalian way of thinking about the state. Postcolonialism, on the other hand, points out that sovereignty as a concept is a product of Western discourse and, along with ideas of the state, was imposed on the colonized world by the colonial powers.

Postcolonialism, then, is a critical theory that questions many of the assumptions that traditional theorists of global politics take for granted.

Postcolonial theorists have also criticized other critical theories, such as Marxism, for its claim that economic class and class struggle lies at the heart of the global system. Instead, they claim that much of global politics and the international system can often only be understood in terms of race.

Nair gives the example of inequality to demonstrate how discourse plays a central role in understanding the postcolonial approach to global politics. If we accept that global inequality exists (after all, we can measure it using a number of indicators which we will discuss in more detail in the thematic study on development) and that these indicators tell us something about how the world is structured, then we need to consider the ideas that make this appear 'normal'. Nair suggests that by doing so, and by focusing on Western discourses of power, we see how characterizations of global poverty are often 'accompanied by images and narratives of non-Western governments and societies as simultaneously primitive, hyper-masculine, aggressive, childlike and effeminate' as part of a Western discourse.

This is closely linked to the work of Edward Said. Postcolonialism draws on Said's concept of 'Orientalism' as a theory. Said claimed that there was a binary way of thinking about 'the Orient'. According to Said, people in Asia were ascribed characteristics – by the West – that were in opposition to what may have been seen as Western characteristics and were therefore more negative. For example, people in Asia may have been considered exotic, emotional or non-rational among other characteristics, in contrast to supposed Western characteristics such as rationality, civilization and modernity. This idea of 'othering' plays a key role in postcolonialism and writers such as Frantz Fanon (see page 45) have written extensively about the way in which colonialism was the way in which a 'patronising and dehumanising relationship between settlers and natives was established … with the former represented as enlightened educators of the latter – animalistic and inferior, childlike populations in need of white stewardship' (Fanon). As some postcolonial theorists suggest, evidence of this unequal power dynamic can be seen in the way in which colonial powers were painted as benevolent for 'gifting' freedom and independence to the people who were colonized, so ignoring the struggle for independence by millions around the world. This is another example of discourse at work.

Some writers, such as Nair and Shampa Biswas, have attempted to use postcolonialism as a way to consider contemporary political events, such as concern over nuclear programmes in Iran and North Korea. US foreign policy discourse tends to frame this in terms of rogue states who cannot be trusted with nuclear weapons for the safety and security of the international community. However, this ignores the fact that the only state ever to have used nuclear weapons is the United States. For Biswas and others, there is an element of hypocrisy here. They see this as a racialized discourse that asks questions such as 'who can be trusted with nuclear weapons?', when really the question, in postcolonial terms, should be, 'who gets to decide who is trusted with nuclear weapons?' (Biswas).

It is also interesting to consider the impact of postcolonialism as a theory in the light of ongoing debates surrounding decolonization, which can be seen as an attempt to alter or challenge Western discourses regarding colonization and empire. This process has been ongoing in a number of Western countries and institutions and has ranged from grassroots protests demanding the removal of statues celebrating those who benefited from the trade in enslaved people to formal attempts by educational institutions to 'decolonize' their curriculum.

ACTIVITY

Research a recent or ongoing attempt to challenge western discourses regarding colonization and empire. You may wish to consider specific cases, such as the activists who threw the statue of the slave trader Edward Colston into the harbour in Bristol, UK, or consider wider debates such as those surrounding the use of language and terminology such as 'Sub-Saharan' to refer to certain countries in Africa.

Postcolonialism, as with many critical theories, may often seem to raise more questions than it provides answers. However, arguably this does not subtract from its value as a theoretical perspective in global politics. Rather, by asking these questions of more established theories and offering an alternative way of considering the world around us it adds value to the subject.

◼ Feminism

Similar to other critical theories such as Marxism and postcolonialism, criticizes parts of the traditional theories of liberalism and realism. However, feminism goes further, as it focuses on both the exclusion of the experience of women from global politics as a discipline and political processes in public life around the world, as well as making significant contributions through an exploration of patriarchy.

◼ **Figure 1.33** Thousands of people took part in the women's march in central London in 2017, just one of many such marches taking place around the world

◆ **Intersectionality** is a term used to describe how a person's social and political identities result in various combinations of oppression, discrimination or privilege. Patriarchy refers to the idea that society is organized alongs lines which benefit men and exclude women from power.

Intersectionality, visibility and the patriarchy

Later work in feminist theory has also focused on the idea of **intersectionality**. This, for example, has highlighted the fact that the lived experience of women is dependent on a number of factors other than gender. For example, the experience of a working-class black woman in an Eastern European state is likely to be significantly different to the experience of a middle-class white woman in south-east Asia, for example.

One of the key strands of feminist theory, then, is concerned with the visibility of women in global politics. Data from the Pew Research Center show that, as of March 2023, 'women currently serve as the head of government in just 13 of the 193 member states of the United Nations and fewer than a third of UN countries have ever had a woman leader' (Clancy and Austin). Heywood and Whitham also point out that 85 per cent of the world's ambassadors are male as well as the fact that the armed forces globally are overwhelmingly male and, therefore, so are the senior strategic decision makers. Yet, women make up around half the global population, which means that this significant under-representation in the sphere of global politics must be due to social and cultural rules as well as historical processes.

Feminists argue that it is patriarchy that is one of the key drivers of this exclusion of women from global politics as it has led male dominance of key institutions at both a state and interstate level as well as at the sub-state level. Behaviour that incorporates what are perhaps regarded as masculine values such as violence and aggression has, some feminist theorists suggested, led to the use of war as a foreign policy tool by states. Furthermore, as Heywood and Whitham suggest, these behaviours are then explained away by theories of global politics such as realism, which are generally constructed by men and, as feminist theorists might argue, for the benefit of men.

Gender-based violence

Feminist theorists also highlight the issue of gender-based violence as one that specifically affects women around the world. This is also a way of shining a light on an international system that 'tacitly accepts a large amount of violence against women as a normal state of affairs' (McGlinchey et al.). Data from the UN show that one in three women worldwide experience physical or sexual violence in their lifetimes. 155 countries have passed laws on domestic violence, and 140 have legislation on sexual harassment in the workplace, which means a significant number have done neither and, in cases where these laws exist, enforcement is often inconsistent (UN Women).

CORE: Understanding power and global politics

ACTIVITY

Research the gender balance amongst key political actors and decision makers in your country. Remember to go beyond the percentage of female versus male politicians and consider how you might broaden your definition of key political actors and decision makers.

Feminist theorists, such as Jacqui True, see this as significant for a number of reasons. First, True has suggested that there are clear links between the violence experienced by women in the private sphere and the violence they experience 'in public, in an increasingly globalized workplace and in times of war'. This is important for an understanding of global politics because it shows that in virtually every society around the world, women face gendered violence, which can range from sexual violence within the home to rape as a weapon of war. This continuum, then, does not fit neatly into categories of war and peace or violence and non-violence and feminist theorists argue that traditional theories of global politics tend to ignore the issue by viewing violence as a matter or state-level security and stability. For feminists, gendered violence is a double-edged sword. Not only is it a human rights issue, but the way in which violence is traditionally thought of ignores the lived experience of millions of women.

Feminist theory in global politics is important because it has demonstrated not only how much work remains to be done in tackling what might be seen traditionally as women's issues, but also the way in which structures of global politics build and continue gendered systems of inequality in which women are made less visible than men.

Constructivism

Constructivism is another critical theory that challenges the more traditional theories of global politics, such as realism and liberalism.

Social constructions

At its most simple, constructivism challenges the assumption that the physical world matters more than the social world. It proposes that global politics is socially constructed through norms, beliefs and discourse. A social construction, then, is a concept that exists not objectively in reality, but as a result of human interaction. We can illustrate this with an example. The act of killing another person is a physically objective act that exists in reality but whether or not this would be considered as murder would depend on a whole range of social factors. Was, for example, the deceased a trespasser? An enemy soldier in wartime? A political prisoner? A child crossing the road? Much would depend on how murder as a concept is socially constructed within the rules and laws of a particular society or social context.

Constructivism poses a challenge to traditional theories of global politics – and to realism in particular – because it questions the very assumptions upon which these theories are built. If realists are, as the name suggests, concerned with reality, then constructivist theorists take issue with the very idea that there is a single objective reality.

Alexander Wendt, a leading constructivist theorist, develops this point in the famous article 'Anarchy is what states make of it'. In it, Wendt develops the idea that states – as well as people – 'act towards objects, including other actors, on the basis of the meanings that the objects have for them' rather than on any objective meaning that these objects possess. According to Wendt, therefore, US military power has a hugely different significance for Cuba than it does for Canada despite the fact that, objectively, the size of US military power is the same regardless.

Equally, Wendt points out that nuclear missiles acquire a different significance for the United States depending on which country possesses them. It is not, therefore, the nuclear missiles themselves – what is referred to as the material structure – that causes them to be more or less threatening to the United States, but the *meaning* that is given to the material structure. This is referred to as the ideational structure. In Wendt's example, the nuclear missiles do not have any meaning except in the social context in which we understand them. In this case, the social context involves considering who is regarded as a friend and an enemy, and by whom.

Social constructions, then, are the first fundamental component of constructivist theory and, as Kaarbo and Ray point out, in constructivism 'there is no certain, permanent, factual reality and, even if there were, physical truths matter less than social constructions'. This can be seen as a direct criticism of traditional theories – realism, in particular – because it suggests that, essentially, global politics is influenced by the way in which states construct the international system than any objective way the system is organized.

Identities and interests

The second important component of global politics for constructivists is identities and interests. Constructivism suggests that states have identities that are constructed through their interaction with other states. Identities in this context, according to Sarina Theys, are 'representations of an actor's understanding of who they are, which in turn signals their interests' (McGlinchey et al.). Constructivists argue that this is important because identities define interests and actions. For example, the identity of a small state may mean that its interests will be more focused on survival in the international system, while the identity of a larger state may influence its interests more in the area of achieving dominance in the military or economic sphere.

Social norms

The third important component of global politics for constructivists is that they see the role of social norms as essential to an understanding of how states operate within global politics. For example, norms against war for offensive purposes or norms against enslaving people are not objective things that exist in and of themselves. Rather, they have been socially constructed, largely through states' behaviour, and now form an important role in framing what is considered acceptable in the international system. So, the international system is created by the international system itself.

The key principle underlying constructivism is that interactions and perceptions are what creates reality instead of it being something that is objective and existing in and of itself. While this is a very simple idea, it offers a substantial challenge to other theories of global politics – particularly the more traditional theories of liberalism and realism – and a radically different way of considering the world.

Discussion point

While constructivism offers a radically different lens for considering the world, its more abstract nature may mean it is less relevant to what we see in the world around us. To what extent is this both an advantage and disadvantage?

1.6.2 Use and applicability of theory to political issues

One of the reasons we use theories in global politics is to attempt to explain what happens in the international system and in the world around us. In particular, we use theories as tools to help us explore political issues. In this section we will look at two examples of how theories can be related to political issues, but it is important to remember that a wide variety of political issues can be explored from any number of theoretical perspectives.

Structural realism and the rise of China

Structural realists have used their theory to consider the rise of China in the international system and whether it will be possible for China to do so peacefully or if the structure of the international system means that conflict with the United States is inevitable. Offensive structural realists, such as Mearsheimer, have argued strongly in favour of the claim that conflict with China is inevitable because of the assumptions that underpin realist thinking. Mearsheimer argues that, because the international system is structured in an anarchic manner, it makes sense for China to increase its power relative to its neighbours. China has done so through growing its economy and developing its military.

According to the structural realist view it also makes sense for China to challenge the United States as a **peer competitor** in the Asia-Pacific region. Through an extensive programme of military expansion, which has included creating new islands in the South China Sea, challenging US-led freedom of navigation exercises, and a phenomenal exercise of soft power through the **Belt and Road initiative**, China has challenged the US as a peer competitor and continues to do so.

None of this is to say that Mearsheimer and his realist colleagues are correct in saying that conflict is inevitable. Ultimately, there is no crystal ball in global politics and we cannot predict the future with certainty. However, structural realism, in this instance, provides us with a framework with which we can ask relevant questions as we seek to understand the power dynamics at play in the Asia-Pacific region and consider the possible consequences.

Feminism and peacekeeping in post-conflict societies

A second interesting application of theory is given by Sarah Smith, who has suggested that feminist theory has an important role to play in challenging our assumptions about peacekeeping in post-conflict societies.

Smith points out that peacekeeping, as security-seeking behaviour, is shaped by masculine ideas of militarized security. This goes far beyond some of the traditional views that we may hold about peacekeeping in global politics, which tends to be considered largely from a gender-neutral perspective. Smith argues that this is insufficient given that 'violence against women often continues in the post-conflict period at rates commensurate to or even greater than during the conflict period. This includes rape and sexual assault, domestic violence and forced prostitution, as well as those selling sex to alleviate financial insecurity' (McGlinchey et al.). For feminist theorists, peacekeeping – like the vast majority of political issues – is intensely gendered. Feminist theory offers a way to take this into account when exploring the issue as opposed to the dominant approach, which often obscures the kinds of violence that disproportionately affects women.

Both of the examples above highlight the ways in which theories can be used to explore real political issues and are not just the preserve of academics in ivory towers.

1.6.3 Bias and limitations of theory in global politics

While we have seen that theories are useful – indeed, essential – if we are to truly explore global politics and make sense of a messy and complicated world, we must accept that all theories are imperfect to differing degrees. After all, if a theory existed that was accurate in accounting for all behaviour and actions at all scales of global politics, then clearly there would be no need for competing theories!

However, as we have seen, there is no grand unifying theory of global politics – and whether one is possible or even desirable is beyond the scope of this textbook. While theories are indeed useful tools for students of global politics, we must also think about the limitations of theory.

◆ A **peer competitor** is a state with the power and/or motivation to challenge another state in the international system. For example, China can be seen as a peer competitor to the United States.

◆ The **Belt and Road initiative** is a system of roads and infrastructure that links 150 countries and international organizations to China, with the aim of increasing trade and economic growth.

These include the following:

- Theories do not often reflect the complicated world we live in.
- Theories cannot explain or address everything.
- Theories fall short when we consider them in relation to ontology (what is true or real), epistemology (how knowledge is created and what is possible to know) and methodology (the procedure we follow to test our arguments or opinions).
- Theories are more like ideologies.

Theories do not often reflect the complicated world we live in

The way in which we compartmentalize different arguments and ideas put forward by theorists into nice, neat, tidy little boxes, that we refer to as theories, is artificial, as this doesn't often reflect the messy and complicated world we live in. Some theorists have attempted to resolve this issue by accepting some parts of a theory and rejecting others. For example, The English School of international relations and its description of the international system as a society of states rather than a system of states is an attempt to combine the realist view of anarchy with the liberal view that international relations are, in a meaningful way, governed by rules. As a result, some writers refer to the view as liberal realism.

In addition, not all those who identify as supporters of a particular theory agree with others within the same theoretical tradition. In fact, some of the most intense debates occur within rather than between different theories.

Theories cannot explain or address everything

Theories cannot – and generally do not attempt – to explain or address everything. As the prominent realist John Mearsheimer noted, in an interview as part of the Theory Talks series at ETH Zürich, 'I'm a realist who believes that one can explain what happens in the world much better with a realist theory than with a liberal theory– which is not to say that realism can explain everything' (Schouten).

Theories fall short in relation to ontology, epistemology and methodology

We can consider the limitations of different theories on the grounds of ontology, epistemology and methodology. Heywood and Whitham refer to these as 'explicit commitments or implicit assumptions' about the social world of global politics':

- Ontology, or what is true or real, refers to questions around what the social world of global politics is actually made up of. What are the building blocks of global politics, for example? Should we, like the realists, be primarily concerned with the way states interact with each other, or should we be more concerned with interdependence and interaction at the sub-state level?
- Epistemology is concerned with how knowledge of global politics is produced. Can we, for example, study global politics in the same way as we study the natural sciences? How do we test or measure our theoretical arguments in an empirical way (based on something that is seen or experienced rather than a theory)?
- Methodology refers to the methods we use as students of global politics. Can we generate objective data about global politics or must we be content with more subjective data? Can we use data to make objective laws about how global politics works or are we limited to subjective interpretations?

Theories are more like ideologies

Finally, some experts argue that what we refer to as 'theories' in global politics are not really theories but 'ideologies'. So, when we talk about Marxism in global politics, for example, we are not really talking about a theory but about a world view or an ideology.

● Chapter summary

In this chapter, we have covered:
- what is meant by theory in global politics
- the ways in which theories can be categorized as explanatory, interpretive or normative, as well as traditional versus critical theories
- the key principles and assumptions that underpin a number of key theories of global politics, including both traditional and critical theories
- the way in which theories can be applied to deepen our understanding of real-world political issues as well as some of the limitations associated with using theories.

REVIEW QUESTIONS

Now that you have read this chapter, reflect on these questions:

- Is it possible to make sense of global politics without theory?

- To what extent have the traditional theories of realism and liberalism been undermined by critical theories?

- Feminist theory attempts to make women more visible in global politics. Why might this be considered necessary and important work?

- Writers such as Frantz Fanon are influenced by their cultural, national and racial identity. How far does this shape the theories they propose and does this matter?

2 Rights and justice

Contested meanings of rights and justice

2.1

By the end of this chapter, you should understand:
▶ contested meanings of rights and justice
▶ definitions, interpretations of and perspectives on rights, including positive and negative rights and cultural relativism
▶ definitions, interpretations of and perspectives on justice, including social justice, political justice, egalitarian justice, cosmopolitan justice, ecological justice and Zulu Ubuntu
▶ theoretical views on rights and justice.

2.1.1 Key concepts of rights and justice

Rights and justice are both concepts that are embedded in our daily lives. As an individual, you probably have expectations of how you should be treated by others. For example, you most likely expect to be safe and to have the same opportunities as those around you. You may feel that someone who has harmed you should have to apologize or even face more severe consequences depending on how badly you have been treated. These assumptions are linked to the idea that individuals have rights and access to justice. But where, specifically, do our ideas of rights and justice come from?

We all live within social groups and those groups impact our understandings of rights and justice. As a small child you were probably exposed to ideas of 'right and wrong' and these ideas may have come from family, school, religion, close friends or the media. Additionally, the wider community we live within has expectations of what people should and should not do, and often, within states, legal systems are based on these shared ideas or morality. On a global scale we can also see that the United Nations (UN) and other intergovernmental organizations (IGOs) and non-governmental organizations (NGOs) have definitive ideas about which rights all human beings deserve. Although there may be varying views on what these rights are, and how justice should be applied, it would be difficult to imagine a well-functioning society where there were no rights and justice at all.

Fundamentally, rights and justice are closely linked to power, which is the key focus of global politics. How people function and interact in any society is directly impacted by how power is distributed and challenged.

In fact, as you make your way through this chapter, you will see that all of the concepts in Figure 2.1 play a role in understanding how rights and justice work in contemporary global politics.

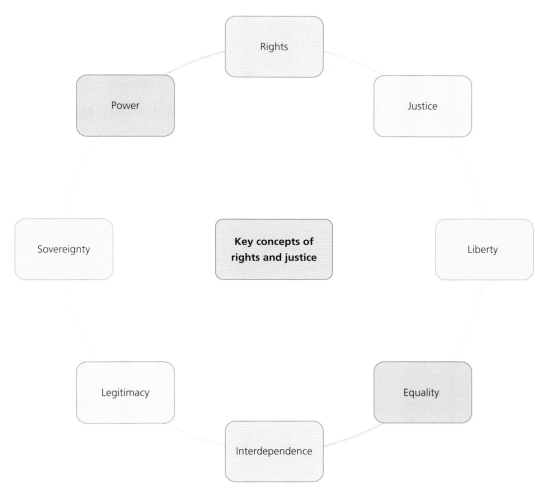

■ **Figure 2.1** Key concepts of rights and justice

■ Key concepts of the course and how they link to this thematic study

It's important to remember that the concepts shown in Figure 2.1 underpin the entire course and connect to all the thematic studies.

Power

Power can be seen as the ability to affect change and is an aspect of relations among people within social organizations. Power is the central concept in the study of global politics and a key focus of all thematic studies of the course, including rights and justice.

Sovereignty

Sovereignty is essentially a state's right to make decisions independently. How states choose to apply and enforce the rights of their citizens is a crucial issue in the study of rights and justice.

Legitimacy

Legitimacy refers to a state or actor being commonly accepted as having the authority to exercise power over others. In matters of rights and justice, the legitimacy of states, courts, IGOs, NGOs, etc. is often called into question.

Interdependence

Interdependence refers to mutual reliance among groups, organizations, geographical regions, etc. Often this is economic in focus, but ideas and values can also be shared along the way, and this can have an impact on the ideas and practices of rights and justice.

◼ Key concepts embedded in many aspects of rights and justice

These concepts are essential to understanding rights and justice as a thematic study. They will be explored and developed extensively throughout this chapter.

Equality

All people have the same intrinsic value. Equality is very closely linked to rights and justice and is one of the most essential concepts to consider in this thematic study.

Liberty

Often divided into two aspects: 'negative liberty' and 'positive liberty'. Negative liberty is freedom from coercion, meaning people should not be forced to do something they don't want to do. Positive liberty refers to people being able to do what they want to do. Liberty is very closely linked to rights and justice, and is one of the most essential concepts to consider in this thematic study.

Justice

This is a complex concept, but many see it as people being treated fairly and getting what they deserve. The concept of justice will be explored in depth throughout this chapter.

Rights

This, too, is a very complex concept, which will be explored in depth during this chapter. As a starting point, we can think of having rights as essential to living a life of dignity and purpose.

2.1.2 Definitions, interpretations of and perspectives on rights

TOK

Your own beliefs about what constitute a 'right' can be characterized as a form of knowledge. 'I know that I have the right to an education' or 'I know that I have the right to be safe from physical attack' are forms of knowledge. They are, therefore, open to genuine questions about whether these knowledge claims are actually true and where you get these claims from. Who (which people) and what (what institutions) have influenced your belief in this context? It's very likely that other people in the world (or maybe even in your local community) will disagree over whether you have these rights, or on how these rights should be realized in political structures.

Rights and history

● Consider the way in which history is taught in your school or community. What facts and events are explored and discussed? Why do you think it is taught this way?

● Now consider your own beliefs about what 'rights' you hold or should hold in your community.

● Discuss the connections between the historical narratives discussed in your history classes and the rights you hold. Do you think those narratives emphasize certain rights over others? Do you think these narratives promote a particular set of rights over others? Do you think these narratives encourage you to hold or defend particular rights?

■ The United Nations and the Universal Declaration of Human Rights

When you ask people what are 'rights' they often think of a document called the Universal Declaration of Human Rights (UDHR). For many political stakeholders and actors concerned with human rights, the UDHR informs how human rights are defined.

Who created the Universal Declaration of Human Rights and why?

During the twentieth century, two world wars brought previously unseen suffering and destruction to many parts of the world, as well as genocide in Europe. There was a strong desire among nations to try to do something to prevent this kind of global conflict from happening again.

Towards the end of the Second World War, from 21 August 1944, representatives from France, the Soviet Union, the United States and the UK met to discuss their vision of what the world would look like once the war was over, and how peace and security for all nations could be prioritized.

These state representatives were members of the Allied forces and they were confident of an impending victory over the Axis powers, which included Germany, Italy and Japan. By 6 October 1944 the Allied group drafted a document known as the 'Proposals for the establishment of a General International Organization'. Negotiations on the future of this organization, which would involve the participation of all nations, continued at the Yalta Conference held on 4–11 February 1945. In attendance were the US president Franklin D. Roosevelt, the UK prime minister Winston Churchill and the Soviet premier Josef Stalin.

This organization became what we now know as the United Nations.

Figure 2.2 From left: Churchill, Roosevelt, Stalin, depicted in a commemorative statue in Yalta, Southern Ukraine

On 24 October 1945 the United Nations came into existence after being ratified by the five permanent members of the Security Council: China, France, the UK, the United States and the USSR.

The purposes of the United Nations, as set forth in Article 1 of the UN Charter are:

● to maintain international peace and security
● to develop friendly relations among nations based on respect for the principle of equal rights and self-determination of peoples
● to cooperate in solving international economic, social, cultural and humanitarian problems and in promoting respect for human rights and fundamental freedoms
● to be a centre for harmonizing the actions of nations in attaining these common ends.

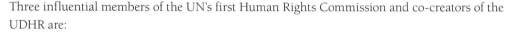

Discussion point

As you can see, the UN Charter specifically mentions focusing on 'equal rights', 'self-determination' (which can be seen as democracy), 'human rights' and 'fundamental freedoms' to maintain peace. These are all terms we associate with human rights. How might this focus on human rights help the world to maintain peace?

In 1948, just three years after the UN's formation, the UN General Assembly (UNGA) adopted the Universal Declaration of Human Rights (UDHR) as a significant and meaningful approach to protecting the safety of people and ensuring lasting peace.

It is worth taking a moment to remember what the global community was facing at the end of the Second World War: the aftermath of the Holocaust, a widespread refugee crisis, and political and economic turmoil inspired many to try to prevent future conflict and to protect the individuals who suffered most. The Human Rights Commission created the UDHR in just under two years, and it has proven to be essential to UN policy and philosophy. The Commission was made up of 19 members from various political, cultural and religious backgrounds to try to ensure that multiple viewpoints were considered. This document has largely defined what many have come to think of as the most essential entitlements and obligations.

Figure 2.3 Peng-chun Chang

Three influential members of the UN's first Human Rights Commission and co-creators of the UDHR are:

Peng-chun Chang, China

Peng-chun Chang was the first delegate from China to the United Nations and was elected vice-chairperson of the UN Commission on Human Rights in 1947. His leadership and contributions to the UDHR are noteworthy. He saw the need to balance respect for others, duties to the community and individual rights, and insisted on the concept of universalism. His understanding of human rights included social, economic, political and civil rights.

Eleanor Roosevelt, United States

Figure 2.4 Eleanor Roosevelt

After a lifetime of humanitarian commitments, the US First Lady Eleanor Roosevelt was the first Chairperson of the Commission on Human Rights. She played a significant role in the drafting of the UDHR, which she submitted to the General Assembly of the United Nations.

Charles Habib Malik, Lebanon

Educated at Harvard, in the United States, Charles Habib Malik was both a philosopher and a diplomat who founded the Philosophy Department at the American University of Beirut. He was religious but set about ensuring that the UDHR successfully applied to all, regardless of religious background. He was described as a major force in the debates that preceded the finalization of the UDHR.

Although diverse points of view were considered, some claim that because the authors of the UDHR were mostly Western or Western-educated men, the UDHR demonstrates a Western approach to rights.

TOK

Given that the UN is a largely 'Western' construct (i.e. it was developed by 'Western' and European powers, despite the fact that China is a member of the UN Security Council), some might argue that the values inherent in the work of the UN are 'Western' in nature. Many even reflect on the International Baccalaureate in a similar way, considering its attitudes towards learning and knowledge as holding a 'Western' perspective. Given that there are many different types of countries, political and educational systems, how might a truly global understanding of 'rights' be maintained by the UN?

■ **Figure 2.5** The first Human Rights Commission of the United Nations, 9 June 1947

The UDHR was adopted by the General Assembly on 10 December 1948. To this day, 10 December is celebrated as Human Rights Day globally. The UDHR has probably had the greatest impact on our modern understanding of what rights are. The declaration lists 30 different rights, which have been simplified in Figure 2.6. The full declaration can be easily accessed online in multiple languages.

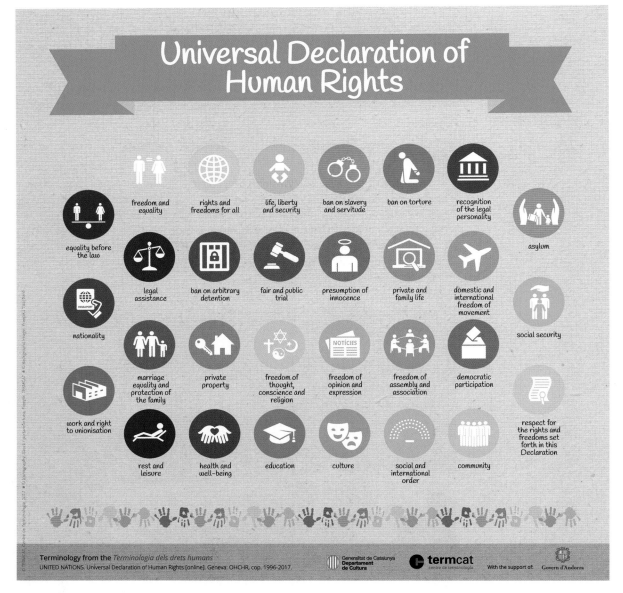

Figure 2.6 Simplified version of the UDHR

As you can see, these rights cover many aspects of our everyday lives. The visuals might help you to remember a few of them, and are great for revision, but it is worth considering them in greater depth, as this will help you to better understand the rights and justice thematic study.

Table 2.1 breaks down the UDHR into six categories:

- civil rights and liberties
- legal rights
- social rights
- political rights
- economic rights
- cultural and solidarity rights.

■ Table 2.1 The six categories of the UDHR

Civil rights and liberties	1	Right to freedom and equality in dignity and rights.
	2	Freedom from discrimination.
	3	Right to life, liberty and personal security.
	4	Freedom from slavery.
	5	Freedom from torture and degrading treatment.
Legal rights	6	Right to recognition before the law.
	7	Right to equality before the law.
	8	Right to a remedy when rights have been violated.
	9	No arbitrary arrest, detention or exile.
	10	Right to a fair trial.
	11	Right to be presumed innocent until proven guilty.
Social rights	12	Right to privacy, a family and a home.
	13	Freedom of movement within a state and the right to leave any country.
	14	Right to asylum from persecution in another country.
	15	Right to a nationality.
	16	Right to marry and start a family.
	24	Right to rest and leisure.
	26	Right to education.
Economic rights	17	Right to own property.
	22	Right to social security.
	23	Right to work for a fair wage and join trade unions.
	25	Right to an adequate standard of living.
Political rights	18	Freedom of beliefs, including religion.
	19	Freedom of expression.
	20	Right to peaceful assembly and association.
	21	Right to take part in government and free elections.
Cultural and solidarity rights	27	Right to participate in your community's cultural life.
	28	Right to a social order in which these rights can be realized.
	29	Duties in the community and responsibility to respect the rights of others.
	30	Freedom from the removal of these rights by the state.

◆ In international law, the expression **non-binding agreements** refers to agreements that contain political or moral commitments but are not legally enforceable. Therefore, if a state breaks the rules of these kinds of agreements it will not face legal consequences. However, the state's legitimacy may be questioned and so they may be effective.

ACTIVITY

Read the original UDHR online at **www.un.org/en/about-us/universal-declaration-of-human-rights**. You can choose to read the document in almost any language. Reading the original document might help you to better understand it.

States' acceptance of the Universal Declaration of Human Rights

The UDHR was voted on and adopted by most countries in the UN General Assembly of 1948. The declaration is a **non-binding** international law, but it has influenced many other binding international covenants, regional conventions and state laws. The UDHR itself is seen as an aspirational document, meaning the global community must always strive to achieve these rights even if it is impossible to imagine a world where every human being has complete access to them.

The UDHR has several key principles, as shown in Table 2.2.

■ **Table 2.2** The UDHR's key principles

◆ **Inalienable** refers to something that cannot be taken away or given away.

Principles	Definition
Universal and **inalienable**	All people everywhere in the world are entitled to these rights simply because they are human, and you can't have them taken away or give them away yourself.
Indivisible	All human rights listed in the document are equal in importance. You can't value some and ignore others.
Interdependent and interrelated	In order for people to reach fulfilment, all of these rights combine to make that possible.
Participation and inclusion	All people have the right to participate in making decisions that affect their lives and/or access information about the decision-making process.
Accountability and the rule of law	States must be accountable if citizens' rights are violated. There has to be a way for individuals to seek justice. Laws, media, civil society and the international community should all hold governments accountable.

■ **Figure 2.7** John Locke

The key principles and links to natural rights and natural law

The key principles of the UDHR are based on the idea that human rights are 'natural' and not dependent on the laws, culture or beliefs of any particular culture or government. These natural rights include many of the rights you see in the UDHR today.

Natural rights have been discussed within Western philosophical circles since ancient times. During the European Age of Enlightenment (seventeenth to eighteenth centuries), the ideas were refined and are the basis for what many consider to be human rights today. Assuming that people have natural rights, the legitimacy of the authority of the state over the individual was widely discussed and debated.

English philosopher John Locke (1632–1704) (see Figure 2.7) argued that natural rights include perfect equality and freedom, and the right to preserve life and property. However, natural rights are not simply a philosophical ideal. These ideas inspired many significant social and political movements that shaped the world we live in today, including the American Revolution, the French Revolution and the abolition of trade in enslaved people in the United States.

Discussion point

Why might some disagree with the assertion that all people on Earth possess natural rights simply because they are human?

2.1.3 Thinking about human rights

Human rights have been debated and discussed for centuries, and there are various ways they are classified.

■ Positive and negative rights

The idea of 'negative' rights is often attributed to the German philosopher Immanuel Kant (1724–1804). His focus, like that of many Western philosophers who considered the idea of rights, was on the individual. The idea of 'positive' rights emerged in the twentieth century.

Table 2.3 gives an overview of both types.

■ **Table 2.3** Positive and negative rights

	Definition	Some examples from daily life	Examples from the UDHR
Positive rights	Positive rights require the authorities, such as governments, to take action. Positive rights therefore place responsibility on those with power.	You have a right to live in a clean environment. You have the right to seek help if you are in danger. You have the right to go to school.	Article 11: Everyone charged with a crime has the right to be presumed innocent until proven guilty according to law in a public trial at which he has had all the guarantees necessary for his defense. Article 26: Everyone has the right to education. Education shall be free, at least in the elementary and fundamental stages. Elementary education shall be compulsory. Technical and professional education shall be made generally available and higher education shall be equally accessible to all on the basis of merit.
Negative rights	Negative rights require those with power to respect individuals' rights simply by doing nothing at all. Negative rights prohibit certain actions by those with power.	You have the right to privacy. You have the right to walk home from school safely. Others should not take things that belong to you.	Article 3: Everyone has the right to life, liberty and security of person. Article 5: No one shall be subjected to torture or to cruel, inhuman or degrading treatment or punishment.

Discussion point

Can you think of any other real-world examples that demonstrate the interdependent nature of negative and positive rights?

◆ **Fraternity** is being a part of a community, looking out for each other.

Positive and negative rights in the real world

In practice it can sometimes be difficult to distinguish between positive and negative rights, and many disagree with this distinction. For example, consider that no one should be treated cruelly or abused. If we think of this as a negative right, we can say that within a prison, for example, the guards should not abuse or mistreat the prisoners. Those in power within the prison should not interfere with the prisoners' negative right to feel safe.

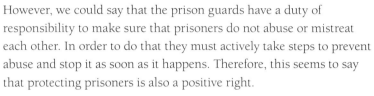

However, we could say that the prison guards have a duty of responsibility to make sure that prisoners do not abuse or mistreat each other. In order to do that they must actively take steps to prevent abuse and stop it as soon as it happens. Therefore, this seems to say that protecting prisoners is also a positive right.

Often, then, positive and negative rights are interdependent when we examine real-world situations.

■ The three generations of human rights

When we discuss human rights, they are often divided up into three categories, called 'generations'. Karel Vasak, the first Secretary-General of the International Institute of Human Rights in Strasbourg, first used this classification in the 1970s. However, the ideas are connected to a long history of Western philosophical traditions.

Vasak was inspired by the revolutions that took place in the United States in 1776 and France in 1789. These revolutions were primarily driven by people demanding rights and questioning the authority of the state. The French Revolution, in particular, is famous for the people's demand of: 'liberté, egalité, fraternité' (liberty, equality and **fraternity**).

■ **Figure 2.8** Government building in France, just one of many that still carry the revolutionary statement 'liberté, egalité, fraternité'

These demands became the foundation of the new French Republic. As seen in Figure 2.8, public buildings in France are adorned with this phrase, demonstrating the importance of these ideals to the French people.

But what exactly are the three generations of rights? Table 2.4 provides an overview.

■ **Table 2.4** The three generations of rights

Generation 1: Liberty	Generation 2: Equality	Generation 3: Fraternity
These are civil and political rights.	These are economic, cultural and social rights.	These are collective rights for all communities, societies and nations. Generation 3 rights are a response to globalization and interdependence.
Some examples include: • freedom from slavery • the right to be treated equally • the right to privacy • protection from being arrested for no reason • the right to a fair trial.	Some examples include: • the right to fair and safe working conditions • the right to decent housing • the right to food, clothing and health care • the right to social security.	Some examples include: • the right for all people to live in a clean environment • the right to economic development • the right to benefit from world trade.

You may have noticed that first generation rights have some similarities to negative rights, while second generation rights are more similar to positive rights. Third generation rights are, however, unique, as they are more focused on the rights of the community rather than the rights of the individual.

Collective rights

Although often when we discuss 'human rights' we are considering the rights of the individual, we should also consider collective rights, which are the rights of groups of people or communities. The collective element of rights is often considered when looking at groups of people who share a cultural or ethnic identity. An example of collective rights would be 'the right to self-determination'.

Sometimes, because of historical events or past conflicts, large groups of people may end up living in a state where they don't identify with the leadership and are possibly mistreated. As a result, they may demand the creation of their own state so that they can preserve their culture, language and heritage and decide who governs them. Examples of groups demanding self-determination include the Palestinian community and the Catalonian people in Spain. When we speak of a group's right to 'self-determination', we mean that those people have a right to decide their own type of government and form a new state if this is what the group wants.

Some of the rights we have looked at so far, such as 'freedom of religion' or 'the right to live in a clean environment', can be seen from both the individual's perspective and the perspective of a wider group of people.

Cultural relativism

So far we have seen that modern conceptions of human rights are closely connected to Western religious, philosophical and political thought. Some people claim that widely accepted ideas of human rights do not always reflect the ethical and social standards of the global community.

Cultural relativists insist that all cultures have unique characteristics and moral codes, and so concepts of 'right' and 'wrong' should be determined by the moral codes of the community or society on a more local scale, not by a universal authority like the UN. They therefore argue that the universality claim of the UDHR is an example of Western values being imposed on the global community.

For example, Article 3 of the Universal Declaration of Human Rights reads: 'Everyone has the right to life, liberty and security of person'. One interpretation of this article that applies to the real world is that the death penalty as a form of punishment should be abolished. After all, people put to death by the state are deprived of their lives. Today, states around the world vary greatly in their use of the death penalty; some have abolished it, some have it but rarely use it, and some use it regularly.

Historically the death penalty, also referred to as capital punishment, was taken for granted and generally not questioned. The assumption was that states had the sovereign right to execute their citizens if they decided it was necessary. However, as we have seen, the power of the state to deprive people of their 'natural rights' was hotly debated during the Age of Enlightenment. Over time, this assumption began to be challenged more frequently and, following the horrors of early twentieth-century genocides, there was plenty of evidence that states could abuse capital punishment. Many concluded that ordinary people should be protected from being put to death by the state. Therefore, Article 3 of the UDHR is often associated with the abolishment of capital punishment.

Cultural relativists may argue, however, that, while most people would agree with Article 3 in principle, it is unfair to make the assumption that all societies and cultures would agree with this interpretation. Some cultural relativists would say that the focus on the abolition of the death penalty is a Western perspective.

The Qur'an, the holy book of Islam, promotes the use of the death penalty under restricted circumstances. States with cultural and legal ties to Islam, such as Saudi Arabia, Iran and Egypt, refuse to abolish the death penalty on the basis of cultural relativism.

Universalism (human rights belong to all people regardless of culture, religion, nationality, etc.) and cultural relativism are two perspectives to consider when examining real-world global political issues of rights and justice.

Discussion point

Several states around the world still retain the death penalty. Other than cultural relativism, what are some other reasons why states might refuse to abolish capital punishment?

2.1.4 Theoretical views on rights and justice

◆ **Multifaceted** means having many sides or parts.

As we see in the core unit and thematic studies of this course, there are overarching theories and models of global politics. These theories are complex, **multifaceted** and often there are differences of opinion even within one school of thought.

This is also true for matters involving rights and justice. A simplified overview, however, can get you started as you explore these theories in greater depth and in the context of your own case studies and examples (see Table 2.5).

■ **Table 2.5** Theoretical views: rights and justice

Theory	Rights and justice	Key thinker
Liberalism	There are rights we possess simply because we are human. Human rights exist independently of whether or not society accepts them. This is a traditional view of rights, and the UDHR exemplifies this school of thought. This viewpoint is very much concerned with the rights of the individual. Liberals see laws and **codification** as essential methods for ensuring that human rights are met.	*International legal universality is one of the greatest achievements of the international human rights movements.* Jack Donnelly, 'The relative universality of human rights'
Marxism	Marxists tend to reject the idea of 'natural rights' and see our conception of human rights as coming from social agreements. They argue that capitalism is a system designed to maximize profit at the expense of workers' rights. Modern human rights instruments make no attempt to change the structural causes of abuse and exploitation in a capitalist society.	*Human rights have purely instrumental value in the political culture; they provide a useful tool for propaganda, nothing more.* Noam Chomsky, 'The possibility of humanitarian intervention'
Postcolonialism	First and foremost, rights must be focused on addressing the injustice seen in society. Postcolonialists are more concerned with what is actually happening in the real world, and use current examples of injustice. In this model, all of us have obligations to ensure that those who are marginalized or oppressed get justice. Postcolonialists are mistrustful of human rights law and see it as ineffective and designed by the elite.	*there is immeasurable distance between what we call 'human rights' and the right of all human; and this distance can begin to be traversed only if we claim the audacity to look at human rights from the standpoint of the historically oppressed groups.* Upendra Baxi, 'From human rights to the right to be human: Some heresies'
Feminism	Feminists believe that any set definition of 'rights' is **imperialistic** in nature. They do believe in rights but question the idea of individual rights. Instead, they look to wider concepts that have more far-reaching impact, such as 'female-**emancipation**'. They look at how this can be best put into practice and reject the idea of universalism. They see that rights laws are sometimes helpful and sometimes ineffectual depending on the situation.	*The feminist movements of today mostly belong to a younger generation, from #MeToo to struggles in Afghanistan and Türkiye and really all over the world. We have the biggest feminist mobilization probably in the history of the world.* Wendy Brown, quoted in Khachaturian, 'Rights without bounds: An interview with Wendy Brown'

You may have noticed one main theory missing from the table, and that is realism. This is because realists largely view rights and justice as irrelevant issues in global politics – not because they are unethical, but because they argue that states make decisions based on national interest and ethics play no role in these decisions.

Discussion point

What role does the state play in protecting and enforcing rights in each of the four theoretical viewpoints?

Adopting one ideology or another has consequences far beyond the limited context of which political beliefs you hold. You might, for instance, favour a particular historical narrative depending on the political ideology you hold, or you might analyse the economic practices of people quite differently depending on whether your political ideology prioritizes individual wealth or collective well-being.

Consider your own views on what you think would be relevant to teach to young students in a history class, or your own views on taxation or how the government should spend its money. Now consider the list of theoretical views in Table 2.5. Do your views on these historical or economic views fit better with one ideology over another?

2.1.5 Definitions, interpretations of and perspectives on justice

There are many approaches to defining the concept of justice. It is an ethical concept and concerns how people as individuals or as part of a society should or should not be treated. It is not easy to provide a 'one size fits all' definition, but justice is often associated with individuals or groups being treated fairly or getting what they deserve.

There are, of course, differences of opinion when deciding what people 'deserve'. For example, some may argue that all people deserve access to clean drinking water, and if you live in a society where this is not the case, then your society is not a just one. Others, including cultural relativists, may argue that the circumstances of that society determine what is considered 'justice'.

In global politics we often associate justice with rights. Thinking back to how rights are defined in the UDHR, we might expect that all individuals have the right to be treated equally by those with power (for example, the government or police) and by other members of their society. When individuals or groups are deprived of their rights, we might expect negative consequences for those responsible. This is also an aspect of justice.

Table 2.6 considers how justice is seen in the real world.

■ **Table 2.6** How justice is seen in the real world

Social justice	Political justice
Social justice concerns comparisons of different people living within a region or state, or globally.	Political justice can concern the power that members of any society have in making decisions and changes to that society.
We can compare all kinds of factors such as: • access to food, water and other necessities of life • access to education, health care and other public services • housing, living conditions and neighbourhood safety • opportunities to work and the ability to live comfortably on these wages.	Authoritarian societies, such as North Korea, have little political justice, as the citizens are unable to share in the decision-making process of the state. Democratic states where all adults can vote are said to have a higher level of political justice.
Ideally, to move towards social justice we want to see fewer differences between what is available to diverse groups and individuals. Of course, in reality, we can see social injustice all around us, from our own communities to the wider global society.	Political justice can also refer to judicial systems within states and how people are treated within those systems. This can be seen by looking at how different groups within a society are treated by the police and within judicial institutions.
It may be impossible to imagine a world with no social injustice but ignoring these inequalities can lead to instability, violence and conflict.	Additionally, if people are persecuted or imprisoned for their beliefs about how a state should be run, this could be considered a political injustice.
	It can be argued that political justice, like social justice, leads to instability, violence and conflict.

Democracy alone is not sufficient evidence of political justice. And frequently, social injustice and political injustice are interdependent. For example, in recent years the United States' judicial and prison system has been criticized extensively by community members and human rights activists concerned about minority ethnic and indigenous Americans' access to justice.

> *Racial discrimination in housing, sentencing, and policing frequently explains why data show stark disproportionalities in justice involvement for people of color, particularly Black people…. people of color are overrepresented in jails, prisons, and non-carceral (non-prison) forms of punishment.*

> Prison Policy Initiative, 'Race and ethnicity'

Table 2.7 is an overview of the current US prison system.

■ **Table 2.7** The US prison system: key statistics in 2023

Category	Data	Source
Percentage of black Americans in the general US population	13%	Census.gov
Percentage of people in prison or jail who are black	38%	Census.gov
Prison incarceration rate for indigenous people versus the nation as a whole	763 versus 350 per 100,000	Prison Policy Initiative
Percentage of people serving life, life without parole or 'virtual life' sentences who are black	48%	The Sentencing Project
Arrest rate for black versus white Americans	6,109 versus 2,795 per 100,000	US Department of Justice Office of Juvenile Justice and Delinquency Prevention
Number of arrests of black Americans in 2018	2.8 million	US Department of Justice Office of Juvenile Justice and Delinquency Prevention
Percentage of people on probation or parole who are black	30%	Prison Policy Initiative

■ **Figure 2.9** People march in a Black Lives Matter protest in Montreal, Canada, on 7 June 2020

● TOK

Social media has become a powerful force in society, providing us with carefully curated views of the world around us. Your own choices about how to consume social media and your stance towards it undoubtedly have huge effects on your political and social values and views.

Many commentators talk about social media 'bubbles', referring to the ways in which social media algorithms suggest to us ideas and content that we are likely to watch. The algorithms pay close attention to how we've used social media in the past, what we've clicked on and how long we've watched before scrolling away in order to identify and present material likely to hold our attention. The effect of this is that we are more likely to consume content that is already something we would be likely to watch and are less often presented with contrasting points of view. This only embeds our own beliefs and ideas, and prevents us from having to think critically about views other than our own.

Try monitoring your own use of social media and consider how often conflicting or contrasting interests, or information are presented to you. If you tend to be more right-leaning in your views, do you see many left-leaning ideas being presented charitably? If you are more left-leaning, how often are you presented with content from right-leaning creators? How do you think this impacts your own outlook on the world?

■ Egalitarian justice

Egalitarian justice is focused on social justice and has a long history in Western philosophical thought. Influential philosophers have debated the meaning of 'justice' over many centuries, and ideas connected to egalitarian justice continue to impact our understanding of rights and justice today, since its influence can be seen in the UDHR and the work of many human rights NGOs.

Some key principles of egalitarian justice include the following:

- All individuals in a society must be treated with equal respect and dignity, no exceptions.
- All people should have equal freedoms and opportunities.
- We are moral beings and have an innate understanding of right and wrong.
- We inhabit a world where people are often seen in terms of economics and politics, but our moral identities cannot be overlooked.

Key theorist

John Rawls (1921–2002)

The political philosopher John Rawls was a well-respected and influential advocate for egalitarian justice.

A society regulated by a public sense of justice is inherently stable.

John Rawls, A Theory of Justice

■ **Figure 2.10** John Rawls

One opposing view of egalitarian justice is that sometimes it is necessary and just to sacrifice the rights of a few people if it provides greater benefit to the larger society. For example, some might argue that, in a society with limited resources, it is best to spend public money educating only the most talented and high-achieving students because in the long run they will benefit society more significantly.

John Rawls's response to this would be:

> *Each person possesses an inviolability founded on justice that even the welfare of society as a whole cannot override. For this reason justice denies that the loss of freedom for some is made right by a greater good shared by others. It does not allow that the sacrifices imposed on a few are outweighed by the larger sum of advantages enjoyed by many.*
>
> *John Rawls*, A Theory of Justice

Rawls would therefore argue that spending public money selectively on only the most talented and high-achieving is morally wrong. Possibly these people are more talented and achieve higher grades because their parents can afford to send them to private school. Whatever the case, an egalitarian would argue that in a just society each person should have access to the same opportunities, and this leads to a happier and more stable society, so all will benefit.

■ Cosmopolitan justice

Like egalitarian justice, cosmopolitan justice is concerned with morality and the obligations found in both social and political justice. Cosmopolitan justice takes the ideas of egalitarian justice further and argues that all people must work at achieving justice for all individuals on a global scale. For practical reasons, IGOs such as the UN and/or perhaps regional IGOs like the African Union (AU) have an obligation to act when needed.

Additionally, in extreme situations, humanitarian intervention can be seen as necessary. Sometimes sovereignty can be seen as an obstacle to justice, and cosmopolitan justice argues that intervening in the affairs of another state is justifiable if:

● the state is structurally 'unjust'; for example, this could mean that a totalitarian regime is in place that is abusing its citizens, or that the state is a failed state struggling to address the needs of its citizens

● the intervention will succeed; this is difficult as it involves predicting the outcome and being assured the intervention will result in justice for the citizens

● all other methods to help have been attempted with no success, and intervention is your last resort.

Cosmopolitan justice in the real world

A real-world example of cosmopolitan justice can be seen when we look at migration, the movement of people within states and between states. Migrants can leave their home countries for many reasons, but in recent decades, more and more people have been forced to leave their homes because of environmental, economic or political instability. The term 'migrant' is a more all-inclusive term that refers to anyone moving from one place to another, but often these people are later classified as 'refugees'.

It is estimated that climate change will push this trend globally and in the coming decades more people may be on the move than ever before in our history. Cosmopolitan justice argues that we are morally obligated to help migrants and refugees, as we are all members of an interdependent global community. To do this, states must cooperate with civil society, including NGOs, regional IGOs and the UN, to rehome migrants and refugees and support them as they build new lives.

As we know, borders are an important element of state sovereignty, and sometimes states and citizens perceive migrants and refugees as a threat to their sovereignty and social stability. As a result, they are often reluctant to accept them or, if they do accept them, they may not grant them legal status. Many migrants then face a life of uncertainty and structural violence.

Conflict is often the source of sudden migration, and the conflicts in Syria and Ukraine have created humanitarian crises in which large numbers of people, desperate to leave their homes, have sought protection from the international community. But which member states of the international community are more likely to have the largest share of responsibility in times of a refugee crisis?

According to the United Nations Refugee Agency:

- 70 per cent of refugees and other people in need of international protection live in countries neighbouring their country of origin.

- 76 per cent of the world's refugees and other people in need of international protection are hosted by low- and middle-income countries. The least economically developed countries provide asylum to 20 per cent of that number.

These statistics are significant because, during any sudden crisis, the neighbouring states of that crisis must initially provide support to the people fleeing. Cosmopolitan justice would then argue that other, more economically developed states must also step in to offer support and provide **asylum** to vulnerable people in need of international protection.

◆ **Asylum** is a place of safety and shelter.

As can be seen in Table 2.8, economically developed states provide the highest amount of funding to help support refugees.

■ **Table 2.8** International funding to help support refugees, 2022

Rank	Donor	Amount (USD)
1	United States	2,195,608,503
2	Germany	536,332,981
3	European Union	255,101,061
4	Private donors in the United States	212,020,330
5	Japan	167,708,064
6	Private donors in Japan	165,678,801
7	Sweden	145,652,735
8	Private donors in Spain	133,916,121
9	Norway	118,176,368
10	Netherlands	110,001,407

UNHCR, *Update on budgets and funding (2022 and 2023)*

However, while many economically developed nations have provided significant financial support to the United Nations Refugee Agency (UNHCR), some wealthy countries host fewer refugees, as seen in Figure 2.11.

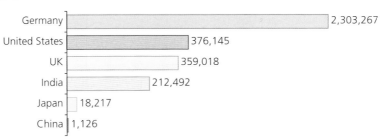

■ **Figure 2.11** Number of refugees and asylum seekers hosted by the world's wealthiest six countries in 2022 (data from UNHCR, *Update on budgets and funding (2022 and 2023)*)

Table 2.9 indicates the top 10 countries in terms of numbers of refugees hosted. Although cosmopolitan justice urges states not to see international borders as walls to exclude people in need, states are entitled to control their borders and who comes and goes. We can see in the table that many low- and middle-income countries host the largest number of people seeking safety, and many are doing so because they are neighbouring countries and have little choice, while more economically developed states provide financial aid but are less likely to host refugees.

■ **Table 2.9** The top 10 refugee host countries in mid-2022

Country	Number of refugees
Türkiye	3,673,808
Germany	2,065,576
Uganda	1,489,559
Pakistan	1,286,262
Poland	1,210,582
Sudan	1,112,303
Bangladesh	929,681
Ethiopia	867,799
Lebanon	835,714
Iran	800,025

UNHCR, *Update on budgets and funding (2022 and 2023)*

Discussion point

As we have seen, more economically developed states donate more money to help refugees, but are also less likely to host them. Does this situation reflect the ideal of cosmopolitan justice?

■ Ecological justice

Ordinarily, in discussions of rights and justice, human beings are the focus. You have probably seen, heard or even participated in some sort of environmental activism. Environmental concerns cross state boundaries and, globally, people are concerned about the state of the environment and its impact on the health and well-being of all of humankind.

Ecological justice advocates that we start considering all living beings, not only people, when taking action to address environmental concerns. Due to the interconnected nature of our global environment, our future cohabitation on this planet depends on us being more conscious and proactive when it comes to practising rights and justice for non-human living beings.

Some people who agree with an ecological justice viewpoint argue that non-human living beings are holders of 'moral considerability', meaning we humans are morally obliged to pursue justice on their behalf, but not only because we will benefit. They believe that human beings have created a world where there simply has not been any consideration for the non-human inhabitants, and this has led to a severe crisis in terms of loss of habitat and mass extinction.

Discussion point

Can you think of an example where private actors/companies, in your city or anywhere else, have been challenged by activists concerned about the welfare of animals?
To what extent do you think the activists are fighting for ecological justice?

Zulu Ubuntu

There are many interpretations of what 'justice' means and how it looks in society. As you examine political issues taking place in different regions of the world, look into what concepts of rights and justice are present and consider the impact they have on politics.

In South Africa, the Zulu people refer to the concept of Ubuntu. Ubuntu has its roots in Zulu African philosophy, in which the idea of community is the essential building block of society.

Desmond Tutu (1931–2021) was a South African religious leader, anti-apartheid leader, human rights activist and winner of the Nobel Peace Prize.

In his memoir, *No Future Without Forgiveness*, Tutu wrote:

> *Ubuntu is very difficult to render into a Western language. ... It is to say, 'My humanity is inextricably bound up in yours.' We belong in a bundle of life.*

■ **Figure 2.12** Desmond Tutu

Nelson Mandela (1918–2013), like Tutu, was a South African anti-apartheid leader, human rights activist and winner of the Nobel Peace Prize. Mandela has been quoted as saying that Ubuntu is not simply about enriching your own life, but also enriching the lives of those living in your community (Modise). It has been adopted as an important philosophy by environmentalists and by those who support a more communal, rather than individual-focused, approach to rights and justice. (For more information on Ubuntu, see pages 287–288.)

Liberty and equality are two of the key concepts of this chapter. They are often seen as interdependent (see Figure 2.16) and are embedded in many real-world human rights political issues. Throughout this chapter we have seen evidence that 'liberty' is about personal freedom and having the ability to make choices and decisions for yourself, while 'equality' is the idea that all human beings have equal worth and value. No matter how you define rights and justice, the concepts of liberty and equality will also be considered.

Extended essay

If you're thinking of writing an extended essay about local or regional interpretations of justice, looking into indigenous people's concepts of justice could be an interesting start. Remember, though, a good extended essay must consider multiple perspectives, and always discuss your ideas and potential research questions with your extended essay supervisor.

■ **Figure 2.13** Nelson Mandela

ACTIVITY

Reflect on how liberty and equality are embedded in the UDHR, cultural relativism, social justice and Ubuntu. What evidence can you find to support the claim that liberty and equality are embedded in most perspectives of rights and justice?

Liberty
Personal
freedom and
decision
making

Equality
All people have
the same
intrinsic value

■ **Figure 2.14** The delicate balance between liberty and equality

 Chapter summary

In this chapter we have covered:
- the meaning of rights and justice, two very complex concepts
- multiple interpretations of rights, justice, liberty and equality
- that in our contemporary world, the United Nations and the Universal Declaration of Human Rights 'definitions' dominate most discussion regarding rights and justice, but there are alternative views to consider and explore within the context of real-world situations.

The following chapters will expand upon some of these viewpoints and give you a better understanding of rights and justice.

REVIEW QUESTIONS

Now that you have read this chapter, reflect on these questions:

■ According to John Rawls, 'A society regulated by a public sense of justice is inherently stable.' Using this quotation and what you have learned in this chapter, write your own definition of 'justice'.

■ What evidence of the importance of liberty and equality can you see in the Universal Declaration of Human Rights?

■ When we talk about 'contested meanings' we're not saying that these different meanings are always in complete opposition to each other. It is important to see that there can be agreement, particularly when looking at real-world examples. For example, in what ways might a cultural relativist view agree with a postcolonialist view of rights and justice? Can you think of a real-world example to support your claim?

Interactions of political stakeholders and actors

SYLLABUS CONTENT

By the end of this chapter, you should understand:
▶ the interactions of political stakeholders and actors in relation to rights and justice, including:
  ▷ the state and national governments
  ▷ intergovernmental organizations
  ▷ regional human rights tribunals
  ▷ civil society organizations (including advocacy)
  ▷ marginalized, vulnerable or most affected groups and individuals
  ▷ private companies and unions.

Look at the list below and think about how each of these stakeholders you were introduced to in Section 1 could be concerned with rights and justice:

● states

● sub-national and local governments

● intergovernmental organizations (IGOs)

● organized civil society (including non-governmental organizations, NGOs)

● private actors/companies

● social movements

● resistance movements

● political parties

● interest and pressure groups

● political leaders

● formal and informal political forums

● the media

● other individual and collective actors.

If we think about real-world examples, we quickly see that many actors and political stakeholders are involved with rights and justice, and they frequently interact with each other, as together they are more effective at bringing about change. For example, if a private company is mistreating its employees, and the local government appears not to be helping, the media may become involved, and the complaints of the workers could be posted online. This might attract the attention of a local NGO concerned with workers' rights, who might further pressure the local government and other political leaders to take action.

■ **Figure 2.15** There is a complex web of interconnections between many stakeholders and actors in global politics

TOK

Now that you've identified the different perspectives of the different stakeholders, consider how those perspectives might be a consequence of the core values, assumptions and relationship to the issues, and how that might have contributed to those perspectives. Are they characterizing the issues in the same way? Why might they differ? How do you think your own perspectives on the issues are influenced by your own assumptions and values? Where do you think those values come from?

2.2.1 The state

The state remains the primary actor in global politics, and this is most certainly true when it comes to rights and justice. After all, the state is responsible for the laws, judicial systems and welfare of its citizens. However, it's important to remember that the interdependent nature of global politics continues to challenge the supremacy of the state when it comes to rights and justice.

Despite the interest and concern of multiple actors, the state/national government does have control over key mechanisms that influence rights and justice. Some of the ways the state can contribute to a society where rights and justice are enforced include:

● ensuring a stable economic and political climate

● allowing people to protest and speak their minds

● allowing citizens to fully participate in government

● creating and/or enforcing laws that promote rights and justice

● allowing NGOs and open communication with international human rights groups

● encouraging and celebrating diversity and respect for all races, socio-economic groups, sexualities and gender identities

● providing clear access to justice in the event that rights are violated.

2.2.2 Intergovernmental organizations

In Section 1, you were introduced to intergovernmental organizations as a group of states or governments that work together on issues of common interest. The main purpose of IGOs is to provide a way for the global community to work together in areas of peace, security, economics and rights and justice. In our interdependent world, IGOs play a significant role in global politics.

The United Nations (UN) is the most influential IGO globally. In order to protect and enforce human rights, it has several mechanisms, or organs, in place, including the International Court of Justice, the International Criminal Court, the UN Human Rights Council and the UN High Commission for Refugees.

Figure 2.16 The Peace Palace (Vredespalais) in The Hague, which houses the International Court of Justice

International Court of Justice

The International Court of Justice (ICJ) is the principal judicial organ of the UN. Its purpose is to settle disputes between states in accordance with international law and to provide legal opinions to the UN and its agencies as requested. There are 15 judges, each serving a nine-year term, elected by the UN General Assembly and the UN Security Council.

The important thing to remember is that this is a court where only states can seek justice. Especially important is that usually both states must be willing to participate and accept that the decision of the court is final and legally binding.

Discussion point

How can resolving disputes between countries in a formal court help to reduce the chance of conflict?

Cases of the International Court of Justice

What kinds of disputes does the court commonly address? Many of the cases brought to the ICJ involve disputes over territory or activities by one state that are perceived to infringe on the sovereignty of the other. Table 2.10 summarizes two of the recently resolved cases.

Table 2.10 Two recently resolved cases of the ICJ

Dates (beginning to end)	States involved	Issue/case name	Decision
2013–22	Nicaragua and Colombia	Alleged violations of Sovereign Rights and Maritime Spaces in the Caribbean Sea (Nicaragua v. Colombia)	Colombia must immediately stop patrolling and trying to control fishing in oil resources in Nicaragua's waters.
1999–2022	Democratic Republic of the Congo and Uganda	Armed Activities on the Territory of the Congo (Democratic Republic of the Congo v. Uganda)	Uganda ordered to pay Democratic Republic of the Congo $325 million (USD) for the occupation (1998–2003) of territory, looting of valuable resources and deaths of 10,000–15,000 people.

Limitations of the ICJ

1 Ordinarily both states must have accepted a declaration recognizing the ICJ's jurisdiction. Currently, less than half of the states represented in the UN recognize the court's jurisdiction. However, the ICJ statute states that the ICJ can override this if the case being proposed shows evidence that the UN Charter or treaties and conventions have been/are being violated.

2 As you can see in Table 2.10, court cases can take a long time to resolve.

3 Once judgments have been made, there is no guarantee that states will comply with the verdict; they may exercise their sovereignty and ignore the recommendations. In such circumstances the case may then be brought to the UN Security Council (UNSC) for consideration. Therefore, the UNSC has more power than the ICJ and can, if it chooses, decide not to enforce the ruling.

Discussion point

Why might the UNSC decide not to enforce a ruling made by the ICJ? Could the structure of the Security Council be an obstacle to justice?

■ International Criminal Court

The International Criminal Court (ICC) came into force in 2002 after 60 states ratified the Rome Statute of 1998. The Rome Statute established the legal conditions and structure of the court. The ICC is the first permanent international criminal court to target individuals guilty of war crimes, genocide and crimes against humanity. Anyone can be tried at the court – heads of states, members of the government and military officials can all face trial. Importantly, victims and the families of the victims of these crimes can participate in the proceedings and request **reparations**.

◆ **Reparations** are payments in either money or resources.

The ICC has jurisdiction over two categories of crimes, which are clearly defined in the Rome Statute:

1 Crimes of concern to the global community including genocide, crimes against humanity and war crimes. These crimes must have occurred after 2002, at which time the court was opened.

2 Crimes of aggression after 1998, at which time 120 states adopted the Rome Statute. This would involve threats against the sovereignty and independence of another state.

The court does not replace national courts within states but is meant to complement them. If the court system within a state is unable or unwilling to prosecute cases, the ICC may do so.

■ **Figure 2.17** The International Criminal Court judges, 2023

How do cases get to the ICC and how is it structured?

There are three ways a case can come to the ICC:

1 State parties to the Rome statute can refer situations to the ICC prosecutor.

2 The UN Security Council can request the prosecutor to launch an investigation.

3 The Office of the Prosecutor may launch an investigation on the basis of information from outside sources.

There is a president and vice-president of the ICC, along with 18 elected judges selected from around the world. Each serve a total of nine years on the court.

● Common mistake

Students often confuse the International Court of Justice (ICJ) and the International Criminal Court (ICC) because they are both courts associated with the United Nations. Always remember that both have distinct purposes and functions: broadly, the ICJ settles disputes between states; the ICC prosecutes individuals accused of international crimes, including war crimes, crimes against humanity and genocide.

Figure 2.18 The UNHRC in session, Geneva, Switzerland

UN Human Rights Council

Its purpose is:

● to work towards ensuring that people know about their rights

● to work towards ensuring that all people can use their rights.

The UNHRC is made up of 47 delegates elected by the UN General Assembly. Each delegate represents a state and is elected to serve a three-year term on the council. In order to attempt to address global disparities in the distribution of power, the UNHRC committee is made up of delegates as follows:

● African States: 13 seats

● Asia-Pacific States: 13 seats

● Latin American and Caribbean states: 8 seats

● Western European and other states: 7 seats

● Eastern European states: 6 seats

HL extension: Poverty

Poverty is often associated with a lack of power and, in order to address this, some IGOs have attempted to give a greater voice to states that are less economically developed. The structure of the UNHRC is an attempt to address this imbalance of power. A possible starting point for a global political challenge case study about poverty could be to look at how structural changes can reduce poverty at a local, state or regional level.

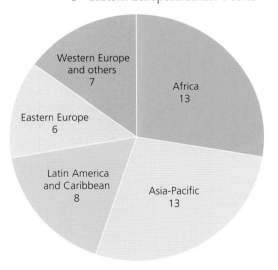

Figure 2.19 The UNHRC committee members

The UNHRC also works collaboratively with a group, or 'think tank', of 18 people who have special knowledge in different areas of human rights issues. They are called the Advisory Committee.

Sometimes, the UNHRC also works with other experts who know a lot about one right or one country. When this happens, it is referred to as 'Special Procedures'.

What does the UN Human Rights Council do?

The UNHRC meets at least three times a year in Geneva, Switzerland. During these sessions, members discuss and debate human rights issues that are of concern generally and human rights issues specific to a particular state. They then negotiate and draft resolutions to address these concerns. Resolutions are documents that explain the human rights concerns and also provide actions that could help to address them. Sometimes NGOs are invited to these sessions to offer their perspectives.

Resolutions could, for example:

- call for an in-depth investigation
- call for other UN agencies and officials to become involved
- call for experts to become involved.

These resolutions are not legally binding.

Other than resolutions, the other main function of the UNHRC is to conduct a Universal Periodic Review. This is an overview of how well each state is doing in fulfilling its human rights obligations.

The UNHRC focuses on issues that are closely aligned to the values of the United Nations. The main areas of focus are shown in Table 2.11.

■ **Table 2.11** Main areas of UNHRC focus

Stated topic	What does it involve?
Civil spaces and democracy	This concerns the right people have to actively contribute to, and participate in, the politics of their communities. Human rights defenders and democracy activists are covered here, as are ordinary people and their right to freedom of expression.
Development and living in dignity	This concerns a wide variety of issues that impact everyday life, including: • environmental sustainability • the right to education and health • the right to clean water • the right to a basic standard of living. The responsibilities of multinational corporations (MNCs) as well as states may come into examination here.
Equality and non-discrimination	Some of the specific areas of focus here include: • racism • gender and women's equality • children and youth • freedom of religion • indigenous people • LGBTQ+ rights • migration • minorities • older people • people with disabilities • albinism.
Justice and the rule of law	This concerns the administration of justice and law, including: • the death penalty, detention and jail conditions • disappearances and executions • enslavement of people • trafficking • terrorism and violent extremism.
Peace and security	This concerns: • conflict prevention • humanitarian emergencies • peacekeeping.

■ **Figure 2.20** The UNHRC focuses on a number of issues, including development and living in dignity

Limitations of the UN Human Rights Council

1 Some of the countries with delegates in the UNHRC have been heavily criticized for their own human rights records. Many of the delegates represent countries that are not democratic, and so human rights activists wonder how we can expect non-democratic states to uphold the values associated with rights and justice. The non-profit organization Freedom House has described the inclusion of known human rights-violating states on the UNHRC as 'foxes in the henhouse', which undermines the credibility and effectiveness of the committee.

2 A second criticism is that the resolutions are not legally binding. Therefore, states may exercise their sovereignty and ignore the recommendations and resolutions of the committee.

■ **Figure 2.21** The United Nations High Commission for Refugees, Geneva, Switzerland

■ UN High Commission for Refugees

In Section 1 we looked at migration as an example of cosmopolitan justice. In this part of the chapter, we are examining how the UN attempts to help refugees, displaced people and asylum seekers.

After the Second World War millions of people were left homeless and displaced. The UN High Commission for Refugees (UNHCR) was established in 1950 by the UN General Assembly to address this problem. The 1951 Refugee Convention has 146 member states (as of April 2023) and establishes the UNHCR's mandate to monitor the implementation of the Refugee Convention.

It remains a global organization designed to protect:

● refugees

● people forcibly displaced within their own states

● those denied a nationality and who are therefore stateless.

Purpose and structure

The purpose of the UNCHR is to protect the rights of refugees and others needing help (see Table 2.12) by working with states to find solutions to problems associated with granting asylum and refugee status. Additionally, it works together with IGOs and NGOs to provide help and material and financial support when needed.

■ **Table 2.12** The different groups of people needing help from the UNHCR

Group	Definition
Refugees	People escaping conflict or persecution. They often risk their lives for a life of uncertainty because circumstances in their own country are too dangerous and intolerable.
Internally displaced people	People seeking safety somewhere else but still within their own country.
Asylum seekers	People seeking international protection from conflict and persecution. These people may have somehow managed to leave their country and are seeking refugee status in a different state.
Migrants	People moving to another country for reasons other than conflict or persecution. Maybe they are seeking educational or work opportunities, or simply seeking a safer and better quality of life.

Figure 2.22 shows the countries where people needed help from the UNHCR in 2020.

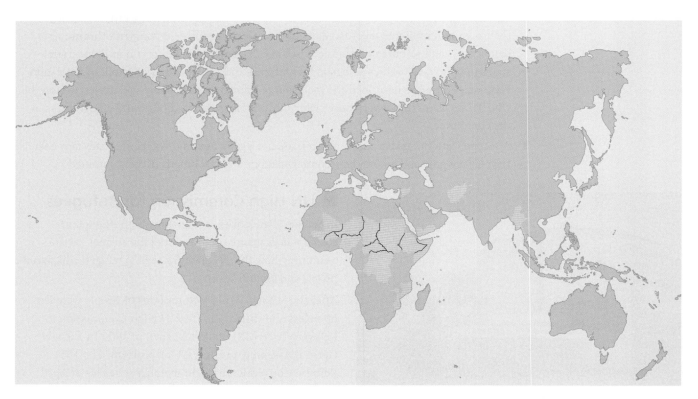

■ **Figure 2.22** The world faces a persistent and devastating refugee and displaced persons crisis impacting people globally. How many of the countries facing this crisis can you identify?

Discussion point

Why are the rights of asylum seekers, displaced people and refugees more difficult to monitor and protect?

Many people fleeing their countries end up being housed in a refugee camp (see Figure 2.23) until alternate arrangements can be made for them to be settled in a new country or return home safely. This process is very challenging and can take many years.

CASE STUDY

The Rohingya crisis

■ **Figure 2.23** A refugee camp in Bangladesh housing Rohingya refugees from Myanmar

In 2017, massive-scale violence and serious human rights abuses forced the Rohingya people, a minority ethnic group, to escape from their homes in Myanmar. Thousands fled by sea to Bangladesh. It is estimated that at one time almost a million Rohingya people found temporary safety in the Cox's Bazar Region of Bangladesh, which was, at that time, home to the world's largest refugee camp.

Some of the immediate needs of refugees addressed at UN refugee camps can be seen in Figure 2.24.

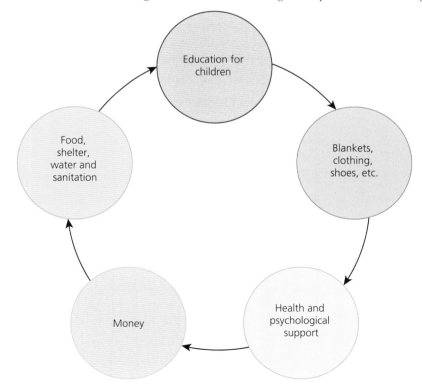

■ **Figure 2.24** The immediate needs of refugees living in refugee camps

Stateless people

It might surprise you to know that there are millions of people who are denied a nationality in the world today. How could this happen?

1 The most common reason is that they were born into a country where the state discriminates against their race, ethnicity, religion, language or gender. The laws in several countries do not allow women to pass on nationality to their children. For example, in Malaysia, if a father denies the child or dies, the children can be left stateless.

2 A child born to illegal migrants may be denied citizenship and left stateless.

3 Some countries revoke citizenship for those who have lived outside the country for an extended period.

4 Sometimes people fleeing war or conflict may lack identity papers proving their nationality and are therefore considered stateless.

5 Many stateless people pass this condition on to their children.

Why is being 'stateless' a problem?

In many ways, without a nationality you have no 'proof' of your existence. Therefore, it is very hard to secure human rights for stateless people and, as a result:

● They are denied the right to education, health care, marriage and job opportunities.

● They cannot travel as they have no right to a passport.

● They are more likely to face discrimination, harassment, human trafficking and slavery.

Challenges to ending statelessness

The right to nationality can only be granted by states themselves. Sovereignty means that states have the right to determine the conditions for nationality in their own countries. The UNHCR works to convince states of the importance of this issue and launches campaigns on social media to persuade ordinary people of the importance of this issue.

Discussion point

What countries refuse women the right to pass their nationality to their children? What NGOs are working to address this problem?

Limitations of the UN Human Rights Council

In recent years, the global community has been confronted with an expanding, and at times overwhelming, refugee crisis. Funding for the work of the UNHCR, which comes from the donations of key donor states, has not kept up with the need. This has placed a great strain on the council and the work it does.

Additionally, because of state sovereignty, the UNHCR can only operate within a country if it is given permission. Once given that permission, the state may place limitations on the work the UNHCR is able to do, and often states will demand financial and political favours in return for cooperation.

■ Regional human rights tribunals

Since the creation of the Universal Declaration of Human Rights, other IGOs have been founded that attempt to address the protection and enforcement of human rights within specific geographical regions. Many of these regional institutions work collaboratively with the United Nations but also attempt to address the specific needs and concerns of the people of their region.

Table 2.13 shows the major global human rights institutions and instruments.

■ Table 2.13 The major global human rights institutions and instruments

Human rights institution	Instrument
African Union	African Charter on Human and People's Rights
Association of Southeast Asian Nations	ASEAN Human Rights Declaration
European Union	Charter of Fundamental Rights
Organization of American States	American Convention on Human Rights, American Declaration of the Rights and Duties of Man
Organisation of Islamic Cooperation	Arab Charter on Human Rights

1950: European Convention on Human Rights

The Convention for the Protection of Human Rights and Fundamental Freedoms, better known as the European Convention on Human Rights, was signed in Rome (Italy) on 4 November 1950 by 12 member states of the Council of Europe and entered into force on 3 September 1953.

It was the first instrument to give legally binding force to many of the rights stated in the Universal Declaration of Human Rights.

It was also the first treaty to establish a supranational organ to ensure that the states complied with the rights stated. By doing this, the Council of Europe (which later evolved into the European Union (EU)) attempted to overcome the obstacle of state sovereignty. The convention was a milestone in the development of international law and the protection and enforcement of rights and justice. Even today, EU members must agree to it and abstaining is not an option.

◆ **Supranational** usually refers to a collective group that is outside of the power of an individual state. The United Nations and the African Union are examples.

The '**supranational** court' mentioned is the European Court of Human Rights in Strasbourg, France. This court is above the laws of any individual state. Ordinary citizens and states can approach the court if they feel the rights as laid out in the European Convention on Human Rights have been violated.

Its judgments are binding, and today there are 46 states within the EU who adhere to its rulings.

1969: American Convention on Human Rights

The American Convention on Human Rights (ACHR) was adopted in 1969 by the Organization of American States. The ACHR formalized the process by which human rights could be monitored and addressed within the Americas.

In general, cases are first brought to the Inter-American Commission of Human Rights by individuals, NGOs and/or state representatives. The function of this commission is not to make judgments but instead to facilitate a 'friendly settlement' between concerned parties. However, if a resolution is not possible, the commission may refer the case to the InterAmerican Court of Human Rights, which is the judicial organ. The judges hold two sessions a year but sometimes meet for emergency sessions as needed. The court can issue 'advisory opinions' but its decisions are non-binding. Only the commission or states can refer a case to this court.

1981: African Charter on Human and Peoples' Rights

The African Charter on Human and Peoples' Rights was adopted by the Organization for African Unity (now the African Union) in 1981. The charter covers civil, political, economic, social and cultural rights. It is a legally binding treaty guaranteeing human rights, however, a member state may ratify the charter but also choose to opt out or declare a 'reservation' of certain clauses. Therefore, state sovereignty remains predominant in decisions regarding human rights, unlike the European Convention on Human Rights. Consequently, this charter rejects the idea of universalism.

The African Court on Human and Peoples' Rights exists to address concerns of individuals and NGOs, but only eight of the 34 member states of the African Union accept the court's legitimacy.

1990: Cairo Declaration

In 1990, the Organisation of Islamic Cooperation (OIC) created the Cairo Declaration. This declaration resembles the UDHR, but at the heart of every article is Islamic Sharia. In 2007, Pakistan's ambassador Masood Khan addressed the UN and said that the Cairo Declaration 'is not an alternative, competing world view on human rights. It complements the Universal Declaration as it addresses religious and cultural specificity of the Muslim countries.' The document is non-binding.

The Cairo Declaration is largely symbolic and has led to no change in legislation. It is rarely discussed publicly, leading many to claim it has little purpose. However, some argue its value is that it gives a voice to a Muslim point of view of human rights.

2012: ASEAN Human Rights Declaration

Adopted on 18 November 2012 in Phnom Penh, Cambodia, the ASEAN Human Rights Declaration is south-east Asia's first regional declaration of human rights. The ASEAN declaration is not legally binding but is considered a framework for member states to follow.

There are 40 articles, which focus on civil, political, economic, social and cultural rights. Additionally, the right to development and the right to peace are specified. Currently there is no court to address violations and, instead, the ASEAN Intergovernmental Commission meets twice a year to discuss pertinent issues surrounding rights as laid out in the declaration.

The following is an overview of ASEAN's purpose:

> *ASEAN Member States share a common interest in and commitment to the promotion and protection of human rights and fundamental freedoms. In accordance with the ASEAN Charter, respect for and promotion of human rights underpin regional cooperation among ASEAN Member States on human rights and its cooperation with relevant national, regional and international institutions and organizations.*

The Association of Southeast Asian Nations website

Table 2.14 shows us the regional approach to human rights.

■ **Table 2.14** Regional human rights at a glance

Organization	Document	Purpose	Is it binding?	Judicial component
Council of Europe	European Convention on Human Rights	Created to provide an effective and binding force for the UDHR	Yes	Yes
Organization of American States	American Convention on Human Rights	To promote individual rights within a democratic framework	No	Yes
African Union	African Charter on Human and Peoples' Rights	To promote and protect basic human freedoms in Africa	No	Yes
Organisation of Islamic Cooperation	Cairo Declaration	To incorporate Islamic law into human rights	No	No
Association of Southeast Asian Nations	ASEAN Human Rights Declaration	To unify states and work towards progressive social development	No	No

2.2.3 Civil society organizations including NGOs that advocate human rights

Although states and IGOs are significant stakeholders in the protection and enforcement of rights and justice, civil society organizations (CSO) also play a crucial role and frequently interact with these stakeholders.

As you learned in the core chapters, 'civil society' is a broad term that covers groups or organizations voluntarily formed by people with a common goal. Non-governmental organizations (NGOs) or community-based organizations are considered CSOs.

The legitimacy of these groups depends upon them being non-profit, independent of government control and without commercial affiliation. They can be organized on a local, national or global level and are driven by common humanitarian goals. CSOs can often monitor rights and justice on a more local level and provide feedback to states, IGOs and ordinary people regarding the current state of rights and justice in a variety of ways and places.

◼ What does it mean to 'advocate' for human rights?

Those who advocate for rights identify problem areas and want those with power to make changes! They do this by advocating; they attempt to 'spread the word' about their concerns to as many people as possible in order to apply pressure to those who have the power to make necessary changes. They do this via the tools of social media, letters, emails or organizing events such as protest marches. Advocacy can be a very effective method of raising public awareness and bringing about change.

Discussion point

What do you think are the strengths and limitations to using advocacy as a way to bring about change?

Amnesty International

Amnesty International is probably the most famous civil society organization in the world. It focuses on human rights, and it has the widest global reach, with offices in Europe, Asia-Pacific, Africa, Latin America and the Middle East. It started in 1961, focusing on the rights of political prisoners – those held in detention for their beliefs.

In 1977, Amnesty International won the Nobel Peace Prize for its contributions to peace and human rights. Over time, it has expanded its areas of focus and some of the issues it monitors include:

- armed conflict
- climate change
- detention
- freedom of expression
- living in dignity
- issues related to refugees, asylum seekers and migrants
- arms control
- corporate accountability
- disappearances

- indigenous rights
- older people's rights
- sexual and reproductive rights
- child rights
- the death penalty
- discrimination
- international justice
- police brutality
- torture.

Looking at the list above, it becomes clear that the goals of Amnesty International and the Universal Declaration of Human Rights have commonalities.

Amnesty International has had special consultative status at the UN since 1964, and has advised and contributed to many facets of human rights issues over the years. However, unlike a state, it cannot vote in the General Assembly and can only advise and advocate. Amnesty International maintains complete neutrality and at times can be a harsh critic of the UN and its agencies. It claims to have over 10 million members, and funding is provided by voluntary contributions from individuals and in some instances businesses they deem ethical.

What does Amnesty International do?

Amnesty International has a wide network of researchers investigating claims of violations. Once satisfied that it has enough evidence, it shares its findings with governments, IGOs and other influential actors in order to bring about change. Additionally, its members organize letter writing, petitions, protests and human rights campaigns worldwide.

Every year it publishes a report, 'The State of the World', in which it highlights human rights violations taking place in all countries of the world. This report is based on extensive research and is an effective way to see trends both globally and regionally, and to 'name and shame' the states violating human rights.

 Extended essay

If you're thinking of writing an extended essay on human rights, the most up-to-date Amnesty International report is an excellent place to get you started. Not only are there global and regional overviews, additionally each state is reported on separately. The report provides valuable background information and an up-to-date picture of the global situation. Remember, though, a good extended essay must consider multiple perspectives, and always discuss your ideas and potential research questions with your extended essay supervisor.

Human Rights Watch

Human Rights Watch (HRW) is another example of a well-known civil society organization concerned with rights and justice. It was founded in 1978 and frequently collaborates with Amnesty International and, like Amnesty International, accepts the basic definitions of human rights as laid out in the UDHR.

In 1997, HRW was awarded the Nobel Peace Prize for its extensive work to end the usage of land mines. HRW researches and documents human rights abuses often by going undercover and speaking directly to people being deprived of their rights. Although it is concerned with all human rights abuses, it tends to focus on specific areas of crisis, including armed conflict and pandemics. It uses social media, videos and published reports to present its findings and advocate for change. Its funding comes from private donations.

Some of the issues it monitors include:

- arms
- economic justice and rights
- LGBTQ+ rights
- technology and rights
- children's rights
- the environment
- refugees and migrants
- terrorism and counter-terrorism

- crisis and conflict
- free speech
- women's rights
- the rights of older people
- torture
- disability rights
- health
- international justice.

THEMATIC STUDIES: Rights and justice

HL extension: Health

Access to affordable and timely healthcare is considered by many to be a right that all people should have. Good health is necessary for a good quality of life. A possible starting point for a global political challenge case study focused on health could be to examine what factors have led to some people not being able to access necessary healthcare in a particular state or community. There may be links to other global political challenges including Poverty, Identity, Technology and/or Equality.

■ **Figure 2.25** Human Rights Watch monitors a range of human rights issues, including the rights of older people

Discussion point

What similarities can you see when looking at the issues covered by both Amnesty International and Human Rights Watch? What differences can you see?

Child Rights International Network

Child Rights International Network is a civil society organization specifically concerned with addressing the rights of children. Traditionally, in most societies, children have been seen as extensions of their parents or guardians, and the responsibility to protect the child is often seen as a private one. The Child Rights International Network challenges this idea and argues that children, like adults, should be seen as individuals with their own autonomy and rights. As vulnerable members of society, many children cannot rely on the protection of adults and therefore there needs to be a greater awareness of how we as a global society can ensure children are safe.

The Child Rights International Network was established in 1990 as a response to the UN Convention on the Rights of the Child (UNCRC). This convention echoes many of the articles of the Universal Declaration of Human Rights while also specifically addressing the rights of children.

Figure 2.26 is a visual summary of the key elements in the UN Convention on the Rights of the Child. To see the full document outlining all of the Articles of the Convention, visit **unicef.org**.

Child Rights International Network aims to:

- monitor patterns of children's human rights challenges globally
- conduct public campaigns focused on raising awareness of children's rights
- challenge violators of children's rights
- engage with relevant professions and other civil society organizations to bring about justice and change.

Protection and support of the family.

Protection from kidnapping, violence and discrimination of any kind.

Protection of culture, identity, religion, privacy and opinions

Protection of basic needs including water, food, clothing, shelter and education.

Special attention is paid to the unique needs of refugee children.

■ **Figure 2.26** Key elements in the UN Convention on the Rights of the Child

Child Rights International has launched campaigns on the issues shown in Table 2.15 based on the rights listed in the UNCRC.

■ **Table 2.15** Child Rights International campaigns based on UNCRC rights

Access to justice	Assisted reproduction+++	Civil and political rights	Children's rights in the digital age	Environment	Military enlistment
Age assessment++	Bodily integrity	Counter-terrorism	Deprivation of liberty	Girls	Sexual violence

++ In some circumstances children are unable to prove they are under 18 (perhaps they are refugees or displaced) and therefore they are considered adults by authorities. This can be harmful as the child may then be deprived of educational opportunities or housed with adults and face potential abuse.

+++ This looks at unregulated surrogacy, embryo screening and other technologies associated with new life from the perspective of the child, rather than the parents.

Child Rights International Network, 'Issues'

Discussion point

The campaign to end military recruitment of under-18s in the UK was launched by the Child Rights International Network. Why, when we already have the UDHR, is it necessary to outline children's rights in a separate document?

Marginalized, vulnerable or most affected groups and individuals

Within most societies there will be those who are seen as or treated differently simply because of who they are.

Marginalization occurs when people are perceived as 'different' by the wider society because of their social identities. Race, gender, sexuality, nationality, social class as well as economic status can all be used as reasons to deny people their basic rights and access to justice. As a result, marginalized people can be considered vulnerable.

It is worth considering that people can also be considered vulnerable due to other factors, such as substance addiction, being elderly, being stateless, being pregnant or, as we saw when examining the work of Child Rights International, being a child. Ultimately, there are groups of people and individuals who are not treated fairly, and addressing this injustice is at the heart of almost all human rights activism.

TOK

One of the impacts of the lack of representation in wider society of marginalized populations is the limiting nature of various forms of knowing and thinking in that society. Often, marginalized communities have important insights, methods and perspectives that would benefit wider society. Historically, for example, women were a marginalized group (lacking a voice or not being able to exercise political will). Many would argue that many areas of knowledge were worse off for not having the voice of women in their fields.

However, since the academic and political world became more welcoming to new voices, new knowledge has been developed. Fields such as psychology, anthropology, history, philosophy, political science and sociology have been deeply enriched by these previously unknown insights.

TOK activity

Research the role of marginalized populations in the communities of knowers related to a favourite subject in your IB subjects. Learn what new questions and insights they might have brought to the discussions of topics in that field and evaluate the effect of those insights.

■ **Figure 2.27** Maina Kiai

Civil society tends to focus on what needs to be done, so sometimes positive achievements can be overlooked. There are human rights activists who acknowledge and celebrate changes that have taken place with regard to vulnerable groups and in particular LGBTQ+ communities. One such activist is Maina Kiai (see Figure 2.27), a Kenyan lawyer who specializes in human rights both in Kenya and globally. He has worked closely with the UN as an expert adviser on the UN Human Rights Council. Additionally, he also works closely with Human Rights Watch, leading their Alliances and Partnerships Program, and was an original member of the Oversight Board of Facebook/Instagram, moderating content for human rights violations.

Maina Kiai has said that, although inequality and discrimination against LGBTQ+ communities continues to exist, the LGBTQ+ rights movement is one of the most successful social movements in recent years. As evidence to support these claims, he points to the widespread acceptance of same-sex marriage in the Global North and observes that traditionally conservative societies such as Uruguay, Argentina and Chile have advocated for LGBTQ+ rights at the international level. Kiai has stated that we must learn from and celebrate the successes of this movement in order to further the rights of other marginalized groups (Hudson).

2.2.4 Private companies and unions

When we think about protecting and enforcing rights and justice we can see how states, regional and global IGOs, human rights tribunals and civil society all have responsibilities and duties. The complex interactions of political stakeholders and actors also must include private companies and unions.

■ Private companies

Private companies come in many forms, from small, family-owned businesses to well-known global multinational corporations (MNCs). Of course, rights and justice should apply within the workplace as they do in the wider civil society, but the enforcement and protection of these rights can sometimes be neglected. The unbalanced power relationship between employer and employee can leave some employees vulnerable to exploitation.

Concepts

Marxism and private companies

Marxists are very concerned with unbalanced power relationships between workers and employers. They argue that capitalism sets up this unfair relationship and that companies, driven by profit, will never put the well-being of the employees first. Workers are therefore considered to be a vulnerable group open to exploitation and abuse. Marxists generally do not put much faith into international agreements as they see the United Nations as an elitist organization protecting the powerful and wealthy.

Marxists are concerned with the rights of workers, but they are not the only ones.

As most, if not all, companies are primarily motivated by profit, ensuring that workers operate in safe conditions, and have adequate rest and paid holidays may mean that some employers worry their profits will be reduced if they comply. The UN has therefore produced Guiding Principles on Business and Human Rights, in which it outlines how the state, business and workers are all interconnected when it comes to ensuring workers' rights.

● TOK

Marxism provides a very particular approach to understanding economic processes and historical facts – aiming to characterize economic and historical forces as being at their heart about economic and class struggle. This very intentional approach helps raise new issues when looking at old content and material. Economists and historians holding different ideological beliefs might have different approaches and ask their own questions of the data.

Figure 2.28 illustrates the interconnected nature of protecting human rights in the workplace.

THE STATE has the responsibility to ensure that workers are treated fairly and are not subjected to human rights abuses. They do this by making and enforcing regulations and laws to protect the well-being of workers.

THE EMPLOYER is responsible for making sure workers are protected from abuse. If abuse does occur, they must act quickly and create polices to prevent such things from happening again.

THE EMPLOYEE must be aware that they can get help if their rights are being abused and that the help can come from the state or state agencies (such as the police) and non-state actors (such as NGOs).

■ **Figure 2.28** The interconnected nature of protecting human rights in the workplace

■ **Figure 2.29** Prince Zeid Ra'ad Al Hussein of Jordan

Prince Zeid Ra'ad Al Hussein of Jordan (see Figure 2.29) was the first Muslim Arab High Commissioner for Human Rights at the UN. He is particularly knowledgeable about, and a strong advocate for, the rights of women, international criminal justice, international law, UN peacekeeping, post-conflict peace-building, international development and counter-nuclear terrorism.

In an article entitled 'Dollars and sense: how – and why – the private sector needs to stand up for human rights', published on the UN's website, Al Hussein wrote:

> *Business cannot thrive in failing societies, where tension spikes and communities bristle with grievances and mutual contempt. Strong civil societies, due process, equality and justice: these are what enable real economic empowerment.*

ACTIVITY

IGO statements on workers' rights

Compare the two statements below on workers' rights and answer the question that follows.

> *[The International Labour Organization (ILO)] affirms the obligations and commitments that are inherent in membership of the ILO, namely:*
>
> *(a) freedom of association and the effective recognition of the right to collective bargaining;*
>
> *(b) the elimination of all forms of forced or compulsory labour;*
>
> *(c) the effective abolition of child labour;*
>
> *(d) the elimination of discrimination in respect of employment and occupation; and*
>
> *(e) a safe and healthy working environment.*
>
> *International Labour Organization, 'ILO Declaration on Fundamental Principles and Rights at Work'*

In what ways does the statement of the ILO agree with the statement of the WTO?

Despite the incentives to provide safe and fair working conditions globally, many workers continue to have their rights denied and receive no protection from the state. MNCs are often criticized for not doing more to protect human rights in states where they operate.

Women are particularly vulnerable to exploitation and abuse of many of their basic human rights. It has been documented that in many parts of the world young women seeking employment in textile industries are often sexually harassed.

However, there there is evidence to suggest that the use of child labour has decreased amongst most multinational companies over the past decade. Although these improvements are hopeful, the protection and enforcement of rights in multinational workplaces remains challenging (Counts).

Extended essay

If you're thinking of writing an extended essay on human rights in the workplace, an evaluation of the successes or failures of IGOs, such as the International Labour Organization, could be an interesting start. Remember, though, a good extended essay must consider multiple perspectives, and always discuss your ideas and potential research questions with your extended essay supervisor.

■ Unions

Traditionally, workers have come together to attempt to advocate for better conditions and treatment by forming or joining existing unions. A union is an organization where workers form a collective with the idea that a group of people with a unified purpose is always more powerful when seeking rights and justice than a lone individual. This is collective bargaining. Through the union, workers can negotiate with employers to improve workplace health and safety, wages, benefits and other work-related rights.

Unions are democratic organizations, and their leaders are elected by members voting. Although some companies welcome unions, many oppose them as they think management can best look after the needs of its workers.

International Trade Union Confederation

According to the 2022 Global Rights Index report of the International Trade Union Confederation, the rights of workers globally have been increasingly threatened in recent years.

Discussion point

Could the COVID-19 pandemic be linked to this increase in the violation of workers' rights?

● Chapter summary

In this chapter we have covered the interactions of political stakeholders and actors, including:

- the state and national governments
- intergovernmental organizations
- regional human rights tribunals
- civil society organizations (including advocacy)
- marginalized, vulnerable or most affected groups and individuals
- private companies and unions.

REVIEW QUESTIONS

Now that you have read this chapter, reflect on these questions:

- In your own words, explain the different purposes of the International Court of Justice and the International Criminal Court.

- To what extent do regional human rights tribunals address the concerns expressed by cultural relativists that rights are too 'Western' in focus?

- Human Rights Watch and Amnesty International are two of the world's largest human rights NGOs. Why do they both support the claim that rights must be viewed as universal?

- What do we mean by a 'marginalized/vulnerable group or individual'?

- What do private companies have to do with rights and justice?

By the end of this chapter, you should understand:
- ▶ the codification, protection and monitoring of rights and justice
- ▶ the international and regional rights frameworks (including the United Nations system and the Universal Declaration of Human Rights)
- ▶ the development of world norms in rights and justice (including Responsibility to Protect – R2P)
- ▶ responses to violations of rights and perceived injustices.

2.3.1 The codification, protection and monitoring of rights and justice

It's important to remember that the most widely accepted international standard of human rights, the Universal Declaration of Human Rights, is aspirational and not legally binding. Although states may support the ideas in principle, they reserve the right to decide how and whether these rights are enforced. Sovereignty is a powerful concept in global politics, and many states are unwilling to concede what they see as control over their territory and population.

However, as we have seen, in our increasingly interdependent world, there are significant challenges to state sovereignty by various political stakeholders and actors. Intergovernmental organizations, regional human rights tribunals, civil society organizations, including non-governmental organizations, social and resistance movements, social media and other groups, all scrutinize states when it comes to rights and justice.

But the state continues to play an essential role in the codification, protection and monitoring of rights and justice, and often, but not always, it willingly cooperates with these stakeholders and actors. Sometimes they cooperate to create or maintain a more stable and just society, but sometimes the state may primarily be motivated by political gain.

■ **Figure 2.30** The codification, protection, and monitoring of rights and justice is the responsibility of all members of society, not just the state

◆ **Codification** is the process of making human rights laws, such as those as seen in treaties and covenants, legitimate and enforceable within the legal systems of states.

■ Codification

Codification provides a formal, legal framework for the protection and enforcement of rights and justice. 'Codifying' rights essentially means making them 'legal'. So, instead of rights being aspirational, they are enforceable and legally binding.

Different ideas of rights and justice usually influence states in terms of what laws they choose to codify. Within the state, there are two main ways rights can be codified:

1 constitutions

2 laws and the judicial system.

1 Constitutions

A constitution is a set of rules that determine how a country or state is run. Almost all constitutions are 'codified', which means they are written down clearly in a specific document called 'the constitution'. Constitutions usually include a preamble, a description of powers of the state, and a guarantee of specific rights for citizens:

Preamble statement

This tells the reader what the purpose of the constitution is. For example, the preamble to the Constitution of the United States:

> *We the People of the United States, in Order to form a more perfect Union, establish Justice, insure domestic Tranquility, provide for the common defense, promote the general Welfare, and secure the Blessings of Liberty to ourselves and our Posterity, do ordain and establish this Constitution for the United States of America.*

Description of powers of the state

This is a detailed description of how power is to be distributed between the three branches of government – the legislature, executive and judiciary – as well as between national and state levels of government. For example, in the Constitution of South Africa:

> *All spheres of government and all organs of state within each sphere must –*
>
> *a. preserve the peace, national unity and the indivisibility of the Republic;*
>
> *b. secure the well-being of the people of the Republic;*
>
> *c. provide effective, transparent, accountable and coherent government for the Republic as a whole;*
>
> *d. be loyal to the Constitution, the Republic and its people;*
>
> *e. respect the constitutional status, institutions, powers and functions of government in the other spheres;*
>
> *f. not assume any power or function except those conferred on them in terms of the Constitution;*
>
> *g. exercise their powers and perform their functions in a manner that does not encroach on the geographical, functional or institutional integrity of government in another sphere; and*
>
> *h. cooperate with one another in mutual trust and good faith by –*
>
> > *i. fostering friendly relations;*
> >
> > *ii. assisting and supporting one another;*
> >
> > *iii. informing one another of, and consulting one another on, matters of common interest;*
> >
> > *iv. coordinating their actions and legislation with one another;*
> >
> > *v. adhering to agreed procedures; and*
> >
> > *vi. avoiding legal proceedings against one another.'*

Guarantee of the specific rights for citizens

This is a guarantee of certain basic rights enjoyed by individual citizens of the country. For example, in the Constitution of Brazil:

> *Article 193. The social order is based on the primacy of labor and aimed at social well-being and justice. The State shall perform the function of planning social policies, ensuring, under the law, the participation of the society in the formulation of these policies, monitoring, control, and evaluation process.*

Constitutions include the most important rules of government, and it is difficult for them to be changed. The constitution is the 'supreme law' of a state and other laws made at all levels of government must not contradict it.

Sometimes the interpretation of constitutions, like the interpretations of the Universal Declaration of Human Rights, are varied and lead to legal cases challenging the constitutionality of existing laws. You may think that constitutions are dusty documents nobody reads, but they can have immense power over judicial systems.

CASE STUDY

Challenges to constitutional law: *Roe* v. *Wade*

The Supreme Court of the United States is the highest tribunal for all cases arising under the Constitution or the laws of the United States. The Court's purpose is to give the American people equal justice under law and it also functions as guardian and interpreter of the Constitution.

In 1970, a Texas woman, referred to as Jane Roe (not her real name), launched a lawsuit against a Texas district attorney, Henry Wade, demanding that women should be allowed to terminate pregnancies without any interference from the state. Roe felt she was denied justice as promised in the US Constitution and in 1973 the case was brought to the US Supreme Court. Roe argued that it was unconstitutional for the state to prohibit abortions because the constitution guarantees liberty to all in the Fifth Amendment: 'nor shall any person … be deprived of life, liberty or property, without due process of law'.

On hearing the case, the US Supreme Court ruled that restricting abortions was unconstitutional because it violated women's constitutional right to privacy, but only if the foetus was under 24 weeks old.

Challenges to the Supreme Court decision

Abortion is a very sensitive and divisive topic in the United States, and the ruling has been challenged on many occasions in the years since by people who believe that the state should seldom or never allow abortions to occur.

A court case regarding the state of Mississippi introducing a ban on most abortions after 15 weeks (not the 24 decided upon during *Roe* v. *Wade*) was brought to the Supreme Court in 2022. The counterclaim on behalf of Mississippi was that the decision of *Roe* v. *Wade* was not based on constitutional law. Mississippi court documents stated, 'The conclusion that abortion is a constitutional right has no basis in text, structure, history or tradition.'

The Supreme Court ruled in favour of Mississippi. Justice Samuel Alito said that the 1973 Roe ruling 'must be overruled' because the Supreme Court judges of 1973 who made the ruling were 'egregiously wrong', the arguments 'exceptionally weak' and so 'damaging' that they amounted to 'an abuse of judicial authority'. Due to the ruling, since 2022, each US state could make its own laws regarding abortion access.

This is a clear example that constitutions, like any form of codification, can be open to interpretation and politicization.

Discussion point

What role do you think 'history and tradition' have played in the divisive opinions about abortion in the United States?

Perspectives

Gloria Steinem on feminism and abortion as a right

Many feminists see reproductive rights as essential rights for all women. They often refer to the 'patriarchy', the system of government and or social order controlled by men for the benefit of men.

Gloria Steinem, a leading American feminist who celebrated the initial *Roe* v. *Wade* ruling in 1973, expressed concern about the 2022 ruling by saying 'the very definition of patriarchy is trying to control women and birth giving' (quoted in Kelly et al.).

A constitution is supposed to provide the fundamental rules and principles that govern a country. One consequence of the overturning of *Roe* v. *Wade* was that some US states quickly changed their own laws to legally restrict abortion access. Human rights activists, legal experts and many women were upset and disturbed by the decision, as they felt the rights of women were being taken away.

A constitution is a 'supreme law' that is very difficult to change or amend, but, as we can see, the interpretation of the constitution can change over time. In democratic states where political parties may come and go, the constitution should offer stability and continuity to the people, so the reversal made by the Supreme Court in the case of *Roe* v. *Wade* was unsettling to many people.

 TOK

One reason why *Roe* v. *Wade* was overturned is because of the wider social, religious and political beliefs of the justices of the US Supreme Court. While they may argue that their job when interpreting the Constitution is to keep their beliefs about non-legal matters off the table, it is a conscious part of choosing justices to consider their wider social, economic, religious and political beliefs. This suggests that, when interpreting law (or any other data for that matter), an individual's own background and beliefs create a sort of lens through which information is analysed, methods are decided upon, and conclusions are formed.

Some areas of knowledge, like mathematics, the natural sciences and history, incorporate methods designed to limit the effect of an individual's wider beliefs, but can only do so to varying degrees.

 Extended essay

If you're interested in constitutional law and its impact on rights and justice, you could start by exploring specific rights promised in a country's constitution and evaluate to what extent various stakeholders in civil society support these rights. This could lead to an interesting research question, but always discuss your ideas with your extended essay supervisor!

2 Laws and the judicial system

Although not all states have constitutions, most do have laws that attempt to govern the activities of citizens in order to create a safe and fair society. Sometimes laws governing behaviour are focused on rights as laid out in a constitution and/or a wider understanding of shared rights and justice. For example, most states have laws regarding marriage, working conditions, discrimination and education, which all impact the rights of citizens and attempt to create a stable society. This is another way that rights and justice are codified; They are made enforceable by other systems within the state, including the police and judicial system.

The state is responsible for ensuring that these systems of law and justice remain impartial, fair and free of corruption. Civil society, the media and other stakeholders often challenge these institutions when rights and justice are ignored or deliberately violated.

Discussion point

What is the impact of police abuse and unlawful killings on the internal legitimacy of a state? Can you think of any examples?

As we have seen, codifying rights essentially means making them 'legal'. So, instead of rights being aspirational, they are enforceable and legally binding. Due to state sovereignty, this is more commonly seen within states in the form of constitutions and laws that guarantee rights and justice. However, we can also see codification at the international level of global politics in the form of treaties, conventions and covenants.

Treaties, conventions and covenants are essentially human rights laws created by IGOs. There is no difference between a treaty, a convention and a covenant, and states can choose whether or not to agree to them. However, if they do agree, these treaties, conventions and covenants become enforceable and legally binding.

Discussion point

If states agree to human rights treaties, to what extent are they sacrificing their sovereignty? One argument that can be made is that states are not giving up their sovereignty because they choose to be a part of these treaties, conventions and covenants. What could be a counterclaim to this?

The United Nations (UN) has developed a wide range of bodies and programmes that take the Universal Declaration of Human Rights one step further by urging states to codify rights, thereby making them more enforceable and legally binding.

There are two ways a state can show its support:

1 **Signing:** the state agrees in principle and will act in good faith but is not yet ready to fully commit.

2 **Ratifying:** the state accepts that it is bound by this treaty and may be subject to consequences if it does not comply.

Over the years there have been several UN human rights treaties, conventions and covenants, as seen in Table 2.16. Although it is expected that you focus on contemporary case studies and examples in your studies, these various human rights codifications continue to have influence in contemporary global political issues. And remember, codification is not a guarantee that the fulfilment of rights and justice will improve, but constitutions, laws and international treaties, declarations, conventions and covenants are all attempts to create fairer and more just societies.

■ Table 2.16 Significant UN human rights treaties, conventions and covenants

Full name	Abbreviation/ acronym	Date came into force	What does it concern?	Status of acceptance
Convention on the Elimination of All Forms of Racial Discrimination	ICERD	1965	This convention further reinforces the principle that discrimination based on race and ethnicity must be banned, and promotes understanding among all races.	Widely accepted. All Security Council members have ratified.
International Covenant on Civil and Political Rights	ICCPR	1966	Many of the same rights seen in the Universal Declaration of Human Rights (UDHR) can be seen here. This covenant is concerned with civil and political rights. A few of these rights concern non-discrimination on the grounds of race, gender and religion, legal rights, and freedom from enslavement.	Widely ratified. Notable exceptions: China (Security Council), Malaysia, Saudi Arabia and Singapore.
International Covenant on Economic, Social and Cultural Rights	ICESCR	1966	Many of the same rights seen in the UDHR can be seen here. This covenant is concerned with economic, social, and cultural rights. Fair working conditions, housing conditions and education are just some of the rights found here.	Widely ratified. Notable exceptions: the United States (Security Council), Nigeria, Saudi Arabia and Singapore.
Convention on the Elimination of All Forms of Discrimination Against Women	CEDAW	1979	The legal, educational, employment and reproductive rights of women are covered here. States must proactively find ways to stop discrimination in public and private life.	Widely ratified since its creation in 1979. Notable exceptions: the United States (Security Council) is one of only seven states not to ratify this convention.
Convention against Torture and Other Cruel, Inhuman or Degrading Treatment or Punishment	UNCAT	1984	This convention specifies that the state must not use torture and abuse, and is particularly targeted at the judicial and prison mechanisms.	Widely accepted. All Security Council members have ratified.
Convention on the Rights of the Child	CRC	1989	Children are recognized as needing extra protection from states due to their vulnerable status. Convention defines those under the age of 18 as 'children' and recognizes that this age group needs special protections, freedoms and rights.	Widely accepted. Notable exceptions: the United States (Security Council) and Somalia are the only states not to have ratified this convention.
Convention on the Protection of Rights of all Migrant Workers and Members of Their Families	CMW	1990	The primary purpose of this convention is to protect workers who are not citizens of the state from exploitation and abuse.	This has not been widely accepted and no members of the Security Council have ratified it.
Rome Statute of the International Criminal Court	ICC	2002	This statute created the International Criminal Court (ICC), explored in Chapter 2.2. The ICC prosecutes individuals for war crimes and genocide.	Widely accepted. Notable exceptions: China and the United States (both on the Security Council) have not ratified this statute. The United States signed but later withdrew its signature.
United Nations Declaration on the Rights of Indigenous Peoples	UNDRIP	2007	This declaration addresses the concerns of a vulnerable group in many societies: indigenous people. It aims to promote reconciliation and end discrimination.	Widely accepted. The United States (Security Council), Canada, Australia and New Zealand (all nations with significant indigenous populations) did not initially endorse, but later changed their positions.

Discussion point

The United States, as a key member of the Security Council, has not ratified the ICESCR, CEDAW, CRC, CMW or the ICC. Does the legitimacy of these human rights covenants and treaties suffer when members of the Security Council do not support them?

Realism and the motivations of states

As mentioned previously, realists are not much concerned with human rights or any international mechanisms to protect rights because they argue the state will always put self-interest first. As evidence, they point to the United States who, they claim, fears any infringement on its sovereignty and consistently prioritizes national interests over international cooperation.

Figure 2.31 covers 18 international human rights treaties and gives a good overview of which states widely support these treaties and which do not.

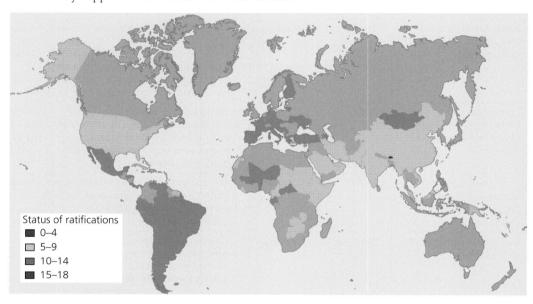

Status of ratifications
- ■ 0–4
- □ 5–9
- ■ 10–14
- ■ 15–18

■ **Figure 2.31** The ratification of 18 international human rights treaties

Consequences for states that violate the UN human rights treaties, conventions and covenants they ratified

According to the Office of the UN High Commissioner for Human Rights (OHCHR), detailed evidence of alleged violations of human rights treaties, conventions and covenants can be presented only after the individual or group has tried and failed to receive justice from the state judicial system. If this has occurred, there are three main ways people can then alert the UN to human rights violations taking place:

1 An individual can directly complain or have someone complain on their behalf (maybe a lawyer or NGO representative). They do this by filling out a detailed form outlining the complaint and then submitting it to those in charge of monitoring the violated treaty, convention or covenant.

2 A state can file a complaint against another state if they have concerns that human rights abuses are taking place.

3 Other stakeholders and actors can alert the appropriate committee with evidence that rights are being systematically violated.

What happens next?

- After being contacted, the committee will alert the state that a complaint has been received.
- An inquiry might take place, which could involve a visit to the state by a UN official.
- Recommendations could then be made, advising the state how to address the concerns.
- The state is then invited to submit evidence that the concerns are being addressed within a fixed time period (usually six months).
- The entire procedure is confidential and dependent on the cooperation of the state.

Is codification effective?

Despite being 'legally binding', many argue that UN human rights treaties, conventions and covenants are ineffective, as the consequences for violating them are at best minimal and state sovereignty remains an obstacle for justice. Critics point out that many states with numerous violations see ratification as a means to legitimacy and so their intention to respect human rights is questionable. For example, some point out that Saudi Arabia ratified CEDAW in 2001 despite women not even having the right to drive at that time.

As a counterclaim to the argument that the seemingly minimal punishment renders many of these agreements ineffective, some argue this is exactly what makes these treaties more attractive and meaningful, as states do not like being 'forced' into complying with international standards. Some human rights activists argue that the lack of force allows states who genuinely want change to do so at their own pace, while also retaining their sovereignty and internal legitimacy.

Whether codification is effective or not, we should question why states might agree to publicly endorse rights that they have no intention of upholding. We will look at this in more detail in Chapter 2.4.

Discussion point

The Convention Against Torture and Other Cruel, Inhuman or Degrading Treatment or Punishment (UNCAT) has been codified and is a 'legally binding' document in most states. To what extent do you think the consequences for violating this convention would prevent human rights violations?

◼ Protection and monitoring

As we have seen, the state plays a crucial role in the codification of rights and justice. Codification, however, is just the first step towards protecting people's rights. Just because rights can be seen in a constitution or legal system does not mean that they are actively monitored or protected.

We often think of rights as something given to us by authorities in power and, while these 'positive rights' are significant, as we have seen, the protection and monitoring of human rights is more complex and involves:

1 states
2 non-state actors
3 other human rights stakeholders.

1 The role of states in protecting and monitoring rights and justice

As previously explained, states have the authority to sign or ratify international and regional human rights treaties, covenants and conventions, and to codify rights. However, none of these actions guarantee that these rights, written on paper, will be protected and monitored in the real world.

So in what ways can a state protect and monitor rights?

Create and/or support human rights commissions

Many states have national human rights institutions to protect and promote human rights within the state. Although the OHCHR encourages such institutions to be set up, states will sometimes do this independently and on their own terms. Ideally, human rights commissions are led by committees of people from many societal groups so that all members of society feel comfortable in approaching them to seek justice.

Human rights commissions have two main purposes:

1 To promote rights education in the community: this can be done in many ways including creating educational materials that can be used in schools and community centres, creating advertisements advocating rights, holding public meetings, or organizing community celebrations of diversity and inclusion. Human rights commissions often partner with civil society and non-government agencies to work toward common goals. The idea is to communicate the values, beliefs and attitudes that help to ensure that all people's rights are protected and that ordinary people, as well as the state, are responsible for protecting rights.

2 To address grievances from groups or individuals that violate the law of the state: the second purpose is to monitor rights by allowing people to seek help if they feel their rights have been violated. For example, if a person was certain that they had been overlooked for a job because of their race, they could appeal for help from the commission, which could then investigate the matter.

The state positively interacts with other political stakeholders and actors

The monitoring of human rights is a complex process and cooperation with civil society and non-governmental organizations (NGOs), such as Amnesty International and Human Rights Watch, can enable the state to better monitor and protect rights.

2 The role of non-state actors in protecting and monitoring rights and justice

We have previously examined what the UN does on the international level, but it is important to consider what regional intergovernmental organizations (IGOS) do to protect and monitor rights and justice.

We were introduced to the main IGOs in Chapter 2.2. Each of the main regional IGOs has a different approach to the protection and monitoring of rights and justice, although the Universal Declaration of Human Rights is used as the starting point in most declarations.

ASEAN and the protection and monitoring of rights and justice

■ **Figure 2.32** The 10 ASEAN member states

The ASEAN Intergovernmental Commission on Human Rights was established in 2009, and in 2012 the ASEAN Human Rights Declaration was adopted unanimously by all 10 member states (see Figure 2.32).

At first glance it may seem as if, structurally, ASEAN is not designed to protect and monitor rights based on its principles and purpose:

● ASEAN has always stated that state sovereignty is non-negotiable and it will not directly interfere with the internal matters of member states. ASEAN has no designs to become a supranational organization.

● Within the region there has been a somewhat lukewarm response to most of the international treaties, covenants and conventions mentioned earlier in this chapter.

● Member states of ASEAN will not publicly criticize each other (no 'naming and shaming', as occurs in the UN).

● There are no special conditions regarding rights placed on joining or remaining in ASEAN (unlike the EU).

● When the ASEAN Intergovernmental Commission on Human Rights was established, only five of the 10 member states had human rights commissions set up to raise awareness of rights and offer assistance to those with concerns or complaints.

Questioning the motives of ASEAN

These factors have led some experts to question the motivations and sincerity of ASEAN with regard to enforcing and monitoring rights and justice in the region. There have been criticisms by those who say ASEAN's focus on human rights is superficial and essentially a way to reduce criticism and demands for reform from civil society and other rights stakeholders and actors. Certainly situations like the Rohingya Crisis in Myanmar have caused widespread condemnation of ASEAN for being slow to respond and address the actions of the Myanmar government. Others have claimed that ASEAN is simply seeking external legitimacy by attempting to appear to be part of the 'global norm' with regard to rights and justice.

However, there are other perspectives to consider. Many welcomed the creation of the ASEAN Intergovernmental Commission on Human Rights and the ASEAN Human Rights Declaration as the most impressive public commitment the region has made towards human rights. As Singapore, Myanmar, Malaysia and Brunei are not signatories to the International Covenant on Civil and Political Rights (ICCPR), their approval of the ASEAN Human Rights Declaration is an indication of support for many civil, political, economic, cultural and social rights. All of this inspires hope in many political stakeholders and actors within the region.

The similarities and differences between the ASEAN Human Rights Declaration and the UDHR

Consider clause 2 of the ASEAN Human Rights Declaration, which implies a sense of universality:

> 2. Every person is entitled to the rights and freedoms set forth herein, without distinction of any kind, such as race, gender, age, language, religion, political or other opinion, national or social origin, economic status, birth, disability or other status.

And now read clause 7:

> 7. All human rights are universal, indivisible, interdependent and interrelated. All human rights and fundamental freedoms in this Declaration must be treated in a fair and equal manner, on the same footing and with the same emphasis. At the same time, the realization of human rights must be considered in the regional and national context bearing in mind different political, economic, legal, social, cultural, historical and religious backgrounds.

Clause 7 is using claims of cultural relativism to suggest that all rights may not be universal and must be considered in the context of the region. This is something to consider when examining regional IGOs' understanding and interpretations of rights.

Discussion point

In global politics, you are encouraged to learn about political issues that are relevant to you and your life. Do you live in an area that is covered by one of the regional IGOs we have looked at? How does that IGO protect and monitor rights and justice in your region?

3 The role of other human rights stakeholders in protecting and monitoring rights and justice

In the era of globalization, within civil society organizations it can be argued that non-governmental organizations (NGOs) are by far the most active and dynamic groups protecting and monitoring rights and justice.

The developments of NGOs over the past several decades has been significant, and over this time their global influence and importance have grown and they contribute hugely to both the national and international arena of global politics. Today, many believe that, without the active involvement of NGOs, the monitoring and protection of human rights would not function well.

You were introduced to Amnesty International, Human Rights Watch and Child's Rights International in Chapter 2.2, but these NGOs are just some of the more famous examples, and there are thousands more at all levels of global politics.

The activities and strategies employed by NGOs include:

- education
- monitoring
- investigating
- documenting
- advocating
- lobbying.

All of these strategies significantly contribute to encouraging the enforcement of rights and justice.

Discussion point

What are the advantages and disadvantages of smaller, regional or local NGOs compared with globally well-known IGOs?

2.3.2 Development of world norms regarding rights and justice

What does the development of world norms mean?

'World norms' implies a common global understanding of rights and justice, and this fits well with the idea that there can be a 'universal' understanding of these concepts. In other words, there can be some rights that apply to all of us, no matter where we come from or what other beliefs we hold. However, it is worth considering that increased interdependence and globalization have allowed for ideas and perspectives to be shared more readily and that the standards of how people should be treated can change and evolve. Is this a counterclaim to the idea of universalism?

■ **Figure 2.33** Even in 2023, people all over the world are still engaged in the fight for gender equality

■ The global community and its impact on norms of rights and justice

As we have seen, IGOs at the international and regional levels can impact world norms on rights and justice. Virtually every UN agency is involved to some degree in the promotion and protection of human rights. Non-binding and legally binding covenants and conventions, both at the international and regional level, offer people an understanding of how they should be treated.

Let's consider the real-life example of the right of gender equality.

In recent decades, gender equality norms have been widely discussed and integrated into international law. The Convention on the Elimination of All Forms of Discrimination Against Women (CEDAW) is often credited with helping to develop a world norm regarding the protection and monitoring of the rights of women. It is an interesting example to consider, because women have traditionally been seen as members of the private sphere of life, and many violations of women's rights are rooted in sociocultural traditions. Can international agreements such as CEDAW cause significant and lasting change within societies?

Some scholars point out that female life expectancy, literacy rates and involvement in government all positively increase with CEDAW ratification, but others argue the relationship is not so linear. They maintain that treaties such as CEDAW work best in societies where there is a *pre-existing public interest in challenging the position women hold in society*. In other words, the society norms were already changing and open to the idea of equal rights for women.

Additionally, we know that international treaties are never enough. To truly protect rights, they must be codified into local and national law, and monitoring and protection by NGOs and civil society are needed. Therefore, the development of world norms is more complex than simply a top-down approach.

Discussion point

Do you think globalization plays a significant role in shifting attitudes towards women within communities? If yes, how?

■ **Figure 2.34** Social media has contributed greatly to the development of world norms regarding rights and justice

■ Social media and their impact on norms of rights and justice

Media in general, and more recently social media, have contributed greatly to the development of world norms regarding rights and justice. Videos and evidence of actions many consider to be violations of rights are instantly and widely circulated and have raised awareness of the mistreatment of marginalized and vulnerable people in particular.

Globally, there has been a focus in recent years on the actions of police and institutionalized racism and the abuse of power. Individuals have filmed and uploaded to global social media

■ **Figure 2.35**
#EndSARSNow trended globally after the 2020 shooting of unarmed protesters in Nigeria

platforms footage of police aggression against unarmed civilians in, among others, the United States, France and Nigeria, sparking widespread outrage and protest.

The hashtags #EndPoliceBrutality and #EndSARSNow trended globally after the 2020 shooting of unarmed protesters in Nigeria. The protest was against the Special Anti-Robbery Squad (SARS), which has been widely criticized, as it allegedly enabled police to extort money from, arrest, torture and kill innocent civilians with impunity.

In many countries around the globe, the actions of police forces and the abuse of police power are being questioned and scrutinized to an extent never seen before, and social media has played a significant role in this movement.

 TOK

How much news about events across the world do you receive via social media? There are a number of TOK-related questions you might ask about this, including:

● To what extent do you think that this information is reliable?
● Do you think the information provided shows a range of analysis or perspectives?
● What perspectives and views are not shown?
● Who are the authors of this information and what is their purpose in presenting the information?
● How are your own ideas on the events you see influenced by the choices of the content creators?

When it comes to writing your TOK exhibition, you might consider using a post from your social media account as an object. Review the TOK IA prompts and see which of them you might explore using social media.

■ New interpretations and the development of world norms regarding rights and justice

Sometimes, the way we interpret rights can change over time. As an example, let's consider Article 16 of the UDHR:

> *1 Men and women of full age, without any limitation due to race, nationality or religion, have the right to marry and to found a family. They are entitled to equal rights as to marriage, during marriage and at its dissolution.*

> *2 Marriage shall be entered into only with the free and full consent of the intending spouses.*

> *3 The family is the natural and fundamental group unit of society and is entitled to protection by society and the State.*

This article was originally intended to address the concerns of women who were often forced into marriage against their will. In the 1940s, there was widespread discrimination against women in matters of marriage and divorce globally, and it is safe to assume that the original authors considered that marriage referred to a union between a man and a woman. However, this interpretation of the article has evolved over time. World norms previously accepted that a marriage only takes place between a man and a woman, but this has been challenged in recent years, and Article 16 has been increasingly interpreted to mean that *everyone* has a right to choose their marriage partner and that gender is not a factor. The United Nations has also urged states to legally accept same-sex unions and have called for the same benefits to all couples regardless of gender.

HL extension: Technology

An interesting starting point for a global political challenge case study focused on technology would be to examine how global norms have been challenged by the use of technology. This technology could be related to the sharing of ideas on social media and how this has impacted our understanding of rights and justice.

We could say in such a case that world norms surrounding marriage have developed in recent years. This does not mean that all people agree with this interpretation, of course, but we can certainly see evidence that there has been an impact globally.

TOK

This could be another example of how background beliefs, this time including social beliefs as they change and develop, provide a lens through which we interpret the world around us. Here, the idea is that attitudes towards the role of women in society have shifted and, with that shift, many interpret the UN Articles or other laws in new ways. Article 16(1) seems no longer limited to a reading suggesting men and women are free to marry one another, but now is open to reading as suggesting men and women are free to marry whomever they wish. Both are available interpretations given the language of the Article, but the second might not have even been considered when initially written.

ACTIVITY

In Figure 2.36, the countries shaded purple are those in which same-sex marriage is permitted (or where it is legal in some jurisdictions).

■ **Figure 2.36** Countries in which same-sex marriage is permitted (or is legal in some jurisdictions), as of January 2024

Looking at the map, what pattern can you recognize about LGBTQ+ rights globally? To what extent do you agree with the claim that world norms regarding same-sex marriage have changed?

2.3.3 Global norms on state sovereignty and the protection of rights: the Responsibility to Protect (R2P) and humanitarian intervention

As noted elsewhere in this textbook, sovereignty remains a key concept in global politics and is often seen as an obstacle to the protection of human rights. In the 1990s, within the borders of Rwanda and Bosnia, horrific crimes were committed against people. The international community, including the UN, seemingly stood by and did nothing to stop them. Many criticized the lack of response and questioned why the UN, an organization founded to prevent crimes against humanity, was unable to intervene.

The idea that sometimes it might be necessary to intervene in a state in cases of extreme human rights catastrophe gained momentum in the late 1990s. This became known as the Responsibility to Protect, or 'R2P'. Prior to R2P, the African Union supported the right of its members to intervene in a member state in cases of war crimes, genocide and crimes against humanity (2002). Additionally, the Rome Statute, which led to the creation of the International Criminal Court in 2002, left room for the UN Security Council to step in in extreme situations, even without the consent of the state.

In 2005, the UN World Summit unanimously accepted 'responsibility to protect populations from genocide, war crimes, ethnic cleansing and crimes against humanity'. The definition of sovereignty, it was agreed, must require the state to take responsibility to protect its residents from atrocities.

◾ The Responsibility to Protect (R2P)

Figure 2.37 illustrates the three pillars of the R2P doctrine.

Pillar I
States have an obligation to protect their citizens from mass atrocity crimes, such as genocide, war crimes, ethnic cleansing and crimes against humanity.

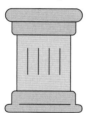

Pillar II
It is the responsibility of the international community to assist states to prevent mass atrocity crimes.

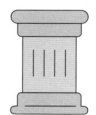

Pillar III
In the event that mass atrocities occur and the state is either unable or unwilling to act, the international community must take timely and decisive action as justified by international law.

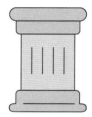

◾ **Figure 2.37** The three pillars of the R2P doctrine

The responsibility to protect embraces three specific responsibilities for the global community:

1 The responsibility to **PREVENT**: to address both the long-term causes and short-term causes of internal conflict and other human created crises putting people at risk.

2 The responsibility to **REACT**: to respond to situations with appropriate measures, which may include using force: sanctions and international prosecution and, in extreme cases, military intervention.

3 The responsibility to **REBUILD**: to provide, particularly after a military intervention, full assistance with recovery, reconstruction and reconciliation, addressing the causes of the harm the intervention was designed to halt or avert.

◾ What is humanitarian intervention?

The term 'humanitarian intervention' specifically refers to the use of military force. It is important to remember that R2P is primarily about the prevention of atrocities and military intervention, although a component of R2P, is the last resort and not undertaken lightly. However, the use of military force and violence inevitably causes death and destruction, which can be seen as contrary to the original stated goals of the UN.

■ What is international humanitarian law?

International humanitarian law is a set of regulations to limit the harm of armed conflict. Of course, any armed conflict violates human rights and causes misery and destruction, but humanitarian law attempts to make rules that states must follow so that the damage can be minimized.

International humanitarian law is meant to protect all people who are somehow involved in the conflict. This applies to everyone, from soldiers to civilians. The type of weaponry used and military tactics that can cause extensive damage are often restricted.

International humanitarian law is part of international law and can be seen in several treaties or conventions. These laws are agreed upon by states and are considered legally binding.

The Geneva Conventions of 1949 have been accepted as law by almost all nations on Earth and they lay out several rules of warfare. Over time, as weaponry has evolved and concepts of rights and justice have expanded, these rules have expanded to include:

- 1972 Biological Weapons Convention
- 1977 Additional protocols for victims of armed conflict
- 1993 Chemical Weapons Convention
- 1997 Ottawa Convention on anti-personnel mines
- 2000 Optional Protocol to the Convention on the Rights of the Child on the involvement of children in conflict.

International humanitarian law applies to interstate conflicts – armed conflict taking place between states. It has limited effectiveness in cases of intrastate conflict because non-state actors make no such international agreements. This is a limitation, as most armed conflicts in the world today are intrastate. (See more on this in Chapter 4.2 in the thematic study on peace and conflict).

As we have seen before and will explore more fully later, 'legally binding' does not mean all states will follow it. Increasingly, those who suffer most during armed conflict are civilians. If we look at real-world examples, we can see that in times of extreme conflict violence it is very difficult to enforce international humanitarian law.

2.3.4 Responses to violations of rights and perceived injustices

In global politics we can see many real-world examples of violations of rights and perceived injustices. This entire section on rights and justice is all about responses to these violations and perceived injustices. Now, it is your turn to investigate responses!

Table 2.17 demonstrates issues that are particularly problematic and of immediate concern to a wide variety of political stakeholders and actors. They are all worthy of investigation and could be useful to both HL students and SL students as real-world examples essential to understanding how global politics works.

■ Table 2.17 Real-world examples of violations of rights and perceived injustices

Violation/ perceived injustice	What is it?	Why is this concerning?
Child soldiers	A child soldier is someone below the age of 18 who is associated with an armed force or an armed group. Although we call them 'soldiers', children of all genders are used in a variety of ways during conflict, for example, as fighters, cooks, spies and manual labourers. They are often forcefully abducted and commonly abused. They are frequently witnesses of, and/or forced to participate in, torture, killings and sexual violence.	Regardless of how these children are used, or what they did, they are seen as victims. They are usually deprived of an opportunity for education and healthy socialization. They often suffer from serious and long-term mental and physical health concerns and find it difficult to rebuild their lives once they are independent of the armed force or group.
Human trafficking	Human trafficking is often described as modern enslavement. People are sometimes tricked into it or they may be forcibly abducted – in all cases, the people are victims. Victims are often transported away from friends and family and subjected to physical, emotional and sexual abuse. Vulnerable people are often targeted, including women and girls, migrant workers, stateless people, LGBTQ+ people, children and youth in the child welfare system, and those who are socially or economically disadvantaged.	Human trafficking is a horrific crime that exploits the most vulnerable in society. Individuals are often threatened and forced to work or provide sexual services. They suffer from long-term mental and physical health concerns and may find it difficult to rebuild their lives if and when they are freed.
Forced labour	Forced labour is work that is performed involuntarily and under threat. Individuals can be threatened with violence or in more subtle ways, such as being told they have a debt to repay, or having their identity papers taken and being told the immigration authorities or police will be called unless they work. Illegal migrants are particularly vulnerable to this kind of abuse, but other vulnerable groups include children and those who are economically disadvantaged.	Like human trafficking, many describe forced labour as a form of enslavement, and the victims often feel they cannot get help from law enforcement without putting themselves in danger of arrest or deportation.
Forced relocation	As we saw in Section 2, sometimes people or groups of people are forced or compelled to leave their homes in order to avoid the effects of armed conflict, situations of violence, violations of human rights or natural or human-made disasters. Forced relocation can occur within a state or across state borders.	Beyond the trauma of having to flee their homes, friends and family, individuals who are forcibly relocated face a life of uncertainty and are vulnerable to long-term physical and mental health concerns.
Denial of prisoner of war rights	The 1949 Geneva Convention states that prisoners of war must be treated humanely, and prisoners of war must not be put in a situation where their life is in danger or their health can be negatively impacted. The reality is, however, that many prisoners of war, in both interstate and intrastate conflicts, face torture, deprivation and/or death.	The horrors of war are no excuse to abuse an 'enemy' who has surrendered and is unarmed. The abuse of prisoners of war can significantly hinder the peace process and the chances of future positive peace.
Violations of freedom of speech	States have a duty to prohibit hateful, discriminatory speech, but many abuse their authority to shut down the voices of those they feel threatened by. NGOs, activists, and journalists are just some of the groups who are silenced. Violating freedom of speech denies people the right to participate openly in civil society.	Silencing people who want to bring about positive change in society creates a climate of fear and oppression, where change by peaceful means is less achievable.
Violations in the name of preventing terrorism	The threat of terrorism has instilled fear in the minds of many people globally. An increasing number of governments are exploiting this fear by expanding their powers and violating rights in order to prevent terrorism. Freedom of speech is a common casualty in the name of preventing terrorism, as is protection from torture and inhumane treatment, freedom of association, and many economic, cultural and social rights, as laid out in the UDHR.	When giving special privileges to agents of the state (for example, the police, military and security forces) to tackle terrorism, constitutional rights and laws that protect citizens have frequently been overruled. Additionally, creating a climate of fear around terrorism has led to an escalation of violence and discrimination against marginalized groups who are perceived to be threatening.
Gender discrimination	We have discussed gender discrimination in several places in this book, and this usually refers to women being treated differently and having less access to rights and justice than men. In recent years, gender discrimination has expanded to be inclusive of non-binary and transgender people.	Worldwide, women's rights issues have evolved in recent years. Women's rights are considered to be fundamental to the fight for democracy, social justice and sustainable development – no matter what the specific context or issue. Non-binary and transgender people are also vulnerable. Essentially, discriminating against people for who they are has negative consequences for all.

Discussion point

Think about which stakeholders and actors within your own community are attempting to improve the rights violations in Table 2.17.

 Chapter summary

In this chapter we have covered:
- the codification of rights and justice
- the protection and monitoring of rights and justice
- international humanitarian law and global norms surrounding rights and justice.

International humanitarian laws and global norms surrounding right and justice may shift and change, and there are many debates and points of view regarding this topic. We will explore this more extensively in the next chapter.

REVIEW QUESTIONS

Now that you have read this chapter, reflect on these questions:
- What are the benefits and limitations of codifying rights?
- How could the interpretation of constitutions change over time?
- How can sovereignty be an obstacle to the protection and monitoring of rights?
- What role do NGOs play in the protection and monitoring of rights?
- What are some examples of 'world norms' in rights and justice?

2.4 Debates on rights and justice

SYLLABUS CONTENT

By the end of this chapter, you should understand:
▶ diverse standards and understandings of rights
▶ the politicization of rights and justice
▶ humanitarian stakeholders and debates surrounding humanitarian intervention
▶ claims on individual and collective rights.

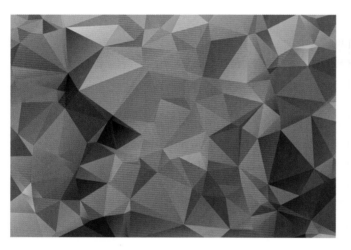

When we think of 'debates' we might think of a formal debate where we have two individuals or teams arguing opposite points of view on a specific topic. Formal debates are often very clear-cut: one side agrees completely and the other is in complete opposition. In global politics, however, debates are not so black and white, and disagreements or differing opinions are more refined and complex. Most rational human beings agree that there are 'good' ways to treat people and that society needs some kind of justice. So when we look at debates, we must appreciate the complexity of the arguments and avoid simplifying the perspectives of various stakeholders and actors.

■ **Figure 2.38** Debates about rights and justice are complex – like this piece of art, there are not simply two points of view but many views, of varying intensity and complexity

 TOK

Looking at debates as a TOK student, you might take time to consider what is happening 'behind' the actual words and ideas being used in the debate. When understanding what each side is saying, you should consider where each side is 'coming from'. Each voice will bring to the debate a whole series of background ideologies, assumptions and beliefs that can be considered the reasons why they hold the views they do. To truly understand what points are being made, take time to understand the core values from which the points in the debate are coming. A debate in the United States about abortion, for instance, might have quite different starting points: arguing for 'freedom of choice' is about the individual liberties of women, while arguing for a 'pro-life' position might come from beliefs about the sanctity of human life.

2.4.1 Diverse standards and understanding of rights

Although the Universal Declaration of Human Rights (UDHR) is by far the most widely accepted international standard of human rights, as we have seen throughout Section 2, there are other standards and understanding of rights as a global political concept. When we examine real-world political issues we should always consider the points of view of various stakeholders and actors to better appreciate the diverse standards and understandings of these issues.

Chapter 2.1 summarizes many different contested meanings of rights and justice, but two of the main opposing viewpoints – universalism and cultural relativism – are embedded in many global political debates on rights and justice.

The following is a brief recap on these two opposing viewpoints.

▦ Universality

There are many who believe that there are certain rights that all people have simply because they are human. There are no exceptions and a person cannot 'give up' these rights or have them taken away for any reason. For example, the United Nations (UN), the UDHR and non-governmental organizations (NGOs) such as Amnesty International support the claim of universality.

They argue that, if you adapt or change rights on the basis of culture, then you are basically allowing states to continue to oppress marginalized groups, such as women or indigenous people, in the name of 'culture'. They dispute the argument that the UDHR is 'Western' because the multicultural committee that created it was designed to prevent this.

▦ Cultural relativism

Cultural relativists disagree with universalists, arguing that cultures differ from one another, and so do the moral frameworks that structure relations within different societies. Cultural relativists are not saying that there are no such things as rights; instead, they are saying that rights should be considered within the context of culture. Some observe that in many cultures the rights of the community are more important than the rights of the individual.

They argue that 'universal' rights are focused on Western-centric values and come from a long Western philosophical tradition. By imposing universalism, the Western world is continuing to try to dominate and control the global community.

2.4.2 The politicization of rights and justice

In rights and justice, politicization means that actors are directed by political motives, rather than being genuinely concerned with rights and justice. Politicization, therefore, is seen when the actions and intentions of stakeholders are centred on gaining or manipulating power. When you examine real-world examples and case studies, you may come across those who seem to be motivated by political gain and those who are not.

> ### Discussion point
>
> Are universalists really just trying to impose Western values on the global community, as claimed by cultural relativists? Are cultural relativists simply opposing universality so that they can pick and choose which rights they support, and oppress some members of their communities? It's not always easy to see the true intentions of actors and stakeholders, but it's also important to remember that there can be a variety of motivations and intentions even within a group.

The absence of politicization is widely considered to be the ideal situation with regard to ensuring the credibility of international organizations (IGOs) concerned with rights and justice. This is the reason why many NGOs focusing on rights and justice avoid any kind of government funding and fiercely value their independence. But for IGOs, avoiding politicization can be difficult as,

■ Figure 2.39 Former UN Secretary-General Kofi Annan

of course, they are groups of states, and it is not always easy for a state to avoid putting its own interests first.

Evidence of politicization can negatively impact the legitimacy of IGOs, and most take the threat very seriously.

In 2006, UN Secretary-General Kofi Annan (see Figure 2.39) attempted to put an end to the politicization that was impacting the legitimacy of the UN Human Rights Commission by establishing the Human Rights Council. The council would conduct independent reviews of the commission to review the decisions and actions of member states to safeguard against politicization. Speaking of the newly formed council, he said:

> It was intended to give concrete form to our shared principles of universality, non-selectivity, objectivity and cooperation. The world looks to the Council to develop a review mechanism that lives up to those ideals.

Discussion point

The European Union and the Council of Europe consider the death penalty to be an example of torture. Do you agree? Why or why not? Are there diverse points of view on this within your class?

■ Why would a state ratify a human rights treaty and then go on to violate it?

As we saw in Chapter 2.3, many international human rights treaties and conventions appear to be widely accepted by the international community. The state is often seen as the most powerful stakeholder in global politics, and it's clear that states do hold great responsibility for the protection and enforcement of rights and justice. Although states may claim to value the rights outlined in treaties and conventions, the abuse of people, corruption, racism and inequality all persist in our world today. While it may be difficult to imagine a world where everyone lives in perfect peace and harmony, it can be confusing when we see many instances of people saying they believe in rights and justice, but acting in ways that seemingly contradict this claim.

On the global political stage, a state may ratify a human rights convention, only to later be accused of violating the treaty. Why might this happen? One reason for this could be that the state has a different understanding of the convention. Maybe the state lacks the resources or will to protect rights. Or perhaps states are attempting to politicize rights and get some sort of advantage by appearing to prioritize their citizens.

In any case, it's worth considering a real-world example in relation to this.

The Convention against Torture and Other Cruel, Inhuman or Degrading Treatment or Punishment

The convention defines torture as the infliction of severe physical or mental pain and suffering in order to get information or a confession, or to intimidate or terrify someone, or as a form of punishment. It does not include pain and suffering that is the result of lawful imprisonment, such as loneliness or depression.

The obligations of the state outlined in the Convention against Torture and Other Cruel, Inhuman or Degrading Treatment or Punishment include the following:

- An obligation not to deport or transfer a person to a state where they would be at risk of torture or ill-treatment (non-refoulement) (Article 3). This article specifically refers to asylum seekers or refugees who have legitimate claims that they will be tortured or mistreated if they are forced to return to their original country of residence.

- Torture will be criminalized under domestic law (Article 4).

- Ensuring that victims of torture can seek justice (Article 14).

- Making sure evidence obtained through torture is not used in any proceedings (the exclusionary rule) (Article 15).

As we noted in Chapter 2.3, this convention has been widely accepted and has been ratified by all permanent members of the UN Security Council (China, France, Russia, the UK, the United States). However, according to many human rights stakeholders and actors, the five permanent members of the Security Council have all violated this convention.

The following case studies outline some of the ways the treaty has been allegedly violated by both China and the United States.

CASE STUDY

China

State	Alleged violation	Response of the state to claims they are violating the treaty
China	There is a long history of the persecution of Muslims in China and, since 2017, there has been widespread concern expressed among human rights activists about the establishment of inhumane forced detention camps and suspected genocide. In a 2022, 45-page UN report, China was condemned for its treatment of the Uyghur people, Kazakh people and other predominantly minority ethnic Muslim groups in China's Xinjiang Uyghur Autonomous Region. The report claimed that there was state-organized mass imprisonment, torture and persecution amounting to crimes against humanity.	China called the report 'a farce' and responded with its own 131-page document claiming it was attempting to combat religious extremism by setting up vocational and educational training centres to help rehabilitate these people. 'To sum up, respecting and protecting human rights is a basic principle enshrined in the Constitution of China', the report states. The report claims anti-China forces in the United States and the West merely pretend to care about human rights and are using the Uyghur issue as a means to destabilize the rule of President Xi Jinping and suppress China.

Could this be an example of China having a different understanding of 'torture'? Possibly. This could also be seen as an example of the politicization of rights and justice.

China, as a permanent member of the UN Security Council, and a world leader, is deeply concerned with external legitimacy. As it has ratified the Convention against Torture and Other Cruel, Inhuman or Degrading Treatment or Punishment, it would not readily admit to violating it. It is also important to remember that there is extensive evidence from a wide variety of sources that extreme human rights violations are taking place against minority ethnic Muslim groups in China.

Politicizing rights means to use them for some reason which connects to power. What examples of politicization of rights can we see in the China example?

1 Many question why it took the UN so long to speak out against China. Could it be because China is very powerful and a permanent member of the UN Security Council? Could power be interfering with rights and justice?

2 China claims that the United States and the West are politicizing human rights as a way to discredit China by attempting to make it look bad on the world stage with false claims.

Discussion point

The relationship between China and the United States has been strained for many years. How might this have impacted China's response to the claims they are committing serious human rights violations against the Uyghur people?

Consider the claims made about another permanent member of the Security Council, the USA.

CASE STUDY

The United States

State	Alleged violation	Response of the state to claims they are violating the treaty
United States	The United States has been widely criticized for its post 9/11 'war on terror'. In 2022, the Watson Institute of International and Public Affairs at Brown University in Boston, in collaboration with Human Rights Watch, released a report stating that the CIA had secretly detained at least 119 Muslim men and tortured at least 39. The military also allegedly held thousands of Muslim men, and in some cases boys, in detention centres, including in Afghanistan, Iraq and Guantánamo Bay, Cuba. Nearly 800 men and boys were held in Guantánamo, and 39 remain detained as of 2023, 27 without criminal charges. Cases of US-facilitated indefinite detention continued under the Obama, Trump and Biden administrations.	Many activists and groups, both inside and outside the United States, have called for an investigation into the actions of the CIA. President Donald Trump used his first TV interview as president in 2017 to say he believes torture 'absolutely' works and that the United States should 'fight fire with fire'. On 26 June 2023, in honour of The International Day of Support for Victims of Torture, President Biden stated: *It is our firm belief as a nation that we must hold ourselves to the same standards to which we hold others. This is why we continue to ensure that torture remains prohibited in all of its forms, without exception.* The statement then goes on to condemn Russia, Syria and North Korea but makes no mention of allegations of torture conducted by the United States.

President Trump's statement clearly prioritizes national interests over any concerns regarding the violation of rights.

President Biden, by contrast, avoids the topic completely, insisting, like the report produced by China, that the United States always prioritizes human rights. By deflecting attention to examples of torture taking place in other countries, Biden is also politicizing rights, the implication being that the United States is still a world leader and other places are far worse. He is using the human rights abuses taking place in Syria, North Korea and Russia for the political gain of the United States. However, many see this stance as hypocritical and a cynical abuse of power.

Discussion point

Would you agree that the response of President Trump supports a realist view of global politics? Why or why not?

Discussion point

In 2023, the Chinese foreign ministry spokesperson Zhao Lijian criticized what he called the horrifying torture of prisoners that had taken place at American 'black sites'. He claimed that Washington had no right to criticize any other country for human rights violations. Do you think this could be another way of politicizing rights? Was Zhao Lijian deflecting attention from what is allegedly happening in China?

Common mistake

As we have seen, particularly with the US example above, debates on rights and justice also take place within states. In states where civil society is more able to openly express opinions and disagree with government policy this can be more obvious, but even in oppressive states there can be evidence of dissent.

It is a common mistake to talk about government policies and positions as if everyone within the state completely supports the government. This is simply not the case and demonstrates a lack of understanding of the complexity of political issues and the debates on rights and justice.

2.4.3 Humanitarian stakeholders

What does 'humanitarian' mean?

What does the term 'humanitarian' mean? Generally, humanitarianism is a general dedication to and belief in the value of all human life. In global politics, it often refers to the international crisis response that has evolved from the founding of the Red Cross (and later Red Crescent) and the first Geneva Convention in 1864. As an organized response to a crisis, humanitarianism means helping people who have been impacted by natural disasters, conflict, famine and health crises, including pandemics.

Humanitarianism can be defined by the following:

- The principles of humanity, neutrality, impartiality and independence are fundamental to humanitarian action.
- Human suffering must be addressed wherever it is found, with particular attention to the most vulnerable.
- Humanitarian aid must not take any side in an armed conflict.
- Humanitarian aid must be given on the basis of need, without discrimination.
- Those who provide humanitarian relief must do so without political, economic, military or other objectives.

Humanitarian stakeholders

There are countless humanitarian agencies operating globally. The following agencies in Table 2.18 are some of the best known. There is frequent cooperation between these groups, NGOs and IGOs.

■ **Table 2.18** A selection of the best-known humanitarian agencies

Agency	Aim
International Committee of the Red Cross (ICRC)	The ICRC was established in 1863. It aims to help people affected by armed conflict. It also responds to disasters in conflict zones because disasters are much worse if they impact a country already at war. It is focused on responding rapidly as emergencies are not always predictable. It operates at the international level. The ICRC closely follows the work of the UN Human Rights Commission, while maintaining its full independence. It has been awarded the Nobel Peace Prize three times.
International Federation of Red Cross and Red Crescent societies (IFRC)	The IFRC is a group of national societies operating globally in over 190 states, reaching over 150 million people per year. It acts at a more regional/local level to provide humanitarian aid. It works together with the ICRC and provides a more local perspective and focus during and after disasters and health emergencies.
Médecins Sans Frontières (MSF) (Doctors Without Borders)	MSF brings medical humanitarian assistance to victims of conflict, natural disasters, epidemics, or those unable to access health care. It operates globally and has worked collaboratively with the ICRC in conflict zones. The organization was awarded the Nobel Peace Prize in 1999.
Oxfam	Oxfam's mission is to fight inequality and end poverty and injustice. Across regions, from the local to the global, it works with people to attempt to make long-term change beyond responding to disasters. It is committed to the universality of human rights and supports the empowerment of women as a means of achieving these aims. Oxfam works in partnership with the UN Sustainable Development Goals.
Save the Children	Save the Children was founded in 1919 as a response to the need to help children suffering from the impact of the First World War. It remains an independent NGO but partners with corporations and foundations and also ordinary people, who provide donations in 120 countries. It operates globally, providing necessities to children caught up in armed conflict as well as helping children in both more and less economically developed nations who are particularly vulnerable. Save the Children created the initial draft for what would become the UN Convention on the Rights of the Child in 1923. As we covered in Chapter 2.3, this was finally realized in 1989 and has been ratified by most states.

■ **Figure 2.40** A medic administers an open-air vaccination to a child during the COVID-19 pandemic

■ The United Nations and humanitarianism

The UN frequently collaborates with independent humanitarian agencies, but also has its own designated agencies. In 2005, a major reform of humanitarian coordination, the Humanitarian Reform Agenda, took place so that all could work more efficiently and collaboratively. From this, the Cluster Approach was developed.

Clusters are groups of humanitarian organizations, both UN and non-UN, in each of the main sectors of humanitarian action, for example water, health and logistics. They are designated by the Inter-Agency Standing Committee (IASC) and have clear responsibilities for coordination, as shown in Figure 2.41.

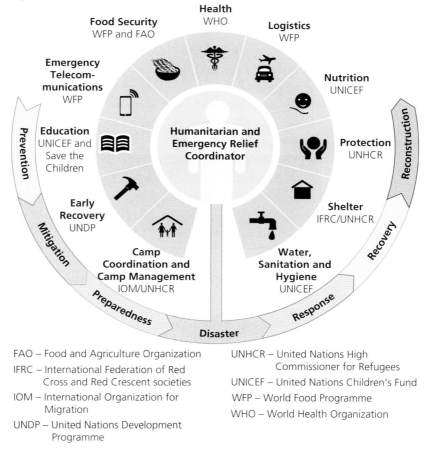

FAO – Food and Agriculture Organization

IFRC – International Federation of Red Cross and Red Crescent societies

IOM – International Organization for Migration

UNDP – United Nations Development Programme

UNHCR – United Nations High Commissioner for Refugees

UNICEF – United Nations Children's Fund

WFP – World Food Programme

WHO – World Health Organization

■ **Figure 2.41** The Cluster Approach (adapted from Humanitarian Response)

2.4.4 Debates surrounding humanitarian intervention

Helping people in times of conflict may not seem to be a very controversial or debatable topic. But, we know that, in real-world situations, it is extremely dangerous to send people into conflict zones. Additionally, to do so may usually mean violating rules of state sovereignty, which is ordinarily perceived as a hostile act.

The international community has long grappled with how to help the marginalized and vulnerable who are caught up in conflict. One aspect of this has been to consider the ethics of using deadly force to protect the rights of those being abused. 'Just war' theory is a Western philosophical guideline for determining when 'war' is acceptable morally. It originated centuries ago among Christian scholars who were troubled with how the violence of war contradicts the teaching of Christianity.

The principles of the 'just war' theory are:

- There must be a just cause.
- Other solutions to the conflict were tried and failed and war was the last resort.
- War is declared by a proper authority.
- There is a reasonable chance of success.
- The methods used are reasonable in order to achieve success – nothing more.

In Chapter 2.3 you were introduced to the idea of humanitarian intervention and the Responsibility to Protect (R2P), which evolved as a response to widespread criticism of the UN for seemingly doing nothing as thousands were killed in Rwanda and Bosnia in the 1990s. In this section, we look at why humanitarian intervention as a component of R2P is widely debated in the international community.

> ## Discussion point
>
> Review the section on Responsibility to Protect (R2P) in Chapter 2.3. What are the similarities between the 'just war' theory and R2P? What might a cultural relativist say about these similarities?

■ Debates on humanitarian intervention and R2P: real-world examples

There are several debates to consider when discussing humanitarian intervention and R2P, but these debates only come to life when you examine real-world examples. Remember, IBDP Global Politics is not focused on theory – you need examples and case studies to support your claims. So, as you consider debates in rights and justice, always think about how examples of this can be seen in our contemporary global political world.

Concerns regarding humanitarian intervention and R2P: the values of the United Nations

The use of military force seems to contradict the core value of the UN Charter, which bans the use of force when it violates state sovereignty. The use of military force to protect the universal rights guaranteed in the Universal Declaration of Human Rights concerns many, as it disregards the essential principles of state sovereignty and UN ideology.

Concerns regarding humanitarian intervention and R2P: loss of life

The use of military force will cause death, destruction and violence. Critics argue it can be very difficult to predict the consequences of using armed force. There is the possibility that it could make the conflict worse and result in causing more human rights violations and loss of life. Armed conflict can quickly escalate in real-world situations and it can be difficult to control the actions of combatants and the evolution of the conflict.

Concerns regarding humanitarian intervention and R2P: politicization

When a state fails to respond to peaceful and diplomatic efforts, the UN Security Council can also employ more forceful measures such as sanctions, arms embargoes or referrals to the International Criminal Court. As a last resort, the Security Council can authorize military action through the UN or a regional organization. Overall, the Security Council has significant flexibility when responding to an R2P crisis in determining how to implement its responsibility.

Critics argue that, although humanitarian intervention requires 'neutrality, impartiality and independence', it appears that the Security Council's members consistently prioritize their own interests. As a result, they have been unable to respond quickly and decisively to major conflicts and human rights crises, including the civil war in Syria, the COVID-19 pandemic, Russia's annexation of Crimea and subsequent invasion of Ukraine, the Rohingya crisis in Myanmar, and reports of extreme violations taking place in North Korea.

■ **Figure 2.42** Protesters against the military coup in Myanmar call for international intervention, Yangon, 12 April 2021

CASE STUDY

Libya and humanitarian intervention

Background

The Arab Spring was a series of anti-government protests, uprisings and armed rebellions that spread across much of the Arab world in the early 2010s. In February 2011, a violent crackdown was launched against protesters in Libya. An estimated 500–700 people were killed over several weeks as the government, led by Muammar Gaddafi, used the military to respond with force.

In response to these attacks, the UN Security Council invoked R2P, authorizing 'humanitarian intervention' to protect the people. In addition to the military action, sanctions against Gaddafi and associates were imposed. The Libyan National Oil Corp and the Central Bank of Libya, among others, had their assets frozen.

A NATO-led alliance of countries started by conducting air strikes against military targets in Libya. After several months of intense fighting, Tripoli was taken over by Libyan rebel forces and the Gaddafi government collapsed in August 2011.

This intervention is generally acknowledged to be the international community's first attempt to use 'humanitarian intervention' within R2P as a way to stop mass atrocity crimes.

Immediate concerns about R2P after the collapse of the Gaddafi government

A number of issues came to light after the Libyan intervention which have caused many to question the new global norm of R2P and to what extent state sovereignty can be ignored.

Many UN member states expressed concern that the strength of military force must, in future, be clearly defined prior to humanitarian intervention. In Libya, it was argued, too much power was given to the states conducting the intervention and not enough safeguards were in place to ensure that all action taken was solely to protect civilians.

Additionally, Gaddafi and the mechanisms of his government were directly targeted, and many felt this was beyond the mandate of R2P. NATO even supplied rebel groups with weapons to fight against Gaddafi forces. China was one state which expressed concern that R2P must not be used as a way to get rid of governments, as this is clearly a breach of sovereignty. Some argue that there were effectively two interventions in Libya: the legal one to avert a massacre of civilians, and the illegal one with the aim of regime change.

Widespread perceptions that the intervention was just a way for Western powers to control Libya's oil reserves demonstrate the cynicism that many have about R2P and the UN in general. Barely two years after the fall of Gaddafi, most viewed the intervention not as a success story but as a case study on how *not* to intervene.

Impact on Libya

It's generally agreed that the involvement of international forces significantly prolonged the conflict and led to further crisis:

1 Large stocks of weapons were quickly looted and sold within the region, contributing to regional instability and violence in places such as Mali.

2 African migrants living in Libya were no longer welcome, leading to tens of thousands of displaced people being left vulnerable to trafficking and abuse.

3 Gaddafi was hunted and his execution filmed and broadcast by NATO. Many say this normalized the unlawful killing of anyone labelled a supporter of Gaddafi's government and contributed further to an atmosphere of chaos and violence.

4 Because Gaddafi had essentially ruled Libya for 42 years, there was no clear plan as to who could take over after his regime was destroyed. This led to armed groups at both the city and regional level attempting to seize power.

UN Support Mission in Libya (UNSMIL)

This mission was set up in 2011 after the fall of the Gaddafi government as a political mission, not a military mission. This means it was established to help Libya with conflict resolution and the transition to a stable form of government, and to promote rights and justice. However, as late as 2023, the UNSMIL issued a statement describing disturbing events including abductions, arbitrary arrests, disappearances of ordinary people and public citizens, and oil fields being shut down by rebel groups.

The description from the UNSMIL clearly describes Libya as a failed state and has caused widespread concern about the unforeseen impact of using humanitarian intervention. However, others argue that Libya was already in crisis prior to the humanitarian intervention of R2P and therefore this cannot be blamed entirely on the intervention.

Perspectives

Claudia Gazzini on humanitarian intervention in Libya

There was no international state building plan except for the idea of let's put in place a UN mission to go and organize elections. There was no strong will or capacity for anything else.

Quoted by Peter Beaumont, '"War weary" Libya reflects 10 years on from Gaddafi and Arab spring'

Claudia Gazzini is the International Crisis Group's Senior Analyst for Libya. She has covered this role since 2012. She was Head of the UN Support Mission in Libya (UNSMIL) 2017–18.

■ **Figure 2.43** Claudia Gazzini

■ Consequences for R2P, humanitarian intervention and world norms of rights and justice

R2P has been invoked in more than 80 UN security resolutions concerning crises in Central African Republic, Côte d'Ivoire, Democratic Republic of the Congo, Liberia, Libya, Mali, Somalia, South Sudan, Syria and Yemen. It is important for us to remember that R2P rarely deploys 'humanitarian intervention'.

Its continued use is the most powerful evidence that global norms of collective obligations to prevent atrocities remain in focus. However, the use of humanitarian intervention has been, and continues to be, heavily scrutinized and debated.

Concepts

Postcolonialism and R2P

Postcolonialists argue that R2P's 'humanitarian intervention' is viewed as anything but humanitarian. Instead, they state, it's nothing but a new name for old forms of violence and domination by powerful states. They point out that it goes against the internationally acknowledged principles of sovereignty and non-intervention, which are supported by the UN Charter. For a long time, the only accepted reason for a state to use armed force against another was for self-defence, but now, according to postcolonialists, we are seeing it used to serve states' self-interested goals.

● Extended essay

If you're thinking of writing an extended essay on the effectiveness of R2P, as a starting point you could investigate a few of the other 80+ instances the UN Security Council has had it invoked. Make sure you discuss any potential research questions with your extended essay supervisor.

Sanctions: why are they controversial?

We have mentioned several times in Section 2 that sanctions are an alternative to the use of military force. They are generally regarded as 'safer' than humanitarian intervention, too.

Sanctions can take a variety of forms including:

- travel bans
- asset freezes
- arms embargoes
- foreign aid reduction
- trade restrictions.

Usually they are used by states or IGOs to try to force a state, group or individual to change their behaviour. Often they are used when there are concerns about human rights abuses.

According to Joseph Nye, sanctions are hard power tactics. They are put in place to modify the behaviour of a group and weaken its power. Some people debate the effectiveness of the use of sanctions, which often end up negatively impacting the population of the state, while others see them as an essential strategy.

Figure 2.44 shows the global sanctions in operation today.

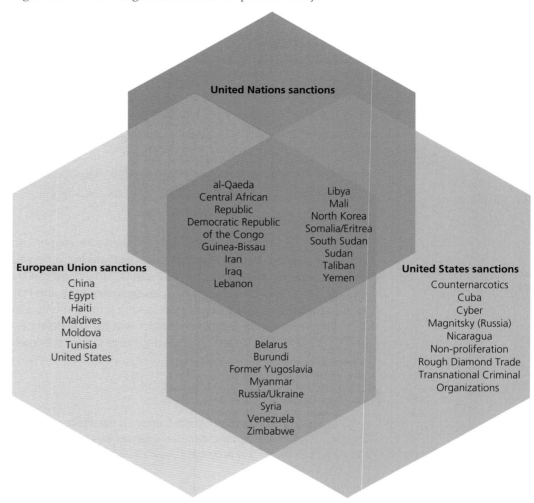

United Nations sanctions

al-Qaeda
Central African
Republic
Democratic Republic
of the Congo
Guinea-Bissau
Iran
Iraq
Lebanon

Libya
Mali
North Korea
Somalia/Eritrea
South Sudan
Sudan
Taliban
Yemen

European Union sanctions

China
Egypt
Haiti
Maldives
Moldova
Tunisia
United States

United States sanctions

Counternarcotics
Cuba
Cyber
Magnitsky (Russia)
Nicaragua
Non-proliferation
Rough Diamond Trade
Transnational Criminal
Organizations

Belarus
Burundi
Former Yugoslavia
Myanmar
Russia/Ukraine
Syria
Venezuela
Zimbabwe

■ **Figure 2.44** Global sanctions in operation today (adapted from Masters, with data from the Council of the European Union and the US Treasury Department)

Discussion point

What real-world evidence can you find that supports the claim that sanctions can be effective? From a TOK perspective, you might include what background assumptions there are about what 'effective' means in your response. What other assumptions about 'effective' might someone who disagrees with you have?

2.4.5 Claims on individual and collective rights

As we have seen throughout Section 2, although the needs of the wider community are considered, the rights of the individual tend to take precedence.

One criticism of the UDHR is that it strongly emphasizes the rights of the individual and therefore represents an inherently 'Western' perspective. Consider the following quotation from Chinese philosopher Lo Chung-shu (1903–85):

> *The basic ethical concept of Chinese social political relations is the fulfillment of the duty to one's neighbour, rather than the claiming of rights. The idea of mutual obligations is regarded as the fundamental teaching of Confucianism.*

Lo is claiming that obligations to the greater society, or the 'collective rights' of the wider society, traditionally take priority in Chinese cultural tradition. Of course, an emphasis on collective rights does not mean that individual rights have no significance, and Lo worked extensively with the UN to see how both collective and individual rights could complement each other.

Once again, we see that debates on rights and justice are not simply black and white.

 TOK

The quotation from Lo Chung-shu is an example of how pre-existing beliefs might affect how we interpret 'rights'. If a collective unit like a family or group is the basic moral structure, then thinking about other political, economic, social or ethical issues might come out quite differently from when we think of the individual as the basic moral concern. This might impact the methods we use when we reason about issues.

Many modern social debates hinge on whether groups or individuals are affected. Debates around '**affirmative action**', for example, are often characterized as being about two competing assumptions. For instance, one might prioritize the group an applicant comes from and support affirmative action in hiring decisions (possibly to the disadvantage of individuals), while the other might prioritize only the individual's own merits, regardless of what group they belong to (despite the advantages that individual might already have being part of a group with high social power).

◆ **Affirmative action** is usually discussed in terms of American case studies and means that an effort has been made to improve educational and employment opportunities for marginalized groups by prioritizing them as applicants.

■ Concerns about prioritizing the 'collective rights' of the majority in a state

Societies that traditionally emphasize collective rights do not necessarily reject the human rights norms of our contemporary global political world. After all, we can see that most states claim to support and respect these norms as members of the UN.

However, one criticism that some have about the emphasis of 'collective rights' is that it assumes some kind of common agreement among all members of society. In our modern world, there are few examples of states in which the population is homogeneous (meaning of one cultural background). Most state populations identify with a variety of cultures, religions, traditions and ways of life.

When we speak of collective rights it implies that decisions are being made about what that society values based on whoever holds the most power. Will the views of the marginalized and vulnerable be considered as part of the 'collective'? This is why some people argue that it is essential to emphasize universalism, and that all people be treated equally by focusing on individual rights.

■ Collective rights for marginalized and vulnerable groups

Another way to consider collective rights is to look at them from the perspective of the marginalized and vulnerable who seek protection of the collective rights of their particular communities. As we saw when discussing trade unions in Chapter 2.2, when a group, rather than just an individual, demands rights it can be more impactful.

Throughout Section 2 we have considered how women and members of the LGBTQ+ communities continue to do just that. Black Lives Matter is another example of people fighting for the collective rights of their community:

Discussion point

Can you think of any marginalized or vulnerable groups from your own country or region who have unified to demand their collective rights? What have they done to bring attention to their cause?

■ Indigenous rights

Historically, indigenous people have faced widespread abuse and oppression. Many groups have struggled to maintain their languages and traditional way of life.

Despite the differences between indigenous populations across the world, many indigenous people experience similar struggles:

- Globally, they are more likely to experience extreme poverty and significantly lower life expectancy rates.

- Indigenous women and girls are particularly threatened by violence and discrimination.

- Climate change has negatively impacted their environments and livelihoods and, although they are seen to hold vital knowledge and expertise on how to adapt and reduce climate disaster risks, their voices are not always heard.

CASE STUDY

Collective indigenous rights

Indigenous people are distinct social and cultural groups who share collective connections to the land and natural resources where they live, or once lived. The land and resources are linked to the indigenous people's identities, cultures and spiritual beliefs. They often have their own leadership systems and maintain a distinct identity from the wider society.

Different general terms and specific names are used to describe indigenous people in different areas of the world. Table 2.19 is a partial list.

■ Table 2.19 General terms and specific names for indigenous people in different areas of the world

Country/Region	Name
China	Ethnic minority
India	Adivasi
Japan	Ainu
Russia and northern Scandinavia	Saami
Botswana	San
Iran, Iraq, Syria, Türkiye	Kurds
North America	Native and First Nations
Australia	Aboriginal
New Zealand	Maori
Mexico and Guatemala	Mayan

Which group(s) identify as indigenous in your state or region?

■ Table 2.20 The world's indigenous people

Country/Region	Percentage of indigenous people
Africa	7%
Arabia	5%
Canada and USA	1%
China	36%
Latin America	8%
South Asia	32%
Southeast Asia	10%

■ Figure 2.45 The indigenous Hmong people of Vietnam in traditional costume

Indigenous rights and the global community

In our more globalized and interdependent world, the struggle to advocate for the collective rights of indigenous people goes beyond state borders. The emergence of the movement for indigenous rights in recent decades represents one of the most significant developments in international rights. Why? Because global norms of sovereignty and individual rights are being challenged on an unprecedented scale.

The creation of the UN Declaration on the Rights of Indigenous Peoples (UNDRIP) in 2007 was the result of cooperation and collaboration between civil society, states, regional IGOs and the UN. In particular, inter-American, African and European human rights systems contributed greatly to the refinement and creation of this declaration.

The central themes of UNDRIP are:

- the right to self-determination, which means indigenous people, as a community, can make decisions about their legal systems, health and education
- the right to land, resources and territory
- the right to be recognized as a distinct group
- the right to be free from discrimination
- the right to protect the environment.

Discussion point

Which of these bullet points challenge(s) global norms of state sovereignty?

● Extended essay

As we saw in Chapter 2.3, the United States, Canada, Australia and New Zealand all voted against UNDRIP in 2007, but later changed their positions. Exploring what contributed to these changes could be the start of an interesting investigation into power and global politics and could lead to an interesting research question for an extended essay. Always discuss your ideas with your extended essay supervisor!

Debates surrounding claims on individual and collective rights

Below are a few of the more common debatable issues on individual and collective rights.

- Different cultures and human conditions can lead to different interpretations of rights and justice, but focusing on individual rights does not acknowledge or respect those differences.

- Modern norms of rights clearly state that all people, regardless of culture, gender, religion, race, etc. have equal rights. So why is it necessary for certain groups to distinguish themselves as requiring collective rights? By claiming some groups deserve 'special' rights, are we actually creating division as well as denying universalism?

- When we discuss the 'collective' rights of a group of people we must remember that even within marginalized groups there can be discrimination. Is it possible that marginalized people within that group, for example women and those who identify as LGBTQ+, could be ignored or forgotten?

- Many point out that there is a place for both individual and collective rights and that they are not in opposition but actually complement each other to make the world a fairer place for all.

Sharia and rights and justice

Sharia means 'the correct path' and it comes from two main sources: the Qur'an and the sayings of the Prophet Mohammed. Sharia guides the personal religious practices of Muslims worldwide, but whether it should influence modern legal and political systems remains a subject of intense debate. Different Islamic scholars, religious leaders and political systems offer differing interpretations of the meaning of Sharia. Many argue that Islamic law is always about the human interpretation of Sharia and therefore must be open to debate and change.

Is the Universal Declaration of Human Rights in opposition to Sharia and Islamic interpretations of rights and justice? As always, the answers are never a clear 'yes' or 'no'.

Perspectives

Dr Khaled Abou El Fadl on Islam and human rights

Dr Abou El Fadl is an expert in Islamic law, offering a unique perspective on the current state of Islam and the West. He is a strong proponent of human rights and is the 2007 recipient of the University of Oslo Human Rights Award, the Lisl and Leo Eitinger Prize. He was also named a Carnegie Scholar in Islam for 2005. He serves on the Advisory Board of Middle East Watch, and was previously on the Board of Directors of Human Rights Watch.

> Political realities—such as colonialism, the persistence of highly invasive and domineering despotic governments, the widespread perception, and reality, of Western hypocrisy in the human rights field, and the emergence and spread of supremacist movements of moral exceptionalism in modern Islam ... are not consistent with a commitment to human rights.

Dr Khaled Abou El Fadl, Human Rights and Responsibilities in the World Religions

---

Sometimes, differing interpretations of Sharia can be in conflict with members of civil society as well as regional and international norms of rights and justice. Two of the more commonly debated aspects of Sharia that are open to debate by Islamic scholars and others include the use of corporal punishment and women's rights.

Corporal punishment and Sharia

One debatable issue with regard to Sharia is if and when corporal punishment should be used. Corporal punishment means inflicting physical suffering as a deterrent, or a way to scare people so that they don't commit crimes. This punishment can include flogging, stoning and amputation.

Most Muslim-majority states do not use corporal punishment anymore. However, Indonesia, Iran, the Maldives and Qatar are among the countries that still carry out floggings, and Iran, Mauritania, Nigeria, Saudi Arabia and Sudan have punished convicted thieves with amputations in recent decades. Additionally, in Afghanistan, the Taliban's interpretation of Sharia means corporal punishment for offences including adultery, drinking alcohol, theft, banditry, religious betrayal and rebellion. (See Robinson.)

However, even within these countries, not everyone supports the interpretation of Sharia that allows the state to use corporal punishment against its citizens. Some would point out that the states justifying the use of corporal punishment are oppressive states ruled by force and violence.

Women's' rights and Sharia

The Qur'an states that women are morally and spiritually equal to men but also indicates that women have specific roles as wives and mothers. Some governments use their interpretation of Sharia to significantly restrict women's rights, dictating what they wear and limiting their educational opportunities and participation in public life.

One such state is Iran, which saw widespread protests in 2022 after Mahsa Amini, a 22-year-old woman, was murdered by morality police for violating the country's strict dress code (she appeared in public without a hijab and with her hair showing). Over 500 people died in these protests and tens of thousands were arrested, indicating that many Muslims do not agree with Iran's strict interpretation of Sharia, which only mentions dressing modestly. Iranian expatriates and many others protested globally to demand justice for Mahsa Amini and to draw attention to Iran's violent regime. The protests indicate that there are widespread debates regarding the rights of women within the Muslim community and it is a mistake to assume that the oppression of women is an accepted aspect of Sharia.

■ **Figure 2.46** A protester holds a poster depicting Mahsa Amini during a protest in Istanbul, Türkiye

Critics argue that extreme modesty rules create inequality by limiting education and employment opportunities for Islamic women. Other laws prevent women from initiating divorce and marriage on their own, contributing to child marriages and gender-based violence.

Additionally, there is significant debate over what the Qur'an teaches compared with what practices come from local customs. For example, Muslim feminists have long argued that sexist interpretations of Sharia come from social norms, not from Islam. As an example, Saudi Arabia cited Islamic law when it finally allowed women to drive in 2018; many welcomed the development but also pointed out that it was the interpretation of Sharia that had changed, not the teachings of Islam, and therefore a lot of the rules that are called 'Islamic' are often local cultural traditions.

Extended essay

If you're thinking of writing an extended essay about cultural relativism and challenges to global norms of rights and justice, one possible place to start could be to investigate different interpretations of Sharia and how political systems interpret these laws. Be aware that debates in this topic are complex and multiple perspectives must be considered. Always consult with your extended essay supervisor about any potential research questions.

Chapter summary

In this chapter we have covered:
- diverse standards and understandings of rights
- the politicization of rights and justice
- humanitarian stakeholders and debates surrounding humanitarian intervention
- claims on individual and collective rights and real-world examples.

REVIEW QUESTIONS

Now that you have read this chapter, reflect on these questions:

■ There are countless acronyms for political stakeholders associated with rights and justice. Many of these acronyms are very similar to each other and it can get confusing, but it's important you use these terms correctly. Make a chart in your notes listing all the acronyms, and their full names and purpose, using Section 2 for reference. Here are a few to get you started:

Acronym	Full name
UDHR	Universal Declaration of Human Rights
ICJ	International Court of Justice
ICC	International Criminal Court

■ What are the arguments in support of using the Responsibility to Protect (R2P)? What are some of the arguments against?

■ Why do humanitarian stakeholders such as Médecins Sans Frontières and the International Red Cross/Red Crescent always try to uphold principles of humanity, neutrality, impartiality and independence?

■ What does 'politicization' of rights and justice mean?

■ What are claims on individual and collective rights? Can you name a few real-world examples?

Exam-style questions: rights and justice

For generic advice on how to structure a response to a Paper 2 question, please see page 402. Remember, Section A questions are rooted firmly in one of the three thematic studies, while Section B questions will require you to integrate content from across the course.

Note, there are always claims and counterclaims expected in a Paper 2-style essay and this guidance identifies some of the claims and counterclaims you may choose to make. These are simply suggestions and you may choose to use other claims if appropriate.

Section A-style question

1 'The contested meaning of rights has contributed to their politicization.' Discuss this view with reference to two specific real-world cases.

■ General advice

In your response you may choose to include a definition of rights as basic claims and entitlements. You may go slightly further and define human rights as those rights that, many argue, one should be able to exercise simply by virtue of being a human being. You could address the fact that the contested nature of rights arises from differing perspectives on the origin, scope and universality of rights, as well as conflicting interests and cultural norms. You should also offer some definition of politicization. This may be done in terms of seeing (different conceptualizations of) rights being used as a political tool in partisan politics to block an opposing party or in identity politics to mobilize support, for instance. The most important thing is to demonstrate an understanding that politicization entails the use or manipulation of rights to achieve a specific goal.

You should be careful to note that the question requires you to refer to at least two specific contemporary real-world examples. These examples can be drawn from different scales such as national and regional. You should make sure that you show understanding of the different ways in which rights can be categorized, such as individual versus collective rights or by making reference to the different generations of rights.

■ Claims

Your claims should support the view that the contested meaning of rights has contributed to their politicization. They may include the following:

- Different conceptualizations of which rights matter most allows some states to refer to the human rights records of other states as a means to rationalize policy decisions (for example, trade preferences), to seek or justify punitive measures (for example, sanctions), or, conversely, to reward (for example, aid packages).

- The language of rights is often untethered to specific legal interpretations and so is too loose to prevent governments from politicizing them in the service of illiberal agendas. For example, Russia referenced the rights of minority ethnic groups in Crimea to justify its 2014 invasion.

- The existence of contested meanings of rights allows political actors to politicize such differences in order to achieve strategic goals, i.e. some have argued that prioritizing human rights over the right of the sovereign state to non-interference in its domestic affairs can allow for regime change under the guise of humanitarian protection, for example the NATO intervention in Libya (2011).

- Many countries in the global south see the existing human rights regimes' focus on individual rights as a Western construct and a tool for continued Western domination. Such a culturally relative perspective argues that cultural differences are politicized and used as a weapon, for example opposition to the International Criminal Court (ICC) within the African Union given the perception of neocolonialism, exemplified by Burundi's withdrawal from the ICC.

- The prioritization of collectivist interpretations of rights may be used to restrict or repress individual human rights, for example the suppression of LGBTQ+ rights in many parts of the world on purported cultural or religious grounds.

- At the national level, contested conceptualizations of whose rights matter provide the grounds for their politicization, for example the Trump administration's vilification of immigrants in the United States by building a wall ostensibly to protect the rights of US citizens, or lockdown restrictions and mandatory quarantine orders during the COVID-19 pandemic.

■ Counterclaims

Your counterclaims should support the view that the contested meaning of rights has not contributed to their politicization. They may include the following:

- Many rights are broadly agreed upon and so are uncontested. For example, the right to life appears in all regional codifications of human rights (the Inter-American Human Rights Convention, the African Charter of Human and People's Rights, etc.).

- The politicization of rights has been driven by a variety of other factors, including social and economic inequality, and the influence of interest groups, for example anti-abortion groups in the United States. Growing income inequality globally has led to an increase in identity politics and the prioritization of 'native' rights over those of immigrants.

- The causal chain may work in the other direction, with increased political polarization in many parts of the world, meaning that adherence to one set of rights helps to identify the boundary of the group and acts as a 'gatekeeper'. For example, many Republican politicians in the United States must subscribe to the inviolability of gun rights.

- Different conceptualizations of rights are interdependent and so the assumption that their meanings are contested might be a false one. For example, civil-political rights often depend upon the fulfilment of economic, social and cultural rights, and vice versa.

- The contested meaning of rights does not necessarily result in their politicization. It can be argued that the ongoing debates and diverse interpretations of rights are a natural part of the process of refining and clarifying the understanding of rights. For example, in the case of *Goodwin* v. *United Kingdom* (2002), the European Court of Human Rights ruled that the right to respect for private life, as guaranteed by Article 8 of the Equality and Human Rights Commission, includes protection for transgender individuals. This decision was a landmark moment in recognizing and affirming the rights of transgender people.

■ Some other possibilities

The examiner will be looking for you to demonstrate a clear understanding of rights and that the contested meanings of rights can be used as a political tool by states and non-state actors. Your response should contain references to specific contemporary real-world examples. Arguments in favour of the claim could note that moral rules, including (human) rights, function within dynamic moral communities and so contestation is inevitable. The political contestation of rights serves as a catalyst for change, pushing societies to address gaps and injustices, for example marriage equality and LGBTQ+ rights. You might make the point that politicians and interest groups may exploit the contested nature of rights to advance their own agendas or to divide society for their own benefit. For example, actors including non-governmental organizations (NGOs) and transnational rights activists often interpret rights through their own political biases, which politicizes human rights dialogues, for example Amnesty International and Human Rights Watch see rights through a distinctly liberal Western lens.

On the other hand, you might choose to highlight the fact that rights are, by their nature, political, and so it is likely that they would be politicized regardless of whether their meaning was contested or not. You could also argue that the contested meaning of rights does not necessarily result in their politicization and that ongoing debates are a natural part of the process of refining and clarifying the understanding of rights. For example, Article 19 of the Universal Declaration of Human Rights (UDHR) enshrines the right to freedom of expression. While this right has been subject to various interpretations and debates worldwide, the objective standard set forth by the UDHR has been instrumental in shaping international human rights law and jurisprudence.

Additionally, you might suggest that the politicization of rights is integral to their understanding, monitoring, protection and enforcement. The contested meaning of rights may provide opportunities for deeper exploration and education about the principles underlying these rights. As different interpretations are presented and debated, it may encourage a more nuanced understanding of these rights. For example, debates around affirmative action policies have prompted discussions about the intersectionality of rights and the historical context of systemic discrimination in both the United States and Europe, while the extension of the right of women to drive in Saudi Arabia was influenced by domestic and international pressure exerted by women's advocates. All of these would be considered valid approaches to tackling this question.

■ Conclusion

You should ensure that your answer leads towards a conclusion on the degree to which you agree with the claim that it is the contested meaning of rights that has contributed to their politicization.

Section B-style question

1 'The most significant cause of rights violations in global politics is structural violence.' Discuss this claim.

Your answer should include a definition of human rights as basic claims and entitlements that, many argue, one should be able to exercise simply because they are a human being. These rights are inalienable and essential for living a life of dignity. The examiner will also be expecting you to provide a definition of structural violence as a form of violence through which some social structure or social institutions may harm people by preventing them from meeting their basic needs and/or from allowing them to realize their full potential. You may also choose to define structural violence in terms of inequalities in the share of power to decide the distribution of resources.

■ Claims

Your claims should support the view that the most significant cause of human rights violations in global politics is structural violence. They may include the following:

- Structural violence constrains human agency to the extent that human needs (food, water, shelter, etc.) cannot be attained. It is therefore the most significant cause of human rights violations, both within a state and between states, for example racial inequality in the United States and the distribution of the global poor.

- Structural violence is responsible for a greater number of human rights violations worldwide given the numbers of starving and diseased people as well as the hundreds of millions still living in absolute poverty. For example, poverty forces many families in the global south to rely on their children's labour to contribute to household income, often resulting in the denial of education, hazardous working conditions and low wages.

- Structural violence violates the right to development, which fully integrates civil and political rights as well as social, economic and cultural rights. Therefore, by perpetuating underdevelopment, structural violence is the most significant cause of human rights violations. For example, in sub-Saharan Africa, structural violence in the form of limited education opportunities disproportionately affects marginalized communities, continuing the cycles of poverty and inequality.

- In a related sense, structural violence is the most significant cause of human rights violations due to its impact on poverty and liberty. Amartya Sen, economist and philosopher much respected for his theories concerning approaches to development, has asserted that severe poverty causes massive under-fulfilment of fundamental social and economic as well as civil and political rights.

- Structural violence in the form of unequal access to education and health care, disproportionate rates of incarceration, restricted voting rights, structural economic inequalities and issues surrounding policing are present in both developing and developed states. For example, African Americans and Native Americans experience disproportionately higher rights of arrest and police violence in the United States.

- Structural violence is the most significant cause of human rights violations as it is entirely avoidable – inequalities associated with class, race, ethnicity, religion, etc. are not natural and betray the fact that an unrealized fundamental human right/need is avoidable.

■ Counterclaims

Your counterclaims should support the view that the most significant cause of human rights violations in global politics is not structural violence. They may include the following:

- Direct violence is a more significant cause of human rights violations in global politics than structural violence as it is more immediately devasting. Furthermore, it is more visible and so potentially pushes global and national actors to address its effects, for example the displacement of millions due to the Syrian civil war.

- While structures and institutions may be significant causes of human rights violations, realists would argue that it is agency – the actual choices actors make to protect/violate human rights – that is more significant.

- By legitimizing structural violence, cultural violence is a more significant cause of human rights violations. That is, cultural violence allows structural violence to become more **intransigent** by providing cover for it to the extent that we are even unaware of the latter's existence.

◆ **Intransigent** means someone or something refusing to change behaviour or attitudes.

THEMATIC STUDIES: Rights and justice

- It may be easier to make legislative changes to institutions to correct structural violence (for example, policing reforms) than to address direct violence such as an inextricable civil conflict (for example, the wars in Yemen or Syria).

- What qualifies as a human rights violation may vary. For example, cultural practices throughout the world systematically discriminate against women where they are denied the vote, suffer from domestic abuse and are excluded from employment opportunities. For example, women in Saudi Arabia still face limited legal protections and societal stigmatization when reporting domestic abuse and gender-based violence.

- An even more extreme view argues that the existence of cultural differences precludes even the notion of human rights violations as there is no such thing as universal human rights. For example, the recognition and protection of LGBTQ+ rights varies significantly across the world due to cultural, religious and societal differences.

◼ Some other possibilities

You should remember to refer to specific examples to support your evaluation of the claim in the question. In support of the claim, you could reference data highlighting growing inequality, both within and between states, as well as any examples demonstrating how certain populations, especially the most vulnerable, experience more constraints and limits on their agency when it comes to fulfilling their human rights. For example, the World Food Programme has noted that poverty and hunger often occur together, with hunger being the number one cause of death in the world, killing more than HIV/AIDS, malaria and tuberculosis combined.

You may also decide to mention other forms of structural violence, for example those that feature in economic, political, medical or legal systems. Arguments against the claim might reference any relevant example of more visible and immediate human rights violations, such as the incarceration of Uyghurs in Xinjiang or the ongoing operation of Camp Delta (Guantanamo Bay). You could also argue that it is neither easy nor accurate to distinguish between different forms of violence and so it may not be the case that any single form of violence is the most significant cause of human rights violations. All of these approaches would be considered valid and given credit by the examiner reading your paper.

◼ Conclusion

Your answer should lead clearly to a conclusion on the extent to which you believe that structural violence is the most significant cause of human rights violations in global politics.

3 Development and sustainability

SYLLABUS CONTENT

By the end of this chapter, you should understand:
▶ contested meanings of development and sustainability
▶ interaction of political stakeholders and actors
▶ the nature, practice and study of development and sustainability
▶ current debates about development and sustainability
▶ the way in which the concepts of development, sustainability, inequality and poverty are interconnected and impact each other.

3.1.1 Key concepts of development and sustainability

Development and sustainability are concepts that affect our daily lives. As an individual, you probably have expectations of access to basic needs such as shelter, food and clothing. You may feel that the government and those in power should be doing more to prevent climate change and protect the environment. You may even see the effects of inequality and poverty in the area in which you live.

This particular thematic study covers the issues of development, sustainability, inequality and poverty, and illustrates how these concepts, as well as being **contested**, are closely related to each other. In this chapter we will explore the different ideas and interpretations of development as well as the related concepts of sustainability, inequality and poverty, and the ways in which these concepts relate to each other.

◆ A **contested concept** is a concept that can be understood in a number of different ways. Contested concepts tend to be multifaceted and multidimensional.

3.1.2 Definitions, interpretations of and perspectives on development

The Society for International Development defines **development** as 'a process that creates growth, progress, positive change or the addition of physical, economic, environmental, social and demographic components'. These features are widely accepted as characteristics of development. However, there is no single agreed definition of development. This is because development is a **multidimensional** concept that can be measured and defined in many different ways.

Historically, development has often been viewed in largely economic terms, in part because it is often relatively easier to measure by using indicators such as gross domestic product (GDP). This allows experts to place countries into broad categories, such as 'more economically developed' and 'less economically developed' (we will discuss some of the problems with categorizing countries in this way later in the chapter).

However, this simplistic approach ignores the multifaceted nature of international development. Development is a contested concept that can be explored and defined in more ways than just economic, including the following:

◆ **Development** is a process that creates growth, progress and positive change.

◆ When something is **multidimensional**, it has many dimensions, aspects or features.

◆ **Sustainable** means able to be maintained or develop at a certain level. Sustainability means to meet the needs of the present without compromising the needs for the future.

- human development
- social development
- environmental development
- **sustainable** development.

A state may be considered economically developed but be much less developed in terms of sustainable or environmental development. China, for example, has seen significant economic growth in recent years but this has come at the cost of significant environmental impact in terms of pollution and resource consumption (Yang and Zhao). Therefore, it is important to remember that these categories do not exist in isolation, and there is a large degree of overlap between them, for example between environmental and sustainable development.

It is also worth acknowledging that countries can experience differing levels of development across different regions. For example, GDP per capita varies across Italian regions from €48,100 in the semi-autonomous province of Bolzano in the north of Italy to as low as €17,300 in the southern province of Calabria, as seen in Figure 3.1.

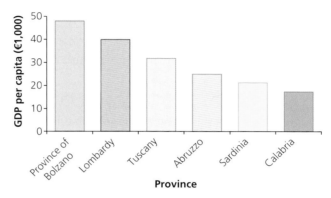

■ **Figure 3.1** GDP per capita in Italian provinces (2019)

 TOK

Consider how the choice of definition might impact the consumers of the arguments. If we include in our definition of GDP sustainable development, then this provides a type of argument highlighting weaknesses, but if the definition focuses more on economics, then the resulting argument could be more charitable. Does this suggest that the definition one chooses is a form of shaping or manipulating the data? What processes and methods are in place in the economics community to mitigate this influence?

At its simplest, we can consider development to be progress towards meeting the basic needs of all members of a society such as food, shelter and clothing. This definition, however, does not reflect the complexity of the concept. For example, what do we consider to be basic needs? Might we, for example, include education as a basic need or perhaps respect for and protection of human rights?

Of particular relevance in recent years has been the emphasis on sustainability as a key component of development. This will be discussed in further detail later in the chapter, but for now we can take sustainable development to mean meeting the developmental needs of a society today without compromising the ability of future generations to meet their development goals. This can take many forms, but the success of Costa Rica in achieving 100 per cent of the energy generation needs through the use of renewable energy is just one example of the ways in which urgent economic and environmental issues can be balanced successfully.

Development can also be considered in terms of independence and self-reliance. In this view, development is a process that countries take responsibility for in order to reduce their dependence and reliance on others. This can range from tackling structural issues within a country, such as corruption and ineffective institutions, to industrial development in order to reduce economic reliance on other states. The extent to which this is possible in a world characterized by complex interdependence remains, as with much in global politics, a source of debate among scholars.

The final factor that complicates our understanding of development is the difficulty in **operationalizing** the concept. This refers to the idea that there is no single unit of measurement of development, in part due to the contested nature of the concept. It means, therefore, that we must use measurable indicators that can be quantified and measured over time that, in turn, tell us something about development. For example, GDP is a common indicator of economic development, while literacy levels and life expectancy are often used as indicators of human development, as can be seen in the Human Development Index (HDI). It is important to note, however, that development indicators do not give the full picture and there are many limitations associated with relying on single indicators when measuring development, as they may fail to take into account the multidimensional nature of the concept.

We can see, therefore, that development is not a simple concept to define due to its multidimensional nature and disagreement as to which indicators most accurately reflect progress towards developmental goals. It is important to bear all of this in mind while exploring this thematic study, as well as the ways in which development relates to the other relevant concepts of sustainability, **poverty** and **inequality**.

● TOK

One way of analysing the idea of 'contested concepts' is to explore which knowledge communities might be involved in the debate. Different communities of knowers might be working from different assumptions and different values and have quite different outcomes in mind. See *Theory of Knowledge for the IB Diploma*, page 45, for a full discussion of knowledge communities and how they can help open interesting TOK discussions. There are strengths and weaknesses to the different communities' approach, as we will explore below.

For example, in what ways might starting from a focus on political development impact the resulting exploration and reasoning of the issues versus an approach focusing on institutional or social or economic development? Are there 'better' or 'worse' approaches and what might go into making a choice between them? How will these choices impact the resulting thinking, conclusions and actions?

■ Four dimensions of development

The subject guide for global politics suggests four possible dimensions to development, although it is important to note that these are not exhaustive and there are other ways in which you can understand development as a concept. These are:

- political development
- social and human development
- institutional development
- economic development.

It is also worth remembering that these four dimensions are, by the very nature of development, interrelated and interdependent.

Political development

Political development can be defined, in broad terms, as the development of the political and social institutions that form the political system of a society.

Democratization

The elements of political development are often considered to involve moving towards greater democracy (**democratization**) and governmental accountability, and increased respect for and protection of human rights.

Democratization is an important element of political development, as can be seen by the fact that the US Agency for International Development (USAID) has set aside $2.8 billion in its 2024 budget to foster democratic governance, counter corruption, and deliver on commitments under the Summit for Democracy and the Presidential Initiative for Democratic Renewal.

The relationship between democracy and development, however, is not clear-cut, and there is debate as to the extent to which democracy is necessary for development. The American lawyer and expert on democracy and foreign policy Thomas Carothers has argued that there are two broad schools of thought:

- Developmentalists argue that authoritarian rule is necessary in order for a poor country to progress towards development. Promoting democracy should be a secondary concern that should come about once development is well underway.

- Pro-democracy voices argue that any country can become democratic, provided that enough of its citizens are in favour, regardless of its level of social or economic development.

It is helpful to consider the different ways in which governments are viewed from these two perspectives, particularly the way in which governments are a problem rather than a solution (according to the pro-democracy perspective). We must then consider the implications this has in terms of donor states directing development to non-state rather than state actors. Bypassing states and channelling development aid through non-state actors such as NGOs can, therefore, be seen as a means of compensating for weak institutions in recipient states (Acht et al.).

Governmental accountability

Greater governmental accountability, in simple terms, refers to the principle that governments and their officials have the responsibility to explain and justify their actions to the people and the electorate. There are a number of different accountability mechanisms, such as free and fair elections and an independent judiciary, along with codes of conduct and mechanisms for citizen input into the decision-making process.

Government accountability is key for political development because, without it, corruption and other practices negatively impacting on development are able to thrive unchallenged. The embezzlement of more than $1 billion from Venezuela's state-owned oil company, Petróleos de Venezuela (PDVSA), from 2014 onwards is an example of how corruption can deny a country access to foreign currency that can otherwise be used to fund investment in health, education and infrastructure.

Governmental accountability also links closely to the idea of democratization as a driver of development. Democratic governments, by their very nature, are more accountable simply due to the fact that they can be voted out by the electorate if their choices and policy decisions do not meet with sufficient approval from the people. As Tusalem points out, 'democratic regimes are known to generate economic progress and development more so than autocracies, thus leading to higher levels of citizen satisfaction with their quality of life'. While this may be good news for democratic governments and global leaders, it is of course possible that the picture is slightly more complicated, as is so often the case in global politics. After all, China is by no means a democratic state yet the rate of development when measured in purely economic terms has been phenomenal in recent years, with GDP per capita ($PPP) rising to $18,200 in 2022 from $1,930 in 1990 (Gapminder).

Respect for and protection of human rights

Increased respect for and protection of human rights can also be viewed as a core element of political development, given the increased prominence that human rights play in contemporary global politics. The UN Office of the High Commissioner for Human Rights (OHCHR) is clear in its claim that development is a human right that belongs to everyone, individually and collectively.

As stated in the UN Declaration on the Right to Development, Article 1(1):

> *every human person and all peoples are entitled to participate in, contribute to, and enjoy economic, social, cultural and political development, in which all human rights and fundamental freedoms can be fully realized.*

Put simply, without states embarking on a pathway to development, all other human rights to which we are entitled cannot be realized effectively.

It is also interesting to note the extent to which overseas development aid is often conditional on recipient governments. This is known as the Aid Conditionality Hypothesis. Douch and Edwards argue that human rights are a clear non-economic component of development that reflects the level of repression and corruption in a country. They go on to claim that, because respect for human rights underpins stronger institutions that reduce repression and corruption, the overall level of development and the effectiveness of overseas development aid is greater in such countries. Therefore, human rights should be used as a tool to both measure development and to assess the effectiveness and impact of aid (Douch et al.).

Discussion point

To what extent, if any, do you believe that development aid should be unconditional? If aid should be conditional, what conditions do you believe should be attached?

Social and human development

Social development can be seen as broadly related to human development and, according to Browne and Millington, can include:

- reduced vulnerability
- inclusion
- well-being
- accountability
- people-centred approaches
- freedom from violence.

Social development is:

> *fundamentally concerned with human rights, formal and informal power relations, inequality and possibilities for building greater equality among individuals and groups within societies.*

> *'Human development' is a process of enlarging people's choices by building human capabilities to lead lives that they value. This involves the capability to lead long and healthy lives, to be educated, to access resources and social protection, and fair employment.*

Evie Browne and Kerry Millington, 'Social development and human development'

Human development, then, is more focused on the individual, while social development can be seen as having much closer links to political and institutional development. As ever, the division between these different types of development is not clear-cut and there is considerable crossover.

For example, human development might include good health and access to knowledge, while the related social development components may include improvements in gender equality and levels of education. Equally, while good health and a high level of education are clearly linked, to an extent, the social and state institutions that provide these services need to be funded and supported at an economic level. As ever in global politics, the picture is messier than we might at first imagine.

Institutional development

What is an institution? Some organizations are not institutions; some institutions are not organizations; while some institutions are organizations and vice versa. So, to take a legal example, while a new law firm is an organization, the law itself is an institution and a court of law would be both an organization and an institution (McGill).

Developing institutions are often priorities for states and non-state actors. We can clearly see this in one of the targets for UN Sustainable Development Goal 16, which seeks to 'develop effective, accountable and transparent institutions at all levels' (UN Department of Economic and Social Affairs).

The Organization for Economic Cooperation and Development (OECD) highlights the important role played by Supreme Audit Institutions (SAIs), which it defines as 'the lead public sector audit organization in a country [whose] principle [sic] task is to examine whether public funds are spent economically, efficiently and effectively in compliance with existing rules and regulations' (Hegarty). The role played by SAIs is vitally important because, by ensuring money is well spent, institutions are more able to contribute to national development and poverty reduction.

However, institutional development presents many challenges, not least of all due to the complex nature of the difficulties faced by institutions. Local and national context will vary hugely from country to country, and causes of inefficiency in public spending, such as corruption, are not always easily rooted out. In Nigeria, for example, according to the UN Office on Drugs and Crime, in the 12 months prior to the 2019 survey, 30.2 per cent of all those who had contact with a public official either paid or were asked to pay a bribe to a public official. Even accounting for the fact this may well be an underestimate, it shows that issues such as corruption can become firmly rooted in a country's culture and the daily lives of its citizens, meaning that, while attempts to tackle this at the institutional level are essential, institutions can never alone be completely successful.

We can also understand institutions to refer to the major bodies – national and transnational – that underpin the development architecture of the global system, such as the **Bretton Woods institutions**.

The role of these institutions is generally to work with states and national-level institutions to strengthen these institutions in order to ensure they function efficiently and effectively to meet the development challenges of different countries. There have been many criticisms made of the Bretton Woods institutions. One of the main criticisms is that the basic principles of these institutions reflect the interests and ideologies of the United States and other Western European states, rather than those of the states they claim to support.

Economic development

We can understand economic development in two main ways.

First, at its most simplistic, we can view economic development as economic growth with the aim of increasing productivity and revenue. Additional components of economic development include the establishment of new industries – often in new and emerging technologies – and economic **diversification** in order to reduce reliance on a single resource.

Second, economic development may also refer to wealth and income distribution within a country. Is wealth shared equally between all inhabitants, or do some groups hold the majority of the wealth while others live in poverty? At some level, these questions are relatively easy to answer as economic development can be more easily quantified than other forms of development (we will discuss this in more detail later in this chapter).

Economic development is influenced by a wide range of factors that include:

● access to resources

● infrastructure

◆ The **Bretton Woods institutions** are the World Bank and the International Monetary Fund, which were set up at the Bretton Woods Conference in 1944 in order to aid global economic recovery and development following the Second World War.

◆ **Diversification** is the process of adding new things, such as resources, products or services, to reduce the risks of an economy, business or organization relying on a single resource.

- debt
- access to capital and credit
- issues surrounding trade, aid and investment
- the role played by vested interests and the **informal economy**.

Economists disagree as to the best ways in which to promote economic development but, in recent years, there has been a growing acceptance of the principles described in the Washington Consensus. These suggest that states should adopt neoliberal market-led reforms in order to reduce poverty and promote growth. However, some economists have criticized this approach. They argue that such policies have inflicted economic pain and hardship in more developing countries without delivering the promised economic growth.

Economic development, however, remains a key concern of policy makers and political leaders worldwide, with significant implications for both state and non-state actors in a world increasingly characterized by globalization and complex interdependence. Evidence of this can be seen in the way in which we attempt to categorize states according to levels of development. The vast majority of economic indexes for measurements (indices) have a significant, if not exclusive, economic component, such as GDP per capita.

Therefore, we can see that development is a much more contested and wide-ranging concept than we might first think. It can be thought of in a number of different ways, including political, social, institutional and economic. The way in which we understand development has implications for the ways in which we attempt to measure the process and solutions that state and non-state actors adopt in order to promote development at different levels.

3.1.3 Definitions, interpretations of and perspectives on sustainability

At its most simple, sustainability is the ability to meet our own present needs without adversely compromising the ability of future generations to do the same.

Sustainability is, therefore, a significant concept when it comes to any inquiry into development, as the two concepts are linked in multiple ways. Indeed, referring to our definition of development in the previous section, we might argue that development neatly encompasses the ability to meet our own present needs.

However, as with most concepts in global politics, sustainability is a contested concept that can be explored and understood in a number of different ways. The subject guide for Global Politics refers to environmental, social and economic sustainability as a starting point and, as with our discussion of development as a concept, the same thing applies here, in that these different forms of sustainability cannot be understood in isolation from each other. Indeed, the relationship between the different forms of sustainability can be viewed as either complementary or contradictory, which raises some interesting questions. Would China, for example, have experienced such sustained economic growth in recent years if there had been an equal emphasis on environmental sustainability? This has been reflected in two main debates:

- the extent to which the three components of sustainability are equally important
- whether environmental sustainability is actually the more fundamental and provides the basis upon which economic and social sustainability can be developed.

THEMATIC STUDIES: Development and sustainability

We can see this reflected in Figure 3.2:

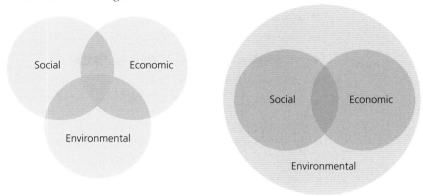

■ **Figure 3.2** Two ways in which the relationship between economic, environmental and social sustainability can be visualized

It is helpful, at this point, to distinguish between sustainability and sustainable development. Sustainability refers mainly to the long-term goal, while sustainable development is understood to mean the process and pathways undertaken in order to achieve this goal.

The importance of sustainability as a component of development can be seen in the UN Sustainable Development Goals, which recognize that:

> *ending poverty and other deprivations must go hand-in-hand with strategies that improve health and education, reduce inequality, and spur economic growth – all while tackling climate change and working to preserve our oceans and forests.*
>
> *United Nations Department of Economic and Social Affairs, 'The 17 goals'*

■ Environmental sustainability

Environmental sustainability is often what first comes to mind whenever we think of sustainability. It can be hard to avoid the images of rainforest deforestation and plastic in the world's oceans from coming immediately to mind. However, as we have discussed, environmental sustainability is just one component of sustainable development, albeit perhaps the most fundamental. Furthermore, in this sense, it is understood as the need to tackle pressing environmental issues that will impact on the ability of future generations to meet their needs by developing sustainable development strategies, such as the use of renewable energy sources rather than fossil fuels.

Clearly, there is a certain degree of tension and incompatibility between economic development and the needs of the environment. Some states have made better progress in balancing these competing demands than others. As is well known, China has undergone phenomenal economic growth in recent years and, as a result, has succeeded in lifting millions out of poverty. However, the environmental costs of doing so at such a pace have not been insignificant. Air pollution contributes to an estimated 1.1 million premature deaths every year in China and an estimated 12 million of the 664 million tonnes of grain produced every year are contaminated by heavy metals, all of which contributes to the significant economic cost, estimated by the Ministry of Ecology and the Environment to be roughly $227 billion in 2010 or equivalent to 3.5 per cent of GDP as a result of unsustainable development (Campbell et al.).

This contrasts with the approach taken by Costa Rica, which has invested significantly in sustainable development and environmental protection with the result that it now generates almost 100 per cent of its energy from renewable sources annually.

There are multiple challenges to environmental sustainability including:

- climate change
- land degradation
- water and air pollution
- decreasing biodiversity
- habitat loss.

It is worth noting that these factors pose challenges for states and non-state actors at different levels. For instance, climate change is clearly a global and transnational political issue that requires states to collaborate in order to tackle it effectively, while other factors such as habitat loss can be more easily tackled at the state and even local levels.

One of the major challenges to tackling issues at the global level can be seen in the ineffectiveness of intergovernmental institutions, such as the United Nations (UN), partly due to the unwillingness or inability of states to act against their own perceived short-term interests. As the UN Environment Programme states, 'collectively, countries are falling short of meeting their new or updated [environmental] pledges with current policies' (United Nations Climate Change).

It can, however, be argued that there is a positive trend towards sustainable development at the local and community levels, with increased awareness of environmental issues and climate change among citizens. This translates into action being taken, albeit at a local and individual level. The challenge of translating this action to the national and global level, however, remains.

Also significant is the fact that the effects of climate change and environmental damage as a result of unsustainable practices disproportionately affect those countries in the global south. Less developed countries, including small island nations who are already facing the very real effects of climate change, such as rising sea levels, raise important issues regarding the responsibility of more developed countries, who are primarily responsible for the vast majority of carbon emissions. As Sengupta argues 'first, the primary responsibility for reducing greenhouse gas (GHG) emissions … rested with the developed world … Second, the emissions of developing countries were still very low and needed to grow to meet their future development [needs] … Third, any formal agreement on climate change needed to provide for technology transfer and funds for developing countries to help them address this challenge' (Ülgen and Sengupta).

■ Social sustainability

While writers such as Magnus Boström suggest it is more difficult to define social sustainability than environmental sustainability, we can use as a starting point the definition provided by the Brundtland Commission, which identifies the key objective of social sustainability as satisfying human needs, including:

- clean water
- nutrition
- a sense of security

- well-being
- justice
- democratic systems of governance
- democratic civil society.

As we can see, some of these needs, such as clean water, are very closely tied in with environmental factors, once again reflecting the interconnected nature of the different components of sustainability.

We can also consider the different elements that make up social sustainability in terms of a hierarchy similar to Maslow's hierarchy of needs (see Figure 3.3). This suggests that states first of all have an obligation to ensure basic needs, such as clean water and adequate nutrition, for its citizens, before factors such as a democratic system of governance and justice.

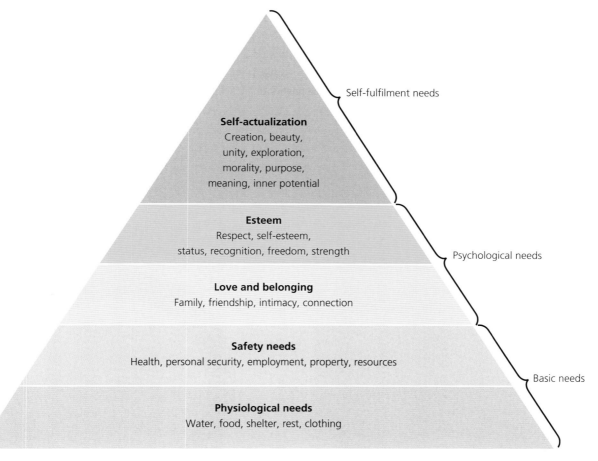

Self-fulfilment needs

Self-actualization
Creation, beauty, unity, exploration, morality, purpose, meaning, inner potential

Esteem
Respect, self-esteem, status, recognition, freedom, strength

Psychological needs

Love and belonging
Family, friendship, intimacy, connection

Safety needs
Health, personal security, employment, property, resources

Basic needs

Physiological needs
Water, food, shelter, rest, clothing

■ **Figure 3.3** Maslow's hierarchy of needs

We can also see that social sustainability has strong links to the ideas associated with institutional and political development, because the creation of strong democratic institutions will promote and aid social sustainability.

Social sustainability for women

Strategies for achieving social sustainability are varied and, as with all strategies for achieving sustainable development, are arguably dependent on the challenges different states face. However, usually they include broadening access to education, particularly for girls, and increasing political participation by women. The impact of doing so can be significant. As research by UNICEF points out, 'Girls who complete a secondary school education earn more, marry later and raise children who are healthier and better nourished. Educated girls are less likely to face discrimination. They are safer and better protected from exploitation and abuse. They invest more in their communities' (UNICEF USA).

This view is reflected in the importance accorded to quality education (SDG 4) and gender equality (SDG 5) in the UN Sustainable Development Goals.

Social justice

Further strategies for sustainable social development include increasing equity between rich and poor, both within and between countries, as a means of promoting social justice. In this context, social justice is defined as the fair distribution of wealth, privilege and opportunities within a society and can therefore be seen as a key component of social sustainability.

■ Economic sustainability

Economic sustainability is the fourth component of sustainability, although there is debate as to its importance relative to environmental and social sustainability. Partly this is because we could, depending on the exact definitions used, see economic sustainability as a component of social sustainability rather than existing as a concept in and of itself, as seen in Figure 3.4.

While it is tempting to adopt the view that economic growth and development will always have a destructive impact on the environment, there are models of economic development that promote a much reduced negative impact. One of these models is the shift towards a 'circular economy', which aims to reduce, reuse, recycle and remake products as much as possible (see Figure 3.5)

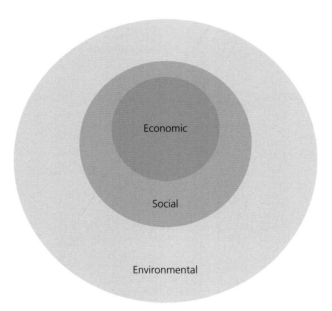

■ **Figure 3.4** Economic sustainability as a component of social sustainability

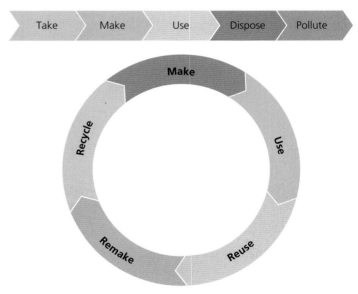

■ **Figure 3.5** Linear versus circular economy models

Economic development as a driver of sustainability

When we think about environmental sustainability, it can be easy to think of economic development only in terms of environmental impact. However, it is important to remember that economic development may be essential in promoting new technology and innovations that can actually improve environmental sustainability. For example, significant investment is often required for large-scale renewable energy generation.

However, most authorities accept that economic growth more often has a negative impact on environmental sustainability, meaning that the challenge for state and non-state actors is to either minimize this impact as much as possible or move to a model in which economic growth is considered secondary to sustainability. This view has significant implications for the relationship between economic development and social sustainability, given the need to tackle challenges such as poverty and global hunger. It is clear that one of the pathways out of poverty is economic development, which is largely the view promoted by the Bretton Woods institutions and other international and intergovernmental organizations. Indeed, the UN's own Sustainable Development Goals (SDGs) identify economic growth as a driver of social progress and well-being (SDG 8) and call for the least developed countries in the world to achieve 7 per cent growth GDP per year.

If, as seems likely, economic development is a driver of social sustainability, then it is significant that many authorities also suggest that environmental sustainability not only can be a neutral factor of economic development but also actively contributes towards it.

Cohen uses the United States as an example and argues that, since the founding of the Environmental Protection Agency (EPA) and the introduction of 'public policies ranging from command-and-control regulations to direct and indirect government subsidies, businesses and governments developed and applied technologies that reduced pollution while allowing continued economic growth'. He goes on to argue that 'clean air and water, healthy food and preserved nature all benefit human health and result in far more economic benefit than economic cost', and gives the example of the rise in property values and the regeneration of New York's West Side following concerted efforts to clean up the Hudson River. Environmental sustainability, therefore, is not an inhibitor of economic development but actively contributes towards it.

Poverty and environmental sustainability

The relationship between poverty and environmental sustainability as an indicator of social development is a two-way process. The Brundtland Commission identified poverty as a cause of environmental problems. However, poverty can also be seen to result from a lack of environmental sustainability (World Commission on Environment and Development).

The non-governmental organization (NGO) Worldvision identifies a number of factors that demonstrate the complicated relationship between poverty and environmental sustainability, as seen in Table 3.1.

■ **Table 3.1** The relationship between poverty and environmental degradation according to Worldvision

Poverty leads to environmental degradation	Environmental degradation leads to poverty
High death rates and lack of security in old age can lead to having more children.	Overcrowded urban areas increase the risk of disease.
Difficulty in meeting community needs often leads to pressure on land, over-exploitation of soil and deforestation.	Shortage of wood for fuel results in higher costs.
Many people living in poverty work the land but lack training in environmental protection, which puts pressure on the land and results in lower crop yields.	Soil erosion and deforestation lead to decreasing crop yields.
Limited access to sanitation leads to poor hygiene practices.	Environmental damage increases the impact of natural disasters such as floods.

World Vision New Zealand, 'Poverty and the environment'

In summary, it is clear, therefore, that sustainability is a contested and multidimensional concept. There remains significant debate as to the relationship between environmental, social and economic sustainability. However, the relationship between these three components is complex and highly interdependent.

3.1.4 Poverty

When we define poverty it is necessary to go beyond simply distinguishing those who are rich from those who are poor. What does it mean to be poor and is this the same as living in poverty? Is the experience of poverty the same regardless of where it occurs in the world? Are there different types of poverty? These are not easy questions to answer.

The World Bank provide us with a useful starting point for a definition of poverty. It states that poverty is a pronounced deprivation in well-being (Haughton and Khandker).

We can also distinguish between **absolute poverty** and **relative poverty**.

◆ **Absolute poverty** is when household income is below a certain level, making it impossible to meet basic needs, such as food, shelter, safe drinking water, education, health care and so on.

◆ **Relative poverty** is when households receive 50 per cent less than the average household income, meaning they have some money, but only enough to cover basic needs.

The World Bank defines extreme poverty as anyone living on less than $2.15 per day, which is an increase from the previous poverty line of $1.90. This reflects the increase in the cost of basic food, clothing and shelter in low-income countries in recent years. Put simply, this means that anyone living on less than this amount per day is considered to be living in extreme, or absolute, poverty. In 2018, according to World Bank data, 719 million people, or over 9 per cent of the world's population, were living in extreme poverty worldwide, although this is likely to be an underestimate (Peer).

However, as with most concepts in global politics, poverty is not necessarily as simple as this. The concept of relative poverty defines poverty in relation to a relative poverty threshold. This approach is used by the European Union, among other organizations, and it considers the poverty line to be 50 per cent or less of the average household income (Heywood). This means that people are considered to be poor if their income is substantially below that of a typical person in their particular country. The concept of relative poverty has implications for governments and policy makers, as reducing relative poverty also requires a corresponding reduction in inequality within a state or society.

These definitions of both absolute and relative poverty tend to focus largely on income and measure poverty in financial terms. However, poverty is a multidimensional concept and can be seen to occur when non-material as well as material needs go unmet. This includes a lack of opportunities and resources.

◼ Poverty as a lack of opportunity

According to the UN, poverty is more than just a lack of income and productive resources to ensure a sustainable livelihood. It includes hunger, malnutrition, lack of access to education and other basic services, and social discrimination, as well as exclusion from decision making.

Poverty is, therefore, a much wider ranging concept than might be first imagined and this is referred to as multidimensional poverty. As Peer points out, a family's income may be above the poverty line but they may still lack access to basic services such as education, electricity or clean water.

The Oxford Poverty and Human Development Initiative (OPHDI) at the University of Oxford supports this multidimensional idea of poverty, and this can be seen in the multidimensional poverty index (MPI). The MPI (see Table 3.2) identifies 10 different indicators across three dimensions and, if three or more are applicable to a household, then that household is considered to be experiencing multidimensional poverty.

Dimension	Indicator	Weighting
Health	Nutrition	1/6
	Child mortality	1/6
Education	Years of schooling	1/6
	School attendance	1/6
Living standards	Cooking fuel	1/18
	Sanitation	1/18
	Drinking water	1/18
	Electricity	1/18
	Housing	1/18
	Assets	1/18

Adapted from the UNDP and Oxford Poverty and Human Development Initiative, 'Global multidimensional poverty index 2023'

The work of Indian economist Amartya Sen has been important in this area. He argues that 'human beings are thoroughly diverse. You cannot draw a poverty line and then apply it across the board to everyone the same way, without taking into account personal characteristics and circumstances' (quoted in Inter-American Development Bank).

For Sen, therefore, poverty means having an income that does not allow the individual to access basic necessities in their particular environment and context, rather than living below an arbitrary poverty line. He gives the example of the disparity of opportunity and different freedoms experienced by men and women to illustrate the multidimensional and interconnected factors impacting on poverty, and points out that a woman with more education tends to have a better-paid job, better control over her fertility, and better health indicators for herself and her children. So, in this example, it is educational opportunity rather than income that causes poverty. This is not to ignore the impact that income often has on educational opportunity, however, which reminds us just how complex and misleading it can be to reduce such a multitude of factors to one simple concept.

Key theorist

Amartya Sen (1933–)

Amartya Sen is an Indian economist and philosopher. He is known for his work on capability theory, in which he argued that development should be understood in terms of the capabilities and freedoms possessed by individuals rather than simply by objective metrics, such as GDP.

Much of his work was influenced by his experience as a nine-year-old when he witnessed at close hand the Bengal famine of 1943. This led him to conclude later that famine arises not because of a lack of food but because of structural inequalities built into the system of food distribution.

■ **Figure 3.6** Amartya Sen

Poverty, human rights and environmental impact

The concept of poverty is not simply related to the thematic study of development, but can also be considered with regard to human rights and environmental impact. As stated by the UN Office of the High Commissioner for Refugees, 'no phenomenon is as comprehensive in its assault on human rights as poverty'.

In addition, poverty can restrict the choices available to individuals, families and communities, leading to negative environmental impact. After all, it is reasonable that a family struggling to put food on the table will be less concerned about the long-term viability of their land compared to their ability to provide for the family in the short term.

The poverty trap

An important concept related to poverty – and a challenge for those concerned with poverty reduction – is that of the poverty trap. Put simply, this is the idea that the mechanisms that cause poverty are self-reinforcing, causing those in poverty to be the ones least able to escape from it.

For example, the resources for escaping poverty, such as a higher level of education, may cost money, which is a resource less likely to be accessible to those in poverty. This means they are more likely to remain in an impoverished position and, consequently, even less likely to accrue (accumulate) the means of escaping the trap, such as education or financial capital.

In summary, poverty reduction can be seen to be a priority of international organizations and governments for a number of different reasons, including the widespread impact of poverty on the ability of families to meet both material and non-material needs. The challenges associated with poverty reduction are significant, given the multidimensional nature of poverty.

The thought experiment then asks what sort of society (with its inequalities) you would want to construct, so that when you join that society you could join any position and feel it was just or fair (even if you'd rather not join in that position). Is the society built in such a way that you'd accept the consequence of joining it as illiterate, or economically poor, or in one political system rather than another? If the society was built to provide fair and just help to those who find themselves disadvantaged, then you might be willing to accept a less advantaged position, knowing that the society would help, or at least that the society, its politics and its economic systems are not unjust. If you would not be happy, however, then you might be admitting that the society is unjust in its allocation of resources. In other words, the inequalities themselves were not just or fair.

The TOK thinking is written into the thought experiment: Rawls accepts the fact that the world has limited resources, and that some will end up with more and others will end up with fewer. He also acknowledges that we cannot help but consider our own desires when we make choices and build knowledge about what is 'best' or 'just' or 'right'. If, however, you can remove that thinking by considering whether you'd be happy to take up any role in that society (poor or rich, or politically weak or powerful, a minority, educated or not) then you might construct a far fairer idea of what is good for society.

Other areas of knowledge also have methods to mitigate the effect of our own particular desires and beliefs. The 'scientific method', peer review, public debate, providing data, freedom of the press and other systems and institutions all help provide a challenge to the ways in which an individual's own subjectivity (their experiences, background and opinions) might shape the knowledge being constructed.

HL extension: Poverty

The idea of the poverty trap provides a possible entry point to HL inquiry into the global political challenge of Poverty. This could be explored through a case study at a number of different scales from the individual family all the way up to the state level.

3.1.5 Inequality

Inequality is the fourth of the concepts underpinning the thematic study of development. it is equally challenging to define as a concept, given its multidimensional nature and the way in which it is thought of differently by different actors.

We can take, as our starting point, a basic definition in which inequality is understood as the state of different individuals and groups not being equal. This, however, raises the immediate question: 'not equal in what, exactly?'. This lies at the heart of debates surrounding inequality and its relationship to both development and sustainability.

Many would argue that inequality refers to economic inequality, and this may be one of the first things that springs to mind – particularly income inequality – when we consider the term. However, we can move beyond simply viewing inequality in economic terms and understand inequality in terms of access to both resources and opportunities.

For example, different levels of access to education for boys and girls in Afghanistan can be seen as a clear example of inequality of opportunity. According to UNICEF, 'the underlying reasons for low girls' enrolment is insecurity and traditional norms and practices related to girls' and women's role in the society'. This influences a number of other factors, such as a lack of female teachers, provision of girls-only schools, and low levels of school attendance by girls, amongst others.

ACTIVITY

Use Gapminder (www.gapminder.org) or World Bank data to identify a country with significant gender disparities in educational access and explore this in more depth as part of a case study.

We can see, therefore, that individuals may experience different forms of inequalities based on different factors such as gender, ethnicity and economic background among others.

■ Economic inequality

The Equality Trust provides a simple definition of economic inequality, stating that economic inequalities are most obviously seen through people's different positions within the economic distribution. It is important not to simply equate economic inequality with income inequality. Rather, it can be seen that there are three main forms of economic inequality: income, pay and wealth.

- Income refers to all money received from employment (wages, salary, etc.) *and* all money from investments (such as interest on savings, dividends on stocks and shares, income from rental properties, etc.), among other sources of income.

- Pay refers to money earned from employment and therefore is different to income. Pay may be in the form of wages, usually paid hourly or daily, or a salary, which is usually calculated annually.

- Wealth refers to the total amount of **assets** of an individual or household, which may include financial assets such as property and land.

This means an individual may earn significantly less than a neighbour or co-worker but, because they own many more assets, they would be more wealthy. Economic inequality, therefore, is a more complicated concept than might appear at first glance.

The causes of economic inequality are not necessarily straightforward and are rooted in the specific circumstances and national contexts of different countries. According to data from the Gapminder Foundation, South Africa has the highest rate of income inequality in the world (as of 2022) with a Gini coefficient score of 0.657 (for an explanation of the Gini coefficient, see page 226). Much of this can be explained in terms of the historical legacy left by **apartheid**, which effectively institutionalized and legitimized inequality through racial segregation. Unequal land distribution under apartheid has persisted to this day and, according to the World Bank, significant inequalities in wealth have contributed to limiting intergenerational economic mobility (World Bank).

Pay inequality as a legacy of apartheid is also a significant issue in South Africa, and this is significant because labour market income – or, put simply, wages and salary – accounts for by far the largest component of household income. Nokulunga Mabuza points out that black South Africans earn around 23 per cent less than white South Africans. However, the causes of inequality go beyond ethnicity, as women, regardless of ethnic background, earn 14 per cent less than men. This suggests that economic inequality in South Africa is multidimensional and impacted by a number of different factors.

The UK has a relatively high level of income inequality compared to most developed countries, yet wealth inequality is still greater. In 2020, the UK Office of National Statistics (ONS) calculated that the richest 10 per cent of households hold 43 per cent of all wealth. The poorest 50 per cent, by contrast, own just 9 per cent. This has implications for efforts to reduce inequality. As the wealthy have seen the value of their assets steadily increase, this has not been matched by wages and salaries, meaning those reliant on income and pay rather than wealth are less able to compete economically and this will, if left unchecked, result in a continuing increase in wealth inequality.

Does it really matter, though, if some are wealthy and others are not? After all, isn't being rich a reward for hard work? And don't the rich drive growth? Some scholars support this viewpoint. For example, Hinds gives the example of Steve Jobs and Thomas Edison: 'who actually created new inventions and enterprises for the sake of putting themselves on the best side of inequality – to make large amounts of money that would increase their income over that of the rest of the population.'

However, there are data to suggest that, when it comes to the economy, inequality inhibits rather than drives growth.

◆ **Assets** are items or resources with economic value owned by a person or business.

◆ **Apartheid** effectively institutionalized and legitimized political and economic inequality through racial segregation in South Africa between 1948 and 1994.

■ **Figure 3.7** Steve Jobs, who founded Apple in 1999 and went on to become a billionaire

THEMATIC STUDIES: Development and sustainability

Analysis by the Organization for Economic Cooperation and Development (OECD) suggests that countries where income inequality is decreasing grow faster than those with rising inequality, and that reducing income inequality in particular would boost economic growth.

Writers such as Stiglitz go further and, focusing on the United States in particular, argue that inequality distorts our society in every conceivable way. He argues that extreme wealth inequality means decisions are taken in the interests of the wealthy in a society, and that governments compete economically to benefit wealthy elites. While this may lead to what we see as economic growth, it does not lead to the provision of economic security, low taxes on ordinary wage earners, good education and a clean environment – things those outside of the wealthy elites care about – because it does not need to.

HL extension: Equality

The concepts of equality and inequality can be seen as two sides of the same coin. Equality can form the entry point for an interesting HL inquiry into the impact of inequality on multiple aspects of the lives of different actors in South Africa society. You may find it useful to explore the differences between inequality of inputs such as educational quality and outputs such as income and life expectancy.

■ Political inequality

Dubrow defines political inequality as the unequal influence over decisions made by political bodies and the unequal outcomes of those decisions. Political inequality is, therefore, closely related to discussions of power, the foundational concept of the global politics course.

Compared to economic inequality, political inequality is a much harder concept to measure. Dubrow offers an interesting analogy and suggests that we can consider state-level politics as a conversation between the government on the one hand and citizens and other actors on the other. Conversation, in this analogy, is broken down into voice and response:

● Voice can be understood as the way in which individuals and groups express what they need and want from their government. Just like in a conversation, voices can be loud or soft, or in a language that the government understands or not. Put simply, some people's voices are heard more clearly by the government than others.

● Response is the way in which the government reacts to the expressed voice.

Political equality and inequality, therefore, can be understood in terms of equality of opportunity. That is to say, do all actors have an equally loud and clear voice?

Equally, we can consider political inequality in terms of outcomes and the extent to which everyone benefits – or at least has the opportunity to benefit – equally from decisions made by the state (Dubrow). It is clear that, around the world, not all individuals and groups have the same political voice, nor do governments make decisions from which everyone has the opportunity to benefit. This is why debates surrounding political inequality matter in global politics.

Unequal influence

We all have some influence over the decisions taken by political bodies on our behalf, although this varies hugely from the limited to the more impactful and formal. Perhaps we might voice dissent or disagreement in a letter to a newspaper, or vote for a political party in a democratic election based on the promises put forward in their manifesto. However, our ability to influence decisions made by political bodies is highly dependent on the local and national context. Arguably, it is easier to have influence over political decision-making in a democracy rather than in an authoritarian state. In addition, our ability to influence political decision-making is dependent on a variety of social factors and economic factors, such as wealth and gender.

Discussion point

In what ways have you exercised influence over political decisions taken by others that impact your life? How effective were you? What factors limited your effectiveness?

Influence in democratic versus authoritarian states

Authoritarian states provide some of the clearest examples of political inequality. In totalitarian North Korea – a state in which influence over government policy is extremely limited to begin with – citizens are classified according to the 'songbun' system. This ranks citizens according to their perceived loyalty to the regime.

Those in the lowest 'hostile' group are denied access to preferred jobs in the military and ruling Korean Workers' Party, and are often forcibly relocated to impoverished and isolated regions of the country.

The country's elite, meanwhile – those with the very highest songbun – are able to live in the capital, Pyongyang, with access to all this entails, including government jobs, imported food and elite schools and universities, according to Human Rights Watch (Robertson).

Songbun status is also partially inherited, in what is similar to a political hereditary caste system. This means that, not only is political inequality structurally embedded in the country's political system, but also individuals are unable to change or improve their status due to perceived anti-government hostility towards their family members.

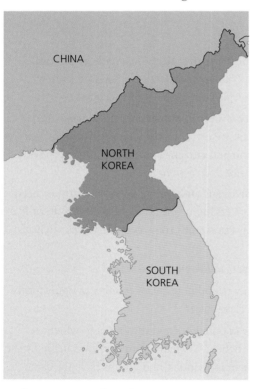

■ **Figure 3.8** Map of North Korea

North Korea is, perhaps, an extreme case, but even in democratic states there is significant inequality with regards to influence over political decision-making. Data presented by the OECD show that there has been a general downward trend in electoral participation in most OECD countries over the last three decades, from around 75 per cent to 65 per cent, although the extent of electoral participation varies largely by country.

There are several reasons to explain different levels of voter turnout, such as whether or not voting is compulsory or the type of electoral system (for example, proportional representation systems tend to attract higher voter engagement). However, the key point is that, in a democracy where low numbers of eligible voters actually vote, their vote is proportionally more impactful than in a system where the views of all citizens are equally weighted. One way of reducing political inequality, therefore, is for governments and states to increase the level of voter turnout, such as through compulsory voting as in Belgium and Australia.

Social and economic factors for political inequality

Political inequality can also be impacted significantly by social and economic factors. For example, data suggest that there is a very strong correlation between income and voting in the United States, where 86 per cent of families with an income of around $150,000 per year voted in the 2016 election compared to only 48 per cent of families in the lowest income bracket (Akee et al.). However, it is important not to assume that having a higher income is the reason people are more likely to vote. It may also be the case that factors that make people more likely to have a high income, such as educational background, make them more likely to vote. It may also be the case that, in countries such as the USA, where people do not get a day off work in order to vote, it is simply not economically feasible for some people to go to the polling booth. As ever, in global politics, the picture is complicated. Nonetheless, the point remains. In simple terms, in the United States people who have a low income are less likely to wield political influence than those with a higher income.

Political inequality can also be seen in the way that certain groups are disengaged and sometimes **disenfranchised** from having influence on the mechanisms of power in a society.

◆ **Disenfranchisement** refers to those who are denied the right to vote. For example, in some US states, those convicted of a felony offence may be disenfranchised.

THEMATIC STUDIES: Development and sustainability

For example, in some countries, those serving prison sentences are unable to vote. The Sentencing Project estimates that, as of 2022, 4.6 million Americans are denied their voting rights as a result of a felony conviction, accounting for over 2 per cent of the US electorate. Clearly this is unequal.

ACTIVITY

Research voting rates by socio-economic class in a country of your choice. What obstacles stop people from voting and how can this be related to the concept of inequality?

It is also worth noting the role played by pressure and lobbying groups in exercising influence on the political decision-making process, which also contributes to political inequality. Quinn et al. point out that in the United Kingdom around £13 million was poured into a growing network of MPs' interest by private firms between 2018 and 2022, including health care bodies, arms companies and tech giants, fuelling concerns over the potential for backdoor influence. Clearly, this level of financial investment is not an option for the average citizen, reinforcing the view that political inequality is an issue.

At an international and global level, political inequality can also be seen as being embedded into the international structure. The veto power according to the five permanent member states of the UN Security Council is an example, as is the fact that the heads of the World Bank and IMF have always been American and European, respectively.

Unequal outcomes

Governments have the ability to make decisions that have a huge impact on the lives of citizens. To what extent do all citizens benefit from these decisions?

◆ According to the World Health Organization, the **healthy life expectancy** is 'the average number of years a person can expect to live in "full health" by taking into account years lived in less than full health due to disease and/ or injury'.

For example, in many countries, there is a huge disparity in government investment in infrastructure and other services by region. In the UK, the government spent £1,212 per capita on transport in London and the South East compared to just £394 per capita in the East Midlands (Clark). Similarly, disparities can be seen in Italy where, in 2022, the **healthy life expectancy** at birth ranges from 65.8 in South Tyrol to a significantly lower 54.4 years in Calabria (Statista).

A particularly startling disparity can be seen in data from the US Federal Bureau of Prisons, which show that almost 39 per cent of prisoners in the federal system are black while the Pew Research Centre points out that around 14 per cent of the country's population are black Americans, suggesting not all are equal before the law.

All of these disparities are, to some extent, the result of political decisions made by policy makers and demonstrate that not only does political inequality of outcome play just as significant a role as inequality of opportunity, but that the two are clearly highly interconnected and involve social and economic factors that may be difficult to separate and quantify.

■ Social inequality

We can define social inequality in terms of members of society having unequal access to society's opportunities, benefits and resources. Social inequality, therefore, is not a standalone dimension of inequality but includes – and is included in – elements of political and economic inequality.

Education

Education is one area in which social inequalities can be seen on a number of different levels. The fact that educational inequalities still persist on a global scale can be seen in the need for the United Nations to include ensuring 'inclusive and equitable quality education and promote lifelong learning opportunities for all' as the fourth Sustainable Development Goal (SDG 4)

(United Nations Department of Economic and Social Affairs, or UNDESA). The COVID-19 pandemic clearly had an adverse impact on progress towards this goal but, even setting this aside, there is still considerable work to be done. According to the UNDESA:

- only one in six countries will meet SDG 4 and achieve universal access to quality education by 2030
- an estimated 84 million children and young people will still be out of school
- an estimated 300 million students will still not have the basic numeracy and literacy skills they need to succeed in life.

Developing countries are adversely impacted by inequalities in education compared to more developed countries, too. This can be seen in indicators such as the percentage of primary aged children enrolled in school, which varies widely between more developed countries, such as Singapore and Sweden, with 100 per cent and 99 per cent enrolment respectively, to South Sudan and Equatorial Guinea, with 35 per cent and 43 per cent respectively (World Bank).

There are a number of factors that impact school enrolment and not all necessarily to do with provision on the part of the state. Often the need for children to work due to poverty or poor health can play a role. As ever, factors are interconnected and complex.

Nonetheless, the point remains that, in general, developing countries experience inequality when it comes to educational opportunities compared to those in developing countries. This does not mean, however, that those in more developed countries do not experience educational inequality – both of opportunity and of outcome. Access to different forms and levels of education, such as private schools or university-level study, is often dependent on an ability to pay, and so is directly impacted by individual or family economic circumstances.

◆ A **lingua franca** is a language that is adopted as a common language by speakers of different languages.

Equally, access to education may be affected by the language spoken by the child, which may disadvantage those students who are not proficient in the language of instruction. According to a report by Al-Jazeera, Nigeria has taken interesting steps to move away from English as a **lingua franca** at the primary level and requires students to be taught in their own local language or first language before this is combined with English as the national language at the secondary level. Given the existence of around 625 local languages in Nigeria, this will provide many challenges but is indicative of some of the unique issues faced by developing countries in reducing educational inequality and therefore promoting development.

Health care

Health inequalities are also a significant form of social inequality, with significant impacts on development. Again, we can see this through the inclusion of health as one of the UN Sustainable Development Goals – in this case, SDG 3, which seeks to ensure healthy lives and promotes well-being for all at all ages. An ambitious goal, perhaps, but, given the stark inequalities in health worldwide, arguably a fundamentally important one.

We will consider the different ways of measuring health as a concept later in the chapter but, regardless of the indicators used, developing countries experience significant inequalities, both in terms of opportunity and outcome.

According to data from the World Bank, the mean life expectancy at birth in high-income countries is 80, compared to only 62 in low-income countries. In some countries, obviously, life expectancy is much lower. In Chad, for example, life expectancy is only 53.

To look at another indicator of health, this time in terms of opportunity rather than outcome, it is interesting to consider the number of doctors per 1,000 people in different countries. Data from the Gapminder Foundation highlight significant inequalities in this indicator, with Italy having

Healthcare provides a
fascinating opportunity
to carry out an HL
inquiry into the global
political challenge
of Health that offers
clear links to equality
as a related global
challenge topic area.
This could take the
form of investigating
health indices and
indicators such as life
expectancy across
different countries
to measure levels of
inequality as a starting
point.

8.01 doctors per 1,000 people while Papua New Guinea and Benin have 0.0661 and 0.0647 doctors per 1,000 people respectively.

While health and education may be the most obvious dimensions of social inequality, we can also identify numerous other ways in which individuals and families experience inequality around the world, from environmental factors such as lack of waste disposal and recycling facilities, to what we might term cultural factors such as religious and linguistic discrimination. As ever in global politics, the world is messy and complicated and the interconnection of different factors all play a role.

3.1.6 Power asymmetries

Asymmetrical power refers to a relationship between two actors in which one, the powerful actor, has control over the outcomes of the other, the subordinate, but not vice versa. Power asymmetry matters in our discussion of inequality because it can be seen as the root cause of much inequality, regardless of whether it is political, economic or social in nature. Indeed, Nicola Phillips argues that inequality arises at the intersections of three dimensions of asymmetry – asymmetries of market power, asymmetries of social power and asymmetries of political power. Put simply, inequality arises when one actor is able to exercise substantially less power in economic, social and political terms. This is represented in Figure 3.9.

ACTIVITY

Use Figure 3.9 as a
template to record
your research on how
different asymmetries
contribute to the
creation of inequality
for different actors in
your country.

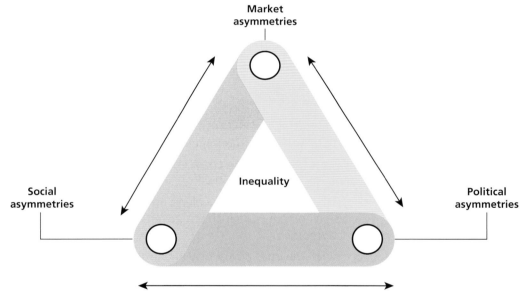

■ **Figure 3.9** Inequality at intersection of three asymmetries (based on Phillips)

Therefore, any discussion of inequality is also a discussion around power. Who has the opportunity to exercise power, what is the outcome, and who benefits?

Actors who benefit from asymmetries of power can be identified at different scales.

On a global scale, it is the more developed countries and what some might refer to as the great powers who are in the dominant position in any power relationship. These countries are able to set the agenda to varying degrees and exert a great deal of power and influence in the global system. Leech and Leech give the example of the disproportionate power exercised over the Bretton Woods institutions by the United States at the expense of other member states as a result of the weighted voting mechanism linked directly to how much money each member contributes.

At a national scale, the role played by powerful multinational corporations (MNCs) can demonstrate huge inequalities of power leading to significant negative outcomes for citizens. Sarah Boseley, writing in the *Guardian* newspaper, identifies at least eight countries in Africa in which large, multinational tobacco companies have 'threatened governments demanding they axe or dilute the kind of protections that have saved millions of lives in the west'. She provides an extract from a memo regarding the Togolese government's plans for plain packaging for cigarettes written by the chief executive of Philip Morris West Africa to the minister of commerce of Togo, to reiterate its concerns following a meeting in 2013: 'As a country whose economy heavily relies on exports, Togo can ill afford to anger its international partners by introducing plain packaging.' To date, cigarettes in Togo only carry text health warnings rather than images, in a country where around 35 per cent of the country is illiterate.

Power asymmetries, therefore, are hugely important to any discussion of inequality, as where social, economic and political asymmetries interact, inequality can be found. This demonstrates the foundational role that the concept of power plays in all aspects of global politics in general, and development and sustainability in particular.

Chapter summary

In this chapter we have covered:
- how the four concepts of development, sustainability, poverty and inequality can be considered to be multidimensional and interrelated
- real-world examples that show how these concepts can be applied to the world around us.

The following chapters will expand upon some of these viewpoints and give you a better understanding of development and sustainability.

REVIEW QUESTIONS

Now that you have read this chapter, reflect on these questions:

- What challenges are posed by the fact that contested concepts are, by their very nature, difficult to define?

- To what extent is it possible to understand one of the four concepts of development, sustainability, poverty and inequality without reference to the other concepts?

- What role does power play in our understanding of the concepts discussed in this chapter?

By the end of this chapter, you should understand:
► the interactions of political stakeholders and actors in relation to development and sustainability, including:
  ▷ state, national and local governments, and agencies
  ▷ civil society
  ▷ international governmental organizations, including international financial institutions
  ▷ vulnerable, marginalized or most affected groups and individuals
  ▷ multinational and transnational companies.

Global politics, fundamentally, is based on interactions between stakeholders and actors related to a political issue. With regard to development and sustainability, the subject guide for IBDP Global Politics suggests five broad categories of actors and stakeholders, as shown in Figure 3.10. It is very important, however, to see these categories simply as a starting point rather than an exhaustive list.

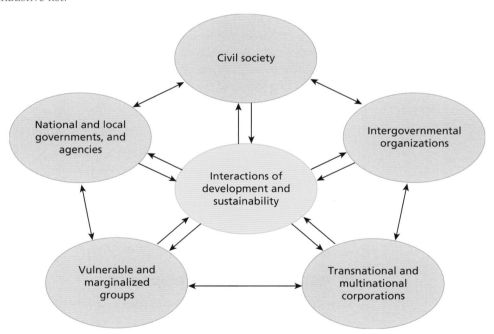

■ **Figure 3.10** Interactions between the five broad categories of actors and stakeholders in development and sustainability

Discussion point

What do we mean by interactions of development and sustainability?

We can define interactions of development and sustainability as:

● the actions taken by political actors

● the goals underpinning them

● the effect this has on other stakeholders, given the fact that they operate in a global system characterized by complex interdependence.

In this chapter you will explore some examples of these interactions and attempt to relate them to the concepts of development, sustainability, poverty and inequality discussed in the previous chapter.

3.2.1 State, national and local governments, and agencies

Development is a concern of national governments at several different levels. While there may be much truth in the realist claim that the primary goal of a state – and therefore the overriding priority of its government – is survival, it can be argued that promoting development is undoubtedly the next most important priority.

There are many different ways in which development can be understood, and different states may accord different weight to different understandings of development. Nonetheless, all states seek to develop, regardless of how they understand the concept, as these quotations from national leaders demonstrate.

US President Joe Biden in 2022:

> *The economic plan we began with in this administration has shown some real results. We've had the strongest job growth on record, the largest decline in unemployment on record, the strongest small business growth in a long time, and the strongest economic growth in 40 years.*

Chinese President Xi Jinping in 2023:

> *High-quality development is the first and foremost task in building a modern socialist country in all respects.*

South African President Cyril Ramaphosa in 2022:

> *we must go back to basics. We must focus on providing quality education, achieving universal health coverage, building the industrial capacity of developing countries through infrastructure development and addressing structural challenges that limit the ability of developing countries to trade.*

■ Approaches to development

Linked with this are fundamental questions as to how these aims can be met while ensuring poverty reduction, considering the need for sustainable practices, and dealing with the many issues surrounding inequality.

States are concerned with development in two main areas:

1 Their own national development

2 Broader issues of international development and poverty reduction.

When discussing the ways in which states promote and work towards national development, it is difficult to make generalizations, given that the priorities of states will vary hugely according to their contexts.

THEMATIC STUDIES: Development and sustainability

China: economic development at a cost?

■ **Figure 3.11** High-rise buildings in Pudong, the central business district of China's economic capital city, Shanghai

In recent years, China has been focused on rapid economic development. According to the World Bank, since China began to open up and reform its economy in 1978, GDP growth has averaged over 9 per cent a year, and more than 800 million people have lifted themselves out of poverty.

There have also been significant improvements in access to health care, education and other services over the same period.

China's exceptional rate of economic growth has been based on significant levels of investment, low-cost manufacturing and a high level of exports, and this has led to what the World Bank has termed the fastest sustained expansion by a major economy in history.

There are several reasons as to why China adopted this economic path:

● The need to lift millions out of poverty: this has a particular urgency in a one-party political system such as China, as the legitimacy of the ruling Chinese Communist Party depends on its ability to provide high living standards for its citizens.

● Simple geopolitical considerations of power: if China seeks to be the regional hegemon in south-east Asia – and all the evidence suggests this is clearly its aim – then significant economic power is required to underpin any increase in military capacity in order to match the United States as a peer rival.

Now, over 40 years since beginning on this path of accelerated economic development, there is evidence that China's economic growth has begun to slow and, according to the US Congressional Research Service, this has been acknowledged by the Chinese government, who have referred to it as the 'new normal' (Morrison). This means that economic development in China moving forward will now need to focus more on private consumption and innovation within China, rather than placing such a huge emphasis on exports.

China's impressive economic growth has also come at the cost of substantial environmental damage in some areas. As the world's largest source of greenhouse gas emissions in recent years, China suffers from notoriously bad air pollution and its carbon-intensive industries have caused additional environmental challenges. This includes water scarcity and soil contamination, according to the Council on Foreign Relations (Maizland).

Furthermore, some have argued that China's economic development has come at significant cost in the areas of political development and human rights. A 2018 report by the NGO China Labor Watch, for example, identifies:

● countless hours of overtime

● contact with dangerous chemicals

● poor wages, barely enough to live on, in Chinese toy factories.

These are just three facets of the abuse of human rights that may take place in the pursuit of economic development.

This does not just show the potential consequences of a focus on economic development to the exclusion of other forms of development, such as political and social. It also provides us with an interesting insight into the interactions between state actors and multinational corporations – that poor working conditions and labour violations are usually a direct result of factories attempting to compete on cost to meet the demands of Western companies for a cheaper product.

Other state and national governments' approaches to development

Other state and national governments have adopted a different understanding of development. They have set priorities and developed policies in ways that reflect this.

For example, Finland, Iceland, Scotland and New Zealand, among others, are all members of the Wellbeing Economy Governments (WEGo) partnership. This is a 'collaboration of national and regional governments interested in sharing expertise and transferrable policy practices to advance their shared ambition of building Wellbeing Economies' (Wellbeing Economy Alliance). Put simply, well-being economies are those which seek to reframe economic policy to deliver quality of life for all citizens in harmony with the environment, rather than focus on economic growth.

Well-being economies seek, through a variety of strategies, to promote development in a way that incorporates social, human, political and environmental development. Strategies used by WEGo partnership countries and others include:

- in Finland, health literacy was incorporated as a compulsory part of the national curriculum from primary through to high school
- in Italy, sustainability and the climate crisis were made compulsory subjects for school children aged between 3 and 19
- in Bhutan, gross national happiness – defined as 'a multidimensional development approach seeking to achieve a harmonious balance between material wellbeing and the spiritual, emotional and cultural needs of society' (Wellbeing Economy Alliance) – is used as a measure of development in place of the purely economic gross domestic product (GDP) measure.

All of these examples highlight that promoting development at the national level involves countries using a range of strategies depending on their own development priorities.

> **ACTIVITY**
>
> Carry out research that identifies the different ways development is understood in a state of your choice and assess the extent to which their development priorities are being achieved.

■ 2 Broader issues of international development and poverty reduction

Discussion point

Before you continue reading, ask yourself this question: If we accept the premise that states act primarily in self-interest, why do they commit such sums to international development aid?

States are also relevant actors when you consider the dimension of international development. Although the numbers are significant, it can be difficult to measure just exactly how much more developed states spend on international development and poverty reduction. This is due to the fact that much spending is often categorized under the catch-all term 'foreign aid', which may include things such as military assistance.

US President Joe Biden requested Congress to approve a 2024 budget of approximately $32 billion for the US Agency for International Development (USAID), while European Union (EU) states claim to be collectively the biggest donor of international aid in the world, providing over €50 billion a year to help overcome poverty and advance global development (European Commission).

It is not simply what we might consider to be the more developed global north that is spending large sums on development aid. According to OECD estimates, China was spending around $2.9 billion on international development by 2020 – perhaps not as much as the United States or EU but not an insignificant amount of money.

Why do states commit such sums to international development aid?

The obvious answer to the discussion point above is that, to a very large extent, it is in their own self-interest to do so. Environmental and sustainability related challenges, such as deforestation and pollution, if not dealt with, have consequences. These are climate change and air pollution, and they cannot be dealt with purely at the national level, requiring states to support one another in tackling them.

Elsewhere, inequality of development, as demonstrated by differences in living standards, can act as a driver of migration; a challenge that many developed states would prefer to resolve at source.

In Mexico, thousands of central American migrants illegally ride freight trains, known collectively as La Bestia (The Beast), to try and reach the US border. According to Amnesty International, while all undocumented migrants are at risk of abuse:

> women and children – particularly unaccompanied children – are especially vulnerable. They face serious risks of trafficking and sexual assault by criminals, other migrants, and corrupt public officials … some human rights organizations and academics estimate that as many as six in 10 women and girl migrants experience sexual violence during the journey.

ACTIVITY

La Bestia is not the only migration route used by undocumented migrants worldwide. Research another migration route and create a case study that explores the motivations and challenges of a migrant along that route.

The factors that drive migrants to take such a risky journey are complex, but relative levels of development in the United States and the origin countries of Central America play a central role, and many migrants are fleeing from what they see as a lack of opportunity and a life of violence and insecurity. Similar migration routes exist across the Mediterranean, where migrants take exceptional risks for what they perceive to be the chance of a better life in Europe.

Less developed countries are also more likely to have higher levels of corruption and weak institutions.

You can now see how it is in the interests of more developed states to tackle issues such as corruption, weak institutions and environmental degradation in developing states, as this also promotes development at home.

ACTIVITY

Use Gapminder (**www.gapminder.org**) to compare corruption with other development indicators, such as environmental degradation. What does this tell us about the impact of corruption on development in different states?

Morality

Morality isn't a concept often discussed in global politics, but it is worth acknowledging that there is almost certainly an element of states seeking to promote development in other states simply because it is seen as the morally 'right' thing to do. Around 31 per cent of donors worldwide give to non-governmental organizations (NGOs) and charities located outside of their country of residence (Nonprofits Source). Clearly, there is a willingness among a significant number of people to support those in need around the world. Democratic governments will be aware that the majority of these people are part of the electorate and so will have an impact on the formulation of governmental foreign and developmental aid policy.

3.2.2 Civil society

Civil society can be defined as 'the associational life operating in the space between the state and market, including individual participation, and the activities of non-governmental, voluntary and community organizations' (CSIDP).

As we have seen, individuals can play a role in promoting development and sustainability and tackling inequality but, by and large, these are collective endeavours. Because civil society can be seen as the place in which individuals and organizations come together to achieve change – and development and sustainability are no exception – it is not surprising that NGOs and civil society organizations (CSOs) have a key role to play. Indeed, as the UN states in an article on 'The UN and civil society', 'The UN recognizes the importance of partnering with civil society, because it advances the Organization's ideals, and helps support its work'.

As we discussed more fully in Chapter 1.1, different NGOs and CSOs have a diverse range of aims and areas in which they work, and operate at many different levels, from the community all the way to being fully international. However, despite the wide range of differences across NGOs and CSOs, there are several commonalities between them that set them apart from either state- or market-based political actors, and that make them uniquely important in the field of development and sustainability:

- They are not beholden to shareholders or commercial concerns in the same way as multinational corporations (MNCs) and transnational corporations (TNCs). This provides them with the space to act outside of purely commercial considerations. Nor are they necessarily bound by considerations of national self-interest in the way that governments and state actors often are.

- They often have access to specific local knowledge and expertise in the countries they operate, in a way that may not always be available to other political actors.

- They are often experts in a particular field, such as humanitarian relief or disaster response.

It is important to note that, while we may think of NGOs and CSOs as independent organizations operating in a separate sphere to state actors, this is not always the case. For example, many governments seek to achieve their developmental objectives through the provision of programme funding for NGOs operating in particular areas.

◼ International Committee of the Red Cross

Established in 1863, the International Committee of the Red Cross (ICRC) is an independent and politically neutral CSO that operates worldwide, helping people affected by conflict and armed violence and promoting the laws that protect victims of war. The ICRC's stated 'exclusively humanitarian mission' is:

> to protect the lives and dignity of victims of armed conflict and other situations of violence and to provide them with assistance.

> The ICRC also endeavours to prevent suffering by promoting and strengthening humanitarian law and universal humanitarian principles.

You can see in this mission statement that there are two clear elements to the work of the ICRC:

1 It is reactive, in that it responds to events and scenarios that hinder development, such as armed conflict.

2 It is preventative, in that it seeks to prevent these situations arising in the first place.

THEMATIC STUDIES: Development and sustainability

As of 2023, the ICRC has over 20,000 staff operating in over 100 countries worldwide. Seven of the countries where the ICRC has key operations are:

● Afghanistan

● Ethiopia

● Sahel

● Sudan

● Syria

● Ukraine

● Yemen.

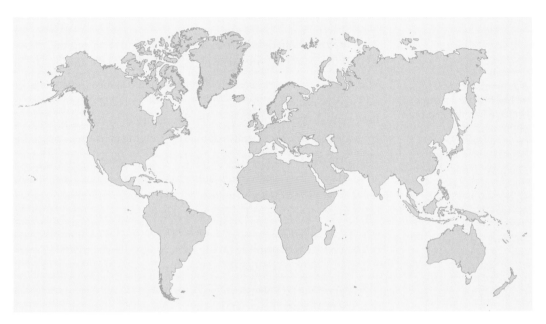

■ **Figure 3.12** Map showing some of the key areas of focus for the ICRC as of 2023

Both the reactive and preventative elements of the ICRC's work can be considered as part of the broader development sphere, but it is also worth distinguishing between developmental and humanitarian projects as they relate to civil society and non-governmental actors. According to People in Need:

● *Humanitarian aid is a rapid intervention designed to save lives, alleviate hardship and get disaster victims back on their feet.*

● *Development aid is an effort to help people in their efforts to lift themselves out of poverty and develop further.*

It is not always easy to distinguish between these two categories in practice, as can be seen in this summary of several key statistics regarding the ICRC's work in Afghanistan in 2022:

● 6,291,645 benefited from medical consultations at the 33 ICRC-supported hospitals.

● 13,981 vulnerable households received multipurpose cash assistance to meet their basic needs.

● 18,732 new patients registered, including 1,456 amputees.

● 362,044 physiotherapy sessions were held.

- 68 visits were made to 22 places of detention holding 12,633 detainees.

- 281 missing persons' fate and whereabouts were clarified.

- 90 human remains of fighters and civilians were retrieved, transferred and returned to their families and communities with the support of the Afghan Red Crescent Society (ARCS) and ICRC-contracted taxi drivers under the Human Remains Transfer Programme.

(It is worth noting that the ICRC is not the same as the Red Cross and Red Crescent Societies. The ICRC is a part of the International Red Cross and Red Crescent Movement, which is comprised of 189 National Red Cross and Red Crescent Societies, as well as the International Federation of Red Cross and Red Crescent Societies.)

■ Médecins Sans Frontières

Médecins Sans Frontières (MSF), also known as Doctors Without Borders, is an NGO based in Paris. It was founded in 1971 by a group of journalists and doctors, and has since grown to over 45,000 staff made up primarily of health professionals, administrative and logistical staff.

The stated aim of MSF is to provide medical assistance to people affected by conflict, epidemics, disasters or exclusion from health care. This can take place over a variety of timescales. For example, MSF has devoted significant efforts to educating individuals and groups in the countries in which it operates about the growing challenges posed by **antibiotic resistance**.

This form of educational outreach that, by its very nature, moves beyond the immediate short term, contrasts with some of the humanitarian response-focused activities carried out by MSF. Examples range from providing immediate medical care in the aftermath of the 2010 earthquake in Haiti to the 2004 Indian Ocean tsunami, and also the response to the 2014 Ebola crisis in West Africa, as covered in Chapter 1.1. In cases such as this, the role of MSF is to support and reinforce local health provision depending on the local context. Given that MSF operates in such a wide variety of different countries worldwide, it often has staff on the ground, ready to respond if needed.

MSF makes it very clear that NGOs, such as itself, and military forces fulfil a different role, and that the distinction between the two is important, especially as both often operate simultaneously in the midst of crises. As Nicolas De Torenté, the executive director of MSF-USA, points out: 'there is a fundamental incompatibility between waging a war (using military or other means, including distribution of relief supplies) and conducting humanitarian action'.

◆ According to MSF, **antibiotic resistance** occurs when the improper use of antibiotics increases antibiotic resistance in bacteria. Examples of improper use include patients buying antibiotics over the counter without a prescription at a pharmacy, doctors prescribing antibiotics when they're not needed, or using the wrong type of antibiotic when they are.

By maintaining its impartiality, MSF is able to do two things in particular:

- First, it is not seen as a party to any conflict and, therefore, is much more likely to be able to access those in need and to support them with the aid needed.

- Second, as a non-conflict actor, MSF is able to call out and highlight abuses of human rights and humanitarian law rather than being seen as a party to such breaches.

It is important to note, however, that not all NGOs working in the development sphere seek to maintain such independence from state actors. Indeed, many NGOs rely heavily on funding from states, while states often fund NGOs in order to pursue their foreign policy objectives. The relationship between state and non-actors is not

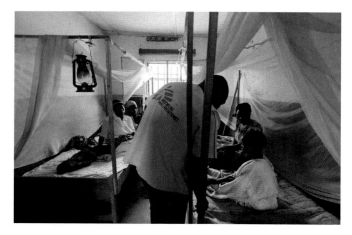

■ **Figure 3.13** Médecins Sans Frontières in operation in a health centre in the Democratic Republic of Congo

THEMATIC STUDIES: Development and sustainability

necessarily straightforward and much depends on the aims and objectives of both, as well as the area and contexts in which they operate. In MSF's case, only around 1 per cent of its funding comes from governments. Indeed, since 2016, it has not accepted funds from the EU, its member states and Norway, in opposition to what MSF views as damaging deterrence policies on migration and the intensification of attempts by these governments to push people away from European shores (Médecins Sans Frontières).

■ International Rescue Committee

The International Rescue Committee (IRC) is a global humanitarian and relief NGO based in New York that operates programmes in more than 40 countries around the world. IRC programmes are both developmental and humanitarian in nature and this can be seen in the following extract from the IRC's website in which the organization identifies ways in which has made an impact in 2022:

- Supported 3,137 health facilities
- Provided 8,013,515 primary health care consultations
- Treated 222,278 children under five for severe acute malnutrition
- Admitted 453,344 children and 106,722 pregnant and lactating women to nutrition programmes
- Built or rehabilitated water supplies serving 3,490,159 people
- Reached 1,421,270 people with cash assistance
- Distributed $109,751,532 in cash or vouchers
- Provided counselling to 43,814 women survivors of gender-based violence
- Supported 122,390 children in IRC safe spaces and other protection programmes
- Enrolled 807,853 children and youth in learning programmes
- Provided 186,491 individuals with livelihood support.

The IRC differs from NGOs like MSF in that a significant proportion of its revenue comes from government funding. According to data from Forbes, approximately $537 million of the IRC's total $1 billion revenue came from governments in 2022 (Forbes Media LLC), which demonstrates the interdependence of state and non-state actors in the development sphere.

Much of the funding is provided by the US government to fund the resettlement programmes run by the IRC in which refugees are supported in building new lives in the United States. Other government funding is provided by government agencies such as the former UK Department for International Development (DfID), which provided the IRC with a grant of £16 million in 2019 for a development project entitled 'Promoting Rights and Supporting Protection Needs in North East Nigeria'.

Receiving funding from state actors can have both advantages and disadvantages for NGOs. Advantages include financial support to achieve the aims of the NGO. A disadvantage might be a decrease in autonomy to comply with conditions imposed by a state donor.

The IRC also provides another interesting example of the interdependence between NGOs and state actors. It was one of 13 international NGOs expelled from Sudan in 2009 in response to the indictment of former president Omar al-Bashir by the International Criminal Court. As non-state actors, NGOs are reliant to a large extent on the goodwill of host governments to allow them to continue operating. Even when they are permitted to operate, they can often face a range of bureaucratic obstacles and harassment that makes it difficult for them to achieve their objectives.

◼ Community Outreach and Patient Empowerment

Not all NGOs operate on such a wide geographic scale as the IRC and MSF. Community Outreach and Patient Empowerment (COPE) is an NGO that works in partnership with the Navajo Nation Community Health Representative Outreach Program to improve the lives of those living with chronic diseases in the Navajo Nation in the United States.

Its stated aim is to:

> *develop programs that address structural barriers to good health, respond to the burden of disease and bridge gaps in the health care system identified by providers, patients and families.*

> Community Outreach and Patient Empowerment, 'Who we are: our work'

This can be seen as almost a rather niche preoccupation compared to the more sweeping concerns of larger NGOs, such as MSF and the IRC.

COPE has a full-time staff of around 15 staff members and they focus on working exclusively with indigenous peoples in the United States. Not only does this demonstrate the different levels and scales at which NGOs operate in tackling issues related to development – in 2019, for example, as part of its food sovereignty programme aiming to make fruits, vegetables and healthy traditional foods accessible and affordable in Native communities, COPE enrolled 274 families in fruit and vegetable prescription programmes and supported 10 community gardens – but it also demonstrates that progress towards meeting development goals can be just as effective at the small-scale community level as it is at the national or international scale.

This comparison between small and large NGOs raises some interesting questions as to which are the more effective and impactful in promoting development and tackling obstacles to the same. There are arguments to be made in favour of both.

Small NGOs are often very efficient. Indeed, given their small size and limited resources, they have no choice but to be efficient if they are to survive and achieve their aims. It could be argued that their small size and relative lack of a complex bureaucracy means that small NGOs are able to respond more quickly and effectively to the needs of those they seek to help.

Smaller NGOs are often more firmly rooted in the communities they seek to serve. COPE, for example, has its headquarters in the town of Gallup, New Mexico, which is part of the ancestral and cultural homeland of the Navajo and Zuni tribes. This can lead to higher levels of trust in small NGOs compared to those which may be seen as outsiders by communities.

However, there are occasions when, perhaps, there are clear advantages to being a larger, well-established international NGO. Brand recognition plays a significant role. NGOs such as MSF and Oxfam are able to leverage this successfully in fundraising, which can exclude smaller NGOs from accessing the same funding. Additionally, as Kate Akhtar of the AIDS Orphan Trust UK points out, 'Not having access to peers easily to bounce ideas around [and] not having budgetary support in the form of finance personnel to support financial aspects of proposal/report writing' are additional ways in which small NGOs often face challenges not encountered by their larger counterparts.

3.2.3 Intergovernmental organizations (including international financial institutions)

An intergovernmental organization (IGO) is defined simply as an international organization made up of national governments. Thus, the United Nations is probably the most obvious example of an IGO in contemporary global politics. Many IGOs have an impact – both positive and negative –

on development, whether through concerted efforts to address development-related issues (for example, the UN Development Programme (UNDP)) or simply through the actions they take (for example, NATO involvement in Afghanistan during the two decades following the September 11 terrorist attack in the United States).

IGOs take many forms and operate at both the international and regional scale. Some IGOs, such as the World Bank, are focused on work related specifically to development and poverty reduction, while others, such as the International Maritime Organization, focus on very specific areas like, in this case, the regulation of shipping. In this section, we will focus on those IGOs that seek to explicitly engage in poverty reduction and development.

■ World Bank

The World Bank, formally known as the International Bank for Reconstruction and Development, is one of five institutions that make up the World Bank Group. For the purposes of simplicity, we will focus on the World Bank itself.

The World Bank is one of the Bretton Woods institutions that came into being in the aftermath of the Second World War. Their goal was to 'formulate the institutional architecture for the post-war international financial and monetary system'.

The stated mission of the World Bank is to reduce poverty and encourage economic growth. The World Bank aims to do this, in simple terms, by:

● lending money to its poorest member states in order to fund development projects

● growing the economies of the poorest member states

● improving the living conditions of the poorest citizens of the member states.

The World Bank itself sees its role within the architecture of global governance as indispensable and claims, perhaps unsurprisingly, that 'without a place like the World Bank from which to borrow money, the world's poorest countries would have few, if any, ways to finance much-needed development projects. The projects are essential to helping people become educated, live healthy lives, get jobs and contribute as active citizens.

However, the World Bank has come in for criticism for a number of reasons, including its organizational structure and its adherence to the **Washington Consensus**.

◆ The **Washington Consensus**, a term coined by John Williamson in 1989, is a set of 10 economic neoliberal policy recommendations for economic reform of developing countries.

The World Bank is set up as a system whereby the voting power of each member state is related to the size of its economy as well as the size of its financial contribution to the Bank in the form of shares. This has resulted in the United States being the largest single shareholder, followed by the United Kingdom, Germany, Japan and France. This allows each of these states to directly appoint one of the Bank's executive directors respectively. The remaining 19 directors are elected by the other member states on a regional basis.

In addition to the significant voting power of the United States, the president of the Bank has traditionally always been a US citizen, who is nominated by the United States. This has led to criticism that the World Bank is more willing to lend to countries friendly to the United States (Clark and Dolan). At the very least, the disproportionate influence in decision-making by a relatively small number of powerful member states gives support to those who would argue that the Bank serves the interests of economically developed countries rather than those it appears to help.

Like all banks, the World Bank's core business is lending money – albeit with a particular aim – and it does so by borrowing the money it lends to developing countries. It can do this because its significant financial reserves mean it is able to borrow money at low interest rates and then lend the money to developing countries at lower interest rates than they would be able to access through a commercial bank.

The Bank's financial reserves come from:

- fees paid by member countries
- contributions made by wealthier member states
- earnings on investments
- the repayment of loans by the countries it lends money to.

As well as lending money, the World Bank also provides other forms of support, such as expertise in particular areas that client states can draw upon.

Naomi Klein has criticized the conditionality that the World Bank attaches to many of the loans it makes and argues that this undermines the Bank's credibility as an institution dedicated to poverty reduction. Writing in the *Guardian* newspaper, she suggests 'the bank's credibility was fatally compromised when it forced school fees on students in Ghana in exchange for a loan; when it demanded that Tanzania privatise its water system; when it made telecom privatisation a condition of aid for Hurricane Mitch; when it demanded labour "flexibility" in Sri Lanka in the aftermath of the Asian tsunami; when it pushed for eliminating food subsidies in post-invasion Iraq'.

■ International Monetary Fund

The International Monetary Fund (IMF) can, in many respects, be seen as the partner institution of the World Bank. Indeed, the two institutions are based in Washington, DC on opposite sides of the same street. The IMF has three stated missions:

1 Furthering international monetary cooperation

2 Encouraging the expansion of trade and economic growth

3 Discouraging policies that would harm prosperity.

It seeks to do so through monitoring economic and financial developments, and advising countries; providing technical assistance and training to help governments to implement sound economic policies; and providing loans and financial aid to other member countries.

It is the provision of loans that has perhaps attracted more criticism than other aspects of the IMF's work and – as with the World Bank – there were often extensive conditionalities attached. In particular, these conditions often required recipient countries to undertake **structural adjustment programmes (SAPs)**.

The use of SAPs by the IMF has been criticized by experts who argue that they reflected Western economic interests and often caused significant harm to the countries they were appearing to help. In particular, what became known as 'shock therapy' market reforms, which reduced government spending, resulted in increased poverty and unemployment.

The IMF has also been criticized for not fully understanding economic and cultural conditions on the ground in the countries to which it provides financial assistance and, as a result, imposes economic conditions on loans that have an unnecessarily adverse effect on the poorest countries. Consequently, the economist Jeffrey Sachs has memorably claimed the IMF's usual prescription is 'budgetary belt tightening to countries who are much too poor to own belts'.

Joseph Stiglitz, the former chief economist to the World Bank, goes further and argues that, 'Modern high-tech warfare is designed to remove physical contact: dropping bombs from 50,000 feet ensures that one does not "feel" what one does. Modern economic management is similar: from one's luxury hotel, one can callously impose policies about which one would think twice if one knew the people whose lives one was destroying.'

◆ **Structural adjustment programmes (SAPs)** are economic policy reforms that states had to adhere to in order to get a loan from the IMF and/ or World Bank.

THEMATIC STUDIES: Development and sustainability

The IMF has also been criticized by those who believe it undermines state sovereignty by requiring governments to adhere to IMF-imposed conditions, leading then Tanzanian president Julius Nyerere to ask, 'who elected the IMF to be the ministry of finance for every country in the world?' (Mwakikagile).

 TOK

Many of the critiques of the IMF covered here show concern for how different cultural understandings might actually hinder the processes aimed at development. Every individual and every institution has a particular cultural history, one that might be significantly different from another. In addition to this, other ideological background beliefs (such as neoliberalism) influence the way in which policy is developed. These insights lead to questions about whether it is possible to genuinely understand one cultural context from the perspective of another, or whether we can step out of our own ideological background beliefs long enough to see the issue from another perspective.

How might your answer to these questions affect what you think about the reliability of knowledge in global politics more generally?

The IMF has also been criticized on similar grounds to criticisms levelled at the World Bank, in that decisions are taken that benefit economically developed member states at the expense of less developed countries. This is partly due to the way voting rights are allocated according to the financial contributions of members, which gives the United States over 16 per cent of the votes. It is also worth noting that, due to tacit agreement between Europe and the United States going back to the foundation of both institutions in 1944, the managing director of the IMF has always been a European, while the position of first deputy director has always been held by a US citizen.

Additionally, both the World Bank and the IMF have been heavily criticized for their adherence to the economic neoliberalism put forward in the Washington Consensus, and critics of both institutions have argued that neoliberal economic policies are designed to benefit Western developed nations above less developed countries. We will discuss neoliberalism as a theory of development in more detail in the following chapter. However, it is worth noting at this point that both the World Bank and the IMF tend to focus on development in largely economic terms while, as we have seen, development can also be considered through other lenses, such as political or human and social development.

■ Inter-American Development Bank

The Inter-American Development Bank (IDB) is an international financial institution made up of 48 member states, although it is somewhat different from the World Bank and the IMF in a number of ways.

First, as the name suggests, it is focused on the Americas. Its aim is to promote development in the region by improving health and education, and advancing infrastructure through the provision of financial and technical support to reduce poverty and inequality.

Second, the membership structure of the IDB is somewhat different from other international financial institutions in the development sphere. It is made up of 48 member states, including several European countries, but only just over half of these countries are eligible to draw on the assistance provided by the Bank. Those countries are mostly located in Latin America and the Caribbean and are known as borrowing members.

Voting rights are based on the number of shares in the Bank held by member states. While the United States has the greatest number of shares, the borrowing members collectively have just over 50 per cent of the total voting rights.

ACTIVITY

Search online at the website of the Inter-American Development Bank to find a breakdown of borrowing and non-borrowing members.

Advantages of membership for non-borrowing members

There are several reasons why states such as Italy and Spain contribute to the IDB, despite not being located in the region.

First, in a global system characterized by complex interdependence, any development in Latin America and the Caribbean will boost opportunities for trade and investment for all IDB member countries.

Second, as the IDB points out, 'membership in the Bank allows non-borrowing countries to substantially leverage their resources and to channel their concerns regarding development issues through the IDB, reaching a larger number of beneficiary countries than would be possible for them through bilateral programs'.

There are also advantages for non-borrowing member states, in that the Bank places restrictions on suppliers for projects it finances and requires that only goods and services from member states are used, and the Bank itself only employs staff from member states.

Advantages of membership for borrowing members

For borrowing member states, the advantages of membership in the Bank are perhaps more obvious. Examples of projects funded by financing from the IDB include:

- support for the expansion of secondary education in Guatemala
- an initial literacy programme for vulnerable communities across the region with no or low online connectivity
- the development of an investment programme in water and sanitation in Ecuador.

All of these projects – in theory, at least – positively impact directly on levels of development, including economic, environmental, human and social development. You will consider issues related to measurement of development in the next chapter but, for now, it is possible to criticize the IDB, given that data from the Bank's own internal evaluation office suggest that only around 53 per cent of projects were considered effective across the four areas in which they are measured by the Bank: relevance, effectiveness, efficiency and sustainability.

The IDB has also been criticized by some for failing to take into account the rights and developmental needs of indigenous people. One example can be seen in a wind farm project funded by the IDB in Oaxaca, Mexico, when the full participation of seven local indigenous communities was not included as part of the project design (Indian Law Resource Center).

3.2.4 Vulnerable and marginalized groups and individuals

As in the wider context of global politics, different groups and actors can have very different experiences of development, poverty and other related concepts. While the world has lifted millions of people out of extreme poverty over the past years, the reality is still the case that, as of 2022, around 8 per cent of the global population still live in extreme poverty (Gapminder) and are therefore disproportionately impacted by poor development of all types. For example, data from the World Bank show that 60 per cent of the global poor are located in sub-Saharan Africa.

It is not simply poverty that is unequally distributed, however. Certain groups are much more susceptible to being impacted by environmental factors related to development. For example, many people living in small island developing states, such as Fiji and the Maldives, are at significant risk from rising sea levels as a result of climate change and global warming, which can be seen as a direct consequence of unsustainable development worldwide.

Different groups are also impacted developmentally by social factors. In Afghanistan, for example, access to education is severely limited for girls and women as a result of restrictions brought in by the Taliban following their return to power in 2021.

Indigenous people can also be seen to be adversely affected by structural inequalities related to development. In the United States, the National Community Reinvestment Coalition points out that, as a population, Native Americans do not have equitable access to affordable, quality housing and are one of the least wealthy groups in the United States. Many also live in rural communities without access to nearby health care and have an average life expectancy that is over five years lower than that of the US population as a whole (Asante).

It is also important to note the interconnectedness of all these factors and to acknowledge the underlying complexity of the picture presented.

◼ Groups affected by extreme poverty

Children

Children are one group that can be seen to be impacted disproportionately by extreme poverty. Data released in 2020 by the World Bank and UNICEF suggest that:

> *Although children make up around a third of the global population, around half of the extreme poor are children. Children are more than twice as likely to be extremely poor as adults (17.5 per cent of children versus 7.9 per cent of adults). The youngest children are the worst off – nearly 20 per cent of all children below the age of five in the developing world live in extremely poor households.*

The impact of extreme poverty on children – an already vulnerable group – can be significant and leave them vulnerable to increased chances of malnutrition, disease and stunted growth, as well as making it more likely that they will miss school, leading to a poorer level of education. This, in turn, can increase the likelihood of being exposed to child labour and violence and, for girls in particular, a higher likelihood of early marriage (Save the Children UK).

This clearly shows the complex relationship between interrelated factors. For example, while poverty contributes to poor educational access and opportunities, a lack of quality education can increase the chance of an impoverished child experiencing poverty as an adult. At its most extreme, the consequences are even more stark and, as UNICEF points out, the poorest children are twice as likely to die in childhood than their wealthier peers.

◆ A **polycrisis** is, according to UNICEF Innocenti, who coined the term, 'multiple, simultaneous shocks with strong interdependencies, intensified in an ever-more integrated world'.

The interconnectivity of threats to children and their impact on opportunities for development has been considered by UNICEF in the light of what it terms a '**polycrisis**'. This is defined as multiple, simultaneous shocks with strong interdependencies, intensified in an ever-more integrated world (UNICEF Innocenti).

Discussion points
Read the UNICEF Innocenti report 'Prospects for Children in the Polycrisis – A 2023 Global Outlook'.

Use the following prompts as the basis for a small group or whole class discussion.

- Do you agree with UNICEF that the world is being affected by a polycrisis?
- What other crises do you think might contribute to a polycrisis?
- For each of the eight trends that make up the polycrisis, UNICEF identify potential responses from actors within the international community. In what ways are these responses already taking place? Who is responsible? How effective are they?

It is also interesting to consider not just the impact of development and poverty on children as a disproportionately impacted group, but also the way in which exploitation of children as a distinct demographic group in some countries has actually contributed to economic development in the short term through the use of child labour.

While children are often forced into child labour as a result of poverty and the need to contribute financially to the family, companies are often only too willing to take advantage of lax regulatory regimes and the relative ease with which child workers can be exploited compared to adults. The International Labour Organization (ILO) points out that:

> Children are easier to manage than adults – although less skilled, they are less aware of their rights, less troublesome, less complaining and more flexible – and ultimately expendable. For some employers they constitute a reserve of casual labour to be hired and fired at will. When their labour is illegal, they and their parents are less likely to complain to the authorities for fear of losing whatever meagre income they bring to their families.

Child labour, therefore, is not only a way in which children are denied their rights, but they are also exploited by unscrupulous employers in order to gain an economic benefit.

■ Groups affected by structural arrangements

The structure of a society also plays an important role in determining which groups benefit the most from development and which groups are disproportionately impacted by inequality and poverty.

In many societies worldwide, women are less likely to access tools and routes out of poverty, such as education and health care, while in other societies there are significant disparities between ethnic groups, which demonstrate the significant role structure plays in development. (For a fuller discussion of structural violence, please refer to the Chapter 4 peace and conflict thematic study on pages 277–278.)

Women

Sustainable Development Goal number five (SDG 5) calls for achieving gender equality and empowering all women and girls. Why does this matter in relation to development? Given that women and girls make up around half the global population, we might expect them to contribute equally to development, as well as being equally impacted by obstacles to development, such as poverty. However, the evidence suggests that women and girls are disproportionately affected by issues such as inequality in the form of unequal access to resources and opportunities.

The scale of the challenges facing women can be seen by the World Economic Forum's (WEF's) Global Gender Gap Report 2023, which suggests that gender parity may not be achieved for a further 131 years at current rates of progress. Much of the reason for this is due to structural inequalities between men and women.

These structural inequalities often arise because of deeply rooted cultural values in different societies that assign different roles to men and women. For example, in many societies it is women who have primary responsibility for domestic labour and giving care. This then impacts on their own individual opportunities for development, such as access to education and the labour market, on a practical level due to the double burden and time constraints experienced by women compared to men. This also highlights the unpaid labour contributing to the development of a national economy that is undertaken by women in the form of unpaid childcare and other domestic tasks that are not rewarded financially in the same way as a job of work outside of the home would be.

Religious belief can also be seen as another cultural norm that underpins structural inequality that discriminates against women. In Saudi Arabia, for example, a strict interpretation of Islam has led to legislation mandating gender segregation in many areas of public life, including at work, limiting opportunities for women to participate in the labour force at the higher rate enjoyed by some other countries. Data from the World Bank show only 28 per cent participation in the labour force by women in 2002 in Saudi Arabia compared to 61 per cent in the Netherlands and 67 per cent in New Zealand.

While it may be tempting to see this as solely down to structural factors related to gender norms, we should be careful not to over-simplify the picture and remember that there are numerous other factors that may play a role. For example, in Mozambique, women's participation in the labour force is 78 per cent, which suggests that poverty may also have a significant role to play.

Discussion point

Access the Global Gender Gap Report 2023 on the World Economic Forum website and consider the relative rankings for Japan, Mozambique, the Netherlands, New Zealand and Saudi Arabia. What questions does this raise about the relationship between gender equality and development?

The UN Development Programme points out that while poverty has a stronger impact on women, the other side of the coin is that empowering women results in greater and faster progress in poverty reduction:

> *Ensuring access of girls and women to primary and higher levels of education, medical care, reproductive health, credit, assets, as well as information on nutrition, on HIV/AIDS, on legal rights and on entitlements are all key elements of a poverty reduction strategy.*

Put simply, focusing development efforts on women and girls will have a greater impact than efforts to promote development that do not take gender as a structural factor into account. We will discuss this in more detail in the following chapter.

ACTIVITY

Using data from the Global Gender Gap Report and other appropriate sources, such as Gapminder, create a series of annotated graphs that show the relationship between development and gender equality. Your annotations should identify:
- what conclusions you have drawn from the data
- the limitations of the data
- links to to both core content and other thematic studies
- other areas for further investigation.

Black Americans

A further example of the role played by structural factors in disproportionately impacting certain groups can be seen by considering the different levels of opportunity and outcomes experienced by black Americans compared to the US population as a whole. Black Americans are more likely to experience less education, less wealth, poorer health and shorter lives than the overall US population.

Hartman et al. provide some stark statistics that highlight just how great these disparities are:

Black women are three to four times more likely to die from pregnancy-related causes than white women.

Black households are two and a half times more likely to experience food insecurity than white households.

On average, black male offenders received federal sentences almost 20 per cent longer than white male offenders for the same crime.

It is clear, therefore, that structural factors have a significant impact on the life chances and outcomes experienced by identifiable groups.

TOK

TOK Internal Assessment Question: 11. Can new knowledge change established values or beliefs?

Facts like those quoted by Hartman above are offered in an attempt to impact people's beliefs about society. However, many people won't accept new facts that conflict with their own understanding of the world. Many of our political beliefs are deeply 'established', meaning they are deeply embedded in our understanding of how the world works. However, part of the method of the 'sciences', and this includes the 'human sciences', of which global politics is one, new data, evidence and perspectives are continually being offered to further confirm or to challenge existing understanding.

In the last half-decade, facts, such as those provided by Reuters, are used to support the view that racism continues to exist in society, and often exists as an 'institutional' feature, that, even though no one individual intends to disadvantage another because of their race, the institutions themselves nevertheless have a built-in bias that leads to the widespread disadvantages outlined above.

Discussion point

What structural disparities do you think exist in your country and how might these differ from other countries?

HL extension: Identity

Gender norms and their impact on inequality and poverty for men versus women provide a possible entry point to HL inquiry into the global political challenge of Identity. You may choose to focus on the way in which this is manifested in a wide variety of aspects in a particular state. Alternatively, it may be interesting to compare a variety of states and explore the extent to which gender norms impact on a specific aspect of life such as access to work or education.

3.2.5 Multinational and transnational companies

Multinational companies (MNCs) and transnational companies (TNCs), as we have seen, are significant actors in contemporary global politics. Their impact on development is significant and can be seen in both positive and negative terms.

The negative impact on economic development

Many MNCs/TNCs can be seen to have a negative impact on economic development due to the way in which they structure their financial affairs in order to avoid paying – or, at the very least, minimize paying – tax in the countries in which they operate. Given that one of the key sources

The relationship
between borders
and the operations
of MNCs provides a
possible entry point
to HL inquiry into
the global political
challenge of Borders.
This could be explored
from a number of
different angles such as
the strategies used by a
particular company to
take advantage of the
benefits of operating
transnationally or the
ways in which states
develop strategies
to assert sovereignty
over such companies
through measures such
as taxation.

of funding for national governments is tax revenue, this has an adverse effect on the amount of money available to fund national development at an economic level.

For example, many MNCs and TNCs make use of what is known as the single unitary principle, which 'allows huge MNCs to dodge their tax obligations by presenting their operations in different countries as completely independent of one another. The principle permits them to shift their profits to countries with low or zero tax rates – and to move their losses into countries where taxes are higher' (Jones). Liu and Otusanya give the example of Zambia as a developing country that is rich in natural resources but receives limited financial benefit from the foreign countries involved in extracting these natural resources, especially copper, due to tax loopholes. As a result, they claim that Zambia misses out on around $3 billion in tax revenues annually, or the equivalent of around 12 per cent of its annual GDP.

This phenomenon of companies moving taxable income to countries with very low – or non-existent – rates of corporate tax is currently embedded in the international tax system and shows the importance of interdependence as a key concept in contemporary global politics. Countries may be responsible for their own system of taxation, but they are also affected by the decisions on taxation made by other countries.

The negative impact on environmental development

MNCs and TNCs have also been accused of having a negative environmental impact in the countries in which they operate. Unsurprisingly, firms tend to have a greater negative impact in countries where environmental protection regulation and legislation is relatively weak.

The Niger Delta region of Nigeria is home to the deep oil and gas reserves that have accounted for more than 70 per cent of foreign revenue earned by Nigeria since the 1970s. It would, perhaps, be obvious to see this as an economic asset and a significant driver of development in the country. However, the environmental impact of oil extraction in the region by foreign companies has been significant and, according to Zahra Rasool, has turned the Niger Delta into one of the most polluted places on Earth. In the period from 2011 to 2022, as Table 3.3 shows, there have been an average of almost 900 spills per year in the region.

■ Table 3.3 Number of spills in the Niger delta 2011–22

Year	Number of spills	Number of major spills
2011	1,058	2
2012	1,135	4
2013	1,647	1
2014	1,517	8
2015	920	4
2016	683	5
2017	599	6
2018	715	0
2019	729	5
2020	440	0
2021	409	2
2022	624	4

Adapted from Nigerian Oil Spill Monitor, 'Oil spill data summary'

This example illustrates the complications that arise from using different definitions of development. Taking a purely economic understanding based around GDP, then the oil industry in the delta region can be seen as a contributor to development. However, taking a broader view of development and including environmental sustainability as well as the impact on local farmers, whose crop yields are massively impacted by oil spills, we can see that the impact on development is much more mixed and that foreign companies appear to be taking advantage of lax regulation and corrupt institutions in order to maximize profit. This is a useful reminder of the power that non-state actors in global politics, such as MNCs and TNCs, are able to exercise in their own interests, in much the same way as discussed in the section on power asymmetries in Chapter 3.1.

The positive impact on development

While it is easy – and perhaps tempting – to focus solely on the negative impact of MNCs and TNCs with regard to development, as ever in global politics the reality is perhaps a little more complex.

Investment by MNCs in developing countries often creates employment opportunities, although sometimes these have been criticized for being low-paid and exploitative of workers in poorer countries. While we have seen that foreign companies will generally do what they can to minimize their tax exposure in host countries, the reality is that almost all MNCs will pay some tax in the host country, which can be used by national governments to fund development. Operations by international companies can also act as a spur for infrastructure development, such as improved transport links like ports and railways.

ACTIVITY

Copy the table below and use it to structure a group brainstorm activity summarizing the positive and negative impact of different types of political actors on development.

Actor	Positive impact	Negative impact
States		
NGOs/CSOs		
IGOs		
MNCs		

Global trade networks

◆ **Global trade networks** are a network of bilateral trading routes and partnerships between states.

MNCs and TNCs are a fundamental part of what are known as **global trade networks**. These are defined simply as a network of bilateral trading routes and partnerships between states. As can be imagined, a world characterized by complex interdependence is reflected in the complexity of global trade networks, as shown in Figure 3.14, which depicts global food trade patterns in 2018.

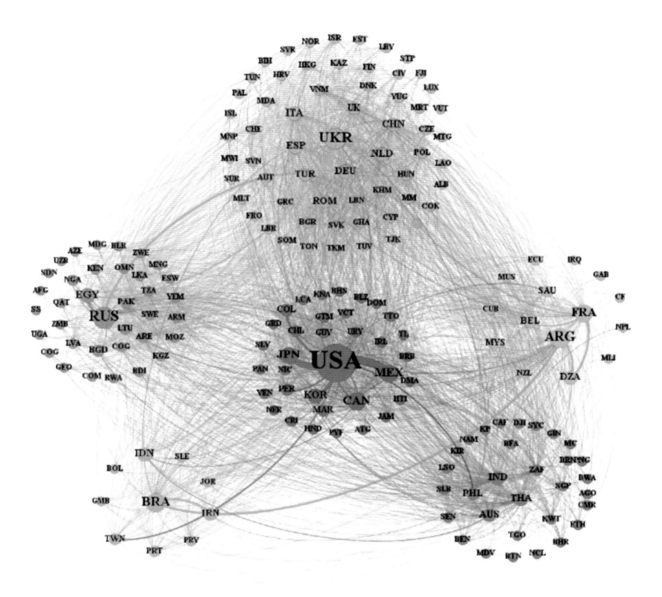

■ **Figure 3.14** Global food trade patterns in 2018 (Jieyong Wand and Chun Dai, 'Evolution of Global Food Trade Patterns and Its Implications for Food Security Based on Complex Network Analysis')

As Dai and Wang point out, 'the increasingly complex food trade network [represented in the image] improves food availability and nutritional diversity; however, the food trade system, led by several large countries, has increased the vulnerability of some countries' food systems and brings about unsafe factors, such as global natural disasters and political instability'. Global trade networks are therefore a useful tool when considering the impact of complex interdependence on development.

We can also acknowledge the importance that states place on developing stronger links with partners within global trade networks as a means of promoting development. One example is China's Belt and Road initiative, which aims to develop infrastructure along the approximate routes of the old silk road and maritime routes between China and the West. While the project, launched by President Xi Jinping in 2013, was originally devised to link east Asia and Europe through physical infrastructure, the Council for Foreign Relations points out that in the decade since, 'the project has expanded to Africa, Oceania and Latin America, significantly broadening China's economic and political influence through a vast collection of development and investment initiatives' (McBride et al.).

In summary, in this chapter we have seen that development and related issues are not simply the concern of state actors, but that non-state actors, such as NGOs, MNCs and IGOs, are also impacted on – and impacted in turn – by development and poverty. Poverty continues to disproportionately impact marginalized and vulnerable groups, and inequality is still an issue of concern around the world.

We have also highlighted the importance of acknowledging the different experiences and contexts of different actors. While state actors, for example, may have similar concerns to other states, they act in their own specific context and make decisions in their own self-interest, reminding us to avoid making broad-brush generalizations.

 Chapter summary

In this chapter we have covered:
- the impact that different political actors – both state and non-state – have on development around the world, including:
  o the state, national and local governments, and agencies
  o civil society
  o international governmental organizations, including international financial institutions
  o vulnerable, marginalized, and other affected groups and individuals
  o multinational and transnational companies
- that this impact can be both positive and negative and takes place at a number of scales, from the very local upwards.

REVIEW QUESTIONS

Now that you have read this chapter, reflect on these questions:

■ What challenges are there with considering different types of actors and their impact on development? For example, do all NGOs have an equally positive impact?

■ Which type of political actor has the most significant impact on development? Why?

THEMATIC STUDIES: Development and sustainability

3.3

Nature, practice and study of development and sustainability

3.3.1 Dimensions and assessment of development and sustainability

 TOK

Many of the following measures of development incorporate different types of data. Some will be economic, some social, some psychological. In the human sciences, the gathering of useful data is a far bigger task than simply looking at the world and measuring what is seen. Decisions about what to observe have to be made ahead of time and the interpretation of what is seen must be made in order to create quantitative data. The Happy Planet Index, for example, attempts to quantify 'experienced well-being'. Do you think that the data being collected in some of these contexts are genuinely observable and measurable? What steps do human scientists take to ensure that their data are reliable?

As you read through these different methods of measurement, consider how, from a 'scientist's' perspective (we are considering the human 'sciences' as an Area of Knowledge after all!), reliable, valid or replicable you think the data are.

■ Gross domestic product

Gross domestic product (GDP) is the total value of all goods and services produced in a country in a given time period (usually over one year) measured in US$ (adjusted for purchasing power parity, which means it takes into account the relative purchasing power of the dollar in different countries).

The main advantage of using GDP as a measure of development is that it is a simple and easy-to-use measure for which the data are widely available. However, GDP can be problematic because it fails to consider the size of the population.

For example, the United States' GDP of $25,462,700 million seems significant and is way higher than, say, Luxembourg, with the much lower figure of $82,274 million. This might lead us to assume that the United States is much more developed than Luxembourg. But if we use the measure of GDP per capita, then we are dividing the total GDP by the size of the population. Essentially, we are imagining that every person in the country has an exactly equal share of GDP.

If we use GDP per capita as a measure, then we see that the United States has a GDP per capita of $76,398 while Luxembourg has almost double the per capita GDP at $142,213. GDP per capita, therefore, is a more useful measure than total GDP, but it has two significant flaws:

- First, GDP only measures economic activity. It takes no account of factors such as human happiness, health and well-being, and makes no mention of the importance of environmental sustainability as a component of development. Essentially, GDP equates development with wealth.

- Second, while GDP per capita attempts to take population size into account, it only tells us how wealth is distributed in an imagined world where every person has an exactly equal share. We know, however, that the world is not like this and wealth is not equally distributed in any society.

TOK

Consider how measuring a per capita GDP might influence how you think about the economic success of a country. What facts are lost when we use a model that suggests each individual has the same amount of money? If this method of measurement masks deep and unjust social, economic and political inequalities, does this mean that the choice of formulation has an ethical dimension?

Gini coefficient

There are several advantages to using the Gini coefficient to tell us about development. The Gini coefficient is one measure we can use to learn more about inequality in a society than we can learn from simply looking at a country's GDP, as it gives us information about how wealth is distributed within a country. It ranges from 0 to 1, where a score of 0 represents perfect equality and a score of 1 represents perfect inequality (see Table 3.4).

■ Table 3.4 Four categories of the Gini coefficient

Tier	Description	HDI
1	Very high human development	0.8–1.0
2	High human development	0.7–0.79
3	Medium human development	0.55–0.7
4	Low human development	<0.55

TOK

What assumptions are built into the idea that 'perfect equality' is equality in which 'wealth is distributed completely equally among all citizens'. Are there other ways we might define 'perfect equality', and what would be the advantages or disadvantages of defining them in that way?

Perfect equality is when wealth is distributed completely equally among all citizens. Perfect inequality happens when all wealth is held by a single individual. As we discussed in Chapter 3.1, South Africa has high levels of inequality and you can see that, in its high Gini coefficient score of 0.657. On the other hand, Norway and Iceland appear to be much more equal societies in comparison, with scores of 0.276 and 0.261 respectively.

However, like GDP, the Gini coefficient is an economic measure and does not tell us anything about social cohesion, environmental impact or whether or not citizens lead happy and fulfilling lives.

Human Development Index

The Human Development Index (HDI), used by the UN Development Programme's Human Development Report Office, tries to go further than single indicators and is an example of a composite index. This means it tries to measure more than just economic growth and instead emphasizes 'that people and their capabilities should be the ultimate criteria for assessing the development of a country' (UNDP).

The HDI measures three different indicators in the broad areas of health, income and education, and places countries in one of four categories as a result (see Figure 3.15).

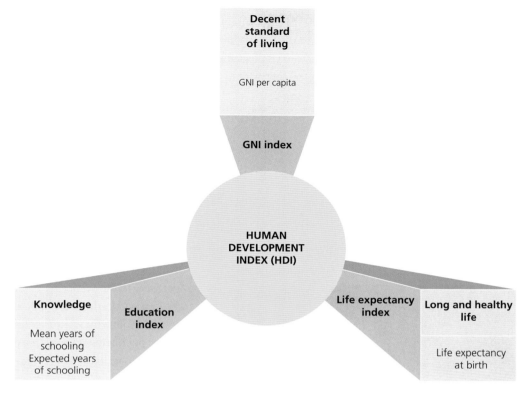

■ **Figure 3.15** The Human Development Index

◆ The **mean** is the average of the numbers, calculated by adding all the numbers and dividing the total by how many numbers there are.

◆ **Gross national income (GNI)** is a measure of all income received by a country from its residents and businesses regardless of whether they are located in the country or abroad.

◆ **Remittances** are funds sent home by individuals, often migrant workers, to support family members in their origin countries.

The HDI, therefore, is based on the principle that development, in practice, is seen in people enjoying long and healthy lives, being knowledgeable and enjoying a decent standard of living.

The index measures the three dimensions through a combination of different indicators:

● A long and healthy life is measured by life expectancy at birth.

● Knowledge is measured by two different indicators: the **mean** years of schooling for adults aged 25 years and over; and by expected years of schooling for children of school-entering age.

● A decent standard of living is measured by **gross national income (GNI)** per capita. This is different to GDP in that it includes all income received by the country from its residents and businesses regardless of whether they are located in the country or abroad. This means that it includes **remittances**, which can often make a substantial economic contribution to developing countries in particular.

■ Happy Planet Index

The Happy Planet Index is another composite index, but its aim is to address what its creators, the New Economics Foundation (a UK-based think tank focused on social, economic and environmental justice) see as the weaknesses of other indices, such as the HDI. These other indices are criticized for not taking sustainability – primarily environmental sustainability – into account, as well as disregarding that the goal for most people is to be happy and healthy rather than rich.

The Happy Planet Index 'measures what matters: sustainable wellbeing for all. It tells you how well nations are doing at achieving long, happy, sustainable lives'. It does so by multiplying the mean life expectancy of residents of a given country by the mean experienced well-being of residents in the same country. This is to calculate what the foundation refers to as 'Happy Life Years'.

The use of experienced well-being as a component of the index is particularly interesting as this is very subjective when compared to more objective data, such as life expectancy. The Happy Planet Index defines experienced well-being as the average of all responses from within the population to a question that asks, if a ladder has steps numbered one to ten from top to bottom, and the top of the ladder represents the best possible life, then which step comes closest to the way you feel about your life? The figure for the Happy Life Years is then divided by the ecological footprint to obtain an overall score for each country (see Figure 3.16).

$$\text{HAPPY PLANET INDEX} = \frac{\text{LIFE EXPECTANCY} \times \text{EXPERIENCED WELL-BEING}}{\text{ECOLOGICAL FOOTPRINT}}$$

■ **Figure 3.16** The Happy Planet Index equation

■ **Figure 3.17** The Happy Planet Index measures well-being and environmental sustainability in a way few other indices do

According to the Wellbeing Economy Alliance (WEAll), who carried out the latest update of the index in 2021, the ecological footprint is the average amount of land needed, per head of population, to sustain a country's typical consumption patterns. As well as the land required to provide renewable resources, such as food, it also includes any land taken up by infrastructure, as well as any land required to absorb carbon dioxide emissions. It is important to note that ecological footprint measures consumption rather than production. We can see this through the example of a television produced in China, but bought and used by someone in France. In this instance, the carbon dioxide associated with manufacturing the television will count towards the ecological footprint of France rather than China. Ecological footprint is expressed using a standardized unit: global hectares.

It is important to note that the Happy Planet Index, despite the name, refers to the 'happiness' of the planet rather than individual measures of happiness. This common misunderstanding has led to criticisms of the index. However, some criticisms of the index are well-founded, such as those related to the very subjective nature of measuring experienced well-being.

On the other hand, the Happy Planet Index has several advantages over more traditional development indices. It includes well-being and environmental sustainability in its measurement in a way few other indices do. The way it is calculated is simple: it focuses more on the end result of economic activity in the shape of life expectancy and satisfaction, rather than viewing economic activity as a means in itself.

■ Social progress indicators

Social progress indicators (SPIs) were developed by the Social Progress Initiative. The 2024 Social Progress Index is made up of 57 different indicators that contribute to measuring development as a multidimensional concept by focusing on **social progress**.

◆ **Social progress** refers to the capacity of a society to: meet the basic human needs of its citizens; establish the building blocks that allow citizens and communities to enhance and sustain the quality of their lives; and create the conditions for all individuals to reach their full potential.

THEMATIC STUDIES: Development and sustainability

The indicators are divided into three broad categories, or dimensions, which are each further divided into four components. Each dimension is built upon an attempt to answer a guiding question, as seen in Table 3.5.

■ **Table 3.5** Social progress indicator (SPI) components

Dimension	Component	Indicators
Basic human needs Does a country provide for its people's most essential needs?	Nutrition and medical care	Undernourishment Depth of food deficit Maternal mortality rate Stillbirth rate Child mortality rate Prevalence of tuberculosis
	Water and sanitation	Basic sanitation service Basic water service Satisfaction with water quality Unsafe water, sanitation and hygiene
	Housing	Access to electricity Dissatisfaction with housing affordability Household air pollution Usage of clean fuels and technology for cooking
	Safety	Feeling safe while walking alone Interpersonal violence Intimate partner violence Money stolen Transportation related injuries
Foundations of well-being Are the building blocks in place for individuals and communities to enhance and sustain well-being?	Basic education	Gender parity in secondary attainment Population with no schooling Primary school enrolment Secondary school attainment
	Information and communications	Access to online governance Internet users Mobile telephone subscriptions World Press Freedom index
	Health	Access to essential health services Equal access to quality healthcare Life expectancy at 60 Mortality 15–50 Satisfaction with availability of quality healthcare
	Environmental quality	Lead exposure Outdoor air pollution Particulate matter pollution Recycling Species protection
Opportunity Is there opportunity for individuals to reach their full potential?	Rights and voice	Equal protection index Equality before the law and individual index Freedom of peaceful assembly Political rights
	Access to higher education	Academic freedom Citable documents Expected years of tertiary schooling Quality weighted universities Women with advanced education

Dimension	Component	Indicators
	Freedom and choice	Early marriage
		Freedom over life choices
		Perception of corruption
		Satisfied demand for corruption
		Vulnerable employment
		Young people not in employment, education or training
	Inclusive society	Acceptance of gay/lesbian people
		Count on help
		Discrimination and violence against minorities
		Equal access index

In order to be included in the model, each indicator must meet two criteria:

1 The measurement procedures used capture what the indicator claims to measure.

2 Each indicator must be measured well, with the same methodology, by the same organization, across all (or essentially all) of the countries in the sample.

One of the key features of the SPI that sets it apart from many other indices is that it measures outcomes – specifically social and environmental – rather than economic factors in order to measure the overall well-being of a society. Furthermore, in common with many other indices, such as the HDI, it attempts to move beyond the merely economic.

However, the index has been criticized by some for using criteria that might be said to be based largely on Western or European values, raising interesting questions about the universality of development and social progress as contested concepts.

■ Human Poverty Index and Global Multidimensional Poverty Index

The Human Poverty Index (HPI), introduced in 1997, was an attempt to enhance the Human Development Index (HDI) by focusing specifically on poverty in terms of deprivation related to three key components of the HDI:

- long and healthy lives
- education
- decent standard of living.

◆ The **OECD countries** are the member states of the Organization for Economic Co-operation and Development, an intergovernmental organization with 38 member countries, founded in 1961 to stimulate economic progress and world trade.

However, as we saw in Chapter 3.1, poverty is a relative concept and what might be considered impoverished in one country may not be the case in another. The HPI attempts to get around this issue by developing two separate indices – one for developing countries (HPI-1) and one for 'more developed' **OECD countries** (HPI-2), in which the indicators used to assess the degree of deprivation for the three different components are slightly different, as seen in Table 3.6.

■ **Table 3.6** The Human Poverty Index (HPI)

	HPI-1 Developing countries	HPI-2 Developed countries
Long and healthy lives	The probability of not surviving to the age of 40	The probability at birth of not surviving to the age of 60
Education	Adult literacy rate	The percentage of adults lacking functional literacy skills
Decent standard of living	The percentage of the population without access to an improved water source and the percentage of malnourished children	The percentage of the population living below the poverty line (below 50 per cent of median household disposable income) and social exclusion, indicated by the long-term unemployment rate

Adapted from UNDP, 'Human Development Index (HDI)' and Oxford Poverty and Human Development Initiative, 'Global Multidimensional Poverty Index'

The HPI was replaced in 2010 by the Multidimensional Poverty Index (MPI). This was partly in response to one of the major criticisms levelled at the HPI, which was that it could not identify specific groups of people because of the way in which it was structured, which meant it *combined average levels of deprivation* for each of the three dimensions. The MPI goes beyond this by assessing poverty at the *individual level*.

The MPI is made up of 10 weighted indicators, and a person's deprivation score is the sum of the weighted deprivations they experience. The global MPI identifies people as multidimensionally poor if their deprivation score is 33.3 per cent or higher (see Table 3.7).

■ **Table 3.7** The Multidimensional Poverty Index (MPI)

Dimension	Indicator	Deprived if living in a household where ...	Weight
Health	Nutrition	any child who is stunted or any child or adult for whom data are available is underweight.	1/6
	Child mortality	any child died in the past five years.	1/6
Education	Years of schooling	no household member has completed six years of schooling.	1/6
	School attendance	any school-aged child is not attending school up to the age at which he or she would complete class 8.	1/6
Living standards	Cooking fuel	the household cooks with dung, wood, charcoal or coal.	1/18
	Sanitation	the household lacks an improved sanitation facility that is not shared.	1/18
	Drinking water	an improved source of drinking water is not available within a 30 minute walk round trip.	1/18
	Electricity	the household lacks access to electricity.	1/18
	Housing	housing materials for at least one of roof, walls and floor are inadequate: the floor is of natural materials and/or the roof and/or walls are of natural or rudimentary materials.	1/18
	Assets	the household does not own more than one of these assets: radio, TV, telephone, computer, animal cart, bicycle, motorcycle or refrigerator, and does not own a car or truck.	1/18

Adapted from Oxford Poverty and Human Development Initiative, 'Global Multidimensional Poverty Index'

The MPI tells you who is poor, but how can this information be used on a national and international scale by governments, IGOs, NGOs and other relevant actors? The MPI value for each country ranges from 0 to 1 and is calculated by multiplying the proportion of the population living in multidimensional poverty by the average deprivation score of those living in multidimensional poverty. Higher scores therefore indicate higher levels of multidimensional poverty.

The importance of the MPI then is that 'by identifying who is poor, the nature of their poverty (their deprivation profile) and how poor they are (their deprivation score), the global MPI complements the international $2.15 a day poverty rate, bringing into view interlinked nonmonetary deprivations' (UNDP and OPHI).

ACTIVITY

Explore the case studies on the 'Global MPI case studies' page of the Oxford Poverty and Human Development Initiative (OPHI) website. For each of the cases provided, reflect on the extent to which you agree they are living in multidimensional poverty and consider what aspects of their lives may not be analysed using this measurement.

Corruption Perceptions Index

As we know, obstacles to development can take many forms and one of these is corruption. However, like many concepts in global politics, corruption can be difficult to measure. There is, after all, no unit of corruption in the same way that we have units for length and weight, for example.

The Corruption Perceptions Index (CPI), published by the NGO Transparency International, is a composite index. It tries to measure the perception of corruption by experts and business leaders based on 13 surveys conducted by various institutions worldwide, including the World Bank, the African Development Bank and the World Economic Forum. To be counted in the CPI, a country must appear in at least three of the 13 sources used by Transparency International, which awards each country both a score and a rank. The score is the 'perceived level of public sector corruption on a scale of 0–100, where 0 means that a country is perceived as highly corrupt and 100 means that a country is perceived as "very clean". A country's rank indicates its position relative to the other countries included in the index' (Transparency International).

Figure 3.18 shows the top 10 and bottom 10 ranked countries in the CPI for 2022.

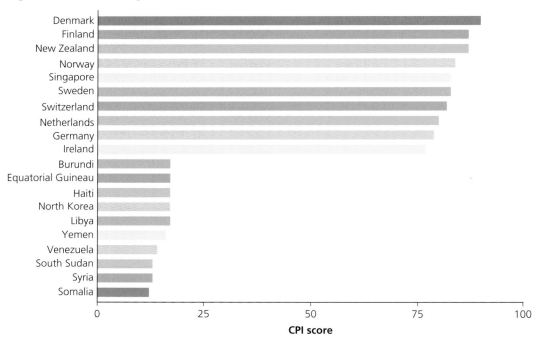

■ **Figure 3.18** Top and bottom ranked countries in the Corruption Perceptions Index (CPI) for 2022

The CPI has been heavily criticized because:

● it measures the perception of corruption rather than corruption itself. This may simply be a result of the fact that corruption is an impossible concept to operationalize. However, it does run the risk of the CPI simply embedding existing prejudices and stereotypes about certain countries and presenting them as fact

● it only addresses public sector corruption and says nothing about the private sector

● corruption is a much too complex and multidimensional issue to be reduced to a single numerical score (Hough).

Environmental Performance Index

The Environmental Performance Index (EPI) and its predecessor, the Environmental Sustainability Index (ESI), were developed by Yale and Columbia universities along with the World Economic Forum.

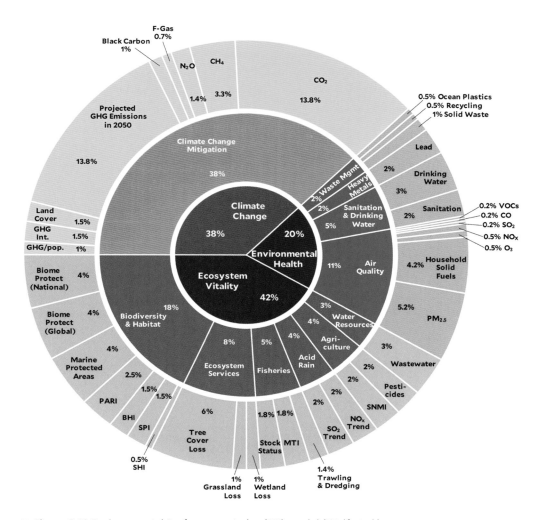

■ Figure 3.19 Environmental Performance Index (EPI) model (Wolf et al.)

The aim of the EPI is to evaluate and assess the environmental sustainability of different countries worldwide. This is distinct from the various indices we have covered so far, in that it focuses specifically on environmental sustainability, which is an issue of increasing concern to contemporary political actors and policy makers worldwide.

The EPI considers 40 performance indicators across 11 issue categories grouped into three policy objectives to rank 180 countries on climate change performance, environmental health and ecosystem vitality. The raw scores are then converted to a percentage, with 100 per cent being the most environmentally sustainable.

The categories and indicators are shown in Figure 3.19, along with the weighting accorded to each component.

The EPI is a significant index for two reasons:

● First, the focus on environmental sustainability reflects the importance of the environment in debates in contemporary global politics and the acceptance that sustainability is central to any understanding of development.

● Second, the wide range of indicators considered by the EPI means that it is a very good example of a composite index that it is not overly reliant on limited data to allocate scores to different countries.

▨ Sustainable Society Index

Similar to the Environmental Performance Index (EPI), the Sustainable Society Index (SSI) attempts to measure the extent to which societies can be considered sustainable. Unlike the EPI, it goes beyond a focus on purely environmental factors.

The SSI takes the Brundtland definition of sustainability, which states that 'sustainable development is development that meets the needs of the present without compromising the ability of future generations to meet their own needs'.

The index, like the social progress indicators, assesses a range of indicators grouped into different dimensions and categories, as shown in Table 3.8.

▪ **Table 3.8** The Sustainable Society Index (SSI)

Dimension	Category	Indicator
Human well-being	Basic needs	Sufficient food
		Sufficient drinking water
		Safe sanitation
	Personal development and health	Education
		Healthy life
		Gender equality
	Well-balanced society	Income distribution
		Population growth
		Good governance
Environmental well-being	Natural resources	Biodiversity
		Renewable water resources
		Consumption
	Climate and energy	Energy use
		Energy savings
		Greenhouse gases
		Renewable energy
Economic well-being	Transition	Organic farming
		Genuine savings
	Economy	GDP
		Employment
		Public debt

The SSI scores each indicator, category and dimension from 0 to 10, with 10 being the most sustainable. However, it does not give an overall index score for each country assessed, which can be seen as a disadvantage of the index.

The SSI is based upon the principle of the triple bottom line. In simple terms, this is the idea that governments and companies must move beyond a simple economic bottom line, which is measured purely in terms of financial profit and loss. Instead, the SSI consists of three bottom lines which must be taken into account:

● people – the social bottom line

● planet – the environmental bottom line

● profit – the economic bottom line.

The SSI, therefore, is another useful index for considering development, specifically in the light of sustainability. However, as with all indices and indicators, it does not tell us the complete picture.

■ Sustainable Governance Indicators

The Sustainable Governance Indicators (SGIs) are a project developed by the Bertelsmann Stiftung in Germany, which examines how effectively governments create and implement effective policies to promote sustainable development as well as advocating for more sustainable governance. It does so through focusing on three main pillars:

- policy performance
- democracy
- governance.

The starting point of the SGI project is the idea that sustainable development and good governance are inseparable. Sustainable development will be impossible to achieve without good governance. The SGI sample is made up of 41 different countries (see Figure 3.20) across the EU and the OECD, which means that, while it is very useful for assessing trends in sustainable development in these countries, it is perhaps not as useful as more wide-ranging measurements with greater international scope.

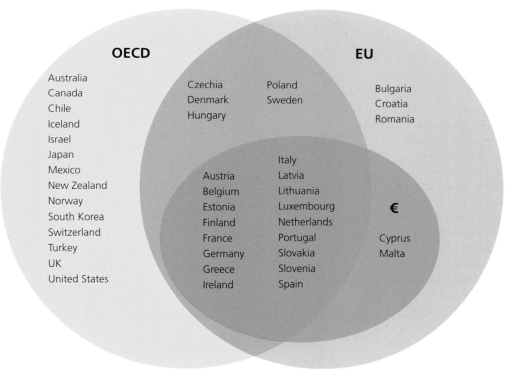

■ **Figure 3.20** Countries covered by the Sustainable Governance Indicators (SGIs) project

The SGI uses a combination of two methods to rate each country. These methods are:

1 Qualitative assessments by country experts that provide a 'thick' description that captures the nuance of the situation. These are, by their very nature, subjective to a certain degree although the methodology used by the SGIs ensures they go through a rigorous peer review.

2 Quantitative data that are gathered from official sources that conform to internationally recognized standards. These, by their nature, are much more objective than the qualitative assessments used. Examples of quantitative indicators include GDP per capita, infant mortality rate and the homicide rate.

The SGI 2022 contains three pillars divided into different categories, each of which are made up of various criteria (see Table 3.9). Each criterion is then measured by a variety of indicators. There are 71 qualitative indicators and 86 quantitative indicators overall.

■ **Table 3.9** Components of the Sustainable Governance Indicators (SGIs)

Pillar	Category	Criteria
Policy performance	Economic policies	Economy
		Labour markets
		Taxes
		Budgets
		Research, innovation and infrastructure
		Global financial system
	Social policies	Education
		Social inclusion
		Health
		Families
		Pensions
		Integration
		Safe living
		Global inequalities
	Environmental policies	Environment
		Global environmental protection
Democracy	Quality of democracy	Electoral processes
		Access to information
		Civil rights and political liberties
		Rule of law
Governance	Executive capacity	Strategic capacity
		Interministerial coordination
		Evidence-based instruments
		Societal consultation
		Policy communication
		Implementation
		Adaptability
		Organizational reform
	Executive accountability	Citizens' participatory competence
		Legislative actors' resources
		Media
		Parties and interest associations
		Independent supervisory bodies

The SGI is a much more complex exploration of the factors impacting sustainable development than many of the indices we have considered in this chapter. This means, perhaps, that we can take seriously its key finding that the main driver for sustainability development is good governance.

However, as with all the methods of measurement, the SGI has its limitations. It can be criticized on the basis that almost half of the indicators it relies on are subjective judgements, albeit made by experts.

In summary, as we have seen, there are numerous ways in which we can attempt to measure and assess different dimensions of development and related concepts, such as inequality and sustainability. These range from economic indicators, such as GDP, to more holistic, composite indicators, such as the HDI and sustainable governance indicators. Each has its own strengths and weaknesses and it is important to understand them in relation to each other.

Discussion point

What are the merits and limitations of each of the indicators discussed above? How might these limitations be overcome or mitigated?

ACTIVITY

Use Gapminder (**www.gapminder.org**) or World Bank open data (**https://data.worldbank.org/**) to create a top and bottom 10 ranking for each of the development indices discussed in this chapter.

What do the different rankings tell you about development and about the strengths and limitations of the different indices?

3.3.2 Pathways towards development and sustainability

While we have seen how most actors regard development as a less important goal, people also don't agree over what development looks like and the best way to achieve it. The debates often take the form of theories of development, which attempt to explain why countries develop in a particular way, or set out the conditions that countries must meet to develop. We will look at three of these theories in this section:

1 Modernization theory

2 Dependency theory (neo-Marxism)

3 Neoliberalism.

◆ The **global north** is a group of countries that have a high level of economic and industrial development, and are typically located to the north of less industrialized nations.

◆ The **global south** is a group of countries that have a low level of economic and industrial development, and are typically located to the south of more industrialized nations.

The questions these theories set out to tackle can be seen to relate to the division of the world into the **global north** and **global south**, as seen in Figure 3.21. These are obviously broad oversimplifications that fail to take into account the complexity of real world conditions but, nonetheless, you can if you choose, divide the world up into two halves – the rich or developed global north and the poor or underdeveloped global south. This then begs the question – why is there an economic gap between the global north and the global south and why, according to some measures, is this gap getting wider? Put in more simple terms, why are some countries richer than others?

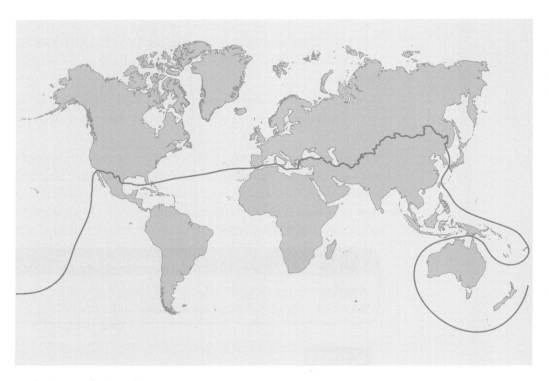

■ **Figure 3.21** The Brandt Line

▉ 1 Modernization theory

Modernization theory is a linear theory of development that has a certain elegant simplicity to it that can be appealing. However, to fully understand why modernization theory might be considered so appealing, we need to go back a little and contemplate the role played by colonialism in the development of different countries.

Colonialism can be seen to have contributed to the creation of the economic gap between the global north and the global south for several reasons. Colonial powers extracted minerals and raw materials from colonies, but the profits from this extraction benefited the colonial power. Any economic expertise developed was largely limited to the colonists and not shared with the people who were colonized. As such, their economies developed in a narrow way, which benefited the needs of the colonists rather than the people who were colonized. In parts of East Africa such as Kenya, for example, coffee and other luxury crops were planted to fulfil a demand by the colonizing power's population.

◆ **Agrarian** refers to land or farming. An agrarian economy is one dependent on maintaining farmland and producing crops.

The process of industrialization in the global north, therefore, was based on the extraction of raw materials from the exploited global south, which led, in turn, to the growth of infrastructure and financial capital in the global north. Both are necessary for continued economic development. The global south, meanwhile, remains in a position where it is largely **agrarian**, with economic and political structures that promote the interests of the global north. Put very simply, the global south lagged developmentally behind the global north.

If this is true, then it seems evident that the end of colonialism would, in effect, free the global south from that which held it back and it would catch up economically with the global north.

Modernization theory, developed by Walt Rostow, attempts to explain why this would be the case.

Modernization theory suggests that all societies move through the same five stages as they develop (see Figure 3.22). However, they may not move through these stages at the same rate. Therefore, at any given point, some societies may be seen as less developed than others.

THEMATIC STUDIES: Development and sustainability

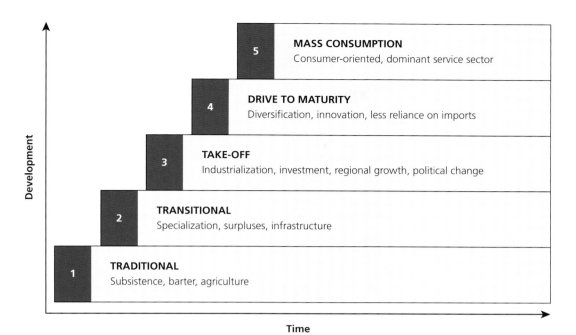

■ **Figure 3.22** The five stages of Rostow's modernization theory

Modernization theory's claim that all countries go through the same stages in the same order, then, suggests that the more industrialized – or economically developed – global north becomes the model that the global south should follow in order to develop. By adopting systems of free enterprise built upon individual initiative, rather than excessive state control, and developing democratic political systems, the global south would begin to replicate the global north. Urbanization would promote economic development through industrialization, as it did in the global north, and these processes would be accelerated by economic interactions between rich and poor countries in the form of aid, trade and investment.

> ## Discussion point
>
> Modernization theory has been criticized from both a neo-Marxist and neo-liberal perspective, and these are discussed in more detail below. However, the simple fact is that the global south did not catch up with the global north as predicted. Do you think this is the most obvious flaw in Rostov's reasoning? And if so, why?

■ 2 Dependency theory (neo-Marxism)

Dependency theory is one of the theories that attempts to explain why there are different levels of development. It offers a pathway to development for less developed countries in a way that modernization theory fails to do.

According to dependency theorists (also known as **neo-Marxists**), the basic exploitative structures of colonialism continued to exist even after the end of colonialism. This means that the neo-imperial relationship between the former colonial powers and former colonies continues to disadvantage countries in the global south. Therefore, dependency theorists claim that the pathway to development lies in changing the international structure of the global economy.

Power is arguably the key concept in global politics, and it plays an important role here. Dependency theorists argue that after developing states, gained independence they were subjected to international power structures. This meant they had to compete in an international structure

◆ **Neo-marxists** are theorists who attempt to build on the work and theories of Karl Marx (1818–1883) to inform their analysis of contemporary global politics. In development studies, neo-Marxists see economic exploitation as central to any understanding of development.

that was dominated by relatively rich and developed states, such as France, the UK and the United States. Domination of the international system was multidimensional, including military, economic and political dimensions.

The main criticism that dependency theory makes of modernization theory is that adopting similar strategies for development as used by countries in the global north is not a realistic option for developing states in the global south. This is because rich countries became rich, in simple terms, by transferring wealth from the global south to the global north. Put another way, rich countries became rich by making poor countries poor(er).

The international system is dominated by rich and powerful countries. This means that the global south cannot escape poverty originating in colonialism because the way that international trade, investment and aid – the three things that modernization theorists claim will accelerate development in less developed countries – are structured actually works *against* the interests of countries in the global south. These exploitative economic structures are also supported by military and political power.

◆ **Commodity concentration** is when poorer countries rely heavily on the export of one or two raw materials or commodities, meaning they are susceptible to changes in the price of this commodity.

◆ **Protectionism** refers to government policies that restrict international trade to help domestic industries. This can be achieved through, for example, tariffs, quotas (placing a limit on the quantity of imports) and embargoes (a total ban on a product if it is deemed dangerous).

It is worth considering just why international trade does not enhance development of countries in the global south according to dependency theorists. Much of this is to do with **commodity concentration**. This is when poorer countries rely heavily on the export of one or two raw materials or commodities. Examples include copper exports from Zambia and mined diamonds from Botswana. This reliance means countries with high commodity concentration are especially susceptible to changes in the price of this commodity.

Poorer countries rely on international trade for a high proportion of their GDP. Many countries in the global south remain economically dependent on one major trading partner who is often the former colonial power, too. Taken together, this means that countries in the global south will remain in an economically subordinate position.

Dependency theorists also argue that richer countries in the global north exploit **protectionism** to their advantage and will not abide by free-trade principles when it is in their own interest to ignore them. For example, the north pushes for free trade on manufactured goods (which it exports) while still pushing to impose tariffs on raw materials, in which the global south enjoys a comparative advantage.

Overseas development aid

We would expect overseas development aid (ODA) to go some way to fixing the initial exploitative transfer of wealth. However, dependency theorists point out that it is yet another form of neo-colonialism that benefits the global north rather than the global south. There are several reasons why this is the case:

● ODA from more developed countries often supports the elites in the less developed countries. The interests of the elites in the global south are often more aligned to the interests of the elites in the global north rather than to their own citizens.

● Aid can often be used to suppress those who would like to achieve increased national autonomy.

● Aid builds up debt that the global south has difficulty repaying. In certain cases, aid may have even been used to suppress populations – as in the case of apartheid in South Africa – meaning citizens are not paying off debts incurred to fund their own oppression.

● Aid is often tied and conditional, which means it can only be spent on goods and services produced by the donor country.

THEMATIC STUDIES: Development and sustainability

The pathway to development for the neo-Marxist dependency theorists, therefore, relies on rebuilding the international structure to remove these exploitative power imbalances between rich and poor states.

◼ 3 Neoliberalism

Neoliberals criticize the dependency theory put forward by neo-Marxists. They argue that as long as the international system is based on economically liberal ideas, it will benefit all countries, both rich and poor.

According to neoliberals the key to economic growth for all countries is international trade based on:

● the principle of **comparative advantage**

● investment by multinational corporations

● the promotion of economic interdependence.

They argue that this will lead to all countries being able to acquire markets, technology and capital. The key difference between neoliberalism and dependency theory is where they see the need for changes to occur:

● Neo-Marxists believe that it is the structure of the global economic system that creates obstacles to development. This is not to say they disregard internal factors, such as the role of the elites, but they see external, structural factors as more important.

● Neoliberals, on the other hand, claim that the changes required for poorer countries to develop are largely internal, such as political and economic changes within countries, in order to remove obstacles to free-market trade.

Neoliberals support reductions in government spending and what are collectively known as **economic liberalization policies**. These policies promote free trade, deregulation and the elimination of subsidies.

The one thing that all three pathways to development have in common is that they all see development in largely economic terms. Development cannot occur without economic growth, which is largely focused on states and institutions.

◆ **Comparative advantage** is an economy's ability to produce a particular good or service at a lower cost than its trading partners.

◆ **Economic liberalization policies** are policies, such as deregulation, privatization and free trade, that major international financial institutions, such as the World Bank and the IMF, insist upon in return for financial assistance and loans provided to developing countries.

Discussion point

What are the limitations of using theories in global politics to make sense of the contemporary world around us?

⦿ TOK

In what ways do different historical narratives fit into our understanding of global politics? Is a historical narrative prioritizing trade and economic growth better than one prioritizing the impact of colonial expansion on indigenous cultures? Each of the different narratives in this section chart a 'pathway towards development and sustainability' but does each consider quite different historical facts?

This is an intriguing example of how different knowledge communities (for example, historians and political scientists) might impact one another. Being a skilled political scientist might mean showing skill in developing, or at least skill in interpreting, different historical narratives. This shows the deep inter-relatedness of different areas of knowledge.

◼ Capability approaches

Capability approaches refer to the theory put forward by Indian economist Amartya Sen (see Key theorist box on page 193). They are important in our discussion of pathways towards development because they attempt to move away from thinking in terms of economic models, such as neoliberalism, towards ideas such as capacity, freedom and choice.

Sen's central argument is that economic development (measured by indicators such as GDP) does not necessarily result in what people would regard as 'good lives'. Sen identifies the concepts of functionings and capabilities as key components of his capability approach:

- Functionings are doings and beings. They are what people do and what people are, and they give value to our lives. Examples of functionings include being:
  - ○ well nourished
  - ○ literate
  - ○ healthy
  - ○ able to work or to rest.

  It is important to distinguish between functionings and commodities. To give an example, being well nourished is a functioning and the commodities used to achieve this might be bread or rice. Similarly, bicycling is a functioning, while possessing a bicycle is a commodity. Achieving a functioning, then, is dependent on an individual making use of whatever commodities are at their command and relies on a number of factors. For example, achieving a state of being well nourished (a being) using bread or rice (commodities) depends on factors such as education, gender, age and climate.

- Capabilities are understood as options to achieve valuable functionings. They refer to the valuable functionings that an individual is able to access. Put simply, they refer to an individual's opportunity to choose. Capabilities, therefore, are best understood as being made up of functionings as well as the individual's freedom to choose from them.

We can use an example to distinguish between functionings and capabilities more clearly. A victim of famine in Yemen and a high school student taking part in a sponsored 24-hour fast can both be considered to be fasting or not eating. However, the key difference between the two is freedom, or lack of opportunity. The famine victim is constrained in their choice (they cannot choose to eat) while the student has the capability to be well-fed and yet chooses not to take advantage of this option.

Sen's capability approach, therefore, is significant because it does not simply focus on economic growth as a pathway to development. Rather, it suggests that any pathway to development and poverty reduction must focus on *improving the capabilities* of individuals.

Sen's work on capabilities has been developed by Martha Nussbaum, who suggests that, because the capability approach focuses on the capability rather than the right of individuals to lead lives that they value, at its heart is a list of capabilities that are central to a good life. Nussbaum argues that 'a life that lacks any one of these capabilities, no matter what else it has, will fall short of being a good human life' and that following the list below, therefore, should serve as both a guide and a standard for those responsible for formulating development policy:

- to live a life of normal length
- to be healthy, including reproductive health, with adequate nutrition and shelter
- to avoid unnecessary pain and have enjoyable experiences
- to use the senses, imagine, think and reason, and have the educational opportunities to be able to fully realize these abilities
- to have emotional attachments to things and people over and above ourselves
- to engage in critical reflection about the planning of our own life and to form an understanding of what is 'good'

- to recognize and show compassion and empathy for others
- to live in relation to animals, plants and the natural world
- to laugh and play, and to enjoy recreational activities
- to live a life with freedom of association and freedom from unwarranted search and seizure.

> ### Discussion point
>
> Nussbaum claims that 'the central goal of public planning should be the capabilities of citizens to perform various important functions'. To what extent do you agree?

3.3.3 Economic, environmental, political, social and institutional factors

There are a number of factors that impact on development; the subject guide for global politics identifies five categories that impact, both positively and negatively, on development and sustainability. They are:

- economic
- environmental
- political
- social
- institutional.

It is important to remember that these different categories and factors should not be understood in isolation – there is a high degree of crossover between all of them. For example, corruption might be understood to be a political factor but it can be seen to have a clear economic and environmental impact in some cases.

> **ACTIVITY**
>
> Before going any further, create a mind map that shows the interrelationship between economic, environmental, political, social and institutional factors that impact on development. Try to include real-world examples to support the points you make. As you read through the following content, you should revisit your mind map and update it accordingly.

■ Economic factors impacting on development

One of the major economic factors impacting on development is the unsustainable levels of debt incurred by countries. This means that money that could otherwise be spent on projects to promote development and reduce poverty and inequality must be used to service a country's debt.

Developing countries, in particular, are often burdened by high levels of debt. This is often known as 'third-world debt' (even though the term 'developing world' is generally preferred to 'third-world'). Third-world debt refers to the high levels of debt that developing countries owe to more developed countries and international finance institutions, such as the World Bank and the International Monetary Fund (IMF). Much of this debt was incurred in the years following former colonized countries gaining their independence, and there are a number of reasons why developing countries took on this debt.

'Third-world' debt

First, many countries sought to shift their economies, from largely agrarian to investing in manufacturing industries. In order to do this, developing countries funded the necessary investment by borrowing from developed countries and international institutions. Banks were all too willing to lend to developing countries due to a widespread belief that national governments would not default on a loan.

However, the global oil crisis of 1973 had a significant impact on the debt incurred by developing countries because, not only were they dependent on oil imports due to their new manufacturing industries, but they were also not in a position to be able to afford oil at the higher price. This required developing countries to borrow yet more money to subsidize the oil imports necessary to keep their manufacturing industries running.

The oil crisis also brought increased interest rates due to high inflation. This meant that, not only were developing countries taking on higher levels of debt, but also the cost of servicing that debt had increased too.

This has led to a situation in today's world in which third-world debt has a significant impact on development. The campaign group Debt Justice estimates that 'based on the amount their governments are spending on debt payments which leave the country, people in 54 countries are currently living in debt crisis'.

Secretary-General of the UN Conference on Trade and Development, Rebeca Grynspan, argued that there is a tendency in the international community to believe that because debts can be paid off after some sacrifice, they are essentially sustainable. Grynspan pointed out that this is 'like saying a poor family will stay afloat because they always repay their loan sharks. To take this view is to overlook the skipped meals, the foregone investment in education and the lack of health spending that forcibly make room for interest payments'.

Clearly, 'third-world' debt impacts on development, and many actors in the international system, including NGOs such as Debt Justice, have argued for either a reduction in or complete forgiveness of this debt. They justify such a claim by pointing out that less developed countries are spending five times more on servicing their debts than they are on dealing with the climate crisis. This is money that could be more effectively used to deal with developmental challenges and to work towards a more sustainable future.

Creation of improved infrastructure

A second way in which economic factors impact directly on development is through the creation of improved infrastructure, such as railways, ports, road networks and electricity grids. According to the Asian Development Bank, infrastructure is crucially important to foster countries' economic development and prosperity. Investments in infrastructure contribute to higher productivity and growth, facilitate trade and connectivity, and promote economic inclusion.

This goes some way to explaining why so many states – both developed and less developed – are prepared to invest such significant sums of money into infrastructure projects. China's significant investment in the Belt and Road initiative is an example of the huge sums of money countries are prepared to invest in infrastructure projects in order to support development. Estimates by the Council on Foreign Relations suggest that the total cost to China could reach as much as $8 trillion. (It should be noted, however, that China also has significant geostrategic power interests in the Belt and Road project, as well as purely developmental and economic concerns.)

So, why are countries so willing to invest such large sums in infrastructure?

Connectivity between high- and low-income regions allows for shared prosperity between the two. This is the rationale behind the development of high-speed rail in countries such as China, France and Italy. However, critics claim that improved connectivity simply makes it easier for human and financial capital to move from low-income to high-income regions, rather than vice versa as intended.

An economic multiplier effect is created by large infrastructure projects, as expenditure and investment equate to income for individuals and businesses. Investing in infrastructure leads to greater reliability in the provision of core services, such as electricity generation, which are essential for development.

As ever, the reality is not as clear-cut as we might first think. How do we measure the supposed economic benefits as a result of infrastructure development? Is it really as high as some claim?

■ Environmental factors impacting on development

We must also take into account the environmental impact of large infrastructure projects. For example, the UK government's decision to expand drilling for oil and gas in the North Sea not only has wider implications for climate change but, should an accident occur on a drilling platform, the environmental consequences are likely to be extreme. Put simply, when things go wrong, they are likely to go very wrong, as was the case in the Deepwater Horizon incident in the Gulf of Mexico in 2010, which led to the discharge of millions of gallons of crude oil into the sea.

There is also the impact on quality of life to consider. A six-lane motorway might improve connectivity between two regions of a country, but what might the impact be on those living along the proposed route in terms of noise and pollution?

We can consider environmental factors impacting in two different ways in particular:

- the impact of environmental factors, such as geographic location and access to natural resources
- the impact of environmental changes over time which have affected development, such as rising sea levels and climate change.

Environmental factors

◆ The **world ocean** is a term used to describe all five of the world's oceans (Arctic, Atlantic, Indian, Pacific, Southern) combined.

Landlocked countries – those countries that are surrounded by one or more states and therefore do not have access to the **world ocean** – face some very specific challenges that can have a significant impact on their development, and this explains why historically many states have gone to great lengths in order to achieve or maintain access to the sea.

According to the UN Office of the High Representative for the Least Developed Countries, Landlocked Developing Countries and Small Island Developing States (UN-OHRLLS), landlocked countries experience an erosion of competitive edge for exports due to the increased costs related to distance and terrain in a way that countries with access to the world ocean do not.

Additionally, the need to cross land borders can add a layer of administration that is costly, bureaucratic and inefficient. Paperwork, customs charges and procedures, as well as heavy traffic, all contribute to these inefficiencies. These delays have a further knock-on effect on trade routes. For example, significant delays in crossing the border between Uganda and Kenya can make it impossible to book a reliable slot ahead of time on ships leaving the Kenyan port of Mombasa.

Landlocked countries also suffer dependency related issues. This means they are dependent on their transit neighbours in three ways in particular:

1 Dependence on transit infrastructure

2 Dependence on political relations with neighbours

3 Dependence on internal peace and stability within transit neighbours.

If any of these three factors is adversely affected, then the subsequent impact on development of the dependent nation can be significant. While some landlocked countries are considered to be highly developed by measures such as the Human Development Index (HDI) – for example, Switzerland and Luxembourg – nine out of the 12 countries with the lowest HDI scores are landlocked. Clearly, being landlocked is a geographic factor that has a significant impact on development.

◆ **Resource endowment** is the number and type of resources a country has for economic activity, such as land, minerals, labour and capital.

Another geographic factor impacting development is **resource endowment**. It is clear that states are endowed with different reserves and types of resources. For example, South Africa is a significant producer of platinum, while Saudi Arabia has huge oil reserves. It might seem obvious that countries with a high level of resource endowment are more likely, therefore, to be highly developed as a result. The United States, for example, is significantly endowed with natural resources:

● US natural resources are equal to approximately $45 trillion.

● The United States has 31.2 per cent of the Earth's coal reserves.

● The United States is among the top five states that are rich in reserves of gold, copper and natural gas.

● 750 million acres of US land are covered with forests, which produce huge amounts of timber (Basic Planet).

It is perhaps unsurprising, then, that the United States ranks as one of the most developed countries in the world.

However, as ever in global politics, it is not quite as straightforward as it might appear. The Democratic Republic of the Congo (DRC) also possesses abundant natural resources, including diamonds, gold, copper, cobalt, cassiterite (tin ore) and coltan, as well as timber, coffee and oil. In addition, the DRC produces 17 per cent of the world's rough diamonds, 34 per cent of the world's cobalt and 10 per cent of the world's copper. It also has 60–80 per cent of global reserves of coltan, which is used in mobile phones and other electronics. It does not, however, score anywhere near as highly as the United States in terms of development, as Table 3.10 shows.

■ **Table 3.10** Comparing development indicators of the United States and the Democratic Republic of the Congo (Gapminder)

	United States	Democratic Republic of the Congo
Life expectancy	79 years	65.7
HDI score	0.921	0.479
Infant mortality rate	5.4	62.4
GDP per capita (USD)	$63,600	$1,070

These hugely different development outcomes, despite both countries having a significant resource endowment, could possibly be explained in terms of a phenomenon known as the 'resource curse'. This is also sometimes referred to as the 'paradox of plenty' or the 'poverty paradox'. It refers to countries with an abundance of natural resources having poorer development outcomes than countries with fewer natural resources.

While the resource curse is not a universal phenomenon by any means – Singapore, for example, has very few natural resources yet scores highly on most development indices – it can be seen in several instances, such as the DRC, and several reasons have been offered by way of explanation, including the way in which resource income is spent, system of government, institutional quality and the types of resources. In many cases, corruption and weak institutions have a significant impact on the inability to maximize exploitation of natural resources effectively.

Environmental changes

Climate change is also a significant factor that impacts on development of countries in a number of different ways.

Rising sea levels are a direct threat to many low-lying countries and communities, such as Kiribati and other Pacific island nations. The rise in sea levels is likely to lead to a loss of land and property, as well as loss of life, due to an increased chance of storm surge flooding. Communities living inland will not be exempt from the impact of rising sea levels either, as the need to abandon or relocate low-lying communities leads to an increase in migration, with the associated challenges that this brings.

Global warming has also impacted significantly on development. As UN Sustainable Development Goal 13 (SDG-13) states, the impact of climate change includes flooding and drought, displacing millions of people, sinking them into poverty and hunger, denying them access to basic services, such as health and education, expanding inequalities, stifling economic growth and causing conflict over increasingly scarce resources.

The relationship between climate change and development raises some interesting issues.

First, we need to consider just how the global north became rich in the first place. In large part, it was due to burning fossil fuels, cutting down forests and farming livestock on a large scale. How, then, do we expect developing countries to react now, when they are told that this is not a viable pathway to development by more developed states that took exactly this pathway?

Second, it is important to consider the way in which development outcomes can have a negative impact on the environment, leading to climate change. There is, in some ways, a direct correlation between increasing affluence and climate changes. For example, global meat production has risen significantly as living standards rise in different regions of the world, as shown in Figure 3.23, which is based on data from the UN Food and Agriculture Organization.

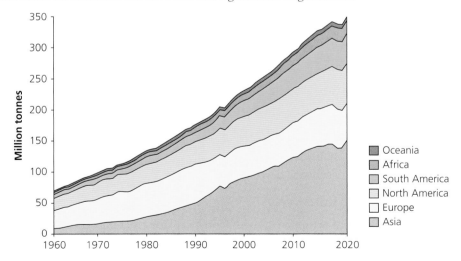

■ **Figure 3.23** Global meat production, 1960–2020 (adapted from Our World in Data, 'Global meat production, 1961 to 2021')

HL extension: Environment

The impact of environmental factors on development provides numerous possibilities for HL inquiry into the global political challenge of Environment. One possible pathway would be to compare the environmental impact of rising sea levels on different low lying states and explore the effectiveness of the different strategies used by states to address this challenge.

■ Political factors impacting on development

The subject guide for IBDP Global Politics identifies ideologies, history and persistence of conflict, stability, accountability, transparency, legal frameworks, political consequences of different development paths, decisions about the allocation of aid, political culture, culture of bureaucracy, and vested interests as some of the many different political factors that impact on development.

Political instability

Political instability can have a significant impact on development. Countries that experience political instability may find it harder to attract foreign direct investment, as many companies are more reluctant to invest in uncertain operating environments. For example, companies are unwilling to open a factory in a country if there is any likelihood of a sudden non-democratic change of government leading to nationalization of their investment.

◆ A **coup d'etat** is the sudden, violent overthrow, or attempted overthrow, of a government by a smaller group.

Moving beyond purely economic considerations, political instability can also have major impacts on human rights which, as we have seen, can be regarded as integral to a broader, more comprehensive definition of development. In a politically unstable country, many governments that come to power may do so due to repression and denial of human rights, as well as through anti-democratic processes such as **coups d'etat**.

It is also important to note that development is a process and not an event, and much development can only take place over relatively long periods of time. Any lack of continuity, therefore, hinders development as an ongoing continual process.

Political instability can also lead to increased tension with other states, particularly close neighbours. Coups d'etat in Mali, Burkina Faso, Guinea and Niger have resulted in all four states being suspended from the regional IGO the Economic Community of West African States (ECOWAS).

Internal conflict is another form of political instability that impacts negatively on development. Long-term conflict in Afghanistan and Syria, for example, has resulted in very low development outcomes, while ethnic and tribal tensions in countries such as Kenya have led to disputed elections and resultant violence that has negatively impacted on development.

Political ideologies

Political ideologies can also have an impact on development as they have a significant effect on the way in which governments allocate financial resources to different sectors. The Juche ideology practised by North Korea – which suggests that a country prospers only through achieving self-reliance in the three realms of political, economic and military independence – is an extreme example of the way in which ideology can impact on the development of a country. As part of the push to military independence and self-reliance, North Korea has adopted a military first policy – Songun – which has led to the government spending between 20 and 25 per cent of GDP on the military, according to data from the US Central Intelligence Agency. Obviously, this would be a huge proportion in any country, but in a country facing developmental challenges to the extent of North Korea, it is a remarkable sum of money that could be spent on improving human and economic development throughout the country.

Corruption

Corruption is another political factor that impacts on development, as it very often occurs due to weak legal systems and enforcement, poor funding of public sector organizations such as the police and judiciary, and very often the government itself is willing to engage in corrupt practices. Transparency International identifies three categories of public sector corruption:

● Grand corruption: 'Acts committed at a high level of government that distort policies or the central functioning of the state, enabling leaders to benefit at the expense of the public good.'

THEMATIC STUDIES: Development and sustainability

- Petty corruption: 'Everyday abuse of entrusted power by low- and mid-level public officials in their interactions with ordinary citizens … often trying to access basic public goods and services.'
- Political corruption: 'Manipulation of policies, institutions and rules of procedure in the allocation of resources and financing by political decision makers, who abuse their position to sustain their power, status and wealth.'

A PricewaterhouseCoopers (PwC) report into corruption in Nigeria suggests that corruption across these three categories has a significant adverse impact on Nigeria being able to reach its potential for a number of reasons.

- Corruption both reduces the tax base from which the government gains revenue and increases the inefficiency of government expenditure. PwC estimates that Nigeria's tax revenues are only around 8 per cent of GDP, which is very low when compared to similar countries.
- Corruption also affects the willingness of many international firms to invest in Nigeria as well as lowering human capital, as fewer people are unable to access education and health care, the poorest people being the most affected.

Tackling corruption in countries such as Nigeria, therefore, is a key component of raising living standards, promoting development and reducing poverty.

■ Social factors impacting on development

The subject guide for IBDP Global Politics identifies values, culture, tradition, gender relations and migration as possible factors that impact on development, although obviously this is not an exhaustive list. It is important to note that factors such as values, culture and tradition are difficult to measure and assess. We also need to be mindful of the need to avoid making ethnocentric and even racist generalizations. Nonetheless, we can see evidence of their impact on development in various examples around the world, from the role of culture as a store of traditional knowledge that can be drawn upon when addressing contemporary challenges, to the economic benefits that culture provides to different countries. For example, in his paper on 'The value of cultural tourism to London', Brian Smith has estimated that cultural tourism was worth £3.2 billion to London in 2013 and supported 80,000 jobs. Clearly this is a significant economic driver of development.

Gender discrimination

Gender discrimination impacts on development in a number of ways. At a purely economic level, female exclusion from the workforce means that the economic and human potential of around 50 per cent of the population is not being fully utilized. This can be seen in states such as Afghanistan, where significant legal barriers to women's employment exist, as well as in countries where social norms and cultural expectations make it harder for women to work. In addition, as the economist Jeffrey Sachs points out, 'Cultural or religious norms may block the role of women … leaving half the population without economic or political rights and without education, thereby undermining half of the population in its contribution to overall development.'

It can also be argued that women's contribution to development is often unrecognized and unacknowledged. Globally, women take on the greatest share of unpaid domestic labour and responsibility for raising children – an essential prerequisite for a country to develop – yet this work is largely unpaid and, to a large extent, invisible in any official statistics. The world development report from the World Bank, 'Gender Equality and Development', identifies four gaps that need to be filled in order to close the development gender gap between men and women:

- human capital
- economic productivity
- access to finance
- empowerment.

Human capital refers to the need to address factors such as access to education and health care. For example, in Malawi, studies show that family obligations often limit participation in education and result in lower skills development for young women (Cho and Kalomba).

Economic productivity can often be lower for women due to structures that directly and indirectly discriminate against women and girls. Often, their access to economic opportunities is limited by their lower levels of access to production inputs, and Kondylis and Jones give the example of female farmers in many countries who have less access to information due to the fact the agricultural networks are dominated by men. The fact that in many countries, particularly in sub-Saharan Africa, women are limited in terms of land ownership, as much land is inherited **patrilineally**, is another example of the way in which gender discrimination impacts on development.

◆ A **patrilineal** society is one in which descent is based on the male line. Patrilineal inheritance, therefore, means property passes from father to son.

Globally, access to finance is often constrained for women when compared to men. In Malawi, it is common in some communities for male relatives to seize a woman's assets on the death of her husband. Additionally, and highlighting the way in which these factors are interrelated, is the impact of lower levels of educational access for girls on female financial literacy.

Kondylis and Jones also highlight the wide range of justifications for empowering women in order to achieve development outcomes, including improving institutional efficiency, especially with regard to resource distribution and what they suggest may be the beneficial impact of female leaders on social norms.

Migration

Migration is another social factor that impacts upon development. While many newspaper headlines make claims about the negative impact of migration, the overall picture is much more nuanced. Indeed, the OECD points out that migration makes significant contributions to economic development in three interrelated areas (Dumont and Liebig):

- The labour market: migrants have accounted for significant increases in the workforce, particularly in the United States and Europe, with increases of 47 per cent and 70 per cent respectively, and fill important niches in both growing and declining sectors of the economy.

- The public purse: despite poorly informed misconceptions, data suggest that migrants contribute more in tax revenue than they receive in benefits from the state.

- Economic growth: migrants are a key way of boosting the working-age population and they arrive with skills that boost the human capital and technological progress of host countries.

It is worth noting that, while much of the discussion around the negative impact of migration focuses on receiving countries, the impact on countries of origin can be significant and can be viewed in both positive and negative terms.

The phenomenon of 'brain-drain', defined as the emigration of a nation's most highly skilled individuals (Gibson and Mackenzie), has often been related to fields such as health care, where highly trained doctors may move abroad from developing countries in search of better pay, improved working conditions and political stability. This obviously then has an adverse effect on the health care system in the country of origin.

However, it is not so straightforward as to say that emigration has a negative impact on countries. Many migrants send significant sums of money in the form of remittances to family and loved ones back home. Indeed, remittances made up 54 per cent of the GDP of Lebanon and 44 per cent of Tonga in 2021, according to data from the World Bank, which also show remittances reaching $630 billion globally in 2022, a significant driver of development.

■ Institutional factors impacting on development

Institutional factors impacting on development refer to the role played by global institutions, such as the World Bank and the International Monetary Fund (IMF), as well as national-level institutions, such as state development agencies and state-level partnerships between countries.

Global institutions

The World Bank and the IMF can have a significant impact on the development of particular countries, and the extent to which this is considered positive or negative is often highly debated. Both the World Bank and the IMF provide loans to countries in need of financial assistance, although the IMF tends to provide short- to medium-term financial assistance while loans provided by the World Bank are generally over the longer term.

Most of the time, financial assistance from both institutions is conditional, meaning that recipient countries must meet certain conditions or make specified changes in order to receive loans. These are known as structural adjustment programmes (SAPs), as the aim is to adjust the structure of the recipient country's economy. SAPs require borrowing countries to implement policies such as privatization of state-owned industries, trade liberalization and the reduction of government deficits, often through decreased government spending.

SAPs have been criticized on a number of grounds. Some commentators make the point that they undermine national sovereignty, as economic policy is being dictated – or at the very least, heavily influenced – by outside actors. This relates to development because, as national budgets and government expenditure are cut as a result of SAPs, it is very often the most disadvantaged groups in a society that are disproportionately impacted by cuts in areas such as education and health care.

SAPs have also been criticized on grounds of postcolonialism, with some arguing that they provide a pathway for multinational companies (MNCs) to extract resources from developing countries.

Privatization – often a key component of SAPs – can also be seen as having a negative impact on development, as the decision to privatize state industries may often be based on poor financial performance of those companies. This fails to take into account service provision and the wider social role played by, for example water companies.

Unsurprisingly, perhaps, both Bretton Woods institutions claim a much more positive impact on development. The World Bank Impact Report for 2022, for example, highlights 34.6 million people covered by social safety net programmes; 16.7 million people provided with essential health, nutrition and population services; and 6.8 million people with access to improved water sources, among other achievements.

National and regional-level institutions

National and regional-level institutions also have a significant impact on development.

The International Fund for Agricultural Development points out that many of the challenges that face poor rural people in many countries, such as remote locations and poor access to basic infrastructure such as banking and internet connectivity, lead to a lack of control over their own livelihoods. These challenges can be overcome, to a large extent, by strong institutions and organizations such as farming cooperatives that can help rural people by: 'giving them direct access to critically needed resources, services and markets; reducing the price of inputs for farmers through larger collective purchases; and acting as a forum for exchanging knowledge and experience, as well as jointly-owned assets, such as equipment and machinery' (Grandval et al.).

Microfinance institutions, such as Grameen, can also impact significantly on development in the poorest countries by offering small loans to people who traditionally would not be able to access credit facilities, such as women in rural areas. Supporters of locally based initiatives such as these argue that they are more able to support communities to develop as they have a more in-depth, local understanding of the issues facing local people and are more empowering for recipients of loans and assistance rather than simply being passive beneficiaries, as may be more likely the case with other forms of overseas development aid.

State-level partnerships can also be considered as an institutional factor impacting upon development. The UN Department for Economic and Social Affairs identifies three forms of cooperation (note, the terms 'north' and 'south' are not used in a geographic sense here, but refer to the global north and the global south):

- North-South refers to a developed country supporting a less developed country economically or with another kind of resource. For example, humanitarian aid after a natural disaster or during a humanitarian crisis is a form of cooperation.

- South-South refers to technical cooperation between countries in the global south and is defined by the UN Department of Economic and Social Affairs as 'a tool used by states, international organizations, academics, civil society and the private sector to collaborate and share knowledge, skills and successful initiatives in specific areas such as agricultural development, human rights, urbanization, health, climate change etc.' The UN Office for South-South Cooperation gives several examples of successful cooperation impacting positively on development, including:
  - Cuba's support in the fight against Ebola in West Africa
  - Mexico's experience in diversifying corn products to improve health and nutrition in Kenya
  - the knowledge of strategies to reduce hunger shared by Colombia to Mesoamerican countries
  - the lessons from Chile to the Caribbean countries on product labelling as a measure to end obesity (UNDESA).

- Triangular cooperation refers to a partnership between two nations in the global south collaborating with a partner in the global north who may or may not be a state actor. For example, the Japan International Cooperation Agency, a Japanese government department, provided financial assistance for de-mining experts from Cambodia to travel to Colombia to share knowledge and expertise.

3.3.4 Links between development and sustainability

While historically much focus on development has been on the economic dimension and considered in the short- to medium-term, there is now much greater awareness of the need to ensure development is not only effective at eradicating poverty and raising living standards, but that it is also sustainable. Much of this change is due to a collective realization that models of development that focused solely on economic growth were unsustainable and led directly to environmental issues such as climate change that, as we have seen, have direct and negative impacts on development.

Perhaps the most obvious manifestation of the relationship between development and sustainability can be seen in the creation and pursuit of the UN Sustainable Development Goals (SDGs). The SDGs are a global development framework that replaced the Millennium Development Goals (MDGs), which expired in 2015, and were formally adopted in a UN resolution known as Agenda 2030.

SUSTAINABLE DEVELOPMENT G⬤ALS

■ **Figure 3.24** The 17 Sustainable Development Goals

In 2017, a further resolution was passed that provides specific targets for each of the 17 goals along with identifying indicators to measure progress towards achieving each goal.

It is important to remember that the targets for each SDG are divided into outcome targets and means of implementation targets. The means of implementation targets were developed later in the process of developing the framework in order to address the concerns of some states as to how the different goals would be achieved.

The SDGs provide a comprehensive framework that attempts to put sustainability at the centre of all forms of development, as well as acknowledging that development cannot be understood or achieved through a purely economic dimension. This can be seen in the targets set for SDG-8, which acknowledges an economic dimension while at the same time acknowledging the importance of labour rights and a safe working environment, which speaks more to a human aspect of development.

It is important to bear in mind that, just as development is not simply economic in nature, sustainability is not confined to an environmental dimension. Indeed, the SDGs clearly show that economic, social and environmental sustainability are key to sustainable development.

This is not to say that the SDGs provide a perfect framework for sustainable development – in fact, they have been criticized on a number of grounds (which we will discuss in Chapter 3.4). They do, however, clearly demonstrate that development and sustainability are inseparable concepts when tackling the challenges in a twenty-first-century world.

ACTIVITY

For a comprehensive list of targets and indicators for each SDG, visit the Sustainable Develpment Goals page on the UNDP website. Research the extent to which each of the targets for one or more of the goals is being met globally.

Discussion point

How can states be persuaded to support the SDGs, even when they may harm their own short-term national interest?

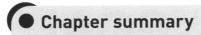

● Chapter summary

In this chapter we have covered:

- the challenges of measuring the contested concepts of development, sustainability, poverty and inequality, along with the advantages and disadvantages of a variety of different indices and indicators
- the arguments put forward by different theorists to propose different pathways towards development
- some of the many different factors that impact on development across a range of categories, and how this impact can be both positive and negative.

REVIEW QUESTIONS

Now that you have read this chapter, reflect on these questions:

- Is it possible or desirable to measure development or other concepts by using a single index or indicator?
- Are all factors impacting on development equally easy to measure? If not, why?
- What are the limitations of each of the proposed pathways to development discussed in this chapter?

Debates on development and sustainability

By the end of this chapter, you should understand:
▶ globalization and development and sustainability
▶ sustainable development
▶ alternative views on development and sustainability.

3.4.1 Globalization and development and sustainability

◆ **Globalization**
describes how the growth and development of trade and technology, and the spread of social and cultural influences, have made the world (states, governments, economies and people) a more connected, interdependent place.

Globalization is another contested concept, but we can take it to mean a process that is based around 'the growing interdependence of the world's economies, cultures and populations, brought about by cross-border trade in goods and services, technology, and flows of investment, people, and information' (PIIE). Much of this is, therefore, very closely related to the concept of complex interdependence, which liberal theorists such as Joseph Nye argue characterize our world in the twenty-first century.

Scholars disagree over whether globalization is a negative process or a force for good in the world. As the International Labour Organization (ILO) points out in its report 'A Fair Globalization: Creating Opportunities for All': 'at one extreme, globalization is seen as an irresistible and benign force for delivering economic prosperity to people throughout the world. At the other, it is blamed as a source of all contemporary ills.'

Bill Etherington, Council of Europe Rapporteur for the Committee on the Environment, Agriculture and Local and Regional Affairs, has argued that globalization is characterized by four trends:

1 Increased flows of commodities and persons

2 Expansion and diversification of financial activities

3 Development of communication, networks, knowledge and relationships

4 Increasing disparities.

These four trends, according to Etherington, pose major challenges and, simultaneously, significant opportunities for both development and sustainability.

The relationship between globalization, sustainability and development is a complex one, but we can identify several ways in which globalization has impacted on both development and sustainability.

■ 1 Increased flows of commodities and persons

Increased flows of people around the world leading to changing patterns of migration has impacted on development, as we saw in Chapter 3.3 under social factors impacting on development. The increasing ease of global travel, particularly air travel and the growing availability of cheap flights, is one way in which globalization can be seen in practice, but this comes at an environmental cost. As of 2018, global aviation (including domestic and international; passenger and freight) accounts for 0.9 per cent of greenhouse gas emissions (which includes all greenhouse gases, not only carbon dioxide) and 2.5 per cent of carbon dioxide emissions (Ritchie). This clearly has a negative environmental impact on development and, in the long term, is unsustainable for the well-being of our planet.

However, not all flows of commodities and people are due to aviation. Around 90 per cent of all freight moved around the world is transported by sea (George). The rise of containerization has been a key component of globalization, enabling goods to be exported and imported around the world, with obvious impacts on development. It is no coincidence that states are prepared to make significant investments into the development of major ports, as they provide a range of development opportunities. For example, the direct and indirect added value of the Port of Rotterdam is €63 billion. This represents 8.2 per cent of the Dutch gross domestic product (GDP) (Port of Rotterdam).

■ **Figure 3.25** The container port at Europoort, Rotterdam, The Netherlands

It is also important to note that, even in an increasingly globalized world, where goods, firms and money remain largely free to cross national borders, the same is not necessarily true for all people. While, for example, citizens of the European Union are free to live and work in any of the 27 member states, the same privilege does not extend to the majority of the global population. Even something as relatively simple as visa-travel is a privilege much more accessible to citizens of the global north.

In order for countries to develop – particularly economically – it is important in a globalized world that they are integrated into global supply chains and trade routes. The phenomenal spending by the Chinese government, for example, on developing the Belt and Road initiative is recognition, on the part of the Chinese, that this is essential to China's development and a way of increasing and exercising soft power in the pursuit of hegemony in the region. The extent to which this benefits all countries equally, however, is debatable. It can be argued that the development of supply and transport infrastructure, such as ports, in developing countries simply assists with resource extraction and exploitation of these countries by the countries of the global north.

Discussion point

One of the key concepts that underpins the global politics course is interdependence. How does interdependence help us to make sense of the relationship between globalization, sustainability and development?

THEMATIC STUDIES: Development and sustainability

■ 2 Expansion and diversification of financial activities

The expansion and diversification of financial activities as a component of globalization has also impacted significantly on development in both positive and negative ways. The closer integration of global banking systems now means it is possible to send and receive money around the world, even for those with traditionally limited access to banking facilities. The rise of mobile money networks, where money can be transferred via mobile phone, has contributed to the ease with which many economic migrants are able to make remittances to families back at home, which can have a significant impact on development at both the community and national level.

Complex interdependence between states and other actors can also be seen in the activities of multinational corporations (MNCs) around the world, in that economic processes in one country can have knock-on effects in other countries. For example, the decision of certain companies to stop or scale back operations in the UK after Brexit has had an impact on employment in certain UK communities.

This level of interdependence could also be seen during the global financial crisis of 2007–09, in which a downturn in the US housing market was a catalyst for a financial crisis that spread from the United States to the rest of the world through linkages in the global financial system. The impact on economic development was significant. Many banks around the world incurred large losses and relied on government support to avoid bankruptcy, leading to millions of people losing their jobs (Reserve Bank of Australia).

Changes to financial systems as a result of globalization also impact on development. As **private financial flows** have increased massively and begun to exceed **official financial flows**, the influence of non-state actors, such as banks and **ratings agencies**, has increased accordingly. The result of this is that private actors now have ever greater influence over the economic policies of states and governments.

Ratings agencies, for example, are able to determine the cost at which national governments are able to borrow money internationally. This is significant because a key principle is that actors in global politics will generally act in their own self-interest. When that self-interest is profit, it is not necessarily the case that this will align with national developmental priorities or sustainability concerns.

◆ **Private financial flows** are financed by private sector resources as opposed to government resources. Private flows, therefore, include remittances sent home by migrants, foreign direct investment and private sector borrowing.

◆ **Official financial flows** relate to official development assistance provided by one state to another.

◆ **Ratings agencies** are companies that independently assess the financial strength of individuals, companies and government entities.

■ 3 Development of communication, networks, knowledge and relationships

The development of communications and knowledge networks as a component of globalization, part of what liberals would see as the multiple channels of complex interdependence, have much potential for positively impacting sustainability.

Increasing internet access, even in less developed countries, through mobile phone networks, means that knowledge and information are now more widely available. Advocates for globalization would argue that this, for example, means that poor farmers in rural communities are now more likely to be able to benefit from improved farming techniques and access to market information.

However, while this may be true in some cases, and is certainly attractive in theory, it is far from universally applicable. The development of communications technology now means it is possible to outsource work to other countries, where labour costs may be lower. For example, some British companies have transferred their telephone call centres to English-speaking countries overseas, such as India. This shows how globalization processes such as these can have a mixed impact on development. While they may contribute to the economic development of the country to which they are relocated, at the same time this can have a negative impact on certain groups of workers in the original country, who may face unemployment. As ever, when we're discussing development, the picture is often more complicated than it might appear at first glance.

Improved communication can also be considered a driver of aspiration. People living in less developed countries now have greater access to, and understanding of, the quality of life enjoyed in more developed countries, and this can lead to pressure on national governments to ensure the same quality of life is available in less developed nations.

However, as has been pointed out by some critics of globalization, this can lead to an increasing cultural homogeneity, where local cultures and traditions are threatened. If we adopt a broad view of development to include respect for local traditions, then the potential negative impact is clear.

■ 4 Increasing disparities

◆ **Disparities** are unequal or unfair differences in levels of treatment.

It is important to acknowledge that, despite the benefits that globalization can bring in terms of trade and investment, these benefits are not equally distributed and there are significant **disparities** in the way in which people around the world have benefited.

While significant disparities remain between different countries, particularly between the global north and the global south, Serbian-American economist Branko Milanovic has considered what inequality between individuals looks like on a global scale in our globalized world. Using the Gini coefficient, his research shows the world is still, unsurprisingly, unequal. The disparities between the richest people and the poorest people are still huge, but Milanovic offers some unexpected findings:

- Two of the main groups benefiting from globalization are the global Top 1 per cent and the emerging middle class in countries like China and India. However, it is interesting – and perhaps unexpected – that the income of this emerging middle class has risen even faster than the Top 1 per cent, and the emerging middle class accounts for around half the global population.

- Milanovic also demonstrates that people in what he terms the 'global bottom' have also experienced increased income as a result of globalization. Admittedly, this has been at a lower rate than the emerging middle class but has, nonetheless, significantly reduced abject poverty. It should be noted, however, that the very poorest 5 per cent of the world's population have been largely bypassed by globalization processes and seen very little benefit. Typically, many of those in the bottom 5 per cent live in conflict affected countries, which serves to highlight the interconnectedness of factors in global politics.

- According to Milanovic, the losers in globalization have been those between the 75th and 90th percentile of global income distribution – the poorest in Western Europe and the lower middle-class in Eastern Europe, for example. These people may not have lost out, but equally they have not seen income rise in any meaningful manner compared to other groups globally.

ACTIVITY

The quotations in Figure 3.26 are all based on responses by participants in the inquiry by the 2004 ILO World Commission on the Social Dimension of Globalization, chaired by Tarja Halonen, President of Finland, and Benjamin William Mkapa, President of Tanzania.

Consider the quotations and, with a partner, reflect on whether or not globalization is a force for good with regard to development and sustainability.

THEMATIC STUDIES: Development and sustainability

'Globalization is the re-colonization of our countries. It is unwanted, foreign and forced on Africa'
Participant from Senegal

'Globalization involves much talk of markets, but in reality very little access, much talk of jobs, but they are somewhere else, and much talk of a better life, but for others'
Participant from the Philippines

'Globalization can lead to greater democracy, education and employment. Whatever the impact of globalization on the continent, Africa cannot advance by isolating itself from the process'
Participant from Uganda

'African solutions for African problems'
Participant from an unnamed African country

'A conversation between a cat and a mouse is not a conversation. It is a deeply undemocratic and disempowering system'
Participant representing an unnamed civil society organization

'Workers can hardly trust the current model of globalization when they see every day a growth of the informal economy, a decline in social protection and the imposition of an authoritarian workplace culture'
Trade union leader from Costa Rica

'Globalization is unequal combat that will lead to certain death. Africa needs to develop a culture of resistance to globalization in order to avoid being reduced to the status of a beggar economy'
African civil society leader

'There is no point to a globalization that reduces the price of a child's shoes, but costs the father his job'
Participant from the Philippines

■ **Figure 3.26** Responses by participants at the International Labour Organization World Commission on the Social Dimension of Globalization (ILO, 'A fair globalization: Creating opportunities for all')

TOK

If you and your partner disagree after you have done the activity, try to identify where your disagreements might originate. Do you think your cultures, personal histories or family histories had any influence on your understanding of globalization? Are you consumers of different types of political or social media? How might these differences shape your understanding of the issues? To what extent are our political views shaped by society, family backgrounds, education or social class?

3.4.2 Sustainable development

While it might be difficult to come up with a comprehensive and universally agreed upon definition of a concept as complex and multifaceted as sustainable development, the Brundtland Commission offers perhaps the most elegant definition as 'development which satisfies the needs of the present generation without endangering the future generations' capacity to satisfy their own' (World Commission on Environment and Development).

However, one of the challenges of this definition is that it is so broad ranging – it covers everything from us as individuals having a responsibility to live within our means, all the way to requiring the global community to live within the sustainable resources of the world. Therefore, this definition covers a huge breadth and scale of activity (Mawhinney).

While it is clear that the Brundtland definition of sustainable development has an obvious environmental component, the definition provided by the World Conservation Union, the United Nations Environment Programme and the World Wildlife Fund offers a more explicit reference to the environment, stating that 'sustainable development means improving the quality of life while living within the carrying capacity of supporting systems' (Munro and Holdgate).

It is not always the case, however, that all ideas of sustainable development include explicit reference to an environmental component. This can be seen in the definition provided by the World Commission on Environment and Development report, 'Our common future', which defines sustainable development as 'development that meets the needs of the present without compromising the ability of future generations to meet their own needs'. Such a definition focuses on the social and economic aspects of development.

Therefore, we can see that there are many different understandings of sustainable development, and we must bear this in mind when exploring debates around this concept.

One of the key issues to address when thinking about social development is the tension that exists between traditional understandings of development and sustainability. In one sense, sustainable development can be understood as an attempt to marry these two competing concerns. Furthermore, as we know from our discussion of development in Chapter 3.1 of this thematic study, there arguably exists a tension between different forms of development. These are simplified into two categories of economic and social development in the model in Figure 3.27, showing the trade-off between development and sustainability. However, as with all models, we need to remember that this is a deliberate over-simplification of a messy and complicated reality.

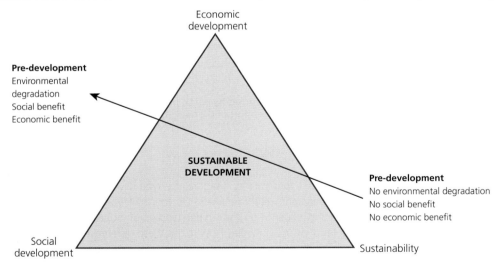

■ **Figure 3.27** The relationship of economic and social development and sustainability as contradictory forces acting upon sustainable development (adapted from Mawhinney)

Discussion point

If sustainable development is an inevitable trade-off between competing priorities, which countries have been most successful in balancing sustainability, economic growth and social growth?

This model suggests, therefore, that there is no perfect solution for achieving perfect sustainable development. Instead, it will always be a trade-off between the competing priorities of sustainability, economic and social development. The concept of sustainable development can therefore be criticized on the grounds that it necessarily seeks to marry the incompatible goals of both development and sustainability, as well as the fact that there still remains a number of different definitions and there is no overarching agreement as to what the concept actually looks like in practice.

THEMATIC STUDIES: Development and sustainability

Criticisms of the UN Sustainable Development Goals

The UN Sustainable Development Goals (SDGs) have attempted to address the issue of incompatible goals and set out a way of achieving development in a way that is sustainable over the longer term. They do this by seeking to address many of the challenges faced in our twenty-first-century globalized world. We discussed the SDGs in more detail in Chapter 3.3, but it is worth considering some of the criticisms that have been levelled at the SDGs again.

The SDGs are not binding on states

This means there is no effective mechanism to penalize states for not acting on the goals. Essentially, then, the SDGs are aspirations rather than goals. It is important to not just agree on what must be done but vital that there is agreement on who will be responsible for it being done. As Thomas Pogge of Yale University points out, 'If no such division of labour is agreed upon, then all we have is a long list of Sustainable Development Wishes along with the pious hope that economic growth and charitable activities will move things far enough in the right direction'. Pogge goes on, however, to concede that the SDGs present an opportunity, in that states are perhaps more likely to accept ambitious targets when there is no binding commitment on them to achieve those targets.

The SDGs are insufficiently ambitious

Progress towards the SDGs is slow and step-by-step, but critics of the goals claim this is not enough. As Charles Kenny points out, 'The eradication of severe poverty worldwide is possible today, so we must eradicate it now, as fast as we possibly can.'

It can also be argued that some of the measurements used in the SDGs are inadequate to achieve meaningful change. For example, SDG-1 seeks to eradicate extreme poverty, defined as people living on less than $1.25 a day. If someone moves from living on $1.25 a day to living on $1.30 a day, then they would no longer be considered to be in extreme poverty. But, really, how much would their quality of life have improved?

Top-down goals that ignore local contexts

Critics of the SDGs point out that a 'one-size fits all' approach will not work in achieving sustainable development. What might work in one local or national context may not work in another, and therefore the SGDs must achieve a balance between the local and global scales.

The SDGs are still based around a neoliberal economic model that favours the global north

Critics of the goals argue, instead, for a fundamental rethink around systems such as trading rules that will involve powerful countries conceding some of the structural power they currently possess. David Taylor notes that this may involve situations whereby 'ensuring the sustainability of one place, one location, one country, might undermine the sustainability of other places'.

The SDGs are based on outdated and dubious assumptions

Aram Ziai has argued that the SDGs are merely a renewal of the Cold War promise made by developed countries to the developing world that 'they could become, with the support of the West, prosperous or developed countries within a capitalist world economic order'. However, Ziai claims that this has only come true for a very small minority of countries and that, in the world of international development, there are no real rags-to-riches stories. Ziai goes on to make the point that while development cooperation has always been driven by the idea that the people in the global south are less 'developed' and are reliant on the expert knowledge of the global north, and that fighting poverty in global capitalism could be a win-win solution for poor and rich countries alike, both were already very dubious assumptions even back in the mid-twentieth century.

Many of the criticisms of the SDGs relate to methodological issues or are on the grounds of effectiveness. They do not necessarily take issue with the notion of sustainable development as a laudable and achievable goal. However, the very notion of sustainable development has been criticized by some writers.

◆ **Poststructuralism** is a perspective that attempts to move beyond making sense of the world in terms of pre-established social structures.

Arturo Escobar, writing from a **poststructuralist** perspective, has criticized the very concept of sustainable development for objectifying both people and nature as well as creating a discourse that assumes both can be managed. In doing so, Escobar raises the question of just how different sustainable development is from plain development. He argues that there is no real difference and that, 'The eco-developmentalist vision expressed in mainstream versions of sustainable development reproduces certain aspects of economism and developmentalism'. Put simply, Escobar is arguing that sustainable development follows the same principles as economic development and does not offer anything new.

Key theorist

Arturo Escobar (1951–)

Arturo Escobar is a Colombian-American anthropologist and Professor Emeritus of Anthropology at the University of North Carolina. His research work has included, among other areas, social movements, anti-globalization movements and post-development theory. He is a major figure in post-development academic discourse.

Escobar rejected the belief that the global south should follow a pathway set by the global north. He began to develop a radical critique of the dominant capitalist model of development through what he refers to as the concept of post-development. For Escobar, post-development is defined by two key elements.

■ **Figure 3.28** Arturo Escobar

- First, it challenges the central premises upon which Western models of development are based, such as economic growth.

- Second, nations in the global south or developing world can – and perhaps more importantly should – put forward alternative models of development that are based around non-Western understandings of what a thriving society looks like.

Some have sought to characterize Escobar's work as proposing alternative models of development. However, he argues that he is advocating for *alternatives to development* – something he suggests is an important distinction. As he points out in his article 'Farewell to development':

> *Over the course of the last few decades, 'development' has undergone multiple modifications, such as sustainable development, participatory development, development with gender equity, integrated rural development, and so forth. All these approaches stay within the conventional understanding of development: they don't constitute a radical departure from the prevailing paradigm.*

Escobar gives the example of the Pacific Coast region in Colombia to demonstrate this point. This is a highly biodiverse region with a significant percentage of the population being indigenous people. He claims that, despite 30 years of research, strategies and interventions to develop the area – including mining and palm oil plantations – poverty, inequality and violence have actually increased. For Escobar, then, the issue is not underdevelopment but excessive development.

Discussion point

To what extent do you agree with Escobar's claim that there is no real difference between sustainable development and simple plain development?

For those who criticize the very concept of sustainable development and, indeed, development itself, what are the alternatives? In the final section of this thematic study we will consider alternative views on development, including degrowth and regenerative approaches.

3.4.3 Alternative views on development and sustainability

■ Degrowth

◆ **Degrowth** argues for shrinking rather than growing economies in order to use less of the world's increasingly scarce resources.

Degrowth, according to the World Economic Forum, is a radical theory that originated in the 1970s and, in simple terms, argues for shrinking rather than growing economies in order to use less of the world's increasingly scarce resources.

One of the key tenets of degrowth theory is that well-being should come before profit and economic growth in all decisions regarding development, sustainability and economics. Some have sought to paint advocates of degrowth as wanting us all to go back to living in caves and, while this may be an amusing image, supporters of degrowth argue that there is a world of difference between this exaggerated, dystopian vision and a sensible set of policies focused on helping economies, citizens and the planet by becoming more sustainable. Degrowth, then, can be distinguished from sustainable development, as it does not make the central claim that economic growth and sustainability are not mutually exclusive.

The term 'degrowth' was first coined by the French intellectual André Gorz, who claimed, in his 1977 essay, 'Ecology and Freedom', that 'lack of realism consists in imagining that economic growth can still bring about increased human welfare, and indeed that it is still physically possible'.

There are three key principles that underpin degrowth as an approach to development and sustainability.

Abolishing economic growth

The first is abolishing economic growth as a development objective. In order to do so, societies must use fewer natural resources and will need to organize and live differently from the way in which we live today. According to ecological economists, degrowth, then, is 'an equitable downscaling of production and consumption that will reduce societies' throughput of energy and raw materials' (Mastini).

◆ **Social metabolism** is the idea that society needs a constant stream of resources, materials and energy from the environment to build, maintain and operate its structures, such as buildings, infrastructure and machinery.

The concept of a **social metabolism** is useful for understanding what this shift might look like. According to the BOKU – University of Natural Resources and Life Sciences in Austria, 'the social metabolism can be seen as a functional equivalent of biological metabolism', and refers to the way in which societies require continuous throughput of materials and energy required to build up, maintain and operate their material stocks (e.g. buildings, infrastructures, machinery, etc.) (Haberl). As Riccardo Mastini points out, this shift towards a degrowth economic model will not only result in a smaller social metabolism but also one with a different structure serving different functions.

Further growth does not increase happiness

The second principle that underpins degrowth is the assumption that above a certain level of growth, further growth does not increase human happiness. This can be seen when we consider some of the costs associated with economic growth from a human perspective – long hours, work-related stress, pollution, traffic congestion, environmental degradation and resource consumption, to name just a few.

Earth's finite resource base

Third, the objective of infinite economic growth scientifically contradicts the fact that we have a finite resource base on Earth upon which we depend.

The question, then, is whether a degrowth economic model is desirable or even possible?

Critics of this approach would argue that much – indeed, almost all – of what makes life worth living is as a result of economic growth. Kelsey Piper argues that it is economic growth that has brought us cancer treatments and neonatal intensive care units, smallpox vaccines and insulin. It is because of economic growth that, in many parts of the world, houses have indoor plumbing and gas heating and electricity. Economic growth means that infant mortality is down and life expectancies are longer than at any time in the past. While Piper does acknowledge that it is also economic growth that means that in an increasingly wealthy world we eat more meat, mostly from factory-farmed animals, emit lots more greenhouse gases, and consume and discard many more resources, she remains unconvinced that degrowth provides an alternative. Instead, Piper argues that many countries have managed to shrink carbon emissions at the same time as growing their economies, and goes on to point out the impracticality of poor countries developing up to a certain level of prosperity and then stopping, while rich countries scale down to the same level.

Supporters of degrowth, on the other hand, argue that it is an essential alternative to our current understanding of sustainable development because of a process known as 'decoupling', which lies at the heart of arguments in favour of sustainable development.

At its most simple, decoupling refers to economic output progressively using less energy and raw materials to achieve the same economic outputs due to increases in efficiency. According to advocates of sustainable development, there is no inevitable clash between economic growth and environmental impact as a result of decoupling. Proponents of degrowth theory, however, say that it is essential that we distinguish between relative and absolute decoupling.

Relative decoupling occurs when there is a decline in the ecological intensity per unit of economic output due to increases in efficiency but, as Mastini points out, the use of energy and raw materials does not decline in absolute terms. This means that ecological impacts still increase, but do so at a slower pace than growth in GDP. This allows us, collectively, to collude in a belief that we are being more sustainable as a society based on a capitalist economic model.

Essentially, resource use and ecological impact may be less per unit of production and consumption but they are still increasing overall. Instead, degrowth advocates claim that we must move towards **absolute decoupling**, where there is an absolute decline in ecological resource use over time.

Prominent advocates of degrowth, such as Sam Alexander of the Melbourne Sustainable Society Institute, have also pointed out that 'doesn't mean we are going to be living in caves with candles. Instead, it might mean people in rich countries changing their diets, living in smaller houses and driving and travelling less.' None of these, while certainly ambitious, are impossible to achieve. The question is whether there is the political will for governments and non-state actors to act against their own short-term self-interest in order to achieve them.

◆ **Relative decoupling** is a term used to describe a decline in the ecological intensity per unit of economic output due to increases in efficiency, but the use of energy and raw materials does not decline in absolute terms.

◆ **Absolute decoupling** is a term used to describe a decline in the ecological intensity per unit of economic output due to increases in efficiency along with an absolute decline in the use of energy and raw materials.

TOK

How do we decide between the opinions of experts when they disagree? Who are the experts in global politics?

These questions come from the IBDP Global Politics specification and might be applied here. Here we are presented with quite different theories and understandings of just what 'development' or 'sustainable development' are meant to mean or meant to achieve. How should we decide between them? The natural sciences have largely agreed upon methodologies and generally accepted practices to answer questions in their communities. In the human sciences, however, it is far less clear how to proceed.

THEMATIC STUDIES: Development and sustainability

◼ Regenerative approaches

◆ Regenerative development is development that uses the resources of the world in such a way that capacity for future growth is increased.

While degrowth theory is a radical alternative to sustainable development, writers such as Medard Gabel have focused on what has become known as **regenerative development**.

Gabel's starting point, in common with degrowth theory, is that sustainable development simply does not go far enough in rethinking what development should be like in order to meet the challenges of today's world:

> *Sustainable development is a half-vast approach to vast problems. Its purpose, to make life on this planet sustainable, is a noble disguise for the maintenance of the status quo. When the status quo includes hundreds of millions of acres of degraded to destroyed farmland and levelled rainforest, depleted to exhausted fisheries and aquifers, toxic-choked streams, decreasing biodiversity, and a changing climate, sustainability is simply not acceptable. In short, sustainable development is like the bromide 'do no evil'; it does not set the bar high enough. We can, and need, to do better than just sustain the unacceptable—or accept the present as the best we can do. Regeneration is the next step along the continuum of measurement tools for evaluating various solutions and strategies for development and solving problems. Regeneration's next step is to posit that solutions make systems better – stronger, more resilient – after use than before, as are soils from lands grown with regenerative agriculture.*

> *From 'Regenerative development: going beyond sustainability'*
> *and private communication*

ACTIVITY

Reflect on the quotation from Medard Gabel, which critiques sustainable development. How far do you think this is a fair criticism of sustainable development, in general, and the UN Sustainable Development Goals, in particular?

If we accept the broad definitions of development as 'the use of resources to improve the well-being of a society' and sustainable development as 'the use of resources to improve society's well-being in a way that does not impact our ability to do the same in the future', Gabel argues that what is really needed is to move beyond these to a model of regenerative development. In this case, regenerative development would be understood as using resources in such a way as to build capacity for future growth.

While sustainable development is widely considered to be an improvement on what we might term plain development, at best it simply maintains capacity. Regenerative development goes further and increases capacity. An example of how this might work in practice can be seen in agriculture where sustainable agricultural practices are a significant improvement on traditional intensive farming that leads to significant soil erosion. Sustainable farming practices keep soil erosion to replacement levels which allow the land to be farmed for generations to come. Regenerative farming practices, however, would allow us to produce food whilst also leaving the plot of land used better off. For example, while sustainable farming happens in a way so that the same quantity of soil is left after harvest, regenerative practices would actually increase the quantity and quality of that same soil. Gabel suggests that this is now both technologically and economically possible.

HL extension: Technology

Regenerative development focuses on increasing capacity and one of the ways in which this can be done is through the use of technology. This is a possible entry point to HL inquiry into the global political challenge of Technology. You may choose, for example, to inquire into how new and emerging technologies are making regenerative development possible in practice and compare different cases around the world.

Advocates of regenerative development argue that it provides a 'frame of reference for looking at the world – at our problems, resources, and options – in a way that can lead to a future of ecosystem health, economic wealth, and human prosperity' (Gabel). However, one of the challenges they face is in explaining exactly how we move beyond this to practical solutions based on more than just a hope and expectation that technology will provide the answers.

Chapter summary

In this chapter we have covered:
- the role played by globalization on both development and sustainability, and identified some of the trends as a result of globalization
- critiques of sustainable development, particularly with reference to the UN Sustainable Development Goals (SDGs)
- some of the alternative models put forward in response to current debates around sustainable development as a concept.

REVIEW QUESTIONS

Now that you have read this chapter, reflect on these questions:
- What role does globalization play in helping us to understand contemporary debates around development and sustainability?
- How do the different understandings of 'globalization' impact your understanding of these contemporary debates?
- To what extent is it possible to measure the impact of globalization on both development and sustainability?
- Are criticisms of the UN Sustainable Development Goals (SDGs) justified, and how far should this impact our support for these goals?
- How convincing are the alternatives to sustainable development, particularly degrowth theory and regenerative approaches?

Exam-style questions: development and sustainability

For generic advice on how to structure a response to a Paper 2 question, please see page 402). Remember, Section A questions are rooted firmly in one of the three thematic studies, while Section B questions will require you to integrate content from across the course.

Note, there are always claims and counterclaims expected in a Paper 2-style essay and this guidance identifies some of the claims and counterclaims you may choose to make. These are simply suggestions and you may choose to use other claims if appropriate.

Section A-style question

1 Evaluate the claim that the challenges of sustainability mean that development may no longer be possible.

■ General advice

Your response to this question should either include a definition or description or demonstrate understanding of sustainability along the lines of 'development that meets the needs of the present without compromising the ability of future generations to meet their own needs'. Your answer should also make reference to the multidimensional and contested nature of development and the different means of measuring it. In defining development, you might identify different types of development: economic, social or political. You might also discuss different models of development and how they are more or less compatible with sustainability.

■ Claims

Your claims should support the view that the challenges of sustainability mean that development may no longer be possible. They may include the following:

● Ambitious economic development (especially if synonymous with growth) and sustainability are seen as in conflict with each other. Recent and growing evidence of climate change has started to alter priorities towards the latter. For example, SDG Watch Europe, a Brussels-based pressure group, argued in 2017 that economic growth is not environmentally sustainable. Further development would only be possible if an economy can be managed without growth.

● Growth and development are funded and fuelled by debt. This is borrowing against a future that can no longer be like the past, meaning that repayment may not be possible. The financial system is already prone to instability caused by financial crises such as the crisis in 2008, the COVID-19 pandemic and the war in Ukraine, which has caused global inflation. Against this background, sustainable development looks riskier.

● It has been argued that all non-renewable resources are finite and that therefore they should not be used. Given current dependence on fossil fuels, minerals and other raw materials, sustainable development is not possible at current rates of consumption.

● Environmental evidence of degradation and the deteriorating quality of the natural environment, such as air and water and prevalence of plastics, has led to arguments that current modes of development have to stop and be reversed.

- Because the ability of the natural environment to absorb high levels of pollutants is increasingly limited, a tipping point may be reached, so it is better to halt development now. Climate change is seen increasingly as evidence that the assimilative capacity of ecosystems is being reached.

- Even if all development – sustainable and otherwise – were to stop now, some indicators such as rising sea level would continue, so development needs not only stopping but also reversing. Climatologists have argued that wealthy nations now need to adopt a degrowth strategy because sustainable development is itself an oxymoron (a contradictory term).

■ Counterclaims

Your counterclaims should support the view that the challenges of sustainability mean that development may no longer be possible. They may include the following:

- The adoption in 2015 of the UN's 17 Sustainable Development Goals for 2030 shows that there is international consensus that development remains possible but by different paths from previously.

- A series of environmental disasters related to climate change, including wildfires, hurricanes and floods, has brought the feasibility of sustainable development towards the top of the academic agenda. For example, Jeffrey Sachs has argued that technology and politics will exist and has linked further development to good governance.

- The UN Decade of Education for Sustainable Development (2005–14) implies that education can change behaviours, values and priorities to make sustainability possible. Outcomes included summits and agreements, such as Rio (2012) and Paris (2015).

- Climate change agreements such as Kyoto and Paris (2015, signed by 196 states) show that such issues are being taken seriously at the highest levels and that the decision to limit global temperature increase to 1.5 per cent shows consensus to reach risk-reducing targets.

- The emergence, adoption and government promotion of new technologies based on renewable energy supplies, such as solar panels and wind turbines, shows that businesses and consumers can respond to altered priorities. For example, in the UK, 2020 was the year that renewable energy generation overtook coal and gas generation. In 2022 Norway generated 72 per cent of its energy from renewables, Sweden 51 per cent and Brazil 46 per cent.

- Actions taken by developed countries show that further development is possible, for example The Netherlands railway running on renewables and Singapore's rooftop SolarNova programme.

■ Some other possibilities

You must remember that the examiner will expect your response to contain references to specific examples. For example, you could consider the arguments over the Amazon fires in 2022, which appeared to have tacit approval from the Bolsonaro administration.

Your response might also address the fact that this is an area of data conflict, where reliability, omission and interpretation of data are highly contestable, as well as referring to recent writing on this debate, for example the idea of Deep Adaptation or lack of political will to confront it, especially among populist leaders.

You might choose to refer to disagreements within the academic professions as mainstream economists try to argue that growth and development can be decoupled from environmental impacts. For example, Kenneth Boulding, an economist, said that, 'anyone who believes that exponential growth can go on forever in a finite world is either a madman or an economist'.

You may choose to make reference to the IPCC's 2018 critical target of 1.5 degrees (formerly 2 degrees) above baseline preindustrial levels and its likely imminent achievement (formerly by 2050 or 2100) as justification for the claim and for urgent action.

■ Conclusion

Your answer must build towards a conclusion that clearly states the extent to which you agree with the claim that the challenges of sustainability mean that development may no longer be possible.

Section B-style question

1 Examine the view that development offers the greatest challenge to state sovereignty.

■ General advice

Your response to this question should either include definitions of development and state sovereignty or these terms should be used in such a way as to demonstrate you understand exactly what they mean. The examiner will expect you to demonstrate that state sovereignty means that a state has the supreme legal responsibility and authority of an independent state to regulate and govern political life within its territory without foreign interference or influence.

Alternatively, you might choose to approach statehood as comprising the four features identified by the UN: functioning government, defined boundaries, a permanent population and the ability to enter international affairs. You should show that you understand development as a multifaceted concept that includes sustained increases in living standards and welfare, leading to higher income, improved services, reduced poverty, inequality and unemployment, and increased sustainability.

■ Claims

Your claims should support the view that development offers the greatest challenge to state sovereignty. They may include the following:

- International trade agreements, a feature of development, can lead to economic integration and therefore the erosion of state borders. For example, the Trans-Pacific Partnership and the EU require states to open their markets to foreign competition, limit their trade barriers and conform to labour or environmental standards. Within the EU, the Schengen Zone allows for freer movement than would be expected between sovereign states.

- Development is associated with the emergence of large multi- and transnational corporations (MNCs and TNCs), which can be larger than the states in which they operate and challenge the sovereignty of states by operating across their borders and influencing their decisions. These huge corporations may demand certain changes before investing within a state, such as tax breaks and regulatory exemptions.

- Globalization, another feature of development, fosters interdependence. For example, it may be hard to establish the 'economic nationality' of a product, such as a car whose components are made in different countries, yet tariffs (which raise taxes) are a part of a state's sovereignty.

- Global flows of goods, people and ideas have led to a weakening of states' power to exercise domestic policies in the face of international influences. For example, protests regarding the wearing of headscarves in Iran.

- Development has also fostered IGOs such as the UN, World Bank, International Monetary Fund (IMF), World Trade Organization and the International Criminal Court, which have created rules and regulations that can supersede domestic laws. For example, the IMF and World Bank can impose policies and conditions on states in return for loans or financial assistance. These may conflict with the state's own goals and thus limit sovereignty.

■ Counterclaims

Your counterclaims should support the view that development offers the greatest challenge to state sovereignty. They may include the following:

- Economic development can greatly enhance the power and influence of a country and therefore allow it to enhance its sovereignty through both hard and soft power. For example, its economic weight might allow it to afford a stronger defence force.

- Development might allow a state to create preferential trade agreements or spheres of political influence or, in historical terms, empires which fortify its sovereignty. For example, home-grown MNCs might actually enhance the sovereignty of their home states. Boeing, a US-based MNC, earns huge income from commercial aviation but works closely with the US government on military and weapons development, boosting its sovereignty. Similarly Huawei, a Chinese MNC, has strong ties to the government and may even use data and information to support it.

- Other factors may offer greater challenges to state sovereignty than development. For example, climate change, a common threat to all states, is forcing cooperation through international agreements, which may limit the sovereignty of individual states and inhibit development that relies on non-renewable resources.

- Other factors that may offer greater threats to state sovereignty than development are terrorism and cyberwarfare, which have made it increasingly difficult for states to maintain control of their information and communications infrastructure.

- States remain free to reassert their sovereignty by withdrawing from international organizations. A relevant example is the UK's withdrawal from the EU.

■ Some other possibilities

You must remember that the examiner will expect your response to contain references to specific examples. For example, you could point to the use of sanctions by IGOs to deliberately limit the sovereignty of states: UN members are not allowed to trade freely with Iran (as of 2023), even though it would be beneficial to both sides. You might choose to consider whether or not NGOs might be included in the list of institutions that potentially diminish sovereignty. Because their goals are often humanitarian, NGOs may highlight the weakness of sovereign states to provide for their people. Oxfam, for example, advocates for the homeless and the involvement of women in positions of power, which gives a type of internal soft power that challenges the state's authority.

■ Conclusion

Your answer must build towards a conclusion that explicitly states the extent to which you agree with the claim that development offers the greatest challenge to state sovereignty.

4 Peace and conflict

4.1

Contested meanings of peace and conflict

SYLLABUS CONTENT

By the end of this chapter, you should understand:
▶ the evolution of peace and conflict studies
▶ contested meanings in peace and conflict studies
▶ definitions, interpretations of and perspectives on:
  ▷ peace, including violence, negative and positive peace, feminist peace, and religious and spiritual peace
  ▷ conflict, including destructive and constructive conflict
  ▷ non-violence, including the different approaches to pacifism.

While the academic field of peace and conflict studies is relatively new, the quest for peace between nations has existed throughout humanity, including among indigenous people, who have provided examples of how peace can be enacted and maintained between nations. Many of these examples occurred long before encounters with colonizers created new conflicts that might have been lessened if the colonizing newcomers had respected, and perhaps even applied, indigenous principles of peace to their interactions.

One historical example of the indigenous enactment of peace is the Great Law of Peace (*Kaianere'ko:wa*). The Great Law of Peace was a complex agreement among five (later six) nations of the Haudenosaunee or Iroquois Confederacy in present-day North America.

The Great Law of Peace (1451 CE) comes from the story of Hiawatha, a Mohawk warrior who wanted to take revenge on Atatarho, a violent chief responsible for the death of his family during a war. Instead, Hiawatha was met by the Great Peacemaker – a spiritual leader named Deganawida. The two then travelled across what is today the American state of New York and the Canadian provinces of Ontario and Quebec to visit all the Haudenosaunee nations to bring about peace and reconciliation among them. The Clan Mothers in each nation influenced their people to accept Hiawatha's message. When the five nations were finally persuaded to make peace, they followed the Peacemaker to a tall white pine tree. The tree was uprooted and warriors from all nations threw their weapons into a hole. The tree was then replanted and became known as the Tree of Peace.

■ **Figure 4.1** The Haudenosaunee Confederacy Flag

The flag of the Haudenosaunee (Iroquois) Confederacy was based on the Great Law of Peace wampum.

Wampums are beads strung together to form a belt so as to tell stories or mark agreements between peoples. Here, the tree represents the Onondaga Nation, where the Peacemaker planted the Tree of Peace and under which the leaders of the original five nations buried their weapons. The white squares represent the other four nations, the Seneca, Cayuga, Oneida and Mohawk peoples. The lines extending from the nations stand for a path other nations might follow if they agree to live in peace and join the Confederacy.

4.1.1 Evolution of peace and conflict studies

The evolution of peace and conflict studies is perhaps best captured by peace and conflict researcher Oliver Richmond, who suggests that the field of study has gone through four phases in its development:

1 Conflict management, which is closely related to the realist perspective of global politics, argues that conflict is an inevitable reality of the anarchical international system. The best that can be hoped for is an absence of war, where relationships between groups and states are managed – a state that Johan Galtung calls 'negative peace'.

2 Conflict resolution, which looked to a more liberal view of conflict that sees a role for regional and international institutions in facilitating peace negotiations and helping to provide for basic human needs that are often the cause of conflict.

3 Developing peacebuilding institutions, different approaches to diplomacy, as well as humanitarian aid, and addressing genocide and other human rights violations.

4 Today a lot of the peace and conflict studies research revolves around multifaceted approaches. These approaches involve peacemaking and peacebuilding through the arts, humanities and storytelling that address challenges faced by the LGBTQ+ community, environmental devastation and issues faced by young people, women, indigenous people and other marginalized groups.

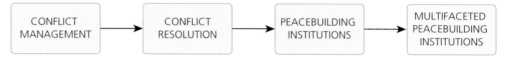

■ **Figure 4.2** The evolution of peace and conflict studies

4.1.2 Contested meanings in peace and conflict studies

Seeking a precise definition of any term has its difficulties. When reviewing literature related to terms like 'peace', 'conflict' and 'violence', the common refrain among theorists is how difficult it is to set out a satisfactory definition of any of these terms.

In your theory of knowledge class, your teacher may have chosen to study the theme of 'knowledge and language', and, as part of your discussions, you might have explored some of the reasons why settling on definitions can be challenging.

One of the reasons it can be difficult to settle on a meaning is the multifaceted nature of words. For example, take a term like peace: does it mean world peace where there is no war? Or does it mean a quiet walk in the forest? Does it mean inner peace where you have achieved, at least for a time, a personal state of calm and satisfaction with your station in life? These questions highlight how language can be vague – the meaning of peace depends on the context. It also demonstrates the ambiguity of language – peace can have multiple meanings instead of a precise, singular meaning.

◆ The **denotation** of a word is its literal or primary meaning, not the feelings or ideas an individual may connect with it.

◆ **Connotations** are feelings or ideas that certain words evoke in individuals, or something suggested or implied by a word.

Furthermore, words have both **denotations** and **connotations**, and can be used and applied in many ways. In the case of peace, it can literally mean there is no conflict between two parties. However, the connotation of two parties peacefully coexisting may mean that not only is there no conflict, but there is also a warmth, kindness and caring nature to their relationship. An element of ambiguity and interpretation built into our language results in a lack of clarity and precision when we attempt to define a word.

Finally, consider that there are more than 7,000 languages spoken in the world today, some of which, like the Inuit of the Canadian Arctic region, do not have a specific word for a term like peace (though they have a number of words that relate well to the idea of peace).

The purpose of this brief introduction to the challenges we face in defining terms in global politics is to highlight that meanings are contested and are rarely, if ever, just a matter of providing a dictionary definition. Figure 4.3 shows you a summary of some of the reasons we have outlined for why language can have contested meanings.

Throughout this chapter, we will endeavour to examine the multifaceted and debated meanings of terms like peace, violence, conflict and non-violence. We will save discussions related to causes of conflict and approaches to resolving conflict to subsequent chapters.

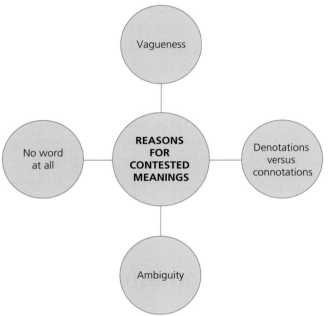

■ **Figure 4.3** The challenge of creating meaning

Discussion point

What are the challenges of defining terms like 'peace', 'conflict' and 'violence' in the context of global politics? How might the multifaceted nature of these terms affect our understanding of global conflicts?

4.1.3 Definitions, interpretations of and perspectives on violence and peace

In this chapter, we will explore the contested meanings of peace, conflict, violence and non-violence. However, as noted above, it is challenging to discuss these terms in isolation as in real-world events they all overlap. To help, we will first explore the notions of violence and peace separately and then bring them together to show how they are linked.

When we look at definitions of peace and conflict, we could start with peace, then look at how peace breaks down and conflicts starts. Is our world essentially peaceful and occasionally interrupted by points of conflict? Or is it filled with conflict and only occasional periods of peace?

As we have discussed throughout this textbook, realists argue that the world is mostly conflict-ridden and that times of peace are only exceptions to the normal state of things. On the other hand, some liberals argue that a state of peace is possible and that international institutions, such as the United Nations or the World Trade Organization, can foster cooperation among states to help to resolve conflicts and so promote peace. Their view is that these types of institutions can set rules and expectations, as well as be a place for discussion and negotiation to occur when conflict arises.

Peace is a multi-layered concept. It represents a condition of harmony, justice and cooperation at every level, from personal to global, where members of a society can flourish at all levels.

- At the community level, peace occurs where justice prevails, rights are respected and individuals can express themselves without fear of retribution. It involves equal access to resources, social services and opportunities for all.

- At the national level, peace can signify a country free of civil strife, with a government that ensures the safety, rights and well-being of its citizens.

- On a global or international level, peace usually means the absence of war or violent conflicts between nations. But it's more than that – it also means international cooperation, respect for international laws, and efforts to address global issues such as poverty and inequality.

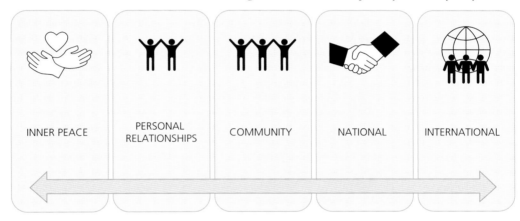

INNER PEACE · PERSONAL RELATIONSHIPS · COMMUNITY · NATIONAL · INTERNATIONAL

■ **Figure 4.4** Peace: a multi-layered concept

ACTIVITY

Create a mind map that explores the spectrum of peace. Include elements like harmony, justice, freedom, cooperation and the absence of war.

◆ **Deprivation** means the absence or too little of something considered to be a basic necessity. An individual can be in a state of deprivation if they have nothing, or too little of a basic necessity.

■ Violence

According to Johan Galtung, peace can be either negative or positive. While the term 'negative' can be confusing, it simply means that the violence has been removed, or it is absent. It does not mean that positive changes have taken place in order to create a more thorough and long-lasting peace in society.

So, we can say that one of the main characteristics of peace is the absence of violence. If that is the case, then our understanding of what peace actually looks like must be based on how we define violence.

Galtung states simply that 'violence is needs **deprivation**'.

Johan Galtung (1930–2024)

Johan Galtung is an influential figure in the academic field of Peace and Conflict Studies. Born in Oslo, Norway, he is often called the 'father of peace studies' due to his groundbreaking work developing theories and methods to understand and resolve conflict.

Galtung began his academic journey in mathematics and sociology, but his experiences growing up during the Second World War and witnessing its devastating effects motivated him to dedicate his life to the pursuit of peace. He established the Peace Research Institute Oslo (PRIO) in 1959, one of the first centres in the world of its kind.

■ **Figure 4.5** Johan Galtung

PRIO focused on researching the conditions for peaceful relations between nations, groups and individuals. In 1964, Galtung founded the now influential *Journal of Peace Research*, which provides a platform for scholars to share their insights on peace and conflict studies.

Galtung has written many books and articles on the development of the foundational concepts of peace and conflict studies, including positive and negative peace, peacebuilding, the three types of violence, and the ABC and PIN conflict analysis triangles.

Direct violence and negative peace

There are several components to direct violence:

- it is intentional and personal
- it is intended to injure or hurt another individual
- it can impact one or many individuals, either physically or psychologically
- those experiencing direct violence may immediately complain, as the violence is instantly recognizable as such and quickly acknowledged as hurtful.

For example, if the people in a state are experiencing injury or even death due to war, they are experiencing direct, personal violence. If we end the war, we remove the possibility of injury or death – the direct violence – and create a 'negative' peace. The peace is seen as negative because the violence causing the damage has been removed, and further possibilities of injury and death due to the actions of the violent actors have been removed.

However, this does not mean that anything has been done to improve the societal structures that may have caused the conflict in the first place. The grievances that may have caused the war in the first place have not been addressed. The term 'negative', therefore, simply means that the peace that is being described is a peace that is only without personal violence.

In short, negative peace is simply the absence of direct or personal violence. However, this is a rather limited understanding of peace and violence. If peace is more than simply not experiencing direct violence but instead involves creating and developing positive structures that make peace long-lasting, then how we define peace and violence will be broader than what negative peace has to offer. Before exploring what might qualify as positive peace, we will look at two aspects of violence that significantly broaden its meaning.

Structural violence

According to Galtung, there are structures in society that cause harm or are unjust. An example of this could be a government that refuses to allow a same-sex couple to marry. In fact, Galtung argues that structural violence is essentially the same as social injustices like this example, so you may find it helpful to think of structural violence in this way.

Structural violence differs to direct violence in the following ways:

● Unlike direct violence, it is difficult to identify an individual or group who is directly aiming to hurt another individual or group in a structurally violent act. Instead, structural violence is built into the structures of society or an organization and reveals itself as unequal power, which results in unequal opportunities. This might mean that resources are unevenly distributed, for example income, educational opportunities or medical services. Therefore, structural violence relates to policy and how those policies limit freedoms and opportunities.

● Because we can clearly see direct violence, it is not unusual for people to pay more attention to it than they do to structural violence. Structural acts of violence are built into the framework of how a society operates, so unlike direct violence, they may sometimes go unnoticed; they may be viewed as the natural state of things.

Structural violence that goes undetected is sometimes referred to as latent or unseen. However, when structural violence is revealed, we say it has manifested itself. When this occurs, the response by those who benefit from the structural violence may be direct violence. This is because they want to ensure that the benefits of structural violence can be maintained. Similarly, those experiencing structural violence may resort to direct violence in order to break down the barriers between their actual circumstances and their preferred circumstances.

CASE STUDY

Migrant labour as direct and structural violence

In some parts of the world, particularly in Middle Eastern countries (for example, Saudi Arabia, the UAE and Qatar) and in south-east Asian countries (for example, Malaysia, Singapore and China), legal structures are put in place by governments to make it easier for employers to exploit migrant workers. They provide a large supply of cheap labour to foster significant economic growth and provide cheap domestic labour in the form of cleaning, cooking and childcare.

Some people argue that this is positive, as migrant workers are able to send remittances back home to their families. As we have seen, this also helps to increase the gross national income (GNI) of the origin country. However, the system is becoming more and more controversial and more people see it as exploitation.

In countries where migrant labour is most popular, there are not many regulations and protections for migrant workers. They often face low pay, bad working conditions and mistreatment from employers. Racial discrimination and gender-based violence are common.

The Kafala system is a programme in some Middle Eastern countries where the government gives local people or businesses permits to hire foreign workers. The sponsor is responsible for the workers' travel expenses and living arrangements. These can range from shared living spaces similar to dorms or, for domestic workers, living in the sponsor's house.

Typically, this system falls under the management of departments dealing with domestic affairs, not those dealing with labour issues. As a result, the workers often do not receive protection from the host country's labour laws. There have been reports of employers taking away passports, visas and mobile phones, and restricting domestic workers to their homes. Workers have to rely on their sponsors to stay in the country legally. However, their status can be revoked by the sponsors for any reason, which puts the labourers at risk. This gives the sponsors a lot of power, which can be misused.

There are also stories of debt bondage. While a lot of host countries require employers to cover recruitment fees, workers often have to pay these. The workers might be required to take out loans to cover the costs of the recruitment fees or travel expenses. It's common for employers to lower or withhold workers' salaries to cover these loans or as a form of punishment.

One example of debt bondage is the brick kiln industry in South Asia, particularly in countries like Pakistan and India. In these regions, labourers, often including entire families, work in brick kilns to repay a loan they have taken from the kiln owner. The terms of these loans are typically very exploitative, with high interest rates and low wages, making it nearly impossible for the workers to repay the debt. The labourers are bound to work at the kiln until their debt is fully paid off, which can take many years, often leading to a cycle of inherited debt that can persist for generations (Reynolds et al.; Anti-Slavery International).

There are also some cases of recruiters using deception or pressure to manipulate workers into forced labour. It is common for workers to be tricked into accepting low wages and poor working conditions by signing contracts, sometimes in languages they do not understand. Non-domestic workers frequently live in cramped living quarters and do not have sufficient health care.

The Middle East is behind other regions in approving international agreements that have the potential to protect workers' rights. For instance, none of the host countries have agreed to the International Labour Organization's Domestic Workers Convention. This convention promises to set a minimum wage, stop forced labour and ensure safe working conditions, among other protections.

We can therefore see the Kafala system as a structure of violence. There is not a single individual that is responsible for the violence. Instead, it is a system that puts structures in place that cause inequality and discrimination. For some, the system is not even questioned. It is considered simply to be the 'way things are', and some people argue that migrant workers should 'just be thankful to have a job'.

In addition to structural violence, the Kafala system creates direct violence. Because of structural violence, employers have the means to engage in direct acts of violence towards workers, for example physical abuse, or causing sleep deprivation, hunger or exhaustion from overwork. Recognizing the inequities and injustice of the system and changing the regulations so that fair wages and working conditions are the norms is what we call 'positive peacebuilding', which we will discuss further later in this thematic study.

HL extension: Poverty and Equality

All three forms of violence reflect, as Galtung has suggested, a deprivation of needs. Structural violence in particular could be a good concept to start from or link to as part of an inquiry into the global political challenges of Poverty and/or Equality. Very often, impoverishment is linked to the structures (or lack thereof) that exist within a society.

Cultural violence

Cultural violence is often confused with structural violence. While structural violence can cause cultural violence and cultural violence can lead to structural violence, they are not the same thing.

Cultural violence is related to aspects of culture, such as religion, art, language, sport and ideology. These can be used to justify or legitimize direct or structural violence. It is important to remember that each feature is an aspect of culture and does not reflect entire cultures.

Galtung explains that cultural violence makes direct and structural violence look or feel right or, at the very least, not feel wrong. Therefore, cultural violence operates as an effective justification tool. This means that instead of creating a needs deficit, like direct and structural violence, cultural violence creates the atmosphere needed to enact direct and structural violence. Cultural violence is the stage on which direct and structural violence is played out.

As Galtung states in his article 'Cultural violence': 'One way cultural violence works is by changing the moral colour of an act from 'red' – wrong, to 'green' – right, or at least to 'yellow' – acceptable.' Galtung shows us how the three types of violence are linked in his Violence Triangle, seen in Figure 4.6.

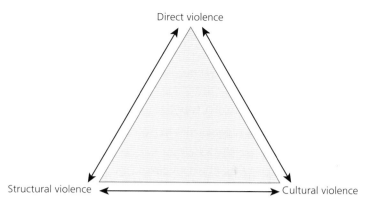

Direct violence

Structural violence ← → Cultural violence

■ **Figure 4.6** Galtung's Violence Triangle

● **Extended essay**

If you are interested in writing an extended essay on peace and conflict, you may want to use Galtung's Violence Triangle as a theoretical foundation for examining a conflict.

While the triangle shows direct violence at the top, none of the three forms of violence is seen as a starting point or end point, and none has priority over another.

For example, if we were to place direct and structural violence at the bottom of the triangle, we could say that it is cultural violence that legitimizes direct and structural violence. If we turned the triangle so that direct violence is at the top, then structural and cultural violence can be viewed as sources of direct violence. Finally, if we turned the triangle one more time so that structural violence is at the top of the triangle, then we could say that structural violence reinforces or causes cultural violence and that the structures in place provide the loopholes or even permission for the acts of direct violence. Because violence can flow in either direction, our figure has arrows pointing in both directions.

Galtung offered examples where acts of violence could be viewed as starting with any of the three types. However, he does state that an act of violence usually tends to move from cultural to structural to direct violence. He explains that the culture preaches, urges us on, and dulls us into seeing structures of exploitation or repression as normal and natural, or worse, we are lulled into not seeing exploitation at all. From this comes direct violence, where oppressed people use direct violence to escape structural violence. This is then met with counter-violence to keep the structures of oppression intact.

We can also think of the three types of violence in this way:

● direct violence is an event
● structural violence is a process or a framework that institutionalizes violence
● cultural violence is a way of thinking.

Consider the real-world example of migrant workers we saw in the earlier case study. You hear a story of a live-in domestic helper that works 14-hour days, is required to sleep on the kitchen floor and earns very little money. This is a direct act of violence by the employers. However, because the worker is a migrant, the owner is not accountable to the country's labour laws. This is a violent structure or framework. However, this does not explain why the employer believes this behaviour is acceptable. Is it because there is prejudice against the migrant workers' culture and migrant workers are seen as less than those of the country in which they are working? Is it because there is a cultural mentality of individualism that encourages citizens to take care of their own (this could be family members or fellow citizens) and neglect those who are seen as different? Perhaps, it is an economic, cultural perspective: work hard, and you too can achieve a position of power where you can choose to pay employees as little as possible.

If, as Galtung has stated, violence creates needs deficits, then perhaps violence can be understood as the shortfall between an individual's current situation and what they need. Of course, the next question is what counts as a need.

Choose a current
conflict and analyse
it using Galtung's
triangle of violence
(direct, structural and
cultural). Present a case
study explaining how
these forms of violence
manifest and interact in
the chosen conflict.

Discussion point

Describe the relationship between direct, structural and cultural violence. How do they interact and influence each other in perpetuating conflict?

Basic human needs

Galtung suggests that we should consider two aspects of needs: one is basic human needs, and the other is ecological balance. Table 4.1 is a summary of his suggestions on human needs only.

■ **Table 4.1** Galtung's suggestions on human needs

Type of need	Suggestions
Security needs	• To avoid direct violence • No individual violence, such as verbal abuse or torture • No collective violence, such as wars
Welfare needs	• Nutrition, water, air, sleep, exercise, shelter • Protection and treatment of disease and illness • Protection against excessive strain or overwork • Opportunities for self-expression, dialogue or education
Identity needs	• Creativity and ways to pursue happiness • New experiences • Affection, belongingness and relationships • Sense of purpose
Freedom needs	• Choice in receiving and expressing information and opinion • Choice of people and places to visit and places to live • Choice of spouse • Choice of way of life

While scholars debate the definition of a need, we could start by suggesting part of David Wiggins' description of a need being seen as someone lacking something that harms their functioning in life as a human being and that whatever they are lacking is integral to that person having a life of minimal value.

On the basis of Wiggins' definition, Brian Orend lists five aspects of human needs:

1 Personal security
2 Material subsistence – having enough resources to meet the minimum standards for maintaining health and well-being, such as food, water, clothing, shelter and sometimes health care and education
3 Basic equality
4 Personal freedom
5 Recognition as a member of the human community.

Actual circumstance versus potential circumstance

Galtung's ideas of violence should be understood in the context of needs (such as those suggested in the list above and in Table 4.1) and not in the context of wants.

For example, if I prevent you from eating junk food, you are not experiencing direct violence. This is a *want*, not a *need*. Related to this is when something unavoidable, like an earthquake, occurs. An earthquake is, currently, an unavoidable natural disaster. While the results of the earthquake may feel violent, any analysis in terms of direct, structural or cultural violence is not required. But, if we could find a way to prevent an earthquake, then an analysis of violence would be appropriate (why didn't the government put measures in place to prevent the earthquake from causing such devastation?) Furthermore, if a government did not put regulations in place, or construction companies were not required to take the appropriate steps needed in order to construct a safe building that would withstand an earthquake, then this would be an example of structural violence. See the Rana Plaza collapse in Bangladesh as an example.

What Galtung suggests, then, is that violence is anything that gets in the way (or increases) the distance between your current or actual circumstance and a potentially better, more peaceful circumstance. So, an act of violence is when a barrier is created (or made larger) so that you are unable to move from your current, unpeaceful situation to a better, more peaceful situation (see Figure 4.7).

'Violence' could be described as a barrier to peace, and the 'perpetrators of violence' are those individuals, groups of people or organizations that uphold or create these barriers to peace. Both direct and structural violence create these needs-deficits.

For example, if the government in your country uses fear of persecution or imprisonment to prevent you from practising your religion or sharing your opinion on, for instance, the state of democracy, then this prevention of freedom of religion or opinion is an act of violence. This [hypothetical!] repression by the state authorities is a barrier between your actual circumstance (no freedom of religion or opinion) and your potential circumstance (being able to practise your religion and express your opinion).

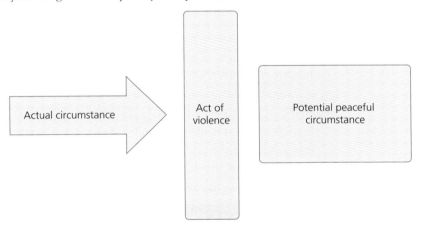

■ **Figure 4.7** Barriers to peace: actual versus potential circumstance

TOK

As you'll see, there are a number of different definitions of 'peace'. That there are different perspectives is not the interesting TOK point (although recognizing the differences is crucial to a TOK analysis!). The interesting point comes when we discuss the impact of those differences on the knowledge produced.

Consider the relative impact of each of the different theories of peace. In what ways do each of the perspectives add new elements to the discussions? Do some perspectives create new conversations that might not have arisen in the other theories?

Consider the different conceptions of peace, presented here. Do you think that some are more effective, or practical, or easier to enact? Compare your decisions with another student and discuss why and where your ideas differ or are similar.

■ Positive peace

While Galtung's perspectives on peace are sometimes presented as a definition, Galtung himself suggests that 'nobody has any monopoly on defining peace'. So, while he does argue that peace is the absence of violence, he further explains that it is 'not a definition' but rather a description of what is absent when peace exists.

If negative peace is the removal of direct, personal violence, then positive peace is the removal of structural and cultural violence. Now that we have offered some possibilities of what structural and cultural violence might be, let's explore what might constitute positive peace.

As Galtung states in his article 'Violence, peace, and peace research', 'The absence of structural violence … we shall refer to as positive peace.' Positive peace includes concepts like legitimacy and justice. An unjust structure or relationship is not peaceful, so in order to achieve positive peace, injustice must be removed. This extends to unjust economic relations between different countries and regions of the world, and between majority and minority groups within a country. It also extends to unjust personal relations between individuals. Furthermore, it applies to some of the ways we group members of society. Positive peace would reflect surpressing the idea that some ethnicities are superior to others, male domination, socio-economic advantages and even the idea that achievement is purely of one's own doing (see Michael Sandel's *The Tyranny of Merit*).

If the opposite of violence is peace, then the opposite of cultural violence would be cultural peace. If there are many examples of direct and structural peace within a culture, then it might be said that it is a peaceful culture.

Ramsbotham et al. have challenged the idea of positive peace, calling it 'deeply problematic'. They explain that 'injustice' is often equated to 'perceived injustice', which broadens the idea of injustice so that it also includes all of politics. They argue that nothing is more characteristic of perceived injustice than violent conflicts where 'all parties genuinely believe that they are victims of injustice and that therefore "justice" is on their side'. Furthermore, some fight against perceived injustice yet use force in order to do so.

That said, there is exploitation and injustice, much of which is built into the structures of society. The exploiters may even be as unaware of the structural injustices that they are taking part in. Consider some of the injustices you have learned about in global politics that you are part of yet were unaware of until now.

Perspectives

Critiques of Galtung's ideas of peace

Dustin Sharp has criticized Galtung's ideas of positive peace.

First, he sees the term 'negative' as somewhat problematic. Negative peace is quite desirable and, in some situations, could be thought of as an incredible achievement. Sharp also wonders if viewing peace as the absence of violence inaccurately suggests that peace cannot exist alongside violence as part of the complex modern societies in which we live. He urges us not to perceive peace and violence as an on-off button.

Second, he questions Galtung's seemingly clear distinction between negative and positive peace. He suggests that they are not distinct because, first of all, negative peace must be established, and then work on positive peace can be started. Instead, 'both might be found to coexist in complex patterns and to varying degrees in the same country or region'. He suggested that it might be best to look at progress towards negative peace and positive peace on their own **continuums** (see Figure 4.8).

◆ A **continuum** is something that keeps on going and changing over time.

Discussion point

Explain Johan Galtung's distinction between negative and positive peace. How do these concepts help in understanding the complexities of peace and violence in global politics?

Instead of looking at negative and positive peace as existing only along one continuum:

Negative peace ⟷ Positive peace

Sharp suggests two continua that might look like this:

Initial stages of negative peace ⟶ Achievement of negative peace

Initial stages of positive peace ⟶ Achievement of positive peace

■ **Figure 4.8** Sharp's negative and positive peace continuums

Sharp argues that the idea of positive peace as social justice is too broad and vague to offer a meaningful vision of peace. He suggests that concepts like positive peace and structural violence could be viewed as loose metaphors instead of a model or descriptions of what peace is.

To avoid this, some scholars have suggested that we should implement specific measures of peacefulness, such as human rights and security, which might be achievable. For example, the Institute for Economics and Peace's (IEP's) annual Positive Peace Report breaks down the concept of positive peace into eight pillars (see Figure 4.9).

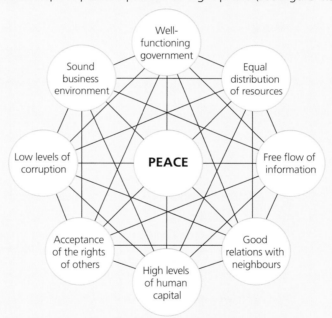

■ **Figure 4.9** The IEP's 'Pillars of Positive Peace' (adapted from Vision of Humanity)

Third, Sharp suggests that the idea that positive peace is the breaking down of structural violence is problematic because it limits the causes of inequalities to societal structures and neglects to include inequalities which may result from things like 'luck, grit, intelligence, individual choices and agency, and many other factors'. He is also concerned that the focus on oppressive social structures may take away from the role that inner peace, relational peace and peaceful interaction with the environment can play in bringing about a truly peaceful society.

Finally, Sharp worries that attempts to enact positive peace as social justice could result in widening intervention to a degree that we find ourselves engaging in acts of neocolonialism. We will explore this concern further when we examine the notion of the Responsibility to Protect (R2P) later in this thematic study.

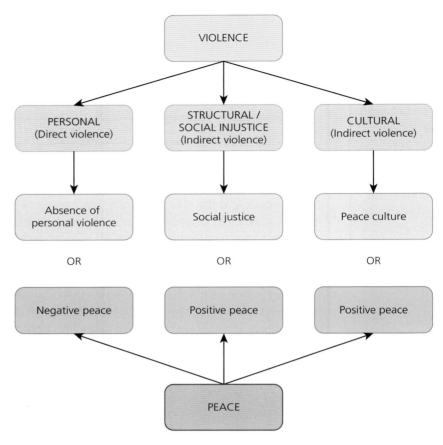

■ **Figure 4.10** Galtung's extended concepts of peace and violence

TOK

Section 4 includes quite a few models of the theories being discussed (for example, Galtung's various models, the IEP's 'Pillars of Positive Peace' and Ramsbotham et al.'s conflict escalation and de-escalation).

All areas of knowledge make use of such visual models in order to help others understand the ideas, but how helpful do you think they are? What do they add that written analysis doesn't offer?

Consider this TOK essay title from May 2023:

'Are visual representations always helpful in the communication of knowledge?'

Reflect on the various models and visual representations used in this textbook. Make a list of ways in which they are helpful and ways in which they might not be helpful. Do they help clarify the ideas, and in what ways? However, do they also shape the knowledge you gain in ways that might not be intentional? Discuss with a partner or develop an outline for an essay on this title to help you practise for your own TOK essay.

■ Peace as balance of power

The balance of power theory of peace suggests that the best way to guarantee national security is to ensure no single country is powerful enough to control others in their region or anywhere in the world. If a country becomes too powerful, it could be seen as a threat that might cause other countries to either band together for protection, boost their own defences or both. The core element of peace as a balance of power is to make going to war too dangerous and, by doing so, maintain peace.

In analysing balance of power approaches to peace, both Henry Kissinger and Hans Morgenthau suggested that there have only been 12 periods where something resembling a balance of power systems has existed in human history, none of which was particularly peaceful. The reason for this may be that the alliances between countries that are created in order to develop balances of power may not be strong enough to ensure some countries don't engage in aggressive foreign policy.

There may be several reasons for this.

● First, there is a tendency of some members of alliances to 'free ride'. This means they do not meet their obligations to maintain their own military at agreed levels. For example, in recent years, most NATO members have not met their minimum military spending expectations.

● Second, small disputes can become larger through 'chaining'. Chaining occurs when alliance members agree that an attack on any member is the same as an attack on all members. This creates situations where one state, perhaps even a weak state, ends up dragging the rest of the alliance into the conflict like prisoners in a chain gang, so creating a much larger conflict than was originally the case.

Instead of adopting the balance of power approach to peace, most states tend to take a more nuanced, multifaceted approach. States may ally or 'jump on the bandwagon' with an aggressor. They might do this in order to share in the benefits of being the victors in the conflict. They may also take this approach in order to avoid being a target of the aggressor nation themselves.

Alternatively, states may find ways to continue the conflict between the states involved in order to see both states weakened, so gathering more power for themselves.

◼ Feminist peace

When we talk about peace and violence in the world, it's not as simple as looking at isolated incidents. Feminist peace research tries to understand how things like gender, where you come from, your class and other parts of who you are can change how power is used in a situation. This type of study isn't just about understanding peace – it's also about trying to make things fairer. By focusing on these issues, we can aim to make a world that is more peaceful for everyone.

People often think about feminism as making sure men and women are treated the same. However, there are many ways to think about this. Some of the most interesting work in feminism and gender studies comes from researchers who look at how different types of unfairness can overlap or 'intersect'. These scholars often show how the overlap of different aspects, like class, race, gender, ethnicity, religion, sexuality and disability, can make oppression worse, making the situation even more challenging for marginalized or vulnerable groups. This approach gives us a fuller understanding of how power is distributed in society. Intersectional feminism shows us that we can't solve one type of unfairness without looking at others. This means *all* forms of discrimination and inequality are connected and should be addressed together.

By thinking about these ideas, we can start to ask new questions about how gender affects peace and conflict. For example, 'Who benefits most from peace?' and 'Do people of different genders experience war and peace differently?' These types of questions let us define peace from a gender-focused viewpoint.

Asking these questions lets us broaden our understanding of peace in various ways:

● It helps us think about how people of different genders experience conflict differently.

● It makes us consider how gender roles in politics, power and security can affect things like war and traditional power structures.

● It also shows us how people of different genders are impacted differently by conflicts and how women are often left out when we try to solve conflicts and establish peace.

One key aspect of studying feminist peace is its focus on freedom and change. The aim is to redefine our idea of peace to include the real-life experiences of people who have lived through conflict and war. This way of thinking challenges the usual way we talk about peace, which is often focused only on the state, and not the individuals within the state. Instead, studying peace through a gender lens shows us the importance of individual experiences and actions. It shows us that big, general ideas about peace are not enough. They often overlook the real, personal experiences that people have, from war to domestic violence to poverty. This way of studying peace pushes us to understand peace in a way that includes these personal experiences.

■ Peace in religious and spiritual traditions

This section will look at peace in the context of several faith traditions, though it will not explore any of their religious practices beyond that.

For many individuals throughout the world, the source of their pursuit of peace is grounded in their faith traditions. As we have done so far, there is value in considering the different theoretical meanings of peace. However, the spiritual foundations of peace that have existed within religious practice for millennia have been the source of efforts to create peace for many.

This is not to say that religion has not played a factor in, or been a cause of, violence and conflict. Among others, Karen Armstrong, in her book *Fields of Blood: Religion and the History of Violence*, explores this question in detail. However, the purpose of this section is to briefly look at how peace is reflected in various faith traditions.

There are two important things to keep in mind whenever we study religious or spiritual traditions.

First, given the nuances within each faith tradition, it is challenging and sometimes impossible to say, for example, 'All Christians believe X.' As a result, we will offer some initial thoughts regarding peace in several spiritual traditions and then offer some examples. You are encouraged to explore the vast literature on peace as it relates to the many faith traditions in our world today.

Second, there are dozens of religions, spiritual traditions and many more denominations within each religion. Trying to touch on all the different traditions would require more space than we have here. As a result, this section will simply be an attempt to provide a starting point for you to explore the various traditions around the world.

● TOK

Religious knowledge systems are hugely complex – far more complex than many people outside any religious knowledge community might realize. A further complication that arises when trying to understand religious knowledge systems is that individuals are enacting the religious practices and beliefs, meaning in many cases the individual's actions seem to contrast with a central tenet (belief) of the religion, and the individual's actions might impact what someone outside the religious tradition says about that tradition.

As with any reflection on the claims of an area of knowledge, you must take into account your own background beliefs and assumptions and consider their impact on how you interpret the claims. In this case, you might disagree with some of these characterizations of religious belief, but you might think about what has impacted this disagreement. Is it based on your understanding of the religious tradition, or on events that might not give you a full picture?

Hinduism

Hindu dharma is a concept of social order and duty that sustains the whole universe. It includes the virtue and discipline of ahimsa. Ahimsa is one of the central ethics of Hinduism, which means that one should avoid both the desire to harm and the act of harming any living thing. Ahimsa is not just non-violence; it means avoiding any harm, whether physical, mental or emotional.

Jainism

Most Jains today live in India. Unlike any other religion, non-violence or ahimsa defines Jainism. The practice of non-violence is linked to the Jain belief that all beings have a soul and, as a result, it is critical to avoid any speech, thought or actions that could cause harm to any living being. Many Jains sweep the ground before them as they walk so they will not accidentally step on an insect and will eat only fruits and vegetables that have already fallen from the vine.

Buddhism

In addition to the Four Noble Truths and Eightfold Path followed by adherents of Buddhism, there are also five ethical precepts, or the Panch Shila, that include **abstaining** from violence. This **prohibition** of violence towards all living beings, or the Dhammapada, is believed to be composed of the Buddha's own words. It instructs followers to avoid acts that cause injury to other beings. The Buddha warns against harsh speech and certain occupations that cause violence to humans and animals, including the trade of weapons and animal slaughter.

◆ To **abstain** from something is to not do it, or have it, especially if it is something considered to be enjoyable.

◆ **Prohibition** is a law or rule that officially stops something happening.

Christianity

Jesus, the central Christian figure, encouraged his followers to 'love our neighbour as ourselves'. He also challenged his disciples and followers in his 'Sermon on the Mount' to love their enemy and actively return good for evil.

> *You have heard that they were told, 'An eye for an eye and a tooth for a tooth.' But I tell you not to resist injury, but if anyone strikes you on your right cheek, turn the other to him too … You have heard that they were told, 'You must love your neighbour and hate your enemy.' But I tell you, love your enemies and pray for your persecutors.*

> *Matthew 5:38–46*

◆ **Mennonites** are a pacifist religious group that have roots in Eastern Europe. They immigrated to the Americas in the late 1800s and early 1900s after facing persecution.

Perhaps the most influential Christian pacifist denomination has been the Society of Friends or Quakers, which arose in the 1600s in England under George Fox and Margaret Fell. Quakers believe that there is 'that of God' or the divine light in all of us. Because humans are seen as part of a collective divinity, it is important to treat all human beings with a degree of respect and kindness that reflects being part of the divine. The **Mennonites** are another pacifist religious group that have roots in Eastern Europe. They immigrated to the Americas in the late 1800s and early 1900s after facing persecution. While they tend not to subscribe to this notion of God, they hold firm to Jesus' teachings and have practised conscientious objection – the refusal to participate in war – throughout the world.

Islam

The term Islam is related to salam, whose root meaning is peace. The essential message of the Qur'an with regard to non-violence and peace is highlighted by teaching that Allah calls on all of humanity, and Muslims in particular, to practise peace and not destroy life. In addition, the Qur'an also stresses the importance of inclusion and respect for others.

Ubuntu

Ubuntu is not a religion but is a philosophy of peace that is practised in parts of Africa. After apartheid ended in South Africa, Desmond Tutu, an Anglican Church minister, and others began a process of truth and reconciliation. As part of this, Tutu emphasized the philosophy of Ubuntu in the context of his Christian faith. He explained that Ubuntu is a South African Zulu proverb that says: 'I am a person through other people. My humanity is tied to yours.'

Tutu explained that Ubuntu is:

> *the essence of being human. … We think of ourselves far too frequently as individuals, separated from one another, whereas you are connected, and what you do affects the whole world. When you do well, it spreads out; it is for the whole of humanity.*

> *Desmond Tutu,* No Future without Forgiveness

In the context of his spiritual practice, Tutu taught that:

> *God wants humans to overcome the divisions they have created between each other. We need to realize that every human being is precious. Then we need to take concrete steps toward reconciliation, which involves confession and forgiveness and making a new start. This is needed on the interpersonal level as well as the international level.*

> *Quoted in Gish and Gish,* Desmond Tutu: A Biography

Figure 4.11 is a collection of quotations from selected religious texts. It is important to note that the wording here might vary slightly depending on the translation, but the core sentiment remains the same.

Hinduism

Consider all creatures of the world as your friend. See all beings as your own self.

As the footprints of all smaller animals are encompassed in the footprint of an elephant, all virtues are included in non-violence.

There is nothing higher than the virtue of non-violence because it comprehends all virtues.

The Hindu epic Mahabharata

Jainism

All breathing, existing, living, sentient creatures should not be slain nor treated with violence, nor abused, nor tormented, nor driven away. This is the pure unchangeable law.

All beings hate pains; therefore, one should not kill them. This is the quintessence of wisdom: not to kill anything.

Sutrakritanga Sutra

Buddhism

All men [beings] tremble at punishment, all men fear death. Likening others to oneself, one should neither slay nor cause to slay. All men tremble at punishment; all men love life. Likening others to oneself, one should neither slay nor cause to slay.

The Dhammapada, *X: 1–2*

All fear death. None are unafraid of sticks and knives. Seeing yourself in others, Don't kill, don't harm.

The Dhammapada, *18*

Judaism

Depart from evil, and do good; seek peace, and pursue it.

Psalm 34: 14

For out of Zion shall go forth instruction and the word of the Lord from Jerusalem. He shall judge between the nations and shall arbitrate for many peoples; they shall beat their swords into plowshares, and their spears into pruning hooks; nation shall not lift up sword against nation, neither shall they learn war anymore.

Isaiah 2:4

Taoism

Weapons are the tools of violence; all decent men detest them.

Weapons are the tools of fear; a decent man will avoid them except in the direst necessity and, if compelled, will use them only with the utmost restraint. Peace is his highest value. If the peace has been shattered, how can he be content? His enemies are not demons but human beings like himself. He doesn't wish them personal harm. Nor does he rejoice in victory. How could he rejoice in victory and delight in the slaughter of men?

Tao Te Ching by Lao Tzu (translated by Stephen Mitchell)

Christianity

Blessed are those who hunger and thirst for righteousness, for they will be filled.

Blessed are the merciful, for they will receive mercy.

Blessed are the pure in heart, for they will see God.

Blessed are the peacemakers, for they will be called children of God.

Matthew 5: 6–9

Do not repay anyone evil for evil, but take thought for what is noble in the sight of all. If it is possible, so far as it depends on you, live peaceably with all … Let us then pursue what makes for peace and for mutual upbuilding.

Romans 12:17–18; 14:19

We utterly deny all outward wars and strife and fighting with outward weapons for any end or under any pretense whatever; this is our testimony to the whole world.

The Quaker George Fox, to Charles II of England in 1660

■ **Figure 4.11** Quotations from selected religious texts

4.1.4 Definitions, interpretations of and perspectives on conflict

Galtung explained that peace theory is closely connected with conflict theory, particularly regarding negative peace.

The term 'conflict' comes from the Latin word *confligere*, which means 'to strike together'. Morton Deutsch refers to conflict as a situation that manifests itself whenever incompatible activities occur. In a general sense, conflict occurs when an individual or a group feels that their position, needs, interests or concerns are being threatened or challenged by another individual or group.

Conflicts can arise from many factors, including:

- differing goals
- personality clashes

- competition for resources
- relationship disputes
- diverse values and beliefs, and even communication styles.

Conflict can also be influenced by history, culture, identity, perspective and technology, and it can occur at all levels of society.

Different types of conflict include:

- internal conflict
- emotional conflict
- conflict between two individuals, or between groups at the community or national level
- conflict beyond the borders of a country where two states enter into conflict, which may draw in other states, nations or groups and create a regional or international conflict.

Today, we also acknowledge that there is conflict between humanity and our environment and ecosystems to the extent that conflict in this context is truly global.

◆ Something is **latent** when it exists, but is hidden or concealed.

Ramsbotham et al. state that conflict is a 'universal feature of human society'. Conflict may develop because of economic differences, social or political changes, or cultural differences. While these conflictual features of society may be unseen, or what peace and conflict theorists often refer to as **latent**, they present themselves when groups or 'parties to conflict' (see Chapter 4.2) are formed that have, or are at least perceived to have, different goals. For example, one group or party may perceive the economic structure of society to be unfair and have the goal of wanting to seek greater equality. However, those parties currently benefiting from the economic structure are likely to want to protect the benefits they are enjoying and perhaps even enhance them.

The identity of the parties to conflict is likely to vary over time, and this can happen for a few reasons.

- The groups' priorities may change. For example, a group may start out focused on protesting about issues related to environmental sustainability but may later find that those battles are more effectively fought in the political arena. There are times when these transitions lead parties to question their mission and conflict strategies.
- The parties to conflict may change. As new parties enter the stage where conflict is played out, this may alter the strategy of some parties, and the groups with whom they are most often in direct conflict.

■ Destructive and constructive conflict

To this point, we have not suggested whether conflict is inherently good or bad; we have only indicated that it is a 'universal feature of human society'. However, theorists like Morton Deutsch have distinguished between destructive and constructive conflict, noting that while destructive conflicts like war and abusive behaviour should be avoided, constructive conflict is important and necessary. It is how we test ideas, put pressure on our tightly held ideals and how we ultimately progress as a society. Remember, a little over 100 years ago, women did not have the right to vote in most countries. Women's suffrage movements rose up and contested this perspective to the point that today, in most countries in the world, women have an equal right to vote.

We will adopt this broad interpretation of conflict, which reflects both destructive and constructive forms of conflict. What we will not include as conflict are sporting events or legal cases where the rules are clearly outlined.

■ What makes for a conflict?

Mack and Snyder suggest that overt or manifest conflict can be identified or characterized by the following four conditions:

1 Two or more parties are involved.
2 The parties have opposing goals.
3 There is a situation where there are limited resources or limited positions available.
4 There is behaviour that is designed to hurt or injure the other, in the broadest sense (it does not have to be only physical hurt or injury).

Without all four of these conditions, Mack and Snyder argue that the conflict will remain latent.

On the other hand, Johan Galtung argued there needs to be three components for there to be a full conflict: attitudes, behaviours and contradictions. While in many cases, parties may have contradicting perspectives on issues, that type of conflict is only latent and only exists as part of the structures that are in place. However, as the dynamic nature of conflict evolves, and attitudes toward other parties grow negative and even hostile and behaviours become oppressive or confrontational, it is at that point that the conflict is no longer latent but has instead become **manifest**. As the conflict gets more intense, the conflict may widen, drawing parties and individuals into the conflict and generating secondary, related conflicts. As the conflict gets more complicated and draws more parties in, it makes it more difficult to identify the core causes of the conflict and makes it harder to resolve.

◆ When something becomes **manifest**, it can be seen clearly (in other words, it is no longer hidden or concealed).

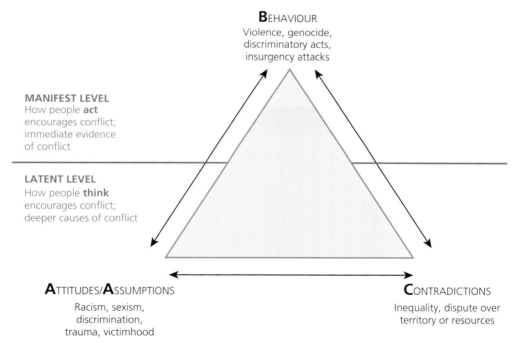

■ **Figure 4.12** Galtung's Conflict, or ABC, Triangle

You may see similarities between Galtung's ABC triangle, as seen in Figure 4.12, and his direct, structural and cultural violence triangle (Figure 4.6). We end direct violence by putting an end to conflict behaviour. We end structural violence by altering or changing the structures that cause the initial contradictions and injustices. We end cultural violence by changing attitudes.

Ramsbotham et al. offer the escalation and de-escalation model shown in Figure 4.13, which reflects how latent contradictions can become full, manifest states of conflict.

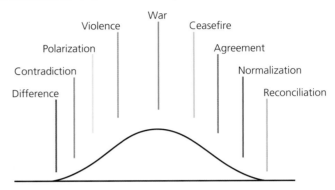

■ **Figure 4.13** Ramsbotham et al.'s conflict escalation and de-escalation model

The world is becoming less accepting of war, particularly actions in war that break international law. More and more people are speaking up against violent behaviours in society, at home and towards animals. Even though we are still dealing with issues of war and violence, we are becoming more conscious of how destructive and ineffective war is and how it creates endless cycles of harm. We are also starting to recognize the impact of war on those not directly involved in the fighting, whether it is the impact on the soldiers themselves through problems like post-traumatic stress disorder or on our environment. We are also becoming more mindful of issues like violence that are built into our social structures and institutions.

The focus of the next section, therefore, is on approaches that are seeking to counter war and violence. Here you will be introduced to possible meanings and descriptions of non-violence and pacifism.

4.1.5 Definitions, interpretations of and perspectives on non-violence

Large peace movements are relatively new and have grown out of the belief that all of humanity ought to work together to live peacefully and that simply by being human, we are equal and deserving of the same rights.

In the United States, during the Mexican–American War in the 1890s, American writer Henry David Thoreau was jailed for refusing to pay a tax, which, in his judgement, indirectly supported that conflict. He wrote about his thoughts on being jailed in his 1849 essay 'Civil Disobedience', which has influenced supporters of non-violent action ever since.

In 'Civil Disobedience', Thoreau argued that citizens of a democracy have a greater obligation to their conscience than to the policies of their government. He wrote, 'If a thousand men were not to pay their tax bills this year, that would not be a violent and bloody measure, as it would be to pay them and enable the State to commit violence and shed innocent blood. This is, in fact, the definition of a peaceable revolution, if any such is possible.' When Thoreau was imprisoned for failing to pay his taxes, his close friend, Ralph Waldo Emerson, visited him in jail where he asked Thoreau, 'What are you doing in here?' Thoreau is reported to have responded by saying, 'Ralph, what are you doing out there?'

In general, non-violence is a philosophy of not resorting to violence as a response to conflict or as a method for overcoming barriers to achieve greater equality. There could be two reasons for taking this approach:

● principled non-violence that grows out of an ethical or religious foundation

● strategic non-violence – taking a non-violent approach because it is the most effective tool to achieve one's desired outcomes.

We will first examine strategic non-violence.

◼ Strategic non-violence

Recently, the work of Maria Stephan and Erica Chenoweth has focused on how effective taking the non-violent approach to conflict and resistance is. During the last 100 years, they found that non-violent resistance campaigns were about twice as effective as violent campaigns. We will explore the logic and reasons why in further detail in Chapter 4.3. What is important to highlight here, though, is that not only does non-violent resistance have a moral foundation, but it also has a tactical rationale.

In defining non-violence, Stephan and Chenoweth, more precisely, refer to it as 'non-violent resistance'. They define it as a 'method of struggle in which unarmed people confront an adversary by using collective action — including protests, **demonstrations**, strikes and noncooperation — to build power and achieve political goals'. Stephan and Chenoweth suggest that the terms civil

◆ **Demonstrations** are public gatherings for people to show their collective stance on a particular issue or cause.

resistance, people power, unarmed struggle and non-violent action are synonymous with (have the same meaning as) non-violent resistance and are sometimes used interchangeably.

While armed struggle used to be the main way in which movements fought for change from outside the political system, this is no longer the case. Instead, the majority of resistance campaigns since the 1900s have used non-violent tactics and, since 2010, the largest number of non-violent campaigns was initiated since 1900.

Why non-violent resistance?

As we have seen, there are both ethical and strategic reasons for adopting non-violent resistance. Erica Chenoweth offers five reasons why actors may be adopting a non-violent approach:

- More people see non-violent resistance as a legitimate and successful method for creating change.
- New information technology makes it easier to learn about events that previously went unreported. As a result, those engaged in civil resistance do not always have to go through the traditional 'gatekeepers' of information. Instead, they can share their message instantly across the globe and, in doing so, quickly generate momentum for their movement.
- The market for violence is drying up. States are not arming **proxy** groups as they did during the Cold War. During the civil war in Yemen, Saudi Arabia's support for the government and Iran's support for the Houthi rebel group have become the exception, not the norm.
- As society has come to value and expect fairness, the protection of human rights and the avoidance of needless violence, international non-governmental organizations (NGOs) – such as the Albert Einstein Institution and Non-violence International – have developed and have begun to speak out and offer tools that can support and educate in the area of non-violent resistance.
- Unfortunately, there may be new motivations to resist. Over the past 10–20 years, democracy has begun to decline. The erosion of democratic rights has provoked mass protest movements in authoritarian countries such as Egypt and Türkiye and democracies such as Poland and the United States. With challenges such as racial justice, climate change, public health, rising inequality and demands for education and opportunity, a growing number of people are turning to non-violent movements. In some ways, Chenoweth suggests, this is both a sign of success and failure. Success in the sense that people have come to believe they can confront injustice using non-violent methods, and failure in that so many issues of injustice remain unresolved.

◼ Principled non-violence and pacifism

Pacifism and non-violence have been written about extensively within peace and conflict studies and, at times, they can seem interchangeable. However, pacifism is typically used in a narrow sense to mean opposition to war, while non-violence is usually more broadly defined:

- Non-violence is a negative term that rejects violence because it is either impractical or morally unacceptable.
- Alternatively, pacifism is more positive in its promotion of peace. The term pacifism comes from the Latin *pacificus*, which means to make, build or create peace.

Pacifism is best understood as a philosophical position that rejects the use of violence on moral grounds – in other words, it is principled non-violence. However, it is important to note that in civil/non-violent resistance campaigns, participants may very well not be pacifists. Instead, they are taking action in opposition to intolerable circumstances and are willing to use the best available method. In this regard, non-violence tends to be more broadly defined and reflects an approach to resistance or advocacy. While these distinctions can help us use the terms more

◆ A **proxy** war is a conflict in which a state attempts to increase its power or influence without taking part in the action, by providing arms or finance to the parties to conflict.

ACTIVITY

In groups, select a recent non-violent movement and analyse the movement based on Chenoweth's five reasons for adopting non-violent approaches. Which ones seem to be the most relevant to the example you have chosen?

THEMATIC STUDIES: Peace and conflict

precisely and effectively, there is no consensus on the usage of these terms among scholars who write about and debate non-violence and pacifism.

Martin Luther King, Jr saw non-violence as a virtue or a philosophical approach when he explained that, 'Non-violence in its truest sense is not a strategy that one uses simply because it is expedient at the moment; non-violence is ultimately a way of life that men live by because of the sheer morality of its claim.' Many advocates of pacifism and non-violence, like Mahatma Gandhi and Martin Luther King, Jr, grounded their approach in their religious practice. That said, opposition to war can also be grounded in nonreligious, moral arguments. Nonreligious pacifists, such as Bertrand Russell and Simone de Beauvoir, took this approach.

In the next section, we will look at the various approaches to pacifism.

Discussion point

What are the distinctions between non-violence and pacifism? Consider their definitions, motivations and how they are applied.

Approaches to pacifism

Personal pacifism

While some pacifists have personally refused to participate in war or violence (to varying degrees) as part of adopting a non-violent way of life, they have not suggested that it be a moral requirement for others. This approach is often called personal pacifism. Unlike absolute or universal pacifism, personal pacifists may not believe that violence is always wrong but instead take the position that it is a morally preferable way of life to which they have committed.

Moral pacifism

General or moral pacifism starts with the idea that all life is sacred (human or otherwise, depending on the kind of pacifist). It assumes that it should be difficult or even impossible to justify taking someone's life and, generally speaking, also unjustifiable to engage in physical violence. As a result, most pacifists would argue that violent responses to conflict, particularly acts of war, are impossible to justify and are immoral. Most pacifists arrive at their position from a moral perspective that does not always allow for quick compromise. This distinguishes committed moral pacifists from pragmatic or relative pacifists (see below).

Anti-war pacifism

As the term suggests, this is only the basic or general idea of pacifism. Many individuals oppose war but argue that they would engage in self-defence if their lives or loved ones were at risk. Peace theorists call this anti-war pacifism, which is likely the most common form of pacifism – a resistance to the impersonal, institutionalized violence of war but a willingness to acknowledge that when it comes to immediate, direct physical threats, self-defence is often warranted.

Some believe that even the use of violence for self-defence is not justifiable. Instead, they argue that every situation can be approached uniquely with various non-violent responses to draw on to defuse tensions and possible acts of physical violence.

Feminist pacifism

People who are both feminists and pacifists think that war and violence are the results of systems that are dominated by men or patriarchal ideas, where the approach is often top-down and forceful. They believe the only way to stop violence and war is to change these systems and make them fairer for everyone. Feminist researchers pay close attention to women's experiences. This is because women tend to be victimized more during war, and they are often the ones responsible for taking care of others. These researchers believe that looking at these experiences can give us new ways of thinking about peace and non-violence.

Universal pacifism

Universal pacifism was made famous by Gandhi. Those who practise this form of pacifism denounce violence in all forms, defending every living thing. They oppose:

- institutionalized violence, as in the military
- violent cultural conventions, such as racism and slavery
- religious concepts, such as holy wars, as well as religious teachings that entrench relationships of domination and hierarchy
- economic violence, like the poverty and hunger worsened by institutions such as the World Bank and the International Monetary Fund
- environmental violence, like the damage done by fracking
- acts of interpersonal violence, such as rape, abuse and neglect.

One radical form of universal pacifism is found among the Jain monks in India that we explored earlier in this chapter.

Pragmatic or relative pacifism

A pragmatic or relativist pacifist might be persuaded to suspend or abandon their convictions if the justification for a certain war is particularly compelling. However, there often seems to be plenty of compelling arguments for reactionary violence, so in general, pacifists seem reluctant to embrace the relativist approach.

Through all these approaches to pacifism, we can see that the appeal is an appreciation of, and care for, life on Earth. Pacifists acknowledge that living things deserve respect and care.

Conscientious objectors

In addition to opposing military policies, pacifists refuse personal participation in wars, most directly by resisting **conscription**. A conscientious objector is an individual who has claimed the right to refuse to perform military service based on freedom of thought, conscience or religion. They often practise tax resistance as well, which frequently takes the form of refusing to pay the proportion of national taxes that goes towards the military.

ACTIVITY

Write a reflection on the different forms of pacifism and consider which one(s) you align with most (if any at all) and why.

◆ **Conscription** is when a state orders people by law to join the armed forces.

Currently and in the past, war resisters have faced persecution, been imprisoned and have sometimes been killed for speaking out against war. However, a small number of countries have accepted the legitimacy of conscientious objectors so long as some form of alternative service is available. In this case, conscientious objectors are assigned to an alternative service as a substitute for military conscription (see Figure 4.14).

A number of organizations around the world celebrate the right to conscientiously object on 15 May as part of International Conscientious Objection Day. On 8 March 1995, a UN Commission on Human Rights resolution stated that 'persons performing military service should not be excluded from the right to have conscientious objections to military service'.

■ **Figure 4.14** Conscientious objectors in Canada loading railroad ties during the Second World War

Critics of pacifism

Critics of both pacifism and non-violence may argue that they are utopian and unrealistic ideals; nice in theory, impractical in reality. However, even if this debatable position is true, there is value in considering how humans might interact, debate, disagree, and even protest so that violence and death are avoided.

Pacifists have also been criticized for being cowards or for being 'free riders' who are able to avoid the moral questions related to war while still benefiting from the security of the military and the willingness of others to fight.

There are also challenges related to prioritizing the importance of avoiding killing. Could there be times when ideals such as justice, freedom and respect ought to be worth a sacrifice as great as giving up one's life or taking the life of another? The value of life is closely linked to the conditions in which people live to the extent that there may be arguments made for violence to protect values. It is this very reason that is sometimes offered as a rationale for humanitarian wars, where the moral costs of forcible intervention are the trade-off so that human rights can be protected and the suffering of citizens can be alleviated.

Mahatma Gandhi and non-violent resistance

Gandhi's approach to non-violence was grounded in the notion of ahimsa, which we explored earlier in this chapter. Its focus is on doing no harm to all living things. But ahimsa is not meek or passive. Rather, it involves active, engaged work towards caring for all living things, including the environment. Gandhi taught that this focus on care for others and the planet may result in suffering. Interestingly, as a young man in South Africa, Gandhi's views of black South Africans were not caring, as he had taught, and were instead quite harmful. However, according to some of Gandhi's biographers his views of black South Africans did evolve positively to the extent that Martin Luther King, Jr took great inspiration from Gandhi in his civil rights work in the United States.

According to Gandhi, this approach to non-violence is not meant to be simply reactive but should instead be proactive. Gandhi emphasized the Hindu concept of satyagraha (holding firmly to the truth, in this case, the truth of non-violence). This pursuit of satyagraha highlighted his emphasis on actively resisting and demanding no harm be done. This distinguished Gandhi's approach to non-violence from passively avoiding conflict at any price.

From the Gandhian perspective, using violent methods can build up resentment and hatred and, in doing so, possibly lay the foundations for even more injustice and more violence. Violent political activists, he argued, can end up making moral compromises to the extent that such compromises may justify almost any means of attaining them.

Gandhi's techniques were not alternatives to fighting, they were an alternative to violent fighting. Through marches, boycotts, picketing, leafleting, strikes, civil disobedience, the non-violent occupation of various government facilities, vigils and fasts, mass imprisonments, and refusal to pay taxes, there was a willingness to fight, just non-violently. Gandhi argued that it took far more strength to be abused by the authorities and respond non-violently, with politeness and courage, than to throw a punch or use a gun.

■ **Figure 4.15** Mahatma Gandhi

Martin Luther King, Jr's strategic and principled approach to non-violent resistance

Martin Luther King, Jr described his 'pilgrimage to non-violence' in his first book, *Stride Toward Freedom*, and in other books and articles. 'True pacifism,' or 'non-violent resistance,' King wrote, is 'a courageous confrontation of evil by the power of love.' King was both 'morally and practically' (what we have called principled and strategically) committed to non-violence. He believed that 'the Christian doctrine of love operating through the Gandhian method of non-violence was one of the most potent weapons available to oppressed people in their struggle for freedom'.

King's practical or strategic experience of leading non-violent protest convinced him that non-violence could become a way of life that could be applied to all situations. King called the principle of non-violent resistance the 'guiding light of our movement. Christ furnished the spirit and motivation while Gandhi furnished the method.'

King's notion of non-violence had six key principles:

- We can resist evil without resorting to violence.
- Non-violence seeks to win the 'friendship and understanding' of the opponent, not to humiliate him.
- Oppose the evil act, not the people committing the act.
- Those committed to non-violence must be willing to suffer without retaliation.
- Non-violent resistance avoids 'external physical violence' and 'internal violence of spirit'. An act of non-violence not only means a refusal to 'shoot [your] opponent but also refuses to hate him'. The resister should be motivated by love.
- The non-violent resister must have a 'deep faith in the future', grounded in the conviction that 'the universe is on the side of justice'.

◆ In Christianity, **agape** is the highest form of love and charity, the fatherly love of God for humans.

King's strategic non-violence was rooted in Christianity. He admired Gandhi and applied Gandhi's ideas to racial issues in the United States because he saw that they were rooted in an ethic of love, **agape**, that was itself an intrinsic part of Christianity.

In saying how he saw Gandhi's approach to non-violence and his Christian theology worked together, King explained:

> Love, for Gandhi, was a potent instrument for social and collective transformation.
> It was in this Gandhian emphasis on love and nonviolence that I discovered
> the method for social reform that I had been seeking for so many months.

Martin Luther King, Jr, 'My pilgrimage to nonviolence'

In King's 'Letter From a Birmingham Jail', where King had been imprisoned for his leading role in anti-segregation protests, he explains the logic behind his beliefs in non-violence and non-violent resistance or direct action. You will notice that this is much more active than the passive, inactive forms of non-violence that adherents have sometimes been accused of.

> You may well ask, 'Why direct action? Why sit-ins, marches, etc? Isn't negotiation
> a better path?' You are exactly right in your call for negotiation. Indeed, this
> is the purpose of direct action. Non-violent direct action seeks to create such a
> crisis and establish such creative tension that a community that has constantly
> refused to negotiate is forced to confront the issue. It seeks so to dramatize
> the issue that it can no longer be ignored. I just referred to the creation of
> tension as a part of the work of the non-violent resister, This may sound
> rather shocking, But I must confess that I am not afraid of the word tension.

THEMATIC STUDIES: Peace and conflict

I have earnestly worked and preached against violent tension, but there is a type of constructive, non-violent tension that is necessary for growth. ...

... One may well ask, 'how can you advocate breaking some laws and obeying others?' The answer is found in the fact that there are two types of laws: There are just, and there are unjust laws. I would agree with Saint Augustine that an unjust law is no law at all.

ACTIVITY

Review Martin Luther King, Jr's six key principles of non-violence. How relevant do you think they are in global politics today?

CASE STUDY

The 2019 Anti-Extradition Bill protests in Hong Kong

In the summer of 2019, Hong Kong saw its largest protests, with as many as 2 million of the 7.5 million residents in the city taking to the streets to demonstrate against a China-backed legislative proposal that would have allowed extraditions (transferring a person accused of a crime) from Hong Kong to China. There were fears that Hong Kong residents could not get a fair trial in mainland China. Incidents of police brutality, including the use of tear gas and rubber bullets, made tensions worse. On 23 October 2019, Chief Executive Carrie Lam withdrew the bill, but the protests, which garnered international attention, continued. Protesters were now asking for further changes, including the resignation of Chief Executive Carrie Lam.

Thomas Yun-tong Tang examined the evolution of violence during the protests and noted that, as the police began to respond violently, Hongkongers located throughout the world began to mobilize so that by the end of the protest there was a total of 178 oppositional actions organized by expatriate Hongkongers and foreign supporters.

As highlighted in Table 4.2, most of the actions taken by protesters in Hong Kong were non-violent in nature, however, instances of violent actions increased five-fold from July to August. Although the protesters became increasingly frustrated by police violence, to a large degree they maintained a non-violent approach in order to damage the legitimacy of the campaign.

■ Table 4.2 Top 20 most frequently used tactics during the Anti-Extradition Bill protests in Hong Kong

Rank	Tactics	Frequency
1	Public assemblies/sit-ins	537
2	Releasing public statements	501
3	Displaying and/or creating physical artifact(s)	359
4	Blockades	333
5	Collective singing	307
6	Damaging property	261
7	Graffiti	210
8	Demonstrations/marching	195
9	Arson	180
10	Signature campaigns	147
11	Mourning and/or worshipping activities	133
12	Human chains	123
13	Promotional activities	107
14	Physical attacks	105
15	Press conferences (for presenting protest claims)	99
16	Spatial occupations	99
17	Displaying and/or creating non-physical artifact(s)	97
18	Disruption (non-physical contact)	96
19	Solidarity building actions (psychological support)	92
20	Non-physical attacks	77

Adapted from Thomas Yun-tong Tang, 'The evolution of protest repertoires in Hong Kong: Violent tactics in the Anti-Extradition Bill protests in 2019'

As more violent actions were used alongside non-violent resistance (arson, physical attacks, damaging property), this resulted in an increase in the use of violent tactics. The increasing violence from the police gave protesters a reason to engage in acts of violence themselves.

As one protester explained, 'Why should we be so lenient to the enemy and so restrictive to ourselves? … We had not caused any fires until the confrontation … on 21 July. On that day, the police kept shooting us with rubber bullets. How could we escape if we did not light a fire as a barricade?'

As there were more incidents of violence by the protesters, this, of course, provided the police with more reason to engage in violence. And so the spiral of violence was initiated, particularly from August to November of 2019. As of September, slogans of 'Hongkongers, resist!' became 'Hongkongers, revenge!' Violence peaked in November, with 109 instances of violent actions.

The protests continued until the outbreak of COVID-19 in early 2020. Then, on 30 June 2020, during the height of the COVID-19 pandemic and with the protests still fresh in their memory, China bypassed the Hong Kong legislature and imposed a national security law on Hong Kong. The legislation essentially criminalizes any dissent by using broad definitions for crimes such as terrorism, subversion, secession and collusion with foreign powers. The law also allows China to establish a security force in Hong Kong and participate in selecting judges who hear national security cases. Decent in Hong Kong has effectively been silenced.

Exploring the causes of conflicts or the efficacy of violent and non-violent protest can form the basis of a strong extended essay.

■ **Figure 4.16** 'If we burn, you burn with us.' Graffiti reflecting the increasing anger towards police violence during the Hong Kong protests

● Chapter summary

In this chapter we have covered:
- evolution of peace and conflict studies
- contested meanings in peace and conflict studies
- definitions, interpretations of, and perspectives on:
  - peace, including violence, negative and positive peace, feminist peace, and religious and spiritual peace
  - conflict, including destructive and constructive conflict
  - non-violence, including the different approaches to pacifism.

The following chapters will expand upon some of these viewpoints and give you a better understanding of peace and conflict.

REVIEW QUESTIONS

Now that you have read this chapter, reflect on these questions:

- What are the two contrasting perspectives presented in the introduction regarding the nature of the world?
- Define and differentiate between direct violence, structural violence and cultural violence according to Johan Galtung's framework.
- Explain Johan Galtung's perspective on the definition of peace and his distinction between negative peace and positive peace.
- What are the critiques of Galtung's perspective on peace, as outlined by Ramsbotham et al. and Dustin Sharp?
- How does the balance of power theory of peace propose to maintain national security, and what are some of the weaknesses or challenges related to this approach?
- Explain the concept of conflict and the different ways in which it manifests.
- According to Deutsch, what is the difference between destructive and constructive conflict?
- Explain Thoreau's argument that citizens have a greater obligation to their conscience than to government policies.
- What is the difference between principled non-violence and strategic non-violence?
- According to Chenoweth and Stephan, what is the strategic rationale for adopting non-violent resistance?
- What is the relationship between pacifism and non-violence?
- What are the key distinctions between various approaches to pacifism? In particular, how do they view violence and conflict differently?
- What role do conscientious objectors play in advocating for pacifist principles?

4.2 Interactions of political stakeholders and actors

By the end of this chapter, you should understand:
▶ parties to conflict
▶ violent and non-violent state and non-state actors
▶ third parties, including negotiation processes, mediation processes and interventions
▶ marginalized, vulnerable and most affected groups and individuals in conflict.

Now that we have explored some of the possible meanings of the various aspects of peace and conflict studies, we will move on to consider the roles of the political stakeholders and actors that may be involved in peace activism, acts of violence, conflict and non-violent resistance.

Furthermore, we will examine some of the intervention processes that third parties may undertake when attempting to resolve disputes between various actors.

4.2.1 Parties to conflict

To ensure that international humanitarian law is applied as widely as possible and does not favour one conflict group or another, the 1949 Geneva Conventions and the Additional Protocols use the general term 'parties to the conflict'. This term refers to anyone, including states and non-state actors, who is involved in a conflict. Today, the phrase 'parties to conflict' has replaced the word 'belligerent' in legal peace and conflict language. Nevertheless, 'belligerent' is often used to name individuals, groups or countries in an armed conflict, so you should be familiar with that term too.

◼ The Geneva Conventions

◆ The **Geneva Conventions** are a set of international treaties that establish legal standards for the humanitarian treatment of individuals involved in armed conflicts. These conventions outline the rights of wounded and sick soldiers, prisoners of war, and civilians, aiming to protect them from unnecessary suffering and inhumane treatment.

The **Geneva Conventions** form the basis of international humanitarian law, or the laws of war or conflict. They set out how wartime prisoners, soldiers and civilians should be treated in war. The conventions were adopted in 1949 in the wake of the Second World War, and were signed and ratified by 196 countries.

There are four Conventions:

● First Convention: protect the sick, wounded, medical and religious personnel during conflict.

● Second Convention: care for the wounded, sick and shipwrecked during war at sea.

● Third Convention: treat prisoners of war with humanity.

● Fourth Convention: protect all civilians, including those in occupied territory.

Three Additional Protocols have since been added, which form additional protection for victims, and medical and religious personnel involved in conflict. Not all countries have ratified all Additional Protocols.

International humanitarian law distinguishes between 'parties to the conflict' and 'high contracting parties'. High contracting parties are countries that have agreed to follow the Geneva Conventions, even if they are not involved in a war. This means that if a high contracting party is attacked by a country that has not agreed to the Geneva Conventions, the high contracting party is still required to follow the rules of the Geneva Conventions.

The Geneva Conventions have also gained customary status, which means that even countries that have not agreed to the Geneva Conventions are still bound to follow most of the rules and may be held accountable in cases where they do not abide by customary international law. This is because customary international law is binding on all countries, regardless of whether countries agree to the customary law.

Why is customary law binding?

There are essentially three reasons why international law that is custom or tradition is binding:

● Customary law is binding because states act or behave as though they are bound by the custom. For example, states don't typically bomb ambulances and hospitals on purpose, and those who do are often seen as lacking humanity. In other words, the custom is not to bomb hospitals, so most parties to conflict abide by this custom.

Some suggest that states choose to be bound by customary law because it serves their interests by ensuring they can live in peace with other states. This manifests itself in two ways. One is a quid pro quo situation (Latin for 'something for something'). In other words, if I abide by international law, I can expect you to do the same. If I start breaking international law, I can expect you to do the same. I also need to remember that if I start breaking international laws, I might draw other actors into the conflict.

● Customary international law is respected for economic reasons. For example, suppose a state starts bombing hospitals and ambulances. In that case, the inhumane nature of such an act may discourage other countries that take international humanitarian law seriously from trading with them.

● Some experts argue that states follow customary law because those customs are right and good and, simply put, they make sense if we are all going to function well in the world together.

There is no requirement for 'reciprocity' in humanitarian law. This means that a country cannot violate the Geneva Conventions because the other side violated them first. All countries are always bound to follow the rules of humanitarian law, regardless of what the other side is doing.

For example, imagine playing a football game with your friends. You agree to follow the rules of the game, but one of your friends starts cheating. You cannot cheat just because your friend is cheating. You are still bound to follow the rules of the game, even if a player or the whole other team is not following the rules (and, typically, they will be punished for breaking the rules). The same is true for humanitarian law. Even if one side in a conflict violates the rules, the other side is still bound to follow them. This is because humanitarian law is designed to protect people caught up in wars, regardless of who is fighting.

Conflicts are not only between recognized countries and their official militaries. Sometimes, conflicts occur between groups like rebels, insurgents or terrorist organizations that are not officially recognized at any level. Because these groups are not officially recognized actors, they cannot sign international agreements related to humanitarian law. Nevertheless, international law applies to everyone, regardless of their legal status.

■ Primary parties to conflict

The 'first' or 'primary' parties in a conflict are the parties (individuals or groups) that oppose one another in the conflict. These are often called the '**disputants**'. The behaviour of primary disputants is clearly **conflictual** as it is easy to identify that they are in conflict with one another and that they

◆ **Disputant** (a person who is involved in a dispute) is another word for the first or primary parties to a conflict.

◆ When someone's behaviour is **conflictual**, it is characterized by conflict or disagreement.

are primary actors in the conflict. A final characteristic of primary disputants is that they have a direct stake in the outcome of the conflict, which is reflected in the intensity of their behaviour.

In real-world examples, there are many possible primary disputants, but one of the most common is disputes between two states, or what we call **interstate conflict**.

In the case of the conflict over the Nagorno-Karabakh region, the two primary disputants were the two states of Azerbaijan and Armenia (see Figure 4.17). As we will learn, military conflict within states – **intrastate conflict** – is much more common than interstate conflicts like this example.

In the case of intrastate primary conflict, like the Sudan example below, the conflict parties are two groups from within the same country. The conflict could be between the ruling government and a rebel faction wanting to displace them or between non-governing groups. For example, during the COVID-19 global pandemic, in several countries, those opposed to vaccine and masking mandates sometimes engaged in non-violent primary conflict with those in favour. These conflicts occurred between protesters and governments, two protesting factions, or even within families and schools.

■ **Figure 4.17** Territory that was the source of the Nagorno-Karabakh conflict (adapted from Armenicum)

Primary conflict parties may manifest as protest groups in many forms. These protest groups may be terrorist groups protesting based on a religious conviction, a social justice group demonstrating for equal rights or, as was the case in Hong Kong, a collection of citizens banding together to speak out against a government policy aimed at limiting their legal rights. Often these protest groups come into conflict with the government because they want a change that the government is unwilling to enact or they want to prevent a change that the government wants to undertake.

Finally, it is important to remember that all of the primary conflict parties noted above are made up of individuals. Each of these individuals has a unique world view and experiences. Because of this, there may be individuals within these groups that come into conflict with other members of the same group. And, as we have all experienced, conflict can come in the form of two individuals. This might be over who gets the last biscuit in the jar, but can also have global political implications. Should two world leaders struggle to get along personally, this may impact whether their countries can negotiate trade or peace agreements.

◆ **Moderates** are a secondary party to conflict. They hope to see their side in the conflict win, but are unlikely to put anything on the line to help them win.

◆ **Hardliners** are a secondary party to conflict. They support their favoured disputant, while also working to recruit and convince others to support their side.

◆ While they may not sympathize with the side they support ideologically in a conflict, **conflict profiteers** supply all manner of resources to their side and are happy to support them because they benefit financially.

◆ **Spoilers** are a secondary party to conflict closely associated with hardliners, but they often use tactics to prevent or take issue with any sort of peace negotiations. They tend to favour violence and hold extreme or radical positions.

◆ **Bystanders** are those who are neither engaged in a conflict nor willing to take a side, speak out against atrocities or actively support reconciliation.

■ Secondary and third parties to conflict

Secondary parties to conflict have an indirect stake in the outcome of the conflict. They often provide assistance or support to their allies in the conflict, but they are not directly involved in the conflict itself. Still, by supporting one of the disputants, secondary parties may benefit in a way that will support them in the future.

Secondary parties can take on a variety of roles:

- They can be **moderates** who hope to see their side victorious in the conflict but are unlikely to put anything on the line to help them win.

- **Hardliners** not only support their favoured disputant but may also work to recruit and convince others to support their side.

- There may be external supporters who have allied themselves with one side in the dispute and may provide diplomatic, economic and/or military aid.
  - ○ Secondary parties that provide diplomatic support may do so by attempting to facilitate mediation between groups. We see that at the United Nations level but also have seen Türkiye and France attempt to help negotiate peace in Russia's war on Ukraine.
  - ○ Secondary parties that provide economic support may do this through financial aid, which may be provided to sustain their preferred combatant during the conflict, or military aid, by providing weapons or even military personnel. Figure 4.18 shows the military and financial aid provided to Ukraine during the first year of the conflict.

- There may also be **conflict profiteers** who supply all manner of resources to one of the sides. They may not be ideological sympathizers with the party they are cooperating with but are happy to support them because they benefit financially. Alternatively, conflict profiteers may be military leaders who benefit from the conflict by gaining prestige and power from their role in the conflict.

- Finally, closely associated with the hardliners noted above are **spoilers**, who often use tactics to prevent or take issue with any sort of peace negotiations. They tend to favour violence and hold extreme or radical positions. They are likely to refuse any compromise and unlikely to change their position. Instead of seeking a resolution to the conflict, they would rather continue to cause their opponents harm or eliminate them entirely through genocide or forced migration.

There are also third parties in conflicts who play a very different role than primary or secondary parties to conflict. Third parties may be mediators, arbitrators or dialogue facilitators actively trying to cool or end hostilities.

Alternatively, there are third parties who are **bystanders** – they are neither engaged in the conflict nor willing to take a side, including being unwilling to speak out against atrocities or actively support reconciliation between the two groups. However, bystanders tend to be pulled into the conflict and forced to join one side or the other, thus polarizing the conflict even further.

Finally, non-combatant third parties, such as children, are negatively affected by inter and intrastate conflict in ways that can be quite long-lasting. We will explore several second and third parties later in this chapter.

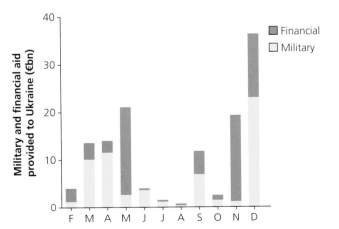

■ **Figure 4.18** Military and financial aid provided to Ukraine in 2022 (first year of the conflict) (adapted from Trebesch et al.)

Conflict parties and the 2023 civil war in Sudan

The primary parties of the 2023 conflict are the Sudan military government, the Sudan Armed Forces (SAF) and the paramilitary group, the Rapid Support Forces (RSF). The conflict began with airstrikes and gunfire attacks by the paramilitary RSF on government sites.

In 2019, former President Omar al-Bashir was overthrown and replaced by the joint leadership composed of the leader of the RSF, General Mohamed Hamdan Dagalo (better known as Hemedti), and the Sudanese military chief Abdel Fattah al-Burhan. Hemedti agreed to take on the role of Deputy Leader and support Burhan as military chief and ruler of Sudan.

The current conflict resulted from discussions regarding the merging of Hemedti's RSF into the national army. This was supposed to be a key step in reinstating the civilian governance of Sudan and determining the power structure in the newly formed hierarchy and who should report to whom.

As explained, there are times when conflict can grow out of disagreements from within a primary party to conflict. Once allies in their opposition to former President Omar al-Bishar, the two primary parties in this conflict are now the SAF and the RSF or, more precisely, Hemedti and Burhan. It is clear that these groups are the primary disputants and that control of the government and leadership of the country are the direct and clear stakes at the heart of the outcome.

Although it has not always been clear, allies or secondary parties of the RSF seem to be the United Arab Emirates (UAE) and Saudi Arabia. The RSF also has good relations with Yemen because Hemedti sent thousands of his RSF mercenaries to Yemen to fight on the government's behalf during its civil war against the Yemenese Houthi rebels allied with Iran.

The indirect benefit the UAE, Saudi Arabia and Yemen may experience if Hemedti is victorious in the conflict is that he may engage in preferential trade and diplomatic relations with them as thanks for supporting him in his rise to power.

In terms of third parties in the conflict in Sudan, at the time of writing, there have been attempts by the United States to broker temporary ceasefires to get supplies to those who need them or get individuals out of the country. In addition, the United Nations, as well as many countries throughout the world, have called for ceasefires.

With this example in mind, you can likely identify the three types of parties to conflict in another inter or intrastate conflict occurring in the world today.

ACTIVITY

Choose a current global conflict, provide a brief background and then highlight the first, second and third parties to the conflict.

4.2.2 Violent and non-violent state and non-state actors

Various state and non-state actors involved in conflicts have different ways of achieving their goals:

- those seeking to achieve their goals by violent means
- those seeking not only to make change non-violently, but also actively attempting to achieve peace.

We will begin this section by looking at violent state and non-state actors, and will conclude this section by exploring non-violent state and non-state actors.

■ Violent state actors

While states themselves are often perceived as violent actors, in many regards, a country like, for example, Ethiopia is not an actor at all. Ethiopia is a diverse geographical region, not an actor. Instead, it is *within a state* where you will find some of the various individuals and groups who act on behalf of (or despite) the citizens and residents of Ethiopia. These actors are often described using the name of a state, like Ethiopia. You may also sometimes read or hear actors described by the capital of a country. For example, the United States is often described as 'Washington' or China described as 'Beijing'. This is because the capital is usually where political decision-making is done – where the actors act. When considering Ethiopia or 'Addis Ababa,' Ahmed Abiy, the president of Ethiopia, has been an actor involved in carrying out acts of violence against the region of Tigray. However, there are also the military leaders and, of course, the soldiers engaging in acts of violence. Furthermore, individuals and organizations are responsible for supplying belligerents with the weapons they will use in the conflict and the food and shelter that will sustain them.

Military actors

One of the most identifiable violent state actors is state militaries. The government of the country supports the military or armed forces. They are specifically designed and trained to engage in combat and defensive operations. Militaries are individuals trained in warfare and are equipped with various weapons, vehicles, aircraft, warships and other forms of military technology to assist them in combat. While a military's primary responsibility is to use violence to defend its country from external threats, violence may also be used within a state to deter and prevent violent actors from within a state and, in some minimal cases, like the war in Afghanistan after the September 11 terror attacks on the United States, some states may use their military to deter possible conflict parties outside of their borders. Depending on each nation's approach, the military may also be used for peacekeeping missions or transporting and distributing humanitarian aid.

Global Firepower (GFP) ranks over 60 factors to determine a state's Power Index score. These factors range from the quantity of military equipment, military budget, number of personnel, geography, logistical capacity, available natural resources and the level of industrialization. The GFP ranking does not consider nuclear capabilities in its assessment, as these are not likely to be used in conventional warfare. This offers a more realistic look at a nation's conventional military capabilities.

As we explored in the section on Power, the rankings might not accurately reflect strategic capabilities, the quality of equipment or personnel, or the actual combat readiness of a state's military. That said, the United States often ranks at the top in the GFP rankings, indicating one of the most powerful militaries in the world. It has the largest military budget, which allows for significant investment in advanced technology, and has a large number of military personnel and advanced military equipment. Furthermore, US military bases and military personal are deployed in a number of countries. Nevertheless, in both Iraq and Afghanistan their powerful military struggled to contain counterinsurgencies.

Who needs a military?

One of the perspectives that is sometimes neglected in peace and conflict studies is whether a military is even necessary. Costa Rica is one of the few countries in the world that does not have a standing army. After the civil war in 1948, the Costa Rican government became the first country in the world to abolish the military, creating the Public Force of Costa Rica. It is divided into three branches: the Civil Guard, the Rural Guard and the Air Force. The Civil Guard is responsible for general law enforcement, while the Rural Guard is responsible for patrolling the borders and dealing with illegal immigration. The Air Force is responsible for search and rescue and providing air support to the other branches of the Public Force.

Costa Rica's abolition of the military reflected its commitment to peace and non-violence. It showed that it believed a standing army was unnecessary to defend the country and that the Public Force would be sufficient to maintain law and order. There was also the practical matter of the costs of maintaining a military, which it was also seeking to avoid.

But what if another country attacked Costa Rica? What would happen? First, it is important to understand that Costa Rica has had no involvement in any international military conflict since the mid-1850s, so conflict involving another state is unlikely. However, Costa Rica is a member of the Organization of American States (OAS), which has a mutual defence treaty. This means that if another country attacked Costa Rica, the other members of the OAS would be expected and obligated to come to Costa Rica's defence. Costa Rica is also a member of the regional Rio Security Treaty, which the United States is a part of. The United States also has a long history of military cooperation with Costa Rica, so in the event of an attack on Costa Rica, the United States would likely provide military assistance.

Paramilitary actors

Paramilitaries and militaries are both armed forces, but they have some critical differences regarding their purpose, legal status and equipment (see Table 4.3). While the following may not be the precise case for every country in the world, you will generally find this to be the case.

■ **Table 4.3** The differences between paramilitaries and militaries

	Paramilitaries	**Militaries**
Purpose	Paramilitaries are often used to carry out tasks that the military or police are unable or unwilling to handle. These tasks might include things like riot control and border security.	Militaries are primarily responsible for defending a country's borders and fighting wars.
Legal status	Paramilitaries are not part of a country's official military, although the government may organize them. Paramilitaries are also not under the same level of control as the military.	Unlike paramilitaries, militaries are part of a country's official armed forces and are under the direct control of the government.
Equipment	Paramilitaries typically use less sophisticated equipment than members of the military. This is because paramilitaries may have a less militarily sophisticated role or receive limited funding from private donors or the government.	Militaries receive funding from the government and often have access to cutting-edge military technology and equipment.

It should be noted that paramilitaries may have a greater likelihood of potential abuse than militaries. One of the reasons for this is that paramilitaries are often not subject to the same level of oversight or accountability as militaries. As a result, we sometimes find that paramilitaries are the source of human rights abuses or engage in illegal activities. For example, in 2014 and 2015, the RSF in Sudan (see Case study on page 306) was accused by Human Rights Watch of a wide range of abuses in the Darfur region of Sudan. This included the forced displacement of entire communities, the destruction of wells, and acts of torture, killings and mass rapes.

A different type of paramilitary example is the Israeli Border Police, known as 'Magav'. Magav was established in 1953 and has been involved in several significant international conflicts and used to assist in natural disasters, such as the 2010 Mount Carmel forest fire. Magav is divided into several branches, including the Border Guard, the Counter-Terrorism Unit and the Civil Guard, responsible for providing security to Israelis during emergencies. Israeli law restricts Magav from using the live ammunition and rubber bullets used by the army. Magav has been criticized for helping to enforce borders between Israel and areas of Palestine that Palestinians and many others throughout the world believe are rightfully theirs. Magav has also been accused of violent overreach by B'tselem, an Israeli human rights organization. B'tselem has received reports of misconduct, including injuries and even killings.

North Atlantic Treaty Organization

The North Atlantic Treaty Organization (NATO) is an international alliance comprising 32 member countries from North America and Europe, with its headquarters in Belgium. The most recent members, Finland and Sweden, joined as a result of the Russian attack on Ukraine.

Because NATO is comprised entirely of, and funded by, member states, it should be viewed as a 'state' actor, not a 'non-state' actor. Created in 1949, NATO was primarily devised as a system of collective defence to provide security from belligerent states, particularly the former Soviet Union. Its most crucial principle is found in Article 5 of the NATO treaty, which states that an armed attack against one member is considered an attack against them all. This Article aims to deter any state or non-state actor from attacking any member of the alliance.

NATO does not possess its own military forces but has a military command structure that plans and executes military operations when needed. However, the member countries contribute all of the military forces and equipment. Typically, NATO operations are undertaken because of the response to collective defence, but operations may also involve intervening in other international crises or supporting peacekeeping missions that are likely to contribute to the collective security of the member nations. While NATO seeks to engage in largely non-violent responses like peacekeeping, it is often viewed as a violent state actor because the organization is founded on responding to a violent attack with violence, if necessary.

NATO engages in the following activities:

● Collective defence: NATO's primary military role is the collective defence of its member nations. This is usually associated with Article 5 of the NATO Charter, which has only been invoked once – in response to the terrorist attacks on the United States on 11 September 2001 (9/11). We will explore this central aspect of NATO in more detail below.

● Crisis management: NATO's role in resolving international crises could impact the security of its member nations. This often involves peacekeeping and counterinsurgency operations (responding to revolutionary activities or uprisings). For example, NATO's involvement in the Balkans in the 1990s and the Afghanistan mission in the 2000s.

● Cooperative security and deterrence: NATO also engages in cooperative security efforts, such as weapons control and disarmament. It regularly holds military exercises to demonstrate its capabilities and deter potential threats.

● Partnership and dialogue: NATO engages in partnership activities and dialogue with non-member countries across the world, and works with other international organizations (IGOs) to promote peace and stability.

● Response to terrorism and cyber threats: due to evolving security challenges, NATO has also committed to helping member states improve their capabilities to counter terrorism and cyber threats.

Collective defence

When NATO members agree that an Article 5 incident has occurred (see quotation below), NATO members can provide any assistance they deem necessary to respond to a situation.

■ **Figure 4.19** US Navy engaged in NATO peacekeeping operations

◆ **Capacity-building** is the process of developing, strengthening and sharing skills, abilities, processes and resources to help support a new or growing organization, especially in the military or international security sectors.

NATO clearly explains that the type of assistance is up to the individual member, given the circumstances. The response of each member does not necessarily need to be military and is dependent on the material resources of each country. As a result, it is left to the judgement of each member country, in consultation with the other members, to determine how it will contribute to the response, keeping in mind that the aim is to 'restore and maintain the security of the North Atlantic area'.

Article 5 reads as follows:

The Parties agree that an armed attack against one or more of them in Europe or North America shall be considered an attack against them all and consequently, they agree that, if such an armed attack occurs, each of them, in exercise of the right of individual or collective self-defence recognized by Article 51 of the Charter of the United Nations, will assist the Party or Parties so attacked by taking forthwith, individually and in concert with the other Parties, such action as it deems necessary, including the use of armed force, to restore and maintain the security of the North Atlantic area.

Any such armed attack and all measures taken as a result thereof shall immediately be reported to the Security Council. Such measures shall be terminated when the Security Council has taken the measures necessary to restore and maintain international peace and security.

CASE STUDY

NATO missions

NATO and Kosovo

As of 2023, approximately 4,200 allied and partner troops are operating in Kosovo as part of NATO's Kosovo Force (KFOR). NATO first entered Kosovo in June 1999 to help end violence between ethnic Albanians and ethnic Serbs. Following Kosovo's declaration of independence in February 2008, NATO agreed to maintain its presence and, for many years, has helped to de-escalate tensions between both sides.

NATO and the African Union

Since 2005, NATO has cooperated with and supported the African Union (AU). NATO and the AU work together to address shared security threats and challenges. NATO works with the AU based on its requests for assistance and also alongside other IGOs, such as the United Nations.

For example, NATO provided air and sea support for AU peacekeepers as part of the AU Mission in Somalia (AMISOM), which started in June 2007. NATO has continued to support the AU in Somalia, including as part of the AU's Transition Mission in Somalia (ATMIS) in 2023. NATO also provides **capacity-building** and expert training to the African Standby Force, which is part of the AU's efforts to develop long-term peacekeeping capabilities.

NATO Air Policing

NATO Air Policing is a peacetime mission that aims to preserve the security of the airspace for NATO members. This involves NATO members working together every hour of every day of the year so that fighter aircraft and crews are ready to react as quickly as possible to airspace

THEMATIC STUDIES: Peace and conflict

violations. Since Russia annexed Crimea in 2014 and its invasion of Ukraine in February 2022, NATO air policing has taken extra measures to secure the Eastern European part of the Alliance.

NATO earthquake relief in Türkiye

Following the earthquakes in Türkiye in February 2023, NATO delivered hundreds of temporary shelters, including tents and shipping containers, to house thousands of displaced people. Several NATO Allies and partners coordinated flights that carried hundreds of tonnes of urgent supplies through NATO's Strategic Airlift Capability (SAC). NATO has built and maintained temporary relief sites that house thousands of people in Türkiye. NATO has also provided medical treatment facilities near damaged hospitals in the area.

NATO funding

In 2006, NATO defence ministers agreed to commit a minimum of 2 per cent of their gross domestic product (GDP) to defence spending to ensure NATO has the resources to address military conflicts. When the North Atlantic Council – NATO's top political decision-making body – unanimously decides to engage in an operation or mission, there is no obligation for all members to contribute unless it is an Article 5 collective defence operation.

The number of NATO members achieving the 2 per cent aim has recently been quite low. It has, at times, been a point of contention, particularly from significant contributors like the United States. However, NATO scholar Garret Martin has explained that US defence needs differ greatly from many NATO members in Europe. He says that, 'The United States is a global military power with global military commitments … NATO and the trans-Atlantic geographical area is only a part of what the United States military does. That's not necessarily true for most of the European members of the alliance' (quoted in Welna). In other words, many NATO members simply don't need to spend on their own militaries to the degree the United States needs to, as illustrated in Figure 4.20.

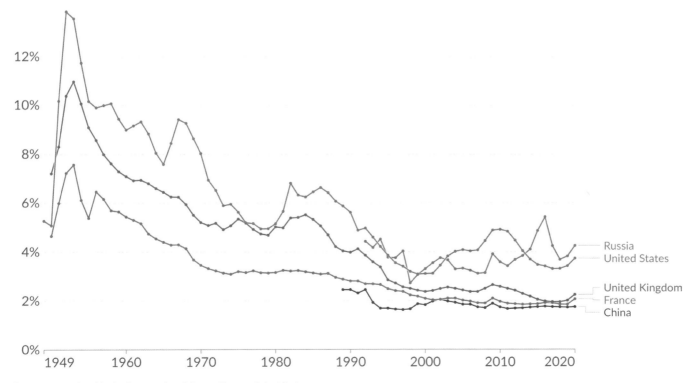

Data source: Stockholm International Peace Research Institute

■ **Figure 4.20** Military expenditure as a share of GDP, 1949 to 2020 (from Our World in Data, 'Military expenditure as a share of GDP, 1949 to 2020')

Violent non-state actors

When it comes to violent non-state actors today, one of the most familiar actors that may come to mind is terrorist groups.

Terrorist and rebel groups

There are dozens of identified terrorist groups in the world today. While there is no agreed upon definition of terrorism, the UN Human Rights Office of the High Commissioner suggests the following, 'As a minimum, terrorism involves the intimidation or coercion of populations or governments through the threat or perpetration of violence, causing death, serious injury or the taking of hostages.' We might add that one other goal of terrorists is to gain public attention.

While we will explore causes and acts of terrorism in more detail in Chapter 4.3, we need to acknowledge that terrorist groups are one of the main violent non-state actors.

While terrorist groups and violent rebel groups are both non-state actors involved in a conflict, they have different characteristics, goals and methods of operation. However, these can be difficult to determine, given the negative connotations of terrorism.

The terms 'terrorism' and 'terrorist' are almost always directed at one's opponent in an effort to delegitimize them and their cause.

TOK

We can see the role of language in shaping our understanding of the world, or how language is shaped by our understanding of the world, by examining the word 'terrorist'.

'Terrorist' has many negative connotations. The person using the term for an opponent tends to disagree with that opponent's ideological or political goals. However, those who agree with the ideological and political goals of the same person might characterize them as 'freedom fighters'. In other words, depending on feelings and attitudes, the language describing the same person changes.

Other examples in modern political debate might include the once neutral term 'illegal alien', which technically means an immigrant who has not entered a country legally. In many political contexts, however, this takes on a strongly negative connotation and a new neutral term has emerged: 'undocumented immigrant'.

In other examples, 'unborn baby' has replaced the more medically neutral term 'foetus' in order to conjure images which might shape your views in the abortion debate.

Consider the use of language in your own political context. Are there terms which do far more than merely identify a group, in that they also provide a 'connotation' or a feeling or attitude that goes along with the identification? What is the effect of that connotation on the political discourse? Are there 'more neutral' terms available?

Violent rebel groups, or insurgents, are typically non-state actors involved in an armed conflict with an established government or ruling power. They are often engaged in a conflict to gain political control of a specific geographic area, such as part of a country or the country as a whole.

◆ **Indiscriminate** means done at random or in a careless way.

While rebel groups may use violent methods, their targets, unlike terrorists, are not **indiscriminate**. Instead, they typically target the military or aspects of the ruling actor's area or means of control. They may attack a weapons depot or the centre of political decision-making in the capital of the country. For rebel groups, indiscriminate acts of terror targeted at civilians could harm the civilians they need support from to take power successfully.

Nevertheless, in practice, the acts carried out by terrorist and rebel groups can blur. A rebel group might engage in acts of terror as part of its strategy, or a terrorist group might evolve into a more conventional rebel group or political entity if it gains legitimacy. For example, the Irish

Republican Army (IRA), originally established in the early 1900s as a paramilitary organization fighting for Irish independence, was often regarded as a terrorist group due to violent tactics, particularly during the period known as 'The Troubles'.

However, the IRA's political wing, Sinn Féin, has since transitioned into a legitimate political party. This transformation was marked by the IRA's eventual ceasefire and the Good Friday Agreement in 1998, which significantly reduced violence and led to power-sharing arrangements in Northern Ireland. Recently, Sinn Féin has gained substantial political ground, as evidenced by their significant electoral successes in both the Republic of Ireland and Northern Ireland, indicating a shift in public perception and legitimization of their role in contemporary Irish politics.

It is important to note that terrorist and rebel groups are usually considered illegal by the governments they oppose, and their use of violence can often lead to significant harm and suffering for civilian populations.

Table 4.4 summarizes the main differences between terrorist and rebel groups.

■ **Table 4.4** The differences between terrorist and rebel groups

	Terrorist groups	**Rebel groups**
Goals	Terrorists aim to achieve their political goals through violence and intimidation.	Rebel groups may use violence to overthrow a government or achieve some other political change.
Targets	Terrorists target civilians, government officials and military personnel.	Rebel groups tend to focus on military and government personnel only.
Methods	Terrorists use suicide attacks, bombings, kidnappings and other indiscriminate violence.	Rebel groups use guerrilla warfare, including ambushes, raids and other conventional military tactics.
Motivation	The motivation for terrorists is some form of religious or ideological extremism.	Rebel groups are likely to have political or economic complaints.

CASE STUDY

The Wagner Group

The origins of the Wagner Group in Russia are unclear, but it seems that the group's leader, Yevgeny Prigozhin, offered to Vladimir Putin to be the CEO of a new mercenary outfit sometime in the 2010s. We do know that the group's military commander, Dmitry Utkin, who had an affinity for Nazi ideology, named the group after Hitler's favourite composer, Richard Wagner.

In September 2015, Russia began militarily intervening in Syria through the Wagner Group. President Vladimir Putin offered the Wagner Group to Bashar al-Assad, the dictatorial leader of Syria facing multiple rebel and terrorist groups seeking to overthrow him. To help Assad regain territory lost in the previous four years, the Russian Air Force was used to bomb from the sky and the Wagner Group worked on the ground.

■ **Figure 4.21** Members of the private military company the Wagner Group

When the Wagner Group helped recapture the Syrian city of Palmyra for Assad in 2016, the value of the Wagner Group grew. As a **mercenary** group, the Wagner Group was not only meant to achieve military victories, but it was also expected to earn money. The Wagner Group worked with the Syrians to share in the profits from the oil fields they seized from Islamic State after their military victories. The mix of military and financial success was something that appealed to other autocratic leaders in Africa, so Wagner sold its services to the Central African Republic, Libya, Mali, Mozambique and Sudan. Leaders in these countries were facing challenges to their power by rebel groups and insurgencies, and the Wagner Group helped prop these leaders up by using indiscriminate violence towards the local population. In exchange for these successes, the Wagner Group took control of natural resources in the mining or timber industries. So prolific was the Wagner Group's integration into the Central African Republic that some groups associated with the Wagner Group attempted to take over the local beer market.

When Putin invaded Ukraine in 2022, the Wagner Group was not part of Putin's initial plans as he had envisioned the invasion being a brief and successful takeover. When the attack on Ukraine looked increasingly unsuccessful, the Wagner Group joined the fight and found a number of early successes. However, as the war has become bogged down and the Wagner Group has suffered casualties, the Group has had to resort to using convicts from Russian prisons.

On 23 August 2023, Yevgeny Prigozhin died in an unexplained plane crash north of Moscow. While the exact cause remains undetermined, there are theories suggesting that the incident could have been an act of targeted killing. As noted, Prigozhin had close ties with Vladimir Putin but shortly before his death had criticized Russia's military leadership and had led a brief revolt against Putin and his military leaders.

◆ In this context, a **mercenary** is a private individual who is hired to fight in a conflict and is motivated by the desire for private gain rather than political or other motivations.

◼ Non-violent state actors

In our exploration of non-violent state actors, we will look at two examples.

- First, we will examine the role of diplomats and how they work non-violently on behalf of states to make change.
- Second, like our investigation into NATO, we will look at UN peacekeepers, who are part of an organization that is viewed as a state actor because it is funded and composed of individual states.

Diplomats

A diplomat is an individual who represents their country and who, when a conflict breaks out or in times of peace, will either defend an act of aggression or a violent response, or threaten or announce consequences for acts of violence.

The work of diplomats is often referred to as 'diplomacy'. This takes place in embassies, consulates, the United Nations and other international agencies. The diplomat plays a non-violent role as a representative of their state, making them a 'non-violent state actor'.

The work diplomats do is often referred to as foreign policy or statecraft. More specifically, according to GR Berridge, 'Diplomats conduct international relations by negotiation rather than by force, propaganda or recourse to law, and by other peaceful means (such as gathering information or engendering goodwill) which are either directly or indirectly designed to promote negotiation.' Similar to what Berridge suggested, diplomats are commonly described as sharing a commitment to peace or international order, and Freeman explained that diplomats behave in this manner as a way of ensuring 'that the functioning of the international state system is sustained and improved'. As a result, much of the work done by diplomats is related to international conflict resolution, which requires skills in negotiation and mediation.

As Figure 4.22 shows, diplomats use a range of tools when practising diplomacy.

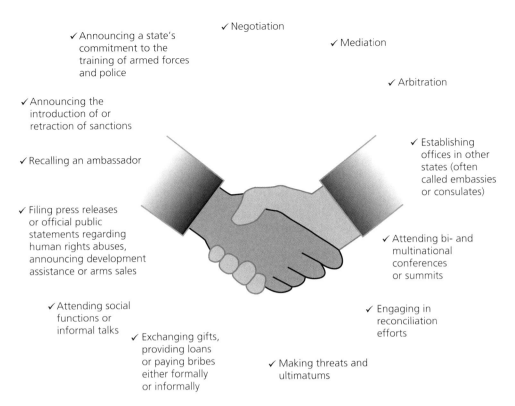

✓ Negotiation

✓ Announcing a state's commitment to the training of armed forces and police

✓ Mediation

✓ Arbitration

✓ Announcing the introduction of or retraction of sanctions

✓ Establishing offices in other states (often called embassies or consulates)

✓ Recalling an ambassador

✓ Filing press releases or official public statements regarding human rights abuses, announcing development assistance or arms sales

✓ Attending bi- and multinational conferences or summits

✓ Attending social functions or informal talks

✓ Engaging in reconciliation efforts

✓ Exchanging gifts, providing loans or paying bribes either formally or informally

✓ Making threats and ultimatums

■ **Figure 4.22** Tools of the diplomat

Diplomacy is often contrasted with war and, therefore, diplomats are contrasted with violent state actors, similar to members of the military. Hamilton and Langhorne have characterized diplomacy as 'the peaceful conduct of relations amongst political entities'. Even though Aron describes diplomacy as 'the art of convincing without using force,' seeing the work of diplomats as fully contrasted with actors using force isn't entirely correct. The notion of 'coercive diplomacy' has been developed to reflect diplomats who need to use threats or limited force to persuade opponents to behave as they would like them to. It is the threat of force or further damage that can make one state comply with another's wishes. Coercive threats used by diplomats are made to either force or compel an opponent to do something, or to stop or deter them from doing something.

Even though war or conflict of some sort may indicate the breakdown or ineffectiveness of diplomacy, to bring the conflict to an end, diplomats will again be required to negotiate or mediate the end of a conflict, as well as maintain peace after an agreement has been signed.

The work of diplomats is only likely to be successful if both sides of the conflict recognize the notion of coexistence or, as Garrett Mattingly stated, 'unless people realize that they have to live together, indefinitely, despite their differences, diplomats have no place to stand'. This acceptance of coexistence is reflective of the reality that states are dependent on one another to survive. This 'norm of coexistence' ensures that conflict can be resolved.

Another critical aspect of the work diplomats do is to keep the lines of communication open. So critical is communication to the work of diplomats, Van Dinh Tran likened it to blood. 'Communication is to diplomacy as blood is to the human body. Whenever communication ceases, the body of international politics, the process of diplomacy is dead, and the result is violent conflict.' In essence, diplomats are messengers, and central to international diplomacy is communication between states. This also means that diplomats need to be effective communicators and be able to understand what other diplomats mean, how to 'read between the lines', or understand what is being said, even though it is not being stated outright.

The principle of diplomatic immunity represents another important aspect of ensuring communication. **Diplomatic immunity** ensures that diplomats are not hurt while negotiating or living in a belligerent country; they are also not held to the laws of the foreign state they may be living in. Ensuring the safety of diplomats is important if relationships between states in conflict are to remain stable. This is also an important step for official relations to develop at the international level and to build the necessary trust to interact with other state or even non-state actors effectively.

So, why do state or non-state actors choose diplomacy? In many ways, the answer is fairly straightforward. Actors tend to resort to diplomacy when the costs of war are much greater than the costs of diplomacy. In comparison to mobilizing armies, the cost of diplomacy is really quite small. It is only when actors see a conflict as so deep-seeded that it cannot be resolved by diplomatic efforts that actors will likely resort to war.

UN peacekeepers

Like diplomats, United Nations (UN) peacekeepers are a good example of (mostly) non-violent state actors. Unless they are peacekeeping under a Chapter VII UN mandate, UN peacekeepers are only permitted to use force if fired upon. Also, the UN has no standing army unassociated with other states. Instead, individual states volunteer military members to assist with peacekeeping missions. Because of this arrangement, UN peacekeepers can often be viewed as non-violent state actors.

We will explore the role of peacekeepers and peacekeeping in more detail in Chapter 4.4. However, here we briefly introduce them as non-violent state actors.

Peacekeepers are often sent to states transitioning from conflict where, with the consent of warring parties, they ensure the parties to conflict are separated, and the peace agreement is being instituted. Today, they often play a central role in monitoring, policing and supporting humanitarian intervention.

With more than 100,000 civilian and military personnel spread across 13 UN missions and a budget of more than $6.5 billion, the UN is starting to face a period of uncertainty due to the size of both the personnel required and the budgetary challenges countries are facing in continuing to fund the forces they are supplying. Furthermore, as states move towards isolationism (they want to engage less with international concerns), we cannot assume that peacekeepers, as non-violent state actors, will be a permanent fixture in global politics.

■ Non-violent non-state actors

In 1991, Joseph Montville coined the term 'Track II diplomacy' to contrast it with the traditional 'Track I' state diplomatic actors we examined above.

Track II diplomacy includes various non-state actors, such as churches, think tanks, humanitarian organizations, and artistic, entertainment, sport and student exchanges. This type of diplomacy is becoming more prominent in the world today.

A second type of Track II diplomacy includes unofficial actors who serve as intermediaries or 'go-betweens' and work with the two conflicting parties. They are intermediary actors who may be former government officials. They may have been asked to participate, and they may participate in so-called 'off-the-record' talks focused on building trust. Finally, there may be a third type of Track II diplomacy that occurs where citizens take the initiative in trying to get official negotiations going.

For example, Pope Francis has tried to encourage both the conflicting parties in Sudan, and Ukraine and Russia, to come to a peace agreement. The Red Cross, as a non-governmental organization, has also played a role in trying to bring conflicting parties together.

In the next section, we will look at several NGOs that are actors on the global political stage. In some cases, they support Track II diplomacy. Still, in other cases, their role is to highlight international law that is being violated or to draw attention to conditions that need to be addressed. In all cases, however, these organizations are non-violent and non-state actors.

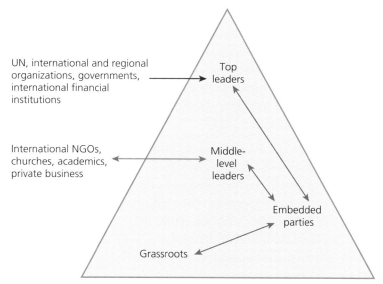

Track I: Negotiation, peacekeeping, arbitration, peace support, mediation with muscle. Exchange and threat power dominate

Track II: Good offices, conciliation, pure mediation, problem-solving. Integrative and exchange power dominate

Track III: Peace constituencies within the conflict, building social cohesion, common ground. Integrative and exchange power dominate

■ **Figure 4.23** The Tracks of Diplomacy (adapted from Ramsbotham et al.)

Non-governmental organizations

Non-governmental organizations (NGOs) are actors that can play a critical role in conflicts. For example, Human Rights Watch and Amnesty International are organizations that have played a central role in highlighting human rights abuses around the world. In 2018, in Myanmar, both organizations exposed the crimes against humanity and possible genocide that the Rohingya people endured, and called for the world to take action.

As actors, NGOs not only publicize the atrocities of war, but they also work to prevent and treat injuries and save combatants from all parties of conflict. Two organizations that have carried out this type of work for decades are Médecins Sans Frontières (Doctors Without Borders) and the Red Cross/Red Crescent. As explained, both organizations take on a neutral role during conflict, treating all those in need. None of these organizations is controlled by, or influenced, by the financial support provided by governments.

CASE STUDY

NGOs addressing human rights violations

Human Rights Watch investigates and reports on abuses throughout the world. It was founded in 1978 as 'Helsinki Watch', when it began investigating rights abuses in countries that signed the Helsinki Accords.

Among other declarations, countries that signed the Helsinki Accords agreed to, 'respect human rights and fundamental freedoms, including the freedom of thought, conscience, religion or belief, for all without distinction as to race, sex, language or religion'.

The work of Human Rights Watch has since expanded to include the investigation and announcement of genocides, governments that take over media organizations, and the arrest of activists and the leaders of political opposition. It also works to address abuses against those likely to face discrimination, including women, LGBTQ+ people and people with disabilities. Particularly in the context of this section, they have attempted to seek justice for those who have experienced war crimes and are not getting justice in their home country.

Human Rights Watch uses in-person interviews, satellite imagery to track the destruction of villages and city blocks, and big data to search for patterns in arrest rates or the deportation of immigrants. It employs over 550 people of more than 70 nationalities, who are country experts, lawyers and journalists, as well as others who target governments, armed groups and businesses in the hope of getting them to change or enforce their laws.

To ensure its independence, Human Rights Watch says, '[We] refuse government funding and carefully review all donations to ensure that they are consistent with our policies, mission, and values. We partner with organizations large and small across the globe to protect embattled activists and to help hold abusers to account and bring justice to victims.'

Besides investigating and meeting with both state and non-state actors in an effort to get them to change, Human Rights Watch also shares widely the stories it has researched with millions of social media users and online followers. As a result of its broad reach, it has found that the news media often share its reports and research, furthering the likelihood that it can meet with governments, the UN, rebel groups, corporations and others to see that policy is changed, laws are enforced and justice is served.

Amnesty International does similar work, except it was founded in 1961 to publicize violations of the Universal Declaration of Human Rights by governments and other actors. It has especially focused on freedom of speech and conscience, and the right not to have to endure torture.

That said, in 2022, Amnesty International shared a detailed report that revealed that the Myanmar military was committing a war crime by laying a massive number of antipersonnel landmines in and around the villages in Kayah (Karenni) State (Amnesty International, 'Armed conflict'). Because landmines can indiscriminately hurt anyone, they have been internationally banned. So while the laying of antipersonnel landlines was not focused precisely on torture, it was an act of violence that Amnesty International felt needed to be publicized.

Medical and humanitarian assistance

The International Red Cross and Red Crescent societies help governments carry out humanitarian work, including providing disaster relief and health and social programmes. During times of war, it assists civilians in need and, where appropriate, supports the army's medical services.

Neutrality is its goal during the conflict as it aims to 'bring assistance without discrimination to the wounded on the battlefield [and to] prevent and alleviate human suffering wherever it may be found'. Its principle of humanity reflects its desire to 'act to prevent and alleviate human suffering [and] respect for human dignity and helping people – regardless of who and where they are – is paramount to everything we do'. In this regard, it doesn't discriminate based on nationality, race, religious beliefs, class or political opinions.

Like Human Rights Watch, the International Red Cross and Red Crescent Movement aim for independence so it can 'resist any interference – be it political, ideological or economic – capable of diverting it from embodying the principles of humanity, impartiality and neutrality'.

We have also previously covered the work of Médecins Sans Frontières (MSF) (Doctors Without Borders) in this book. MSF 'provides medical assistance to people affected by conflict, epidemics, disasters, or exclusion from health care'. Like the Red Cross and Red Crescent Societies, it is guided by impartiality, independence and neutrality.

The core focus of its work is to ensure rapid and effective responses. MSF keeps pre-packaged kits so that its teams can offer rapid lifesaving assistance. This includes surgical kits, inflatable hospitals and cholera kits. It can treat millions of patients every year because it has a large network of supplies and a robust logistical system.

These are just some examples of the hundreds of thousands of NGOs that are working to make the lives of people around the world safer through a variety of non-violent means. You should research some of the NGOs that do good work in your area and perhaps take the opportunity to join them in their work.

> **Discussion point**
>
> To what extent are non-violent approaches more effective in resolving conflict than violent approaches?

> **ACTIVITY**
>
> Explain the characteristics of violent and non-violent actors, both state and non-state. How do their methods and goals differ?

4.2.4 Marginalized, vulnerable and most affected groups and individuals during conflict

In this chapter, we have so far explored the interactions of actors in peace and conflict. These are the individuals or groups who engage in conflict. But as we know, conflict also involves stakeholders – the individuals or groups who, while not involved in the conflict, still have a genuine stake in what the outcome of the conflict will be.

■ The impact of conflict on civilians

◆ A **civilian** is a person who is not a member of the armed or police forces, nor actively engaged in conflict.

In recent years war has become more dangerous for civilians. For example, from 1990 to 2000, out of the 4 million people who died because of wars worldwide, 90 per cent were **civilians**. With fighting shifting from remote battlefields to cities with large populations, civilians have been at a greater risk of injury or death due to civil or interstate war.

Wars in Ukraine, Yemen and Syria have destroyed entire cities, resulting in the deaths of hundreds of thousands of civilians and the displacement of millions more. So significant was the impact on civilians during the civil war in Syria that the UN commissioned an Independent Institution of Missing Persons in the Syrian Arab Republic 'to clarify the fate and whereabouts of all missing persons … and to provide adequate support to victims, survivors and the families of those missing'.

Civilian deaths are not just a result of modern warfare or unintentional impacts from war. Civilians are also targeted deliberately by opposing parties. In fact, between 1989 and 2010, in more than a hundred civil wars, 50 per cent of government forces and 60 per cent of rebel groups deliberately attacked civilians. Alexander Downes says there are several reasons for this:

- It is a desperate response by one party of conflict to reduce its own military casualties.
- A party wants to seize enemy territory.
- When gaining territory is the goal, the population of the land the party is targeting is viewed as a threat, and the aggressive party may target the civilians to remove them from the land it is pursuing.
- When performing poorly, parties may view civilians as legitimate targets to force the opposing party to give up.
- Others have found that civilians are targeted as punishment for collaborating with or assisting the enemy party.

■ Protecting civilians during war

As we saw earlier, international humanitarian law is in place to provide guidance or rules in times of war. These laws include protecting civilians and their property, and combatants are not permitted to target or indiscriminately attack civilians deliberately. This means that no matter the reasons for targeting civilians during war, it is against international law and, therefore, a war crime.

Furthermore, parties cannot, for example, drop large bombs hoping to hit something strategic and in the process cause civilian casualties. This is considered an 'indiscriminate' attack.

■ **Figure 4.24** The impact of war on civilians: this apartment building in Ukraine was destroyed by a Russian missile strike

The Geneva Conventions

As we discussed at the beginning of this chapter, the Geneva Conventions are four treaties adopted in 1949 (with additions or 'protocols' added in 1977 and 2005) and signed by 196 countries. They are the central rules of war that seek to manage the conduct of armed conflict and minimize the impact war has on civilians.

Allen Weiner, the director of the Stanford Program in International and Comparative Law, said that according to the Geneva Conventions, 'civilians can be targeted, but only for such time as they are directly taking part in hostilities. So while a civilian shoots at you, they become a permissible target. When they return home, they cease to be a permissible target under the law of armed conflict' (quoted in El-Bawab).

According to the Geneva Conventions, all parties must abide by the principles of 'distinction', 'proportionality' and 'precautions' during an armed conflict. These three principles are used to guide parties during the conflict.

Distinction

It is the conflict parties' responsibility to distinguish between civilians and combatants, and civilian and military infrastructure. Essential infrastructure, such as roads, hospitals and schools, must not be targeted. This is why there was such uproar when the Russian military hit dozens of Ukrainian hospitals and the Kakhovka dam during the war Russia initiated in 2022. Not only did this break international law, but also it was the responsibility of the Russian military to know that the building they hit was a hospital. Israel continues to argue that Hamas has used hospitals as bases of operation and access points for tunnels, and patients as human shields. While both are brutal, the Russian example seems to be a more straight forward example of a complete lack of discrimination.

The International Committee of the Red Cross (ICRC) has said that the use of 'weapons with wide area effects must be avoided in populated areas' (quoted in El-Bawab).

Proportionality

This prohibits states from launching attacks against military targets if the attack is likely to result in accidental loss of civilian life, injury to civilians or damage to civilian objects.

Precaution

This requires the parties to take constant care to spare civilians and their objects, which includes doing everything possible to make sure that targets are military objects, and giving advance warning of attacks that may affect the civilian population when possible.

The consequences for breaking the rules of war include prosecution by international courts, such as the International Criminal Court. Also, governments are obligated to (must) prosecute any citizen who commits a war crime. Allen Weiner explained that, 'A lot of militaries do actually prosecute their own people if they violate the rules' (quoted in El-Bawab).

 Extended essay

If you are considering writing an extended essay on peace and conflict, examining the extent to which the Geneva Conventions have been violated in a particular conflict could be the basis of a good analytical essay.

◼ Indirect impact of violence

Hunger

Not all civilian casualties result from direct violence, in fact, many of the casualties grow out of indirect causes, such as hunger due to lack of access to basic food supplies. In 2019, 10 of the world's 13 most urgent food crises were in conflict zones. Grocery stores in these countries are unable to stock the food to sell. What they can get is often very expensive, to the extent that a meal can cost more than a day's wages. For example, the cost of a plate of bean stew in South Sudan, where there has been intermittent civil war since 2013, is equivalent to $348. As a result, nearly half a billion people go hungry in conflict zones.

Poverty

Poverty can also result from destruction because things like farming, manufacturing or services cannot be performed. This might mean a lack of access to goods and services, or the workers are no longer able to produce the goods or services because the structures (farms, factories, etc.) have been destroyed. In addition, medical facilities may be destroyed, or there are simply so many casualties they overwhelm the health care system.

◼ Vulnerable groups during conflict

During conflicts a number of vulnerable groups face increased risks, and these include, among others: children, women and people with disabilities.

Children

According to Amnesty International, in 2021, more than 19,000 children were recruited as child soldiers, killed or maimed, subjected to sexual violence, or abducted in armed conflicts. The greatest number of these UN-verified violations occurred in Afghanistan, the Democratic Republic of the Congo, Israel and the Occupied Palestinian Territories, Myanmar, Somalia, Syria and Yemen.

In 1999, the UN Security Council issued its first resolution on children and armed conflict. Then, in 2005, the Security Council created a Monitoring and Reporting Mechanism (MRM) to document and report on six grave violations against children in armed conflict. The goal of the MRM was to create a way for the Secretary-General to list state military and non-state groups committing these violations.

The six grave violations are:

1 recruitment and use of children by armed actors
2 the killing and maiming of children
3 sexual violence
4 abduction of children

5 attacks on schools and hospitals

6 denial of access to humanitarian aid.

All but denial of access to humanitarian aid are triggers for the listing of an armed actor.

Today, the nature of conflict is such that schools are being targeted and we are seeing increasing abduction and enslavement of girls. Furthermore, the battlefields are no longer as clear as they once were, resulting in wars being fought among civilian populations where children are present and consequently harmed. Children suffer differently than adults as a result of conflict. Not only are they, in many cases, physically weaker, but also their physical, mental and psychosocial development is in process and impeded by war.

The impacts on children abducted and manipulated into being child soldiers can be even worse. Former child soldiers are routinely stigmatized, which means many of the children who do survive being soldiers face unimaginable mental, psychological and physical trauma that is left unaddressed.

For example, Boko Haram, a terrorist group operating in northern Nigeria, has forced children to witness and commit atrocities. According to Amnesty International, during attacks, Boko Haram fighters have often forced children to witness the killing or abduction of their parents and siblings.

Sexual violence towards women and girls

In many conflicts, fighting forces continue to use sexual violence against women and girls to deliberately inflict lasting physical and psychological damage. Amnesty International has documented how Ethiopian troops and militia, Eritrean soldiers and fighters from the rebel group, the Tigray People's Liberation Front, have subjected women and girls to rape, gang rape, sexual slavery, sexual mutilation and other forms of torture.

People with disabilities

People with disabilities fleeing violence experience challenges beyond those faced by people without a disability. Some face exhausting journeys without the necessary devices to assist them, like wheelchairs or crutches. As a result, they become dependent on their families or friends.

Sometimes, people with disabilities are left behind as their families or friends flee violence. Others cannot undertake journeys to flee because it would be simply too difficult or would worsen their health or impairment.

Even camps for displaced people provide challenges for people with disabilities. For example, design flaws in toilets and their location can strip people with disabilities of their independence and dignity. During the civil war in Yemen, a 75-year-old man with limited mobility explained that he had to have his sons take him to the toilet by dragging him.

Family members and friends are impacted as well. Some have to sell belongings or delay rent to pay for costs associated with supporting a friend or family member with a disability.

In summary, we can see that there are many actors and stakeholders involved in conflict. What is important to remember is that while there are a number of actors in conflict, such as members of the military, protesters, government officials or even members of the UN, there are also stakeholders – those impacted by the conflict but not directly involved in it. It is important that they are considered as we further explore the nature, practice and study of peace and conflict.

ACTIVITY

Compare and contrast the roles and activities of three NGOs in assisting vulnerable groups during conflict. You may wish to look at some of the examples suggested in the text and/or explore examples beyond those suggestions.

Chapter summary

In this chapter we have covered:
- parties to conflict
- violent and non-violent state and non-state actors
- third parties, including negotiation processes, mediation processes and interventions
- marginalized, vulnerable and most affected groups, and individuals in conflict.

REVIEW QUESTIONS

Now that you have read this chapter, reflect on these questions:

- Explain the difference between 'parties to the conflict' and 'high contracting parties', as defined in international humanitarian law.
- What are the three reasons given for why customary law is binding in the international context?
- Describe the various types of primary disputants that can be involved in conflicts.
- What are the potential advantages and disadvantages of Costa Rica's unique approach toward maintaining national security?
- Explain the various roles and activities that NATO engages in beyond collective defence.
- How do the concepts of 'coercive diplomacy' and 'norms of coexistence' challenge and complement the traditional understanding of diplomacy as a purely peaceful means of conflict resolution?
- Explain the concept of 'Track II diplomacy'.

4.3

Nature, practice and study of conflict

SYLLABUS CONTENT

By the end of this chapter, you should understand:
- types of conflict
- conflict dynamics and causes of conflict
- the legitimacy of conflict
- whether or not non-violence is successful.

In this chapter, we will explore the nature of conflict by first looking at what commonly causes conflict in the global political arena. From there, we will consider the different types of conflict in two contexts.

We will look at types of conflict in the context of its location, and then we will explore how conflict manifests itself in both violent and non-violent ways. Finally, we will look at several debates on the effectiveness of violent and non-violent protest and various justifications or arguments in favour of using violence in a conflict.

4.3.1 Types of conflict

There are many types of conflict in our world today. There can be conflict over which movie to stream, what to have for dinner or which television show to watch. However, in global politics, we want to limit our scope of conflict types to state and (usually) large non-state actors, like non-governmental organizations (NGOs).

Before examining the causes of conflict, we will explore the various types of conflict. There are four main types of conflict in global politics: interstate, intrastate, non-state and extrastate.

■ **Figure 4.25** The remains of a Russian Army armoured column in Bucha, Ukraine, after it was attacked by Ukrainian forces, 1 March 2022

■ Interstate conflict

Interstate conflict occurs between two or more internationally recognized sovereign states. This type of conflict may involve traditional warfare between organized militaries, though it could also involve trade conflict. For example, Russia and Ukraine are engaged in interstate military conflict. In contrast, the United States and China have been engaged in conflict over the trading regulations that exist in each country.

In interstate conflict, the objectives are usually quite clear. Typically, goals involve territorial acquisition or a desire to affect policy in another state. For example, Russia wanted to acquire part or all of Ukrainian territory, with President Vladimir Putin stating, 'Ukraine is not just a neighbouring country for us. It is an inalienable part of our own history, culture and spiritual space.' The Chinese Commerce Ministry stated that the United States was 'artificially hindering global economic and trade exchanges and cooperation' as the US began to limit trade with China.

■ Intrastate conflict

Intrastate conflict, often called civil war or internal conflict, occurs within the borders of a single sovereign state. Intrastate conflict usually involves the government and a non-state actor. These actors may be rebel groups, terrorist groups, ethnic or religious groups, or even lobby groups.

Unlike interstate conflict, the objectives of intrastate conflict can be more complex. They may include any combination of political, economic, social, ethnic or religious grievances. Furthermore, intrastate conflicts may be more asymmetrical, where power between the two groups is unevenly distributed (not equal) than in interstate conflicts. Often, the state will have economic and military advantages and the non-state actor may need to resort to tactics such as guerrilla or cyber warfare. As is often the case, this can blur the distinction between combatants and non-combatants. Because of this, non-combatants can end up being casualties, so creating even more animosity between groups.

While intrastate conflict typically occurs within a state's borders, these types of conflicts can also draw state and non-state actors from outside the country into the conflict. For example, peacekeeping or peacemaking missions, militia groups or the militaries of other states may become involved in an interstate conflict. In cases where the militaries of other states are drawn into the conflict, these intrastate conflicts are referred to as internationalized civil conflicts.

CASE STUDY

Inter- and intrastate conflicts

Ethiopia

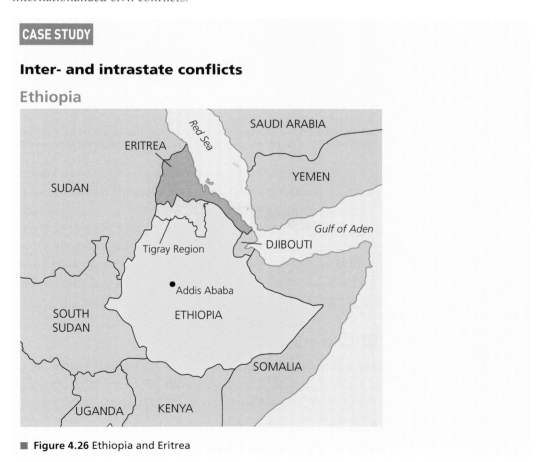

■ **Figure 4.26** Ethiopia and Eritrea

In November 2020, the internationalized civil conflict between the government of Ethiopia and the Tigray People's Liberation Front (TPLF) broke out, resulting in hundreds of thousands of civilian and combatant deaths. Tigrayans have attempted to establish an independent state as far back as the 1200s. In 1991, the TPLF overthrew the government and took control of the capital of Ethiopia, Addis Ababa. The TPLF's removal from power in 2018 led to tension between it and the central government, and by 2020, they were at war. While a ceasefire agreement was signed in November 2022, there continue to be instances of conflict between the two sides that threaten the peace. What made this conflict an 'internationalized' civil war was the involvement of the Eritrean military acting on the side of the Ethiopian government.

Ukraine

■ **Figure 4.27** The areas shaded orange show the extent of Russian incursion into Ukraine since February 2022 (as of February 2024). Crimea was invaded and annexed by Russia in 2014.

In contrast, Russia's invasion of Ukraine is likely the best current example of an interstate conflict. Russia initiated a full-scale invasion of Ukraine on 24 February 2022. Like the intrastate conflict in Ethiopia, this war has resulted in hundreds of thousands of deaths, and also the largest flow of refugees within Europe since the break-up of Yugoslavia in the 1990s. President Putin's ambitions in Ukraine include a desire to gain both territorial and governmental control. However, Ukraine has mounted a strong and sustained defence, and there are increasing suggestions that this may become a protracted war that may very well end in some form of a stalemate.

■ Non-state conflict

As the term suggests, a non-state conflict is a conflict between two organized groups, neither of which is the state. A non-state conflict can occur within one country or across borders. The Uppsala Conflict Data Program (UCDP) categorizes three types of non-state conflict groups:

● formally organized non-governmental groups

● informally organized groups, which may be composed of supporters of political parties

● informally organized groups that engage in communal conflicts – conflicts that are organized around a common identity, such as a religion or ethnicity.

Non-state conflicts may be related to territorial disputes, competition over resources, ethnic or religious tensions, or power struggles among the non-state combatants. The non-state violence in Mexico that has resulted in tens of thousands of casualties represents what non-state conflicts look like. In recent years, the data collected by the UCDP have indicated that Mexico has had the greatest number of deaths resulting from non-state conflict. For example, in 2022, there were more than 14,000 battle-related deaths involving 24 cartels or cartel factions. Cartels like the Sinaloa Cartel, Juarez Cartel and Los Zetas have fought to control drug trafficking routes.

■ Extrastate conflict

An extrastate conflict, like an intrastate conflict, involves a state and a non-state entity. However, the critical difference that makes it an extrastate conflict is that it occurs outside the state's borders and may not be confined to the territory of one state.

The non-state actors in an extrastate conflict could be rebel groups, transnational terrorist organizations or liberation movements operating from neighbouring countries. Like many previous types of conflicts we have explored, extrastate conflicts may be driven by ideological differences, control of resources or territory, or long-term historical animosities.

Perhaps the most well-known example of an extrastate conflict has been between the United States and the al-Qaeda terrorist group. While al-Qaeda was responsible for the attack on United States territory on 11 September 2001, the conflict evolved into an extrastate conflict such that the United States pursued members of al-Qaeda in many countries, including Afghanistan and Pakistan. Similarly, many other states worldwide have engaged in conflict with the terrorist group Islamic State, particularly in Iraq and Syria.

Many of the causes of conflict result in one or more of these types of conflict, so as we begin to explore conflict dynamics, you will want to remind yourself of the differences between the types of conflict, as we will be referring to them often.

Discussion point

What are the similarities and differences between each of the different types of conflict?

4.3.2 Conflict dynamics and causes of conflict

Like many aspects of global politics, it is often difficult to separate one thing from another, and the same is true when we consider 'conflict dynamics' and 'causes of conflict'. In many ways, the dynamics and causes of conflict are interchangeable. The Cambridge dictionary refers to dynamics as 'forces or processes that produce change inside a group or system'. This is very similar to what we are discussing when we look at the causes of conflict. What are the forces, structures, elements or processes at play within society that cause conflict?

During this section, we will explore the various dynamics that cause conflict, such as identity, interests, human needs, greed and grievances. Through this, you will begin to see that many of these causes and dynamics of conflict blend together or do not exist in isolation. When causes do not blend together, we sometimes find that they often play off each other, resulting in multifaceted causes of conflict.

■ Nested Model of Conflict

There are several theories and approaches to understanding conflict. One of these is Máire A. Dugan's Nested Model of Conflict (see Figure 4.28). Here, Dugan presents conflicts within a framework of circles. Each circle represents a different level or type of conflict, and each level of conflict 'nests' within a broader context. Understanding the different nested levels increases the likelihood of finding a resolution to the conflict.

The Nested Model of Conflict has the following levels:

● The issues circle represents the immediate causes or triggers of the conflict. They are the specific disputes or disagreements that are usually visible and obvious.

● The relationship circle represents relational conflicts, either past or current, that may be contributing to the conflict. These can be things like miscommunication or a history of negative interactions.

● The third circle represents the sub-systemic structures. This refers to the structural frameworks where conflict may occur or impact the issues or relational conflicts already at play. These structures can include various things like rules, established hierarchies or the structure of political or economic systems. Sub-systems like these examples may be a contributing factor in the conflict. This circle is not unlike Galtung's idea of structural violence, which we discussed in Chapter 4.1.

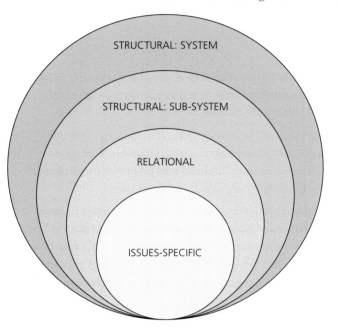

■ **Figure 4.28** Dugan's Nested Model of Conflict

● Sub-systemic structures often reflect broader norms and cultural values that are part of the largest circle, called the systemic structure. These are deeply embedded and are similar to Galtung's idea of cultural violence (see Chapter 4.1). Like cultural violence, they are so deeply ingrained that they can be difficult to change.

Rather than just providing a range of conflict categories, Dugan's model highlights the interconnectedness of these categories, or circles. The more specific categories are embedded or 'nested' within the broader ones and may reflect some broader conflicts. Likewise, broader systemic conflicts may echo the more specific categories beneath them. For example, a relational conflict will involve specific issues; a conflict involving sub-systems will encompass both relational aspects and specific issues; and, at the most expansive level, a system-wide structural conflict will impact and be evident in all other forms of conflict.

ACTIVITY

Use the Nested Model of Conflict to analyse a current conflict in the world today.

● TOK

The TOK course offers a way to compare how different knowledge communities produce knowledge: the Knowledge Framework. The four elements are scope, perspective, methods and tools, and ethics.

You can find links between the Global Politics course and TOK by thinking about how political communities (political scientists) construct knowledge. In this case, we might think of the Nested Model of Conflict as a method or tool for a political scientist to build knowledge about different types of political conflict. If political science is a form of human science (studying the political behaviours and ideas of human beings), then the methods used in this science would have close connections to the scientific method. While the scientific method might be more familiar in the natural sciences (biology, physics, chemistry), it is still applicable when studying different types of human behaviours, such as political behaviour. If this is true, the methods should be based on observational experimentation and prediction, and provide explanatory power, meaning a successful model will show clear cause and effect relationships between the various elements.

So what are the predictions provided by the Nested Model of Conflict? What observations would you expect to see when applying the model to a genuine conflict? Do you observe what was predicted? Does the model help offer a reliable explanation of the conflicts to which it is applied?

These reflective or critical questions can be applied to any of the theories offered in the Global Politics course and help you to engage in a critical way with the material ... just like an expert political scientist would!

CASE STUDY

The Nested Model of Conflict and the civil war in Yemen

Let's use the civil war in Yemen as an example of how the Nested Model of Conflict can be applied.

The issue or immediate cause of the conflict was the takeover of Sanaa, the capital, by the Houthi rebels in 2014. This was a reflection of a long-standing relational conflict between the Houthi (mostly Shia Muslims) and the Yemeni central government (predominantly composed of Sunni Muslims).

Many sub-systemic structures may have influenced the issues and relational conflicts. However, two examples are the weak government structure and the weak economic structures, which included Yemen being one of the poorest countries in the Middle East, with unemployment, food insecurity and lack of resources contributing to economic discontent.

Finally, the broader structural dynamics included the cultural-religious divide between Shia and Sunni Muslims and historical influences, including the fact that Yemen was composed of two separate nations (North and South Yemen) before its unification in 1990. This unification attempted to bring together different political systems and cultures.

Using the Nested Model of Conflict, we can see how immediate issues (like the takeover of the capital) are deeply tied to long-standing relational conflicts (such as religious and political tensions). These relational conflicts are influenced by sub-systemic factors (like economic challenges) and broader systemic structures (like regional religious dynamics).

◼ Identity conflict

Individual and social identity theories help explain shared group conflicts based on how people define themselves. For example, when citizens of a country feel threatened or attacked in a way that challenges or minimizes their identity as citizens of that country, this can result in a type of group conflict called identity conflict.

Identities are unique to each individual but are also in a constant state of flux, or change. Aspects of a person's identity may emerge while other elements develop or change, while other aspects of a person's identity may even disappear. Consider age – we are often identified or categorized according to our age. Are you an adult, a teenager or a child? As we grow and mature, our biological and social characteristics change, along with our identity. Of course, age is not our only source of identity as an individual. Our identity may be tied to sex, gender, ethnicity, religion, sexual orientation, class, nationality and much more. On a social level, our identity may be connected to shared language, faith, economic status or even food.

Because identity includes ethnicity, religion, culture and language, it gives individuals a sense of belonging, purpose and recognition. So, when an individual feels that one or more of these identity elements are under threat, conflict is inevitable. Protecting one's identity is a basic human need, which means that threats to identity are a significant source of conflict in our world today.

Groups not only have cultural or religious bonds but may also have historical bonds, some of which may involve collective memories of past injustices. These historical tensions may be related to land claims, previous state policies that discriminated against one group, or unfair economic policies. The animosity that grows out of these historical injustices can bond one group together and create or continue identity-based tensions between groups.

In the context of global politics, we want to understand how identity acts as a cause of the four types of conflict you have already been introduced to.

One of the ways in which identity can be a source of conflict in global politics is related to the categorizations of groups. When individuals form groups, they see themselves as part of these groups. Because of the many reasons we listed above, they feel a sense of belonging because they identify with the individuals with whom they have one or more of these elements. This is often called the 'in-group', or the group they are 'in' with or a part of. In contrast, the 'out-group' refers to groups perceived as different or separate from the in-group. This creates an in-group–out-group dynamic, sometimes resulting in conflict. When this dynamic occurs, those in the in-group view those in the out-group as 'the other'. This process of 'othering' can go so far as to involve a dominant in-group or majority group defining the out-group as distinctly different and even inferior to itself. Focusing on differences and using those differences breaks down any sense of similarity or connectedness between people. This can reinforce group identities, hierarchies and social boundaries, which may in turn reinforce that the out-group is different or 'not like us'. This can lead to negative stereotypes that may result in misperceptions, misunderstandings, prejudice and discrimination. In extreme situations, out-group members may be seen as less than human, which may easily justify physical and structural acts of violence against the out-group.

Finally, as the world becomes more interconnected, individuals may be drawn even more to their various identities to distinguish themselves or embrace their unique characteristics to in a world that may seem increasingly similar.

Resolving identity-based conflict

Jay Rothman developed the ARIA framework (see Figure 4.29), a process for resolving identity-based conflicts. The framework has four phases:

1 **A**ntagonism

2 **R**esonance

3 **I**nvention

4 **A**ction.

1 Antagonism

The antagonism phase aims to bring suppressed differences to the surface and analyse where the source of the hostility comes from. Participants are asked to share their frustrations and grievances. Facilitators are present to set boundaries and keep the venting from getting out of control.

2 Resonance

Next is the resonance phase, where participants identify common needs and shared interests. Instead of focusing on the frustrations aired at the antagonism stage, parties identify commonalities, take responsibility for areas where they may have perpetuated or caused the conflict, and try to understand the other party's perspective. Ultimately, participants aim to move from an 'us versus them' attitude towards a 'we' attitude.

3 Invention

The resonance phase leads to the invention phase, where the parties in conflict work together to find solutions that meet both parties' needs and interests. This can, of course, be quite challenging. However, reflecting back on the resonance phase, where shared needs and interests were identified, can help the parties progress towards possible solutions.

4 Action

Finally, the fourth phase is the action stage, where participants develop a method to implement the solutions they agreed upon as part of the intervention phase. In this phase, the parties must first decide on the scale of their action. A smaller-scale start can be helpful because it can be easily managed, and if successful, this smaller achievement can build trust in working on larger solutions and actions. Critical to this phase, no matter the scale, is to address who is involved in the action, what the action is, why that action is being taken and how the action is going to be carried out.

The ARIA framework is cyclical, as a breakdown in any of the four phases may result in participants cycling back to previous stages. The framework is, of course, not guaranteed to be successful, but it is an effective tool for attempting to resolve identity-based conflicts.

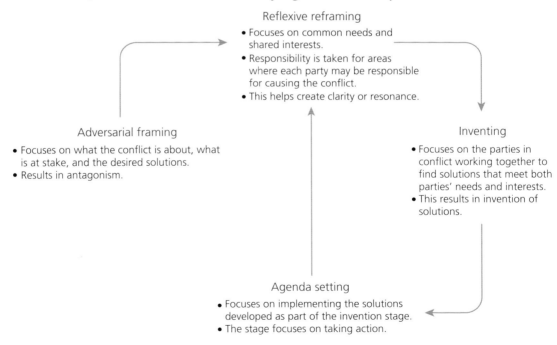

■ **Figure 4.29** The ARIA framework for attempting to resolve identity-based conflicts

Francis Fukuyama and Stacey Abrams on identity politics

Identity politics refers to political stances and movements that prioritize the concerns and interests of various identity groups. These groups might identify with a particular ethnicity, gender, sexual orientation, religion or group that comes together around the desire for a particular right or freedom. The various groups that are part of the identity politics debate can span the political spectrum, from indigenous groups focused on land claims agreements to gun owners who defy limits on gun ownership. When identity groups feel unrecognized, discriminated against or the victims of injustice, they demand public acknowledgement of, and action on, the injustices or discrimination they feel they are experiencing. They are seeking an adjustment to the current power relationships.

One of the main debates related to identity politics is whether it worsens conflict between groups by highlighting differences, or whether the recognition and celebration of unique identities make identity politics an effective tool for drawing attention to inequity, injustice and discrimination.

Stanford international relations scholar Francis Fukuyama (1952–) suggested that, historically, the identity politics that emerged in response to the discrimination and exclusion of black, indigenous or LGBTQ+ communities has been important and valuable. However, he argued more recently that identity politics has become a force that can undermine national unity and sow division. He explained that this is not only the case in the United States, but that identity politics also exists throughout Europe, China, India and Russia.

Central to Fukuyama's argument is that when identity becomes the main focus of a political issue, it threatens the possibility of achieving a common, unifying narrative, which all democracies need to function effectively.

Democracies, he argues, is strained when citizens prioritize subgroup identities over national identity. Perhaps he put it most succinctly when he suggested the following two options. Society could 'demand that [it] treat its members the same way it treat[s] the members of dominant groups, or it could assert a separate identity for its members and demand respect for them as different from the mainstream society' (quoted in Abrams).

In contrast to Fukuyama's position, political activist, politician and lawyer Stacey Abrams (1973–) argued that identity politics does not threaten democracy. Instead, identity is fundamental to democracy. Identity, she suggests, is not a tool for division, rather, it serves as a means for marginalized groups to voice their concerns and secure their rights.

Abrams argues that identity has always been at the forefront of political issues. She states that recognizing and addressing particular groups' unique challenges does not mean that broader universal rights and freedoms are de-emphasized. Furthermore, being a supporter of voting rights, she sees recognizing and responding to the specific needs of various identity groups as a way to engage previously disengaged voters. She sees identity politics as a way to enrich and strengthen democracy, not, as Fukuyama suggests, diminish it. Society, she argues, becomes more inclusive and just by giving voice to marginalized groups and addressing their specific concerns.

● HL extension: Identity

With Identity being one of the eight global political challenges, you may want to use some of the theory and content explored here to support your inquiry. Whether you are looking at exploring possible approaches to addressing/resolving identity conflict or at the causes of identity conflict, this section could be a good place to start.

ACTIVITY

Research a current identity conflict. Based on what we have discussed, what makes it an identity conflict? Next, apply the ARIA framework to a current identity conflict in the world today. How might it work well? Where do you think it may break down?

TOK

Central to this discussion is a TOK question about who belongs to the community that is constructing knowledge and how the knowledge constructed ultimately affects various groups. These issues might be seen as a debate about whose voice belongs to the group of knowledge producers and what types of evidence is appropriate in the production of that knowledge. Fukuyama's position seems to seek a narrow view that the most appropriate evidence is that which is common to most groups, while Abrams seems to suggest that a wider range of evidence, including voices of power-minorities, is appropriate.

■ Interest-based conflict

One cause of many conflicts is a desire to defend an individual or group's interests. Issues causing interest-based conflict usually relate to economic and power differences. Economic conflict may be connected to competition for limited resources and markets. It may also simply come from a desire to achieve greater economic dominance. This type of competition may result in groups coming into conflict with one another as they compete for economic superiority.

In global politics, power conflicts arise when states or groups aim to enhance their influence and dominance over one another. However, as we learned, power can be used in various ways. Some states use hard power: negative tactics, including economic or military threats, violence, or other forms of deception and manipulation. In contrast, other states or groups might choose to use soft power: approaches that rely on persuasive arguments, sharing credible information or working cooperatively with other groups to achieve success for both groups.

Escalation of conflict

Conflicts between political actors are not usually about one thing. They can mix the many issues we have explored so far. All the factors that cause conflict between individuals or groups usually make conflicts grow bigger and more aggressive. This growing tension is called escalation. As conflicts escalate, responses may become more aggressive. This also causes escalation, as tension grows due to animosity towards each side's increasingly aggressive response.

Morton Deutsch explained that if groups act cooperatively, they are, unsurprisingly, more likely to solve their conflicts. However, if they behave competitively, they are more likely to worsen conflicts. Deutsch calls this cycle of competitive behaviour 'malignant social conflict'. He explains that this happens because groups cling to their perspectives and misunderstand each other, allowing groups to justify taking bigger, more aggressive action, and so escalating the conflict even further.

CASE STUDY

Identity and interest-based conflicts

Conflict resolution theorist Jay Rothman argued that identity-based conflicts are often mistaken for disputes over resources. When the focus of the cause of a conflict is misunderstood, then efforts to settle the conflict often fail because they are targeting the wrong issue. He explains that identity-based conflicts are about people's beliefs, religion, culture or ethnicity. In contrast, interest-based conflicts may be over things like land or money.

A recent example of the difference between the two is the identity conflict between the Uyghur Muslims and the Chinese government in Xinjiang and the interest-based trade conflict between the United States and China.

The identity-based conflict between the Uyghur Muslims and the Chinese government in the Xinjiang region of China is very difficult to resolve. The Uyghurs are a Turkic ethnic group who have lived in Xinjiang for centuries. They have their own language, culture and religion. Recently, the Chinese government has accused the Uyghurs of **separatism** and terrorism. The government has detained hundreds of thousands of Uyghurs in so-called 're-education camps', where allegedly they have been subjected to forced labour, political indoctrination and torture. The Uyghurs have also been prevented from practising their religion freely and subjected to cultural assimilation measures.

This identity-based conflict is based on the Uyghurs' religion, culture and ethnicity, making it difficult to resolve. On the one hand, the Chinese government sees the Uyghurs as a threat to national security and is trying to assimilate them into the Han Chinese majority. On the other hand, the Uyghurs are fighting for their right to practise their religion freely and preserve their culture.

Regarding the trade conflict between China and the United States, the two countries have different interests in trade. The United States has said it wants to protect its jobs, and China has said it wants to protect its market share. However, they also have some common interests, such as wanting to promote economic growth. This makes it possible for the two countries to negotiate a solution to their conflict that meets the interests of both sides.

Interest-based conflicts tend to be easier to resolve because there is more room for compromise. In an interest-based conflict, the two sides can often find a solution that meets their needs, even if it does not give them everything they want. In an identity-based conflict, however, the two sides often fight for things they believe are essential to their identity, so finding a solution that both sides can accept is more difficult.

■ Human needs theory of conflict

The human needs theory of conflict suggests that people have basic human needs that must be met to maintain harmony so that conflict does not ensue. While scholars don't agree on all the elements that qualify as human needs, they do agree that human needs must be satisfied in order to resolve or transform a conflict. For example, John Burton of George Mason University in the United States argues that basic needs, such as identity, recognition and security, must be met; otherwise, conflict will likely result. For example, if a group feels their identity is not recognized or respected, they may feel the need to fight for it. Some argue that this approach is too simplistic and does not consider the complex factors that can contribute to conflict. Others argue that even a list clarifying human needs can be too vague and that it is not clear how to measure whether or not a need is being met.

As we saw in Chapter 4.1, Johan Galtung has an extensive list that goes beyond the elements suggested by Burton. Both Burton and Galtung suggest that when universal, basic needs are satisfied, people function well together.

In some ways, this approach reflects a blend of the two types of conflict we have discussed so far – identity and interests. However, Burton argued that these elements go much further than how we choose to identify, or the interests we desire or feel are being threatened. Instead, human needs sit at the core of who we are and what is necessary if we are to develop as human beings. Burton explains that interests are tangible things that may be able to be traded or compromised; needs, such as identity and security, cannot be compromised or negotiated.

As a result, when human needs are threatened, conflict is likely to result.

Needs and values

The importance of values being central to the causes of conflict is also relevant when discussing needs. There are times when conflict will result from a clash between differing values. Conflict is likely to result when individuals, communities or states, for example, have fundamentally different views on the best way to live.

You might also note that some of the needs listed in Figure 4.30 relate to our values – things like identity, cultural security and freedom may relate to the things we value, or reflect what we believe is the best way to live.

Even if we look at values and needs differently, they are similar in that values tend to be constant and rarely negotiable. If the central issues in a conflict are closely related to one's needs or values, the issues are likely to be difficult to resolve or even **intractable**. Negotiating in interest-based conflicts may help progress. However, seeking a negotiated resolution to conflicts involving human needs or value differences is unlikely to succeed.

◆ **Intractable** means very difficult or maybe even impossible to manage or fix.

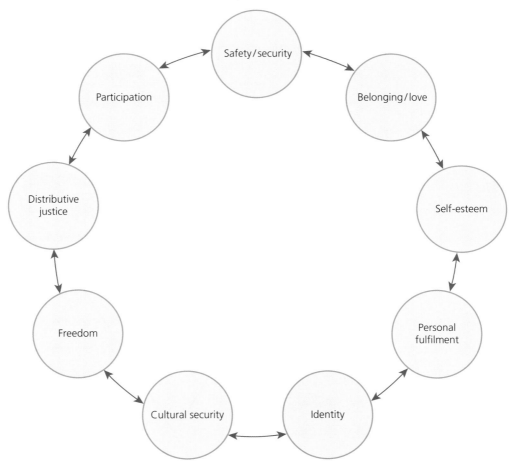

■ **Figure 4.30** Burton and other needs theorists have argued that human needs, such as those listed here, are essential to human development. They also suggest that they should not be viewed in order, with one having priority over the other

■ The positions, interests, needs approach to understanding conflict

Having explored interests and needs, we can now turn our attention to the positions, interests, needs (PIN) approach to conflict resolution. This approach recognizes the difference between the three elements, and the non-negotiable nature of needs.

Positions

Positions are the claims or demands that parties make in a negotiation. It is what a party says they want. However, focusing solely on positions can often lead to a deadlock in negotiating the end of a conflict. If this is the only thing considered, the parties might stick to their positions without considering potential alternatives or the underlying reasons for their demands. It is for this reason the model suggests exploring interests.

Interests

The interests of the parties to conflict are the reasons behind their positions. Interests explain the 'why' behind the 'what'. For example, suppose a party's position is that they want a particular piece of land. In that case, their interest might be that they are seeking the land because they are interested in gaining access to water available on the land. By identifying and addressing the underlying interest – the desire to access a water source – the parties can explore alternatives that might not have been apparent when only the parties' positions were considered.

Needs

However, the parties must understand each other's needs and values before exploring positions or interests. As we explored in the previous section, these are the fundamental, non-negotiable requirements that must be met for a solution to be acceptable. Both parties need to be aware of these so that any solution can be built around the needs of both parties. Identifying any shared or uniting needs and values will also help with negotiations for a settlement.

The idea behind the PIN approach to conflict resolution (see Figure 4.31) is to move beyond the surface-level demands and explore each party's deeper motivations and essentials. By understanding and addressing these underlying factors, negotiators can often find win-win solutions, or at least solutions that are more acceptable to all parties involved.

> **ACTIVITY**
>
> Choose a current conflict and apply the PIN model to it. Does it help you to better understand what might be the causes of the conflict?

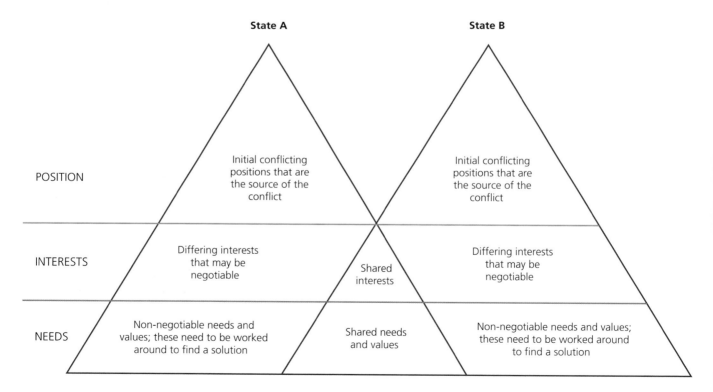

■ **Figure 4.31** The PIN approach to conflict resolution

THEMATIC STUDIES: Peace and conflict

Table 4.5 shows us how we can use the PIN model to better understand the conflict between Russia and Ukraine.

■ **Table 4.5** Applying the PIN model to the conflict between Russia and Ukraine

PIN model element	Russia	Ukraine
Positions	Russia has taken the position that it is invading Ukraine to 'demilitarize and denazify' the country.	Ukraine has assumed that Russia is waging an unprovoked war of aggression.
Interests	Russia's interests in the conflict may include security, influence and economic gain.	Ukraine's interests may include sovereignty, independence and territorial integrity.
Needs	Russia's needs may include security from NATO expansion and a buffer zone between itself and the West.	Ukraine's needs may include security from Russian aggression and the right to self-determination. Their shared need is security.

■ Ideology as a cause of conflict

Another possible cause of conflict is ideology. Ideology is rather a broad idea, but essentially we can say that it may involve some or all of a person's beliefs, values and ideas that together form their world view and affect their actions. Ideological belief systems or world views help individuals or groups make sense of the world and influence their perception and behaviour.

Differences in belief

As we have already discussed, identity conflicts arise from differences in beliefs, ranging from minor preferences to major ideological divides. In global politics, these differences can be about the methods or goals. For example, within organizations or governments, disputes might emerge over decision-making processes or what outcomes are prioritized. On a larger scale, global conflicts can stem from cultural or religious ideological differences, as well as the best strategies to handle global issues or what priorities to set. The challenge of peace and conflict is how dominant groups address these differences. Do they impose their ideological perspective or aim to promote mutual respect and harmony?

One of the ways political actors can come into conflict with one another is as a result of their ideology. When the perspectives of two or more actors on what the world ought to look like clash, there is likely to be conflict. In many cases, an actor's view of the world is tied to their individual and/or group identity. Like many causes of conflict, there are likely to be several interconnected factors. For example, in many countries, we increasingly see individuals' identities – how they see themselves and describe themselves – as a reflection of their political ideology. In this regard, not only is one's ideology a reflection of what they believe the political or social world ought to look like, it is also deeply connected to who they are.

Disagreements over how resources are governed

Ideology can also be the source of how resources are allocated and how society is governed. Disagreements over resource allocation and governance can also be a source of conflict. One way we see this is through tax dollars. A person with one particular ideological perspective may wish to see their tax dollars spent on resources for the underprivileged, public health care, education and so on. In contrast, a person with a different ideological perspective may want to see a decrease in taxation and the privatization of health care and education. Here, we see how resources (in this case, tax dollars) and governance (decisions regarding how the tax dollars are used) can be a source of conflict.

Ideologies that claim exclusivity

Another reason we find ideology at the centre of conflict is that there are ideologies that claim both exclusivity and opposition. This means that some people groups believe that their ideology is the right and only way to view the world. When other individuals or groups suggest an alternative social or political approach, they are 'incorrect'. Their position and possibly even the people with these alternative perspectives must be defeated. This creates an oppositional, or 'us versus them', dynamic, where opposing ideologies are not only viewed as different but as a threat.

When you consider that someone's identity can be wrapped up in their ideology, you quickly see how ideology can cause conflict. Because ideology can be so personal, it can be a source of mobilizing one side over another. Suppose one side views the ideology of another as limiting their freedoms or restricting their financial security. In that case, it can be a major source of anger, frustration and animosity towards those with that ideological position. Again, we see how the causes of conflict influence one another. Identity, interests, values and perceived needs can all impact ideological conflict.

Perspectives

Paul Collier and Anke Hoeffler on greed versus grievance

The greed versus grievance question related to causes of conflict is a framework scholars use to analyse the root causes of intrastate conflicts, particularly civil wars. The debate attempts to determine whether economic motives (greed) or political and societal concerns (grievances) are the primary causes of intrastate conflicts.

Some see greed as a cause of conflict because of the potential economic benefits that may result from success in the conflict. From this perspective, the goal of the conflict is control of resources, territory or other financially beneficial assets. Scholars and policy makers point to many wars where control over valuable resources like diamonds, oil or minerals has played a significant role in causing the conflict. For example, one of the causes of the conflict in Yemen is the competition to control Yemen's oil and gas resources. These resources are essential to the Yemeni economy, and control over them is a major source of power and influence within the country.

Greed

Paul Collier and Anke Hoeffler are key figures in the 'greed versus grievance' debate on the causes of civil wars and conflicts. Collier and Hoeffler argue that the primary motivators for many civil wars are not political or ethnic grievances but rather economic opportunities. They suggest that rebellions often occur when rebel groups perceive that they can gain financially from conflict, especially when the state is weak or there are valuable resources to be controlled.

According to Collier and Hoeffler's research, countries largely dependent on exporting resources like minerals and oil are at a significantly higher risk of experiencing civil wars. These resources can help finance rebel groups and so are a reason for engaging in conflict. This is not to say that Collier and Hoeffler reject the existence or importance of political or ethnic grievances; they simply believe that these grievances are rarely the main motivators for a conflict.

However, critics of the greed argument suggest that this oversimplifies the complex causes of civil conflict. There is little dispute that economic factors may play a role in the conflict, but it is rare for them to be the only or central cause. Grievances arise when governments fail to meet the needs of the people they govern, or fail to build trust with them. Sometimes, this is related to a lack of legitimacy or simply incompetent governing.

When thinking about whether greed or grievance causes conflict, we can look more closely at the civil war in Yemen. While control over the lucrative oil industry plays a role in the conflict, many other historical, political, religious and economic causes exist, including the following:

- Yemen was historically divided into two separate nations, and while they unified in 1990, there are still significant underlying differences.
- The Houthi rebels who follow the Shia branch of Islam are on one side of the conflict, while Yemen's Sunni majority is on the other. However, this identity and ideological factor alone would also oversimplify the conflict.
- During the Arab Spring of 2011, pro-democracy protesters demanded the end of the 33-year rule of President Ali Abdullah Saleh. While a deal was finally negotiated to transfer power to Vice-President Abd Rabbu Mansour Hadi, Hadi's proposals for reforms to the constitution and the budget were rejected by Houthi rebels from the north.
- Yemen is one of the poorest countries in the Middle East, and water scarcity, declining oil revenues, unemployment and limited access to basic services are also sources of conflict.
- The conflict in Yemen is often viewed as a proxy war between Saudi Arabia, the United Arab Emirates (backed by the United States and other countries) and Iran.

This example explains why singling out any one cause of a conflict is almost always an oversimplification. However, does this mean that the other side of the debate, grievance, is the best explanation for what causes intrastate conflict?

Grievance

Those who take the grievance perspective as the cause of civil conflict argue that intrastate conflict arises from historic and deep-seated political, ethnic, religious or social grievances. They suggest that marginalized or persecuted groups rise up against dominant powers (for example, the government or rich business owners) not primarily for economic gain (greed) but instead to address social, political or economic injustices. When looking at the various causes of the civil war in Yemen, we can see how political, social and economic injustices may have led to the conflict.

Scholars who criticize the grievance perspective argue that many so-called grievance-driven wars also contain elements of greed. For example, when looking at Yemen, while the Houthi rebels may have had political, social and religious reasons for engaging in conflict with the Hadi-led government, control over the substantial oil and natural gas resources in Yemen also played a role.

Recently, scholars have reflected on some of the debates over the greed and grievance arguments. They argue that the distinction between greed and grievance is too simplistic. Intrastate conflict is too complex to separate greed and grievance from each other. They further argue that what may start as a grievance-driven conflict can evolve into a greed-driven conflict, as groups seek resources to sustain their efforts or become attracted to the economic benefits of war.

One of the reasons this debate is so important is that understanding whether greed or grievance is the root cause of a conflict can influence how actors respond to conflicts. If greed is driving the conflict, then actors such as the United Nations or other states might respond by cutting off economic resources to warring factions. If grievance is driving the conflict, then solutions to the conflict may involve addressing underlying political or social issues.

The feminist perspective on the causes of conflict

To be 'feminist' in any authentic sense of the term is to want for all people [to have] liberation from sexist role patterns, domination, and oppression.

bell hooks, Feminism is for Everybody

Feminist scholars examine conflict through the lens of gender power relations and dynamics. They explore how conflict shapes, and is shaped by, gender. This way of looking at conflict helps feminists to analyse the power relations and structural inequalities that other approaches to conflict may overlook.

Feminist international relations theorists, like Cynthia Enloe, argue that militarism and conflict are intimately tied to masculine identities. War and preparations for war can be seen as arenas where masculinity is proven and asserted. This link between masculinity and militarism can drive states to be aggressive and pursue wars to present their 'masculine credentials' on the global stage. Women are under-represented in political decision-making processes, and feminists argue that the lack of a feminist lens on conflict-related policy decisions may make conflict more likely.

Feminists argue that economic structures perpetuate gender inequalities, and that this can indirectly contribute to conflict. Women are often underpaid and undervalued. This means states may miss out on their economic growth potential, which, as we have already explored, can be a major cause of conflict.

Finally, feminist scholars emphasize the importance of an intersectional approach. They argue that factors like ethnicity, class and gender intersect and overlap, creating a web of oppression that can worsen grievances and ultimately contribute to conflict. Ignoring this can lead to an incomplete understanding of the causes of conflict.

Institutions as a cause of conflict

Institutions are the main way humans interact within and between states. Examining the nature, design and quality of these institutions can help us to understand the causes of conflict. Institutions can influence whether a conflict starts, how long it lasts, and the quality of and commitment to conflict resolution.

Institutions also determine how power and resources are shared among various groups in a society and how decisions are made. Flawed or biased institutions might exclude certain groups from power, leading to unequal access to resources and input into political decision-making. This has the potential to lead to grievances that can spark conflict.

Institutions play a role in creating and enforcing norms. For example, when institutions fail to enforce international norms, such as opposing territorial aggression, this can encourage states to pursue aggressive international policies that lead to interstate conflict. In contrast, strong institutions that have the power and legitimacy to enforce norms can act as a deterrent to territorial aggression.

These institutions can also act as mediators and arbitrators, and help conflicting parties seek ways to avoid or end conflicts. In this way, the quality, power and legitimacy of institutions can either be a cause of conflict or a way to prevent conflict.

ACTIVITY

Now that we have considered several causes of conflict, choose a current conflict (it could be one you explored as part of some of the activities above) and determine to what extent the conflict seems to have its foundations in each of the causes we have discussed. It could be to a limited extent, some extent or a significant extent. As you complete this activity, recall the debate on greed versus grievance – rarely is it a single cause.

Discussion point

Consider the conflicts occurring in the world today. Can you identify any patterns or triggers that often cause conflict?

THEMATIC STUDIES: Peace and conflict

4.3.3 The legitimacy of conflict

One of the central elements of peace and conflict studies is the legitimacy of various types of conflict. Before exploring how various forms of conflict look, we need first to examine how conflict can be legitimized. We will first look at what might be justifiable reasons for engaging in conflict and then explore justifiable actions during conflict.

■ 'Just war' theory

'Just war' theory seeks to ensure wars are morally justifiable and that they are conducted in a just way. 'Just war' theory can be traced back to various sources, including ancient Indian and Chinese writings. However, its most well-known roots lie in Greek and Roman writing and Christian theology. Most famously, in the 1200s, St Thomas Aquinas explored what makes a just war in his best-known work *Summa Theologica*.

'Just war' theory can be divided into two main components:

- jus ad bellum, or the right to go to war
- jus in bello, or right conduct during war.

Both Latin terms come from the work of Aquinas and St Augustine, both of whom explored justifications for war and just behaviour during war.

Jus ad bellum

Jus ad bellum explores the morality of going to war. It contains several key criteria. There is much debate around each criterion, so do not assume everyone agrees, understands and has the same position on what each criterion means.

The three key conditions are:

- Just cause: there must be a good reason to go to war. The example most often used is self-defence, although there could be other reasons. The UN Charter allows member states to use force in self-defence against an armed attack. This justification requires that the threat be imminent (likely to happen soon), and the use of force must be proportionate (discussed in more detail below) and necessary. In addition, a state can legally intervene in another state if explicit consent is given. For example, the government of one state might invite another country's military to help suppress a rebellion.

- Legitimate authority: typically, this means that the war must only be entered into by a legitimate and recognized authority. As legitimacy isn't always clear, agreement on what it means to be a legitimate authority is also up for debate. However, an internationally recognized head of state is a reasonable starting point. In addition, the UN Security Council has the authority to determine threats to international peace and security and take both non-military and military action in response. When the Security Council adopts a resolution under Chapter VII of the UN Charter, it can authorize member states to use force.

- Just intentions: the warring state must have the right intentions and be engaged in war for the purpose of seeking justice as opposed to its own self- or national interest. There is, of course, the challenge of determining someone's intentions and also what seeking justice looks like. For example, humanitarian intervention to prevent or stop human rights violations, such as genocide, seems to meet 'just intentions'. However, beyond crimes against humanity, do other humanitarian crises warrant intervention, and at what point are these interventions simply thinly disguised colonial interference?

Since the end of the Second World War, three other conditions have typically been included in 'just war' theory:

- Probability of success: there should be a reasonable chance of success in achieving the war's aims. However, this may be quite difficult to determine with all of the complexities of war.

- Last resort: war should only be waged after all peaceful alternatives have been exhausted. The question of what qualifies as a peaceful alternative is also up for debate – it may be impossible to exhaust all of the alternatives. Still, it could mean that war is never justifiable, as there could arguably always be a peaceful alternative.

- Proportionality: the harm caused by the war must be proportionate to (in balance with) the good that is expected to be achieved. However, it is extremely difficult, if not impossible, to determine whether the harm inflicted will be equal to the good achieved before conflict happens.

Jus in bello

Jus in bello, or justice in war, explores what kind of conduct should be allowed during war. Jus in bello is based on the principle of distinction, which means that only combatants, not civilians, should be targeted.

Since the Peace of Westphalia concluded the Thirty Years' War in 1648, there has been a sustained push to establish international law and enforce wartime laws and standards of military behaviour.

Jus in bello is now known as international humanitarian law (which we covered in Chapter 2.3). While international law provides legal rules and regulations for the conduct of war and is designed to protect civilians, it can never cancel out the many negative impacts of war that civilians must endure.

◆ When something is **prohibited** it is formally banned by law or another authority.

The most important sources of jus in bello are the Geneva Conventions of 1949 and their Additional Protocols of 1977 and 2005 (see Chapter 4.2). These treaties set out detailed rules governing the conduct of war, including protecting civilians, prisoners of war and medical personnel (together known as non-combatants). International law also **prohibits** the use of poison gas and biological weapons.

The key principles of jus in bello are as follows:

- The principle of distinction prohibits the targeting of civilians during war.

- The principle of proportionality prohibits the use of excessive force in relation to the anticipated military advantage.

- The principle of precaution requires combatants to take all possible precautions to avoid or minimize harm to civilians and non-combatants.

- The protection of prisoners of war: prisoners of war must be treated humanely and not be subjected to torture or cruel, inhumane or degrading treatment.

- The protection of medical personnel and facilities: medical personnel and facilities must be protected and not targeted during the course of the war.

Criticism of 'just war' theory

While 'just war' theory has influenced the study of peace and conflict, it has also been criticized for a number of reasons. First, as we suggested in our description of jus ad bellum, many terms are ambiguous, vague and unclear. For example, does an imminent attack provide just cause to engage in war? The idea that a state does not need to wait for an armed attack to occur further confuses the question, depending on how the term 'imminent' is defined.

ACTIVITY

Apply jus ad bellum and jus in bello to one conflict occurring in the world today.

THEMATIC STUDIES: Peace and conflict

However, these are not the only criticisms. As we saw in the core chapters of this textbook, realist international relations scholars argue that international politics is driven by power dynamics and national interest, not by principles of justice and fairness. As a result, they see 'just war' theory as idealistic and not reflective of how decisions about war and peace are made in the real world.

Pacifists have also found fault with 'just war' theory. They argue that 'just war' theory can too easily be used to justify violence. They state that violence, even if morally justifiable, continues the cycle of violence.

Similarly, there are the concerns of feminist and intersectional scholars who argue that 'just war' theory often overlooks the impacts of war on women, children and members of other marginalized communities. They suggest that a more nuanced understanding of the impact of war on various communities is necessary before discussing what makes for a just reason or just behaviour during war.

There are also some practical critiques of 'just war' theory. Some argue that 'just war' theory is too focused on the state and that with the rise of non-state actors, civil wars and guerrilla warfare, 'just war' theory seems dated. Furthermore, with the rise of non-traditional forms of war, the distinctions between combatants and non-combatants have been blurred, making some of the ideals of jus in bello all the more difficult to achieve. There is the question of whether 'just war' theory can address the invention of new warfare technologies, such as drones and cyber-attacks. For instance, does a cyber-attack that cripples infrastructure but doesn't directly kill anyone constitute a 'just cause' for war?

Recently, there's been an emphasis on ensuring justice after conflicts, or jus post bellum (justice after war). This includes things like war crime trials, reconstruction and reconciliation, some of which we will explore in Chapter 4.4. Applying either jus ad bellum or jus in bello to a current or recent conflict would make for a strong extended essay.

Discussion point

Do you think 'just war' theory is an effective approach to determining the legitimacy of war?

◼ Religious and cultural justifications for war

Religious justifications

While theologians founded some of 'just war' theory, it is not primarily viewed with religion in mind. Religious justifications have been used, sometimes intersecting with political, economic or territorial motives.

Some of the religious justifications or arguments in favour of war include certain religious traditions that believe that they are required by the supreme or spiritual being they worship to wage war against enemies or defend believers from persecution or threats to the religion itself. These reasons have been used to justify wars against religious minorities and those perceived as threats to their faith.

Wars have also been waged to maintain the religious purity of a spiritual community, or to suppress beliefs that run contrary to what the religious authorities are teaching. There are also cases where territories, buildings or monuments considered sacred or central to religious traditions can become causes for religious-based conflict. Wars may be justified to protect or reclaim these sacred sites or regions.

It is important to note that, while these justifications do exist, they often do not represent mainstream views within any particular religious tradition. Many spiritual traditions emphasize peace and reconciliation, and interpretations used to justify war are often rooted in broader political power dynamics.

Cultural justifications

Cultural justifications for war can be complex and multifaceted and may also be connected to religious justifications for war. Like religious justifications for war, it is important to note that while these justifications may arise from certain cultural contexts, they do not necessarily represent any particular culture.

One of the cultural justifications for conflict may be a historical narrative of past wrongs, invasions or occupations. Leaders can use these historical incidents to mobilize support for war and to legitimize wars of revenge or reconquest. Similarly, cultural narratives can heighten land disputes, particularly if the land where the dispute occurs has a cultural, historical or spiritual significance.

Like religious justifications for violence, if a culture perceives itself or its values as being threatened, it may resort to violence as a means of preservation. In contrast, the desire to spread cultural values and systems can sometimes lead to aggressive expansion or provide an argument for the military necessity of spreading these values and systems to other cultures.

TOK

Making sense of the different causes and justifications for conflict and war might prove a challenge. One way to develop a clear understanding of the differences is to break down each of the positions into the four elements of the TOK Knowledge Framework: Scope, Methods and Tools, Perspectives and Ethics

First, try to identify the central core of the position – what is the position looking for when analysing conflict? This will be the *scope* of the position. Is this particular style of justification primarily looking at the effect of institutions? Or cultural beliefs? Or religious beliefs? These would the differences indicated by the main headings above.

Then you might consider how the different justifications would measure or observe different evidence to build their justifcation. This will relate to the *methods and tools* of the position. What observations are needed to build the position? What is included or excluded in the evidence or analysis?

Even within the different justifications there is likely to be some disagreement, and these might be considered the *perspectives* within each position. For example, not all analysts within the 'institutional position' will necessarily agree on the relative effects of the institutions, so what are the choices within these positions?

Finally, what *ethical* values are driving the justification? Is there a critique or assumption about how the conflicts are resolved, based on how they originate? Are some of the justifications designed to draw out moral values in their arguments? What other areas of knowledge (economic, social, cultural, religious) might be relevant or be affected by this position?

This sort of analysis can show where the similarities and differences lie amongst the different positions and can help you to develop your understanding and critical evaluation of them.

HL extension: Security and Borders

While the security of borders often links the global political challenges of Security and Borders, it is important to note that issues of security also include the social, cultural and economic aspects of global politics. Much of this section on conflict dynamics and the causes of conflict could be a starting point for an inquiry into the elements of security. You could also look for ways in which your inquiry links to global political challenges like Identity, Poverty and Borders. Remember, part of the Paper 3 expectations requires you to be able to address links between the global political challenges.

4.3.4 Forms of conflict

At the beginning of this chapter, we explored four different types or locations of conflict. Now that we have considered a variety of causes and justifications for conflict, we will take an introductory look at various forms of conflict. This section is by no means an attempt to explore all aspects of the many forms of conflict between political actors. Instead, it is a brief survey of a number of relevant forms of conflict that will emerge throughout your study of global politics. You are encouraged to use this introduction to these forms of conflict as an entry point for further inquiry.

■ Symmetric and asymmetric conflicts

We examined power asymmetries in Chapter 3.1; you can refer to this as a reminder of what the term means before jumping into how power asymmetries affect conflict.

We often see conflicts between relatively similar parties when looking at interstate or even intrastate conflict. While it would be incorrect to suggest that Russia and Ukraine have the same military capacities, through support from allies, the conflict has resulted in a relatively symmetric conflict.

However, conflict may also arise between a much stronger and a much weaker majority and minority party, each with different capacities. There are times when this asymmetry lies at the heart of the conflict. Instead of differences in interests or needs, the asymmetrical structures or roles of the groups can seemingly only be changed through conflict.

For the weaker or smaller party to succeed in an asymmetric conflict, it needs to seek the support of a third party to assist or engage in unconventional tactics that can challenge the more dominant party.

Figure 4.32 illustrates how Adam Curle visualized the process of moving from unpeaceful to peaceful relationships. This may require an overt (or visible) conflict, so that people become aware of the power imbalance or injustices.

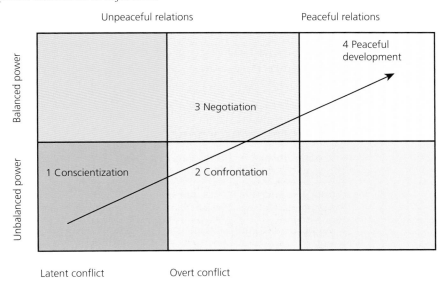

■ **Figure 4.32** Transforming asymmetric conflict (adapted from Ramsbotham et al.)

- Stage 1 of transforming asymmetric conflict involves a 'conscientization', or education stage, where people organize themselves in a way they feel will allow them to articulate their grievances effectively.
- Stage 2, confrontation, involves those who feel oppressed or want a change confronting those in power and demanding changes.
- Stage 3, negotiation, is where the parties to conflict agree to seek a way to resolve the conflict. This may involve creating a more equitable (equal) relationship or meeting needs.
- Stage 4, resolution, is where the parties find a way to re-balance the asymmetric relationship. This means more equity, justice or needs are met, and a peaceful (or at least more peaceful) relationship can happen.

Another tactic is to strengthen and empower the weaker party, where the weaker party withdraws from the asymmetrical relationship and seeks to construct a different structure altogether.

Next, we will explore forms of conflict that are asymmetric in nature, and the various tactics that have been used to either repair unpeaceful relations or to withdraw and attempt to rebuild independently from the current power structure.

■ Guerrilla warfare

◆ **Militia groups** act like armies, but their members are not professional soldiers.

◆ An **insurgent** is a person who is fighting against the government or armed forces in their country.

The term 'guerrilla' comes from the Spanish *guerra*. Guerilla means 'little war' and refers to the use of hit-and-run tactics by small, mobile groups of fighters who use their knowledge of the land and sympathetic local populations to fight a larger and less mobile traditional military. Guerrillas are often made up of local **militia groups**, **insurgents** or members of liberation movements. It is an inherently asymmetric form of warfare that recognizes the group's inability to defeat its opposition's superior forces in open battles. So, the group resorts to tactics that limit traditional military advantages.

Guerrilla warfare relies on ambush tactics meant to surprise the opposition, after which the guerrilla soldiers quickly retreat before opposition reinforcements arrive. Guerrilla warfare seeks to disrupt the opposition's supply chains, communication lines and infrastructure. The group's knowledge of the land allows it to carry out many tactics while evading the opposition's forces. Furthermore, guerrillas rely on local populations for supplies, intelligence and recruits. The relationship with local communities may be because they support the movement, but their support may also result from being coerced into assisting the guerrilla campaign.

A defining characteristic of guerrilla warfare is that it tends to be prolonged since it is a war of attrition. This is war where each side aims to wear down the enemy over time. Key to the success of a guerrilla campaign is adaptability and willingness to quickly change tactics based on the situation and movements of the opposition.

■ Counterinsurgency (COIN)

Counterinsurgency, often called COIN, refers to the strategies and operations undertaken by a government or occupying power to suppress, weaken or eliminate an insurgency. An insurgency may use guerrilla tactics, but its goal tends to be more comprehensive than guerrilla warfare in that it aims to control the resources of a country at least partially or completely and challenge the authority and control of an established government or administration.

COIN operations have military and civil dimensions; they aim to defeat the insurgency militarily and win the 'hearts and minds' of the population. In this way, protecting and winning over the population is more important than defeating the insurgents.

A counterinsurgency must effectively counter the information and propaganda the insurgency shares to achieve this goal. A COIN must also 'clear-hold-build':

● clear an area of insurgents (a COIN operation must be careful not to use indiscriminate force as this is likely to alienate the local population)

● secure the area to prevent the return of insurgents

● build up and renew a legitimate political, social and economic infrastructure and in doing so garner public support.

This must include cultural sensitivity to local customs and grievances to avoid alienating the population and encourage cooperation. This is only likely to be successful if the state's security forces and governance structures carry out most of the COIN work. External forces can be supportive, but local legitimacy is key to a successful counterinsurgency.

One of the biggest challenges to a successful COIN operation is distinguishing combatants from non-combatants. This is challenging because insurgents often blend in with the civilian population. COIN can also be long and drawn out. This means that counterinsurgency requires a long-term commitment to funding, including advisory and military support.

Counterinsurgency in Afghanistan

After the terrorist attacks on the United States on 11 September 2001, the United States led a coalition to overthrow the Taliban government in Afghanistan, which had provided safe haven to the al-Qaeda terrorist organization behind the attacks. The Taliban regime was quickly toppled, but soon after, the Taliban and other groups started an insurgency against the newly established Afghan government and its international backers.

In 2009, the United States adopted a comprehensive COIN strategy, emphasizing the need to protect the Afghan civilian population over killing insurgents. In addition, it focused on building up Afghan governance capacities and promoting economic development in the

■ **Figure 4.33** Afghan citizens being evacuated from Afghanistan after the United States withdrew and the Afghan government collapsed

country. However, despite years of effort and significant investment, the COIN strategy faced many challenges and by 2021, the United States and its NATO allies fully withdrew their combat troops from Afghanistan. At the same time, the Afghan government collapsed, and the Taliban rapidly took control over most of the country, effectively ending a two-decade-long COIN effort.

There were several reasons for the failure, many of which reflect what a COIN operation must avoid in order to be successful:

● Afghanistan's complex social, tribal and ethnic dynamics meant that a one-size-fits-all COIN approach was ineffective.

● The Afghan government was unable to provide basic services and significant corruption failed to develop public trust.

● The United States and its NATO allies also faced the challenge of the Taliban receiving support and sanctuary from neighbouring countries, most notably Pakistan. This made it very difficult to eliminate their networks.

● The United States and its allies were unprepared to commit the necessary resources and time to defeat the insurgency.

■ Terrorism

Terrorism, characterized by violence and often targeting non-combatants, is one of the more well-known examples of asymmetrical warfare. Terrorism is asymmetrical because it uses tactics to challenge more powerful opponents. Instead of engaging in direct, traditional combat, terrorists use surprise attacks and guerrilla tactics, target civilians and exploit media coverage. These methods aim to disrupt, demoralize and create fear to achieve their goals against a stronger, more powerful opponent. As with other forms of irregular or asymmetric warfare, terrorism is designed to achieve political change or is used by groups who feel that violence is the only way to preserve their traditions.

Terrorist attacks are designed to be dramatic events undertaken to capture attention and create fear. Terrorists may be able to exaggerate their strength and the threat they pose by engaging in acts of terror. However, terrorism varies significantly in its specific goals, tactics and location (see Table 4.6).

■ **Table 4.6** Types of terrorism

Location	• Domestic
	• International
Motivation	• Political: overthrow a government or changing government policy
	• Religious: establish a religious state; advance a particular religious tradition or practice; prevent or make changes to society so they are more in line with the religious perspective
	• Ideological: achieve ideological goals, such as promoting a particular political or social ideology
	• Nationalist or separatist: achieve nationalist goals, such as gaining independence for a particular nation or ethnic group
	• Narco-terrorism: carried out by drug cartels to further their role in the drug trade
	• Eco-terrorism: targets industries or entities they see as harming the environment
	• Cyber-terrorism: uses digital tools and the internet to infiltrate or attack digital infrastructures or data systems, with the aim to either cause damage, or create disruption or fear
Targets	• Civilians: to create fear and panic
	• Government officials: to intimidate or assassinate
	• Military personnel: to weaken a government's security forces
	• Infrastructure: to disrupt the economy and cause chaos
	• Religious sites: to provoke religious conflict or to attack a particular religious group

Beyond the asymmetrical nature of terrorism, the reason individuals or groups resort to terrorism is a matter of perspective. Those sympathetic to terrorist causes suggest that violence is the only option to draw attention to their cause. The need to highlight their complaint is so critical that even the death of innocent people is seen as a means to an end. These causes may be ideological, ethnic and religious exclusion or persecution.

Those targeted by terrorists see little, if any, justification for acts of terror. For them, there is no rationale strong enough to justify killing and injuring innocent civilians.

Terrorism is rarely an effective mode of asymmetrical conflict. It rarely gains support from the broader population needed for an effective insurgency. In fact, the methods used by terrorists often alienate potential supporters of their cause. Terrorist groups also struggle to find support because their causes tend to be more radical and, as a result, have little widespread appeal.

Particularly since the terrorist attacks on 11 September 2001, several approaches have been taken to address terrorism. These include:

● education, aiming towards deradicalization of extremist beliefs

● legal changes that have enhanced border controls and tracking of terrorist activities

● attempts to address socio-economic disparities that can increase the appeal of extremist beliefs

● international cooperation, where countries have sought to work together to stamp out terrorism, a form of violence that does not respect borders.

■ Cyber conflict

Cyber conflict or cyberwar is when state or non-state actors use digital tools to attack, defend or exploit the information systems of a party they are in conflict with. Cyber conflict can seek to damage or disrupt critical digital infrastructure or gain access to sensitive data. This form of conflict is relatively new, and it shifts the conflict from traditional battlefields to cyberspace.

Cyberwar is not limited to states. Non-state actors, including terrorist groups, hacktivist collectives and criminal organizations, also use cyberwar tactics. Terrorists might aim to cause

ACTIVITY

Research a current example of each of the violent forms of conflict listed in 4.3.4.

widespread panic by disrupting utilities, while hacktivists might breach data systems to make political statements or expose perceived injustices, and criminal organizations could engage in cyberwarfare to profit from stolen data.

A distinct feature of cyberwar is its asymmetric nature. Even smaller states or loosely affiliated groups with limited resources can launch potent cyber-attacks, levelling the playing field against more technologically advanced or larger opponents. As the world becomes more interconnected, the potential for cyberwarfare to have profound economic, political and social implications grows, as does the need to protect actors and stakeholders from cyber-attacks.

4.3.5 Non-violent forms of conflict

In this final section of the chapter we will look at brief descriptions of various non-violent approaches to conflict.

As we saw in Chapter 4.1, there are many reasons to engage in a peaceful approach to conflict – see page 298 for Martin Luther King, Jr's six key principles of non-violent action. Table 4.7 outlines the main forms of non-violent conflict, their purpose and examples of each form.

■ **Table 4.7** The main forms of non-violent conflict

	Definition	Purpose	Examples
Demonstration	A public gathering for people to show their collective stance on a particular issue or cause	To display support or opposition to a particular cause publicly, raise awareness about an issue, and potentially influence public opinion and policy	Marches, rallies, vigils, public art installations
Protest	Usually includes a public demonstration but is also a public expression or declaration of objection or disapproval of a policy. Protests are often carried out in opposition to something a person is powerless to prevent or avoid	To publicly highlight or state a formal objection to an issue or a formal request for something supporting an issue. This differs from a demonstration in that demonstrations reflect an action being undertaken	Sit-ins, road blockades, riots when protests turn violent
Boycott	A call to abstain from using, buying or dealing with a person, organization or country as an expression of protest against their policies or actions	To exert economic pressure on businesses or other actors and, in doing so, force them to reconsider their policies or practices deemed unjust or harmful by those boycotting	Boycotting the purchase or use of a product, or an event
Petition	A formal written request, typically signed by many people, appealing to an authority or the owners of a business or organizers of an event to start or refrain from doing something	To show a collective demand for change	Online petitions on platforms like **avaaz.org**, physical petitions handed to elected officials
Strike	A work stoppage caused by the mass refusal of employees to attend to their jobs	To pressure employers, usually for better working conditions, wages or benefits	Nurses' strikes for better pay, miners striking against unsafe working conditions
Civil disobedience	A public refusal to obey certain laws or requirements of the government without resorting to physical violence	To challenge or protest unjust laws or practices and bring attention to their injustice non-violently	Historical examples include Rosa Parks refusing to give up her bus seat in Montgomery, Alabama and Mahatma Gandhi's Salt March in colonial India. More recently, in Iran, after the death of Mahsa Amini, protesters refused to wear their legally prescribed headscarves in protest against the harsh consequences of not wearing a headscarf.

■ **Figure 4.34** Members of the environmental activist group Just Stop Oil glue themselves to the wall in London's National Gallery after throwing tomato soup on Vincent Van Gogh's 'Sunflowers'. The group has used a variety of non-violent tactics, including sit-ins and traffic obstruction, to deliver its message

ACTIVITY

Research a current example of each of the non-violent forms of conflict listed in 4.3.5.

Discussion point

Do you think that Chenoweth and Stephan's work will change the nature of conflict in global politics?

The efficacy of non-violence

Maria Stephan and Erica Chenoweth found that 'during the period of 1900 to 2006, non-violent resistance campaigns were about twice as effective as violent ones in achieving their goals'. They also found that 'these trends hold even where most people expect non-violent resistance to be ineffective— for instance, against dictatorships and highly repressive regimes'.

Chenoweth and Stephan found that non-violent campaigns tend to attract a more diverse set of participants. This larger participation means more individuals can protest for change, which can positively impact the outcome for the protesters. They explain that when peaceful protests successfully overthrow authoritarian regimes, they are more likely to form democracies and uphold human rights.

Chenoweth and Stephan also suggest that the traditional reliance on violence and military use might be more because of familiarity than actual effectiveness. There is also the multi-trillion dollar military industry that likely has influence over governmental policy decisions.

Recently, non-violent resistance has overtaken armed conflicts as the primary method of global protest. From 1900 to 2019, research highlighted 628 significant mass movements aiming to overthrow national leaders or establish territorial autonomy. Contrary to many stereotypical images of freedom fighters, less than half (303) of these movements resorted to violence. The majority (325) leaned heavily towards peaceful protest.

The preference for non-violent resistance has especially surged in the last 50 years. Chenoweth found that violent uprisings have fallen since the 1970s, whereas non-violent protests have grown. This was particularly evident from 2010 to 2019, which saw the highest number of non-violent protests since 1900, with 96 significant non-violent movements.

Not everyone agrees with the findings of Chenoweth and Stephan. Kai Thaler, a professor of global studies at the University of California, Santa Barbara, argues that many movements use a blend of peaceful mass demonstrations and violence, making it difficult to differentiate between the two. He further argues that some degree of violent resistance might be essential in stricter authoritarian environments to counter aggressive or violent forces. Thaler explains that while the data might suggest that non-violent resistance is generally more successful, this cannot be generalized to fit every scenario. In fact, he suggests that recommending non-violence without understanding a specific social or political context could be bad advice, as there are times when violence is necessary.

Non-violent resistance can bolster both national and global credibility, putting more strain on those being targeted. If a regime uses violence against peaceful movements, it can backfire. Such actions can rally the public to support the protesters or result in supporters of the regime turning their backs on them. Finally, if a regime uses violence, this could draw international criticism, potentially resulting in sanctions or support for the protesters.

Chapter summary

In this chapter we have covered:
- types of conflict
- conflict dynamics and causes of conflict
- forms of conflict
- whether or not non-violence is successful.

REVIEW QUESTIONS

Now that you have read this chapter, reflect on these questions:

- Define interest-based conflict and explain how economic and power differences can contribute to such conflicts.

- Provide two examples of conflicts in global politics that can be attributed to economic competition and power struggles among states or groups.

- Use Morton Deutsch's 'malignant social conflict' concept to explain why competitive behaviour can lead to bigger and more aggressive conflicts over time.

- Explain the Positions, Interests, Needs (PIN) approach to conflict resolution and how understanding these elements contributes to more effective conflict resolution strategies.

- Provide an example of how political ideology can lead to conflicts. Discuss the challenges of addressing conflicts driven by ideological differences.

- Analyse the strengths and limitations of the 'just war' theory presented in the text. Consider the perspectives of critics who argue that the theory is outdated in the context of non-state actors and evolving warfare technologies. To what extent is 'just war' theory a useful tool to determine the legitimacy of war?

- Explain the differences between symmetric and asymmetric conflicts and provide real-world examples of each.

4.4 Debates on peace and conflict

SYLLABUS CONTENT

By the end of this chapter, you should understand:
▶ types of peacemaking, including barriers to conflict resolution and methods to prevent and deter conflict
▶ debates on UN peacekeeping and the principles of intervention
▶ the effectiveness of peacebuilding efforts.

4.4.1 Peacemaking

The previous chapters in this thematic study have focused on the nature and practice of conflict, and now we will consider how peace is made when actors engage in conflict. We will focus on finding peace in violent conflict, but you should remember that ending non-violent conflict also requires resolution. In fact, many approaches to peacemaking, peacekeeping and peacebuilding can be transferred to non-violent conflict. Whether a conflict is violent or non-violent, ceasing hostilities, understanding the issues at the heart of the conflict and finding compromise is the only way to move from negative to truly positive peace.

The United Nations (UN) defines peacemaking as 'measures to address conflicts in progress and usually involves diplomatic action to bring hostile parties to a negotiated agreement'. It explains that the UN Secretary-General may try to help **facilitate** the resolution of the conflict. However, peacemaking is not limited to the Secretary-General or the UN. Peacemakers may also be diplomats representing a state or groups of states, or regional organizations like the African Union or NATO. Finally, there are also unofficial peacemakers like non-governmental organizations (NGOs) or prominent individuals like the Pope or Dalai Lama that may try to intervene to achieve a **peace agreement**.

◆ To **facilitate** is to make something (an action or process) possible or easier.

◆ A **peace agreement** is a formal document, or set of documents, produced after discussions between two or more parties engaged in conflict have taken place and an agreement has been reached to end the conflict.

Discussion point

Reflect on some of the current conflicts in the world today. What do you think needs to be included in peace agreements so that the root causes of the conflicts can be addressed?

 TOK

What is the difference between political science and politics?

The United Nations seems to be playing two roles here. First, as political scientists, the UN has observed and analysed the nature of actual conflict and diplomatic action to identify a pattern of past behaviours and to devise a definition of 'peacemaking' in order to describe those behaviours. Political scientists, in other words, identify abstract principles and concepts based on observed human behaviour in an attempt to find patterns and describe them. This is why political science can be categorized under the 'human sciences'. It is the application of the scientific method to human political behaviour. However, unlike the application of the scientific method when describing natural phenomena, it is far more difficult to engage in direct experimentation. What other differences might you uncover when comparing the natural sciences and human sciences (particularly political science)?

In addition to the UN engaging in political science, the UN Secretary-General as an individual political actor must now engage with other political actors and enact and seek to realize the aims of the principles (like 'peacemaking') described by the political scientists. Rather than simply observing and describing, a political actor's role is to engage in political systems for sometimes quite narrow ends. Their job is to use political systems to excise, distribute and manage the power entrusted to them. When individuals are voting, legislating, campaigning, voting or facilitating peace agreements, they are engaged in politics.

Create a grid with the traditional elements of the scientific method in the first column (observing, hypothesizing, predicting, experimenting, analysing, reflecting, evaluating, sharing, repeating, etc.) and then the different sciences you explore in TOK or your wider education (chemistry, physics and biology in the natural sciences, and economics, psychology and human geography in the human sciences). For each science, explore how that science uses the concepts in the first column. Now consider how political science might fit and develop a justification for including political science as a legitimate human science.

■ **Figure 4.35** FARC rebel commander Rodrigo Londono celebrates after signing a peace agreement with President Juan Manuel Santos during a ceremony on 26 September 2016 in Cartagena, Colombia. The agreement ended 50 years of armed conflict between the Colombian government and rebel forces

■ Barriers to conflict resolution

In Chapter 4.3, we learned about identity conflict and how conflict connected to strong values and perceived needs is especially difficult to resolve. However, according to Ramsbotham et al., there are several other barriers to making peace during a conflict:

- The economic destruction brought on by war may result in resentment.
- Violence creates a number of groups that benefit from the continuation of war.
- Soldiers have employment through the military and see it as a way of life.
- Warlords benefit from the economic resources and profit from those resources.
- Leaders who have pursued the war may be concerned that they will be held accountable by international criminal courts, their own local population or the judicial system.
- Leaders may also see a reduction in status or prominent roles if war were to come to an end.
- Parties who have put in a lot of money and human sacrifice may want to continue pursuing war because of their investment in the conflict.
- Leaders face the challenge of hardliners who want to continue to pursue victory.

These issues will likely prevent actors from starting the negotiations, and many of these must be overcome before negotiations begin.

■ What is negotiation?

One of the ways to define war and violent conflict is as a negotiation failure. Negotiation, according to William Zartman, is the 'process of combining conflicting positions into a joint agreement', with successful negotiation resulting in the prevention or resolution of violent conflict. Belligerents seek negotiation primarily because the cost of continued conflict or unsolved problems is too great.

Negotiation is actually three sets of negotiations: negotiations to negotiate, negotiations to end the conflict (violent or not), and negotiations to implement the agreement. The process of navigating these three negotiations operates under a set of norms known as the Ethos of Equality. The parties

■ **Figure 4.36** Relative or zero-sum gains are where any gain to one party is a loss to the other, much like the scale seen here. Weight added to one side will decrease the weight on the other. All gains are measured by the losses to the other party

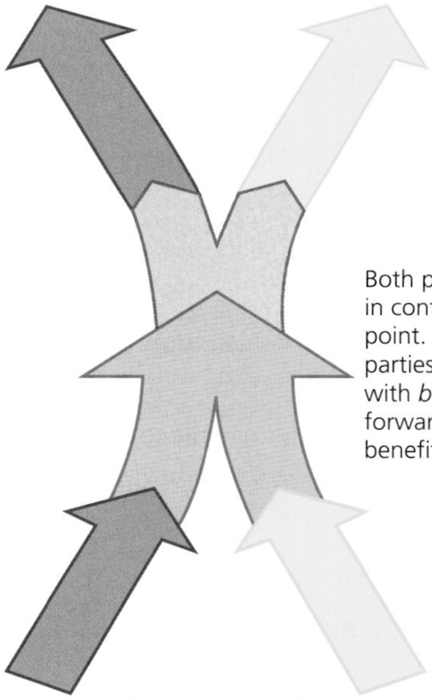

Success in these negotiations does not rely on one party gaining something at the other party's expense.

Both parties find themselves in conflict with one another at one point. Through negotiations, the parties can come to an agreement with *both* benefiting and moving forward, although they may have benefited in different ways.

Both parties come from different places.

■ **Figure 4.37** Absolute gains move in the way these arrows do – both parties come from different places but find themselves in conflict with one another at one point. Through negotiations, the parties can come to an agreement, with both benefiting and moving forward, often in different ways

negotiating are equal because each party has a veto. This means they can say 'no' to any proposed agreement. This ethos also extends to concessions that are part of any negotiation – in other words, if I agree to give up something, I expect you to do the same. These ethos are essential to successful negotiations. When they are ignored, negotiations are likely to break down.

However, all negotiations are asymmetrical (unequal) to some degree; there is no absolute equality in the real world. This means that one party may have more power than the other. Parties that see themselves as close to equal to the other party will seek to maintain or increase that equality as part of the negotiations. While we might think that the closer in equality (near-symmetry) two parties are, the easier the negotiations will be, studies have shown the opposite to be true. If the gap between the two is too small, parties will likely let the unresolved conflict or problem continue. They may even get stuck in an S5 situation (soft, stable, self-serving stalemate).

Asymmetrical conflicts, where one party has significantly more power than the other, are more likely to come to a negotiated agreement. Both parties know their roles and goals, and they seek solutions that will benefit both.

Alternatively, in near-symmetrical conflicts, any gain by one party is seen as something that will come at the other party's expense. As a result, it is difficult to get either side to 'give in' because gains are seen as **relative** (also referred to as a zero-sum game), where any gain to you is a loss to me (see Figure 4.36).

On the other hand, **absolute gains** allow both sides to gain relative to their unique roles and goals, not relative to each other. Absolute gains are more reflective of the arrows seen in Figure 4.37. Both parties come from different places but find themselves in conflict with one another at one point. Through negotiations, the parties can come to an agreement, with both benefiting and moving forward, although they may have benefited in different ways. Success in these negotiations does not rely on one party gaining something at the expense of the other party.

◆ **Relative gains**, sometimes called a zero-sum game, are when any gain to one side in a negotiation is a loss to the other.

◆ **Absolute gains** allow both sides in a negotiation to reach their goals. Success in these negotiations does not rely on one party gaining something at the expense of the other party.

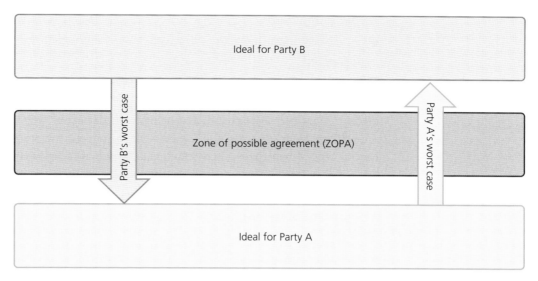

Figure 4.38 Concession requires each of the parties to get to the 'zone of possible agreement' (ZOPA)

Compensation

Compensation involves both parties bringing as many options to the negotiation as possible. For example, if both sides want all of a piece of land, there will be little to negotiate. However, if one side can bring into the negotiations other pieces of land to compensate the other side with, or if there is a desirable trade agreement, such as freeing of political prisoners, signing on to international human rights or sustainability treaties, then there are things that could be used to compensate the other side for the land they desire.

Construction

Construction refers to reframing the conflict or its solution in a way that both parties can see an outcome that might be beneficial to both sides.

One of the most challenging negotiation issues today involves the nature of the parties. Negotiating with diverse parties without clear leadership makes the neat two-party negotiations that our processes above assume more difficult. In addition, sometimes the 'party' does not have a clear sense of what it wants, just that it is upset with the current state of affairs. Finally, parties may not know how to negotiate and be unwilling to consider concession, compensation or construction. In these cases, conflict is referred to as intractable, or very difficult to manage or resolve.

■ What is mediation?

Bercovitch et al. define mediation as a process of conflict management that 'involves the intervention of an outsider – an individual, a group or an organization, with values, resources and interests of their own – into a conflict between two or more states or other actors'. The person (or group) who undertakes this task is called a mediator. The mediator can be an individual or representatives of a group or state.

■ The mediation process

Mediation continues or extends negotiations when the two parties negotiating cannot find a way forward on their own. Instead, they need a third party to assist in finding a resolution, or at least a situation they can both live with.

Therefore, mediators:

- aim to help conflicting parties to achieve a better outcome than they could achieve by themselves
- assist the belligerents in changing their perceptions or behaviour, without resorting to physical force or having the matter turned over to the judicial system.

Mediators may use various methods to achieve a settlement between the conflicting parties. These may include suggestions for a settlement or finding a compromise. Some mediators may be neutral, while others (particularly representatives of other states) may not be neutral at all. The reality of international mediation is complex and often changing.

According to Bercovitch, any mediation situation involves the following four elements:

1 Parties in conflict
2 A mediator
3 A process of mediation
4 The context of mediation.

Mediation versus arbitration

You may have heard of the term 'arbitration'. This also refers to when parties are seeking assistance in resolving a conflict. However, mediation differs from arbitration in that mediation is 'non-binding'. In other words, mediators are simply there to assist belligerents in *finding a solution*; there is no requirement for the belligerents to then adopt or accept the suggestions or approaches offered by the mediators. Mediators are not there to pass judgement and decide on what the conditions will be moving forward – the belligerents are not 'bound' or tied to the mediator's decision.

On the other hand, when two parties decide to involve an arbitrator, they agree to adhere to and follow whatever the arbitrator decides. The arbitrator is there to make a final decision, and their decision is binding; both sides are tied to whatever decision the arbitrator makes.

Mediation, then, is a procedure that is part of the negotiation process. Mediation is meant to be adaptive and responsive to the situation of the parties in conflict.

To summarise, Bercovitch explained that the main features or characteristics of mediation are as follows:

- Mediation is an extension and continuation of peaceful conflict management.
- Mediation is a voluntary form of conflict management that is a non-violent and non-binding intervention.
- Mediators enter a conflict, whether internal or international, to affect it, change it, resolve it, modify it, or influence it somehow.
- Mediators are not without bias. They bring with them, consciously or otherwise, their ideas, assumptions, knowledge, resources and interests of their own or the group or organization they represent.
- The actors involved retain control over the outcome of their conflict (though not always the mediation process itself). They have the freedom to accept or reject mediation or mediators' proposals.

Parties' motivation

Now that we have an understanding of what mediation is, let's consider what the parties' motivations for mediation might be. To start, the belligerents may be finding the conflict expensive and costly politically (they are beginning to lose support as a result of the conflict).

ACTIVITY

William Zartman emphasizes the ethos of equality in successful negotiations. However, negotiations are often asymmetrical in nature. Discuss how the ethos of equality and asymmetry can coexist in a negotiation process. Provide an example to illustrate your answer.

In the case of particularly violent conflict, there is the moral element of wanting to bring an end to the death and destruction that often goes along with conflict.

Conflict parties seek mediation because:

- mediation may help them to reduce the risks of the conflict getting worse and get the belligerents closer to a settlement
- the mediator will actually influence the other party towards their perspective on the issue
- they may see mediation as a public declaration of their commitment to the international norm or expectation that conflict be resolved peacefully
- they may want the mediator to be blamed (instead of themselves) for the conflict not being resolved
- the mediator may monitor and make sure that the other party is holding up its end of the agreement.

Whether we are studying interstate or intrastate conflicts, it is important to remember that once a mediator is involved, they become an actor in the conflict. This involves interests, costs and potential rewards. To be effective, mediators must understand this reality.

■ Forms of mediation

We have examined the processes of negotiation and mediation. Now we look at the different types of peacemakers and who is involved in moving a conflict towards peace.

Non-governmental mediation

International mediation of conflicts has come to include many different organizations and individuals. NGOs, religious bodies, academics and individual mediators can play an important role in the peacemaking process. Still, because it tends to happen behind the scenes or as part of training programmes, it is difficult to fully document the extent of non-governmental influence on ending conflict.

ACTIVITY

The following is a partial list of NGOs that have assisted in peacemaking:
- The African Center for Constructive Resolution of Disputes (ACCORD)
- The Carter Center
- The Community of Sant'Egidio
- The Harvard Negotiation Institute
- The Institute for Multi-Track Diplomacy
- International Alert
- Search for Common Ground.

Research one or several of these institutions to find out how they have been involved in peacemaking and whether or not it was successful.

United Nations mediation

It will come as no surprise that the UN often plays an important role in peacemaking. The legitimacy of the organization and the Secretary-General, in particular, can influence peacemaking efforts.

While the UN is not always successful in its efforts to make and keep peace, it is, however, the central international institution through which armistices (ceasefires) are arranged and peacekeeping operations are organized and enacted. It also facilitates and monitors elections and demilitarization of conflict parties.

Regional mediation: the African Union

As an organization, the African Union (AU) often engages in mediation and negotiation efforts directly or in collaboration with other international and regional organizations like the UN and NATO. To support these efforts, the AU Commission has a 'Peace Fund' that is used to provide the financial resources needed for diplomacy, mediation and peace support operations.

Mediation by governments

The role of governments as peacemakers is a complex one, as they usually get involved because of their national priorities. Whether the conflict is having an economic impact or because they have national security concerns (or both), the line between their role as mediators and interested parties becomes unclear. Should a government engage in forceful coercion, it becomes one of the actors in the conflict.

However, while the reasons for mediation may be self-serving, they can help bring credibility to the process by providing economic or security guarantees as part of a peace agreement. They can also contribute to any peacekeeping mission or coordinator that follows the peacemaking process.

 TOK

Even though mediators are acting as individuals (therefore acting as political actors), they are nevertheless acting on principles developed by political scientists. However, they might be influenced in their work by their own biases, interests, costs and potential rewards. In the natural sciences, the method calls for steps such as peer review, repeatability and responsible publishing of results to mitigate the influence of personal bias. What tools are available to the political scientist or the political actor to ensure that their own biases don't adversely affect the knowledge they produce? Is it even an aim or goal to limit the effect of this in the political sciences?

◼ Successful mediation

For success to be achieved, conflict parties and mediators must identify an acceptable negotiation formula and commit themselves to the process. They also need to find a way to manage the spoilers (see Chapter 4.2), so those outside the negotiations do not upend the process.

If parties are not ready for negotiation, there are other methods for preventing and deterring conflict:

- actors can seek ways to support those in favour of peacemaking and work to find ways for changes to be made to politics that are significant sources of the conflict
- parties from both within and outside the conflict can explore opportunities to change structural elements that create asymmetries that contribute to the conflict
- raising awareness of the conflict and building relationships with conflict actors may help not only to create external pressures to seek peace but also to ensure that when combatants are ready to make peace, there is a relationship in place so peace can be successfully negotiated.

We will discuss some of these in more detail in the section on Peacekeeping later in this chapter.

Subjective considerations

- Fairness: Mediation can be subjectively considered successful when the parties feel or express satisfaction with the process or the outcome of the mediation. Fairness is, of course, subjective; it depends on one's perspective. However, fairness tends to suggest that the agreement's procedure and outcome were equitable for both parties.
- Effective: Another possible indication of mediation success is whether the agreement was effective. Effectiveness is a measure of the results achieved and can be seen by the extent to which change was brought about or by the new forms of behaviour the parties have agreed to.

- Efficiency: Efficiency addresses issues such as the cost of the conflict management or mediation process. We might also consider the extent of the resources that were devoted to the mediation process, how quickly an agreement was arrived at, and how disruptive or difficult the negotiation was.

◼ Treaties

Peace treaties are formal agreements to end a conflict that include peace terms. Terms can include:

- territorial adjustments
- reparations (payments for the costs incurred due to the conflict)
- disarmament (a method for setting aside the weapons used in the conflict)
- the return of prisoners of war.

In many ways, treaties are the symbolic indication that peace has been made, as they:

- act as an agreement to end the hostilities
- keep the peace
- offer a way for peace to be maintained well into the future.

Some agreements may provide for a temporary armistice or truce, though this should not be confused with a more comprehensive peace treaty.

Government representatives typically sign treaties but, in the case of democracies, treaties need to be ratified or confirmed by a governing body like a parliament. This makes the treaty a binding international agreement. Violations can have diplomatic consequences that may even result in renewed hostilities.

Finally, peace treaties may help support the next steps in the peace process. The treaty may include peacekeeping agreements, such as inviting a UN or regional peacekeeping mission to support the peace. Peace treaties may also include peacekeeping elements such as disarmament, demobilization and reintegration (DDR) of combatants, as well as peacebuilding processes like truth and reconciliation commissions, and reconstruction and development efforts.

An example of a peace agreement is the one signed in 2016 by the Colombian government and the Revolutionary Armed Forces of Colombia (FARC). This agreement aimed to end one of the world's longest-running conflicts, which had lasted for over 50 years and resulted in significant loss of life and displacement.

As part of the agreement, the FARC agreed to lay down their arms and demobilize their forces. This process was to be monitored and verified by the United Nations. The agreement provided a pathway for the FARC to transition into a legitimate political movement, allowing them to participate in Colombia's political system. It also included measures for land reform and rural development, aiming to address issues of land rights and economic disparities that were root causes of the conflict. The agreement also established mechanisms that included international support and oversight for the implementation and verification of the agreement.

4.4.2 Preventing and deterring conflict

In the next couple of sections, we will explore ways to prevent the need for peacemaking in the first place and methods to encourage actors to engage in peacemaking sooner than they otherwise might.

◼ Sanctions and embargoes

Sanctions and embargoes are foreign policy tools that can pressure a country to change its behaviour and end a conflict. However, they often prove to have the opposite effect.

Sanctions

Joseph Nye defines sanctions as measures of encouragement or punishment designed to reinforce a decision or make a policy authoritative. Sanctions can be specific and target several areas, including economic, diplomatic, military, sports-related or even cultural elements. Sanctions may also target specific businesses or individuals or the origins of a product. Typical sanctions include:

- freezing of assets
- restricting trade in specific goods or services
- travel bans on key individuals.

Sanctions are not only used by states; organizations may also invoke sanctions.

For example, in 2022, after the Russian invasion of Ukraine, the Cannes Film Festival banned Russian delegations from attending the festival. FIFA banned the Russian national team from continuing to compete for a spot in the 2022 Men's World Cup. A rather common political and diplomatic sanction also occurred when the United States and its allies expelled Russian diplomats from their countries.

In the case of human rights violations, a state may target individuals and goods. On 21 June 2022, the United States Uyghur Forced Labour Prevention Act banned the import of products made with Uyghur forced labour. The United States also imposed sanctions on four Chinese officials they felt were responsible for the abuses. These sanctions were coordinated with the EU, Canada and the UK. The sanctions included travel and economic restrictions.

Embargoes

An embargo is a specific type of sanction on a country that can be comprehensive (covering all goods and services) or selective (targeting specific commodities like oil or weapons). Embargoes are more encompassing and less precise than a sanction. However, because an embargo is a type of sanction, you may sometimes read of an embargo being used as a sanction. For example, in 2006, in response to Iran's nuclear program, the UN sanctioned Iran by imposing an embargo on the supplying, selling or transfer of arms or related materials to or from Iran.

Like sanctions, embargoes are usually implemented as punishment or as a diplomatic tool to pressure another country to change its behaviour or policies. This may be done in the economic or military context. For example, the United States has imposed a comprehensive embargo on North Korea since 1950. The embargo prohibits all trade and financial transactions between the United States and North Korea, with limited exceptions for humanitarian aid. This embargo is one of the world's most comprehensive and long-standing. The current aim of the embargo is to pressure North Korea to abandon its nuclear and ballistic missile programmes. However, like the US embargo on Cuba, it has resulted in limited changes to the policies of either country.

How successful are sanctions and embargoes?

ACTIVITY

Research a current example of a set of sanctions or embargoes and assess how effective they have been in changing the behaviour of the target country.

Sanctions and embargoes can hurt some of the least empowered of a population. Inflation and lack of access to medical supplies and food can result in humanitarian crises. Joseph Nye explained, 'General sanctions are a blunt instrument in which the suffering may be borne by the poor, most vulnerable, and powerless rather than the elites that make decisions in autocratic countries.' Instead, he recommended 'smart sanctions that would target elites rather than the general public'.

The success of sanctions then depends on how 'success' is defined. If the goal is complete policy change, then the success rate is lower and, as Nye has indicated, more harmful. However, if the goal is more modest or specific, the success rate is better, though not high.

THEMATIC STUDIES: Peace and conflict

Election observers
are not new in the
international context,
nor are they new in
the domestic context,
but they are becoming
more and more the
protectors of partisan
political movements
(a political role), rather
than tools to ensure
political legitimacy
(a role required by
political science).
Consider debates in
the state and national
elections in the USA,
and evaluate whether
the role of the election
observer is still about
ensuring political
legitimacy or to drive
narrow political ends.

◆ **Nonpartisan** means
not biased towards a
particular political party.

◼ Election observers

International election observers play an important role in helping to prevent and deter conflict. They can do this by ensuring that elections are transparent, fair and credible. The presence of election observers adds a significant element of legitimacy to an election, so that when one side feels frustrated that their preferred party or candidate did not win, they can, if the election observers are trusted, rest in the knowledge that the election was conducted according to international standards and the country's own legal framework.

Election observers are not only involved in monitoring the procedures on the election day. They often:

- provide training years in advance
- investigate voter registration and campaigning
- participate in the voting process and counting.

Observers are trained to spot and report irregularities, such as voter intimidation, ballot stuffing (an individual voting more than once), or using state resources for campaign purposes. Following an election, observer teams release a report with their findings that often includes recommendations for how the electoral process can be improved in the future.

How successful are election observers?

The effectiveness of international election observers can vary based on their mandate's scope, expertise and impartiality. One of the concerns critics of election observers have is that the presence of international observers can result in an election appearing legitimate when it is, in fact, flawed.

CASE STUDY

The Carter Center

The Carter Center was founded in 1982 by US President Jimmy Carter and his wife Rosalynn Carter. It has trained impartial, credible election observers to support states in ensuring quality, legitimate elections. The Carter Center has monitored 114 elections in Africa, Latin America and Asia since 1989.

To ensure the election observation is helpful and perceived as **nonpartisan** and legitimate, the Carter Center requires an invitation from the country's current leaders and also that they are welcomed by the other major political parties.

The Carter Center explains its process as starting 'long before election day'. It:

- uses experts and long-term observers to analyse election laws
- assesses voter education and registration
- evaluates fairness in campaigns
- monitors the impact of social media.

The Center goes on to explain 'On election day, observers assess the casting and counting of ballots. After the election, observers monitor the tabulation process, electoral dispute resolution, and the publication of final results.' The Center then reports all of its findings in public statements.

Roles of Election Observers

THE CARTER CENTER

	Nonpartisan Observation	Partisan Observation	Election Protection
Demonstrates the community's interest and support for elections that are credible, transparent, accessible to all voters, and that represent a true democratic process	✓	✓	✓
Reinforces the efforts of civil society and voting rights groups in the electoral process and increases the credibility of their work	✓	✓	✓
Protects, advances, and defends the right to vote	✓	✓	✓
Works to ensure the right of access the ballot	✓	✓	✓
Systematically collects data and publicly reports on adherence to election law during absentee voting, in-person voting, and vote tabulation	✓		
Provides an *impartial* assessment of the electoral process – analyzing its strengths and weaknesses	✓		

■ **Figure 4.39** The key similarities and differences between the work of nonpartisan, partisan and election protection observers (The Carter Center)

■ Preventing arms proliferation

Preventing arms proliferation is a multifaceted challenge that requires international cooperation and a combination of diplomatic, legal and enforcement mechanisms. There are several ways that the international community typically goes about preventing the spread of both conventional arms and weapons of mass destruction (WMDs).

One of the primary methods of trying to prevent and deter conflict in the area of arms is by negotiating and signing international treaties and conventions. A few examples of the types of agreements that have been negotiated to prevent conflict are listed below:

● The Treaty on the Non-Proliferation of Nuclear Weapons (NPT) aims to prevent the spread of nuclear weapons and technology, promote peaceful uses of nuclear energy, and further the goal of nuclear disarmament.

- The Biological Weapons Convention (BWC) prohibits producing and possessing biological weapons.
- The Chemical Weapons Convention (CWC) aims to eliminate an entire WMD category by prohibiting the production, stockpiling and use of chemical weapons.
- The Arms Trade Treaty (ATT) sets standards for the international trade of conventional arms to prevent illicit trade and diversion to unauthorized users.
- The 'Ottawa Treaty' or Convention on the Prohibition of the Use, Stockpiling, Production and Transfer of Anti-Personnel Mines and their Destruction aims to eliminate the use of anti-personnel landmines worldwide. These mines are notorious for causing civilian casualties, often years after conflicts have ended. Landmines also inhibit economic development because the areas that have been mined are too dangerous to use.

To further the enforcement of treaties, organizations such as the International Atomic Energy Agency (IAEA) conduct inspections to verify that member states comply with treaties related to atomic energy. They ensure that nuclear materials are not diverted for weapons use and that nations adhere to non-proliferation commitments. Another area where states have worked to cooperate is in the area of disarmament initiatives, where the goal is to reduce existing stockpiles of weapons, often nuclear weapons. They do this so they will not be used in the future and also to ensure that they do not fall into the hands of actors who may be eager to use them.

Non-proliferation does not only need to be the work of international agreements or organizations. Instead, countries implement export controls to regulate and restrict the transfer of sensitive weapon technologies, materials and weapons. As noted previously, various states and other international actors can impose sanctions on states, businesses, organizations or individuals violating non-proliferation agreements. States can also cooperate by sharing intelligence about potential proliferation activities to prevent illegal arms transfers or help detect agreement violations.

While these approaches to preventing and deterring conflict have helped limit arms proliferation, there are still many non-state actors, including criminal and terrorist organizations, and some states that operate outside the treaties and organizations that attempt to limit the proliferation of weapons. As a result, there is still much to do in this regard, even if the mechanisms in place have made some progress.

ACTIVITY

Research the UN Charter. Does the term 'peacekeeping' appear in the charter? What are the three fundamental principles that define UN peacekeeping operations?

4.4.3 Peacekeeping

We examined the UN in detail in Chapter 2.1, and you may wish to refer back to remind yourself of the organization's formation and primary goals. For the purposes of this section, we will focus on the UN's role in peacekeeping.

The origins of UN peacekeeping can be traced back to the UN's founding ideals. The goal of preventing future wars drove the establishment of the UN in 1945 following the Second World War, and the UN Charter states that the organization's primary goal is to maintain international peace and security.

■ Types of UN peacekeeping

There are two main types of UN peacekeeping missions:

- Chapter VI missions are consent-based and focus on the peaceful resolution of disputes.
- Chapter VII missions have broader **mandates** that can include the use of force in response to threats to peace or acts of aggression.

Chapter VI missions

Peacekeeping missions established under Chapter VI of the charter usually involve deploying UN forces to observe and report on the situation without the mandate to use force unless it is in self-defence or defence of the mandate. The forces' main role is often interpositional. This means they place themselves between conflicting parties to deter violence.

Chapter VI missions are usually known as 'traditional' or 'consent-based' missions because they generally operate with the consent of the conflicting parties.

The main challenge for Chapter VI peacekeeping operations is that they can often be difficult to conclude. For example, the UN Peacekeeping Force in Cyprus was set up in 1964 to prevent further fighting between Greek and Turkish Cypriot communities, and the mission's mandate as just been extended to 2024.

Also, despite their peaceful intent, peacekeepers can be the target of violence. As part of the UN peacekeeping mission in Mali, there were 309 fatalities before the mission was terminated (at Mali's request) in June 2023.

Chapter VII missions

Chapter VII gives the UN Security Council the power to take collective action when there is a threat to international peace and security. Measures under Chapter VII can range from economic sanctions to full-scale military interventions.

Peacekeeping or peace enforcement missions established under Chapter VII are usually given mandates that allow the use of force beyond self-defence to achieve their objectives. These missions can be established even without the host country's consent if the UN Security Council deems the situation a threat to international peace and security.

Some of the most notable Chapter VII missions over the years are shown in Table 4.8.

■ **Table 4.8** Most notable Chapter VII missions

Name of mission	Year(s) in operation
UNOSOM I and II in Somalia	1992–93 and 1993–95
UN Protection Force in the former Yugoslavia (UNPROFOR)	1992–95
United Nations Interim Administration Mission in Kosovo (UNMIK)	1999–
African Union - United Nations Hybrid Operation in Darfur (UNAMID)	2007–20
United Nations Organization Stabilization Mission in the Democratic Republic of the Congo (MONUSCO)	2010–
United Nations Multidimensional Integrated Stabilization Mission in Mali (MINUSMA)	2013–

■ Criticisms of UN peacekeeping

There are a number of criticisms of UN peacekeeping operations.

Broad and overly ambitious mandates

For example, in the Democratic Republic of the Congo, given the geography and challenges of moving throughout the country, UN peacekeepers have found it incredibly challenging to protect civilians.

Mismanagement and failure to act when civilians are threatened

A 2014 report by UN internal investigators found that UN peacekeepers only responded to one in five cases where civilians were threatened and failed to use force in deadly attacks. *The Economist* states that one of the biggest reasons for failing to respond is that the countries who contribute troops restrict how they can be used.

Human rights abuses by peacekeepers

Peacekeeping troops have faced accusations of violating human rights, with numerous claims of sexual abuse and exploitation. Recently, the UN recalled several Gabonese peacekeepers from the Central African Republic, initiating an inquiry due to accusations of sexual exploitation and abuse by peacekeepers. Even though there has been an increase in UN inquiries regarding such claims in the past few years, very few have culminated in legal proceedings, and there have been no public convictions. UN peacekeepers have legal immunity in the countries they serve, which places the responsibility on their home countries to pursue any potential legal action.

ACTIVITY

Research a current UN peacekeeping mission. What is its UN mandate? How successful has it been? What criticisms has it faced?

Lack of financing

Some critics of UN peacekeeping contend that given their varying degrees of success, missions are not cost-effective and are overly dependent on a handful of primary donors.

The veto

Furthermore, others highlight how the veto held by the Security Council's permanent members can hinder or dilute peacekeeping directives. In the case of the Darfur region of Sudan, where ethnic cleansing unfolded in the 2000s, the use of the veto or the threat of its use by some permanent members led to delays in an international response. This resulted in a less effective and slower deployment of peacekeeping forces. When resolutions are likely to be vetoed by one of the permanent members, other members may resort to drafting a watered-down resolution that is more acceptable. In the case of Darfur, imposing sanctions or deploying peacekeepers were often tempered to avoid vetoes, ultimately leading to a less forceful international response. The delayed and diluted response of the international community, partly due to the dynamics of the Security Council's veto power, resulted in hundreds of thousands of people being killed and millions displaced.

■ Reform of UN peacekeeping

In 2018, UN Secretary-General Antonio Guterres launched the Action for Peacekeeping (A4P) initiative, which focuses on developing more targeted peacekeeping mandates with clear political strategies, improving the safety of peacekeepers as well as civilians in mission areas, and better training troops. Also, in response to the reports of sexual exploitation and abuse by peacekeepers, the Security Council unanimously adopted a resolution targeting improved leadership and accountability.

Other suggestions from experts and scholars to address some of the criticisms of UN peacekeeping include the following:

- The UN should more closely coordinate regional organizations such as the AU to complement one another and avoid unnecessary overlap in their missions.
- Countries with advanced militaries should help to train and equip troops that are increasingly coming from countries with less developed militaries.
- Inclusivity should be encouraged by employing more women peacekeepers. Evidence has shown that missions are more effective when there are more women peacekeepers.
- Major powers should do more than fund missions. Instead, they should ensure missions are tailored to their environments and guided by clear, inclusive political strategies.

UN Organization Stabilization Mission in the Democratic Republic of the Congo (MONUSCO)

■ **Figure 4.40** UN peacekeepers in the Democratic Republic of the Congo

The Democratic Republic of the Congo (DRC) has been plagued by a series of conflicts involving various rebel groups, ethnic tensions and struggles over the country's vast mineral wealth. The United Nations Organization Stabilization Mission in the Democratic Republic of the Congo (MONUSCO), originally established as MONUC in 1999 and later renamed in 2010 with an updated mandate, is one of the largest and longest-standing UN peacekeeping missions. Its main objectives have been to protect civilians, support the government's stabilization and peace consolidation efforts, and ensure the implementation of the Peace, Security and Cooperation Framework for the DRC and the region.

MONUSCO has made progress in protecting civilians from violence, particularly in areas with active conflicts. The mission has also played a key role in the disarmament and demobilization of several rebel groups. MONUSCO provided logistical and security support during the DRC's elections, helping ensure a relatively peaceful electoral process. Interestingly, MONUSCO was the first UN peacekeeping mission authorized to use surveillance drones so that real-time intelligence could be provided to help enhance the protection of civilians.

Nevertheless, MONUSCO has also faced its challenges. The DRC's large size and challenging geography, combined with limited infrastructure, have made it difficult for peacekeepers to access and operate in many areas. There are also many different armed groups that have complicated disarmament efforts and the overall stabilization of the country. MONUSCO has also been plagued by peacekeepers facing accusations of misconduct, including sexual exploitation and abuse. In some cases, the mission's cooperation with the Congolese national army, which has also been accused of human rights abuses, has posed legitimacy challenges.

4.4.4 Intervention in conflict

Discussion point

All that is required for evil to triumph is that good [people] do nothing.

Commonly attributed to Edmund Burke

When considering Burke's quotation and the violent conflict that exists in the world today, when studying peace and conflict, it is reasonable to ask, what role, if any, should the use of armed force play in conflict resolution?

◆ A **pretext** is a pretend reason given to justify doing something to conceal the real reason.

The issue of forcible intervention is perhaps the key question that divides those working in peace and conflict studies. As we consider the call to action by Burke, we will begin this section by exploring the crime of genocide, sometimes called the 'crime of crimes', as a **pretext** for considering when and how to overcome evil and what those actions should look like.

Genocide

The 1948 UN Convention on the Punishment and Prevention of the Crime of Genocide (the Genocide Convention) technically obligates state parties to 'punish' and to 'prevent' genocide where it occurs. Unfortunately, since the convention was put in place, there have been several genocides. Clearly, prevention has been poor, though there has been some work done in the area of punishment.

During and after the Nazi Holocaust, Raphael Lemkin, a Polish international lawyer, coined the term genocide. It combines the Greek word *genos* (race, nation or tribe) and the Latin *cide* (killing). Lemkin wrote that the main goal of genocide was the destruction of nations and ethnic groups. He defined genocide as 'a coordinated plan of different actions aiming at the destruction of the essential foundations of the life of national groups, with the aim of annihilating the groups themselves'. These statements form the core of the common notion of genocide as group annihilation. The two key elements of the definition of genocide, then, are the actions taken to destroy groups and the intent or purpose of annihilating groups.

For Lemkin, genocide involved not only killing but also a variety of acts that aimed to destroy part or all of a particular group. Lemkin listed acts of genocide that ranged from forced sterilization, abortion, infection to deliberate separation of families.

Lemkin did not see all of the elements of his description become part of the final convention. Still, most of the central elements are contained in the UN conventions that define genocide as the 'intent to destroy, in whole or in part, a national, ethnical, racial or religious group'.

For actions to be called genocide, there must be evidence of a deliberate, often planned, campaign of violence with the purpose of destroying part or all of a group. As the definition notes, only national, ethnical, racial or religious groups are protected. Other groups, such as political or gender groups and people with disabilities, are not explicitly protected by the UN definition.

As we have noted, genocide does not have to mean the destruction of an entire group. The definition specifies a group's 'partial' destruction, which courts have since interpreted to mean that a 'substantial' part of the group must be destroyed. However, that term, too, remains unclear.

The convention also lists a number of different methods of genocide. These include killing, causing serious physical or mental harm, inflicting 'conditions of life calculated to bring about its physical destruction in whole or in part,' preventing birth and transferring children.

When considering intervention in genocide, the UN convention holds those who signed and ratified the convention responsible to 'undertake to prevent' genocide. However, what undertaking to prevent means is unclear. Article VIII of the convention does say that parties 'may call upon the competent organs' of the UN to take action under the charter to prevent and suppress acts of genocide. Therefore, the convention implies that states may intervene, even against the wishes of a sovereign state, to stop genocide. However, the language in the convention is rather limited in describing mechanisms, policies and procedures that states must take to prevent genocide.

In contrast, the convention says relatively more on the issue of punishment.

- There are five specific charges and conditions for extradition.
- Individuals may be punished whether or not they are public officials.
- States that signed the convention must create laws that outlaw genocide.
- Domestic or international courts must try those charged with genocide.

Principles of intervention

With the convention calling upon states to intervene, the related question is: when? At what point must intervention occur? As we explore this question, there is value in starting with the work of Ramsbotham et al., who outline several different principles to consider when intervening in a conflict.

- The principle of impartiality: whatever role an intervener plays, conflict resolution is incomplete unless the interests of all those affected are considered.

- The principle of mutuality aims to make sure that the intervention is seen to be likely to do more good than harm from the conflict party's perspective.

- The principle of sustainability suggests that interveners who are not prepared to commit to the intervention, which includes the required resources, should not undertake the intervention in the first place.

- The principle of complementarity asks that the various intervening organizations ensure that, where appropriate, their work complement one another instead of overlapping (making for inefficiencies) or competing to achieve the same result.

- The principle of reflexivity asks interveners to look at themselves and reflect on their motives, aims and interests. They should consider who they represent (both culturally and organizationally), what they advocate for, and why. Finally, they should consider what resources they bring to support the intervention.

- The principle of consistency: given similar circumstances, interveners should respond similarly, no matter where the crisis occurs. This helps to avoid accusations of bias and hypocrisy.

- The principle of accountability asks the intervenors to reflect on the successes and failures of the interventions. What changes must be made to make an intervention more effective next time?

The Responsibility to Protect

We discussed the Responsibility to Protect (R2P) in detail in Chapter 2.3 in the thematic study on rights and justice, and you should refer back to this to remind yourself of the main goals of R2P. Here, we look at R2P in relation to the UN Convention on Genocide.

The convention suggests that the international community has a responsibility to protect others. The parameters for doing so were unclear, however, in response to the failure to protect populations during the genocides in Rwanda and at Srebrenica during the 1990s, more clarity was created as part of the R2P.

R2P was developed to not only respond to instances of genocide but also to actively attempt to prevent them from happening in the first place. The terminology used in R2P is meant to de-emphasize intervention and instead focus on the international community's responsibility to protect populations from having to experience crimes against humanity.

As we saw in Chapter 2.3, R2P is a political commitment, unanimously adopted by heads of state and government at the 2005 UN World Summit. It aims to prevent and stop four specific crimes:

- genocide
- war crimes
- crimes against humanity
- ethnic cleansing.

R2P states that every state has the responsibility to protect its populations from these crimes, and the international community has the responsibility to encourage and support states in protecting populations living within their borders. Critical to R2P is that if a state is failing to protect their population from genocide, ethnic cleansing, war crimes and crimes against humanity, then the international community must respond. Importantly, however, any military response to interventions can only be carried out when the UN Security Council authorizes them.

The four crimes can be summarized as follows:

■ **Table 4.9** The Responsibility to Protect: definitions of the four crimes

Crime	Definition
Genocide	*Acts committed with intent to destroy in whole or in part a national, ethnic, racial or religious group, including:* *(a) killing members of the group* *(b) causing serious bodily or mental harm to members of the group* *(c) deliberately inflicting on the group conditions of life calculated to bring about its physical destruction in whole or in part* *(d) imposing measures intended to prevent births within the group* *(e) forcibly transferring children of the group to another group.* *UN Convention on the Prevention and Punishment of the Crime of Genocide 1948, Article 2*
War crimes	*Serious violations of the laws and customs applicable in international armed conflict, including grave breaches of the Geneva Conventions.* *Statute of the International Criminal Court, Article 8*
Crimes against humanity	*Acts committed as part of a widespread or* **systematic** *attack directed against a civilian population.* *Rome Statute of the International Criminal Court 1998, Article 7*
Ethnic cleansing	*Rendering an area ethnically* **homogeneous** *by using force or intimidation to remove persons of given groups from the area.* *Letter from the Secretary-General of the UN to the President of the UN Security Council, 9 February 1993*

◆ **Systemic** describes something that relates to or affects an entire system, often implying a deep-rooted, ingrained issue within a complex network or structure.

◆ **Homogeneous** refers to a group that is composed of elements that are all of the same or a similar kind or similar in their composition or character.

R2P is primarily focused on prevention as it is more effective and typically less expensive than response. The first report of the Secretary-General on R2P suggested that R2P be implemented via a three pillar strategy (see Figure 2.37 in Chapter 2.3).

Criticisms of the Responsibility to Protect

Initially, states were critical of how R2P could be used to justify the 'use of force' and worried that this could be used to infringe upon national sovereignty. The concern was that R2P could be used as a cover for military and humanitarian intervention aimed at regime change. Recently, criticism has focused on the failure of states to live up to the R2P commitment to preventing atrocities.

While R2P is often conflated with military intervention, timely and substantial responses to the four crimes can include a range of coercive and non-coercive tactics, some of which we have discussed in this chapter. These include diplomacy, mediation, public advocacy, humanitarian assistance, protection of refugees and displaced persons, monitoring, fact-finding and verification missions, peacekeeping, sanctions, embargoes and peacebuilding. Military intervention is only one of the tools actors can use to prevent the four crimes, and it should only be considered as a UN tool of last resort; military intervention is only meant to be used when all other measures have been exhausted.

For example, during the 2017 'clearance operations' in Myanmar, critics were calling for an 'R2P military intervention' even though it was unclear if a military option could resolve the issues in Myanmar or prevent future atrocities. Intervention itself, military or otherwise, is not at the heart of R2P. Instead, prevention lies at the core. When intervention is considered, it should be done, similarly to what is outlined in 'just war' theory, only as a 'last resort'. Once 'all peaceful alternatives have been considered', only then should the following questions related to 'just war' theory (pages 338–339) be explored:

- Just cause: Is there a good reason to intervene? Are crimes against humanity immanent?
- Just intentions: What are the intentions of the intervention? Is the intervention for the purpose of seeking justice and not self-interest?
- Legitimate authority: Is the intervention condoned and supported by an international governmental organization like the United Nations?
- Probability of success: Is there a reasonable chance of success in achieving the aims of the intervention?
- Proportionality: Is any harm that is likely to be caused by the intervention proportionate to (in balance with) the good that is expected to be achieved by the intervention?

Again, to be clear, any use of force without the consent of the UN Security Council cannot be undertaken on the grounds of R2P.

CASE STUDY

R2P in action

Myanmar

The government of Myanmar had failed Pillar I of the R2P doctrine by not protecting its population. There had been government-led discrimination against the Rohingya by denying them a right to citizenship since at least 1982. In addition, there were restrictions on marriages and reproductive rights, as well as restrictions on religious and economic freedoms. The government had also limited access to much-needed humanitarian assistance. These policies perpetuated an environment where other groups within Myanmar and the military were encouraged to abuse and discriminate against the Rohingya. Despite all of the warning signs, the international community failed to address the abuses faced by the Rohingya.

After the 'clearance operations' by the Tatmadaw (military of Myanmar) in August 2017, when over 700,000 Rohingya fled Myanmar to escape acts of genocide being committed against them, there was limited response by the international community. Initially, some sanctions were imposed by the governments of the United States, Canada, the EU and Australia, but little otherwise. In 2022, Gambia stepped in when other international powers would not and brought the case of the genocide to the International Court of Justice.

The failure of the international community to respond to acts of genocide does not necessarily mean that the doctrine of R2P has failed. In the case of Myanmar, it could be argued that it was a failure by all actors to take the necessary steps to prevent genocide from being committed against the Rohingya.

Question: When genocides occur, does it mean that R2P has failed or has the international community failed to enact R2P?

Answer: António Guterres argued in his 2019 report on R2P that 'there is a growing gap between our words of commitment and the experience of protecting vulnerable populations'. Nevertheless, in the context of the genocide in Myanmar, critics have reasonably asked whether the atrocities in Myanmar were a failure of R2P.

Côte d'Ivoire

In Côte d'Ivoire, violence escalated after the presidential elections in November of 2010 between then-President Gbagbo and Alassane Ouattara. Gbagbo had refused to accept defeat, and violence broke out, with supporters of both men attacking communities based on ethnic identity and perceived political support.

The African Union and ECOWAS both suspended Côte d'Ivoire's membership. They sent mediation teams to Côte d'Ivoire seven times, and the United States and EU imposed sanctions on members of Gbagbo's government. R2P was also invoked in statements by the UN High Commissioner for Human Rights and the UN's special advisers on preventing genocide.

When these efforts failed and violence broke out, the Security Council passed Resolution 1975 authorizing the UN peacekeeping mission in the country (UNOCI) to use 'all necessary means to carry out its mandate to protect civilians under imminent threat of physical violence … including to prevent the use of heavy weapons against the civilian population'.

After a five-day operation, Gbagbo surrendered. This was widely considered an effective application of R2P's third pillar: if a state is manifestly failing to protect its population, the international community must be prepared to take appropriate collective action in a timely and decisive manner.

While R2P is the central international agreement created to prevent crimes against humanity, genocide and ethnic cleansing, time will tell if it is an effective conflict prevention model and whether the international community is willing to enact all three pillars.

Discussion point

Considering our discussion of genocide and the responsibility to protect, do you think the value of R2P outweighs its weaknesses? Are there ways in which R2P could be strengthened or adjusted to be a more useful tool?

● HL extension: Borders

The section on intervention in conflict would be an ideal starting point for an inquiry into the global political challenge of Borders. However, it is recommended that you review Chapter 1.3 on sovereignty as well. The two notions are closely linked and together they will give you a good foundation for exploring political issues related to infringing sovereign borders. Any conflict or humanitarian crisis in the world today is likely to give rise to the question of whether global political actors ought to intervene for the sake of others.

'Just war' theory for Responsibility to Protect

Ramsbotham et al. argued that if military force is for purposes beyond national security, then traditional just war criteria on their own are not enough. Instead, the just war criteria must be expanded to include conflict resolution intervention principles.

They explain that if:

> just war is to become a just intervention, this requires two major revisions: first, the just war criteria themselves need to be adapted and second, additional criteria must be added to them, including the entirely new category of jus post bellum (justice after war). What happens after using military force is integral to overall judgements about whether such force was justified in the first place. This can no longer depend only on the prior 'good intentions' of the interveners, as in traditional jus ad bellum criteria.

Responsible sovereignty

The idea of responsible sovereignty was first proposed by Francis Deng and his colleagues at the Brookings Institution in the 1990s. The concept was further developed as part of the International Commission on Intervention and State Sovereignty (ICISS) report on the R2P.

Deng and his colleagues argued that the traditional concept of sovereignty, which gives states absolute authority over their territory and people, is no longer adequate in a world where states are increasingly interdependent and where the security of individuals is not always guaranteed by their own governments.

Deng and his colleagues proposed that sovereignty should be seen as a responsibility, not a right. States, they argued, have the responsibility to protect their people from harm. They are also responsible for cooperating to address common challenges like violence, poverty and environmental degradation.

4.4.5 Peacebuilding

Now that we have explored possible approaches to making peace and then keeping peace, it is time to consider how to build peace. The process of developing a positive peace so that the likelihood of conflict is minimized is central to peacebuilding.

In their work on conflict resolution, Ramsbotham et al. developed several models to describe the dynamics of conflict escalation and de-escalation. We looked at the first in Chapter 4.3. Now we will examine Ramsbotham's hourglass model (see Figure 4.41).

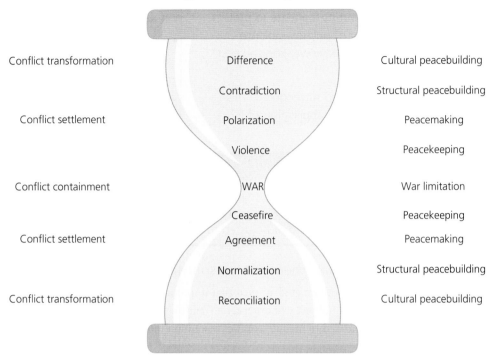

■ **Figure 4.41** Ramsbotham et al.'s hourglass model of conflict escalation and de-escalation

Throughout the chapters in this thematic study on peace and conflict, we have journeyed from the causes of violence and conflict to the types of conflict that occur, and in this chapter, we have explored how conflict de-escalates and peace is made, kept and now built.

- The hourglass model helps us to visualise this journey: how conflicts evolve, intensify and potentially get resolved over time:
- The top bulb of the hourglass represents the escalation phase of a conflict. During this 'entry phase,' the conflict starts, parties become polarized, tensions rise and the possibility of violence increases.
- The neck, or the narrowest part of the hourglass, represents the peak or climax of the conflict. Parties at this stage have a decision to make: continue to engage in conflict or find a way to de-escalate and resolve the issue.
- The bottom bulb of the hourglass represents the de-escalation phase of the conflict and the subsequent peacebuilding efforts. They specifically focus on structural peacebuilding or the reconstruction of societal infrastructures, including political frameworks and economic systems, with an aim toward a more just, equitable and sustainable society. The de-escalation stage also includes cultural peacebuilding, which focuses on changing the perceptions and attitudes of the parties. Cultural peacebuilding aims to try and heal traumas, foster reconciliation and create a culture of peace through education and dialogue. These characteristics of structural and cultural peacebuilding make the likelihood of conflict decrease.

Peacemaking and peacekeeping have a somewhat longer history than peacebuilding. Johan Galtung brought the idea of peacebuilding to the forefront in his 1975 essay 'Understanding Peacebuilding', when he argued that peace is about abolishing structural violence and the root causes of war, such as oppression and domination. He further developed these ingrained attitudes that are at the root of conflict in his 1990 academic article 'Cultural Violence'. To build peace, not only does direct violence need to be eliminated, but so do the structures and attitudes that foster the violence in the first place. The goal of peace (re)building is to rebuild structures and cultures that are a solid foundation for peace to flourish.

In 1992, the UN released the 'Agenda for Peace' report, which helped popularize the idea of peacebuilding. Like Galtung suggested, the report emphasized the main reasons behind conflicts. It discusses creating strong systems that help maintain peace and prevent future conflicts. The report mainly focuses on peace efforts after a conflict has happened, although some experts believe it should cover all stages of conflict, including prevention and conflict management.

When scholars write about peacebuilding, they often note that there is not a clear definition. Still, at its core, peacebuilding refers to efforts to prevent the outbreak or recurrence of violent conflict by promoting conditions that will make for sustainable peace.

Several elements help reduce the risk of lapsing or relapsing into conflict. The UN's involvement in peacebuilding, especially through its Peacebuilding Commission, emphasizes the importance of a comprehensive approach to ending violence, addressing the root causes of conflict, and creating lasting peace and development. We will now examine these core elements of peacebuilding in more detail.

■ Core elements of peacebuilding

De-escalation

Initially, there needs to be a de-escalation stage that involves peacemaking and assistance in keeping any peace that has been agreed. To effectively de-escalate, there must be a disarmament, demobilization and reintegration (DDR) stage. This involves the disarmament of former combatants, demobilization and reintegration into civilian life.

Once the immediate violence has ceased and the process of DDR is completed, there can be a more robust conflict transformation process. This is where peacebuilding really begins. The underlying causes of the conflict need to be addressed. Doing so may require dialogue processes, negotiations and mediation efforts to find solutions to the root issues. Central to this and other aspects of peacebuilding is fostering respect for and protection of human rights.

Rebuilding infrastructure/reforming institutions

There also needs to be a focus on rebuilding the physical, economic and social infrastructures that may have been damaged during the conflict. However, as we saw earlier, rebuilding these infrastructures, particularly the social, political and economic, as they were before, is likely to result in recurring conflict. Instead, institutions need to be reformed to address the issues identified as being at the core of the conflict.

This may mean that the political and electoral systems need reform or reimagining. Perhaps laws need to be passed to create greater social equality. There may need to be reforms to the judicial system so perpetrators are brought to justice and the rule of law is the norm. Reforming both military and police forces to ensure they are there to protect all citizens without discrimination or abuse is an important aspect of the peacebuilding process.

Post-conflict societies often face devastated economies, as well. Economic reconstruction will involve the actual reconstruction of buildings that have been destroyed, but this is only the first step in rebuilding an economy that may require job creation, so there is a return to or creation of productive, sustainable economic activity.

ACTIVITY

Choose a conflict that has been resolved and apply the conflict escalation and de-escalation tools to it.

ACTIVITY

What are the core elements of peacebuilding discussed in this chapter? How do these elements contribute to sustainable peace after a conflict?

Restructuring these elements of society, some of which may require institutional reforms and cultural/educational efforts so that they are more inclusive, representative and accountable, is a critical step in peacebuilding.

Addressing injustices

Finally, addressing injustices can be crucial in preventing future conflicts, and creating war crimes tribunals can be helpful in creating post-conflict justice. However, it is not only retribution that is needed; past traumas should also be addressed through reconciliation mechanisms. The creation of truth and reconciliation commissions (TRCs) (see below) helps foster healing and forgiveness so that the process of rebuilding trust can start.

■ Conflict resolution and international legal institutions

There are a variety of legal mechanisms to ensure perpetrators are held responsible for crimes and to help in the peacebuilding process. In this section, we will examine several of these bodies.

International criminal tribunals

International criminal tribunals are judicial bodies established to prosecute individuals responsible for serious violations of international law, such as war crimes, crimes against humanity and genocide. These tribunals can be established by the UN, other international organizations or through international agreements.

Notable international criminal tribunals include the following:

- The International Military Tribunals in Nuremberg and Tokyo were established after the Second World War to prosecute Nazi and Japanese war criminals.

- The International Criminal Tribunal for the Former Yugoslavia (ICTY) was established by the UN Security Council in 1993 to prosecute crimes committed during the Balkan conflicts of the 1990s.

- The International Criminal Tribunal for Rwanda (ICTR) was created in 1994 by the UN to prosecute those responsible for the genocide that took the lives of more than 800,000 Tutsis, Twa and moderate Hutus in just 100 days.

- The Special Court for Sierra Leone was established in 2002 to prosecute those responsible for committing crimes against humanity during the civil war from 1991 to 2002.

Criminal tribunals primarily aim to hold those responsible for major breaches of international law to account. The act of getting justice on an international platform can also serve as a symbolic gesture, recognizing the suffering of victims. In this regard, it is both a tool of justice and a method of punishing perpetrators. However, punishment is not only for the purposes of retribution but also to deter potential future offenders from committing similar crimes. But, critics argue that pursuing justice may hinder peace processes, especially if key negotiation actors face potential prosecution.

Beyond punishment and deterrence, war crimes tribunals serve several other roles.

- They can help strengthen the rule of law by demonstrating that no one is above the law and that international law violators will be prosecuted for their crimes.

- They also highlight that there is a mechanism to hold criminals accountable and that violent or arbitrary forms of retribution, which are likely to hinder the peacebuilding process, are unnecessary.

- Targeting and incarcerating key perpetrators of violence tribunals can potentially play a role in stabilizing conflict zones.

- Tribunals play a role in creating a detailed and authoritative record of events, which can be essential for future generations and preventing any denial.

Discussion point

What are some of the criticisms levelled against UN peacekeeping missions?

THEMATIC STUDIES: Peace and conflict

International Criminal Court (ICC)

The International Criminal Court is an intergovernmental organization (IGO) and permanent international tribunal in The Hague, Netherlands. It is responsible for prosecuting individuals for grave crimes of international concern, including genocide, war crimes, crimes against humanity, and the crime of aggression. The ICC was established by the Rome Statute that came into force on 1 July 2002. (The ICC doesn't have retroactive jurisdiction. It can only prosecute crimes committed after 1 July 2002, when the Rome Statute was enacted.) Countries that have ratified this treaty are considered State Parties and are bound by its provisions.

Beyond being bound by the provisions of the Rome Statute, the ICC can exercise its jurisdiction if:

● the accused is a national (slightly broader than a citizen) of a state that has signed and ratified the Rome Statute (a State Party) or a state that has accepted the ICC's jurisdiction. For example, the United States may accept the ICC's jurisdiction over a case even though they have not signed the Rome Statute

● the crime occurred on the territory of a State Party or a state that has accepted the ICC's jurisdiction.

The UN Security Council refers a situation to the ICC. In this case, it would not matter the accused's nationality or where the crime occurred.

Prosecution

The ICC operates on a principle of 'complementarity', which means it will only prosecute cases when national courts are unwilling or unable to do so. Unlike other international tribunals, the ICC can initiate prosecutions on its own authority, based on referrals from countries or the UN Security Council. When referrals are sent to the ICC, the Office of the Prosecutor conducts investigations and decides whether to bring charges against individuals.

As a tool to help elevate the rule of law, the Rome Statute states that even senior government officials, including heads of state, are not immune from prosecution by the ICC. For example, the ICC issued a warrant for the arrest of Omar Al Bashir, the former President of Sudan, for five counts of crimes against humanity, two counts of war crimes and three counts of genocide.

Criticism of the International Criminal Court

The ICC has faced several criticisms since its establishment, including its slow proceedings and the high cost of its operations relative to the number of convictions. Other critiques have focused on accusations of bias, lack of credibility and questions regarding the limited scope of the court.

One of the most prominent criticisms is the suggestion that the ICC disproportionately targets African leaders. Many cases before the ICC have had connections to African countries, leading to perceptions of bias. The AU has expressed concerns about this perceived focus on the continent, with some countries threatening to withdraw and Burundi actually withdrawing.

The ICC relies on member states' cooperation to arrest and transfer suspects. However, there have been instances where indicted individuals have travelled internationally without arrest, or states have refused to hand over suspects, undermining the court's credibility. The court's credibility is also undermined by some major powers, like the United States, Russia and China, who have not ratified the Rome Statute, limiting the court's reach and influence. However, as noted previously, these powers can still influence the ICC through the Security Council. So, while they are not subject to the Rome Statute, they can still benefit from the court when convenient.

Finally, some critics argue that the ICC's jurisdiction should be expanded to include other significant international crimes, such as terrorism or environmental crimes. Others believe that the court's current mandate is already too broad.

The International Court of Justice

The International Court of Justice (ICJ), sometimes referred to as the World Court, is the principal judicial organ of the UN. You would have read about it already in Chapter 1.5.

TOK

A political scientist might argue that despite the accusations of bias, inefficient costs and lack of credibility, an effective global judicial system in a truly global society requires something like the International Criminal Court. The criticism might be *political* in nature (and emanate from a particular 'side'), but it might also be from a political science perspective (so would consider whether the *system* needs such a component, regardless of the individual decisions set forth).

Would you agree or disagree that the ICC is required? And would this be from the perspective of a political actor or a political scientist?

◼ Restorative justice

Restorative justice is a philosophy and approach that seeks to address the harm caused by criminal or wrongful acts through a process of reconciliation. Unlike retributive justice, which focuses primarily on punishment, restorative justice focuses on healing, reintegration and community involvement.

Originating with earlier cultures concerned with human dignity and reintegrating individuals into communities after wrongdoing, restorative justice is an alternative for addressing harm promptly and caringly. This is only possible when all parties involved are committed to restoring relationships, trust and the community that someone's actions have harmed. Even though the retributive justice of a court may have served justice, this does not mean that healing has occurred and relationships have been restored.

The UN has recognized the power of restorative justice. In July 2002, UNESCO adopted a resolution to guide member states in encouraging restorative justice in policy and practice. UNICEF has also provided an international definition of restorative justice that emphasizes repairing the harm caused by a crime and restoring harmony as much as possible between offender, victim/survivor and society.

The practice of restorative justice is often called an intervention, and it takes place as a group meeting to explore who has been harmed beyond the identified victim(s). These meetings do not occur until the perpetrator acknowledges their role in the harm.

There are five critical questions to ask when planning a restorative justice process:

1 Who has been hurt?

2 What are their needs?

3 Whose obligations are these?

4 Who has a stake in the situation?

5 What is the appropriate process to involve stakeholders in an effort to put things right?

Reimer et al., Transformative Change

◼ Truth and reconciliation commissions

Truth and reconciliation commissions (TRCs) are set up to investigate and report on past injustices and human rights abuses in societies that have experienced prolonged periods of conflict or authoritarian rule. Unlike international criminal tribunals, which are focused on prosecuting perpetrators, TRCs aim to uncover and acknowledge the truth of what happened during these periods.

The key features of a TRC include:

- Fact Finding: TRCs investigate past abuses, often through public hearings where victims give testimonies about their experiences.

- Recommendations: TRCs usually produce a final report detailing their findings. The report may also include the recommendation of measures to break the cycle of abuse, suggest reparations for the victims and provide suggestions for reconciling fractured individual and group relationships.

- Timebound: TRCs are usually temporary bodies established for a limited period of time.

- Amnesty: In some cases, TRCs might offer amnesty to those who admit to their crimes. The challenge of incorporating amnesty is balancing truth-telling with a desire for accountability.

◆ To make a person **assimilate** is to force them to conform with the customs and attitudes of a dominant social group or nation.

TRCs can play an important role in peacebuilding by providing a platform to acknowledge past wrongs and act on recommendations for building positive peace. Furthermore, TRCs validate the experiences of victims, which can be a crucial step in the healing process. Unfortunately, TRCs face criticism of failing to produce the desired effect when their recommendations are ignored or not fully implemented. There is also a perception that TRCs might be used to avoid genuine accountability or as a political stunt to avoid taking real action or responsibility for the violence and abuse.

CASE STUDY

The Canadian Truth and Reconciliation Commission

■ **Figure 4.42** The Canadian Truth and Reconciliation Commissioners lift a star blanket to unveil their final report of the TRC. Canadian indigenous archivist Elizabeth Kawenaa Montour explained that among the Dakota/Lakota/Nakota peoples, it is believed that when you are wrapped in a star quilt, your ancestors are among you and with you

A good example of a relatively recent TRC (the final report was submitted in 2015) was the Canadian Truth and Reconciliation Commission, established in 2008 as part of the Indian Residential Schools Settlement Agreement. Its mandate was to document the history and lasting impacts of the Indian Residential School system, a network of schools funded by the Canadian government and operated by Christian churches. The system forcibly separated indigenous children from their families, with the aim to **assimilate** them into Euro-Canadian culture. It operated for over 100 years, with the first residential school opening in the late 1800s. The TRC aimed to facilitate reconciliation among former students, their families and broader Canadian society.

The Canadian TRC reflected the key features of truth and reconciliation commissions and its role as a peacebuilding mechanism:

- Fact-Finding: over its six-year mandate, the TRC held events across Canada where survivors shared their experiences. The Commission collected statements from over 6,500 witnesses, revealing the truth about the residential school system and its terrible impacts on indigenous people and their culture.

- Recommendations: the TRC released a final 2015 report detailing its findings and presenting 94 Calls to Action.

- Timebound: the TRC operated from 2008 to 2015, a clearly defined period during which it held seven national and many community events.

4.4.6 Debates on peace and conflict: effectiveness of peacebuilding efforts

■ The 'liberal peacebuilding' model

One of the main criticisms of peacebuilding efforts is the so-called 'liberal peacebuilding' model. This emphasizes democratic governance, market-oriented economic reforms and the rule of law on peacebuilding.

While many of these goals may be appealing, critics argue that imposing these Western-centric models might not always be suitable for post-conflict societies and may lead to superficial or unstable peace. This is not to say that democratic governance may not one day be suitable, it just may not be culturally suitable at the time. The move from an authoritarian to a democratic model can be jarring and complex. When focused on building peace, such a monumental move may not be suitable.

■ Perceived neocolonialism

In addition, there is further debate regarding the balance between external actors and local ownership in peacebuilding. Critics point out that externally driven peacebuilding can be perceived as neocolonialism. While the need for external expertise and resources may have value, the need for ownership of the peacebuilding process by those rooted in the culture is necessary for a solid foundation of positive peace to be formed.

■ Timing challenges

Other critics argue that peacebuilding efforts often focus too much on short-term stabilization (creating a stable negative peace) rather than addressing the long-term structural issues we noted earlier in this section (positive peace).

Another timing challenge is the debate on the right sequencing and timing of peacebuilding activities. For example, should the DDR of combatants occur before or after the work of TRCs? Structuring a successful peacebuilding effort highlights the importance of a jus post bellum strategy.

■ Overlap of multiple actors

The many actors involved in peacebuilding, like the UN, IGOs, NGOs and offers of assistance from other countries can lead to coordination challenges, overlap or even contradictory efforts. Critics have pointed to this heavy involvement by multiple actors as a cause of the high costs of maintaining these supports. This again highlights that local initiatives focused on locally driven peacebuilding would be more effective, practical and cost-effective.

■ Measuring peacebuilding

Perhaps the biggest challenge is actually quantifying the success of peacebuilding. Is a stable peace all that is necessary for us to declare that the peacebuilding process has been successful, or is that just good peacemaking and peacekeeping? How close to positive peace do we need to state that the peacebuilding has succeeded?

While these debates highlight peacebuilding challenges, they also underscore the challenges of transitioning from conflict to sustainable peace. As we discussed at the start of this thematic study on peace and conflict, achieving even some degree of positive peace is a difficult task and the challenges and criticisms that the peacebuilding movement faces are a further indication of how challenging it is. But if we are to achieve a peaceful world, this also highlights how important it is to meet this challenge.

Chapter summary

In this chapter we have covered:
- types of peacemaking and barriers to conflict resolution
- debates on UN peacekeeping and the principles of intervention
- the effectiveness of peacebuilding efforts.

REVIEW QUESTIONS

Now that you have read this chapter, reflect on these questions:

- What are the differences between treaties, sanctions and embargoes in the context of conflict resolution?

- What is the role of international election observers in preventing and deterring conflict? Are they always effective, or can their presence sometimes give a false sense of legitimacy to flawed elections?

- How do Chapter VI and Chapter VII missions differ in the UN Charter?

- What is the Responsibility to Protect? What criticisms and challenges does the R2P doctrine face in its implementation?

- What are the key features of Truth and Reconciliation Commissions?

For generic advice on how to structure a response to a Paper 2 question, please see page 402. Remember, Section A questions are rooted firmly in one of the three thematic studies while Section B questions will require you to integrate content from across the course.

Note, there are always claims and claims counterclaims expected in a Paper 2-style essay and this guidance identifies some of the claims and counterclaims you may choose to make. These are simply suggestions and you may choose to use other claims if appropriate.

Section A-style question

1 Examine the claim that intrastate conflict impacts marginalized groups more significantly than interstate conflict.

◼ General advice

You need to demonstrate an understanding of the nature and practice of both intrastate conflict and interstate conflict and how each type of conflict may impact the lives of marginalized, vulnerable non-combatants. Remember to show that you understand the difference between the two types of conflict mentioned in the question. Intrastate conflict describes sustained political violence taking place within a state, usually between the state itself and armed non-state actors. Interstate conflict takes place between two states. You should also demonstrate your understanding that marginalized, vulnerable non-combatants could be those in society who are treated differently due to their race, gender, sexuality, nationality, social class and/or economic status. You may choose to show how different people can be considered vulnerable due to other factors, such as substance addiction, being older, being stateless, being pregnant or being a child. Your aim in this essay is to evaluate whether the impact on these people is more significant in the case of intrastate or interstate conflict.

Some areas to consider addressing in your answer include distinguishing between contested meanings of conflict (for example, latent and overt) and contested meanings of violence (for example, direct, structural and cultural) and reflecting on how they differ in terms of the impact on the lives of marginalized groups. You might also choose to discuss causes of conflict as socio-economic divisions within society can be the cause of intrastate conflict.

◼ Claims

Your claims should support the view that intrastate conflict impacts marginalized groups more significantly than interstate conflict. They may include the following:

- Marginalized groups (such as LGBTQ+ groups) are more vulnerable to discrimination and abuse, and internal conflict within a state can sometimes be caused by or elevated by this discrimination and abuse even to the point of genocide, for example Myanmar and the Rohingya people.

- Violent non-state actors are likely to use violence, with vulnerable people often the victims. For example, Christian civilians frequently terrorized and attacked by non-state Defenders Front (FPI) in Indonesia.

- Intrastate conflict can disrupt day-to-day life significantly (for example, cutting off access to schools/education, restricting access to food, disrupting transportation, preventing access to health care), making life even harder for vulnerable populations (for example, the impoverished). There has been a significant increase of attacks on schools in Burkina Faso, Niger and Mali by multiple non-state armed groups as of 2023, for example.

- It's possible to lead a relatively normal life in the case of interstate conflict if the violence is not nearby, but this is not normally the case of intrastate conflict. For example, in Kyiv, there have been long periods of relative normalcy even though the war between Russia and Ukraine rages on in the eastern part of Ukraine.

- State sovereignty may prevent vulnerable groups from appealing for help from the international community/NGOs.

◼ Counterclaims

Your counterclaims should support the view that interstate conflict impacts marginalized groups more significantly than intrastate conflict. They may include the following:

- International sanctions (particularly economic) imposed by the international community in response to an interstate conflict can cause a dramatic reduction in necessary goods and services and vulnerable people are most impacted. Russia and Haiti are possible examples.

- Women are often the targets of sexual violence including rape in the event of interstate conflict. For example, during the Russian invasion of Ukraine women were targets for sexual abuse.

- The scale of interstate conflict can mean more sophisticated weaponry and bombing campaigns have a greater impact on all including those in marginalized groups. For example, in Ukraine, older people and people with disabilities have been unable to seek shelter during Russian bombing raids and are unable to access basic needs such as food and water.

- States may use the interstate conflict as an excuse to imprison or terrorize groups because of their race or nationality or perceived association with the state in conflict. For example, the ongoing Armenian /Azerbaijan conflict has left vulnerable ethnically Armenian people living in the Azerbaijan-controlled area outside Nagorno-Karabakh. Hate-speech against Armenians is seen in state-sanctioned media, peacebuilding initiatives involving civil society have been blocked and physical assaults have occurred.

- Marginalized groups are more frequently forced to flee states to seek asylum in interstate conflict because this kind of conflict is more likely to involve conventional warfare, which is more destructive and damaging to infrastructure, for example Ukraine, South Sudan, Yemen, Iraq.

◼ Some other possibilities

It is important that you consider diverse perspectives in your answer. You might present an argument that both types of conflict impact marginalized groups significantly and in similar ways and therefore the claim is false. This is possibly easier to argue but does not mean you cannot come down on one side or the other.

The examples you use should provide examples of both types of conflict and a consideration of how marginalized people, in particular, are impacted. Remember, in global politics, examples should be contemporary.

Most intrastate conflicts today involve stakeholders from outside the state so you may choose to explore if any modern conflict ever truly be 'intrastate'. Equally, you might choose to focus on intrastate conflict examples that have escalated to the point of genocide. Examples may include Myanmar and the Rohingya people, and Darfur. Marginalized groups including migrants have been the targets of violent terrorist acts in several countries including Germany and Canada and these provide interesting cases to explore, as do the fact that the Taliban in Afghanistan has targeted women as a distinct group.

Examples of intrastate conflicts involving violent non-state actors severely impacting marginalized groups could include Syria, where thousands have been forced to flee their homes and women and children have been particularly victimized. Examples of interstate conflicts could include the Russia-Ukraine war, Saudi-Arabia-Yemen conflict and the Azerbaijan-Armenia conflict.

■ Conclusion

Your answer must build towards a conclusion that explicitly states the extent to which you agree with the claim that intrastate conflict impacts marginalized groups more significantly than interstate conflict.

Section B-style question

1 'Conflict always violates human rights.' Evaluate this statement.

■ General advice

It is important that your response shows an understanding of the concepts of human rights and conflict: human rights being the basic claims and entitlements many argue are entitled to all people; and conflict as actual and perceived opposition between individuals and/or groups that can be either violent or non-violent. You should discuss how conflict may violate human rights, such as through repression, collateral damage, forced relocations and in creating refugees. Most importantly, you must evaluate the likelihood that conflict always violates human rights, and whether it is possible to have conflict without human rights violations.

In your answer, you should show you can distinguish between types of conflict (for example, interstate conflict, ideological conflict) as well as types of violence (for example, direct violence, structural violence) and reflect on how they differ in their effect on human rights. You might also decide to show how human rights have been categorized to provide insight into how first-generation human rights, such as the right to life, differ from second- or third-generation rights, such as the right to a healthy environment, before linking this to types of conflict.

■ Claims

Your claims should support the view that conflict always violates human rights. They may include the following:

- Conflict involving direct violence violates bodily integrity and therefore it is impossible to have conflict without violating human rights (for example, Syria, Ukraine, domestic violence).

- Conflict often has spillover effects (for example, health issues, refugees), which are impossible to eliminate completely and result in human rights violations (for example, displaced older people and people with disabilities are unable to receive health care in Afghanistan, Cameroon, the Central African Republic, Israel/Palestine, Jordan, Lebanon, South Sudan, Syria and Ukraine, and children of refugees are unable to receive an education).

- Unintended consequences of conflict often result in the violation of human rights. For example, peaceful protest marches can be overtaken by violent mobs (France, USA); police can overreact to peaceful protestors using tear gas and depriving them of their right to free speech; destruction of infrastructure can lead to mass unemployment and homelessness.

- In violent conflict, it is impossible to remove the potential for mistakes, from friendly fire to incorrect targeting, resulting in violations. For example, Russia claims to have accidentally hit a Ukrainian school killing over 60 people in an air strike in May of 2022.

- Structural or cultural violence is a form of conflict that guarantees human rights violations. For example, maternal mortality rates of black women in the United States are three times higher than white women; Afghanistan's treatment of women under the Taliban; India's caste system.
- Conflict can be undertaken to protect human rights but is still conflict and violates human rights (for example, R2P in Libya).

■ Counterclaims

Your counterclaims should support the view that conflict does not always violate human rights. They may include the following:

- Lower-level conflicts, such as interpersonal conflicts, don't necessarily entail the violation of human rights.
- Traditional military conflict is fought between states and their militaries and therefore there is no expectation that human rights would be violated in such conflicts.
- There are international laws protecting human rights during time of military conflict, from rights of combatants to those of civilians and non-combatants. International humanitarian law finds its sources in treaties and in customary international law (for example, The Hague Regulations respecting the Laws and Customs of War on Land; the Geneva Conventions and the threat of being held accountable at the International Criminal Court can deter the violation of human rights in military conflict).
- Non-violent conflict can be a useful mechanism for bringing about social change and improving human rights, for example social movements, resistance movements such as Black Lives Matter, or Greta Thunberg's School Strike for Climate protests.
- IGO's and civil society including NGOs can intervene in cases of conflict to protect human rights (for example, shelters for victims of domestic abuse, legal aid for workers deprived of wages or benefits, access to vaccines and medical care, R2P, etc.)
- Some conflicts arise in response to human rights violations and although these may violate some human rights in the short term, the aim is to make lasting change that will improve human rights in the long term (for example, Tulip Revolution in Kyrgyzstan 2005, Iceland's Kitchenware Revolution in 2008, the Iranian Green Movement in 2009).

■ Some other possibilities

You should include contemporary examples to support the points you make and explicitly link these to the relationship between conflict and human rights, such as: violent conflict and physical integrity in Syria, South Sudan and Yemen; political conflict in various forms such as economic sanctions' effect on human rights in Iran and Venezuela; and religious and/or ideological conflict and the right to self-determination (for example, the Rohingya people in Myanmar) or the right to freedom of movement (for example, the Islamic religious police in Saudi Arabia). All of these would be considered valid examples by the examiner and given credit.

You could effectively use violent conflicts to support the claim and non-violent conflicts to offer a counterclaim or alternate perspective.

Cultural relativism could be used to support the idea that there are multiple interpretations of human rights, but this is not to say that those who question the Universal Declaration of Human Rights don't believe in any human rights at all. Therefore, even when considering that there are differing interpretations of human rights, you must still answer the question using real-world examples and by examining multiple perspectives.

Conclusion

Your answer must lead towards a conclusion that explicitly states the extent to which you agree with the statement that conflict always violates human rights.

5 The IA engagement project

Introduction to the project

IBDP Global Politics requires that all students complete an internal assessment (IA) called the engagement project. Your completed IA will be a written report examining a political issue of your choice, but the written report is not simply a research paper. Research does play a part, but 'engagement' implies that you are actively involved with the political issue beyond the necessary research.

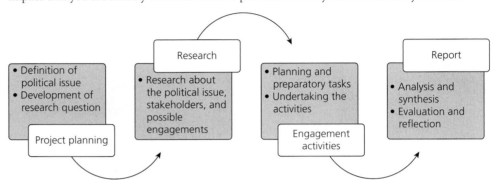

■ **Figure 5.1** The IA engagement project

Figure 5.1 gives an overview of the process you will go through as you work your way towards the finished report. The engagement project is not something you can complete in one evening, or even in one weekend, because it requires you to go out in the real world and actively engage with a political issue.

Both HL and SL students complete the engagement project and go through the same process as seen in Figure 5.1, but there are a few differences:

HL	SL
Time requirement: 35 hours of teaching time	Time requirement: 25 hours of teaching time
Word count of the written report: 2,400 The following are not included in the word count: • Acknowledgements • Contents page • Tables of statistical data • Diagrams or figures • Equations, formulae and calculations • Citations (which, if used, must be in the body of the written report) • References (which, if used, must be in the footnotes/endnotes) • Bibliography • Appendices	Word count of the written report: 2,000 The following are not included in the word count: • Acknowledgements • Contents page • Tables of statistical data • Diagrams or figures • Equations, formulae and calculations • Citations (which, if used, must be in the body of the written report) • References (which, if used, must be in the footnotes/endnotes) • Bibliography • Appendices
30 marks Worth 20 per cent of your final grade	24 marks Worth 30 per cent of your final grade
HL students have the same requirements as SL students but they do an 'extra' component. HL students must undertake further research so that they can make an informed recommendation for a plan of action.	

■ Where do I begin?

First, we need to define what is a 'political issue'.

A political issue is a situation that deals with how power is distributed in society. In other words, who in society has power and who does not? How does the distribution of power impact people's lives? Who is trying to resist change and who is trying to bring about change? Political issues can be seen when looking at all levels of society: global, regional and local levels.

A common misconception is that political issues only involve very high-profile people and institutions. However, there are many actors and stakeholders involved in political issues and, as a student, some of them are more easy to approach than others:

- states
- sub-national and local governments
- intergovernmental organizations (IGOs)
- organized civil society, including non-governmental organizations (NGOs)
- private actors/companies
- social movements
- resistance movements
- political parties
- interest and pressure groups
- political leaders
- formal and informal political forums
- the media
- other individual and collective actors.

Although it is important that we learn about high-profile global political issues, the engagement project is an analysis of power and agency at a **LOCAL** or **COMMUNITY** level.

So, before thinking about your own engagement project, it is important that you first consider what is going on in your own wider community (not confined to the school community). Are there any political issues of particular concern? What are people talking and complaining about? Who are the actors and stakeholders involved?

The engagement project requires you to do some preliminary research into one or more of these political issues and, with more knowledge about the issues, choose the one you think is best and try to formulate a research question.

■ Brainstorm and do some preliminary research

Preliminary research is the research you do before deciding on a research question for your engagement project. Don't assume there will be a lot of information on any particular topic and make sure you spend some time looking into potential political issues. You can talk to your teacher, find local newspaper articles, investigate civil society organizations that are active in your area, look into any social movements actively engaged in your areas of interest, and so on. Additionally, look through this textbook and see how your ideas are connected to the core and thematic studies sections.

Example of a way to get started:

Brainstorm potential political issues that you are interested in exploring	Preliminary research and questions to consider	Consider the engagement: what can you do?
Examples of things I might see in my community: • racism against immigrants • a shortage of affordable housing • not everyone has clean drinking water • the transportation system is unsafe for women travelling alone • if people can afford it, they send their children to private schools not public ones • transgender people are not allowed to legally change their gender. (This is a hypothetical list. Look for genuine issues in your own community.)	From the ideas I have brainstormed, what could be the political issues? What evidence can I find that these issues exist? Who has power in these issues and who does not? Is the power economic, political, social or cultural? Is the power structural or relational? What is the impact on the wider community? Do these issues connect to the IBDP Global Politics course content? Is it safe for me to investigate this political issue? Who are the actors and stakeholders involved in these potential political issues and is it realistic for me to contact them?	What could I realistically and safely do to become actively involved? What could be my research question(s)?

What are the kinds of things I could do?

Once you have decided on your political issue you must then see how you can become involved in order to better understand this issue. Sometimes students do several activities when investigating their engagement project; attending a meeting or participating in a protest march are fine, but those activities alone probably wouldn't help you to effectively analyse and evaluate the political issue. Often, students will supplement this kind of activity by volunteering in some way or interviewing the different actors and/or stakeholders involved. Sometimes, however, students are able to spend an extended period of time involved with their engagement and extra activities are not necessary. This kind of commitment usually involves an extended volunteer session, where you might help address the political issue in some way. For example, if you are looking at discrimination against refugees, you could attempt to volunteer with a local government agency or civil society organization that helps refugees. No matter what you do, it will require planning ahead and you will face rejection, so always have a backup plan.

Creativity Activity Service (CAS)

Other subjects you take and CAS activities you do may inspire an idea about an engagement activity. For example, you may have service in a retirement home for the elderly and that has made you think about how elderly people are treated in your community, leading to an interesting political issue. You cannot, however, use the time you spent doing your service as an engagement. This is called 'double-dipping' and it means you cannot use the same activity or written work for two different diploma requirements. Be very careful of this, as it would be considered a case of academic dishonesty if you did so.

■ Ethical issues

The number one priority when considering what engagement activity you may take part in is your safety and the safety of people involved in your engagement. Do not put yourself at any kind of risk or harm and make sure you consult with your teacher closely to ensure that they also agree that the engagement is safe. Respect the laws and cultural norms of the location where the engagement will take place.

If you interview people or collect data from them, these data (for example, their responses, names, email address, occupation, etc.) must be kept private and only used in the final engagement report. Treat these people with respect and let them read what you have written, so they can see that they've been represented accurately. Do not be confrontational or abusive in any way.

You may not lie to people or deceive them in any way. This deception extends to you making up data or exaggerating your engagement. This would be considered academic dishonesty and you will face serious consequences.

Avoid interviewing children (under the age of consent in your location – consult with your teacher). If you do interview children, then the parents must give their written consent, so in order to avoid this time-consuming and potentially problematic issue, interview adults only. Additionally, do not interview people who are not in a sound state of mind. You should also avoid using relatives as interview subjects, but if that is not possible you must declare they are a relative.

■ What are some of the obstacles I might face with my engagement?

Problem	What can I do?
I have sent out many emails to different individuals and organizations to try to to set up an engagement but no one gets back to me.	This will happen – be prepared! Always have a few backup plans and make sure you give yourself a generous timeline. The people you are contacting are probably very busy people and emails are easy to ignore. Try phoning them or visiting in person. If they reply with a definitive 'no', accept it and move on to your backup plans.
My engagement activity wasn't what I thought it was going to be and I learned nothing about the political issue.	Try to keep an open mind and think about what you did learn from the experience. Possibly you may want to revise your research question? Can you politely contact the person who helped you set up the engagement activity and ask for an interview? Once again, look at backup plans.
I've done a few things but I'm not sure if it's enough.	First of all, ask your teacher for guidance. It is difficult to exactly define when 'enough' has been done but, generally speaking, think about what you have learned about your political issue. Has your engagement(s) provided you with enough knowledge, supplemented with research, to write a report that meets the criterion?

Always remember:

- Consult with your teacher regularly and update them on your progress.
- Be polite and show gratitude to anyone you contact.
- Contact people well in advance of when you would like to do the engagement.
- Be flexible and adaptable.
- Always have a few backup plans.

◼ What comes after my engagement is complete?

You will undertake more research during/after you have completed your engagement. What kind of research?

● Seek background information on the actors, stakeholders and organizations involved with your political issue.

● Establish links between your engagement activity and the key concepts and topics covered in the course.

● Also, remember that your engagement might provide you with just one perspective on the issue (maybe more, depending on what you do). Research is needed to explore other perspectives on the political issue. The strengths and limitations of varying points of view should be considered.

● Secondary material should be used. Newspapers, online academic journals, textbooks, images and audiovisual clips would all be acceptable types of secondary material.

Note: HL students have to conduct extra research to present balanced and informed recommendations.

Remember, the IA engagement project is not primarily a 'research paper' because the focus is on your own engagement. The research helps you to better understand and explore the political issue embedded in your engagement.

◼ What are the important components of the finished report?

The written report combines what you have learned from your engagement and research to provide an answer to your research question about your political issue. You should clearly state your political issue and also explain why you wanted to get involved in this particular engagement and issue.

You need to present your writing in a clearly organized way. An introductory paragraph, several main body paragraphs and a conclusion that summarizes your findings are essential. There is no 'official' format required, but make sure your report follows a clear structure. It is not recommended that you divide your report into sections, with each section representing a different assessment criterion. Your report should cover the criteria but in an authentic and integrated way.

Your engagement project will have involved research, so in-text citations/references and a work cited/bibliography page will be necessary. The style of referencing you use is up to you but it must be consistent. Check with your teacher for more details.

 **Top tip!**

Be careful not to have too much description of your engagement in the report. It is good for you to briefly explain what you did, but focus on what you learned about your political issue, not the mechanics of what happened. If you look at the mark scheme you won't see 'Description of the Engagement' emphasized. In fact, too much description can lead to very low marks in 'Criterion C: Analysis and synthesis'.

◼ Deconstructing the assessment criteria

Make sure you review the assessment criteria and markbands to ensure that you are meeting the requirements:

Overview

Criterion	Description	Marks
A	Explanation and justification	4
B	Process	3
C	Analysis and synthesis	8
D	Evaluation and reflection	6
E	Communication	3

Total: 24 marks

Criterion A: Explanation and justification (4 marks)

- Does the report clearly identify and explain a political issue?
- Does the report explain why the candidate decided to conduct particular engagement activities?

Marks	Level descriptor
0	The work does not reach a standard described by the descriptors below.
1–2	The report includes a limited explanation and justification of the engagement project. • A political issue is identified, but not explained. • There is a limited explanation of the importance and suitability of the project. • The engagement activities are described, but their relevance is not justified.
3–4	The report includes an explanation and justification of the engagement project. • A political issue is identified and explained. • There is an explanation of the importance and suitability of the project. • The engagement activities are explained and their relevance is justified.

Criterion B: Process (3 marks)

- Does the report evidence a well-developed process of research and engagement?

Marks	Level descriptor
0	The work does not reach a standard described by the descriptors below.
1	The report demonstrates a limited research and engagement process.
2	The report demonstrates an adequate research and engagement process.
3	The report evidences a well-planned and integrated research and engagement process.

Criterion C: Analysis and synthesis (8 marks)

- To what extent is the political issue analysed, with reference to the specific context of the engagement?
- To what extent does the report capture and synthetize diverse perspectives of sources and engaged stakeholders?

Marks	Level descriptor
0	The work does not reach a standard described by the descriptors below.
1–2	The report is mostly descriptive. • There is a vague reference to relevant course concepts and content. • The political issue is identified, but not analysed. • There is no synthesis of perspectives.
3–4	The report presents limited analysis and synthesis of the political issue. • The analysis demonstrates a limited understanding of relevant course concepts and content. • Analysis of the political issue is limited. • There is limited synthesis of the perspectives of stakeholders and sources.
5–6	The report presents an adequate analysis and synthesis of the political issue. • The analysis demonstrates understanding of relevant course concepts and content. • The political issue is partially analysed. • Perspectives of stakeholders and sources are partially synthetized, but not always clear.
7–8	The report presents an effective analysis and synthesis of the political issue. • The analysis demonstrates a good understanding and application of course concepts and content. • The political issue is clearly analysed. • There is an effective synthesis of the perspectives of involved stakeholders and sources.

Criterion D: Evaluation and reflection (6 marks)

- Is there an evaluation of the selected sources and the conducted engagement activities?
- Does the report evidence the candidate's critical reflection about the project as a learning experience?

Marks	Level descriptor
0	The work does not reach a standard described by the descriptors below.
1–2	The report demonstrates limited evaluation and reflection. • There is limited reflection on the engagement project as a learning experience. • The research and engagement activities are not evaluated. • No personal positions and biases related to the political issue are identified.
3–4	The report demonstrates an adequate evaluation and reflection. • There is some reflection on the engagement project as a learning experience. • Some of the research and engagement activities are evaluated. • Some personal positions and biases related to the political issue are identified.
5–6	The report evidences a critical evaluation and reflection. • There is a reflection of the engagement project as a learning experience. • The research and engagement activities are evaluated. • Personal positions and biases related to the political issue are explained.

Criterion E: Communication (3 marks)

● Are the information and points presented in the report communicated clearly?

Marks	Level descriptor
0	The work does not reach a standard described by the descriptors below.
1	Communication is limited. The organization and clarity of the report are limited and do not support understanding.
2	Communication is adequate. The report is adequately organized and supports understanding.
3	Communication is effective. The report is well-organized and coherently supports understanding.

■ Common requirements for HL and SL students

Criteria broken down:

A: Explanation and justification (maximum 4 marks)

This is not simply you describing your political issue and your engagement. You must link the two and show the examiner how your engagement was a good choice in order to better understand the political issue. Your engagement must be succinctly explained: express yourself clearly and briefly; leave out any unnecessary details. In other words, get to the point.

B: Process (maximum 3 marks)

Here we see how good research can help your understanding of the political issue, which is embedded in your engagement activity. Part of the research process will involve finding out information that is not really appropriate to your political issue; don't include this kind of information! Once again, be succinct and clearly connect the research to your engagement and political issue.

C: Analysis and synthesis (maximum 8 marks)

Analysis means that you will move beyond simply summarizing your research and what you did for the engagement. You must also consider and evaluate the perspectives of multiple sources, including your own. The final written report must not be descriptive.

Synthesis in this context means that you are effectively combining information from a variety of sources. So, for example, you should consider how you can incorporate the key concepts and the course content of IBDP Global Politics into your essay. Be very careful to avoid throwing random course concepts/content into your essay that don't connect with your political issue. This is clearly 'box ticking' and the opposite of synthesis.

As you can see this criterion is the most heavily weighted and it is important you pay special attention to it. Don't be descriptive! Throughout your report, from start to finish, there should be analysis and synthesis.

D: Evaluation and reflection (maximum 6 marks)

This is an opportunity for you to critically and honestly reflect on and evaluate your engagement activity as a learning experience. Additionally, you should evaluate the sources you have used. For example, if you conducted an interview with an actor or stakeholder involved in a political issue, carefully consider both the value of this information and the limitations. Be honest and consider your own personal position on the issue – did it change as the process evolved?

E: Communication (maximum 3 marks)

It should be every student's goal to score 3/3 on this criterion as it is achievable with a little effort. This is about the organization and structure of your IA engagement project. Remember, there is no prescribed organizational style BUT your report must be clearly organized. You are communicating with an examiner and they rely on you presenting a neatly structured report. Introductory paragraphs, main body paragraphs, conclusions, correctly formatted in-text citations and a bibliography/work cited page will all help with this communication.

■ HL students' extra requirement

Criterion H is for HL students only!

H: Recommendation (maximum mark 6)

As a higher level student, you are expected to go one step further by proposing a recommendation. This recommendation is based on all of the evidence, research, engagement, evaluation and analysis you have completed. It is not simply your personal opinion and it must be consistent with the rest of your report.

■ Final thoughts on the IA engagement project

Students who take IBDP Global Politics appreciate that they have the freedom to explore political issues that are of importance to them. The engagement project gives you an opportunity to investigate and engage with power and politics within your own community and you should embrace this opportunity. If you choose to do something because it's easy but have little personal interest in the issue, then you are passing up an amazing opportunity. Choose something you have a strong personal interest in and enjoy enriching your knowledge of the issue!

6 Assessment guidance

Paper 1 guidance

Summary

Length: 1 hour 15 minutes

Number of sections: One – consisting of four source-based questions

Number of questions answered: You must answer all four questions

Type of questions: Compulsory structured questions

Total marks for this paper: 25 marks

Weighting: Paper 1 is worth 30% of your final grade at SL and 20% at HL

Question 1

▪ What does Question 1 look like?

From the Global Politics Guide: *tests understanding of a source. This can be demonstrated, for example, by identifying specific elements present in a source or by describing or summarizing information included in a diagram or table.*

Question 1 tests a student's understanding of source material. The command terms you are likely to find in Question 1 are: 'identify' or 'describe', though it is possible to also see 'outline' or 'define'.

Question 1 can be asked with reference to an image, chart, graph, political cartoon or excerpt of text. Typically, there have been visuals, but that doesn't mean that Question 1 couldn't be asked on the basis of a written component. In the case of a written source, you can use both the text of the source and the caption describing the source (usually located immediately above the source).

▪ The basics

Marks: 1 mark for each accurate point, up to a maximum of 3 marks.

Length: Spend no longer than five minutes on this question after you have finished reading or examining it.

Structure:

● Point form.

● Write no more than two sentences for each point, typically one is fine.

● Leave an empty line between each point so that it is clear that you have made three distinct points.

Using quotations: While using quotations in this question is acceptable (if it is text-based, of course), they should be kept short – no more than four to five words – and seamlessly incorporated into your response. Examiners want to see if you understand the text, not that you are good at plucking out quotations that correlate to the question that has been asked. In short, keep quotations to a minimum or refrain from using them at all.

■ Constructing the response

Let's look at constructing a response to Question 1 in the context of this possible question:

With **reference to Source A**, identify three ways in which **international governmental organizations can influence global politics**.

There are really two components to this question. First, you need to reference something that is said or displayed in the source. Second, whatever you have referenced needs to be connected to the topic of the question, which in this case is the influence that international governmental organizations have on global politics. In other words, as highlighted in the bold phrases above, you need to ensure you are answering the question that is being asked by making specific reference to both something in the source and connecting that to the topic of the question. As long as this is done, you should find success on what is a rather straightforward question.

Question 2
■ What does Question 2 look like?

From the Global Politics Guide: *The second question tests application of knowledge to the context of a source/sources. Students should primarily focus on the source/sources but should also draw on other supporting examples from their study of global politics.*

Question 2 *tests understanding of a source. This can be demonstrated, for example, by identifying specific elements present in a source or by describing or summarizing information included in a diagram or table.* The command term most often encountered has been 'explain', but you may also see 'analyse', 'distinguish' or 'suggest'.

■ The basics

Marks: 4

Length: Take no longer than 10 minutes for this question.

Structure:

● Two paragraphs, two to three sentences each. Each paragraph is essentially worth 2 marks each for a total of 4 marks.

● You should leave a line between each paragraph so that it is clear that you have made separate points.

● Like Question 1, using quotations in this question is acceptable, but for this question should be seen as more of a 'must do' if it is a written source. However, like Question 1, the quotations should be kept short – no more than four to five words – and seamlessly incorporated into your response. Again, examiners want to see if you understand the text, not that you are good at selecting quotations that correlate to the question that has been asked.

■ Constructing the response

Let's look at constructing a response to Question 2 in the context of this possible question:

Using Source B and one example you have studied, **explain the reasons** why non-governmental organizations may only possess soft power.

In order to 'explain' or 'analyse' this question you will need to go beyond a brief point form of response as in Question 1.

Question 2 requires a little more depth – an explanation. You might take the following approach:

1 Select a good example from Source B.

2 Explain how the example chosen demonstrates 'reasons why non-governmental organizations may only possess soft power'.

3 Choose a good example from something you studied.

4 Explain how the example from something that was studied demonstrates 'reasons why non-governmental organizations may only possess soft power'.

Note: Points 1 and 2 should constitute one paragraph of two sentences (three maximum). Points 3 and 4 should constitute the second paragraph.

It is important to highlight the connection between the command term 'explain' and the actual explaining you are meant to do in the second part of each of the two points/paragraphs. If you don't 'explain' the reasons why 'non-governmental organizations may possess only soft power' you will not achieve full marks.

Question 3

■ What does Question 3 look like?

From the Global Politics Guide: *the third question tests the comparison and/or contrast of the views, ideas, claims and information presented in two of the sources. Candidates should focus on comparing and/or contrasting specific points in the sources but may make use of their wider study of global politics to provide context, if relevant. Candidates should organize the material into a clear, logical and coherent response. For the highest marks, a detailed running comparison and/or contrast is expected.*

Students may be asked to:

● contrast – that is, identify the differences between the two sources

● compare – that is, identify the similarities between two sources

● both 'compare and contrast'.

■ The basics

Marks:

● Students receive 2 marks for each point they make, up to a maximum of 6 marks. Each point is worth 2 marks. See the 'constructing your response' section to ensure you understand the level of detail required to earn both points.

● If students are asked to compare, only compare; if you are asked to contrast, only contrast. There are no points for contrasting when the question is asking you to compare or vice versa. Remember: contrast = different; compare = similar.

Length: 15–20 minutes

Structure:

● Three paragraphs, three to four sentences each. Each paragraph is worth 2 marks each, for a total of 6 marks.

● Leave a line between paragraphs so that each point is distinct from the next.

Using quotations: Using quotations in this question is valuable but, as with Questions 1 and 2, they should be kept short (four to five words) and be seamlessly incorporated into the response. The quotations you use should assist in demonstrating a comparison or contrast; they are not meant to stand on their own.

■ Constructing the response

- Like Question 1, you can use both the text of the source and the caption describing the source (located immediately above the source) to develop a response. Both components are understood to be part of the source and can be used.

- As noted in the quotation from the Global Politics Guide, one of the things that is asked for in this question is a 'detailed running comparison/contrast', but what does that mean? Simply put, it means to compare or contrast the sources with one another immediately. For example, Source B says 'X' while Source D says 'Y'.

  ○ In the case of a contrast question, you are **not** to list all of the things stated in one source and then, in the next paragraph, list all of the contrasting points from the second source. This would **not** be a running commentary.

  ○ If a compare and contrast question is asked, you should do two of either compare or contrast and one of the other – that is two compares and one contrast, or two contrasts and one compare.

  ○ Again, the examiner is looking for a running comparison and contrast. For example: 'Source B is similar to Source D in that Source B says, [insert short quotation from Source B here] and Source D says that [insert short quotation from Source D here]. These sources are similar in that they both [explain in your own words how they are similar].'

  ○ Now, skip a line and start a new paragraph that reads, 'On the other hand, the sources differ in that Source B argues that, [insert short quotation from Source B here] while Source D says that [insert short quotation from Source D here].' Then, once again, summarize the difference you just highlighted in your own words.

  ○ In both examples we can see how both Sources B and D compare and contrast and are seamlessly integrated with one another. This is a good example of what 'running commentary' would look like in a compare and contrast question.

- It is essential to reiterate the importance of specifically addressing the question that is being asked. For example, in a question like 'contrast the views of Source B and Source D regarding the effectiveness of non-violence in addressing global issues', you need to focus specifically on the 'effectiveness of non-violence in addressing global issues'. Nothing else is relevant, only evidence and analysis that addresses the issue of effectiveness. Even if there are really good contrasts between the two sources, if the contrasts aren't related to the effectiveness of non-violence, then they are not relevant.

- As with all four of the questions in this paper, you should highlight or circle the specific topic/issue on the exam that the question is asking you to address, so you remain focused on mining the source for material that is only related to what the question is asking for.

A sample point of contrast that would achieve 2 marks:

When considering the effectiveness of non-violence, Source B takes a positive approach when it states that 'non-violent protest has been shown to be four times more effective in achieving the desired results than violent protest'. In contrast, Source D explains that each conflict is different and that just because statistics demonstrate that non-violence is more effective it 'does not mean non-violence will always be the most effective approach'. In summary, Source B sees non-violence, statistically speaking, as more effective, while Source D thinks each conflict is unique so non-violence isn't always going to be the right choice.

Question 4

◼ What does Question 4 look like?

From the Global Politics Guide: *Question 4 tests the evaluation of sources and synthesis of source material and previous knowledge. Candidates should evaluate the sources and synthesize relevant evidence from them with their own knowledge about the prescribed content of the course. Candidates should organize the material into a clear, logical and coherent response.*

The remaining command terms for Assessment Objective 3 are: 'discuss', 'evaluate', 'examine', 'justify', 'recommend' and 'to what extent'. Question 4 will use one of these command terms as part of the prompt. The commonality between all six is that you are being asked to do an analysis of a global political issue.

◼ The basics

Marks: This question is out of 12 marks and marked using a rubric.

Length: 30–35 minutes – you will note that the timing suggestions for all four questions do not add up to the 1 hour and 15 minute exam. This attempts to account for additional factors such as transitioning between questions, moving to a second writing booklet and reading the sources (you should be able to read through all of the sources once during your five minutes of reading time at the start of the exam).

Structure:

- Brief introduction indicating how you plan to address the question. Two to three sentences, maximum.

- Two to four body paragraphs, depending on the time available. One or two paragraphs focused on the reasons why you agree with the question/prompt and one or two paragraphs on the reasons why you disagree with the question/prompt.

- A brief concluding paragraph that summarizes the main ideas of the points made and your final position on the question.

◼ Constructing the response

- The first thing to notice about this question is which of the four core concepts the question is focused on – power, sovereignty, legitimacy and/or interdependence. Paper 1 will focus on the core concepts of the course though you will likely need to also draw on prescribed content from other aspects of the course.

- This is a mini-essay, where you will need to fully and explicitly answer the question. This is really the only major piece of advice for this question and it is often a significant challenge for not only this question but other assessment elements of the course, like Paper 2. If you address, analyse and construct your response around the question that is being asked, you are likely to do well.

- Aside from clearly addressing the question, you need to blend your own knowledge and the sources together as part of each point that is made. You should not discuss the sources and your own knowledge separately. This will not help you meet the top end of the markbands.

- You should try to use all of the sources as part of your mini-essay, with a firm minimum of three.

- Always use DASK when writing your response to this question:
  - Ensure you look at the question from **D**ifferent perspectives.
  - **A**nalyse/**A**nswer the question.
  - Use the **S**ources and your own **K**nowledge.

◼ Breaking down the Question 4 rubric

The following is based on the Paper 1, Question 4, 10–12 markband. The phrasing for each of the three markband descriptors is in italics, followed by an interpretation.

The response shows an in-depth understanding of the demands of the question:

- This defers from the 7–9 band which uses the term 'adequate'. Much of the difference between 'adequate' and 'in-depth' has to do with the advice given above on the importance of answering the question. Essentially, what you are writing needs to be clearly linked to/focused on the question that is being asked.

- For example, '*Using at least three sources and your own knowledge, evaluate the claim that soft power is the preferred tool for states in twenty-first-century world politics.*' The key term here is 'preferred tool'. Everything you write should focus on this part of the question. The examiner should see 'preferred tool' appear in your response many times. Doing this will be the start of demonstrating that you have an in-depth understanding of the question.

Relevant and accurate knowledge is used effectively throughout:

- The 'relevant' part of 'relevant and accurate knowledge' is also an important consideration for the examiner. Just doing an information dump or name/term dropping all things related to the concept the paper is based on isn't going to result in you achieving the higher markbands. The information needs to be used effectively to help you answer the question.

- Of course, the information needs to not only be 'relevant' but also 'accurate'. The poor and often inaccurate use of theoretical perspectives, such as realism and liberalism or what constitutes soft or hard power, is pervasive across IBDP Global Politics assessments, including Paper 1. Using any idea or theory accurately is an important factor in achieving top marks.

There is effective synthesis of own knowledge and source material, with appropriate examples integrated in the response:

- The top band is asking for an 'effective synthesis of own knowledge and source material', which essentially means that you need to not only be able to use the sources in your response but also to integrate your own knowledge alongside your use of the sources (see point 3 in the 'constructing the response' section). Using both a source and seamlessly integrating appropriate/good examples from your own knowledge into the point you are trying to make will ensure 'effective synthesis'.

- The 'appropriate examples integrated' phrase is going to be connected to the integration of your own knowledge. Do the examples you chose relate well to the question that is being asked? Are the examples 'events occurring approximately over the past two decades'?

Different perspectives on the question, are explored and evaluated:

- An alternative perspective doesn't have to be the exact opposite of a previous point; a different viewpoint is also fine.

- At the 10–12-mark level, each perspective needs to not only be explained or 'explored' (which would be enough for the 7–9 markband) but also 'evaluated'. Part of achieving top marks and meeting the expectations of this band requires you to evaluate the quality of the argument or perspective you are exploring. You might ask yourself, 'what makes the argument I have presented particularly strong or, where are there weaknesses in this argument?' Not only should you offer different perspectives at this level, but you must also evaluate the validity or quality of the perspectives.

Ultimately, Paper 1 is a fair paper and you should be able to achieve well if you follow the advice provided here.

Summary

Length: 1 hour 45 minutes

Number of sections: Two – Section A consisting of three questions from the three thematic studies and Section B consisting of three integrating questions that draw on content from across the course

Number of questions answered: You must answer two questions in total – one essay from Section A and one essay from Section B

Type of questions: Essay

Total marks for this paper: 30 marks

Weighting: Paper 2 is worth 40% of your final grade at SL and 30% at HL

What does a top level Paper 2 essay look like?

Each question on Paper 2 will be marked out of a maximum of 15 marks according to generic markbands and level descriptors. This means that the description of a top level essay – an essay that scores from 13 to 15 marks – will be the same regardless of the question. The examiner will also be provided with question-specific guidance that identifies some of the content they might reasonably expect to see depending on the question set. Obviously, it is unreasonable to expect students to memorize all the descriptors for the different levels – your teacher will be able to provide you with a copy of the generic markbands – but, because you are aiming to align as far as possible with the top level descriptor, it makes sense to be as familiar with it as possible. The earlier in the course you begin doing this, the more comfortable you will feel walking into the exam room and feeling like you are ready to write an essay that matches this description.

The top level descriptor for a Paper 2 essay states that:

- The demands of the question are understood and addressed, and possible implications are considered.
- The response is well structured, balanced and effectively organized.
- Arguments are clear, coherent and compelling.
- All of the main claims are justified and evaluated.
- Relevant and accurate knowledge is used effectively throughout the response.
- Supporting examples are effectively developed.
- Diverse perspectives are explored and evaluated.

Applying the criteria

Let's take a closer look at what these different points actually look like in practice.

The demands of the question are understood and addressed, and possible implications are considered

The key word here is 'demand'. Are you doing exactly what the examiner is asking of you? For example, if the question reads, 'evaluate the claim that challenges of sustainability means that development may no longer be possible', are you actually evaluating the claim as stated in the question? Or, as sometimes happens, are you simply writing down everything you can remember from the past two years that is related to the concepts of development and sustainability? It is also important that you consider any implications arising from the question. These are other issues that might follow on from the points you make but which are not necessarily stated in the question. However, you must be careful that you do not allow yourself to be side-tracked from your focus on the question.

The response is well structured, balanced and effectively organized

Is your essay organized into paragraphs and does it address both claims and counterclaims? Remember, an essay in global politics is essentially an argument, and your task is to address both sides of that argument.

Arguments are clear, coherent and compelling

It is not enough simply to list evidence that supports the claim or counterclaim. Instead, the examiner will expect you to go further and show why your arguments are strong and make sense. The words clear and coherent are also important. Make sure the examiner can see how each point you make relates to your essay as a whole and keep your language simple and to the point.

All of the main claims are justified and evaluated

You cannot just include a claim and leave it to the examiner to decide if it is a good one or not. You must explain why you have included the claim and evaluate it. This means you need to say how effective it is as either a claim or counterclaim. How might it be criticized? What weaknesses does it have?

Relevant and accurate knowledge is used effectively throughout the response

You must be familiar with the course content and the related concepts. For example, there is no excuse in a global politics exam for not having a good grasp of sovereignty as a concept. Equally, if you are going to refer to treaties etc., while nobody will expect you to memorize the Universal Declaration of Human Rights (1948) in full, you should be able to demonstrate familiarity with its key provisions.

Supporting examples are effectively developed

This is where your case study knowledge is essential. It is not enough to simply 'name-drop' examples. You must show you know exactly what is going on in your case study and, just as importantly, show how it is relevant to answering the question.

Diverse perspectives are explored and evaluated

The world is a diverse place and different actors have different motivations and interests. Different theories attempt to explain the same thing in different ways. You should be sure that you do not rely on just one perspective when writing your essay. The word 'evaluated' appears again at this point because it is important. It is not enough to simply offer different perspectives. Make sure you address their strengths and weaknesses.

Structuring your essay

◼ Introduction

Start by unpacking the question. You might choose to identify the key political issue around which it revolves, for example. This would also be a good time to define – accurately, of course – any of the key terms in the question. If you are intending to use any theories or theoretical approaches in your essay, you should make this clear at this point. You don't need to go into a lot of detail but you should let the examiner know what will be coming up and why it is relevant.

State your thesis. Your thesis is a claim that summarizes the argument you are making. For example, if the question is 'Conflict always violates human rights. Evaluate this statement', then your thesis may be that this is untrue and conflict does not always violate human rights. Your introduction is also a smart place to do a bit of 'signposting'. This is basically a sentence or two that briefly explains how you will test or defend your thesis. For example, you might write something like, 'In this essay, I will argue that conflict does not always violate human rights and will support this with reference to conflicts including …'

◼ Body

You should be aiming to include around five or six body paragraphs. Remember, you do not have a lot of time to do this, which is why your paragraphs should be very tightly focused. It is also why it is so important to practise writing timed essays throughout the course. Like all skills, essay writing can be learned but it cannot be learned the night before the exam.

Here is a suggested structure for a body paragraph but, remember, you need to adapt depending on your writing style and the demands of the question. Nonetheless, this provides a useful starting point.

- Your first sentence should be a topic sentence that introduces your argument and is clear, concise and to the point. Remember, given the tight time constraints, every word must count.

- Your second sentence should link your topic sentence to a specific global politics concept. This may be one of the four key concepts – power, sovereignty, legitimacy or interdependence – or may be another relevant concept, such as peace, sustainability or globalization, for example.

- You should then introduce the real-world example you are using to support your point and state, clearly, how it relates to your topic sentence and the argument you are developing.

- Now you begin to develop your example and argument. Tell the examiner why this argument and example are relevant. Explain how it deepens your understanding of the topic and political issue. If you are referring to theories – and remember, you should only do so when they are relevant; do not attempt to 'jam' them in where they do not fit – then this is the place to do it. If your paragraph is a claim, then be sure that one of your counterclaims offers an evaluation of what you have said. If the paragraph is a counterclaim, then you should include a brief evaluation at this point.

- Now answer the question the examiner will be asking themselves while reading your paragraph – 'so what?'. The best way to think of this is as almost a mini-conclusion to your paragraph. You need to show what the impact of your paragraph is on your thesis.

- Finally, you should include a linking or 'signposting' sentence. Think of this as the part where you let the examiner know about the next argument coming in their direction. One way to do this is to include the same – or similar – keywords as in the first sentence of the following paragraph.

■ Conclusion

Pull all of your arguments together and prioritize them. Look back at the points you have made and state which ones are the most convincing. This is why it is so important to clearly articulate how you are evaluating each point you have made. Finally, and this might seem obvious but you would be amazed at how often some students forget, answer the question!

● Five top tips!

1 Read the question very carefully and remember to read between the lines. What are any implications of the question that are not stated explicitly? Most of all, remember to answer the question as it is stated and not how you wish it had been stated.

2 Do not start writing as soon as the reading time finishes. Take five minutes to write a plan so you are clear on exactly what the structure of your essay is going to be.

3 Make sure you support the points you make with detailed examples. This is how you show that you really know what you are talking about. As far as possible, try to include relevant numbers and dates.

4 Be consistent. Your thesis, arguments and conclusion should also be sending the same message. It is no good getting halfway through your essay and wondering what your argument is going to be. You need to know, before you put pen to paper, exactly what your conclusion is going to be and how you are going to get there, which is why making an essay plan is so important.

5 Write in academic, formal English. This means no slang such as 'gonna', and writing in the third person. For example, instead of writing 'I think' you might write 'the evidence suggests …'

Summary

Length: 1 hour 30 minutes

Number of sections: One – consisting of stimulus material, which may be in the form of text, data, diagrams and/or infographics, and four questions

Number of questions answered: You must answer all of the questions – 1, 2a, 2b and 3

Type of questions: Stimulus-based questions

Total marks for this paper: 28 marks

Weighting: Paper 3 is worth 30% of your final grade at HL

What is Paper 3 assessing?

Paper 3 is a stimulus-based paper and is focused on the HL extension global political challenges. In order to address the assessment criteria effectively you will be required to draw on your knowledge of course concepts, content and contexts, as well as drawing upon the research of multiple case studies that you have carried out during the course.

■ The global political challenges and HL topic areas

- Borders
- Security
- Environment
- Health
- Identity
- Technology
- Equality
- Poverty

The stimulus material included in the paper is intended to encourage you to focus on a particular topic or item for analysis or discussion. The relevant evidence that you draw upon to support your answers will mostly be based on the case studies you have researched. Therefore, it is essential that you take the requirement to investigate and explore a variety of case studies during the course seriously. Your teacher will support and guide you during this process.

■ Example stimulus material

The following example is similar to the type of stimulus material you may be presented with in Paper 3. Remember, however, that the stimulus material may take forms other than text.

While global problems are a feature of our contemporary world, so too are the solutions. Much of the time, the causes of these global problems are clear to see and numerous actors – from scientists to policy think-tanks – provide governments with data, theories, evidence and analysis in order to offer solutions. These global problems, however, are often not easily addressed. They are interconnected on a number of different levels and are fast growing, and states cannot collaborate quickly enough to address them.

In terms of global policy, we can distinguish between 'trans-governmentalism', which refers largely to government-led processes of international public policy, and 'transnational policy processes', which refers more to processes in which non-state actors take the lead. As Diane Stone suggests, the word 'transnational' is likely to be encountered much more than the terms 'international' or 'intergovernmental'. She distinguishes between these terms by pointing out that 'transnational' acknowledges the central role played by non-state actors, such as civil society actors (CSOs), multinational corporations (MNCs) and the scientific community in global policy making, while 'intergovernmental' focuses on the formal political relationships between states such as intergovernmental organisations (IGOs).

Essentially, the complex interdependence that characterizes contemporary global politics has led to an increase in both the number and types of actors involved in the creation and implementation of global policy. State actors now work hand in hand with non-state and private actors in the sphere of global policy.

Question 1

There are three marks available for this question and it requires you to demonstrate that you understand and can analyse the stimulus material, as well as demonstrate knowledge of global political challenges. The command term for this question will ask you to 'analyse', 'distinguish', 'explain' or 'suggest'. You should pay close attention to the command term and ensure that you do exactly what is required. For example, if the question asks you to distinguish between two terms in the stimulus material then you should make sure you make clear the differences between them rather than identifying any similarities. Question 1 will usually ask you to refer to one or more examples. This is where you will begin to draw upon your knowledge of the case studies you have researched. Be sure to develop your examples by offering a proper explanation or contextualization that shows why they are relevant, rather than merely mentioning them in passing.

◼ Example question

The following is an example of a Paper 3 Question 1:

Using at least two examples, distinguish between *transnational* and *intergovernmental* political processes.

Question 2a

There are four marks available for this question and it requires you to demonstrate your knowledge and understanding of, as well as ability to analyse, an identified political issue. As with Question 1, the command terms will ask you to 'analyse', 'distinguish', 'explain' or 'suggest'. The question will also ask you to make explicit reference to a political issue identified in one of the case studies you have researched. For example, the question may ask, *'With explicit reference to a political issue identified in one of your researched case-studies, explain the involvement of two types of political actors'.*

To be successful in answering Question 2a, there are a couple of things you should bear in mind:

- You must address the demands of the question. This means you do exactly what the command term is asking you to do. For example, if the command term is 'explain' then you are required to give a detailed account including reasons or causes.

- You must provide a clear analysis of a political issue and demonstrate relevant and accurate knowledge of the context. This means going beyond simply identifying the political issue – although you should certainly do this as well – and break down the issue to identify the key elements and show why they are relevant and important. You might do this by addressing relevant perspectives and actors, causes, consequences and impacts, and any significant recent developments.

The top-level descriptor for Question 2a states:

- The demands of the question are addressed.
- The response provides a clear analysis of a political issue.
- Relevant and accurate knowledge of the context is demonstrated.

■ Example question

The following is an example of a Paper 3 Question 2a:

With explicit reference to a political issue identified in one of your researched case-studies, explain the involvement of three types of actors or stakeholders.

Question 2b

There are six marks available for Question 2b. The command term for this question will be 'recommend', which means 'present an advisable course of action with appropriate supporting evidence/reason in relation to a given situation, problem or issue' and requires you to build upon your answer for the previous question by providing a recommendation of a possible course of action or solution to the identified political issue.

In order to answer this question successfully, you must:

- present a clear and well-supported recommendation; you should state your recommendation clearly towards the start of your answer
- ensure that your recommendation addresses the identified political issue effectively
- identify relevant actors and stakeholders
- make sure that you have identified and considered any implications and possible challenges or unintended consequences to your recommendation and, where appropriate, offered solutions or mitigations.

There are a few possible ways in which you can ensure that you demonstrate that you are doing all of these things, but it may be helpful to consider the following guiding questions:

- What other cases have you researched where similar solutions have been introduced successfully or unsuccessfully?
- Have there been any previous proposals or calls to action by specific stakeholders involved in the political issue? If so, were these proposals developed or calls to action heeded? Why? Why not?
- Are there any theoretical approaches or models of analysis that favour certain approaches for this particular political issue?
- Are there any elements (frameworks, mechanisms or agreements) that may already be in place that could facilitate implementation of suggested measures? How might this work in practice?

The top-level descriptor for Question 2b states:

- A clear and well-supported recommendation is presented.
- The recommendation addresses the identified political issue effectively.
- Implications and possible challenges or unintended consequences are considered.

■ Example question

The following is an example of a Paper 3 Question 2b:

Based on the political issue identified in 2(a), recommend a course of action that would increase the influence of a specific non-state actor.

Question 3

This question is worth 15 marks and is based on the guiding lines of inquiry for the HL extension. The question will require you to demonstrate synthesis and evaluation of researched case studies and global political challenges. As you will see in the feature box, the guiding lines of inquiry emphasize the interconnected nature of the seven global challenge topic areas and you should expect this interconnectedness to form a central focus of your answer to Question 3.

■ Guiding lines of inquiry for the HL extension

- What connections can be established between the global political challenge(s) and the core topics?
- What connections can be established between the global political challenge(s) and the thematic studies?
- To what extent are the global political challenges interconnected? What are some of the links in how they are studied and/or addressed?
- How are the global political challenges perceived and addressed in different contexts?
- What are some of the frameworks, systems, organizations and mechanisms put in place for addressing global political challenges?
- How can looking at specific cases from different topic areas change the way global political challenges are perceived or addressed?

Question 3 will ask you to refer explicitly to one or more of the case studies you have researched, as well as one or more of the HL topic areas. It is very important that you read the question carefully so that you know exactly what the examiner will be expecting you to refer to in your answer. The top-level descriptor for Question 3 states:

- The demands of the question are understood and addressed, and possible implications are considered.
- The response is well structured, balanced and effectively organised.
- Arguments are clear, coherent and compelling.
- All of the main claims are justified and evaluated.
- Relevant and accurate knowledge is used effectively throughout the response.
- Supporting examples are effectively developed.
- Diverse perspectives are explored and evaluated.

This is the same top-level descriptor as the Paper 2 essay. You can refer to the Paper 2 guidance on page 402 for some pointers on unpacking these criteria.

◼ The importance of interconnectedness

Question 3 will be focused on the interconnectedness of one or more case studies with one or more global challenge topic areas. Exactly how you tackle this will depend on the exact wording of the question, but it may be helpful to consider the following guiding questions:

- Are there any common or contributing causes, particular perspectives or approaches that tie them together?

- Are there any contradictions in how the political issue in the different cases and/or global challenge topic areas are addressed by affected stakeholders?

- How are you evidencing specific knowledge from the selected case(s)?

- How are you demonstrating a good understanding of how each global political challenge may be examined?

- Are you going to use a case study first approach? This involves exploring the case studies in depth while evidencing identified links to and across global challenge topic areas. Or will you use a global challenge first approach? This would involve explaining connections between the topic areas in general before illustrating them through your selected case(s).

◼ Example question

The following is an example of a Paper 3 Question 3:

The stimulus mentions the 'interconnected nature' of global problems.

With reference to one of your researched case studies, examine the links between at least two of the HL topic areas.

● Five top tips!

1 Allocate your time according to the marks available. You will have 90 minutes to answer all four questions on this paper, but you should ensure that you spend an appropriate amount of time on each.
2 Plan your answers before committing pen to paper. This is particularly important for the questions that require an extended response. Time spent planning is rarely time wasted.
3 Focus on the command terms. It is essential that you do exactly what the question is asking you to do and the command terms are the way in which the examiner makes this clear to you. For example, 'recommend' is a different instruction to 'explain'.
4 Go beyond simply mentioning the case studies you have researched. It is not enough just to name a particular case. You must explain why it is relevant and demonstrate that you have an in-depth understanding of the case studies you are using. Remember, analysis and evaluation are keys to success and you must resist the urge to simply describe every detail of what you know about your case studies.
5 Remember the importance of interconnectedness with relation to case studies, global challenge topic areas and political issues. It is essential that you articulate links between these clearly and explicitly.

Glossary

Absolute decoupling A decline in the ecological intensity per unit of economic output due to increases in efficiency along with an absolute decline in the use of energy and raw materials.

Absolute gains Allow both sides in a negotiation to reach their goals. Success in these negotiations does not rely on one party gaining something at the expense of the other party.

Absolute poverty When household income is below a certain level, making it impossible to meet basic needs, such as food, shelter, safe drinking water, education, health care, and so on.

Abstain To abstain from something is to not do it, or have it, especially if it is something considered to be enjoyable.

Affirmative action When an effort has been made to improve educational and employment opportunities for marginalized groups by prioritizing them as applicants.

Agape In Christianity, the highest form of love and charity, the fatherly love of God for humans.

Agrarian Land or farming. An agrarian economy is one dependent on maintaining farmland and producing crops.

Antibiotic resistance Occurs when the improper use of antibiotics increases antibiotic resistance in bacteria. Examples of improper use include patients buying antibiotics over the counter without a prescription at a pharmacy, doctors prescribing antibiotics when they're not needed, or using the wrong type of antibiotic when they are.

Apartheid System of government that effectively institutionalized and legitimized political and economic inequality through racial segregation in South Africa between 1948 and 1994.

Assets Items or resources with economic value owned by a person or business.

Assimilate To force a person to conform with the customs and attitudes of a dominant social group or nation.

Asylum A place of safety and shelter.

Belt and Road initiative A system of roads and infrastructure that links 150 countries and international organizations to China, with the aim of increasing trade and economic growth.

Binding When a law is binding, the state's actions must support the promises made in the law, otherwise it will face consequences.

Bretton Woods institutions The World Bank and the International Monetary Fund, which were set up at the Bretton Woods Conference in 1944 in order to aid global economic recovery and development following the Second World War.

Bystanders Those who are neither engaged in a conflict nor willing to take a side, speak out against atrocities or actively support reconciliation.

Capacity-building The process of developing, strengthening and sharing skills, abilities, processes and resources to help support a new or growing organization, especially in the military or international security sectors.

Civilian A person who is not a member of the armed or police forces, nor actively engaged in conflict.

Codification The process of making human rights laws, such as those as seen in treaties and covenants, legitimate and enforceable within the legal systems of states.

Commodity concentration When poorer countries rely heavily on the export of one or two raw materials or commodities, meaning they are susceptible to changes in the price of this commodity.

Comparative advantage An economy's ability to produce a particular good or service at a lower cost than its trading partners.

Compensation Something that is done or given to make up for the damage or loss of something else.

Conflict profiteers Those who may not sympathize with the side they support ideologically in a conflict but supply all manner of resources to their side and are happy to support them because they benefit financially.

Conflictual Behaviour characterized by conflict or disagreement.

Connotations Feelings or ideas that certain words evoke in individuals, or something suggested or implied by a word.

Conscription When a state orders people by law to join the armed forces.

Contested concept A concept that, while there is generally broad agreement about its definition, can be defined in a number of different ways. Contested concepts tend to be multifaceted and multidimensional.

Continuum Something that keeps on going and changing over time.

Coup d'etat The sudden, violent overthrow, or attempted overthrow, of a government by a smaller group.

Customary international law Formed not by written or codified laws, but by existing practices or customs accepted by international states.

Degrowth Argues for shrinking rather than growing economies in order to use less of the world's increasingly scarce resources.

Democratization The process of transition to a more democratic society or system.

Demonstrations Public gatherings for people to show their collective stance on a particular issue or cause.

Denotation A word's literal or primary meaning, not the feelings or ideas an individual may connect with it.

Deprivation The absence or too little of something considered to be a basic necessity. An individual can be in a state of deprivation if they have nothing, or too little of a basic necessity.

Development A process that creates growth, progress and positive change.

Diaspora A large group of people living somewhere that is not their original homeland. Sometimes these people have moved by choice, but other times they may have been forced to relocate.

Digital government Also known as e-government. The use of technological communications, such as smartphones and the internet, to provide public services to citizens and other persons in a country or region.

Diplomatic immunity Special rights given to diplomats working in a country that is not their own, such as freedom from legal action. It also ensures they are not hurt or harmed while living and working there.

Disenfranchisement Refers to those who are denied the right to vote. For example, in some US states, those convicted of a felony offence may be disenfranchised.

Disparities Unequal or unfair differences in levels of treatment.

Disputants A person who is involved in a dispute. Another word for the first or primary parties to a conflict.

Diversification The process of adding new things, such as resources, products or services, to reduce the risks of an economy, business or organization relying on a single resource.

Economic liberalization policies Policies, such as deregulation, privatization and free trade, that major international financial institutions, such as the World Bank and the IMF, insist upon in return for financial assistance and loans provided to developing countries.

Emancipation Freedom, liberty.

Facilitate To make something (an action or process) possible or easier.

Failed state A state that has lost the ability to govern but still has some sort of external sovereignty. There may be uncontrolled violence, government collapse and/or a general breakdown of systems within the state.

Fraternity Being a part of a community, looking out for each other.

Geneva conventions A set of international treaties that establish legal standards for the humanitarian treatment of individuals involved in armed conflicts. These conventions outline the rights of wounded and sick soldiers, prisoners of war, and civilians, aiming to protect them from unnecessary suffering and inhumane treatment.

Genocide The deliberate killing of one ethnic, racial or religious group, with the aim of destroying that group.

Global governance The systems and institutions of decision-making and cooperation among state and non-state actors that facilitate collective action on global political issues.

Globalization Describes how the growth and development of trade and technology, and the spread of social and cultural influences, have made the world (states, governments, economies and people) a more connected, interdependent place.

Global north A group of countries that have a high level of economic and industrial development, and are typically located to the north of less industrialized nations.

Global south A group of countries that have a low level of economic and industrial development, and are typically located to the south of more industrialized nations.

Global trade network A network of bilateral trading routes and partnerships between states.

Gross domestic product (GDP) The value of goods and services produced in a country in one year.

Gross national income (GNI) A measure of all income received by a country from its residents and businesses regardless of whether they are located in the country or abroad.

Hardliners A secondary party to conflict. They support their favoured disputant, while also working to recruit and convince others to support their side.

Healthy life expectancy According to the World Health Organization, 'the average number of years a person can expect to live in "full health" by taking into account years lived in less than full health due to disease and/or injury'.

Hegemony Occurs when one state is politically, economically and militarily dominant over other states.

Homogeneous A group that is composed of elements that are all of the same or a similar kind or similar in their composition or character.

Hybrid multilateralism An approach to global governance that involves increased participation by non-state and civil society actors and moves beyond simple state-level cooperation.

Imperialistic In politics, refers to how the definition of rights is decided by powerful stakeholders and this definition is forced on others.

Inalienable Something that cannot be taken away or given away.

Indigenous A person or people living in an area or a land from the earliest times, before the arrival of colonists.

Indiscriminate Done at random or in a careless way.

Inequality The unfair situation in society in which some people have more opportunities, money and a better standard of living than others.

Informal economy Those economic activities that, if formally recorded, would add value to an economy in the form of GDP and tax revenue.

Insurgent A person who is fighting against the government or armed forces in their country.

Interdependence Can be defined as the mutual reliance between and among groups, organizations, geographic areas and/or states on access to resources that sustain living arrangements.

Intersectionality How a person's social and political identities result in various combinations of oppression, discrimination or privilege.

Interstate conflict Armed conflict taking place between two or more states.

Intractable Very difficult or maybe even impossible to manage or fix.

Intransigent Someone or something refusing to change behaviour or attitudes.

Intrastate conflict Armed conflict taking place within states between two or more groups from within the same country.

Judicial precedent Lower courts have to follow the decisions of the higher courts. It is common in many national legal systems.

Knowledge communities A group of people who share similar knowledge, beliefs, assumptions or opinions.

Latent Hidden or concealed.

Legitimacy Conformity to the law or to rules.

Lingua franca A language that is adopted as a common language by speakers of different languages.

Mandate An official order or permission to act. For example, UN peacekeeping missions are mandated to enter a country as a peacekeeping force.

Manifest Seen clearly (in other words, it is no longer hidden or concealed).

Market cap The total value of a company's shares of stock.

Mean The average of the numbers, calculated by adding all the numbers and dividing the total by how many numbers there are.

Mennonites A pacifist religious group that has roots in Eastern Europe. They immigrated to the Americas in the late 1800s and early 1900s after facing persecution.

Mercenary A private individual who is hired to fight in a conflict and is motivated by the desire for private gain rather than political or other motivations.

Militia groups Like armies, but their members are not professional soldiers.

Moderate A secondary party to conflict. It hopes to see its side in the conflict win, but is unlikely to put anything on the line to help them win.

Multidimensional Has many dimensions, aspects or features.

Multifaceted Having many sides or parts.

Mutually assured destruction The concept that two superpowers can destroy each other with nuclear weapons. Therefore, it acts as a deterrent to nuclear attack.

Neo-marxists Theorists who attempt to build on the work and theories of Karl Marx (1818–1883) to inform their analysis of contemporary global politics. In development studies, neo-Marxists see economic exploitation as central to any understanding of development.

Non-binding agreements In international law, agreements that contain political or moral commitments but are not legally enforceable. Therefore, if a state breaks the rules of these kinds of agreements it will not face legal consequences. However, the state's legitimacy may be questioned and so they may be effective.

Nonpartisan Not biased towards a particular political party.

OECD countries Member states of the Organization for Economic Co-operation and Development, an intergovernmental organization with 38 member countries, founded in 1961 to stimulate economic progress and world trade.

Official financial flows Official development assistance provided by one state to another.

Operationalization Turning abstract conceptual ideas into measurable observations. For example, we may not be able to see the concept of development, but we can see it in action – it may be operationally defined in terms of economic growth, educational achievement and life expectancy among others. These are known as development indicators.

P5 The five permanent members of the UN Security Council – China, France, Russia, the UK and the United States.

Patrilineal A patrilineal society is one in which descent is based on the male line. Patrilineal inheritance, therefore, means property passes from father to son.

Peace agreement A formal document, or set of documents, produced after discussions between two or more parties engaged in conflict have taken place and an agreement has been reached to end the conflict.

Peer competitor A state with the power and/or motivation to challenge another state in the international system. For example, China can be seen as a peer competitor to the United States.

Polycrisis According to UNICEF Innocenti, who coined the term, 'multiple, simultaneous shocks with strong interdependencies, intensified in an ever-more integrated world'.

Poststructuralism A perspective that attempts to move beyond making sense of the world in terms of pre-established social structures.

Poverty A state or condition in which a person does not have the financial resources and essentials for a certain standard of living.

Pretext A pretend reason given to justify doing something to conceal the real reason.

Private financial flows Financed by private sector resources as opposed to government resources. Private flows, therefore, include remittances sent home by migrants, foreign direct investment and private sector borrowing.

Prohibited Formally banned by law or another authority.

Prohibition A law or rule that officially stops something happening.

Protectionism Government policies that restrict international trade to help domestic industries. This can be achieved through, for example, tariffs, quotas (placing a limit on the quantity of imports) and embargoes (a total ban on a product if it is deemed dangerous).

Proxy In reference to war, a conflict in which a state attempts to increase its power or influence without taking part in the action, by providing arms or finance to the parties to conflict.

Ratings agencies Companies that independently assess the financial strength of individuals, companies and government entities.

Regenerative development Development that uses the resources of the world in such a way that capacity for future growth is increased.

Relative decoupling A decline in the ecological intensity per unit of economic output due to increases in efficiency, but the use of energy and raw materials does not decline in absolute terms.

Relative gains Also zero-sum game. When any gain to one side in a negotiation is a loss to the other.

Relative poverty When households receive 50 per cent less than the average household income, meaning they have some money, but only enough to cover basic needs.

Remittances Funds sent home by individuals, often migrant workers, to support family members in their origin countries.

Reparations Payments in either money or resources.

Resource endowment The number and type of resources a country has for economic activity, such as land, minerals, labour and capital.

Retaliatory capacity The ability to respond to a nuclear attack with powerful nuclear retaliation against the attacker.

Rogue state A state threatening world peace and not cooperating with the international community.

Separatism The desire of a group of people within a country to separate from the rest of the country due to cultural, religious, political, ideological or other reasons.

Social metabolism The idea that society needs a constant stream of resources, materials and energy from the environment to build, maintain and operate its structures, such as buildings, infrastructure and machinery.

Social progress The capacity of a society to: meet the basic human needs of its citizens; establish the building blocks that allow citizens and communities to enhance and sustain the quality of their lives; and create the conditions for all individuals to reach their full potential.

Spoilers A secondary party to conflict closely associated with hardliners, but they often use tactics to prevent or take issue with any sort of peace negotiations. They tend to favour violence and hold extreme or radical positions.

Structural adjustment programmes (SAPs) Economic policy reforms that states had to adhere to in order to get a loan from the IMF and/or World Bank.

Supranational A collective group that is outside of the power of an individual state. The United Nations and the African Union are examples.

Sustainable Able to be maintained or develop at a certain level. Sustainability means to meet the needs of the present without compromising the needs for the future.

Systemic Something that relates to or affects an entire system, often implying a deep-rooted, ingrained issue within a complex network or structure.

Washington Consensus A term coined by John Williamson in 1989 referring to a set of 10 economic neoliberal policy recommendations for economic reform of developing countries.

World ocean Describes all five of the world's oceans (Arctic, Atlantic, Indian, Pacific, Southern) combined.

Index

manifest 291

marginalized peoples 84, 131–2, 155, 160–1, 167, 216–20, 319–22, 332, 343, 380–2

market cap 48

marriage
    forced 148
    same-sex 132, 148–9

Marx, Karl 83

Marxism 45, 83, 85, 106, 132

Maslow's hierarchy of needs 189

mean 227

means of production 83

Mearsheimer, John 77–80, 89–90

Médecins Sans Frontières (MSF) 19, 160, 210–11, 317–19

media 17–19, 28, 59

mediation 355–9

medical assistance 318–19

'melting pot' metaphor 46

Mennonites 287

mercenaries 314

methodology 90

Mexico 327

Microsoft 48

middle classes, emerging 258

migrants/migration 46, 110–12, 122, 141, 164, 207, 250, 277–8, 381
    see also asylum; refugees

Milanovic, Branko 258

militarism 340

military actors 307–8

military capacity 78, 79

military force, efficacy 82–3

military intervention 150–1, 369–71

military power 22–3, 28–9, 40, 82–3

militia groups 346

minority interests 56, 123

misinformation 19, 47

moderates 305

modernization theory 237, 238–9, 240

monarchies 52, 55

Montevideo Convention (1933) 3, 4, 36–7

'moral considerability' 112

morality 207

movements 13–14, 15, 16, 60

multidimensional 180

multidimensional poverty index (MPI) 192–3, 230–1

multifaceted 105

multilateralism 64, 73–4

multinational corporations (MNCs) 251, 257
    and development 220–4, 269, 270
    and global governance 72
    and legitimacy 60
    and liberalism 81
    and neo-Marxism 84
    and power 202
    and rights and justice 132, 134
    see also transnational corporations

multiple channels 81

'multiple issues' 82

Muslims 157–8, 170–2, 329, 333–4
    see also Islam

mutually assured destruction 80

Myanmar 123, 317, 318, 369, 370

Nagomo-Karabakh conflict 304

Nair, Sheila 84, 85

nation states 4

nationalism 5, 46–7, 80, 348

natural resources 246–7, 263

needs 334–7
    basic 181, 229, 280
    Maslow's hierarchy of 189

negotiation 353–4

neo-Marxism/neo-Marxists 83–4, 239–41

neocolonialism, perceived 378

neoliberalism 237, 241, 261

networks 74, 222–4, 257–8

New Zealand 45, 56

Nicaragua 65, 117

Nigeria 18, 200, 221–2, 249

non-binding agreements 101

non-governmental organizations (NGOs) 10–11
    and conflict 383
    and development and sustainability 208, 210–12
    and Ebola 19
    and legitimacy 60
    and liberalism 81
    and non-violence 294, 317–19
    and rights and justice 94, 127–32, 146, 155, 159–60
    types 11

non-state actors
    and conflict 326–7, 363
    and development and sustainability 224
    and global governance 71–2
    and legitimacy 59–60
    and liberalism 81
    non-violent 316–19
    and rights 143, 144–5
    violent 312–14, 380
    see also specific non-state actors

non-violence 274, 287–8, 293–9, 308
    and conflict 349–50
    non-violent non-state actors 316–19
    non-violent state actors 314–16
    principled 294–9
    strategic 293–4

nonpartisan 361–2

norms 26–7, 30, 76, 87–8, 340
    and conflict 328
    cultural 219
    gender 219
    and legitimacy 50–1
    and rights/justice 146–51, 165–7, 170–2
    world (global) 35, 39, 146–51, 165–7

North Atlantic Treaty Organization (NATO) 9, 29, 73, 163–4, 213, 285, 309–11, 347
    air policing 310–11

North Korea 63, 198

nuclear weapons 63, 80, 82, 85, 87, 362–3

Nussbaum, Martha 242–3

Nye, Joseph 21–6, 28, 30, 61, 81, 165, 360

Office of the United Nations High Commissioner for Human Rights (OHCHR) 70, 133, 142–4, 161, 183–4, 312, 370

oil industry 221–2, 314, 338, 339
    oil crisis 1973 244
    oil spills 221, 222, 245

one-party states 6

ontology 90

operationalization 182

opportunity 192–4, 219, 222, 229–30, 242

order 53

Organisation for Economic Co-operation and Development (OECD) 185, 197–8, 206, 230, 235, 250

Organisation of Islamic Cooperation (OIC) 125, 126

Organization of American States 125, 126

Orientalism 85

'Original Position, the' 194–5

othering 85, 330

out-groups 330

outcomes 21, 22, 23, 24–5

Oxfam 160

P5 62–3, 67

pacifism 287, 294–9

paramilitary actors 308–9, 313

parliamentary systems 57

participation 102, 198

'parties to conflict' 290, 302–6

patriarchy 86, 139

patrilineal society 250

peace 98, 120, 271–383
    agreements 352
    as balance of power 284–5
    contested meanings of 271–383
    debates on 352–79
    exam-style questions 380–3
    feminist 285–6
    multifaceted approaches to 273, 275
    negative 276, 282–3
    peacebuilding 273, 371–9
    peacekeeping 67, 89, 363–6
    peacemaking 352–9
    positive 282–4
    in religious and spiritual traditions 286–9
    and stakeholder-actor interactions 302–23
    and the United Nations 66–7, 69–71

Peace of Westphalia 1648 34–5, 37

peer competitors 89

people with disabilities 322

persons, flow of 255–6, 269

Pettit, Phillip 56

police 147–8, 299

policies 236

political ideology 248

United Nations Environment Programme 188, 260

United Nations Framework Convention on Climate Change (UNFCCC) 63, 73

United Nations General Assembly (UNGA) 62, 66–9, 98–9, 117, 119, 121, 128

United Nations High Commission for Refugees 111, 116, 121–4, 194

United Nations Human Rights Commission 98, 99, 156, 160

United Nations Human Rights Council (UNHRC) 69–70, 116, 119–21, 124, 131, 156

United Nations Office for South-South Cooperation 250

United Nations Secretariat 68–9

United Nations Security Council (UNSC) 62–3, 66–9, 98, 117–18, 141, 150, 157, 162–3, 199, 321–2, 341, 364–5, 370–1, 375

United Nations Support Mission in Libya (UNSMIL) 164

United States 215, 360
  and aid 206, 207
  and China 89, 325, 333, 334
  and collective security alliances 73
  Constitution 138
  and economic cooperation 74
  and identity 46
  and the Iran nuclear deal 25
  and the justice system 107–8
  and military power 307
  and NATO 311
  and natural resources 246
  and nuclear weapons 85, 87
  and political parties 6
  and power 27, 28, 30, 31
  and rights 70, 157–9
  and sanctions 166
  and Somalia 41–2
  and sovereignty 36

and the subprime mortgage crisis 72
  and terrorism 327
  and the United Nations 97–8
  war on terror 347
  and the World Bank 213

Universal Declaration of Human Rights (UDHR) 97–102, 104–5, 107, 109, 124–7, 129, 136, 138, 140, 144–5, 148, 154–5, 162, 166, 170, 175, 318, 383

universal periodic review (UPR) 70–1

universalism 104–5, 145–6, 155, 170

Uppsala Conflict Data Program (UCDP) 326–7

Uyghur Muslims 157–8, 333–4

values 5, 27, 51–2, 155, 162, 328, 335

Varieties of Democracy (V-Dem) 58

vetoes 365

violence 274–89, 291–300, 353, 372, 380, 382–3
  cultural 278–82, 284, 291, 296, 328, 373, 383
  direct (personal) 276, 277–82, 284, 291, 296
  gender-based 86–7, 89, 172
  indirect impact 321
  and resistance movements 14, 15
  sexual 322, 381
  and state sovereignty 41
  structural 175–7, 277–84, 291, 372–3, 383
  violent non-state actors 312–14, 380
  violent state actors 307–11
  see also non-violence

visibility 86

voting 198–9, 290, 332, 361–2
  see also elections

vulnerable people 131–2, 161, 167, 216–20, 321–2

Wagner Group 313–14

Walt, Stephen 78

war 292–3, 295, 307, 315
  and civilians 319–22
  cultural/religious justification 343–4
  cyber warfare 30
  guerrilla warfare 346
  `just war' theory 161–2, 341–3, 370–1
  proxy 294
  see also conflict

war crimes 150, 369, 374, 375

Washington Consensus 213, 215

wealth 48, 196–7

Weber, Max 53–4

Weiner, Allen 320–1

well-being 227–8, 229, 234

Wellbeing Economie 205

Wendt, Alexander 87

Westphalia, treaty of (1648) 3, 4

women 189–90
  discrimination against 249–50
  exclusion from work 249
  and poverty 218–19
  rights 134, 138–9, 143, 147–8, 152, 171–2, 217–19, 290, 295–6
  role in global politics 86
  and sexual violence 322, 381

World Bank 22, 192, 199–200, 205, 213–15, 217, 251

World Economic Forum (WEF) 17, 218–19, 263

World Health Organization (WHO) 19, 161

world ocean 245

world order 41

World Trade Organization (WTO) 9, 30, 63, 134

Yalta Conference 1945 97

Yemen 294, 306, 329, 338–9

Zeid Ra'ad Al Hussein, Prince 70, 133

Ziai, Aram 261

Zulu people 113

Acknowledgements

Ben Fugill

I would like to thank my wife, Dyonne, without whose encouragement and support this book, and much else, would never have been possible.

Jane Hirons

Thank you to my family, Gordon, Sophie and Madeline, for their constant love, support and encouragement.

Brian Hull

I would like to thank my wife, Theresa, my two daughters, Alyssa and Joelle, my father and mother, and my best friend, Jonny. I appreciated your patience and encouragement throughout the writing of this book.

The Publishers would like to thank the following for permission to reproduce copyright material.

Photo credits

Goals web site: https://www.un.org/sustainabledevelopment/. The content of this publication has not been approved by the United Nations and does not reflect the views of the United Nations or its officials or Member States; **p. 256** © Tjeerd/stock.adobe.com; **p. 262** © UNC-Chapel Hill; **p. 271** © Eduard Borja/stock.adobe.com; **p. 272** © Himasaram/ Zscout370/Wikipedia; **p. 276** © Leber/Ullstein bild/Getty Images; **p. 296** © Brian Hull; **p. 297** © Dinodia Photos/Alamy Stock Photo; **p. 300** © Brian Hull; **p. 310** © Alejandro/stock.adobe.com; **p. 313** © ARKADY BUDNITSKY/EPA-EFE/Shutterstock; **p. 320** © Rospoint/stock.adobe.com; **p. 324** © Geopix/Alamy Stock Photo; **p. 347** © Planetpix/US Air Force Photo/Alamy Stock Photo; **p. 350** © ZUMA Press, Inc./Alamy Stock Photo; **p. 353** © Planetpix/Presidenciamx/Alamy Stock Photo; **p. 354** © Phonlamaiphoto/stock.adobe.com; **p. 362** © The Carter Center, www.cartercenter.org; **p. 366** © Justin Kabumba/Associated Press/Alamy Stock Photo; **p. 377** © Adrian Wyld/The Canadian Press/Alamy Stock Photo; **p. 385** © Malik E/peopleimages.com/stock.adobe.com; **p. 395** © Chinnapong/stock.adobe.com.

Text credits

p. 13 Adapted from Wykis, 'The stages of social movement', reproduced under CC BY-SA 4.0; **p. 161** Adapted from Humanitarian Response (2020), 'What is the Cluster Approach?', reproduced under CC-BY 4.0; **p. 184** E. Browne and K. A. Millington (2015), 'Social development and human development', GSDRC/HEART, © DFID Crown Copyright 2015 Licensed under the Open Government Licence: www.nationalarchives.gov.uk/doc/open-governmentlicence; **p. 200** (a) World Bank, 'School enrolment, primary (% net)', World Bank Open Data (2020), (b) World Bank, 'Life expectancy at birth, total (years)', World Bank Open Data (2021), both reproduced under CC-BY 4.0; **p. 202** S. Boseley (2017), 'Threats, bullying, lawsuits: tobacco industry's dirty war for the African market'. *Guardian*, 12 July, reproduced courtesy of Guardian News & Media Ltd under their Open Licence terms, www.theguardian.com/info/2022/nov/01/open-licence-terms; **p. 205** World Bank, 'China Overview: development news, research, data', World Bank Open Data (2023), reproduced under CC-BY 4.0; **p. 214** N. Klein (2007), 'Naomi Klein: The World Bank has the perfect standard bearer', *Guardian*, 26 April 2007, reproduced courtesy of Guardian News & Media Ltd under their Open Licence terms, www.theguardian.com/info/2022/nov/01/open-licence-terms; **p. 218** International Labour Organization (2023), 'Why do employers outside the family hire children?', reproduced under CC-BY 4.0; **p. 221** S. Jones (2015), 'Tax dodging by big firms "robs poor countries of billions of dollars a year"', *Guardian*, 2 June, reproduced courtesy of Guardian News & Media Ltd under their Open Licence terms, www.theguardian.com/info/2022/nov/01/open-licence-terms; **p. 247** Our World in Data, 'Global meat production, 1961 to 2021', reproduced under CC-BY 4.0; **pp.248–249** Transparency International (2011), 'What is public sector corruption? Blog – Transparency.org', 5 December 2011, reproduced under CC BY-ND 4.0; **p. 256** H. Ritchie (2020), 'Climate change and flying: what share of global CO2 emissions come from aviation?', Our World in Data, 22 October, reproduced under CC BY-ND 4.0; **p. 265** © Medard Gabel, 'Regenerative Development: Going Beyond Sustainability', Fall | Winter 2015; **p. 284** © J. Galtung (1969). Violence, Peace, and Peace Research. Journal of Peace Research, 6(3), 167–191. doi:10.1177/002234336900600301; **p. 292** © Martin Luther King, Jr, *Where Do We Go From Here: Chaos or Community?*, 1967, Beacon Press; **pp. 292, 317, 345, 372** © O. Ramsbotham, T. Woodhouse, and H. Miall (2016), *Contemporary Conflict Resolution* (4th ed.). Cambridge, UK: Polity Press; **p. 298** © Martin Luther King, Jr. (2018) 'Letter from Birmingham Jail', April 1963. Penguin; **p. 304** Adapted from Armenicum (2006), 'The Nagorno-Karabakh conflict', reproduced under CC BY-SA 3.0; **p. 311** Our World in Data, 'Military expenditure as a share of GDP, 1949 to 2020', reproduced under CC-BY 4.0.

The terms of the Creative Commons Attribution-ShareAlike 3.0 International license (CC BY-SA 3.0) can be found at https://creativecommons.org/licenses/by-sa/3.0/deed.en. The terms of the Creative Commons Attribution 4.0 International license (CC-BY 4.0) can be found at https://creativecommons.org/licenses/by/4.0/. The terms of the Creative Commons Attribution-NoDerivs 4.0 International licence can be found at https://creativecommons.org/licenses/by-nd/4.0/deed.en. The terms of the Creative Commons Attribution-ShareAlike 4.0 International license (CC BY-SA 4.0) can be found at https://creativecommons.org/licenses/by-sa/4.0/deed.en.

IB material has been reproduced with kind permission from the International Baccalaureate Organization.